Orchid Species Culture

Orchid Species Culture

Pescatorea
Phaius
Phalaenopsis
Pholidota
Phragmipedium
Pleione

by
Margaret L. Baker
and
Charles O. Baker

TIMBER PRESS
Portland, Oregon

© 1991 by Timber Press, Inc.
All rights reserved.

ISBN 0-88192-189-0 (cloth)
ISBN 0-88192-208-0 (paper)
Printed in Singapore

TIMBER PRESS, INC.
9999 S.W. Wilshire
Portland, Oregon 97225

Library of Congress Cataloging-in-Publication Data

Baker, Margaret L.
    Orchid species culture : Pescatorea, Phaius, Phalaenopsis,
Pholidota, Phragmipedium, Pleione / by Margaret L. Baker and Charles
O. Baker.
        p.   cm
    Includes bibliographical references.
    ISBN 0-88192-189-0
    1. Orchid culture. 2. Orchids. 3. Species.   I. Baker, Charles
O. II. Title
SB409.B25 1991
635.9'3415—dc20   90-22011
                                              CIP

This book is dedicated with love to my father, Joe Vergeer, for teaching me to understand growing plants, and to the memory of my mother, Ruth Ronald Vergeer, for teaching me to ask questions and search for answers.

—M. L. B.

Contents

Prologue 1

1 Sample Format and General Cultural Recommendations
    General Information 5
    Cultural Recommendations 7
    Plant and Flower Information 18

2 *Pescatorea*
    General Information 23
    Species Culture 24

3 *Phaius*
    General Information 31
    Species Culture 33

4 *Phalaenopsis*
    General Information 65
    Species Culture 69

5 *Pholidota*
    General Information 111
    Species Culture 112

6 *Phragmipedium*
    General Information 139
    Species Culture 141

7 *Pleione*
    General Information 159
    Species Culture 161

Appendix A: Orchid Growing Problems
    I. Preventing Disease 179
    II. Identifying and Treating Plant Problems
        Glossary of Terms 181
        Guide to Symptoms 182
        Pathogens 191
        Pests 219
        Nutrients 226
    III. Using Chemicals Safely 233

Appendix B: Unit Conversions and Formulas for Greenhouse Management . . 237

Bibliography
    References 241
    List of Sources 248

Prologue

This is the first volume in a planned series of books on the cultivation of individual orchid species. The subject was last addressed systematically 100 years ago, when James Veitch and Sons Royal Exotic Nursery, in Chelsea, London, published a series of booklets titled *A Manual of Orchidaceous Plants*. The series, published between 1887 and 1894, contained information on native habitat and climate for individual species then cultivated in England. This information, comprehensive for its time, is as valuable today as it was in the 1890s. But in the century since it was compiled, the number of orchid species under cultivation world-wide has multiplied manyfold, and enormous amounts of new information on habitat and climate have become available. Excellent work has been done in the areas of taxonomy and general orchid culture, but no one has focused on the cultivation of individual species and pulled together the mass of species-specific data, including information on weather and habitat.

Our goal has been to make species culture information readily available, easy to use, and as complete as possible. The cultural guidelines were developed from data we originally compiled to help us grow our own, ever-increasing collection of orchid species. The guidelines are based on climate data for each species' native habitat together with cultivation notes and growers' observations, which are included when available. These notes were primarily gleaned from the books listed in the Bibliography, but observations based on personal experience as well as on the expertise of other species growers are also included.

As our fascination with orchid species grew, we turned to books for information to help us cultivate our plants. Our library increased rapidly, as did our feeling of frustration. Locating specific cultural information for a particular species often involved hours of reading. Despite our numerous books, we frequently found that the only mention of a particular plant was a comment that it was "tricky to grow" or "difficult to maintain in cultivation," or that it came from somewhere in Brazil.

We reluctantly concluded that the only source for the information we needed to grow our species well was weather data from the species' original habitats. After researching the plants' native habitats, we acquired global tropical and subtropical climate records to use as the basis for developing our own guidelines. Frequently the temperatures recorded at the nearest weather station were for an elevation different from that of the habitat. Consequently, it required adjusting to reflect the probable temperatures at the elevation where the plants were actually found. Standard atmospheric lapse-rate formulas were used to calculate these probable temperatures.

While the initial impetus for this undertaking was our desire to grow some of the difficult species, we quickly found the information so helpful that we extended our research to include the more easily grown species in our collection. All plants were healthier when the growing conditions were modified to approximate the environmental conditions indicated by the weather data. Whenever a particular plant languished or failed to bloom, it became an easy process to determine what cultural changes were needed.

In addition, the climate information is especially helpful when acclimating a recently imported plant. By knowing the seasonal climatic conditions in the plant's original habitat, we can provide a gradual transition during the time required for it to adapt to the seasons in the Northern Hemisphere, resulting in a dramatic reduction in the number of plants lost to stress.

The weather records are equally useful whenever we deal with reluctant hybrids. By referring to the growing and habitat conditions required by the parent species, we often discover clues to the hybrid's hereditary cultural requirements and possible bloom initiators.

When a flower illustration intrigues us, we turn to this compiled information to decide if we should acquire the plant. Can we provide the environment the plant needs to thrive? How long do the flowers last? Are they fragrant? How large are the flowers relative to plant size? While complete data is not available for all species, the compiled information has proved helpful in a variety of ways.

We believe that as growers we have a responsibility to help reduce whatever pressure our hobby is exerting on populations of wild plants and their natural habitats. Every species grower can contribute to the effort by refusing to purchase wild plants, by growing his or her own species well, and by propagating and making species seedlings available to others as inexpensively as possible.

The world's tropical rainforests are being destroyed at appalling speed, and at the current rate of destruction, many species' natural habitats will soon be beyond salvage. Orchid species growers have a unique opportunity to help preserve a genetic resource that may become the only source of orchid plant material available to future generations.

We sincerely hope that others will join us in making this series of orchid culture books an ongoing project. With this compilation of information as a starting point, perhaps we all can expand our knowledge of how best to grow our orchid species and benefit from each other's experience. To that end, we would appreciate hearing from anyone with additional habitat details or information concerning propagation, the time required for species seeds to be sufficiently mature to be sown using green-pod techniques, or the growing time required for seedlings to reach blooming size. Accounts of personal growing experience, either successful or disastrous, would also be most helpful. Any additional information received will be added to later editions and made available at the earliest opportunity.

Included for each species is a list of references that may be consulted for taxonomic information, additional habitat details, or plant illustrations such as botanical drawings or photographs. The plant names listed under the category "AKA" (Also Known As) are synonyms established by taxonomists and were compiled from the works listed in the Bibliography. After encountering differences of opinion among experts, we decided to select a single botanist as our primary guide for each genus. When a recent review of a genus was available, we chose it as our guide for those species. If a recent review was unavailable, we depended upon a variety of publications, listing the species and synonyms as we found them. Throughout, our aim has been to provide cultural, not taxonomic, information.

Since many orchid reference books are out of print, this and subsequent volumes could not have been compiled without help from the librarians of numerous herbaria, colleges, and universities which lent the material needed. Special appreciation is extended to the Los Angeles State and City Botanical Garden Library, the Marion Ownbey Herbarium Library in Pullman, Washington, and the library staffs of Blue Mountain Community College in Pendleton, Oregon, and the Multnomah County Library in Portland, Oregon, all of whom have been particularly helpful. Their patience and assistance have been invaluable.

We wish to thank Robert M. Hamilton and our son Bruce Baker for their suggestions and reasonably patient proofreading, Charles Jackson for his suggestions on *Phragmipedium* culture and Appendix A, and Dr. J. A. Fowlie, Editor of the *Orchid Digest*, for his help and encouragement. We would like to express special appreciation to Karen Kirtley for her untold hours of effort and many valuable suggestions. Responsibility for any errors, however, remains ours alone.

The following words are attributed to the 18th-century Swedish botanist Carl Linnaeus. They express sentiments we humbly share:

> *If you have remarked errors in me, your superior wisdom must pardon them. Who errs not while perambulating the domain of nature? Who can observe everything with accuracy? Correct me as a friend, and I as a friend will requite with kindness.*

1
Sample Format and General Cultural Recommendations
General Information

SUBFAMILY: *Botanical name of subfamily.*

TRIBE: *Botanical name of tribe.*

SUBTRIBE: *Botanical name of subtribe.*

GENUS: *Botanical name of genus.*

SPECIES: *Botanical name of species.* The International Code of Botanical Nomenclature considers formally described hybrids as species. Artificial hybrids are not included, but natural hybrids, which are sometimes sold as species, are listed alphabetically with their parentage indicated. The information provided for parent species may be consulted for cultural information.

AKA (*Also Known As*): *Other names used over the years and now considered synonymous.* As growers, we generally find name changes more frustrating than illuminating, and from our vantage point they sometimes appear frivolous and unnecessary. However, since beginning this work with individual species, we have come to appreciate some of the problems the taxonomist faces. The more widespread or variable a species is, the greater the number of names given to it. Botanical explorers and early taxonomists did not have the communication systems and computer technology available today and generally described each species as they found it in their area. Even today, taxonomists are plagued with genuine differences of opinion as well as missing or incomplete type specimens. Many of the original specimen collections have been damaged or lost to war, insects, or neglect.

Again, the synonyms here are not included for taxonomic purposes, but to help growers who are using outdated books that may discuss a plant under another name. They may also be helpful when a species is sold under different names.

ORIGIN/HABITAT: *The points of origin, used as the basis for selecting appropriate weather records.* We have included available notes on the species' natural habitat when this information was available. Habitat elevations are usually approximated, and all figures are rounded for ease of use.

CLIMATE: *The climate in each species' native habitat.* All temperatures are as correct as possible for the habitat

of the species and may be used as shown; they do not require modification by the grower.

The first paragraph in this category gives the World Meteorological Organization station number, station name, latitude, longitude, elevation, and record temperatures, which are given as recorded at the station. If both station and habitat elevation are given, all temperatures are calculated to the nearest tenth of a degree in both Fahrenheit and Celsius and reflect the probable climate at the orchids' elevation. Growers should take care to avoid record temperatures and calculated extremes, since *plants may not survive exposure to the extremes.* Record temperatures do not take into account the strong influence of local terrain and microclimate within the orchid habitat. Consequently, they can be considered approximations only, and they are included to indicate how precise environmental control should be for each plant, not to serve as norms in plant culture.

Temperatures in the climate tables are rounded to the nearest whole degree Fahrenheit and to the nearest tenth of a degree Celsius. (Note, however, that Celsius temperatures were computed from *unrounded* Fahrenheit figures, an approach that increases the accuracy of the Celsius temperatures, but may result in seeming discrepancies when the rounded Fahrenheit temperatures and Celsius "equivalents" appear side by side.)

If a plant is growing and blooming well in an artificial environment, the conditions are obviously adequate, and altering them might not be beneficial. In such cases, plants which have been propagated and raised in a greenhouse may have adapted in order to survive. However, if a plant is not thriving or blooming satisfactorily, growing conditions should be gradually modified to more closely resemble those in its natural habitat.

Weather records provide seasonal temperature ranges, rainfall patterns, and day/night temperature fluctuations (diurnal range). These components describe a generally appropriate growing environment. The records do not necessarily reflect the exact conditions in the orchids' microclimate and should be used as a guide only. No attempt should be made to duplicate climate exactly since all the information is averaged. Most species will be healthiest if rainfall cycles and seasonal temperature ranges are at least approximated in cultivation. However, species which are difficult to cultivate will be healthiest in a growing environment that recreates the conditions in their native habitat as closely as possible.

A climate table is provided for each species; the month in which the observations were made corresponds to the month given in the table for the hemisphere in which the station is located. These tables are structured so that they may be used by growers world-wide, and we hope readers will find them genuinely easy to use. As many have discovered, some of the excellent cultural information written for growers in the Southern Hemisphere is awkward for those who live north of the equator, where seasons are opposite, or who think in terms of degrees Fahrenheit (°F) and inches (in.). Conversely, it is cumbersome for those who measure temperature in degrees Celsius (°C) and rainfall in millimeters (mm) to adapt cultural information written for growers in the United States.

To use the climate tables, orchid growers north of the equator should start with the line labeled "N/HEMISPHERE," the seasonal guide at the top of the table. All numbers in the columns below apply to the months shown on the top line. Temperature is given in both °F and °C, and rainfall in both inches and millimeters. The months shown on the line labeled "S/HEMISPHERE," the seasonal guide at the bottom of the table, reflect the corresponding seasons south of the equator. Southern growers need only read the chart from bottom to top to find the same information available to top-to-bottom readers in the North. The seasonal guides for both Northern and Southern Hemispheres begin and end in midwinter.

N/HEMISPHERE   JAN FEB MAR APR MAY JUN JUL AUG SEP OCT NOV DEC: *Calendar guide for the Northern Hemisphere.*

°F AVG MAX: *Average maximum temperature per month expressed in degrees Fahrenheit.*

°F AVG MIN: *Average minimum temperature per month expressed in degrees Fahrenheit.*

DIURNAL RANGE: *Range between day and night temperatures expressed in degrees Fahrenheit.* Diurnal range is often overlooked when plants are cultivated outside their natural habitat. The diurnal fluctuation can be critical for some species, and this range, rather than absolute low temperatures, is often the factor that induces flowering. Unless night temperatures decline by approximately the number of degrees indicated, the plants are unable to rest, and some chemical functions are inhibited.

Diurnal range is determined by many factors, chief among which is the characteristic of different materials to transfer heat at different speeds. Solid surfaces, like the earth, gain and lose heat more rapidly than the surrounding air. As a result, maximum heating or cooling occurs during clear, calm weather when the process of heat absorption or radiation is undisturbed. (It is this differing rate of heat loss that causes surface frost to form even when air temperatures do not fall to freezing.) Conversely, the difference between day and night temperatures is lowest during windy, overcast weather because both wind and clouds moderate temperatures by altering the amount of radiational heating and cooling that can occur. Wind moderates temperatures by mixing the surface air layer with higher air layers, thereby slowing the rate at which the earth is warmed or cooled. Clouds influence temperatures by allowing the passage of a portion of the incoming energy from the sun (short-wave radiation). The incoming radiation is absorbed, warming the earth's surface. Energy is then reradiated by the earth in the form of long-wave radiation, which is unable to penetrate clouds. This causes the phenomenon known as the "greenhouse effect," since clouds act in the same manner as the skin on a greenhouse by preventing the loss of heat.

RAIN/INCHES: *Average monthly rainfall expressed in inches.* Average rainfall figures are an important indication of suitable watering patterns, showing whether a plant requires high or low moisture levels as well as indicating seasonal increases and decreases in available moisture. Precise rainfall measurements are valid only for the location where the observations were made and cannot accurately be adjusted for elevation, since local terrain is an important determining factor.

HUMIDITY/%: *Average monthly relative humidity expressed as a percentage.* In the tropics, extremes normally range at least 10% above and below the average. High humidity during a period of low rainfall indicates that some moisture is probably available in the form of dew, fog, mist, or low clouds.

BLOOM SEASON: *Probable bloom times.* An asterisk (*) marks the months when blooming occurs. Multiple asterisks indicate a higher incidence of blooming. Records of blooming in the wild and collection reports were used when available, but our primary source of information was the extensive work done by Robert M. Hamilton and published in 1988 in *When Does It Flower?* In preparing his volume, Hamilton compiled bloom reports for greenhouse-cultivated plants in the Northern Hemisphere.

DAYS CLR @ 7AM, 8AM, 2PM, 4PM, and so on: *Average number of clear (CLR) days per month at the hour indicated.* A day qualifies as clear when visibility is 3 miles (4.8 km) or greater and when clouds cover 0.3 or less of the sky. Because the records do not take into account the transparency of the clouds, the sun may seem quite bright even though the weather cannot be classified as clear.

While the information is valid only for the station where the observation was taken, it indicates general patterns of high and low available light. When combined with seasonal light variations, the data provide an indication of the time of day and season when a species is most likely to benefit from increased or decreased light, another factor often critical for blooming. Unfortunately, the information is frequently unavailable, and the time when observations are made varies from one location to another. Some stations report sky cover once a day, while others report several times daily. Whenever possible, records are included for morning and afternoon since orchid habitats frequently have morning fog or afternoon clouds.

RAIN/MM: *Average rainfall per month expressed in millimeters.*

°C AVG MAX: *Average maximum temperature per month expressed in degrees Celsius.*

°C AVG MIN: *Average minimum temperature per month expressed in degrees Celsius.*

DIURNAL RANGE: *Range between day and night temperatures expressed in degrees Celsius.*

S/HEMISPHERE   JUL AUG SEP OCT NOV DEC JAN FEB MAR APR MAY JUN:
Calendar guide for the Southern Hemisphere

Cultural Recommendations

The information in this section has been especially tailored to meet growers' needs. Most growers do not work with precision equipment in sophisticated laboratories, hence they are not concerned with fractional degrees of temperature. Accordingly, all temperatures have been rounded to the nearest whole degree. Temperatures are given first in °F, with °C in parentheses.

A healthy, well-grown plant generally escapes most insect and disease damage, while a plant under stress is very susceptible to additional harm from disease and insects. Normally, plant stress is caused by poor cultural and environmental conditions. Some general symptoms of plant stress are included throughout the volume under the heading "Plant and Flower Information." Genus-specific indicators are included in the "General Information" at the beginning of each chapter.

LIGHT: *Approximate light levels, expressed in footcandles (fc).* These light levels may be used as a starting point, but it is important to watch each plant carefully and to modify the light at the first indication of stress (as described under the heading "Leaves" below). Light levels should always be changed gradually.

Plants generally utilize morning light most effectively, since their metabolism is frequently most active in the morning; but as with most rules, there are exceptions. If the habitat climate shows frequent morning overcast, then the plant may benefit from higher light in the afternoon.

Greenhouse plants should be watched carefully during seasonal shifts in light patterns to guard against the possibility of sunburn. Species grown in light which is too low may not bloom, but low light seldom causes the serious damage that can result from excessively high light.

Cultivated species may adapt to different light conditions, but they are unlikely to thrive and may not bloom unless they receive light at the appropriate levels and times. The most widely distributed species are those most likely to be adaptable to various light levels. The following generally accepted cultural divisions describe light levels:

Very high. Over 5000 footcandles—nearly full sun except at midday, when full summer sun in most latitudes may reach 10,000 fc. Full sunlight through clean fiberglass is usually 5000–7000 fc on a clear day.

High. 4000–5000 footcandles—bright light, just under 50% of the full midday sun. Although most plants utilize light most efficiently at 5000 fc, many orchids use light most efficiently at much lower levels.

Intermediate. 1800–4000 footcandles—dappled sunlight.

Low. 1000–1800 footcandles—reduced sunlight, so that if a hand is passed over the leaves it does not produce a shadow.

Very low. Less than 1000 footcandles—deep shade.

Light can be measured with a light meter. If no direct-reading light meter is available, footcandles may be measured with a 35 mm camera that has through-the-lens metering. The procedure is simple. First, set the camera for a film speed of ASA 25 and a shutter speed of $\frac{1}{60}$ second. Center the needle in the viewfinder by adjusting the camera's f/stop while focusing on a clean, white sheet of paper which has been placed where the plant actually grows. Then convert the f/stops to approximate footcandles as follows:

f/2:	f/2.8:	f/4:	f/5.6:	f/8:	f/11:	f/16:
100 fc	200 fc	370 fc	750 fc	1500 fc	2800 fc	5000 fc

When artificial lights are used in the growing area, the f/stop readings may be quite low and yet the light may be adequate. Artificial light is constant, whereas natural light fluctuates during the day as the wind moves leaves and clouds causing shadows.

Orchids grown in the home normally require supplemental lighting. Fluorescent lights are most frequently used in a one-to-one ratio of cool-white and Gro-Lux bulbs which provide nearly full-spectrum light. Growers also successfully use the newer "full-spectrum" fluorescent and high-intensity lights. Halide lights should be combined with sodium bulbs since alone they are deficient in red portions of the light spectrum, which prevents flowering in some species. Artificial lights are easily controlled by timers to provide seasonal fluctuation, increasing and decreasing light levels each month. Most species do well with 11–14 hours of light, which the following schedule provides:

Jan. (Jul.)	6:30 a.m. –6:00 p.m.	Jul. (Jan.)	5:00 a.m.–7:00 p.m.
Feb. (Aug.)	6:00 a.m. –6:00 p.m.	Aug.(Feb.)	5:30 a.m.–6:30 p.m.
Mar. (Sep.)	5:30 a.m. –6:00 p.m.	Sep. (Mar.)	5:30 a.m.–6:00 p.m.
Apr. (Oct.)	5:30 a.m. –6:30 p.m.	Oct. (Apr.)	6:00 a.m.–6:00 p.m.
May (Nov.)	5:00 a.m. –7:00 p.m.	Nov.(May)	6:30 a.m.–6:00 p.m.
Jun. (Dec.)	5:00 a.m. –7:00 p.m.	Dec. (Jun.)	6:30 a.m.–5:30 p.m.

Seedlings need very low light, starting at 200 fc when they are just out of the flask. During the following years, light should gradually be increased to mature-plant levels as the plants reach blooming size.

Studies indicate that seedlings grow more rapidly if given 14–16 hours of light year-round. However, extending light in the general growing area may adversely affect blooming in mature plants. Consequently, either seedlings should be grown in a separate area, or the light should be blocked from other plants in the same area. See the discussion of bloom initiators under "Flowers" later in this chapter.

TEMPERATURES: *Correct growing temperatures and diurnal range for the species during periods of active growth.* Unless the plant is unusually adaptable, temperatures outside the recommended range will cause plant stress and lead to disease. Changes should be introduced gradually, allowing the plant time to adjust. This is true even for plants being grown at temperatures outside the range found in their natural habitat and not thriving.

Newly imported plants often require months to become acclimated to their changed environment. Once the plant is placed in the location with the best possible conditions, it should not be moved around within the greenhouse. Each position in the greenhouse has its own microclimate to which the plant adapts little by little. Anytime a plant is moved, it must adjust to slightly different conditions, and the acclimating process is slowed.

Plants gain and lose water through their leaves. High humidity provides necessary moisture, while low humidity allows cooling through the evaporative process. When temperatures are high, humidity levels must be optimized in order to maintain the proper balance between the plants' need for moisture to replace the water lost through transpiration and the plants' need for the cooling that evaporation provides. When air movement is adequate, this balance is less critical.

Air circulation is important, as it moves fresh air over the leaves, renewing available carbon dioxide near the leaf surfaces. In fact, air circulation may be the single most important factor in preventing disease. Moving air is critically important in hot or excessively humid environments because it moves the thin layer of moisture-laden air from around the leaf, allowing additional evaporation and the associated cooling to continue. Air movement is sufficient if plants gently wave in the circulating air.

Orchid growers frequently use the terms *warm*, *intermediate*, and *cool* to indicate the temperatures required during a plant's growing season. The following table defines the generally accepted divisions and includes suggested temperature ranges for *very warm* and *very cool* categories.

	Daytime Highs		Nighttime Lows	
Very warm	Above 85°F (29°C)		68–75°F	(20–24°C)
Warm	75–85°F	(24–29°C)	62–68°F	(17–20°C)
Intermediate	65–80°F	(18–27°C)	55–62°F	(13–17°C)
Cool	60–75°F	(16–24°C)	50–55°F	(10–13°C)
Very cool	Below 65°F (18°C)		Below 50°F (10°C)	

These categories provide a convenient means of indicating an appropriate temperature range, and the classifications work well for some species. To illustrate, temperatures for a low-elevation equatorial plant can accurately be described as *very warm* throughout the year. The categories could describe any species' requirements, but unfortunately, variations in day, night, summer, and winter conditions are seldom specified by means of this shorthand. A plant requiring a wide diurnal range might be classified as needing *warm* days and *cool* nights, or a plant requiring a winter rest might be designated as needing *intermediate* summers and *very cool* winters. The slight expansion of the shorthand reflected in the table above could dramatically reduce the number of plants lost through ignorance and vastly increase orchid growers' enjoyment of species.

Nearly all plants require at least a variation of 10°F (6°C) between day and night temperatures. Note that habitats vary widely in diurnal range, and individual species have distinct requirements.

Seedlings are healthiest when grown at temperatures in the middle of the range recommended for mature plants.

HUMIDITY: *Correct relative humidity levels for the species.* Relative humidity is a ratio between the amount of water vapor present and the amount the air can hold at a given temperature. Warm air is able to hold more water vapor than cold air before becoming saturated (100% relative humidity). Therefore, if water vapor remains constant, relative humidity will decrease as the temperature rises. Conversely, relative humidity will increase as temperatures decline. If air coming in contact with a cold surface causes the temperature to fall to the point where relative humidity becomes 100%, the water vapor condenses (becomes liquid), resulting in nighttime condensation in the greenhouse, morning dew, or the beads of moisture on a glass containing a cold drink. Humidity records do not reflect the influence of a plant's microclimate. Higher relative humidity is generally found near streams, in marshes, or in dense undergrowth.

Even when relative humidity above 75–90% is indicated by the climate table, a midafternoon reading of 50% is usually appropriate, though the ideal level depends to a large extent on the diurnal range in the greenhouse. Optimum relative humidity is generally as high as possible during the day, short of levels that produce condensation as temperatures decline. Each grower will need to devise his or her own optimum midday humidity levels.

If low humidity is a problem, moisture in the greenhouse can be increased by using evaporative coolers, spraying the floor, or misting the air. Humidity can be increased in a small area, or in the home, by using humidity trays. These should be larger in diameter than the plants. Heavy wire mesh may be used to keep the plants above the water, or the trays may be filled with gravel so that the pots never stand in water.

A plant's ability to utilize water vapor directly from the air depends upon the temperature. Absorption is most efficient when temperatures are 43–82°F (6–28°C), with optimum efficiency at 70°F (21°C). Outside this temperature range, the capacity for absorption decreases rapidly.

Recommended relative humidity levels may be designated as follows:

Very high	*80% or more*	*Intermediate*	*50–70%*
High	*70–80%*	*Low*	*Below 50%*

Seedlings will be healthiest when grown at the highest humidity levels indicated for the species.

WATER: *Water requirements for the species.* These are indicated by the rainfall patterns shown in the climate tables, which should be approximated in cultivation. The cycles need not be exact, and growers should modify them to meet their plants' needs. However, if wet/dry cycles exist in nature, cultivated plants will benefit from a dry period, or at least a drier rest.

Orchids should generally be kept moist during the growing season. Overwatering can be fatal since air around the roots is just as vital as moisture. Both overwatering and deteriorating medium result in insufficient air around the roots, creating a situation conducive to root rot. It is particularly important to avoid excess water when temperatures or light levels are low.

As a general rule, potted orchids should be watered or misted weekly to biweekly in winter unless they require a dry rest, in which case they should be misted only enough to prevent desiccation. Watering should be increased to approximately twice weekly during periods of active growth. Plants mounted on slabs or rafts require daily misting during dry winter weather, while they may need misting several times a day during hot, dry summer weather.

Warmer temperatures, higher light, and lower relative humidity all increase a plant's need for moisture. The opposite is also true: high relative humidity, low light, and low temperatures all reduce the need for water at the roots. Optimal frequency of watering varies with the species, the season, and the environment.

The average relative humidity in the growing area is an excellent indication of the total moisture available to the plants. Since midday readings are normally the lowest and the first to reflect a decline in available moisture, growers use them most often to show when plants need water. For example, if midday readings have averaged 50% but suddenly fall to 35–40%, the grower knows that the plants will benefit from an immediate increase in humidity. This can be achieved by misting the greenhouse walks or running an evaporative cooler. In addition, the grower should plan a thorough watering for the following morning.

The following tips on watering may be helpful to growers:

- Water or mist plants early in the morning. This helps prevent disease by allowing the foliage to dry before evening.

- In winter, water on mornings when the day will be bright and sunny.

- If plants become too dry, water them several times in quick succession until the medium is resaturated.

- Water plants in new medium often. New medium drains rapidly, providing better root aeration, but it requires more frequent watering.

- Decrease water slightly as the medium ages and begins breaking down.

- Do not mist leaves if light levels are high. Water droplets refract and intensify the light, which may cause tissue damage.

- Never use chemically softened water, as the salts used in the softening process accumulate in the pot and may kill the plant.

- Use water that is slightly acid (5.5–5.8 pH), which most orchids prefer.

- Water plants in small pots faithfully, since they dry out more rapidly than those in larger pots, seedling trays, or community pots.

- Water seedlings and young plants carefully. They should never be allowed to dry out.

FERTILIZER: *Recommended strength, plus type and frequency of application.* Excess fertilizer is more harmful to orchids than a slight deficiency, particularly when light levels are low or the plants are dry. Symptoms of nutrient and trace-element deficiencies are discussed in depth in Appendix A.

Essential plant nutrients are classified as either macronutrients or micronutrients. Macronutrients, required in relatively large amounts, include carbon (C), hydrogen (H), and oxygen (O), which are available directly from the atmosphere, together with nitrogen (N), phosphorus (P), and potassium (K), which are usually applied as fertilizer. The last 3 nutrients are listed as percentages in the above order on commercial fertilizer containers. Thus, 30–20–10 contains 30% nitrogen, 20% phosphorus, and 10% potassium, while 10–10–10 contains equal parts of these elements. Other nutrients required in moderately large amounts are calcium (Ca), magnesium (Mg), and sulfur (S).

Micronutrients, or trace minerals, are also necessary for good plant growth, but in much smaller amounts—sometimes in quantities as small as a few parts per billion. These trace minerals include boron (B), chlorine (Cl), cobalt (Co), copper (Cu), iron (Fe), manganese (Mn), molybdenum (Mo), and zinc (Zn). Organic media usually provide sufficient trace elements for orchids, but some growers prefer to make an application of trace minerals in spring and another in midsummer. Growers using non-organic media should either select a fertilizer containing trace elements or periodically apply trace minerals, since they are not otherwise available to the plants. Most commercial fertilizers formulated for indoor plants contain trace minerals even though they may not be listed on the label. (Fertilizer labeling laws in the United States require manufacturers to guarantee the analysis shown on the label. Because the manufacturers are reluctant to guarantee the exact levels of micronutrients, they simply do not list them.)

Plants grown in soft-water areas are more likely to benefit from applications of trace elements than those grown in hard-water areas. Extreme caution should be exercised when applying supplementary trace minerals since an excessive amount can do more damage than a deficiency. Trace elements should never be applied at a higher rate or more frequently than recommended.

Fertilizing dry plants may cause root damage. This can be avoided by always saturating the medium before applying fertilizer, or by using very dilute solutions.

An unhealthy salt buildup is also indicated by discolored root-tips or by white deposits on the leaves or the surface of the pot. A potentially toxic salt accumulation may be prevented by allowing some water (10% of the volume of the pot) to drain through each time the plant is watered, and by flushing or leaching the medium with large quantities of water every few weeks. Plants growing in hard-water areas may be healthier if the pots are flushed more frequently. Species extremely sensitive to salt accumulations may be flushed at every watering.

The pot should be watered at least an hour before it is to be flushed, allowing time for moisture to dissolve the salt crystals. Then an amount of water equal to twice the volume of the pot should be run through the pot. For example, a 6 in. (15 cm) pot holds approximately 2.5 qts. (2.4 liters) of water, so 5 qts. (4.7 liters) should be used to flush the pot. Flushing should be done before fertilizer is applied.

Since orchids are supremely efficient at absorbing nutrients, all fertilizers must be applied in weak solutions. They should be mixed at 10–50% of the strength recommended for garden plants.

Orchid growers in the Northern Hemisphere are sharply divided over the use of organic fertilizers. This will surprise growers from other parts of the world, who use dilute manure tea almost exclusively for both terrestrial and epiphytic orchids. The key to success with any fertilizer is sufficient dilution. Different types of fertilizers have distinct advantages and disadvantages.

Organic fertilizers are particularly beneficial since they contain natural trace minerals, they are less likely to destroy helpful microorganisms, and they reduce the risk of salt buildup. However, growers may find the odor objectionable. Commercial compounds such as fish fertilizer should be mixed at $\frac{1}{4}$–$\frac{1}{2}$ the recommended strength, or $\frac{1}{10}$ the recommended strength if used as a foliar spray. Manure tea is recommended by many growers, but it is difficult to ascertain the strength of the dilution. As a consequence, organic fertilizers are frequently mixed and applied at or near garden-plant strength, causing severe injury to orchids.

Composted manure (the type purchased in bags at gardening stores) may be made into manure tea as follows. These guidelines do not apply when using fresh manure.

• Measure the small amount of composted manure necessary to produce fertilizer of the desired strength.

  1 tsp. per gal. (3.8 liters) is approximately equivalent to commercial fertilizer mixed at $\frac{1}{10}$ tsp. per gal. (3.8 liters).

  2.5 tsp. per gal. (3.8 liters) is approximately equivalent to commercial fertilizer mixed at $\frac{1}{4}$ tsp. per gal. (3.8 liters).

5 tsp. per gal. (3.8 liters) is approximately equivalent to commercial fertilizer mixed at ½ tsp. per gal. (3.8 liters).

- Mix the manure with 1 cup (236 ml) of water, and allow it to steep overnight or longer.
- Strain the liquid, then add enough water to make 1 gal. (3.8 liters) of fertilizer solution.

The following ratios of nitrogen, phosphate, and potassium are approximate values for manure of different types.

Manure	% Nitrogen	% Phosphate	% Potassium
Chicken	30	14	7
Cow	10	3	8
Hog	13	7	11
Horse	15	5	13

Chemical compounds are readily available, clean, odorless, and easier to dilute to a specified level. However, if used in excess, they destroy microorganisms critical to plant health, and they are more likely to result in excessive salt buildup.

Delayed-release fertilizers should not be used with most orchids.

REST PERIOD: *Recommended conditions during the resting phase of the annual growth cycle.* As always, changes in growing conditions should be introduced gradually, allowing the plants time to adjust. Some species are healthiest if growing conditions are maintained year-round, while for other species a rest period is as vital as light, air, or water. Since rest-period conditions often induce the formation of flowers, information on bloom initiators is also included here.

When an unusually cool or unusually dry rest period is indicated by the climate in the species' native habitat, the plants may be healthier in cultivation if given a rest not quite so long, so dry, or so cold. In fact, the microclimate in the native habitat may prevent exposure to extreme conditions. Plants in the wild normally have extremely long roots which collect and store moisture when it is available, whereas cultivated plants have shorter roots which provide less insurance against drought.

Fertilizer should always be reduced during the rest period. Plants need less food when they are not actively growing or when light levels are low. In addition, they use nitrogen less efficiently when temperatures are cool. Continued applications of fer-

tilizer during the rest period only contribute to salt buildup in the medium and do not benefit the plant.

Whether orchids require a rest period is another subject on which growers are sharply divided. In our view, if a plant is growing and blooming well, the growing conditions should not be changed whatever they happen to be. However, when a plant is not thriving, conditions should be altered in the direction indicated by the climate in the plant's native habitat.

The relationship between temperature and water is critical. If plants which adapt to a variety of conditions are grown in warm temperatures, then watering should be continued but perhaps reduced during winter. *If temperatures are cool, water must be reduced.* As a general rule, the cooler the temperatures, the lower the plant's water requirements.

Growers in tropical and subtropical regions may instinctively take advantage of microclimates in their growing area by placing cool-growing plants near an evaporative cooler, by placing low-light species under a bench, by reducing water in winter when days are cooler, by increasing diurnal range through less intensive heating or cooling, by removing shading in winter, and by tending to select species which do well in their conditions. All these techniques may be applied deliberately when cultivating subtropical to temperate-zone orchids in warm climates.

Growers in cooler regions also use microclimates in their growing areas by placing plants requiring high light near a south (or north in the Southern Hemisphere) wall, by setting cool-growing plants near the floor and warm-growing plants near a heater, by reducing water dramatically when humidity is high, and by choosing to grow plants which do well in their area. Again, these are techniques that growers may apply deliberately.

Many orchids which grow well where nights are warm may also grow well at cooler temperatures. While low-altitude equatorial species are unlikely to survive drying, cold nights, or a wide diurnal range, others, such as high-altitude species of *Pleione*, simply will not survive without a cool, dry rest, and many *Cymbidium* species will not bloom without cooler temperatures or an increase in diurnal range. Reading about attempts by growers in low-elevation, tropical climates to induce flowering in cool-growing *Cymbidium* by icing their plants is enough to bring a smile to a temperate-zone grower, while endless discussions regarding techniques for maintaining warm night temperatures are of little interest to growers closer to the equator.

Greenhouse heating costs are a definite concern for most growers in seasonal, temperate latitudes, just as cooling is a consideration for growers in hot climates. By concentrating on adaptable species or those that require the least heating or cooling, growers can dramatically reduce overhead costs. For example, in the maritime Pacific Northwest region of the United States and Canada, the cost of heating increases 3–5% for each additional 1°F (0.6°C) of heat maintained in winter, which means that if plants will grow well at 50°F (10°C) but a minimum temperature of 60°F (15.6°C) is being maintained, the cost of heating the greenhouse is 30–50% higher than it needs to be. Growers in other parts of the world or in other climatic regions may have a different cost basis, but the principle is the same and applies to the costs of summer cooling as well.

GROWING MEDIA: *Recommended media and repotting schedules, based on reports from successful growers.* Growers in different areas use various media, their choice frequently reflecting local availability and cost. No one medium is ideal for all plants or for growers in every area. Mixes that work well in dry climates may retain too much water for areas with high relative humidity, while mixes designed to encourage rapid drainage in a moist environment may cause similar plants to become desiccated in areas with low atmospheric moisture.

A medium must drain quickly so that roots are never soggy, but it should retain enough moisture to keep the roots damp between waterings. A rapidly draining medium is preferable in areas with high relative humidity, while a moisture-retaining medium is advantageous in areas with low atmospheric moisture.

A single-ingredient medium is generally easier to manage than a mixture. Also, equally sized particles provide more air circulation than mixtures of fine and coarse materials, since the smaller pieces fill the air spaces between larger chunks.

The acidity or alkalinity of an orchid medium, indicated by its pH, is a variable often overlooked by growers, although it may play a critical role in whether a plant does well in a particular medium.

Under acid conditions, some nutrients, including calcium, phosphorus, and magnesium, undergo chemical changes allowing them to combine with other elements, thereby forming compounds which make them unavailable to the plants. As a result, plants grown in an overly acid environment may be deficient in these nutrients. Other nutrients become more available to plants under acid conditions. Manganese and aluminum, for instance, are so highly soluble in an acid environment that a plant may absorb them in toxic levels. Deficiencies may occur when some nutrients are displaced by excessive quantities of other nutrients, rather than as a result of an actual shortage.

Excessive alkalinity also affects the availability of nutrients. Deficiencies of boron, copper, iron, manganese, phosphorus, and zinc are common in alkaline soils.

The pH scale is the standard means of indicating the relative acidity or alkalinity of any substance. The scale ranges from 0 (acid) to 14 (alkaline), with 7 being neutral. It is logarithmic, like the Richter scale used to indicate the strength of an earthquake. Consequently, a pH of 5 is 10 times more acid than a pH of 6, and 100 times more acid than a pH of 7.

Technically, pH indicates the concentration of hydrogen ions in a given amount of water rather than the acidity of the medium itself. Thus, in the case of plant medium, what is actually measured is the number of hydrogen ions that can move from the medium to the water which clings to the surface of that medium.

The range of pH that is normally of interest to most plant growers is 5–8 (pH 5.5–6.5 for orchid growers). However, some orchid species grow in very acid habitats with readings as low as 3.5.

Very little work has been done relative to the pH requirements of individual orchid species, but descriptions of the natural habitat often give clues to the acidity or alkalinity in the plants' microclimate. Acidic or low pH conditions may be indicated by the presence of certain plants, such as moss, mountain laurel, oak trees, pitcher plants, and rhododendrons. In general, acid habitats tend to be wet: bogs and marshes are usually the most acid. At the other extreme, alkalinity or high pH is common in dry areas. Under extremely alkaline conditions, mineral salt deposits may form a surface crust. In most cases, alkaline soils occur when the base material is high in lime.

Soil pH is normally measured by adding distilled (neutral) water equal to 2.5 times the volume of the soil being tested, then obtaining a value using either a pH meter or litmus paper. This technique is not practical when dealing with orchid potting materials such as chunky bark or cork, but if the material is pulverized, it might be used. An alternate technique is to collect the water that runs out of the pot (since what matters is the pH at the roots) and to measure its pH.

The pH may be adjusted when a plant's pH requirement is known. Water may safely be acidified by adding citric acid at the rate of approximately $1/4$–$1/3$ tsp. per gal. of water (250 mg per liter) until the desired pH is reached. Potting medium may be made less acid by sprinkling dolomite lime on the surface of the pot.

The acidity in fir bark or sphagnum is desirable for most orchids, which generally prefer an acidic medium. When using an inert medium, it is best to select a fertilizer that provides the proper acidity. It should be noted that the medium becomes more acid as decomposition takes place. Consequently, plant growth often slows as a medium breaks down. This occurs not only because air is less available to the roots, but also because the medium may become too acid for the plant to utilize nutrients properly.

Commonly used media are listed below, with observations on the advantages and disadvantages of each.

Activated charcoal retains moisture, does not break down, improves aeration, absorbs excess salts and chemical contaminants, and helps produce a healthier plant when added to potting mixes. Some growers feel that charcoal absorbs salts and chemical contaminants so efficiently that in time, water released by the charcoal may be toxic to the plant. They recommend replacing the charcoal every year. *Vanda* and *Oncidium* species are sometimes grown in charcoal alone, but 10–20% charcoal and 80–90% other ingredients is a more usual ratio for most orchids.

Coconut husks and fiber work well in the tropics but for unknown reasons are less satisfactory in temperate-zone greenhouses. This material retains large amounts of moisture and contains high levels of nutrients, so that additional fertilizer is not needed. The fibers tend to become tightly packed, restricting aeration.

Cork slabs and nuggets are often used with orchids that must dry out between waterings. The cork may be mixed with activated charcoal. It breaks down slowly unless attacked by insects such as sow bugs and millipedes, which pulverize it in short order. The best results are reported in temperate zones, because cork often breaks down within a year in warm climates.

Cypress-bark slabs are used for mounting orchids. The material is decay-resistant.

Fir bark, with a pH of 5, is the most frequently used medium in North America because it is readily available and moderately inexpensive. In tropical climates, however, it tends to break down rapidly. Bark is available in graded sizes; as a general rule, the finer a plant's roots or the higher a plant's moisture needs, the smaller the bark should be. Before it is used for potting, bark should be soaked in water at least 3 hours, and preferably 24 hours, to allow it to absorb moisture. Watering dry bark after potting is not sufficient. If bark alone dries out too quickly, then perlite, sphagnum moss, or chopped tree-fern may be added at a ratio of approximately 4 parts bark to 1 part moisture-retentive medium.

Gravel and lava rock permit rapid drying, but plants in these media must be faithfully watered. They also require a complete fertilizer which includes trace minerals. Many epiphytic orchids will grow in almost anything that provides excellent drainage.

Oak or beech leaves are sometimes added to terrestrial mixes. The leaves are collected fresh and should be shredded before they are added to the medium. The addition of fibrous loam or screened, composted manure (not garden soil) is also suggested for these mixes, but these ingredients break down in about 6 months so should be used in a small quantity relative to coarse grit or sand.

Osmunda is acid, with a pH of 4.3. The woody-fibered root of the osmunda fern, it was used almost exclusively for many years, but it has become prohibitively expensive. It provides a good balance of air and water, breaks down slowly, and supplies many nutrients. In fact, when this medium is used, fertilizer should not be applied more than once a month. On the negative side, it is somewhat difficult to repot plants in osmunda without damaging the roots. The medium should be soaked before it is used for potting.

Peat moss, ancient sphagnum from peat beds, is normally acid, with a pH of 3.5–5.0, but is sometimes almost neutral. It is available in milled, coarse, or chunky forms. The moss itself contains few nutrients. Once moist, it can hold 10–20 times its weight in water; but when dry it tends to shed water, making it difficult to remoisten. It is sometimes included in terrestrial mixes but is seldom used with epiphytic orchids except as chunks..

Perlite (sponge rock), with a pH of 7.0–7.5, increases both water retention and aeration. It contains no essential elements and does not hold nutrients. Perlite does not decompose, helps keep the medium open, and holds amazing quantities of water on its surface. This water is released as the surrounding medium dries out and is available when the plant needs moisture. The perlite stays cool in a warm environment, which should be helpful for plants requiring cooler temperatures.

Perlite is available in several sizes, but coarse or chunky forms known as sponge rock are most often used for orchids. Perlite should be purchased with care since fluoride levels range from 1–17%, and high fluoride is toxic, causing severe leaf-tip burn. Perlite is frequently included as an additive to increase water retention. Increasingly, it is being used alone, and growers report excellent root growth in this medium. A complete fertilizer with trace minerals should be used for plants in perlite, as with other non-organic media.

Redwood bark is very acid, with a pH of 3.5, which inhibits fungus growth. It is sometimes used as a medium but is more often a component in mixes. It absorbs moisture rapidly and stays very wet. The pH may be raised by adding a mixture of 50% dolomite lime and 50% powdered oyster shell at the rate of ½ lb. per cubic ft. of medium (8 kg per cubic m).

Rice hulls, with a pH of approximately 5.5, are often included in medium mixes, though they become too tightly packed when used alone. The hulls break down slowly, keep terrestrial mixes open, retain moisture, and provide a long-lasting source of potassium. Rice hulls have proved particularly beneficial in seedling mixes.

Rock wool is sterile, has a pH of 5.5, and does not decompose. It is available in several forms with varying capacities for holding and repelling water. Insects and snails avoid the material, but mice love it. When shredded rock wool is used, it is usually mixed by volume with 30% styrofoam beads, which help keep it from becoming too tightly packed. Covering the surface of the pot with small gravel helps prevent the growth of moss or foul-smelling black algae which may grow on the rock wool.

Plants in this non-organic medium must be fertilized faithfully during periods of active growth, and trace minerals should also be applied 1 or 2 times during the summer. However, determining the appropriate fertilizer can be difficult. Urea-based fertilizers are washed out before breaking down enough to be used by the plant. Reports indicate that during dark winter weather, fertilizer is absorbed, changing the electrical conductivity and doubling the strength of the fertilizer.

Sphagnum moss, with a pH of 3.5, is frequently recommended as a medium, and both live and dried strands are used with orchids. While sphagnum may be used alone for some species, it tends to become tightly packed, so it is usually cut into short pieces and mixed with other ingredients such as perlite or tree fern.

When live sphagnum is included in the potting mix, baskets are highly recommended, but white or translucent plastic pots may also be used. The diffused light transmitted by the light-colored plastic is needed to keep the moss inside the pot alive. In dark pots, only the surface layer of moss continues to live. Both chlorine and concentrated fertilizers kill the moss. Watering with rainwater eliminates the problem, and tap water may be used if it has been held in an open container at least 24 hours, allowing the chlorine to escape from the water.

When the moss is kept alive, it produces natural fertilizers adequate for most orchids, and many growers use no additional fertilizer. If fertilizer is added, the plants should be foliar fed with a dilute solution (0.1 tsp. per gal. or 3.8 liters) of fish fertilizer or an equally dilute solution of manure tea. Chemical fertilizer may be used as a foliar feed, but it is more damaging to the moss than organic fertilizers. Even dilute fertilizers should not be applied directly to the moss.

Orchids appear to benefit from the use of live sphagnum moss, providing that the plant needs the constant moisture necessary to keep the moss alive. Sphagnum works well where low humidity is a problem, particularly if coarse perlite or charcoal is added to increase aeration and drainage. It is an excellent medium for species with high annual rainfall in their natural habitats. Live moss tends to become tightly packed when used alone, so most growers prefer to mix it with other ingredients.

Live sphagnum moss is extremely useful in revitalizing weak or sickly plants or establishing back bulbs or small plant divisions. To treat a weak plant, soak it in Natriphene* for an hour or more, then place it on top of live moss in a clear, covered container or plastic bag with optimum growing temperatures for the species. This treatment is often very successful. It was formerly thought that the acidity of sphagnum helped prevent disease, but there are indications that the live moss may also produce a beneficial natural fungicide.

Tree-fern fiber, from large, tropical tree ferns, is frequently used with good success, either alone or mixed with other media. This material is slow to break down even in warm climates, and though it appears very porous, it holds a surprising amount of water. It should not be used for species that require rapid drying. Like fir bark, it should be soaked before it is used for potting.

Vermiculite is an expanded mica that holds tremendous quantities of water for long periods of time. It has a neutral pH of 6.5–7.2, is light and sterile, and contains a high level of magnesium and potassium. It can be a beneficial addition to terrestrial mixes for plants which live in bogs, experience flooding, or require constant moisture. It stays too wet, however, to be suitable for use with most epiphytic orchids. Fertilizer should be decreased if vermiculite is used, since this medium absorbs large quantities of nutrients whenever fertilizer is applied. Small quantities of vermiculite in seedling mixes could help prevent the media from drying out. Horticultural-grade vermiculite should be used since other grades may be excessively alkaline.

Walnut shells mixed with charcoal and perlite are used successfully by some growers. Nut shells should be avoided in areas with soft water and high humidity, where they rapidly deteriorate and become covered with a fungal growth which prevents air from reaching the roots.

Orchids are usually grown in pots or baskets, but pendent plants and those requiring additional air circulation are healthier if mounted on rafts or hanging plaques if humidity is high or the plant is misted faithfully. Rafts are plaques which are laid horizontally on the bench.

A variety of containers are used for potting, including open baskets, unglazed clay pots, and most commonly, plastic pots. Each type of container has advantages and disadvantages. Baskets allow the greatest air circulation and dry most rapidly. Clay pots provide some evaporative cooling and some air transfer through the porous clay; because of their weight, they are preferable for top-heavy plants. Plastic pots are lightweight and easy to clean and sterilize for reuse. However, when plastic is used, moisture retention may be excessive and air circulation is poor. The pot used to hold a medium is usually not critical, though some species do poorly without ample air to the roots, while others do poorly if allowed to dry out.

Plastic pots should be modified with extra drainage holes to increase air circulation and prevent the medium from becoming stale. The extra holes can easily be punched with a hot soldering iron. Because the fumes are noxious, this should be done outside or in a well-ventilated area. A 4 in. (10 cm) pot should

---

* Throughout this volume, mention of a trademark or proprietary product does not constitute a guarantee or warranty of the product by the publisher or authors and does not imply its approval to the exclusion of other products.

have about 1 sq. in. (2–3 sq. cm) of drainage, or 8–9 holes ⅜ in. (1 cm) in diameter. A 6 in. (15 cm) pot needs drainage increased to about 2 sq. in. (5 sq. cm) or about 20 holes. Increasing root aeration will probably eliminate most problems associated with root rot.

Repotting is best done when the plant resumes active growth in the spring or summer, preferably just as new roots begin to grow, but it is sometimes delayed until immediately after flowering. Exceptions are noted for individual species. Generally, if new leaves are growing, so are the roots. Withholding water for a few days before repotting makes the roots of most species more flexible and less prone to injury. After repotting, plants should be rested without food or water for 7–10 days, which will allow any bruised or broken roots to heal. During this period, the foliage may be misted if necessary to prevent desiccation. When watering is resumed, using a hormone and vitamin B-1 solution such as Superthrive will encourage new growth.

Most orchids respond well to new medium and grow more vigorously if repotted annually. The inevitable exceptions are noted for individual species. Orchids generally outgrow their pots in 18–24 months, which is about how long fir bark lasts before breaking down. Some growers suggest mixing about 20% old medium with 80% new bark to increase the moisture retention of the new mix. However, medium should not be reused unless it has been sterilized or is known to be free from disease and insects.

Seedlings should be potted in a relatively fine medium such as ⅛–¼ in. (3–6 mm) bark, and they will grow most rapidly if repotted annually. Physan should not be used when deflasking as it adversely affects some seedlings.

MISCELLANEOUS NOTES: *Supplementary information.*

Orchid diseases are treated comprehensively in Appendix A.

Sterilizing is the best means of preventing disease, which is frequently transmitted from plant to plant by repotting in contaminated pots. Tools and fingernails may also carry disease pathogens. Through careless cultural practices, growers may carry diseases from one plant to another, often without realizing that a plant being cut or examined is diseased. Fingernails are frequently the culprit.

Everything that comes in contact with a diseased plant should be sterilized before each reuse. Sterilization procedures are discussed in detail in Appendix A under the heading "Preventing Disease."

Mineral or fertilizer salt deposits on pots or humidity trays may be dissolved with oxalic acid, which is available from commercial janitorial suppliers. Once the deposits have been dissolved, the pots and trays should be rinsed and sterilized.

Mycorrhizae play an important but little-understood role in orchid culture. The seeds of virtually all plant genera contain nutrients adequate to sustain the plantlets through the stages of germination and production of their first true leaves, after which time the seedlings can produce adequate food supplies independently. Orchid seeds, however, are tiny and contain none of the nutrients necessary for the seedlings to survive. As a consequence, following germination, the developing protocorms are totally dependent upon fungi to supply their food until they are able to produce their own through photosynthesis.

This unusual characteristic of orchid seed, the essential mycorrhizae, and the symbiotic relation between the two became apparent when growers found that orchid seeds grew only when sown around a mature plant. The seedlings needed to be infected with fungus from the adult plant in order to obtain food for survival. The situation changed when a sterile germinating method was developed. Growers using this technique provide nutrients the protocorm can use directly, thereby eliminating the need for fungi.

More recently, plant scientists have discovered that mycorrhizae are essential to the health and survival of many higher order plants. In fact, as research on this topic is extended, it appears that essentially all higher plants require and develop symbiotic relationships with one or more mycorrhizal species. At present, however, we have little information on the specific requirements of adult orchids.

Plant scientists know that protocorms cannot survive without the fungi, and that the relationship continues throughout the life of the orchid. But research has not yet revealed whether the relationship is necessary for the health or survival of mature orchids, since attempts to confirm this have been inconclusive. Interesting questions have been raised, and avenues of speculation opened; but additional research will be necessary before we know whether plant-mycorrhizal relationships play an important role in orchid culture.

If information bearing on the mycorrhizae associated with particular orchid species becomes available, it will be included in species listings under "Miscellaneous Notes."

Plant and Flower Information

PLANT SIZE AND TYPE: *General information on size and growth habit*. Like the information under "Cultural Recommendations," the information in this section has been especially tailored to the needs of growers. Because growers are not ordinarily concerned with fractional measurements, all figures have been rounded to the nearest whole number. Measurements are given in inches with metric equivalents in parentheses.

Measurements of plant size refer to the vegetative growths and do not include the height of the inflorescence. When a plant's growth habit is such that a height measurement is not an appropriate indicator of size (as for *Phalaenopsis)*, the plant is described as "large," "moderate," or "small" in relation to other members of the same genus.

Plants are identified as sympodial (having multiple growths) or monopodial (having a single growth) and as epiphytic (tree-growing), lithophytic (rock-growing), or terrestrial (ground-growing). Because size is influenced by maturity, adaptability, and growing environment, cultivated plants may be various sizes and still be healthy.

Poor overall growth usually indicates a cultural problem. It is frequently the result of root deterioration caused by overwatering, insufficient air to the roots because of deteriorated medium, or salt buildup. Unhealthy plants should be unpotted and examined carefully. Damaged roots should be removed, the plant repotted in new medium, and attention paid to providing the best possible environment for the species. When a plant's root system is inadequate or the environment is too cool, the plant may be unable to utilize available food. Unfortunately, growers often respond to poor growth by increasing water and fertilizer, which not only fails to solve the problem but compounds it by contributing to salt buildup.

The following plant and root abnormalities indicate common cultural problems. (See Appendix A for a more complete list of symptoms indicating problems with pathogens, pests, or nutrients.)

Black root-tips are usually caused by salt buildup.

Discolored root-tips indicate damage from salt buildup.

Hard, wrinkled plants result from high light and inadequate moisture.

Poorly developed roots may occur when trace minerals are inadequate.

Root rot is a common and very serious problem caused by overwatering. It often occurs when the medium breaks down and watering is not decreased. Since damaged roots provide an entry point for disease organisms, symptoms of root rot may first be noticed on other plant parts. Anytime a symptom might be related to root deterioration, the plant should be removed from the pot and the roots checked for rot. If the roots are soft or black, all damaged areas should be trimmed back to healthy tissue, and the plant should be soaked in Natriphene at least an hour. After a thorough soaking, the plant should be repotted in fresh medium.

Short roots may indicate excessive water or fertilizer.

Smaller new growths are more likely to result from inappropriate growing conditions than from insufficient fertilizer.

Soft plants may result if light is too low, if humidity is too high, or if too much nitrogen has been given. Such plants seem to be more prone to attack by disease organisms.

PSEUDOBULB: *Length and general description*. This category is omitted from the listings when all members of a genus are monopodial or without pseudobulbs, but it is included if any plants in the genus have pseudobulbs. When a species grows directly from a rhizome or the root ball, without a pseudobulb, "N/A" indicates that the category of information is not applicable.

Wrinkled pseudobulbs indicate water deprivation over a prolonged period. Newer pseudobulbs will become plump when adequate moisture is available to the plant, but older back bulbs may remain wrinkled. With time, back bulbs eventually lose

LEAVES: *Number, size, and general appearance.* Size measurements refer to length or height rather than width. Leaf information was usually derived from taxonomic descriptions, but information from other sources is also included.

Leaf size and appearance frequently provide the first indication that a plant is stressed. Most successful growers pay very close attention to their plants, examining them frequently in order to observe the first, subtle indications of problems. Every grower would do well to follow this practice, since many problems are easily corrected if detected early.

The following symptoms signal common cultural difficulties. (See Appendix A for a more comprehensive list of symptoms indicating problems with pathogens, pests, or nutrients.)

A brown, discolored patch, usually round, on a curved leaf surface is probably the result of sunburn. The damaged area should be removed, as it offers a point of entry for disease organisms.

Dark green or limp leaves often indicate that the plant is receiving insufficient light or too much nitrogen.

Discolored or damaged leaf surfaces may be caused by ethylene gas but usually result from spider-mite damage.

Heavy leaf loss on orchids that are normally evergreen is a sign of significant stress. But even plants that have lost all their leaves may recover providing their roots are still healthy and they are given the treatment described under "Growing Media" above.

Leaf-tip die-back occurs when insufficient moisture reaches the leaves. The obvious solution is to water more frequently. However, inadequate moisture to the leaves may also occur if the plant has been overwatered to the point of causing root loss. Treatment is suggested above, in the discussion of root rot under "Plant Size and Type."

Leaf-tip die-back also results from hard water, overfertilization, and excessive salt buildup. Excessive salts become concentrated in the tips of the leaves. If the salts have formed white deposits on the leaves, pot, or medium, salt buildup is the most likely cause of the leaf-tip problem.

Pale, yellow-green leaves usually result from high light or insufficient nitrogen. High light is the probable cause if the leaves also appear somewhat dry or wrinkled. Nitrogen deficiency is indicated when the older leaves become yellow. This may result either from an inadequate supply of nitrogen or from a cultural problem which limits the plant's ability to use this nutrient. Possible causes include root damage, cool temperatures, or imbalance of plant nutrients. Rarely, high levels of ethylene gas cause similar symptoms. Ethylene gas is discussed under the heading "Flowers" below, since symptoms of contamination are usually noticed first as *sepal wilt* in the blossoms.

Red-tinged leaves often indicate that the plant has been exposed to maximum light levels, and additional light could be extremely harmful.

Small leaves on normally large-leaved species may indicate a lack of nitrogen, root loss, or damage from salt buildup.

Spotting on the leaves is usually caused by a fungus (see Appendix A).

Wrinkled or hard leaves result when light levels are excessive or watering is insufficient.

INFLORESCENCE: *Length and appearance of the flower spike.* When a species produces multiple spikes per growth, this information is noted.

The following abnormalities in the flower spike signal cultural problems.

Crooked inflorescences may result if a plant's orientation to the light source is changed while the spike is growing, as the spikes usually grow toward the light.

Excessively long spikes may indicate that light is insufficient.

Unusually short spikes may indicate excessively high light levels.

Seedlings will be healthier if the first flower spike is removed soon after the flowers open, directing the plant's energy towards growth rather than maintaining an early bloom.

FLOWERS: *Approximate number of blooms per inflorescence, size of blossoms, and general appearance.* All information refers to flowers on a healthy, mature plant.

When exact bloom counts are not available, relative number is indicated by a term such as "few" or "many." Unless otherwise noted, diameter measurements are given for flower size.

Descriptions of shape, general form, texture, and color are based on information from a variety of sources. These are not intended to describe any particular flower but merely to indicate what might be expected.

This section also includes information on whether buds open simultaneously or sequentially as well as any available information on how long the blooms generally last.

Reported fragrance is described when possible. Fragrance is frequently dependent on light, temperature, and time of day as well as personal preferences and individual sensitivity to particular scents. A fragrance that is nearly overpowering to one person may be only faintly detectable to another, just as a fragrance that is pleasant for one may be unpleasant for another.

Intense flower color is more likely when light levels at the high end of the appropriate range are combined with temperatures at the low end of the appropriate range. Once flowers are open, a combination of lower light and cooler temperatures helps the blooms stay in good condition. When plants are grown under artificial lights, flower color in some species may be somewhat muddy rather than bright and clear.

Flowers, like other plant parts, may hold clues to the plant's health. The following symptoms indicate culture-related problems which make a plant more susceptible to disease or insect damage.

Black spots or streaks on flower sheaths are caused by a fungus that may also rot the flower buds. Affected sheaths should be removed, and the buds treated with a contact fungicide (see Appendix A). Buds will normally continue to develop unless they have also been infected. Infection may be prevented by increasing air circulation, keeping humidity somewhat low, and avoiding overhead watering when plants are in sheath.

Brown spots on the blossoms may be caused by water droplets as a result of careless watering or condensation resulting from excessively high humidity.

Bud drop may be caused by ethylene gas (see *sepal wilt* below) but is more likely to result from low light, wide temperature fluctuations, low relative humidity, or temperature shock, which often results from the use of water colder than the environment. The water used for warm-growing species should be at least 62°F (17°C).

Lack of blooms usually results from inappropriate growing conditions. Unfortunately, the precise bloom triggers have not been determined for most orchid species. The individual climate table and the discussion of bloom initiators included in species listings will hopefully assist in determining the most probable critical factor.

Malformed flowers are often caused by exposure to harmful chemicals, but they may also be caused by genetic disorders which cannot be corrected.

Rapid, premature wilting of flowers results when the flowers are pollinated or the pollinia are removed by insects or by accident.

Sepal wilt is nearly always caused by ethylene gas, which is emitted as a result of incomplete combustion of an open flame. A defective heater is normally the source of the problem, but the gas is also produced in abundance by chrysanthemum flowers and ripening fruit, especially apples. In fact, all flowers produce some ethylene as they mature, and this gas causes them to wilt naturally with age. High levels will cause the blooms to age prematurely. Unopened buds are generally not affected unless contamination is severe.

Yellow buds in winter usually indicate inadequate light.

Insufficient winter rest may result in no blooms the following season. Temperature, light, and water cycles are often critical to a species' ability to initiate blooms. Some crop plants are known to require a specific number of hours during which temperatures are below a particular level before the plants produce the hormones necessary to initiate flowering. Other species require a sudden drop in temperatures, while still others depend on an alternating pattern of wet and dry periods.

Many plants respond to increases and decreases in seasonal light levels, which may result from seasonal fluctuations, a distinct pattern of clear days, or high average light levels (for example, some require at least 10 hours of bright light during winter). Because particular light wavelengths may be critical, some plants are difficult to grow under artificial lights. Even plants which need low light levels may require light for a minimum number of hours each day in winter. Light is available 11–13 hours a day throughout the year near the equator, while it may be available only 7 hours a day during midlatitude winters.

Recent research has shown that photoperiodicity may be defined more accurately as the plant's response to hours of darkness rather than its response to hours of light, as was previously thought. Some plants are unable to produce the hormones required to initiate blooms unless they spend the necessary number of hours in darkness. Although experiments have not been conducted with orchids, some species might fail to bloom if the growing area is exposed to nighttime light.

It is interesting to note that growers who supplement the hours of light in temperate latitudes report greater success when light is extended in late afternoon than when it is extended in the early morning.

Insufficient nutrients or trace minerals may result in a plant's being unable to produce flowers. However, fertilizer should not arbitrarily be increased until other environmental conditions have been carefully analyzed. The number of flowers produced by a weak plant normally declines over time.

HYBRIDIZING NOTES: *Chromosome counts and dominant hybridizing characteristics.* The length of time required for seeds to mature refers to the time necessary for the seeds to become sufficiently viable to be used in green-pod culture, which eliminates the need for presterilization. Changes in the appearance of the capsule may indicate that the seeds should be sown immediately; otherwise they will become contaminated and need to be sterilized before being flasked.

Using the climate tables as a guide, growers can select parent plants that will contribute tolerance of warm or cool temperatures to hybrids.

Because seeds may not be viable or pods may fall off prematurely, attempts to propagate plants may fail, particularly attempts to make intergeneric hybrids. Fred Hillerman, author of *An Introduction to the Cul-*

tivated Angraecoid *Orchids of Madagascar* (1986), developed the following technique, which reportedly improves the success rate and has helped him get viable seeds after numerous failed attempts.

- Following the normal procedure, remove the pollen from the pod parent, then load its stigma with pollen from the donor parent.
- Add a small amount of pollen from the receiving plant or its sibling to help prevent rejection.

Unfortunately, when using this technique, growers often cannot be certain that a cross has taken until the plants bloom. However, if the vegetative growth habits of the parents are quite different, the success or failure may be apparent when the seedlings develop leaves.

REFERENCES: *Numbers corresponding to entries in the Bibliography.* Readers seeking additional information may consult the selected sources listed at the close of this volume.

PHOTOS/DRAWINGS: *Numbers corresponding to entries in the Bibliography.* Here readers will find references to species illustrations. Italic type indicates that the photograph or drawing is reproduced in *color.* Standard type indicates a black-and-white photo or a botanical drawing. This category is not included in synonym listings or for species not recently collected.

Throughout this volume, "N/A" indicates that the information was not available or that the category of information was not applicable.

Synonyms and natural hybrids are listed separately in alphabetical order. Synonyms are followed by a cross-reference to the species or genus name that is now considered valid. Natural hybrid names are followed by a listing of the hybrid's parents.

2
Pescatorea
General Information

SUBFAMILY: Vandoidea.

TRIBE: *Maxillarieae*.

SUBTRIBE: *Zygopetalinae*.

GENUS: *Pescatorea* Rchb.f.

AKA: Most *Pescatorea* species were originally classified as *Zygopetalum*. In *Orchids of Panama*, Louis Williams and Paul Allen write that the separation of species in the closely allied genera of the *Zygopetalum* alliance, which includes *Bollea, Chondrorhyncha, Huntleya, Kefersteinia, Pescatorea, Warczewiczella, Zygopetalum*, and now *Zygosepalum*, is "considered by many to be a matter of individual opinion." Consequently, the species have been rearranged frequently over the years. An indication of how closely the genera are related is the natural hybridization between *Pescatorea klabochorum* and *Bollea coelestis*.

As our authority, we have used Dr. J. A. Fowlie's review of the genus *Pescatorea*, in *Key and Annotated Checklist to the Genus* Pescatorea in the April 1968 issue of *Orchid Digest*, pages 86–91.

SPECIES: In this small genus, only the 6 species described in detail in the following pages have been recently collected or are likely to be available for cultivation.

ORIGIN/HABITAT: The range for *Pescatorea* is quite limited, being confined to fairly similar habitats in Costa Rica, Panama, Colombia, and Ecuador.

CLIMATE: All species are found in tropical rainforest climates at moderately high elevations.

Cultural Recommendations

LIGHT: 2000–4000 fc, though some growers recommend light as high as 5000 fc. Light should always be diffused; sunburn on the leaves may cause serious injury. *Pescatorea* are better able to handle higher light when temperatures are appropriate for the species, moisture levels are high, and air circulation is excellent.

TEMPERATURES: *Pescatorea* species generally require uniform temperatures throughout the year, since the climate of most natural habitats has very little seasonal fluctuation even at higher elevations. Several sources of growing information suggest winter lows of 50 °F (10 °C). It is unknown whether the plants regularly survive this regime or whether this recommendation is what makes them difficult to maintain. The climate tables for individual species provide more accurate average winter temperatures.

HUMIDITY: Very high—80–90% is common in the natural habitat. If misting is used to cool a greenhouse, *Pescatorea* benefit from being placed where they will be exposed to the drifting mist. Cultivated plants are healthiest when high humidity is combined with excellent air circulation.

WATER: Plants should be kept evenly moist year-round. *Pescatorea* species have no means of water storage so are very intolerant of drying. Water should be reduced slightly if temperatures are low for the species. Water should not be allowed to stand on new growths or flower spikes, which are very susceptible to rot, particularly when exposed to stressful temperatures.

FERTILIZER: A ¼-strength solution is recommended with every second or third watering, while a ½-strength solution may be applied biweekly to monthly.

If live sphagnum is used in the medium, a very dilute solution of organic fertilizer, 0.1 tsp. per gal. (0.1 tsp. per 3.8 liters), may be applied as a foliar feed at every watering. When the moss is kept alive, it will normally produce sufficient nutrients for orchids, and very little additional fertilizer is required.

REST PERIOD: With slight modifications, growing conditions should be maintained year-round.

GROWING MEDIA: A medium that allows the roots to remain damp without becoming soggy.

Sphagnum-covered rafts are excellent, providing that moisture can be maintained. Baskets filled with sphagnum, osmunda, or chopped tree-fern are also satisfactory.

Pescatorea tend to do poorly when confined in pots of any kind, particularly in a bark-based medium. However, some growers report success potting in straight perlite.

Plants should be repotted infrequently, and then only when new roots are beginning to grow. The plants are notoriously slow to recover if roots are damaged.

MISCELLANEOUS NOTES: Growing instructions are few and far between for these species. *Pescatorea* are difficult for many growers to maintain in cultivation. Careful attention should be paid to the environmental requirements of each species.

Plant and Flower Information

PLANT SIZE AND TYPE: *Pescatorea* species are sympodial epiphytes producing numerous growths that form dense clumps when grown well. New growths arise directly from the root crown.

PSEUDOBULB: N/A.

LEAVES: The somewhat soft and fragile evergreen leaves are folded along the center vein, distichous, and loosely arranged in open fans. The number of leaves varies depending on overall plant health and vigor.

The following leaf symptoms may reveal cultural problems:

Brown leaf tips are probably an indication of insufficient water. *Pescatorea* are unusually sensitive to drying out, particularly if salt levels are high. Flushing the pots regularly will help prevent salt buildup.

Leaf drop results anytime a plant is stressed by inadequate growing conditions. To prevent additional damage, the conditions should be modified to more closely approximate the plant's natural habitat.

Spider mites frequently damage the leaves, making it difficult to maintain the plants in a healthy condition.

INFLORESCENCE: Short and usually slender, the multiple inflorescences are one-flowered, emerging from the leaf axils near the base of the plant.

FLOWERS: *Pescatorea* generally have showy, waxy, heavily textured, fragrant, long-lived flowers.

HYBRIDIZING NOTES: Normal chromosome counts have not yet been determined.

REFERENCES: 57, 113, 206.

PHOTOS/DRAWINGS: See species listings.

Species Culture

Pescatorea backhousiana Rchb.f. No origin or habitat information is available. This may have been a natural hybrid between unidentified *Pescatorea* and *Bollea* species. REFERENCES: 57, 210.

Pescatorea bella Rchb.f. Reportedly from Colombia, with no additional information available. This may have been a natural hybrid between *Bollea coelestis* and an unidentified *Pescatorea*. REFERENCES: 57, 112, 210.

Pescatorea cerina Rchb.f.

AKA: *Huntleya cerina, Pescatorea costaricensis.*

ORIGIN/HABITAT: Costa Rica to Colombia on the Pacific slopes. It is found on trees in wet, highland cloudforests, at 3000 ft. (914 m) or higher, usually in shady pockets of debris.

CLIMATE: Station # 78793, David, Panama, Lat. 8.4°N, Long. 82.4°W, at 89 ft. (27 m). Temperatures are calculated for 3000 ft. (914 m), resulting in probable extremes of 90°F (32.2°C) and 50°F (10.0°C).

N/HEMISPHERE	JAN	FEB	MAR	APR	MAY	JUN	JUL	AUG	SEP	OCT	NOV	DEC
°F AVG MAX	81	83	84	83	80	78	78	78	78	76	77	78
°F AVG MIN	57	58	59	62	61	61	61	61	60	60	60	59
DIURNAL RANGE	24	25	25	21	19	17	17	17	18	16	17	19
RAIN/INCHES	4.0	0.4	1.0	3.1	10.9	13.8	11.3	12.6	12.2	18.9	10.2	4.5
HUMIDITY/%	78	67	68	77	85	88	88	88	88	90	89	86
BLOOM SEASON		*	*	*	**	***	**	**	**	**	**	**
DAYS CLR @ 7AM	13	13	18	9	2	2	1	1	1	0	1	6
DAYS CLR @ 1PM	5	9	14	3	0	0	1	0	0	0	0	0
RAIN/MM	102	10	25	79	277	351	287	320	310	480	259	114
°C AVG MAX	27.4	28.6	29.1	28.6	26.9	25.8	25.8	25.8	25.8	24.7	25.2	25.8
°C AVG MIN	14.1	14.7	15.2	16.9	16.3	16.3	16.3	16.3	15.8	15.8	15.8	15.2
DIURNAL RANGE	13.3	13.9	13.9	11.7	10.6	9.5	9.5	9.5	10.0	8.9	9.4	10.6
S/HEMISPHERE	JUL	AUG	SEP	OCT	NOV	DEC	JAN	FEB	MAR	APR	MAY	JUN

Cultural Recommendations

LIGHT: 2000–2400 fc. Excessive light may be detrimental.

TEMPERATURES: Days average 76–80°F (25–27°C), and nights average 60–61°F (16°C), with a summer diurnal range of 16–19°F (9–11°C). Many cultural guidelines list this species as a cool grower, but the climate records suggest an intolerance to extremes. Constant moderate temperatures may be important to plant health.

HUMIDITY: 85–90% throughout the year. The lower average humidity and rainfall shown in the climate table during Jan.–Apr. (Jul.–Oct.) are near sea-level readings. They do not reflect the constant moisture found in the cloudforests at higher elevations.

WATER: Plants should be constantly moist while actively growing. Daily misting is suggested. The rainfall pattern is wet/dry, but the dry period is extremely short.

FERTILIZER: ¼ strength, applied every second or third watering.

REST PERIOD: Days average 78–84°F (26–29°C), and nights average 57–59°F (14–15°C), with a winter diurnal range of 21–25°F (12–13°C). Water should be reduced slightly for 2 months, but the medium must not be allowed to dry out. The increasing number of clear days in the plant's natural habitat indicates a potential for higher light.

GROWING MEDIA: Sphagnum-covered rafts, providing that moisture can be maintained. Chopped sphagnum mixed with tree fern or perlite may be used if potting is necessary to maintain moisture. Repotting is best done only when necessary and then only if new root growth is evident.

MISCELLANEOUS NOTES: Although it is a slow grower, this is one of the more adaptable species.

Plant and Flower Information

PLANT SIZE AND TYPE: A moderately sized sympodial epiphyte which forms a large clump.

LEAVES: 4–6 per growth. The arching, linear-lanceolate leaves arise from the root crown, are 7–12 in. (18–30 cm) long, and are loosely arranged in a fan.

INFLORESCENCE: Several. The one-flowered spikes are 3–4 in. (8–10 cm) long and arise from leaf axils at the base of the plant.

FLOWERS: 1 per inflorescence. The blossoms are 3 in. (7.5 cm) across, with a fleshy, heavy texture. The very fragrant, long-lasting flowers have white to light citron-yellow or straw-colored sepals and petals, somewhat blotched with greenish yellow at the base. The rich yellow lip is marked with red-brown, has a large yellow callus, and is recurved at the margins.

HYBRIDIZING NOTES: N/A.

REFERENCES: 14, 57, 112, 148, 174, 205, 206, 211, 212.

PHOTOS/DRAWINGS: *14, 57, 94, 148, 211.*

Pescatorea cochlearis Rolfe. Reportedly collected in the mountains between the provinces of São Paulo and Minas Gerais, Brazil. It has not been found

recently, and no habitat information is available. REFERENCES: 57.

Pescatorea coronaria Rchb.f.

AKA: N/A.

ORIGIN/HABITAT: Pueblorrico District in Choco, Colombia. *P. coronaria* is a rare species about which little is known. A few plants are reported in cultivation. Dr. Fowlie reports that it is always found with *Huntleya gustavi* at 5000–6000 ft. (1524–1829 m).

CLIMATE: Station # 80144, Quibdo, Colombia, Lat. 5.7°N, Long. 76.6°W, at 177 ft. (54 m). Temperatures are calculated for an elevation of 5000 ft. (1524 m). Records of extreme temperatures, humidity, and sky cover are not available for this station.

N/HEMISPHERE	JAN	FEB	MAR	APR	MAY	JUN	JUL	AUG	SEP	OCT	NOV	DEC
°F AVG MAX	67	67	68	69	69	69	70	70	70	69	68	67
°F AVG MIN	58	58	58	59	58	59	58	58	58	57	57	57
DIURNAL RANGE	9	9	10	10	11	10	12	12	12	12	11	10
RAIN/INCHES	3.8	7.3	6.8	8.7	7.1	7.7	8.8	9.1	13.0	9.6	11.0	8.1
HUMIDITY/%	N/A											
BLOOM SEASON					*	*	*					
DAYS CLR	N/A											
RAIN/MM	97	185	173	221	180	196	224	231	330	244	279	206
°C AVG MAX	19.5	19.5	20.0	20.6	20.6	20.6	21.2	21.2	21.2	20.6	20.0	19.5
°C AVG MIN	14.5	14.5	14.5	15.0	14.5	15.0	14.5	14.5	14.5	13.9	13.9	13.9
DIURNAL RANGE	5.0	5.0	5.5	5.6	6.1	5.6	6.7	6.7	6.7	6.7	6.1	5.6
S/HEMISPHERE	JUL	AUG	SEP	OCT	NOV	DEC	JAN	FEB	MAR	APR	MAY	JUN

Cultural Recommendations

LIGHT: 2000–3600 fc. Diffused light is preferred.

TEMPERATURES: Days average 67–70°F (20–21°C), and nights average 57–59°F (14–15°C), with a diurnal range of 9–12°F (5–7°C) throughout the year.

HUMIDITY: The heavy rainfall indicates that humidity should be very high.

WATER: Plants should be kept moist throughout the year. Warm water, about 70°F (21°C), is highly recommended. The rainfall pattern is wet year-round, although the habitat is slightly drier in Jan. (Jul.). Growers report that *Huntleya gustavi* (which grows with *Pescatorea coronaria*) grows well when exposed to drifting mist.

FERTILIZER: ¼ strength, applied every second or third watering, or ½ strength, applied monthly when plants are actively growing.

REST PERIOD: A slight decrease in the diurnal range of 9–10°F (5–6°C) is indicated, but temperatures are nearly constant all year. Water and fertilizer may be reduced slightly when plants are not actively growing, but the medium should not be allowed to dry out.

GROWING MEDIA: Some growers recommend tree-fern or sphagnum-covered rafts, providing that moisture can be maintained. Others report that *Huntleya gustavi* does well in horticultural perlite, so that medium may also work well for *Pescatorea coronaria*. Repotting is best done immediately after plants flower when new roots are beginning to grow.

MISCELLANEOUS NOTES: Growers report that *Huntleya gustavi* can be grown at night temperatures of 55 °F (13 °C) and day temperatures of 95 °F (35 °C), although the elevation range for *Pescatorea coronaria* may be more limited, suggesting that 95 °F (35 °C) should be considered an extreme and avoided if at all possible.

Plant and Flower Information

PLANT SIZE AND TYPE: A sympodial species.

LEAVES: N/A.

INFLORESCENCE: Each growth may produce several one-flowered spikes which emerge from the base of the plant.

FLOWERS: The blossoms are 3 in. (8 cm) across. The sepals and petals are purplish with green or white at the apices, while the lip is paler, sometimes nearly skin-colored. The callus is dark carmine with 21 radiating ribs, and the lip is covered with warty protuberances which are in turn covered with hairlike projections.

HYBRIDIZING NOTES: N/A.

REFERENCES: 57, 169.

PHOTOS/DRAWINGS: 57.

Pescatorea costaricensis. See *P. cerina.* REFERENCES: 57.

Pescatorea dayana Rchb.f.

AKA: *Zygopetalum dayanum.*

ORIGIN/HABITAT: Two distinct varieties are recognized, growing in somewhat different climatic areas. Var. *rhodacra* originates near Darien, Panama, at 2800 ft. (853 m), while var. *candidula* grows east of Narino, Colombia, at 4300 ft. (1310 m).

CLIMATE: Station # 78806, Howard AFB, Panama, Lat. 8.9 °N, Long. 79.6 °W, at 51 ft. (16 m), is the station closest to Darien. Temperatures are calculated for an elevation of 2800 ft. (853 m), resulting in probable extremes of 88 °F (31.1 °C) and 57 °F (13.9 °C).

N/HEMISPHERE	JAN	FEB	MAR	APR	MAY	JUN	JUL	AUG	SEP	OCT	NOV	DEC
°F AVG MAX	80	81	82	82	79	78	78	78	77	76	77	78
°F AVG MIN	65	65	66	66	67	66	66	66	65	65	65	65
DIURNAL RANGE	15	16	16	16	12	12	12	12	12	11	12	13
RAIN/INCHES	0.9	0.9	0.9	3.2	7.7	6.3	6.4	5.4	5.3	7.8	9.8	5.0
HUMIDITY/%	75	74	71	74	81	82	83	84	86	86	85	81
BLOOM SEASON			**	*	*	**	*	*	**	**		
DAYS CLR @ 7AM	17	14	11	6	1	0	1	1	0	1	2	9
DAYS CLR @ 1PM	4	3	2	1	0	0	0	0	0	0	0	1
RAIN/MM	23	23	23	81	196	160	163	137	135	198	249	127
°C AVG MAX	26.6	27.2	27.7	27.7	26.1	25.5	25.5	25.5	25.0	24.4	25.0	25.5
°C AVG MIN	18.3	18.3	18.8	18.8	19.4	18.8	18.8	18.8	18.3	18.3	18.3	18.3
DIURNAL RANGE	8.3	8.9	8.9	8.9	6.7	6.7	6.7	6.7	6.7	6.1	6.7	7.2
S/HEMISPHERE	JUL	AUG	SEP	OCT	NOV	DEC	JAN	FEB	MAR	APR	MAY	JUN

Cultural Recommendations

LIGHT: 2400 fc. Diffused light is preferred.

TEMPERATURES: Days average 76–79 °F (24–26 °C), and nights average 65–67 °F (18–19 °C), with a diurnal range of 11–13 °F (6–7 °C). Extremes vary only a few degrees from average growing temperatures, indicating an intolerance to wide temperature fluctuations.

HUMIDITY: 75–85%.

WATER: Year-round moisture is available in the higher-elevation habitats, but the amounts are lower during the winter. The rainfall pattern is wet/dry.

FERTILIZER: ¼ strength, applied every second or third watering.

REST PERIOD: Winter days average 78–82 °F (25–27 °C) in this habitat, with constant night temperatures near 65 °F (18 °C) and a slightly increased diurnal range of 15–16 °F (8–9 °C). Water should be reduced for 2–3 months, but the medium should never become dry.

GROWING MEDIA: Sphagnum-covered rafts, providing that moisture can be maintained. Chopped tree-fern or perlite may be used for potting. Repotting is best done only when necessary and then only if new root growth is evident.

MISCELLANEOUS NOTES: Adaptable in cultivation. The 2 recognized varieties of this species originate in areas with somewhat different temperature regimes. The climate table is for the habitat of *P. dayana* var. *rhodacra*. Conditions for *P. dayana* var. *candidula* are somewhat cooler, so the climate conditions for *P. lamellosa* might produce a healthier plant. One grower reports that his plants (which may be *P. dayana* var. *candidula*) regularly survive winter lows of 35 °F (1.7 °C) if they are kept dry when temperatures are below 45 °F (7 °C).

Plant and Flower Information

PLANT SIZE AND TYPE: A moderately sized sympodial epiphyte.

LEAVES: 6–8 per growth. The leaves are usually 10–15 in. (25–31 cm) long but may reach a length of 24 in. (61 cm).

INFLORESCENCE: Several. Each growth may produce multiple one-flowered spikes which are 4–5 in. (11 cm) long. They emerge from the base of the plant.

FLOWERS: 1 per inflorescence. The long-lasting, fragrant flowers are 3–3.5 in. (8–9 cm) across with a fleshy, waxy texture. The concave sepals and petals are milk-white and dilated at the apex. They may be marked with green at the apex in var. *candidula* or with purplish rose in var. *rhodacra*. The lip may be white or various shades of violet-purple and is marked with striking violet streaks which radiate from the extremely large, red-to-violet callus.

HYBRIDIZING NOTES: N/A.

REFERENCES: 14, 57, 112, 148, 174, 205, 206, 211.

PHOTOS/DRAWINGS: *14*, *57*, 211.

Pescatorea dormaniana Rchb.f. Not recently collected, this species was described without origin or habitat information. REFERENCES: 57.

Pescatorea euglossa. See *P. wallisii*. REFERENCES: 57.

Pescatorea fimbriata. See *P. lehmanni*. REFERENCES: 57.

Pescatorea gairiana. Now known as *Pescabollea gairiana*, this is a natural hybrid between *Pescatorea klabochorum* and *Bollea coelestis*. REFERENCES: 57. PHOTOS/DRAWINGS: *57*.

Pescatorea klabochorum Rchb.f.

AKA: N/A.

ORIGIN/HABITAT: Ecuador and west of Queremal, Colombia, at 4500 ft. (1372 m).

CLIMATE: Station # 80336, Tumaco, Colombia, Lat. 1.8 ° N, Long. 78.8 °W, is coastal with an elevation of 7 ft. (2 m). Temperatures are calculated for an elevation of

4500 ft. (1372 m), resulting in probable extremes of 75 °F (23.9 °C) and 49 °F (9.4 °C).

N/HEMISPHERE	JAN	FEB	MAR	APR	MAY	JUN	JUL	AUG	SEP	OCT	NOV	DEC
°F AVG MAX	67	67	68	69	68	67	67	67	67	67	66	67
°F AVG MIN	60	60	61	61	61	60	60	60	60	60	60	60
DIURNAL RANGE	7	7	7	8	7	7	7	7	7	7	6	7
RAIN/INCHES	16.9	11.7	9.6	14.6	17.4	12.0	7.7	7.3	7.3	5.9	4.9	7.0
HUMIDITY/%	87	87	87	87	88	88	87	87	87	87	86	86
BLOOM SEASON		*	*	*	**		*	***	**	**		
DAYS CLR @ 7AM	1	0	1	1	1	1	1	1	1	1	1	2
DAYS CLR @ 1PM	3	2	3	3	2	3	2	2	1	3	1	2
RAIN/MM	429	297	244	371	442	305	196	185	185	150	124	178
°C AVG MAX	19.5	19.5	20.1	20.7	20.1	19.5	19.5	19.5	19.5	19.5	19.0	19.5
°C AVG MIN	15.7	15.7	16.2	16.2	16.2	15.7	15.7	15.7	15.7	15.7	15.7	15.7
DIURNAL RANGE	3.8	3.8	3.9	4.5	3.9	3.8	3.8	3.8	3.8	3.8	3.3	3.8
S/HEMISPHERE	JUL	AUG	SEP	OCT	NOV	DEC	JAN	FEB	MAR	APR	MAY	JUN

Cultural Recommendations

LIGHT: 2400 fc. Diffused light is preferred, as clear days in the habitat are exceedingly rare.

TEMPERATURES: Days average 66–68 °F (19–20 °C), and nights average 60–61 °F (16 °C) throughout the year. These temperatures result in an extremely limited diurnal range of 6–8 °F (4 °C). Probable extremes vary only 10 °F (5.5 °C) from the average growing temperatures.

HUMIDITY: 85–90%.

WATER: Constant moisture is preferred, although the habitat is slightly drier in early winter. The rainfall pattern is wet all year.

FERTILIZER: ¼ strength, applied every second or third watering.

REST PERIOD: None. Growing conditions should be maintained year-round.

GROWING MEDIA: Sphagnum-covered rafts, providing that moisture can be maintained. Chopped tree-fern or perlite may be used if plants must be potted. Repotting is best done only when necessary and then only if new root growth is evident.

MISCELLANEOUS NOTES: Considered difficult by many growers, this plant does not tolerate temperature extremes, wide diurnal range, or drying, but it is very free-flowering if well grown.

Plant and Flower Information

PLANT SIZE AND TYPE: A moderately sized sympodial plant that may be either epiphytic or semiterrestrial.

LEAVES: Several per growth. The lanceolate foliage is 12–15 in. (30–38 cm) long, folded along the center line, and distichously arranged in an open fan shape.

INFLORESCENCE: Several. The flower spikes are short, with flowers held near the base of the leaf fan. *P. klabochorum* can be very free-blooming.

FLOWERS: 1 per inflorescence. Heavily textured and very long-lasting, the extremely fragrant flowers are among the finest of the genus. Blossoms are 3.5–4.0 in. (9–10 cm) across. The sepals and shorter petals are spreading, white at the base, and incurved at the chocolate-purple tips. The lip is cream, white, or yellow at the margins, with parallel purple ridges on the midlobe. The callus is yellowish with orchid-lavender markings. Flowers are variable in size and color.

HYBRIDIZING NOTES: N/A.

REFERENCES: 57, 112, 148, 205, 206, 211.

PHOTOS/DRAWINGS: *57, 158,* 205, 211.

Pescatorea lamellosa Rchb.f.

AKA: N/A.

ORIGIN/HABITAT: Colombia to Ecuador on the slopes of the Andes at 4000–6560 ft. (1219–2000 m). The lowest elevation recorded is 3500 ft. (1067 m) in the Narino Province of Colombia.

CLIMATE: Station # 80336, Tumaco, Colombia, Lat. 1.8° N, Long. 78.8°W, at 7 ft. (2 m). Temperatures are calculated for an elevation of 4500 ft. (1372 m), resulting in probable extremes of 75°F (23.9°C) and 49°F (9.4°C).

N/HEMISPHERE	JAN	FEB	MAR	APR	MAY	JUN	JUL	AUG	SEP	OCT	NOV	DEC
°F AVG MAX	67	67	68	69	68	67	67	67	67	67	66	67
°F AVG MIN	60	60	61	61	61	60	60	60	60	60	60	60
DIURNAL RANGE	7	7	7	8	7	7	7	7	7	7	6	7
RAIN/INCHES	16.9	11.7	9.6	14.6	17.4	12.0	7.7	7.3	7.3	5.9	4.9	7.0
HUMIDITY/%	87	87	87	87	88	88	87	87	87	87	86	86
BLOOM SEASON				*	*	*	*					
DAYS CLR @ 7AM	1	0	1	1	1	1	1	1	1	1	1	2
DAYS CLR @ 1PM	3	2	3	3	2	3	2	2	1	3	1	2
RAIN/MM	429	297	244	371	442	305	196	185	185	150	124	178
°C AVG MAX	19.5	19.5	20.1	20.7	20.1	19.5	19.5	19.5	19.5	19.5	19.0	19.5
°C AVG MIN	15.7	15.7	16.2	16.2	16.2	15.7	15.7	15.7	15.7	15.7	15.7	15.7
DIURNAL RANGE	3.8	3.8	3.9	4.5	3.9	3.8	3.8	3.8	3.8	3.8	3.3	3.8
S/HEMISPHERE	JUL	AUG	SEP	OCT	NOV	DEC	JAN	FEB	MAR	APR	MAY	JUN

Cultural Recommendations

LIGHT: 2000–3000 fc. Diffused light is preferred, as clear days are rare in the habitat.

TEMPERATURES: Days average 66–69°F (19–20°C), and nights average 60–61°F (16°C), with an unusually low diurnal range of 6–8°F (3–4°C). Extremes vary about 10°F (5.6°C) from the average growing temperatures, indicating an intolerance to wide temperature fluctuations.

HUMIDITY: 85–90%. *P. lamellosa* prefers to grow over water, where humidity is constantly high. Drifting mist may be particularly beneficial.

WATER: Plants should be constantly moist while actively growing. The rainfall pattern is wet/wetter.

FERTILIZER: ¼ strength, applied every second or third watering.

REST PERIOD: None. Growing conditions should be maintained throughout the year.

GROWING MEDIA: Sphagnum-covered rafts, providing that moisture can be maintained. Chopped tree-fern or perlite may be used if plants are potted. Repotting is best done only when necessary and then only if new root growth is evident.

MISCELLANEOUS NOTES: *P. lamellosa* is not often found in cultivation.

Plant and Flower Information

PLANT SIZE AND TYPE: A 15 in. (38 cm) sympodial epiphyte.

LEAVES: Several per growth. The narrowly lanceolate leaves are about 12–16 in. (30–40 cm) long.

INFLORESCENCE: Several. The stout, erect spikes are usually 4 in. (10 cm) long, each producing a single flower.

FLOWERS: 1 per inflorescence. Waxy, long-lasting, and very fragrant, the flowers are 2 in. (5 cm) across with cream-to-yellowish sepals and petals. The lip has a very large, yellow-to-orange callus, nearly half covered by brownish lamellae.

HYBRIDIZING NOTES: N/A.

REFERENCES: 57, 205.

PHOTOS/DRAWINGS: N/A.

Pescatorea lehmanni Rchb.f.

AKA: *P. fimbriata*.

ORIGIN/HABITAT: Extremely wet, humid cloudforests in the coastal mountains of southern Colombia and northern Ecuador, at 3500–4500 ft. (1065–1372 m).

The plant usually grows near water on moss-covered, horizontal tree limbs.

CLIMATE: Station # 80336, Tumaco, Colombia, Lat. 1.8°N, Long. 78.8°W, at 7 ft. (2 m). Temperatures are calculated for an elevation of 4000 ft. (1219 m), resulting in probable extremes of 77°F (25.0°C) and 51°F (10.6°C).

N/HEMISPHERE	JAN	FEB	MAR	APR	MAY	JUN	JUL	AUG	SEP	OCT	NOV	DEC
°F AVG MAX	69	69	70	71	70	69	69	69	69	69	68	69
°F AVG MIN	62	62	63	63	63	62	62	62	62	62	62	62
DIURNAL RANGE	7	7	7	8	7	7	7	7	7	7	6	7
RAIN/INCHES	16.9	11.7	9.6	14.6	17.4	12.0	7.7	7.3	7.3	5.9	4.9	7.0
HUMIDITY/%	87	87	87	87	88	88	87	87	87	87	86	86
BLOOM SEASON		**	**		**	**	**	*	*	**	**	
DAYS CLR @ 7AM	1	0	1	1	1	1	1	1	1	1	1	2
DAYS CLR @ 1PM	3	2	3	3	2	3	2	2	1	3	1	2
RAIN/MM	429	297	244	371	442	305	196	185	185	150	124	178
°C AVG MAX	20.5	20.5	21.0	21.6	21.0	20.5	20.5	20.5	20.5	20.5	19.9	20.5
°C AVG MIN	16.6	16.6	17.1	17.1	17.1	16.6	16.6	16.6	16.6	16.6	16.6	16.6
DIURNAL RANGE	3.9	3.9	3.9	4.5	3.9	3.9	3.9	3.9	3.9	3.9	3.3	3.9
S/HEMISPHERE	JUL	AUG	SEP	OCT	NOV	DEC	JAN	FEB	MAR	APR	MAY	JUN

Cultural Recommendations

LIGHT: 2400–3600 fc. In nature, plants are usually found in fairly bright, diffused light.

TEMPERATURES: Days average 68–71°F (20–21°C), and nights average 62–63°F (17°C), resulting in a limited diurnal range of 6–8°F (3–4°C) throughout the year. Extremes vary about 10°F (5.5°C) from the average growing temperatures, indicating an intolerance to wide temperature fluctuations.

HUMIDITY: 85–90%. Drifting mist may be particularly beneficial.

WATER: Plants should be constantly moist. The rainfall pattern is wet/wetter.

FERTILIZER: ¼ strength, applied biweekly to monthly.

REST PERIOD: None. Growing conditions should be maintained year-round.

GROWING MEDIA: Tree fern, sphagnum moss, osmunda, and perlite have all been used successfully. Repotting is best done only when necessary and then only if new root growth is evident.

MISCELLANEOUS NOTES: One grower reports that his plants regularly survive winter lows of 35°F (1.7°C), providing they are kept dry at temperatures below 45°F (7°C).

Plant and Flower Information

PLANT SIZE AND TYPE: A moderately sized sympodial epiphyte.

LEAVES: 10 per growth. The leaves are 12–18 in. (30–45 cm) long, narrow, elliptic-lanceolate, distichous, and arranged in a fan.

INFLORESCENCE: Several. Each one-flowered, horizontal spike is 4–6 in. (10–15 cm) long. In cultivation, plants may bloom several times during the year, making them seem nearly ever-blooming.

FLOWERS: 1 per inflorescence. The long-lasting, waxy, fragrant flowers are 2.5–3.5 in. (6–9 cm) across. The somewhat cupped blossoms are white, with numerous parallel lines of plum-purple extending along most of the length of the sepals and petals, sometimes merging to almost hide the white. The oval lip is whitish cream to deep mauve with long hairs, while the yellow callus is trimmed with red. Color, size, and markings are variable.

HYBRIDIZING NOTES: N/A.

REFERENCES: 40, 57, 112, 205, 206, 211.

PHOTOS/DRAWINGS: 40, *57, 169*, 211.

Pescatorea roezlii. See *P. wallisii.* REFERENCES: 57.

Pescatorea ruckeriana Rchb.f. Taxonomists now feel this may have been a natural hybrid between an unidentified *Pescatorea* and a *Bollea*. No recent collections have been made, and habitat information is unavailable. REFERENCES: 57, 211.

Pescatorea russelliana Rchb.f. No recent collections have been made, and habitat information is unavailable. REFERENCES: 57, 211.

Pescatorea triumphans Rchb.f. No recent collections have been made, and habitat information is unavailable. REFERENCES: 57, 211.

Pescatorea wallisii Linden and Rchb.f.

AKA: *Bollea schroederiana, Pescatorea euglossa, P. roezlii, Zygopetalum wallisii.*

ORIGIN/HABITAT: Western Ecuador in tropical rainforests at 230–4000 ft. (70–1219 m).

CLIMATE: Station # 84139, Cuenca, Ecuador, Lat. 2.9°S, Long. 79.1°W, at 8291 ft. (2527 m). Temperatures are

Pescatorea wallisii

calculated for an elevation of 4000 ft. (1219 m), resulting in probable extremes of 95°F (35.0°C) and 43°F (6.1°C).

N/HEMISPHERE	JAN	FEB	MAR	APR	MAY	JUN	JUL	AUG	SEP	OCT	NOV	DEC
°F AVG MAX	79	80	83	84	85	85	83	84	83	83	81	80
°F AVG MIN	61	60	62	63	60	63	64	65	65	64	63	61
DIURNAL RANGE	18	20	21	21	25	22	19	19	18	19	18	19
RAIN/INCHES	0.9	1.1	1.6	3.1	1.8	2.5	2.0	1.8	3.2	4.3	4.3	1.7
HUMIDITY/%	73	75	74	76	74	74	75	76	76	77	77	75
BLOOM SEASON		*		*	*		***		*			
DAYS CLR @ 7AM	4	2	4	4	5	1	2	1	2	1	2	3
DAYS CLR @ 1PM	5	5	3	2	5	2	4	1	2	1	2	2
RAIN/MM	23	28	41	79	46	64	51	46	81	109	109	43
°C AVG MAX	26.2	26.8	28.4	29.0	29.5	29.5	28.4	29.0	28.4	28.4	27.3	26.8
°C AVG MIN	16.2	15.6	16.8	17.3	15.6	17.3	17.9	18.4	18.4	17.9	17.3	16.2
DIURNAL RANGE	10.0	11.2	11.6	11.7	13.9	12.2	10.5	10.6	10.0	10.5	10.0	10.6
S/HEMISPHERE	JUL	AUG	SEP	OCT	NOV	DEC	JAN	FEB	MAR	APR	MAY	JUN

Cultural Recommendations

LIGHT: 2400–3600 fc. Growers report that plants do well at these light levels. Diffused light is preferred.

TEMPERATURES: Days average 83–85°F (28–30°C), and nights average 60–65°F (16–18°C), with a summer diurnal range of 18–19°F (10–11°C). The diurnal range is wider than for most *Pescatorea* species. These temperatures represent the cool end of the spectrum in the plant's natural habitat, so plants should also tolerate warmer averages.

HUMIDITY: 75–85%. *P. wallisii* grows in the mistforest zone, where humidity is higher than that shown in the climate table.

WATER: Plants should be constantly moist. The rainfall shown in the climate table does not reflect the amount of moisture found in the plant's microclimate. The rainfall pattern is wet/dry.

FERTILIZER: ¼–½ strength, applied every second or third watering.

REST PERIOD: Days average 79–85°F (26–29°C), with uniform nights near 60°F (16°C), resulting in a winter diurnal range of 20–25°F (11–14°C). Water should be reduced for 1–2 months, but plants should not be allowed to dry out.

GROWING MEDIA: Sphagnum-covered rafts, providing that moisture can be maintained. Chopped tree-fern or perlite may be used when plants are potted. Repotting is best done only when necessary and then only if new root growth is evident.

MISCELLANEOUS NOTES: Climate records indicate that the plants should be fairly adaptable to greenhouse conditions but might not tolerate the narrow diurnal range required by most *Pescatorea* species.

Plant and Flower Information

PLANT SIZE AND TYPE: A variably sized sympodial epiphyte.

LEAVES: 6–8 per growth. The distichous leaves are normally 10 in. (25 cm) long but may reach a length of 24 in. (61 cm).

INFLORESCENCE: Several. The flower spikes are 5–7 in. (12–17 cm) long. Each spike produces a single blossom, but the plants can be in flower most of the year.

FLOWERS: 1 per inflorescence. Long-lasting and extremely fragrant, the flowers are 3–4 in. (7–10 cm) across. The elongated sepals and petals are sharply reflexed at the margins, making them appear quite narrow. They are cream-white with blue-violet to violet-rose markings at the tips. Plants from higher elevations have darker markings. Color remains constant even when the plants are greenhouse-grown. The white callus is striped with rose.

HYBRIDIZING NOTES: N/A.

REFERENCES: 40, 57, 206, 211.

PHOTOS/DRAWINGS: 40, 57.

3
Phaius
General Information

SUBFAMILY: Epidendroidea.

TRIBE: *Arethuseae.*

SUBTRIBE: *Bletiinae* or *Phaiinae.*

GENUS: *Phaius* Loureiro.

AKA: Some authorities place *Phaius* in the subtribe *Bletiinae,* while others place these species in their own subtribe *Phaiinae.* The genus is closely related to *Calanthe.*

Several species have recently been transferred from the genus *Gastrorchis.* Other genus names have been used over the years, but *Phaius* appears in most current literature. (The genus name may be spelled *Phajus,* but the International Orchid Commission's 1985 *Handbook on Orchid Nomenclature and Registration* spells it *Phaius.*) Several species were originally classified as *Bletia* and *Calanthe.* Other names that are no longer used in current literature include *Limodorum* and *Hecabe.*

SPECIES: Estimates of genus size range from 30–50 species. Since there has been no recent review of the genus as a whole, the species included here are based on individual floras, *Index Kewensis* (1983), and original species descriptions. The following references were used for species in their authors' areas. J. Bosser reviewed the Madagascar *Phaius* in *Revision du genre* Phaius *Lour.* (1971). Java species are covered in *The Genus* Phaius *in Java* (1980) by J. B. Comber, and *Phaius* from Thailand were reviewed by Dr. Gunnar Seidenfaden in *Orchid Genera in Thailand, XIII. Thirty-three Epidendroid Genera* (1986). Philippine *Phaius* are based on *Orchidiana Philippiniana* (1984) by Dr. Helen L. Valmayor.

ORIGIN/HABITAT: *Phaius* habitats are widespread, ranging from Africa to the Philippines and including Southeast Asia, China, India, Australia, and many Pacific islands. The plants most often grow in shady, primary-forest areas.

CLIMATE: Tropical to subtropical climates are common throughout the range, but high-elevation habitats may have temperatures approaching those of moderate temperate zones.

Cultural Recommendations

LIGHT: 1800–4000 fc, or 60–75% shade is appropriate in most midlatitude areas. Light should be diffused or dappled. Species growing in dense forests should be started in low light, which may gradually be increased. Most *Phaius* grow well in *Cattleya* light at 2400–3000 fc.

TEMPERATURES: Intermediate to very warm growing temperatures predominate during the growing season in most *Phaius* habitats, but the diurnal range may be highly variable. Individual climate records provide the best cultivation guidelines.

HUMIDITY: Moderate to high levels are preferable when plants are actively growing or whenever temperatures are warm.

WATER: *Phaius* generally require ample moisture so should be watered freely while actively growing. Sufficient moisture is needed to keep the medium constantly wet, but not soggy.

In cultivation, leaves and young growths are highly susceptible to rot; thus water should not be allowed to touch them, particularly if temperatures are inappropriate. Excellent air circulation helps prevent disease.

FERTILIZER: *Phaius* are rapid growers requiring ample nutrients and may generally be treated more like a potted garden plant than an orchid.

Weekly applications of an organic fertilizer such as weak manure tea are used very successfully in Southeast Asia, but a balanced chemical fertilizer mixed at ½ the recommended strength may also be used. Ample fertilizer, short of burning the plant, improves overall plant vigor as well as flower color.

REST PERIOD: Variable. Some species are truly tropical, requiring constant growing conditions, while others must be given a winter rest with cooler, drier conditions. Many *Phaius* tolerate winter temperatures of 40°F (5°C), and some survive drops to below freezing. Individual climate records are the best guide to rest requirements.

Most species are somewhat adaptable. Moisture and fertilizer requirements decrease in direct proportion to declining temperatures. What may initially appear to be discrepancies in cultural instructions from equally successful growers are usually resolved by factoring in this guideline.

Spring flowers are normally initiated by the change in conditions following a rest period.

GROWING MEDIA: A mix of equal parts soil, rotted cow manure, and peat or sphagnum moss is used successfully. A top dressing of additional rotted cow manure is added each spring when growth resumes.

A soilless mix of ⅓ fine fir bark, ⅓ perlite, ⅙ sand, and ⅙ peat moss is an alternate medium if growers object to using manure. However, fertilizer must be faithfully applied since few nutrients are available from this medium.

Phaius are easily grown in the garden in dappled shade areas if suitable weather conditions prevail, but excellent drainage and ample moisture must be available.

Plants grown in the greenhouse should be potted in large containers which are adequate for about 2 years' growth. Large pots are also needed to provide stability to the taller species. *Phaius* will outgrow their pots in 2–3 years and may easily be divided if they become too large. However, growers recommend repotting annually and report that small divisions produce more blossoms than large clumps. Divisions should be no smaller than 3 growths; 5–6 growths normally continue to bloom. Repotting is best done in early spring as new growth resumes and should be avoided before the winter rest.

MISCELLANEOUS NOTES: New plants will start from the dormant buds on the flower spikes, as with many *Dendrobium* species and *Doritis phalaenopsis*. One technique is to cut the flower stem after flowers have withered and lay it on the surface of a flat filled with moist, sterile sand. Next, cover the flat with a glass or plastic sheet to retain the moisture and place in an area with low light and appropriate temperatures. An alternate method is to place the cut stem in a plastic bag with sphagnum moss moistened with distilled water. The buds should start to swell within a few weeks, and plantlets will be large enough to be individually potted within a few months.

Plant and Flower Information

PLANT SIZE AND TYPE: Sympodial, *Phaius* are normally terrestrials, but at least one species is epiphytic. Plant size is highly variable.

PSEUDOBULB: Pseudobulbs are most often small, but *Phaius* have variable growth habits. New growths may arise either from buds at the base of old pseudobulbs, from cormlike rhizomes, or from elongated, fleshy, knobby rhizomes which resemble iris tubers.

LEAVES: Large, plicate, and arching, the often ruffled foliage makes most *Phaius* attractive plants, even when not in bloom. *Phaius* usually have evergreen leaves, though some are deciduous.

Leaf abnormalities may be caused by infestations of red spider, thrips, and green fly, to which some *Phaius* are highly susceptible. The leaves may respond to other cultural problems with symptoms similar to those of *Phragmipedium* discussed in Chapter 6, since species in both genera often have thin, plicate leaves.

INFLORESCENCE: Flower spikes are most often tall and erect, with flowers arranged in a raceme on the apical portion of the spike. Depending on the species, the spikes may emerge from buds at the base of the pseudobulb, directly from the rhizome, or from nodes at the base of the stem.

Developing spikes are often brittle and easily broken. They should be supported with a stake if they are very tall, if they produce numerous blooms, or if they will be exposed to windy conditions.

FLOWERS: Generally large and fragrant, the fleshy, long-lasting flowers turn grey with age or if bruised. Color intensity is variable and is influenced by the availability of nutrients.

HYBRIDIZING NOTES: Chromosome counts are variable and are included with individual species listings. Seeds normally mature 120–150 days after pollination, but the fruit should be picked for flasking as soon as it begins turning yellow and before it opens.

REFERENCES: 20, 21, 27, 31, 35, 113, 177, 197, 206, 211.

PHOTOS/DRAWINGS: See species listings.

Species Culture

Phaius actinomorphus T. P. Lin

AKA: *Calanthe actinomorpha.*

ORIGIN/HABITAT: Endemic to Taiwan, it grows in moist, shady forests at 2600 ft. (792 m) and prefers northern (shady) exposures.

CLIMATE: Station # 46749, Taichung, Taiwan, Lat. 24.2°N, Long. 120.6°E, at 369 ft. (112 m). Temperatures are calculated for an elevation of 2600 ft. (792 m), resulting in probable extremes of 90°F (32.2°C) and 27°F (-2.8°C).

N/HEMISPHERE	JAN	FEB	MAR	APR	MAY	JUN	JUL	AUG	SEP	OCT	NOV	DEC
°F AVG MAX	61	62	67	72	78	80	82	82	81	77	71	65
°F AVG MIN	45	47	51	57	64	67	69	68	66	60	54	49
DIURNAL RANGE	16	15	16	15	14	13	13	14	15	17	17	16
RAIN/INCHES	1.5	2.3	1.9	4.3	7.1	12.6	8.6	15.7	5.8	0.7	0.6	0.8
HUMIDITY/%	82	84	83	84	83	84	82	84	83	80	79	82
BLOOM SEASON												**
DAYS CLR @ 8AM	5	5	4	4	4	4	2	5	5	11	10	9
DAYS CLR @ 2PM	9	9	8	7	4	2	2	1	8	14	14	12
RAIN/MM	38	58	48	109	180	320	218	399	147	18	15	20
°C AVG MAX	15.9	16.5	19.2	22.0	25.4	26.5	27.6	27.6	27.0	24.8	21.5	18.1
°C AVG MIN	7.0	8.1	10.4	13.7	17.6	19.2	20.4	19.8	18.7	15.4	12.0	9.2
DIURNAL RANGE	8.9	8.4	8.8	8.3	7.8	7.3	7.2	7.8	8.3	9.4	9.5	8.9
S/HEMISPHERE	JUL	AUG	SEP	OCT	NOV	DEC	JAN	FEB	MAR	APR	MAY	JUN

Cultural Recommendations

LIGHT: 1200–2000 fc. Low, diffused light, which may be increased gradually.

TEMPERATURES: Summer days average 77–82°F (25–28°C), and nights average 60–69°F (15–20°C), with a diurnal range of 13–15°F (7–9°C).

HUMIDITY: 80-85%.

WATER: Ample moisture is needed when plants are actively growing. The rainfall pattern is wet/dry.

FERTILIZER: ½-strength, applied weekly during periods of active growth.

REST PERIOD: Winter days average 61–72°F (16–22°C), and nights average 45–57°F (7–14°C). The simultaneous decline in both day and night temperatures results in little change in the average diurnal range. In cultivation, water should be reduced, particularly when temperatures are coolest; but the constantly high humidity levels in the habitat indicate that some moisture is always available, so plants should not be allowed to wither. Fertilizer should be reduced anytime plants are not actively growing. Light levels may be raised to simulate the increased number of clear days in the habitat.

GROWING MEDIA: A fertile terrestrial mix that retains moisture but does not become soggy.

MISCELLANEOUS NOTES: *P. actinomorphus* blooms during the winter dry season when temperatures are cooler. The precise bloom trigger has not been identified.

Plant and Flower Information

PLANT SIZE AND TYPE: A 16–24 in. (40–60 cm) sympodial terrestrial.

PSEUDOBULB: A swelling at the base of the stem.

LEAVES: 3–5 per growth. The variable, light green, oblong-lanceolate leaves are 8–22 in. (20–56 cm) long.

INFLORESCENCE: 20 in. (50 cm) long. The spikes are densely flowered on the upper portion and arise from the base of the pseudobulb.

FLOWERS: The numerous, nodding yellow flowers barely open. In photographs, they appear to be self-pollinating.

HYBRIDIZING NOTES: N/A.

REFERENCES: 122, 132.

PHOTOS/DRAWINGS: 132.

Phaius albus. Now considered a synonym of *Thunia alba.* REFERENCES: 122.

Phaius amboinensis (Zipp.) Blume

AKA: *Bletia amboinensis, Phaius zollingeri. P. papuanus* is considered a variety of *P. amboinensis,*

ORIGIN/HABITAT: Indonesia, New Guinea, and many Pacific islands, where it grows at low elevations in forest humus.

CLIMATE: Station # 97230, Bali, Indonesia, Lat. 8.7°S, Long. 115.2°E, at 16 ft. (5 m). The record high is 97°F (36.1°C), and the record low is 63°F (17.2°C).

Phaius amboinensis

N/HEMISPHERE	JAN	FEB	MAR	APR	MAY	JUN	JUL	AUG	SEP	OCT	NOV	DEC
°F AVG MAX	87	86	88	89	91	90	90	89	90	91	90	88
°F AVG MIN	68	71	71	71	72	71	73	73	73	72	72	70
DIURNAL RANGE	19	15	17	18	19	19	17	16	17	19	18	18
RAIN/INCHES	3.8	1.5	4.4	8.0	7.9	14.7	15.9	8.4	8.1	5.0	1.6	2.0
HUMIDITY/%	74	72	72	72	73	76	76	78	77	75	76	75
BLOOM SEASON					*	*	**	*	*			
DAYS CLR @ 8AM	8	7	9	8	5	4	6	3	3	10	8	9
DAYS CLR @ 2PM	13	14	16	10	6	2	5	3	5	10	12	12
RAIN/MM	97	38	10	122	201	373	404	213	206	127	41	51
°C AVG MAX	30.6	30.0	31.1	31.7	32.8	32.2	32.2	31.7	32.2	32.8	32.2	31.1
°C AVG MIN	20.0	21.7	21.7	21.7	22.2	21.7	22.8	22.8	22.8	22.2	22.2	21.1
DIURNAL RANGE	10.6	8.3	9.4	10.0	10.6	10.5	9.4	8.9	9.4	10.6	10.0	10.0
S/HEMISPHERE	JUL	AUG	SEP	OCT	NOV	DEC	JAN	FEB	MAR	APR	MAY	JUN

Cultural Recommendations

LIGHT: 1800–2400 fc. Light should be diffused or barely dappled, and direct sunlight avoided.

TEMPERATURES: Summer days average 89–91°F (32–33°C), and nights average 71–73°F (22–23°C), with a diurnal range of 15–19°F (8–11°C). The average diurnal range fluctuates only 4°F (2°C) through the year.

HUMIDITY: 70% throughout the year.

WATER: Ample moisture is needed while plants are actively growing. The rainfall pattern is wet/dry, but the relatively stable humidity levels in the habitat indicate that some moisture is continuously available.

FERTILIZER: ½ strength, applied weekly when plants are actively growing.

REST PERIOD: Winter temperatures are marginally cooler with little change in the average diurnal range. Fertilizer and water should be reduced when plants are not actively growing, but the plants should not become dry. In the habitat, light is somewhat higher in winter, but whether this is important in cultivation is unknown.

GROWING MEDIA: A fertile terrestrial mix with good drainage. Repotting is best done in early spring.

MISCELLANEOUS NOTES: N/A.

Plant and Flower Information

PLANT SIZE AND TYPE: A sympodial terrestrial 3 ft. (90 cm) tall.

PSEUDOBULB: 18 in. (46 cm) long. The stemlike pseudobulb is square in cross section.

LEAVES: Many, all along the stem. The elliptic leaves are thin, plicate, dull green, and eventually deciduous.

INFLORESCENCE: 30 in. (76 cm) long. The spikes emerge from internodes on the lower portion of the stem, well above the surface of the ground.

FLOWERS: 3–7. The delicately fragrant blossoms are 4 in. (10 cm) across. They may be uniformly white, or the lip may be pale to bright yellow with white in the center.

HYBRIDIZING NOTES: N/A.

REFERENCES: 31, 112, 122, 164, 175.

PHOTOS/DRAWINGS: *31*, 164, 175.

Phaius augustinianus Klotz. Authorities indicate that this was the same as *P. cupreus*, a doubtful species not mentioned in recent literature. REFERENCES: 122.

Phaius australis. See *P. tankervilleae*. REFERENCES: 122, 131, 205.

Phaius bensoniae. Now considered a synonym of *Thunia alba*. REFERENCES: 122.

Phaius bernaysii. See *P. tankervilleae*. REFERENCES: 122.

Phaius bicolor. See *P. tankervilleae*. REFERENCES: 122, 168.

Phaius blumei. See *P. tankervilleae*. REFERENCES: 122, 168.

Phaius boreensis J. J. Smith. Described as originating in Borneo, with few additional details given. This plant is unlikely to be available for cultivation. REFERENCES: 122.

Phaius bracteosus. See *P. flavus*. REFERENCES: 122.

Phaius calanthoides. Now considered a synonym of *Cephalantheropsis halconensis*. REFERENCES: 203.

Phaius callosus (Blume) Lindley

AKA: *P. hasseltii, P. kuhlii. P. callosus* var. *ecalcaratus* is now considered a separate species.

ORIGIN/HABITAT: Malaya and Indonesia. In Java, it grows at 4000-5000 ft. (1219-1524 m) in shady mountain forests.

CLIMATE: Station # 96755, Bogor, Indonesia, Lat. 6.5°S, Long. 106.8°E, at 558 ft. (170 m). The record high is

96 °F (35.6 °C), and the record low is 66 °F (18.9 °C). This adaptable plant grows well in both the lowlands and hills of its native habitat, so the weather records have not been adjusted.

N/HEMISPHERE	JAN	FEB	MAR	APR	MAY	JUN	JUL	AUG	SEP	OCT	NOV	DEC
°F AVG MAX	86	87	88	88	87	85	84	84	85	86	87	86
°F AVG MIN	73	73	73	74	74	74	74	74	74	75	75	74
DIURNAL RANGE	13	14	15	14	13	11	10	10	11	11	12	12
RAIN/INCHES	2.1	1.0	0.5	5.0	8.1	18.8	23.7	20.2	14.4	12.0	11.9	3.4
HUMIDITY/%	72	68	65	66	74	79	84	84	81	79	77	75
BLOOM SEASON											**	**
DAYS CLR @ 7AM	14	14	14	11	5	3	1	2	4	6	10	12
DAYS CLR @ 1PM	9	10	8	5	1	1	0	0	1	1	3	7
RAIN/MM	53	25	13	127	206	478	602	513	366	305	302	86
°C AVG MAX	30.0	30.6	31.1	31.1	30.6	29.4	28.9	28.9	29.4	30.0	30.6	30.0
°C AVG MIN	22.8	22.8	22.8	23.3	23.3	23.3	23.3	23.3	23.3	23.9	23.9	23.3
DIURNAL RANGE	7.2	7.8	8.3	7.8	7.3	6.1	5.6	5.6	6.1	6.1	6.7	6.7
S/HEMISPHERE	JUL	AUG	SEP	OCT	NOV	DEC	JAN	FEB	MAR	APR	MAY	JUN

Cultural Recommendations

LIGHT: 1200–2400 fc. Diffused or barely dappled light is preferred; direct sunlight should be avoided.

TEMPERATURES: Days average 84–88 °F (29–31 °C), and nights average 73–75 °F (23–24 °C), with a low summer diurnal range of 10–13 °F (6–7 °C). Temperatures at higher elevations are a few degrees cooler with a similar diurnal range and limited seasonal fluctuation. The plant should readily tolerate average lows near 60 °F (16 °C).

HUMIDITY: 65–85%.

WATER: Ample moisture is needed in the active growing season. The medium should be wet, but not soggy. The rainfall pattern is wet/dry.

FERTILIZER: ½ strength, applied weekly when plants are actively growing.

REST PERIOD: Growing temperatures should be maintained, with a slight increase in diurnal range; but water should be reduced to occasional misting, and fertilizer may be reduced or eliminated when the plant is not actively growing. In the habitat, humidity is 65–75% during the dry period, indicating a continuing supply of moisture. Light should be increased somewhat, as skies in the natural environment are frequently clear in winter.

GROWING MEDIA: A fertile terrestrial mix with good drainage. Repotting is best done in the spring when new growth starts.

MISCELLANEOUS NOTES: Bloom initiators have not been identified. In Northern Hemisphere cultivation, *P.*

callosus blooms Nov.–Dec. (May–Jun.), but it reportedly blooms in the spring and summer in its natural habitat.

Plant and Flower Information

PLANT SIZE AND TYPE: A large sympodial terrestrial.

PSEUDOBULB: 3 in. (8 cm) long and clustered.

LEAVES: 3–4 per growth. The leaves are 24 in. (61 cm) long and emerge from ground level.

INFLORESCENCE: 24 in. (61 cm) long. The erect spike arises from the base of new pseudobulbs.

FLOWERS: 7–10. The wide-opening blossoms are 4 in. (10 cm) across, fragrant, long-lasting, and brightly colored. Sepals and petals are white on the backside, and reddish to yellowish brown inside. The white or yellowish lip is ruffled along the margin and marked with purple in front.

HYBRIDIZING NOTES: N/A.

REFERENCES: 2, 68, 112, 118, 122, 175.

PHOTOS/DRAWINGS: *27, 68,* 175.

Phaius candidissimus. Now considered to belong in the genus *Thunia*. REFERENCES: 122.

Phaius carronii. See *P. tankervilleae*. REFERENCES: 122, 168.

Phaius celebicus Schlechter

AKA: Dr. Seidenfaden considers it possible that *P. celebicus* is conspecific with *P. flavus*.

ORIGIN/HABITAT: Sulawesi (Celebes) Island, Indonesia, and perhaps the Ibo Mountain range in New Guinea. It grows in humus in the high-elevation forests on Gunong Mahawo at 3940 ft. (1201 m).

CLIMATE: Station # 97014, Manado, Indonesia, Lat. 1.5 °N, Long. 124.9 °E, at 264 ft. (80 m). Temperatures are calculated for an elevation of 3950 ft. (1204 m), resulting in probable extremes of 85 °F (29.4 °C) and 53 °F (11.7 °C).

N/HEMISPHERE	JAN	FEB	MAR	APR	MAY	JUN	JUL	AUG	SEP	OCT	NOV	DEC
°F AVG MAX	73	73	73	74	75	75	75	77	77	77	75	74
°F AVG MIN	61	61	61	61	62	61	61	61	61	60	61	62
DIURNAL RANGE	12	12	12	13	13	14	14	16	16	17	14	12
RAIN/INCHES	18.6	13.8	12.2	8.0	6.4	6.5	4.8	4.0	3.4	4.9	8.9	14.7
HUMIDITY/%	84	83	83	83	81	80	75	72	75	77	82	83
BLOOM SEASON												**
DAYS CLR @ 8AM	4	3	6	11	11	12	12	12	14	17	12	8
DAYS CLR @ 2PM	1	1	1	2	1	3	3	4	4	4	1	1
RAIN/MM	472	351	310	203	163	165	122	102	86	124	226	373
°C AVG MAX	22.7	22.7	22.7	23.2	23.8	23.8	23.8	24.9	24.9	24.9	23.8	23.2
°C AVG MIN	16.0	16.0	16.0	16.0	16.6	16.0	16.0	16.0	16.0	15.5	16.0	16.6
DIURNAL RANGE	6.7	6.7	6.7	7.2	7.2	7.8	7.8	8.9	8.9	9.4	7.8	6.6
S/HEMISPHERE	JUL	AUG	SEP	OCT	NOV	DEC	JAN	FEB	MAR	APR	MAY	JUN

Cultural Recommendations

LIGHT: 2000–3000 fc. Low to intermediate diffused light is suggested. The light is bright during the clear summer mornings, but afternoons are cloudy, and plants grow in shady forest habitats.

TEMPERATURES: Summer days average 75–77°F (24–25°C), and nights average 61–62°F (16°C), with a diurnal range of 14–17°F (8–9°C). Extremes vary less than 10°F (6°C) from average growing temperatures, indicating an intolerance to wide temperature fluctuations.

HUMIDITY: 70–85%.

WATER: Plants should be kept moist. The rainfall pattern is wet/wetter.

FERTILIZER: ½ strength, applied weekly during the growing season.

REST PERIOD: A review of the climate indicates that the actual rest period may end in Oct. (Apr.), at which time the following conditions occur simultaneously: average night temperatures are lowest, moisture increases after the short dry season, and light is highest based on the number of clear days. It is interesting to note that blooming occurs 2 months later.

Except for a single month, winter days average 73–74°F (23°C), and nights average 61–62°F (16–17°C), with a slightly lower diurnal range of 12–13°F (7°C). The decreased diurnal range results from cooler days, not cooler nights. Rainfall in the habitat is greatest in winter, but water should probably not be increased in cultivation. Fertilizer should be reduced when the plants are not actively growing. Light is lowest in winter.

GROWING MEDIA: A fertile terrestrial mix with good drainage.

MISCELLANEOUS NOTES: The Dec. (Jun.) bloom season given in the climate table is based on reports from the habitat.

Plant and Flower Information

PLANT SIZE AND TYPE: An erect, 28 in. (70 cm) sympodial terrestrial.

PSEUDOBULB: 2 in. (5 cm) long. The cylindrical pseudobulbs are erect and arise from a short rhizome.

LEAVES: 3 per growth. The leaves are 10–14 in. (25–36 cm) long, lanceolate, and erect.

INFLORESCENCE: 20 in. (51 cm) long. The erect spike emerges from the base of the pseudobulb and is somewhat laxly flowered on the apical third.

FLOWERS: 4–6. The yellow flowers are 2.5 in. (6 cm) across and described as similar to those of *P. flavus* Lindley, with technical differences. The lip is deeply ruffled.

HYBRIDIZING NOTES: N/A.

REFERENCES: 163, 168.

PHOTOS/DRAWINGS: N/A.

Phaius columnaris Tang and Cheng

AKA: N/A.

ORIGIN/HABITAT: Northern Guangdong Province, China, at 755 ft. (230 m). It is usually found in limestone areas under forest trees.

CLIMATE: Station #59046, Liu-Chow, China, Lat. 24.3°N, Long. 109.3°E, at 322 ft. (98 m). Temperatures are calculated for an elevation of 750 ft. (229 m), resulting in probable extremes of 100°F (37.8°C) and 26°F (-3.3°C).

N/HEMISPHERE	JAN	FEB	MAR	APR	MAY	JUN	JUL	AUG	SEP	OCT	NOV	DEC
°F AVG MAX	58	59	68	76	83	89	92	91	90	82	71	63
°F AVG MIN	41	45	54	62	69	74	76	75	72	63	54	46
DIURNAL RANGE	17	14	14	14	14	15	16	16	18	19	17	17
RAIN/INCHES	0.9	2.2	4.1	3.9	8.2	7.8	13.3	8.8	1.3	4.2	2.0	1.4
HUMIDITY/%	66	73	79	78	78	78	78	77	70	66	73	73
BLOOM SEASON				**	**							
DAYS CLR @ 7AM	4	2	2	2	3	3	3	8	8	10	8	9
DAYS CLR @ 1PM	8	5	4	4	2	2	2	5	8	10	10	11
RAIN/MM	23	56	104	99	208	198	338	224	33	107	51	36
°C AVG MAX	14.2	14.8	19.8	24.2	28.1	31.4	33.1	32.5	32.0	27.5	21.4	17.0
°C AVG MIN	4.8	7.0	12.0	16.4	20.3	23.1	24.2	23.7	22.0	17.0	12.0	7.5
DIURNAL RANGE	9.4	7.8	7.8	7.8	7.8	8.3	8.9	8.8	10.0	10.5	9.4	9.5
S/HEMISPHERE	JUL	AUG	SEP	OCT	NOV	DEC	JAN	FEB	MAR	APR	MAY	JUN

Cultural Recommendations

LIGHT: 2000–3000 fc.

TEMPERATURES: Summer days average 76–92°F (24–33°C), and nights average 62–76°F (16–24°C), with a diurnal range of 14–16°F (8–9°C) which fluctuates only 5°F (3°C) during the year. *P. columnaris* should be very tolerant of hot summer weather.

HUMIDITY: 70–80%.

WATER: Ample moisture is needed in the active growing season. The medium should be moist, but not soggy. The rainfall pattern is wet/dry.

FERTILIZER: ½ strength, applied weekly when plants are actively growing.

REST PERIOD: Winter days average 58–76°F (14–24°C), and nights average 41–54°F (5–12°C). The diurnal range varies less than might be expected since the high and low temperatures decline simultaneously. The climate data indicate a 2–3-month winter dry period, but the high humidity in the habitat indicates that some moisture is continuously available in the form of dew, fog, and low clouds. Cultivated plants should receive occasional light mistings, particularly on bright, sunny days. In the habitat, light is higher in early autumn when clear weather occurs most frequently. This plant survives cold, dry winters.

GROWING MEDIA: A fertile terrestrial mix with good drainage.

MISCELLANEOUS NOTES: *P. columnaris* is described as easy to cultivate.

Plant and Flower Information

PLANT SIZE AND TYPE: A lithophyte or terrestrial 24–32 in. (60–80 cm) tall.

PSEUDOBULB: 6–10 in. (15–25 cm) long. The unusual column-shaped, olive-green pseudobulbs are ridged with 9 nodes, making the plant easy to identify even when not in bloom.

LEAVES: 6 per growth. The leaves are 12–24 in. (30–60 cm) long, arching, papery, ovate-lanceolate to oblong, and pointed at the apex.

INFLORESCENCE: 9 in. (23 cm) long. The stoutly erect spike arises from the pseudobulb's basal nodes.

FLOWERS: 10–20. The creamy white blossoms are 2.5 in. (6 cm) across, succulent, and not wide-opening. Flowers are held in a drooping cluster at the tip of the inflorescence. The lip is toothed, deeply ruffled, and marked with rich yellow-orange to orange-red.

HYBRIDIZING NOTES: N/A.

REFERENCES: 122, 196.

PHOTOS/DRAWINGS: *196.*

Phaius cooperi Rolfe.

Described in 1910 with the habitat given as unknown, this plant is not mentioned in recent literature and is unlikely to be available for cultivation. REFERENCES: 122, 160.

Phaius corymbioides Schlechter.

No information could be located. This plant is not mentioned in recent literature and is unlikely to be available for cultivation. REFERENCES: 122.

Phaius crinita. See *P. mishmensis.* REFERENCES: 122, 168.

Phaius crispus. See P. flavus. REFERENCES: 122, 168.

Phaius cupreus Rchb.f. AKA: *P. augustinianus.*

Reportedly collected in Java. J. J. Smith, however, considered it a questionable species. It is not mentioned in recent literature and is unlikely to be available for cultivation. REFERENCES: 122, 175.

Phaius daenikerii Kraenzlin

AKA: Also spelled *P. daenikeri.*

ORIGIN/HABITAT: Endemic to New Caledonia. It grows at 2460–3940 ft. (750–1201 m), usually among rocks in humid forest areas.

CLIMATE: Station # 91592, Noumea, New Caledonia, Lat. 22.3°S, Long. 166.5°E, at 246 ft. (75 m). Temperatures are calculated for an elevation of 3000 ft. (914 m), resulting in probable extremes of 90°F (32.2°C) and 43°F (6.1°C).

N/HEMISPHERE	JAN	FEB	MAR	APR	MAY	JUN	JUL	AUG	SEP	OCT	NOV	DEC
°F AVG MAX	67	67	69	71	74	77	77	76	76	74	70	68
°F AVG MIN	53	52	54	56	59	61	63	64	63	61	57	55
DIURNAL RANGE	14	15	15	15	15	16	14	12	13	13	13	13
RAIN/INCHES	3.6	2.6	2.5	2.0	2.4	2.6	3.7	5.1	5.7	5.2	4.4	3.7
HUMIDITY/%	73	70	69	67	68	69	71	74	75	76	73	73
BLOOM SEASON	*					*			*			
DAYS CLR @ 11AM	7	9	9	15	12	10	7	6	7	7	7	7
DAYS CLR @ 5PM	7	11	6	11	7	6	5	4	4	5	3	7
RAIN/MM	91	66	64	51	61	66	94	130	145	132	112	94
°C AVG MAX	19.4	19.4	20.5	21.6	23.3	25.0	25.0	24.4	24.4	23.3	21.1	20.0
°C AVG MIN	11.6	11.1	12.2	13.3	15.0	16.1	17.2	17.7	17.2	16.1	13.8	12.7
DIURNAL RANGE	7.8	8.3	8.3	8.3	8.3	8.9	7.8	6.7	7.2	7.2	7.3	7.3
S/HEMISPHERE	JUL	AUG	SEP	OCT	NOV	DEC	JAN	FEB	MAR	APR	MAY	JUN

Cultural Recommendations

LIGHT: 1800–3000 fc. Days are frequently clear, indicating fairly high light. However, the humid forest microclimate suggests lower light.

TEMPERATURES: Summer days average 74–77 °F (23–25 °C), and nights average 60–64 °F (16–18 °C), with a diurnal range of 13–16 °F (7–9 °C) which fluctuates only 4 °F (2 °C) throughout the year.

HUMIDITY: 70–75%.

WATER: Ample moisture is needed during periods of active growth, but the medium should not be soggy. Monthly rainfall amounts are relatively low and consistent throughout the year, with the greatest rainfall occurring in late summer and early autumn. Moisture may be more available than the climate records indicate, since the habitat is described as humid forests. However, rain in this region normally falls as heavy showers, and *P. daenikerii* might be healthiest if it is thoroughly saturated then allowed to almost dry before additional water is applied.

FERTILIZER: ½ strength, applied weekly while the plant is actively growing.

REST PERIOD: Winter days average 67–70 °F (19–21 °C), and nights average 52–59 °F (11–15 °C). Day and night temperatures decline simultaneously, resulting in little change in the limited diurnal range of 13–15 °F (7-8 °C). Water and fertilizer should be reduced during periods of slow growth or lower temperatures.

GROWING MEDIA: A fertile terrestrial mix with good drainage.

MISCELLANEOUS NOTES: The bloom season shown in the climate table is based on collection records. *P. daenikerii* may be free-flowering, but flower initiators are unknown. The plant and flower information provided in Nicolas Hallé's *Flore de la Nouvelle Calédonie et Dépendencies* (1977) is extremely sketchy.

Plant and Flower Information

PLANT SIZE AND TYPE: A 16–20 in. (40–50 cm) sympodial terrestrial or lithophyte.

PSEUDOBULB: N/A.

LEAVES: 2–3 per growth.

INFLORESCENCE: N/A.

FLOWERS: 5–12. The blossoms are fragrant, but the scent is sometimes described as unpleasant.

HYBRIDIZING NOTES: N/A.

REFERENCES: 107, 122.

PHOTOS/DRAWINGS: 107.

Phaius dodgsonii. Now considered to belong to the genus *Thunia*. REFERENCES: 122.

Phaius ecalcaratus J. J. Smith. Once considered a variation of *P. callosus*, it was described in 1911 as originating in Indonesia. This plant is not mentioned in current literature and is unlikely to be available for cultivation. REFERENCES: 122.

Phaius epiphyticus Seidenfaden

AKA: N/A.

ORIGIN/HABITAT: Endemic to Thailand, where it is found near Loei at 4600–5000 ft. (1402–1524 m).

CLIMATE: Station # 48353, Loei, Thailand, Lat. 17.5 °N, Long. 101.5 °E, at 817 ft. (249 m). Temperatures are calculated for an elevation of 4500 ft. (1372 m), resulting in probable extremes of 94 °F (34.4 °C) and 22 °F (-5.6 °C).

N/HEMISPHERE	JAN	FEB	MAR	APR	MAY	JUN	JUL	AUG	SEP	OCT	NOV	DEC
°F AVG MAX	73	77	82	85	81	79	78	77	76	75	75	72
°F AVG MIN	40	46	53	58	61	62	62	62	61	57	52	44
DIURNAL RANGE	33	31	29	27	20	17	16	15	15	18	23	28
RAIN/INCHES	0.2	0.8	1.4	3.6	6.9	6.8	5.0	8.3	8.8	4.3	0.8	0.1
HUMIDITY/%	62	60	59	62	75	77	77	79	82	79	74	69
BLOOM SEASON	N/A											
DAYS CLR @ 7AM	1	1	1	2	1	0	1	0	0	1	1	1
DAYS CLR @ 1PM	22	14	8	5	2	0	0	1	1	5	11	15
RAIN/MM	5	20	36	91	175	173	127	211	224	109	20	3
°C AVG MAX	22.7	24.9	27.7	29.4	27.1	26.0	25.5	24.9	24.4	23.8	23.8	22.1
°C AVG MIN	4.4	7.7	11.6	14.4	16.0	16.6	16.6	16.6	16.0	13.8	11.0	6.6
DIURNAL RANGE	18.3	17.2	16.1	15.0	11.1	9.4	8.9	8.3	8.4	10.0	12.8	15.5
S/HEMISPHERE	JUL	AUG	SEP	OCT	NOV	DEC	JAN	FEB	MAR	APR	MAY	JUN

Cultural Recommendations

LIGHT: 1800–2000 fc. Diffused or barely dappled light is recommended. Direct sunlight should be avoided.

TEMPERATURES: Days average 75–85 °F (27–29 °C), and nights average 58–62 °F (16–17 °C), with a summer diurnal range of 15–18 °F (8–10 °C).

HUMIDITY: 60–80%.

WATER: Ample moisture is needed when plants are actively growing. Mounted plants should be misted frequently, and potted plants should be kept moist. The rainfall pattern is wet/dry.

FERTILIZER: ¼–½ strength, applied weekly to biweekly—less fertilizer than is suggested for terrestrial *Phaius*.

REST PERIOD: Days average 72–77°F (22–25°C), and nights average 40–46°F (4–8°C) for about 3 months, with a diurnal range of 28–33°F (16-18°C). A less severe rest, however, might prove sufficient in cultivation. Fertilizer should be eliminated when the plants are not actively growing. For 3–5 months, water should be reduced to occasional light mistings. Frequent morning fog, dew, and low clouds in the habitat provide moisture despite low rainfall. Humidity averages may be reduced to 60–70%. Light levels are slightly higher in winter due to clear afternoons. Habitat records indicate that the plant tolerates short periods below freezing, but severe temperatures are best avoided in cultivation.

GROWING MEDIA: Cultural records are lacking, but plants should probably be slabbed with a layer of sphagnum or potted in a bark mixture. Repotting would best be done as growth resumes in the spring.

MISCELLANEOUS NOTES: N/A.

Plant and Flower Information

PLANT SIZE AND TYPE: A sympodial epiphyte that is unusually small for the genus.

PSEUDOBULB: Branching.

LEAVES: 1–2 per growth. The leaves are 4–8 in. (10–20 cm) long, plicate, and persistent.

INFLORESCENCE: Length unknown. The spikes arise from nodes on the pseudobulbs.

FLOWERS: 2–3. The small flowers are 1.2 in. (3 cm) across. The sepals and petals are sulphur-yellow, and the lip sidelobes have a faint, reddish-purple tint.

HYBRIDIZING NOTES: N/A.

REFERENCES: 122, 168.

PHOTOS/DRAWINGS: 168.

Phaius flavus (Blume) Lindley

AKA: *Bletia woodfordii, Hecabe lutea, Limordorum flavum, Phaius bracteosus, P. crispus, P. flexuosus, P. indigoferus* Blume non Hassock, *P. maculatus, P. minor, P. platychilus, P. somai, P. undulatomarginata, P. un-dulatomarginatus, P. woodfordii (woodfortii).* Dr. Seidenfaden considers it possible that *P. celebicus* is conspecific with *P. flavus.*

ORIGIN/HABITAT: This widespread plant grows in Thailand, Malaya, the Philippines, China, Japan, and Taiwan. In India, it grows in swampy places. It usually grows above 4000 ft. (1219 m), and in western Java it is found at 5800 ft. (1768 m).

CLIMATE: Station # 48327, Chiang Mai, Thailand, Lat. 18.8°N, Long. 99.0°E, at 1100 ft. (335 m). Temperatures are calculated for an elevation of 4000 ft. (1219 m), resulting in probable extremes of 99°F (37.2°C) and 28°F (-2.2°C).

N/HEMISPHERE	JAN	FEB	MAR	APR	MAY	JUN	JUL	AUG	SEP	OCT	NOV	DEC
°F AVG MAX	75	80	85	86	84	80	79	77	78	79	76	74
°F AVG MIN	46	47	52	60	64	64	64	65	63	61	56	47
DIURNAL RANGE	29	33	33	26	20	16	15	12	15	18	20	27
RAIN/INCHES	0.3	0.4	0.6	2.0	5.5	6.1	7.4	8.7	11.5	4.9	1.5	0.4
HUMIDITY/%	73	65	58	62	73	78	80	83	83	81	79	76
BLOOM SEASON	**	**	***	**	*		*	**		*		*
DAYS CLR @ 7AM	5	5	2	2	1	0	0	0	0	1	3	3
DAYS CLR @ 1PM	9	8	4	2	0	0	0	0	0	0	1	3
RAIN/MM	8	10	15	51	140	155	188	221	292	124	38	10
°C AVG MAX	24.1	26.9	29.7	30.2	29.1	26.9	26.4	25.2	25.8	26.4	24.7	23.6
°C AVG MIN	8.0	8.6	11.3	15.8	18.0	18.0	18.0	18.6	17.5	16.4	13.6	8.6
DIURNAL RANGE	16.1	18.3	18.4	14.4	11.1	8.9	8.4	6.6	8.3	10.0	11.1	15.0
S/HEMISPHERE	JUL	AUG	SEP	OCT	NOV	DEC	JAN	FEB	MAR	APR	MAY	JUN

Cultural Recommendations

LIGHT: 1500–2400 fc. Diffused light is appropriate, since clear summer days are exceedingly rare in the habitat. Direct sunlight should be avoided.

TEMPERATURES: Days average 77–86°F (24–30°C), and summer nights average 63–65°F (18–19°C), with a diurnal range of 12–20°F (7–11°C). The warmest temperatures occur in late spring, before the onset of the summer monsoon. Both highs and lows are more moderate after the start of the summer wet season. While *P. flavus* is wide-ranging, it is always found in the hills, which suggests that either night temperatures or the diurnal range are important factors.

HUMIDITY: 75–85%.

WATER: Ample moisture is needed in the active growing season. The medium should be wet, but not soggy. The rainfall pattern is wet/dry.

FERTILIZER: ½ strength, applied weekly during periods of active growth.

REST PERIOD: Winter days average 75–80°F (24–27°C), and nights average 46–52°F (8–11°C). The winter diurnal range is 27–33 °F (15–18 °C). During late winter and early spring, humidity readings fall to 58–65%, indicating dramatically reduced moisture in the habitat. For 4 months, water should be reduced to occasional light misting, simulating the moisture available from morning dew, fog, and low clouds. Fertilizer should be eliminated. In the habitat, winter light may be slightly higher, but it may not be critical in cultivation.

GROWING MEDIA: A fertile terrestrial mix with good drainage. Plants are best repotted while new roots are actively growing.

MISCELLANEOUS NOTES: Flower initiators are unknown. In Northern Hemisphere cultivation, heaviest blooming occurs during the winter rest period, but the bloom time is highly variable in the native habitats.

Plant and Flower Information

PLANT SIZE AND TYPE: A 24–36 in. (60–90 cm) sympodial terrestrial that may reach a length of 60 in. (150 cm).

PSEUDOBULB: 4–6 in. (10–15 cm) long. The large, closely spaced pseudobulbous stems are cylindrical or conical and taper at the apex.

LEAVES: 4–8 per growth. The leaves are 12–20 in. (30–50 cm) long, ovate to lanceolate, plicate, and normally dark green. They are often spotted with yellow or white variegations. Leaf bases overlap and alternate along the stem.

INFLORESCENCE: 18–24 in. (46–60 cm) long. The erect spike arises from the base of the stem or side of the pseudobulb. Flowers are arranged in a crowded raceme.

FLOWERS: 10–15. Each showy, fragrant blossom is about 3 in. (8 cm) across and lasts about 2 weeks. The oblong sepals and petals are erect to spreading and range from light to bright yellow or greenish white. Ruffled, tubular, and covered with hairs, the lip may be yellow or pink with brown, red-brown, or orange markings on the ridges and along the margin. Flowers are extremely variable in size and coloring.

HYBRIDIZING NOTES: N/A.

REFERENCES: 9, 20, 24, 31, 91, 112, 118, 132, 148, 157, 167, 168, 175, 203.

PHOTOS/DRAWINGS: 24, *27*, *31*, *132*, 168, 175.

Phaius flexuosus. See *P. flavus*. REFERENCES: 122.

Phaius formosus. Apparently a horticultural name rather than a valid species. REFERENCES: 122.

Phaius fragilis L. O. Williams

AKA: N/A.

ORIGIN/HABITAT: Endemic to the Philippines, where it is found in the mossy forests of many islands at 2950–4920 ft. (899–1500 m).

CLIMATE: Station # 98754, Davao, Philippines, Lat. 7.1 °N, Long. 125.6 °E, at 88 ft. (27 m). Temperatures are calculated for an elevation of 4000 ft. (1219 m), resulting in probable extremes of 84 °F (28.9 °C) and 52 °F (11.1 °C).

N/HEMISPHERE	JAN	FEB	MAR	APR	MAY	JUN	JUL	AUG	SEP	OCT	NOV	DEC
°F AVG MAX	74	75	77	78	77	75	75	75	75	76	76	75
°F AVG MIN	59	59	59	60	61	60	60	60	60	60	60	59
DIURNAL RANGE	15	16	18	18	16	15	15	15	15	16	16	16
RAIN/INCHES	4.8	4.5	5.2	5.8	9.2	9.1	6.5	6.5	6.7	7.9	5.3	6.1
HUMIDITY/%	81	82	78	79	82	83	84	83	83	82	82	82
BLOOM SEASON				*	*	*	*	*				
DAYS CLR @ 8AM	5	7	9	9	6	4	5	4	5	7	6	6
DAYS CLR @ 2PM	3	1	3	4	2	2	3	2	2	2	2	2
RAIN/MM	122	114	132	147	234	231	165	165	170	201	135	155
°C AVG MAX	23.4	23.9	25.1	25.6	25.1	23.9	23.9	23.9	23.9	24.5	24.5	23.9
°C AVG MIN	15.1	15.1	15.1	15.6	16.2	15.6	15.6	15.6	15.6	15.6	15.6	15.1
DIURNAL RANGE	8.3	8.8	10.0	10.0	8.9	8.3	8.3	8.3	8.3	8.9	8.9	8.8
S/HEMISPHERE	JUL	AUG	SEP	OCT	NOV	DEC	JAN	FEB	MAR	APR	MAY	JUN

Cultural Recommendations

LIGHT: 1500–2400 fc. Diffused or barely dappled light is recommended, as clear days are rare in the habitat. Direct sunlight should be avoided.

TEMPERATURES: Days average 74–78 °F (23–26 °C), and nights average 59–61 °F (15–16 °C), with a summer diurnal range of 15–16 °F (8–9 °C). The limited summer temperature range indicates a probable intolerance to wide temperature fluctuations. The extreme temperatures vary just a few degrees from the average growing temperatures.

HUMIDITY: 80%.

WATER: The medium should be kept moist. The rainfall pattern is wet all year, with even heavier rainfall in the mountains where the plant grows.

FERTILIZER: ½ strength, applied weekly when plants are actively growing.

REST PERIOD: Growing temperatures should be maintained year-round. The diurnal range increases to

18 °F (10 °C) for 2 months in the spring. The probable extreme low is just a few degrees below the average low. Fertilizer should be reduced, but plants should be kept moist all winter.

GROWING MEDIA: A fertile terrestrial mix with good drainage. Repotting is best done when roots begin active growth.

MISCELLANEOUS NOTES: Summer blooming may be triggered by increased hours of light or the slight increase in the diurnal temperature range. The bloom season shown in the climate table is based on collection records since no cultivation records were available.

P. fragilis could be difficult to cultivate. The limited habitat suggests that careful attention should be paid to its cultural requirements.

Plant and Flower Information

PLANT SIZE AND TYPE: A moderately sized, 16 in. (40 cm) sympodial terrestrial.

PSEUDOBULB: Stemlike.

LEAVES: Number unknown. The leaves are 3–13 in. (8–33 cm) long and variable in shape, ranging from lanceolate to broadly elliptic-ovoid.

INFLORESCENCE: 10 in. (25 cm) long.

FLOWERS: Number unknown. The blossoms are 2–3 in. (5–7 cm) across and white, with a yellowish center and a delicate texture.

HYBRIDIZING NOTES: N/A.

REFERENCES: 203.

PHOTOS/DRAWINGS: N/A.

Phaius françoisii (Schlechter) Summerhayes

AKA: *Gastorchis françoisii*.

ORIGIN/HABITAT: Endemic to the humid forests of the Mandraka valleys in central Madagascar at 3940–5250 ft. (1201–1600 m).

CLIMATE: Station # 67109, Arivonimamo, Malagasy, Lat. 19.0 °S, Long. 47.2 °E, at 4757 ft. (1450 m). The record high is 90 °F (32.2 °C), and the record low is 30 °F (-1.1 °C).

N/HEMISPHERE	JAN	FEB	MAR	APR	MAY	JUN	JUL	AUG	SEP	OCT	NOV	DEC
°F AVG MAX	68	71	74	78	79	79	79	78	77	77	73	70
°F AVG MIN	46	46	48	52	56	58	59	58	59	55	51	47
DIURNAL RANGE	22	25	26	26	23	21	20	20	18	22	22	23
RAIN/INCHES	0.2	0.5	0.2	2.5	5.1	8.3	12.8	8.2	8.6	1.4	0.7	0.4
HUMIDITY/%	68	67	62	64	68	70	73	75	73	73	73	69
BLOOM SEASON								**	**	*		
DAYS CLR @ 3AM	3	10	5	10	5	3	4	3	1	8	11	5
DAYS CLR @ 3PM	2	6	3	7	2	1	0	1	0	3	6	4
RAIN/MM	5	13	5	64	130	211	325	208	218	36	18	10
°C AVG MAX	20.0	21.7	23.3	25.6	26.1	26.1	26.1	25.6	25.0	25.0	22.8	21.1
°C AVG MIN	7.8	7.8	8.9	11.1	13.3	14.4	15.0	14.4	15.0	12.8	10.6	8.3
DIURNAL RANGE	12.2	13.9	14.4	14.5	12.8	11.7	11.1	11.2	10.0	12.2	12.2	12.8
S/HEMISPHERE	JUL	AUG	SEP	OCT	NOV	DEC	JAN	FEB	MAR	APR	MAY	JUN

Cultural Recommendations

LIGHT: 1800–2400 fc. Low to intermediate diffused light is suggested by the humid forest habitat.

TEMPERATURES: Days average 77–79 °F (25–26 °C), and nights average 56–59 °F (13–15 °C), with a summer diurnal range of 18–23 °F (10–13 °C).

HUMIDITY: 65–75%.

WATER: Ample moisture is needed in the active growing season. The medium should be kept moist, but not soggy. The rainfall pattern is wet/dry, but humidity remains moderately high.

FERTILIZER: ½ strength, applied weekly when plants are actively growing.

REST PERIOD: A 4–5 month cool, dry rest is indicated. In the habitat, winter days average 68-74 °F (20–23 °C), and nights average 46–51 °F (8–11 °C), with a diurnal range of 22–26 °F (12–14 °C). However, Kew Gardens successfully cultivates *P. françoisii* with winter highs of 68–74 °F (22–23 °C) and lows of 55 °F (13 °C), for a diurnal range of 13–19 °F (7–11 °C). After the leaves drop, water should be reduced to occasional mistings, and fertilizer eliminated. In the habitat, the number of clear days increases, indicating higher light, but whether this is important in cultivation is unknown.

Flowering occurs at the end of the growing season.

GROWING MEDIA: A fertile terrestrial mix that retains moisture. Kew Gardens uses a mix of 2 parts peat and 1 part each of leaf-mold, sand, and charcoal. Plants are best repotted as growth resumes in the spring.

MISCELLANEOUS NOTES: *P. françoisii* is a handsome foliage plant which is attractive even when not in bloom, yet it is infrequently collected and seldom cultivated outside Madagascar.

Plant and Flower Information

PLANT SIZE AND TYPE: A 24 in. (61 cm) sympodial terrestrial.

PSEUDOBULB: The rhizome is cormlike.

LEAVES: 2–3 per growth. The glossy leaves are 12–16 in. (30–40 cm) long, bright green, broadly oval-lanceolate, pointed, plicate, suberect, and deciduous.

INFLORESCENCE: 14–36 in. (35–90 cm) long. The spike emerges from the base of the growth and is somewhat laxly flowered.

FLOWERS: 7–12 normally, and rarely, as many as 25. The showy blossoms are 1.5–2.5 in. (4–6 cm) across and last 3–5 weeks. Pink to deep rose on the back, the narrow sepals and smaller petals are white to pink on the inside. The lip is red to red-violet, and the sidelobes are longer than the midlobe. The pubescent, V-shaped callus is surrounded by yellow hairs. Flowers are highly variable in size and color.

HYBRIDIZING NOTES: *P. françoisii* is known to hybridize naturally with *P. humblotii*.

REFERENCES: 21, 35, 117, 121, 122.

PHOTOS/DRAWINGS: N/A.

Phaius geffrayi J. Bosser

AKA: N/A.

ORIGIN/HABITAT: Madagascar, at 3280 ft. (1000 m) in moist, shady forest areas on Mt. d'Ambre.

CLIMATE: Station # 67009, Diego Suarez, Malagasy, Lat. 12.3°S, Long. 49.3°E, at 95 ft. (29 m). Temperatures are calculated for an elevation of 3280 ft. (1000 m), resulting in probable extremes of 87°F (30.6°C) and 52°F (11.1°C).

N/HEMISPHERE	JAN	FEB	MAR	APR	MAY	JUN	JUL	AUG	SEP	OCT	NOV	DEC
°F AVG MAX	73	73	73	75	77	79	77	78	77	77	74	74
°F AVG MIN	58	58	59	61	63	64	64	64	64	64	63	60
DIURNAL RANGE	15	15	14	14	14	15	13	14	13	13	11	14
RAIN/INCHES	0.2	0.2	0.2	0.4	0.9	4.9	10.4	8.1	7.2	2.3	0.3	0.3
HUMIDITY/%	65	65	66	69	73	76	82	83	81	76	69	67
BLOOM SEASON	N/A											
DAYS CLR @ 3AM	21	21	21	21	14	11	10	9	10	13	19	20
DAYS CLR @ 3PM	10	14	16	19	12	4	2	1	1	7	13	12
RAIN/MM	5	5	5	10	23	124	264	206	183	58	8	8
°C AVG MAX	23.0	23.0	23.0	24.2	25.3	26.4	25.3	25.8	25.3	25.3	23.6	23.6
°C AVG MIN	14.7	14.7	15.3	16.4	17.5	18.0	18.0	18.0	18.0	18.0	17.5	15.8
DIURNAL RANGE	8.3	8.3	7.7	7.8	7.8	8.4	7.3	7.8	7.3	7.3	6.1	7.8
S/HEMISPHERE	JUL	AUG	SEP	OCT	NOV	DEC	JAN	FEB	MAR	APR	MAY	JUN

Cultural Recommendations

LIGHT: 1200–2000 fc. Diffused or barely dappled light is recommended. Direct sunlight should be avoided.

TEMPERATURES: Summer days average 75–79°F (24–27°C), and nights average 63–64°F (17–18°C). The average temperatures vary only 6°F (3°C) between summer and winter, and the diurnal range of 11–15°F (6–8°C) fluctuates only 4°F (2°C).

HUMIDITY: 70–80%.

WATER: Ample moisture is needed during periods of active growth. The rainfall pattern is wet/dry, but the moisture in the plant's microclimate is probably greater than the rainfall amounts recorded at the lower-elevation weather station.

FERTILIZER: ½ strength, applied weekly when plants are actively growing.

REST PERIOD: Winter days average 73–75°F (23–24°C), and nights average 58–60°F (15–16°C). The probable extreme low is just 6°F (3°C) below the average winter low. In cultivation, water should be decreased to occasional misting for 4–6 months, and fertilizer eliminated when the plants are dormant. In the habitat, winter light is high and clear days are common, but whether this is important in cultivation is not known.

GROWING MEDIA: A fertile terrestrial mix with good drainage. Repotting is best done in early spring as plants resume growth.

MISCELLANEOUS NOTES: N/A.

Plant and Flower Information

PLANT SIZE AND TYPE: An erect, moderately sized sympodial terrestrial.

PSEUDOBULB: Small and round.

LEAVES: 3–6 per growth. The leaves are 8–18 in. (20–45 cm) long, erect to arching, and linear to oblong, with gently wavy margins.

INFLORESCENCE: The spike arises laterally. The flowers, which open simultaneously, are arranged in a terminal raceme.

FLOWERS: 5–12. Individual blossoms are 2.0–2.5 in. (5–6 cm) across. Initially greenish white, they turn yellow with age. The lip is smooth and has no callus. Floral bracts are persistent.

HYBRIDIZING NOTES: Flowers are often self-pollinating.

REFERENCES: 21, 122.

PHOTOS/DRAWINGS: N/A.

Phaius gibbosulus H. Perrier. Not mentioned in current literature, this plant is unlikely to be available for cultivation. REFERENCES: 122.

Phaius giganteous. See *P. tankervilleae.* REFERENCES: 122.

Phaius gracilis Hayata. See *P. mishmensis.* REFERENCES: 122.

Phaius gracilis (Lindley) S. S. Ying. Now considered a synonym of *Cephalantheropsis gracilis.* REFERENCES: 203.

Phaius graeffi Rchb.f. Collected in Samoa and Fiji. This species was re-collected by a U.S. exploring expedition, but habitat was not described. The plant is unlikely to be available for cultivation. REFERENCES: 122, 153.

Phaius grandiflorus. See *P. tankervilleae.* REFERENCES: 122, 168.

Phaius grandifolius. See *P. tankervilleae.* REFERENCES: 122, 168.

Phaius gratus Blume. Ambon Island. This plant is not mentioned in current literature and is unlikely to be available for cultivation. REFERENCES: 122.

Phaius hainanensis Tang and Cheng

AKA: N/A.

ORIGIN/HABITAT: Hainan Island, China, in the South China Sea. It grows in rock crevices at 3608 ft. (1100 m).

CLIMATE: Station # 59948, Yulin, Hainan, China, Lat. 18.2°N, Long. 109.5°E, at 43 ft. (13 m). Temperatures are calculated for an elevation of 3600 ft. (1097 m), resulting in probable extremes of 85°F (29.4°C) and 31°F (-0.6°C). Since rainfall records are not available for Yulin, the rainfall recorded at Station # 59758, Hai-Kou, Hainan, China, Lat. 20.0°N, Long. 110.4°E, is given. Because of topography, there is probably more rain at the habitat elevation than the climate table indicates, but the patterns are no doubt similar.

N/HEMISPHERE	JAN	FEB	MAR	APR	MAY	JUN	JUL	AUG	SEP	OCT	NOV	DEC
°F AVG MAX	65	66	70	74	77	77	76	76	75	73	71	67
°F AVG MIN	51	55	60	64	67	67	67	66	65	61	58	54
DIURNAL RANGE	14	11	10	10	10	10	9	10	10	12	13	13
RAIN/INCHES	1.0	1.2	1.8	3.8	6.2	8.1	8.5	7.4	10.1	6.7	3.2	1.9
HUMIDITY/%	68	74	77	78	80	83	83	84	84	77	74	72
BLOOM SEASON					**							
DAYS CLR @ 7AM	6	7	4	5	3	1	3	2	3	9	11	8
DAYS CLR @ 1PM	13	9	8	10	6	3	4	3	3	9	11	9
RAIN/MM	25	31	46	97	158	206	216	188	257	170	81	48
°C AVG MAX	18.5	19.0	21.3	23.5	25.1	25.1	24.6	24.6	24.0	22.9	21.8	19.6
°C AVG MIN	10.7	12.9	15.7	17.9	19.6	19.6	19.6	19.0	18.5	16.3	14.6	12.4
DIURNAL RANGE	7.8	6.1	5.6	5.6	5.5	5.5	5.0	5.6	5.5	6.6	7.2	7.2
S/HEMISPHERE	JUL	AUG	SEP	OCT	NOV	DEC	JAN	FEB	MAR	APR	MAY	JUN

Cultural Recommendations

LIGHT: 2000–3000 fc is suggested.

TEMPERATURES: Summer days average 74–77°F (24–25°C), and nights average 64–67°F (18–20°C), with a diurnal range of 9–10°F (5–6°C).

HUMIDITY: 78–84%.

WATER: Despite the wet/dry rainfall pattern, the medium should remain moist throughout the year.

FERTILIZER: ½ strength, applied weekly when plants are actively growing.

REST PERIOD: Winter days average 65–70°F (19–21°C), and nights average 51–60°F (10–16°C), with a diurnal range of 10–14°F (6–8°C). Water and humidity should be reduced for 3–4 months, but the plant should not be allowed to dry out, since moisture from fog and dew is available in the habitat. Winter light is higher in the habitat..

GROWING MEDIA: A fertile terrestrial mix with good drainage.

MISCELLANEOUS NOTES: *P. hainanensis* is reportedly easy to cultivate.

Plant and Flower Information

PLANT SIZE AND TYPE: The 20–32 in. (50–80 cm) plant is described as semiterrestrial.

PSEUDOBULB: 2.0–3.5 in. (5–9 cm) long. The oval-to-conical pseudobulb is dark green.

LEAVES: 4–6 per growth. The arching leaves are pointed, 10–14 in. (25–70 cm) long, oblong-ovate to broadly lanceolate, and slightly undulate at the margins with black, hairlike scales.

INFLORESCENCE: 16 in. (40 cm) long, erect, and stout. The spike emerges from the side of the pseudobulb.

FLOWERS: 8–12. The creamy white blossoms are 3.0–3.5 in. (8–9 cm) across. The oval-lanceolate sepals and petals have a hooklike projection at the apex. The lip is funnel-shaped, marked with yellow in the center, and becomes deep yellow with age.

HYBRIDIZING NOTES: Seed capsules open in Dec.–Jan. (Jun.–Jul.).

REFERENCES: 122, 168, 196.

PHOTOS/DRAWINGS: *196.*

Phaius halconensis. Now considered a synonym of *Cephalantheropsis halconensis.* REFERENCES: 203.

Phaius hasseltii. See *P. callosus.* REFERENCES: 122.

Phaius hookerianus Rchb.f. Described in 1856. Habitat is unknown. References: 122.

Phaius humblotii (Rchb.f.) Summerhayes

AKA: Also spelled *P. humbloti. P. schlechteri* is now considered a color variation of *P. humblotii.*

ORIGIN/HABITAT: Endemic to Madagascar and the Cormoro Islands in wet, semideciduous forests at 3280–4920 ft. (1000–1500 m). Var. *schlechteri* is found at 3936–6560 ft. (1200–2000 m) in mossy forests.

CLIMATE: Station # 67009, Diego Suarez, Malagasy, Lat. 12.3°S, Long. 49.3°E, at 95 ft. (29 m). Temperatures are calculated for an elevation of 4000 ft. (1219 m), resulting in probable extremes of 85°F (29.4°C) and 50°F (10.0°C).

N/HEMISPHERE	JAN	FEB	MAR	APR	MAY	JUN	JUL	AUG	SEP	OCT	NOV	DEC
°F AVG MAX	71	71	71	73	75	77	75	76	75	75	72	72
°F AVG MIN	56	56	57	59	61	62	62	62	62	62	61	58
DIURNAL RANGE	15	15	14	14	14	15	13	14	13	13	11	14
RAIN/INCHES	0.2	0.2	0.2	0.4	0.9	4.9	10.4	8.1	7.2	2.3	0.3	0.3
HUMIDITY/%	65	65	66	69	73	76	82	83	81	76	69	67
BLOOM SEASON					**	**	**	**	*	*		
DAYS CLR @ 3AM	21	21	21	21	14	11	10	9	10	13	19	20
DAYS CLR @ 3PM	10	14	16	19	12	4	2	1	1	7	13	12
RAIN/MM	5	5	5	10	23	124	264	206	183	58	8	8
°C AVG MAX	21.7	21.7	21.7	22.8	24.0	25.1	24.0	24.5	24.0	24.0	22.3	22.3
°C AVG MIN	13.4	13.4	14.0	15.1	16.2	16.7	16.7	16.7	16.7	16.7	16.2	14.5
DIURNAL RANGE	8.3	8.3	7.7	7.7	7.8	8.4	7.3	7.8	7.3	7.3	6.1	7.8
S/HEMISPHERE	JUL	AUG	SEP	OCT	NOV	DEC	JAN	FEB	MAR	APR	MAY	JUN

Cultural Recommendations

LIGHT: 1500–2500 fc. Diffused or barely dappled light is preferred. Direct sunlight should be avoided.

TEMPERATURES: Summer days average 75–77°F (24–25°C), and nights average 59–62°F (15–17°C), with a diurnal range of 13–15°F (7–8°C) which fluctuates only 4°F (2°C) through the year.

HUMIDITY: 70–80% during the wet summer growing season.

WATER: Ample moisture is needed in the season of active growth. The medium should be wet, but not soggy. The rainfall pattern is wet/dry.

FERTILIZER: ½ strength, applied weekly when plants are actively growing.

REST PERIOD: Winter days average 71–72°F (22°C), and nights average 56–59°F (13–15°C), with a diurnal range of 11–15°F (6–8°C). Day and night temperatures decline simultaneously, resulting in little change in the diurnal range. Growers report that the plant survives temperature drops to 40°F (4°C) during the dormant season, providing it is dry. Light may be increased; fertilizer should be reduced. For 6 months, rainfall in the habitat nearly ceases and humidity is also lower, so conditions in cultivation should be much drier, with water reduced to occasional misting to simulate the moisture available from dew, fog, and low clouds. Flowers are initiated by the rest-period conditions.

GROWING MEDIA: A fertile terrestrial mix with good drainage. Repotting is best done in spring, just as plants resume active growth.

MISCELLANEOUS NOTES: Var. *schlechteri* grows at higher elevations and may be healthier if temperatures are 5–8°F (3–4°C) cooler than those shown in the climate table.

Each pseudobulb produces a single inflorescence and 2 buds which become new growths.

Plant and Flower Information

PLANT SIZE AND TYPE: A sympodial terrestrial, it grows 18–32 in. (46–80 cm) tall and forms a large clump.

PSEUDOBULB: 1.5 in. (4 cm) across and nearly round.

LEAVES: 2–4 per growth. The evergreen leaves are 14–16 in. (36–38 cm) long, broadly lanceolate, plicate, glossy, and bright green.

INFLORESCENCE: 14–15 in. (36–38 cm) is the normal length, but the spikes sometimes grow to 36 in. (91 cm). They emerge from the base of new pseudobulbs.

FLOWERS: 7–15. The long-lasting flowers are 2.5 in. (6 cm) across and open over a period of 4 weeks. The sepals and much broader petals are red to rose, occasionally marked with white blotches. The ruffled lip is a deeper rose-crimson with a yellow callus.

HYBRIDIZING NOTES: N/A.

REFERENCES: 21, 35, 117, 182, 205, 211.

PHOTOS/DRAWINGS: 21, 117, 205, 211.

Phaius incarvillei. Also spelled *P. incarvillae* and *P. incarvillie*. See *P. tankervilleae*. REFERENCES: 122.

Phaius indigoferus is sometimes listed as a synonym for *P. flavus*. REFERENCES: 168.

Phaius indigoferus Hassock

AKA: Often generically listed as a synonym for *P. flavus*. However, in his work with Thai orchids, Dr. Seidenfaden has maintained the 2 species as separate.

ORIGIN/HABITAT: Thailand and Vietnam, in mountain forests at 4264 ft. (1300 m).

CLIMATE: Station # 48353, Loei, Thailand, Lat. 17.5°N, Long. 101.5°E, at 817 ft. (249 m). Temperatures are calculated for an elevation of 3500 ft. (1067 m), resulting in probable extremes of 97°F (36.1°C) and 25°F (-3.9°C).

N/HEMISPHERE	JAN	FEB	MAR	APR	MAY	JUN	JUL	AUG	SEP	OCT	NOV	DEC
°F AVG MAX	76	80	85	88	84	82	81	80	79	78	78	75
°F AVG MIN	43	49	56	61	64	65	65	65	64	60	55	47
DIURNAL RANGE	33	31	29	27	20	17	16	15	15	18	23	28
RAIN/INCHES	0.2	0.8	1.4	3.6	6.9	6.8	5.0	8.3	8.8	4.3	0.8	0.1
HUMIDITY/%	62	60	59	62	75	77	77	79	82	79	74	69
BLOOM SEASON	N/A											
DAYS CLR @ 7AM	1	1	1	2	1	0	1	0	0	1	1	1
DAYS CLR @ 1PM	22	14	8	5	2	0	0	1	1	5	11	15
RAIN/MM	5	20	36	91	175	173	127	211	224	109	20	3
°C AVG MAX	24.5	26.7	29.5	31.2	29.0	27.9	27.3	26.7	26.2	25.6	25.6	24.0
°C AVG MIN	6.2	9.5	13.4	16.2	17.9	18.4	18.4	18.4	17.9	15.6	12.9	8.4
DIURNAL RANGE	18.3	17.2	16.1	15.0	11.1	9.5	8.9	8.3	8.3	10.0	12.7	15.6
S/HEMISPHERE	JUL	AUG	SEP	OCT	NOV	DEC	JAN	FEB	MAR	APR	MAY	JUN

Cultural Recommendations

LIGHT: 1800–2500 fc. Diffused or barely dappled light is recommended. Direct sunlight should be avoided.

TEMPERATURES: Summer days average 80–88°F (27–31°C), and nights average 61–65°F (16–18°C), with a 15–27°F (8–15°C) diurnal range. In the habitat, the warmest season occurs in early spring. Probable extreme temperatures indicate a tolerance of both summer heat and winter cold.

HUMIDITY: 75–80%.

WATER: Plants should be constantly moist while actively growing. The rainfall pattern is wet/dry.

FERTILIZER: ½ strength, applied weekly during the season of active growth.

REST PERIOD: Winter days average 75–80°F (24–27°C), and nights average 43–56°F (6–13°C), with a diurnal range of 23–33°F (13–18°C). The calculated extreme low is below freezing, but such temperatures should be avoided since details regarding the microclimate are not available. Light should be increased to correspond with the high number of clear afternoons in the habitat. For 3–5 months, water should be restricted to occasional misting, simulating the early morning dew, fog, and low clouds in the natural habitat. Fertilizer should be eliminated.

GROWING MEDIA: A fertile terrestrial mix with good drainage. Repotting is best done in the spring.

MISCELLANEOUS NOTES: Because the stems run along the surface of the ground before becoming erect, this plant requires a particularly large container.

Plant and Flower Information

PLANT SIZE AND TYPE: A sympodial terrestrial.

PSEUDOBULB: The pseudobulbs are stemlike and sharply square in cross section.

LEAVES: 2–4 per growth. The leaves are large, plicate, and wavy at the margins.

INFLORESCENCE: Tall and erect, the spike emerges from the leaf axis halfway up the stem.

FLOWERS: 3–7. The blossoms are 1.25 in. (3 cm) across with sharply pointed sepals and petals. White on the backside, they are brownish and yellow on the front. The yellow lip is marked with red-brown stripes and covered with long, thin, white hairs.

HYBRIDIZING NOTES: N/A.

REFERENCES: 31, 168, 175.

PHOTOS/DRAWINGS: *31*, 168, 175.

Phaius klabatensis J. J. Smith. Described as originating on Sulawesi (Celebes) Island, Indonesia. This plant is unlikely to be available for cultivation. References: 122.

Phaius kuhlii. See *P. callosus*. REFERENCES: 168.

Phaius labiatus J. J. Smith. Described as originating in Sumatra. This plant is not mentioned in current literature and is unlikely to be available for cultivation. REFERENCES: 122.

Phaius leucophoeus. See *P. tankervilleae.* REFERENCES: 168.

Phaius linearifolius Ames

AKA: N/A.

ORIGIN/HABITAT: Bontoc, Philippines, where it grows in the hills near streams at 3936–5412 ft. (1200–1650 m).

CLIMATE: Station # 98328, Baguio, Philippines, Lat. 16.4°N, Long. 120.6°E, at 4962 ft. (1512 m). The record high is 84°F (28.9°C), and the record low is 46°F (7.8°C).

N/HEMISPHERE	JAN	FEB	MAR	APR	MAY	JUN	JUL	AUG	SEP	OCT	NOV	DEC
°F AVG MAX	72	73	76	77	76	75	71	71	71	73	74	74
°F AVG MIN	55	56	58	60	61	61	60	60	60	60	59	57
DIURNAL RANGE	17	17	18	17	15	14	11	11	11	13	15	17
RAIN/INCHES	0.9	0.9	1.7	4.3	15.8	17.2	42.3	45.7	28.1	15.0	4.9	2.0
HUMIDITY/%	83	83	83	85	89	90	93	93	92	89	86	84
BLOOM SEASON						**	**					
DAYS CLR	N/A											
RAIN/MM	23	23	43	109	401	437	1074	1161	714	381	124	51
°C AVG MAX	22.2	22.8	24.4	25.0	24.4	23.9	21.7	21.7	21.7	22.8	23.3	23.3
°C AVG MIN	12.8	13.3	14.4	15.6	16.1	16.1	15.6	15.6	15.6	15.6	15.0	13.9
DIURNAL RANGE	9.4	9.5	10.0	9.4	8.3	7.8	6.1	6.1	6.1	7.2	8.3	9.4
S/HEMISPHERE	JUL	AUG	SEP	OCT	NOV	DEC	JAN	FEB	MAR	APR	MAY	JUN

Cultural Recommendations

LIGHT: 1800–2400 fc. Diffused or dappled light is recommended. Sky-cover records are unavailable, but high elevations are typically cloudy in this region.

TEMPERATURES: Days average 71–76°F (22–25°C), and nights average 60–61°F (16°C), with a summer diurnal range of 11–14°F (6–8°C).

HUMIDITY: 80–90%.

WATER: Ample moisture is needed in the active growing season. The medium should be wet, but not soggy. The rainfall pattern is very wet/dry.

FERTILIZER: ½ strength, applied weekly when plants are actively growing.

REST PERIOD: Winter days average 72–77°F (22–25°C), and nights average 55–58°F (13–14°C), resulting in a winter diurnal range of 17–18°F (9–10°C). For 2–4 months, water and fertilizer should be reduced, but humidity should remain high throughout the year.

GROWING MEDIA: A fertile terrestrial mix with good drainage. Repotting is best done in the spring when new growth resumes.

MISCELLANEOUS NOTES: Flowering occurs in the middle of the growing season.

Plant and Flower Information

PLANT SIZE AND TYPE: A sympodial terrestrial approximately 24 in. (61 cm) long.

PSEUDOBULB: N/A.

LEAVES: 4–6 per growth. The linear, prominently veined leaves are about 21 in. (53 cm) long.

INFLORESCENCE: 24 in. (61 cm) long. The flowers are arranged in a loose apical raceme.

FLOWERS: 6–15. The blossoms are 2.5 in. (6 cm) across and predominantly yellow, except for brownish markings on the lip midlobe. Lip margins are ruffled and irregularly toothed.

HYBRIDIZING NOTES: N/A.

REFERENCES: 203.

PHOTOS/DRAWINGS: N/A.

Phaius longibracteatus Frappier ex Cordem. Not mentioned in current literature and unlikely to be available for cultivation. REFERENCES: 122.

Phaius longicornu. See *P. tankervilleae.* REFERENCES: 168.

Phaius longicruris Z. H. Tsi. Information on plant and habitat is unavailable. This plant is unlikely to available for cultivation. REFERENCES: 122.

Phaius longipes. Now considered a synonym of *Cephalantheropsis gracilis.* REFERENCES: 203.

Phaius luridus Thwaites

AKA: N/A.

ORIGIN/HABITAT: Sri Lanka (Ceylon). Endemic and rare; when found, it is usually in moist, shady lowlands.

CLIMATE: Station # 43466, Colombo, Sri Lanka, Lat. 6.9°N, Long. 79.9°E, at 27 ft. (8 m). The record high is 99°F (37.2°C), and the record low is 59°F (15.0°C).

N/HEMISPHERE	JAN	FEB	MAR	APR	MAY	JUN	JUL	AUG	SEP	OCT	NOV	DEC
°F AVG MAX	86	87	84	88	87	85	85	85	85	85	85	85
°F AVG MIN	72	72	74	76	78	77	77	77	77	75	73	72
DIURNAL RANGE	14	15	10	12	9	8	8	8	8	10	12	13
RAIN/INCHES	3.5	2.7	5.8	9.1	14.6	8.8	5.3	4.3	6.3	13.7	12.4	5.8
HUMIDITY/%	70	69	69	72	77	79	78	77	77	77	76	72
BLOOM SEASON								**	**			
DAYS CLR @ 5PM	11	10	9	6	3	2	2	2	1	2	4	7
RAIN/MM	89	69	147	231	371	224	135	109	160	348	315	147
°C AVG MAX	30.0	30.6	28.9	31.1	30.6	29.4	29.4	29.4	29.4	29.4	29.4	29.4
°C AVG MIN	22.2	22.2	23.3	24.4	25.6	25.0	25.0	25.0	25.0	23.9	22.8	22.2
DIURNAL RANGE	7.8	8.4	5.6	6.7	5.0	4.4	4.4	4.4	4.4	5.5	6.6	7.2
S/HEMISPHERE	JUL	AUG	SEP	OCT	NOV	DEC	JAN	FEB	MAR	APR	MAY	JUNE

Cultural Recommendations

LIGHT: 1200–2400 fc. Diffused or barely dappled light is recommended. Direct sunlight should be avoided.

TEMPERATURES: Summer days average 84–88°F (29–31°C), and nights average 76–78°F (24–26°C), resulting in a low diurnal range of 8–10°F (5–6°C).

HUMIDITY: 70-80%.

WATER: Ample moisture is needed during the active growing season. The medium should be wet, but not soggy. The rainfall is seasonal, with a wet/wetter pattern. Rainfall is lowest in winter and also low in late summer.

FERTILIZER: ½ strength, applied weekly when plants are actively growing.

REST PERIOD: Winter days average 84–88°F (29–31°C), and nights average 72–74°F (22–23°C), with an increased diurnal range of 10–15°F (6–8°C) resulting from slightly warmer days and cooler nights. In the habitat, clear days occur much more frequently in winter. Water and fertilizer should be continued cautiously, as the plant could be subject to rot if temperatures are below its preferred range. Flowering occurs in late summer, just before heavy rains begin.

GROWING MEDIA: A fertile terrestrial mix with good drainage. Repotting may be done anytime active growth is evident.

MISCELLANEOUS NOTES: The limited habitat and unusually warm temperatures indicate that *P. luridus* could be very difficult to maintain in cultivation.

Plant and Flower Information

PLANT SIZE AND TYPE: A moderately sized sympodial terrestrial.

PSEUDOBULB: Inconspicuous.

LEAVES: 4–5 per growth. The oblong-lanceolate leaves are 12–18 in. (30–45 cm) long.

INFLORESCENCE: 8–10 in. (20–25 cm) long. The spike arises from the lower leaf axils, near the apex of the pseudobulb.

FLOWERS: 10–14. The blossoms are 2 in. (5 cm) across. The yellow sepals and petals are striped lengthwise with red. The undulate lip is marked with 2 red blotches and has 2 wrinkled ridges.

HYBRIDIZING NOTES: N/A.

REFERENCES: 34.

PHOTOS/DRAWINGS: 34.

Phaius luteus (Ursch and Genoud) J. Bosser

AKA: Originally described as *Gastorchis luteus*.

ORIGIN/HABITAT: Madagascar, southeast of Moramanga in humid forests at 2952 ft. (900 m).

CLIMATE: Station # 67143, Mananjary, Malagasy, Lat. 21.2°S, Long. 48.4°E, at 16 ft. (5 m). Temperatures are calculated for an elevation of 2952 ft. (900 m), resulting in probable extremes of 88°F (31.1°C) and 36°F (2.2°C).

N/HEMISPHERE	JAN	FEB	MAR	APR	MAY	JUN	JUL	AUG	SEP	OCT	NOV	DEC
°F AVG MAX	66	66	68	70	74	75	76	76	75	73	70	68
°F AVG MIN	50	50	52	55	58	60	62	62	61	59	55	51
DIURNAL RANGE	16	16	16	15	16	15	14	14	14	14	15	17
RAIN/INCHES	6.4	5.3	4.3	2.9	6.5	8.9	15.8	15.6	18.8	10.0	7.9	9.3
HUMIDITY/%	86	84	83	82	82	84	84	84	85	85	86	86
BLOOM SEASON			**	**								
DAYS CLR	N/A											
RAIN/MM	163	135	109	74	165	226	401	396	478	254	201	236
°C AVG MAX	19.1	19.1	20.2	21.3	23.5	24.1	24.6	24.6	24.1	23.0	21.3	20.2
°C AVG MIN	10.2	10.2	11.3	13.0	14.6	15.7	16.8	16.8	16.3	15.2	13.0	10.7
DIURNAL RANGE	8.9	8.9	8.9	8.3	8.9	8.4	7.8	7.8	7.8	7.8	8.3	9.5
S/HEMISPHERE	JUL	AUG	SEP	OCT	NOV	DEC	JAN	FEB	MAR	APR	MAY	JUN

Cultural Recommendations

LIGHT: 2400 fc. Light should be diffused or barely dappled. Direct sunlight should be avoided.

TEMPERATURES: Summer days average 74–76°F (24–25°C), and nights average 58–62°F (15–17°C). These average temperatures indicate a probable intolerance to hot summers. The diurnal range of 14–16°F (8–9°C) fluctuates only 3°F (2°C) throughout the year and is slightly lower in summer when rainfall is highest.

HUMIDITY: 80–85%.

WATER: Ample moisture is needed in the active growing season. The medium should be moist year-round. The rainfall pattern is wet/wetter.

FERTILIZER: ½ strength, applied weekly when plants are actively growing.

REST PERIOD: Winter days average 66–70°F (18–21°C), and nights average 50–55°F (10–13°C), with a diurnal range of 14–17°F (8–9°C). Plants require less frequent watering during the cooler winter, but the habitat is always moist and humidity high. Fertilizer should be reduced unless active growth is evident.

GROWING MEDIA: A fertile terrestrial mix with good drainage. Repotting is best done as plants break dormancy or immediately after flowering.

MISCELLANEOUS NOTES: N/A.

Plant and Flower Information

PLANT SIZE AND TYPE: The erect, moderately sized, sympodial plants are normally terrestrial, but they also grow epiphytically at the base of moss-covered tree trunks.

PSEUDOBULB: 1 in. (2.5 cm) long and ovoid.

LEAVES: 3–4 per growth. The leaves are 8–16 in. (20–40 cm) long, arising directly from the apex of the pseudobulb. Light green and narrowly lanceolate, the foliage is thinly textured.

INFLORESCENCE: 14–18 in. (35–45 cm) long. Each growth may produce 4–5 laxly flowered spikes, which arise from between the leaves.

FLOWERS: 5–10 per inflorescence. The flowers are 1.5–2.5 in. (3.5–6.0 cm) across. The greenish-yellow blossoms are marked with bright yellow in the center of the lip.

HYBRIDIZING NOTES: N/A.

REFERENCES: 21, 117.

PHOTOS/DRAWINGS: 21.

Phaius lyonii Ames

AKA: N/A.

ORIGIN/HABITAT: Endemic to the Philippines, where the plants are widely distributed in both open and shady glades at 1968–2788 ft. (600–850 m).

CLIMATE: Station # 98325, Dagupan, Philippines, Lat. 16.1°N, Long. 120.6°E, at 7 ft. (2 m). Temperatures are calculated for an elevation of 2300 ft. (701 m), resulting in probable extremes of 96°F (35.6°C) and 50°F (10.0°C).

N/HEMISPHERE	JAN	FEB	MAR	APR	MAY	JUN	JUL	AUG	SEP	OCT	NOV	DEC
°F AVG MAX	81	82	86	88	87	86	82	82	82	83	82	81
°F AVG MIN	61	61	64	66	67	67	67	67	67	66	64	62
DIURNAL RANGE	20	21	22	22	20	19	15	15	15	17	18	19
RAIN/INCHES	0.4	0.6	0.9	2.9	8.8	12.9	23.1	21.5	15.8	7.1	3.1	0.8
HUMIDITY/%	73	70	71	71	75	82	84	85	85	79	76	75
BLOOM SEASON			*	*	*	*	*	*	*			
DAYS CLR @ 8AM	15	15	19	21	17	9	4	4	4	12	14	15
DAYS CLR @ 2PM	14	15	17	17	11	5	2	3	2	10	11	12
RAIN/MM	10	15	23	74	224	328	587	546	401	180	79	20
°C AVG MAX	27.5	28.0	30.2	31.4	30.8	30.2	28.0	28.0	28.0	28.6	28.0	27.5
°C AVG MIN	16.4	16.4	18.0	19.1	19.7	19.7	19.7	19.7	19.7	19.1	18.0	16.9
DIURNAL RANGE	11.1	11.6	12.2	12.3	11.1	10.5	8.3	8.3	8.3	9.5	10.0	10.6
S/HEMISPHERE	JUL	AUG	SEP	OCT	NOV	DEC	JAN	FEB	MAR	APR	MAY	JUN

Cultural Recommendations

LIGHT: 2000–3600 fc. Dappled light is indicated, as the preferred habitat is fairly open. However, clear summer days are uncommon, and at higher elevations they occur less frequently than the climate table indicates.

TEMPERATURES: Summer days average 81–88°F (28–31°C), and nights average 66–67°F (19–20°C), with a diurnal range of 15–20°F (8–11°C).

HUMIDITY: 70–80%.

WATER: Ample moisture is needed in the active growing season. The medium should be wet, but not soggy. In the habitat, the rainfall pattern is wet/dry, but the high humidity levels indicate that some moisture is available from dew, fog, or mist even during the dry season.

FERTILIZER: ½ strength, applied weekly when plants are actively growing.

REST PERIOD: Winter days average 81–88°F (27–31°C), and nights average 61–64°F (16–18°C), resulting in a diurnal range of 20–22°F (11–12°C). Water should be reduced for 3–4 months since rainfall in the habitat is much lower in winter. The medium should be kept slightly moist by misting occasionally, for humidity levels in the habitat indicate that some moisture is available throughout the year. Fertilizer may be eliminated when plants are not actively growing. Light should be increased to reflect an increased number of clear winter days.

GROWING MEDIA: A fertile terrestrial mix with good drainage. Repotting is best done as active growth begins.

MISCELLANEOUS NOTES: Flowering occurs in spring while the plants are actively growing, but bloom initiators have not been indentified. Since cultivation bloom records are unavailable, the bloom period shown in the climate table represents the months during which plants have been collected.

Plant and Flower Information

PLANT SIZE AND TYPE: A medium-to-large sympodial terrestrial.

PSEUDOBULB: 1 in. (2.5 cm) long. New growths arise from a fleshy, elongated rhizome.

LEAVES: 4–6 per growth. The elliptic-lanceolate leaves are 20 in. (51 cm) long.

INFLORESCENCE: 20 in. (51 cm) long. The spike emerges from the base of the pseudobulb.

FLOWERS: 5–7. The flowers are 2.5 in. (6 cm) across. The sepals and petals are yellow on the front and white on the back, and the lip is purplish.

HYBRIDIZING NOTES: N/A.

REFERENCES: 203.

PHOTOS/DRAWINGS: N/A.

Phaius maculatus. See *P. flavus.* REFERENCES: 168.

Phaius mannii Rchb.f.

AKA: *Index Kewensis* (1983) indicates that this species is synonymous with *P. wallichi,* which is now generally accepted as conspecific with *P. tankervilleae.* However, recent work indicates that *P. mannii* may not be conspecific.

ORIGIN/HABITAT: Mayombe (Mayamba), Zaire, near Mt. Madiakoko. Neither habitat information nor elevation was recorded.

CLIMATE: Station # 64210, N'Djili/Kinshasa, Zaire, Lat. 4.4°S, Long. 15.4°E, at 1014 ft. (309 m). The record high is 95°F (35.0°C), and the record low is 56°F (13.3°C).

N/HEMISPHERE	JAN	FEB	MAR	APR	MAY	JUN	JUL	AUG	SEP	OCT	NOV	DEC
°F AVG MAX	80	82	84	85	85	85	86	87	88	88	84	80
°F AVG MIN	64	66	70	71	72	72	73	72	72	72	72	67
DIURNAL RANGE	16	16	14	14	13	13	13	15	16	16	12	13
RAIN/INCHES	0.4	0.1	1.3	3.5	9.3	6.7	5.0	5.6	6.7	8.4	5.4	0.2
HUMIDITY/%	78	73	74	79	82	83	82	80	80	82	83	81
BLOOM SEASON	N/A											
DAYS CLR @ 7AM	5	5	3	2	0	0	1	1	1	1	1	3
DAYS CLR @ 1PM	10	10	8	3	3	4	2	4	2	3	5	9
RAIN/MM	10	3	33	89	236	170	127	142	170	213	137	5
°C AVG MAX	26.7	27.8	28.9	29.4	29.4	29.4	30.0	30.5	31.1	31.1	28.9	26.7
°C AVG MIN	17.8	18.9	21.1	21.7	22.2	22.2	22.8	22.2	22.2	22.2	22.2	19.4
DIURNAL RANGE	8.9	8.9	7.8	7.7	7.2	7.2	7.2	8.3	8.9	8.9	6.7	7.3
S/HEMISPHERE	JUL	AUG	SEP	OCT	NOV	DEC	JAN	FEB	MAR	APR	MAY	JUN

Cultural Recommendations

LIGHT: Low, diffused light is suggested until the plant is well established. Without habitat or cultural information, this is the prudent approach.

TEMPERATURES: Summer days average 85–88°F (29–31°C), and nights average 72–73°F (22–23°C), with a summer diurnal range of 13–16°F (7–9°C). Extremes vary only a few degrees from the average growing temperatures, indicating an intolerance to wide temperature fluctuations. Summer days are frequently over 90°F (32°C).

HUMIDITY: 70–85%.

WATER: Plants should be kept moist during the active growing season. Warm water, about 70°F (21°C), is highly recommended. The rainfall pattern is wet/dry.

FERTILIZER: ½ strength, applied weekly when plants are actively growing.

REST PERIOD: For 3–4 months, winter days average 80–84°F (27–29°C), and nights average 64–67°F (18–19°C), with a diurnal range of 13–16°F (7–9°C). Rainfall in the habitat is negligible in winter, so water should be reduced and fertilizer eliminated, but humidity should remain high.

GROWING MEDIA: A fertile terrestrial mix. Repotting is best done as roots begin new growth.

MISCELLANEOUS NOTES: N/A.

Plant and Flower Information

PLANT SIZE AND TYPE: A 12 in. (30 cm) sympodial terrestrial.

PSEUDOBULB: N/A. New growths arise from a creeping rhizome.

LEAVES: 5–7 per growth. The leaves are 5–9 in. (13–23 cm) long, elliptical, pointed, and plicate.

INFLORESCENCE: 4 in. (10 cm) long. It emerges from between the leaves.

FLOWERS: 5–10. The blossoms, which do not open fully, are 2.5–5.0 in. (6–13 cm) across. The pointed sepals and petals are rose to red, and the pointed lip is white.

HYBRIDIZING NOTES: The chromosome count for *P. mannii* is 2n = 28, differing from counts available for *P. tankervilleae*.

REFERENCES: 92, 122, 168.

PHOTOS/DRAWINGS: 92.

Phaius marshalliae. Now considered a synonym of *Thunia alba*. REFERENCES: 122.

Phaius mindorensis Ames

AKA: N/A.

ORIGIN/HABITAT: Philippines, on Mt. Halcon on Mindoro, and on Mt. Makiling on Luzon, in mossy forests at 3280–4690 ft. (1000–1430 m).

CLIMATE: Station # 98427, Manila, Philippines, Lat. 14.5°N, Long. 121.0°E, at 74 ft. (23 m). Temperatures are calculated for an elevation of 4000 ft. (1219 m), resulting in probable extremes of 88°F (31.1°C) and 45°F (7.2°C).

N/HEMISPHERE	JAN	FEB	MAR	APR	MAY	JUN	JUL	AUG	SEP	OCT	NOV	DEC
°F AVG MAX	73	75	78	80	80	78	75	74	75	75	74	73
°F AVG MIN	56	56	58	60	62	62	62	62	62	61	59	57
DIURNAL RANGE	17	19	20	20	18	16	13	12	13	14	15	16
RAIN/INCHES	0.9	0.5	0.7	1.3	5.1	10.0	17.0	16.6	14.0	7.6	5.7	2.6
HUMIDITY/%	77	73	70	68	71	81	84	86	87	84	82	79
BLOOM SEASON			*								*	
DAYS CLR @ 8AM	6	9	14	14	10	3	2	1	1	6	7	6
DAYS CLR @ 2PM	3	6	10	10	8	2	1	1	0	2	2	3
RAIN/MM	23	13	18	33	130	254	432	422	356	193	145	66
°C AVG MAX	22.8	23.9	25.6	26.7	26.7	25.6	23.9	23.4	23.9	23.9	23.4	22.8
°C AVG MIN	13.4	13.4	14.5	15.6	16.7	16.7	16.7	16.7	16.7	16.1	15.0	13.9
DIURNAL RANGE	9.4	10.5	11.1	11.1	10.0	8.9	7.2	6.7	7.2	7.8	8.4	8.9
S/HEMISPHERE	JUL	AUG	SEP	OCT	NOV	DEC	JAN	FEB	MAR	APR	MAY	JUN

Cultural Recommendations

LIGHT: 1800–2400 fc. Diffused or barely dappled light is indicated. Direct sunlight should be avoided since the plant grows in mossy forests.

TEMPERATURES: Summer days average 74–80°F (24–27°C), and nights average 62°F (17°C), with a diurnal range of 12–18°F (7–10°C).

HUMIDITY: 70–85%.

WATER: Ample moisture is needed in the active growing season. The medium should be wet, but not soggy. The seasonal rainfall pattern is wet/dry, but rainfall amounts are probably greater in the mountainous habitat.

FERTILIZER: ½ strength, applied weekly when plants are actively growing.

REST PERIOD: Winter days average 73–78°F (23–26°C), and nights average 56–58°F (13–15°C), with a diurnal range of 16–20°F (9–11°C). For 3 months, water should be reduced to occasional misting, and humidity may be lowered to 68–75%. Fertilizer should be eliminated until growth resumes. Increasing clear weather suggests that light levels in the habitat are highest during late winter and early spring.

GROWING MEDIA: A fertile terrestrial mix with good drainage. Repotting is best done in the spring when new growth begins or immediately after flowering.

MISCELLANEOUS NOTES: The bloom season shown in the climate table is based on collection times, which indicate that flowering probably occurs near the end of the dry season during a period of increased light.

Plant and Flower Information

PLANT SIZE AND TYPE: A sympodial terrestrial or epiphyte, one of the smallest of the genus.

PSEUDOBULB: Stems are slender and branching.

LEAVES: 3–4 per growth. The lanceolate leaves are 4–7 in. (10–18 cm) long.

INFLORESCENCE: Length unknown. The spikes are described as slender and covered with hairs.

FLOWERS: 10–12. The small blossoms are 0.5 in. (1.3 cm) across. They are white in the bud stage, turning yellow when the blossoms open. The fan-shaped lip is toothed on the sidelobes.

HYBRIDIZING NOTES: N/A.

REFERENCES: 203.

PHOTOS/DRAWINGS: N/A.

Phaius minor. See *P. flavus*. REFERENCES: 168.

Phaius mishmensis (Lindley) Rchb.f.

AKA: *Calanthe crinita, Phaius crinita, P. gracilis, P. roseus*.

ORIGIN/HABITAT: Widely distributed throughout Southeast Asia and the Pacific islands. In Taiwan, it is found in semishade in broadleaf forests below 3000 ft. (914 m). In Vietnam, it is found near Dalat at 4920 ft. (1500 m).

CLIMATE: Station # 48881, Dalat, South Vietnam, Lat. 11.1°N, Long. 108.1°E, at 3156 ft. (962 m). Temperatures are calculated for an elevation of 4920 ft. (1500 m), resulting in probable extremes of 87°F (30.6°C) and 37°F (2.8°C).

N/HEMISPHERE	JAN	FEB	MAR	APR	MAY	JUN	JUL	AUG	SEP	OCT	NOV	DEC
°F AVG MAX	74	76	78	79	78	75	75	74	74	74	73	73
°F AVG MIN	50	51	53	56	59	59	59	59	59	57	54	52
DIURNAL RANGE	24	25	25	23	19	16	16	15	15	17	19	21
RAIN/INCHES	0.2	0.9	1.6	4.6	9.1	6.1	7.7	8.2	10.1	9.7	2.7	1.3
HUMIDITY/%	68	64	65	71	78	81	82	83	84	82	76	73
BLOOM SEASON	*						*	*	*	*	*	*
DAYS CLR @ 7AM	13	13	13	9	5	3	2	2	2	5	7	10
DAYS CLR @ 1PM	8	8	8	2	0	0	0	0	0	1	3	4
RAIN/MM	5	23	41	117	231	155	196	208	257	246	69	33
°C AVG MAX	23.4	24.5	25.7	26.2	25.7	24.0	24.0	23.4	23.4	23.4	22.9	22.9
°C AVG MIN	10.1	10.7	11.8	13.4	15.1	15.1	15.1	15.1	15.1	14.0	12.3	11.2
DIURNAL RANGE	13.3	13.8	13.9	12.8	10.6	8.9	8.9	8.3	8.3	9.4	10.6	11.7
S/HEMISPHERE	JUL	AUG	SEP	OCT	NOV	DEC	JAN	FEB	MAR	APR	MAY	JUN

Cultural Recommendations

LIGHT: 2000 fc initially. The deciduous forest and semi-shade habitats indicate that summer light should be low, but optimal levels for cultivation are unknown.

TEMPERATURES: Summer days average 73–79°F (23–26°C), and nights average 57–59°F (14–15°C), with a diurnal range of 15–19°F (8–10°C).

HUMIDITY: 70–80%.

WATER: Ample moisture is needed in the active growing season. The medium should be moist. The seasonal rainfall pattern is wet/dry.

FERTILIZER: ½ strength, applied weekly during the growing season.

REST PERIOD: Winter days average 73–76°F (23–24°C), and nights average 50–54°F (10–12°C). Warmer days and cooler nights increase the diurnal range to 21–25°F (12–14°C). For 2–3 months, water and fertilizer should be reduced and light may be increased slightly. Since the habitat is always in the hills, winter temperatures or diurnal range may be important to plant health.

GROWING MEDIA: A fertile terrestrial mix with good drainage. Repotting may be done in late winter or early spring.

MISCELLANEOUS NOTES: The bloom season is apparently influenced by local climate, but flower initiators are unknown. Records indicate that blooming extends over 2–3 months.

Plant and Flower Information

PLANT SIZE AND TYPE: A 24–56 in. (60–140 cm) sympodial terrestrial.

PSEUDOBULB: Obscure.

LEAVES: 6–8 per growth. The wavy, plicate leaves are 6–12 in. (15–30 cm) long. The foliage is thick and lustrous, elliptic to lanceolate, and alternates along each side of the upper portion of the stem.

INFLORESCENCE: 12–24 in. (30-60 cm) long. The spikes, often more than one per growth, emerge from leaf axils halfway up the stem. They tend to be deflexed and are laxly flowered at the apex.

FLOWERS: 7–9 per inflorescence. The flowers are 1.75–2.0 in. (4–5 cm) across and do not open fully. They may be delicate rose, dark red, or purplish brown, often becoming orange-red with age. The lip may be white or pink and is speckled with purple. The spur is yellowish to bright yellow.

The Taiwan plant, often called *P. gracilis*, usually has greenish-yellow sepals and petals and a white-to-dark-yellow lip.

HYBRIDIZING NOTES: The chromosome count is 2n = 42.

REFERENCES: 14, 20, 91, 119, 132, 157, 168.

PHOTOS/DRAWINGS: *14*, *20*, *27*, *132*, *168*.

Phaius montanus Schlechter

AKA: N/A.

ORIGIN/HABITAT: Endemic to New Guinea, it grows on sharp ridges in the mistforest zone in the Finistère Mountains at 2624–4264 ft. (800–1300 m). It is frequently found rooted in humus between large stones in semiopen, bushy places.

CLIMATE: Station # 94027, Lae, New Guinea, Lat. 6.7°S, Long. 147.0°E, at 33 ft. (10 m). Temperatures are calculated for an elevation of 3280 ft. (1000 m), resulting in probable extremes of 91°F (32.8°C) and 54°F (12.2°C).

N/HEMISPHERE	JAN	FEB	MAR	APR	MAY	JUN	JUL	AUG	SEP	OCT	NOV	DEC
°F AVG MAX	72	72	73	75	76	77	77	78	77	76	74	73
°F AVG MIN	61	61	61	62	63	63	64	64	64	63	62	61
DIURNAL RANGE	11	11	12	13	13	14	13	14	13	13	12	12
RAIN/INCHES	17.6	19.8	13.4	14.7	9.4	4.6	3.1	4.0	3.9	8.6	13.6	17.4
HUMIDITY/%	87	88	85	83	83	83	82	80	82	84	85	87
BLOOM SEASON	*	*		*					*			
DAYS CLR @ 10AM	2	2	2	3	2	1	1	0	0	2	3	3
DAYS CLR @ 4PM	3	3	2	3	1	0	0	0	0	1	3	3
RAIN/MM	447	503	340	373	239	117	79	102	99	218	345	442
°C AVG MAX	22.4	22.4	22.9	24.0	24.6	25.2	25.2	25.7	25.2	24.6	23.5	22.9
°C AVG MIN	16.3	16.3	16.3	16.8	17.4	17.4	17.9	17.9	17.9	17.4	16.8	16.3
DIURNAL RANGE	6.1	6.1	6.6	7.2	7.2	7.8	7.3	7.8	7.3	7.2	6.7	6.6
S/HEMISPHERE	JUL	AUG	SEP	OCT	NOV	DEC	JAN	FEB	MAR	APR	MAY	JUN

Cultural Recommendations

LIGHT: 2400–3600 fc. Diffused light or dappled shade is recommended. The plant grows in open areas, but clear days are rare in the habitat.

TEMPERATURES: Summer days average 75–78°F (24–26°C), and nights average 62–64°F (17–18°C), with a diurnal range of 13–14°F (7–8°C).

HUMIDITY: 80–85%.

WATER: Moisture should be provided year-round. The rainfall pattern is wet/wetter, and even higher levels of moisture are available in the mistforest.

FERTILIZER: ½ strength, applied weekly when plants are actively growing.

REST PERIOD: Winter days average 72–75°F (22–24°C), and nights average 61–62°F (16–17°C), with a diurnal range of 11–13°F (6–7°C). Rainfall is highest in winter, but unless temperatures are carefully maintained, water should not be increased in cultivation. The habitat is very humid throughout the year.

GROWING MEDIA: A fertile terrestrial mix with good drainage. Repotting is best done immediately after flowering, when roots are actively growing.

MISCELLANEOUS NOTES: N/A.

Plant and Flower Information

PLANT SIZE AND TYPE: A 24–30 in. (61–76 cm) sympodial terrestrial.

PSEUDOBULB: Length unknown. It is described as many jointed.

LEAVES: 4–6 per growth. The erect-spreading leaves are 28 in. (71 cm) long.

INFLORESCENCE: 30 in. (76 cm) long. The spike is erect and laxly flowered on the apical third.

FLOWERS: 6–15. The long-lasting flowers are 3 in. (8 cm) across and were described by R. R. Schlechter, who was not inclined to use superlatives, as truly beautiful. The sepals and petals are yellowish on the outside and brown on the inside. The white lip is marked with red at the apex, and the column is rose-red.

HYBRIDIZING NOTES: N/A.

REFERENCES: 122, 164.

PHOTOS/DRAWINGS: 164.

Phaius monticola. See *P. robertsii.* REFERENCES: 107.

Phaius nanus Hooker f. Found in West Bengal, India. Information on habitat elevation is insufficient to allow the selection of weather records. This plant is unlikely to be available for cultivation. REFERENCES: 122, 157.

Phaius neocaledonicus Rendle

AKA: N/A.

ORIGIN/HABITAT: Endemic to New Caledonia and highly localized, it is usually found at 328–1312 ft. (100–400 m) in small areas of dense forest.

CLIMATE: Station # 91592, Noumea, New Caledonia, Lat. 22.3°S, Long. 166.5°E, at 246 ft. (75 m). Temperatures are calculated for an elevation of 1000 ft. (328 m), resulting in probable extremes of 97°F (36.1°C) and 50°F (10.0°C).

N/HEMISPHERE	JAN	FEB	MAR	APR	MAY	JUN	JUL	AUG	SEP	OCT	NOV	DEC
°F AVG MAX	74	74	76	78	81	84	84	83	83	81	77	75
°F AVG MIN	60	59	61	63	66	68	70	71	70	68	64	62
DIURNAL RANGE	14	15	15	15	15	16	14	12	13	13	13	13
RAIN/INCHES	3.6	2.6	2.5	2.0	2.4	2.6	3.7	5.1	5.7	5.2	4.4	3.7
HUMIDITY/%	73	70	69	67	68	69	71	74	75	76	73	73
BLOOM SEASON	*	*									*	*
DAYS CLR @ 11AM	7	9	9	15	12	10	7	6	7	7	7	7
DAYS CLR @ 5PM	7	11	6	11	7	6	5	4	4	5	3	7
RAIN/MM	91	66	64	51	61	66	94	130	145	132	112	94
°C AVG MAX	23.1	23.1	24.2	25.3	27.0	28.6	28.6	28.1	28.1	27.0	24.7	23.6
°C AVG MIN	15.3	14.7	15.8	17.0	18.6	19.7	20.8	21.4	20.8	19.7	17.5	16.4
DIURNAL RANGE	7.8	8.4	8.4	8.3	8.4	8.9	7.8	6.7	7.3	7.3	7.2	7.2
S/HEMISPHERE	JUL	AUG	SEP	OCT	NOV	DEC	JAN	FEB	MAR	APR	MAY	JUN

Cultural Recommendations

LIGHT: 1200 fc initially. Despite the relatively high number of clear days in the habitat, the plant grows only in dense forests.

TEMPERATURES: Summer days average 81–84°F (27–29°C), and nights average 66–71°F (19–21°C), with a diurnal range of 12–16 °F (7–9 °C) which fluctuates only 4 °F (2 °C) during the year.

HUMIDITY: 70–75% is indicated in the climate table, but levels may be higher in the dense forest habitat.

WATER: Moisture should be provided year-round. The rainfall pattern is moderate all year, with late summer and early autumn the wettest period.

FERTILIZER: ½ strength, applied weekly when plants are actively growing.

REST PERIOD: Winter days average 74–77 °F (23–25 °C), and nights average 59–64 °F (15–18 °C), with a diurnal range of 13–15 °F (7–8 °C). Winter rainfall occurs intermittently as showers, and plants in cultivation may be healthiest if allowed to become slightly dry before being watered. In the habitat, light is highest in early spring.

GROWING MEDIA: A fertile terrestrial mix with good drainage.

MISCELLANEOUS NOTES: Blooming occurs after the period of greatest rainfall, when light is lowest. The limited distribution of this species and the fact that it is highly localized indicate it could be difficult to maintain in cultivation.

Plant and Flower Information

PLANT SIZE AND TYPE: The plant is described as very similar to *P. robertsii*, but no measurements are available.

PSEUDOBULB: Small, arising from a short rhizome.

LEAVES: 2 per growth. The leaves are oval, plicate, and pointed.

INFLORESCENCE: Tall and erect to arching, the spike emerges from bract-covered nodes near the base of the stem.

FLOWERS: 5–12. The white flowers apparently open sequentially, and the 3-lobed lip is speckled with pale rose.

HYBRIDIZING NOTES: N/A.

REFERENCES: 122, 107.

PHOTOS/DRAWINGS: 107.

Phaius niveus.

Now considered a synonym of *Thunia alba*. REFERENCES: 122.

Phaius occidentalis Schlechter

AKA: N/A.

ORIGIN/HABITAT: Uganda, Africa, where it is found in sphagnum swamps along Lake Nabugabo at 3608–4592 ft. (1100–1400 m). It is also found growing in marshy places in Angola, Malawi, Zaire, Zambia, and Zimbabwe.

CLIMATE: Station # 63705, Entebbe, Uganda, Lat. 0.2 °N, Long. 32.5 °E, at 3789 ft. (1155 m). The record high is 92 °F (33.3 °C), and the record low is 51 °F (10.6 °C).

N/HEMISPHERE	JAN	FEB	MAR	APR	MAY	JUN	JUL	AUG	SEP	OCT	NOV	DEC
°F AVG MAX	80	80	80	78	78	77	77	77	77	78	79	79
°F AVG MIN	63	63	64	64	64	63	61	61	62	63	63	63
DIURNAL RANGE	17	17	16	14	14	14	16	16	15	15	16	16
RAIN/INCHES	2.6	3.5	6.2	10.1	9.7	4.6	3.0	3.0	3.1	3.7	5.1	4.5
HUMIDITY/%	78	78	80	83	83	82	81	81	80	79	79	79
BLOOM SEASON		*								*	*	
DAYS CLR @ 8AM	1	1	1	1	1	3	1	2	2	1	1	2
DAYS CLR @ 2PM	2	3	4	2	2	4	3	4	4	2	1	1
RAIN/MM	66	89	157	257	246	117	76	76	79	94	130	114
°C AVG MAX	26.7	26.7	26.7	25.6	25.6	25.0	25.0	25.0	25.0	25.6	26.1	26.1
°C AVG MIN	17.2	17.2	17.8	17.8	17.8	17.2	16.1	16.1	16.7	17.2	17.2	17.2
DIURNAL RANGE	9.5	9.5	8.9	7.8	7.8	7.8	8.9	8.9	8.3	8.4	8.9	8.9
S/HEMISPHERE	JUL	AUG	SEP	OCT	NOV	DEC	JAN	FEB	MAR	APR	MAY	JUN

Cultural Recommendations

LIGHT: 2000–3000 fc is recommended. Direct sun should be avoided.

TEMPERATURES: Summer days average 77–78 °F (25–26 °C), and nights average 61–64 °F (16–18 °C), with a diurnal range of 14–16 °F (8–9 °C).

HUMIDITY: 78–83%.

WATER: Plants should be kept constantly moist. The rainfall pattern is wet/wetter, and even in this climate, the plant grows in swamps and marshes.

FERTILIZER: ½ strength, applied weekly when plants are actively growing.

REST PERIOD: Essentially none—growing conditions should be maintained throughout the year. The record temperatures are within 12 °F (7 °C) of the averages, and the diurnal range varies only 3 °F (2 °C) during the year.

GROWING MEDIA: A fertile, sphagnum-based terrestrial mix with good drainage. Repotting is best done in early spring.

MISCELLANEOUS NOTES: *P. occidentalis* could be difficult to maintain without careful attention to its cultural requirements. In general, plants that need extremely high moisture are often subject to rot if temperatures are outside their preferred range or if air circulation is inadequate.

The flowering time shown in the climate table is based on collection reports and probably extends from Oct.–Feb. (Apr.–Aug.). Bloom initiators are unknown.

When dried or bruised, all plant parts turn blue-green to grey .

Plant and Flower Information

PLANT SIZE AND TYPE: An erect, 24 in. (61 cm) sympodial terrestrial.

PSEUDOBULB: None.

LEAVES: 6 per growth. The leaves are 8–16 in. (20–41 cm) long, erect-spreading, elliptical, and arranged in a false rosette.

INFLORESCENCE: 28 in. (71 cm) long. The flower spike arises from the apex of the tuber, and the flowers are clustered at the top of the inflorescence.

FLOWERS: 5–15. The flowers are 1.5–2.5 in. (4–6 cm) across. The white sepals and petals do not open fully. The lip is also white, with 3 hairy keels and red-brown spotting at the base. The callus is yellow. Flowers quickly turn blue-green when damaged.

HYBRIDIZING NOTES: N/A.

REFERENCES: 92.

PHOTOS/DRAWINGS: 92.

Phaius pallidus. See *P. pauciflorus.* REFERENCES: 118.

Phaius papuanus. See *P. amboinensis.* REFERENCES: 164.

Phaius paradoxus. Now considered a synonym of *Megastylis paradoxa.* REFERENCES: 107.

Phaius pauciflorus Blume

AKA: *P. pallidus* is now considered a variety of *P. pauciflorus.*

ORIGIN/HABITAT: Malaya, Sumatra, and Java. The plants are found in forests at 2624–4920 ft. (800–1500 m).

CLIMATE: Station # 96755, Bogor, Indonesia, Lat. 6.5°S, Long. 106.8°E, at 558 ft. (170 m). Temperatures are calculated for an elevation of 3000 ft. (914 m), resulting in probable extremes of 88°F (31.1°C) and 58°F (14.4°C).

N/HEMISPHERE	JAN	FEB	MAR	APR	MAY	JUN	JUL	AUG	SEP	OCT	NOV	DEC
°F AVG MAX	78	79	80	80	79	77	76	76	77	78	79	78
°F AVG MIN	65	65	65	66	66	66	66	66	66	67	67	66
DIURNAL RANGE	13	14	15	14	13	11	10	10	11	11	12	12
RAIN/INCHES	2.1	1.0	0.5	5.0	8.1	18.8	23.7	20.2	14.4	12.0	11.9	3.4
HUMIDITY/%	72	68	65	66	74	79	84	84	81	79	77	75
BLOOM SEASON	*						*					
DAYS CLR @ 7AM	14	14	14	11	5	3	1	2	4	6	10	12
DAYS CLR @ 1PM	9	10	8	5	1	1	0	0	1	1	3	7
RAIN/MM	53	25	13	127	206	478	602	513	366	305	302	86
°C AVG MAX	25.5	26.1	26.6	26.6	26.1	25.0	24.4	24.4	25.0	25.5	26.1	25.5
°C AVG MIN	18.3	18.3	18.3	18.9	18.9	18.9	18.9	18.9	18.9	19.4	19.4	18.9
DIURNAL RANGE	7.2	7.8	8.3	7.7	7.2	6.1	5.5	5.5	6.1	6.1	6.7	6.6
S/HEMISPHERE	JUL	AUG	SEP	OCT	NOV	DEC	JAN	FEB	MAR	APR	MAY	JUN

Cultural Recommendations

LIGHT: 1800–2400 fc. Diffused or barely dappled light is recommended. Direct sunlight should be avoided.

TEMPERATURES: Summer days average 76–80°F (24–27°C), and nights average 65–67°F (18–19°C), with a diurnal range of 10–15°F (6–8°C). The warmest months occur in spring before the onset of the summer monsoon. The extremes vary only slightly from the average growing temperatures, indicating that the plant is unlikely to be tolerant of wide temperature fluctuations. *P. pauciflorus* may adapt to slightly warmer or cooler conditions if they are uniform.

HUMIDITY: 75–85%.

WATER: Plants should be kept moist during the active growing season. The rainfall pattern is very wet/dry, but the dry period in the habitat is short, and humidity remains high.

FERTILIZER: ½ strength, applied weekly when plants are actively growing.

REST PERIOD: A gentle, 2–3 month rest is indicated, with a slightly higher diurnal range of 13–15°F (7–8°C) which results primarily from warmer days rather than cooler nights. Water should be restricted to occasional misting, humidity reduced, and light increased.

GROWING MEDIA: A fertile terrestrial mix with good drainage. Plants may be repotted anytime new growth is commencing. The stems run along the surface of the ground before becoming erect, so the plant requires a particularly large container.

MISCELLANEOUS NOTES: Bloom initiators have not been identified, and cultivation bloom records are limited.

In its natural habitat, *P. pauciflorus* is reported to bloom during the summer and is described as free-flowering.

Plant and Flower Information

PLANT SIZE AND TYPE: A 24–40 in. (61–101 cm) sympodial terrestrial.

PSEUDOBULB: None. The stem is angled near the base.

LEAVES: Number unknown. The plicate foliage is 5–12 in. (13–30 cm) long and appears on the apical portion of the stem.

INFLORESCENCE: 7 in. (18 cm) long. The spikes, often more than one, arise along the stem from internodes below the leaves, or from the axils of lower leaves.

FLOWERS: 4–6 per inflorescence. The flowers are 2.5 in. (6 cm) across and remain somewhat closed. The wide petals and narrower sepals are white. The lip is marked with a yellow blotch and rows of red spots.

HYBRIDIZING NOTES: N/A.

REFERENCES: 31, 112, 118, 175.

PHOTOS/DRAWINGS: *31*, 175.

Phaius peyrotii J. Bosser

AKA: N/A.

ORIGIN/HABITAT: Endemic to Madagascar, it grows in shady forests at 2952–3608 ft. (900–1100 m).

CLIMATE: Station # 67143, Mananjary, Malagasy, Lat. 21.2°S, Long. 48.4°E, at 16 ft. (5 m). Temperatures are calculated for an elevation of 3000 ft. (914 m), resulting in probable extremes of 88°F (31.1°C) and 36°F (2.2°C).

N/HEMISPHERE	JAN	FEB	MAR	APR	MAY	JUN	JUL	AUG	SEP	OCT	NOV	DEC
°F AVG MAX	66	66	68	70	74	75	76	76	75	73	70	68
°F AVG MIN	50	50	52	55	58	60	62	62	61	59	55	51
DIURNAL RANGE	16	16	16	15	16	15	14	14	14	14	15	17
RAIN/INCHES	6.4	5.3	4.3	2.9	6.5	8.9	15.8	15.6	18.8	10.0	7.9	9.3
HUMIDITY/%	86	84	83	82	82	84	84	84	85	85	86	86
BLOOM SEASON	N/A											
DAYS CLR	N/A											
RAIN/MM	163	135	109	74	165	226	401	396	478	254	201	236
°C AVG MAX	19.0	19.0	20.1	21.2	23.4	24.0	24.5	24.5	24.0	22.9	21.2	20.1
°C AVG MIN	10.1	10.1	11.2	12.9	14.5	15.6	16.8	16.8	16.2	15.1	12.9	10.6
DIURNAL RANGE	8.9	8.9	8.9	8.3	8.9	8.4	7.7	7.7	7.8	7.8	8.3	9.5
S/HEMISPHERE	JUL	AUG	SEP	OCT	NOV	DEC	JAN	FEB	MAR	APR	MAY	JUN

Cultural Recommendations

LIGHT: 1800–2400 fc. Diffused or barely dappled light is recommended, since the plant grows in shady forests.

TEMPERATURES: Summer days average 74–76°F (23–24°C), and nights average 58–62°F (14–17°C), with a diurnal range of 14–15°F (8°C). Plants may not adapt to high summer temperatures, as the probable extremes are just 12°F (7°C) above the highest averages.

HUMIDITY: 80–85%.

WATER: The plants should be kept moist, but not soggy. The rainfall pattern is wet/wetter.

FERTILIZER: ½ strength, applied weekly while plants are actively growing.

REST PERIOD: Winter days average 66–70°F (19–21°C), and nights average 50–55°F (10–13°C), with a diurnal range of 15–17°F (8–9°C). The simultaneous decline in both day and night temperatures results in little change in the diurnal range. In cultivation, water should be reduced, but the medium should not be allowed to become dry. In the habitat, rainfall is lowest in early spring.

GROWING MEDIA: A fertile terrestrial mix with good drainage. Repotting is best done in early spring, when active growth resumes.

MISCELLANEOUS NOTES: N/A.

Plant and Flower Information

PLANT SIZE AND TYPE: A 10–12 in. (25–30 cm) erect sympodial terrestrial.

PSEUDOBULB: 1 in. (2.5 cm) long. The oblong pseudobulbs are small and inconspicuous.

LEAVES: Number unknown. The leaves are 8–14 in. (20–35 cm) long, arching, ovate-lanceolate, and deeply ruffled at the margins.

INFLORESCENCE: 10–12 in. (25–30 cm) long. The spike emerges laterally from the stem.

FLOWERS: 3–5. The flowers are 2 in. (5 cm) across and open sequentially. The sepals and smaller petals are pale rose on the back and violet on the front.

HYBRIDIZING NOTES: N/A.

REFERENCES: 21.

PHOTOS/DRAWINGS: 21.

Phaius philippinensis N. E. Brown

AKA: N/A.

ORIGIN/HABITAT: Mindanao, Philippines, at 3000–4000 ft. (914–1219 m), where it grows in mossy bogs.

CLIMATE: Station # 98325, Dagupan, Philippines, Lat. 16.1°N, Long. 120.6°E, at 7 ft. (2 m). Temperatures are calculated for an elevation of 3500 ft. (1067 m), resulting in probable extremes of 92°F (33.3°C) and 46°F (7.8°C).

N/HEMISPHERE	JAN	FEB	MAR	APR	MAY	JUN	JUL	AUG	SEP	OCT	NOV	DEC
°F AVG MAX	77	78	82	84	83	82	78	78	78	79	78	77
°F AVG MIN	57	57	60	62	63	63	63	63	63	62	60	58
DIURNAL RANGE	20	21	22	22	20	19	15	15	15	17	18	19
RAIN/INCHES	0.4	0.6	0.9	2.9	8.8	12.9	23.1	21.5	15.8	7.1	3.1	0.8
HUMIDITY/%	73	70	71	71	75	82	84	85	85	79	76	75
BLOOM SEASON	*		*	*						*	*	*
DAYS CLR @ 8AM	15	15	19	21	17	9	4	4	4	12	14	15
DAYS CLR @ 2PM	14	15	17	17	11	5	2	3	2	10	11	12
RAIN/MM	10	15	23	74	224	328	587	546	401	180	79	20
°C AVG MAX	25.3	25.8	28.0	29.2	28.6	28.0	25.8	25.8	25.8	26.4	25.8	25.3
°C AVG MIN	14.2	14.2	15.8	16.9	17.5	17.5	17.5	17.5	17.5	16.9	15.8	14.7
DIURNAL RANGE	11.1	11.6	12.2	12.3	11.1	10.5	8.3	8.3	8.3	9.5	10.0	10.6
S/HEMISPHERE	JUL	AUG	SEP	OCT	NOV	DEC	JAN	FEB	MAR	APR	MAY	JUN

Cultural Recommendations

LIGHT: 2000–3000 fc. Diffused or barely dappled light is indicated. Direct sunlight should be avoided.

TEMPERATURES: Summer days average 78–84°F (26–29°C), and nights average 62–63°F (17–18°C), with a diurnal range of 15–22°F (8–12°C). Seasonal changes are minor, indicating a probable intolerance to wide temperature fluctuations.

HUMIDITY: 80–85%.

WATER: Ample moisture is needed throughout the year. The medium should be kept moist. Although the rainfall pattern is very wet/dry, the mossy-bog habitat indicates that moisture requirements are high year-round.

FERTILIZER: ½ strength, applied weekly when plants are actively growing.

REST PERIOD: Winter days average 77–82°F (24–26°C), and nights average 57–60°F (14–16°C), with a diurnal range of 19–22°F (11–12°C). Fertilizer should be reduced when the plant is not actively growing, but water and humidity should remain fairly high despite the low winter rainfall in the habitat. The plants should tolerate higher light in winter.

GROWING MEDIA: A fertile, sphagnum-based terrestrial mix with good drainage. Repotting should be done immediately after flowering.

MISCELLANEOUS NOTES: Bloom records are based on months when collections were made. Flowering time may range from Oct.–Apr. (Apr.–Oct.), or the plant may be free-flowering. As is true with many bog plants, cultivation could be difficult.

Plant and Flower Information

PLANT SIZE AND TYPE: A moderately sized sympodial terrestrial.

LEAVES: 2 per growth. The leaves are 9–15 in. (23–38 cm) long, lanceolate, plicate, and bright green.

PSEUDOBULB: Small, arising from an iris-type rhizome.

INFLORESCENCE: 7 in. (18 cm) long.

FLOWERS: Few. The flowers are 2.5 in. (6 cm) across, long-lasting, leathery, and spreading, but they do not expand fully. The sepals and petals project upwards and are white on the outside and red to orange-brown on the inside, with a narrow, yellow picoteed margin. The trumpet-shaped lip is recurved at the margins, is white when it first opens, and turns yellow with age.

HYBRIDIZING NOTES: N/A.

REFERENCES: 2, 203, 211.

PHOTOS/DRAWINGS: 211.

Phaius pictus T. E. Hunt

AKA: N/A.

ORIGIN/HABITAT: Australia, on the Cape York Peninsula, where it grows on the floor of warm rainforests from near sea level to 2500 ft. (0–762 m).

CLIMATE: Station # 94283, Cooktown, Australia, Lat. 15.5°S, Long. 145.2°E, at 24 ft. (7 m). Temperatures are calculated for an elevation of 1000 ft. (305 m), resulting in probable extremes of 101°F (38.3°C) and 58°F (14.4°C).

N/HEMISPHERE	JAN	FEB	MAR	APR	MAY	JUN	JUL	AUG	SEP	OCT	NOV	DEC
°F AVG MAX	76	77	79	82	85	86	86	85	83	82	79	77
°F AVG MIN	63	64	67	70	72	72	72	72	72	70	67	65
DIURNAL RANGE	13	13	12	12	13	14	14	13	11	12	12	12
RAIN/INCHES	0.9	1.2	0.6	1.0	2.5	6.6	14.4	13.7	15.3	8.8	2.8	2.0
HUMIDITY/%	73	69	68	67	68	71	75	76	77	75	74	75
BLOOM SEASON					*							
DAYS CLR	N/A											
RAIN/MM	23	30	15	25	64	168	366	348	389	224	71	51
°C AVG MAX	24.3	24.9	26.0	27.7	29.3	29.9	29.9	29.3	28.2	27.7	26.0	24.9
°C AVG MIN	17.1	17.7	19.3	21.0	22.1	22.1	22.1	22.1	22.1	21.0	19.3	18.2
DIURNAL RANGE	7.2	7.2	6.7	6.7	7.2	7.8	7.8	7.2	6.1	6.7	6.7	6.7
S/HEMISPHERE	JUL	AUG	SEP	OCT	NOV	DEC	JAN	FEB	MAR	APR	MAY	JUN

Cultural Recommendations

LIGHT: 1800–2400 fc. Diffused or barely dappled light is preferred. Direct sunlight should be avoided.

TEMPERATURES: Summer days average 82–86°F (28–30°C), and nights average 70–72°F (21–22°C), with a diurnal range of 11–14°F (6–8°C) which varies only 3°F (2°C) through the year.

HUMIDITY: 70–75%.

WATER: Ample moisture is needed in the active growing season. The medium should be wet, but not soggy. The rainfall pattern is wet/dry.

FERTILIZER: ½ strength, applied weekly when plants are actively growing.

REST PERIOD: Winter days average 76–82°F (24–28°C), and nights average 63–67°F (17–19°C), with little change in the diurnal range. Despite the wet/dry rainfall pattern recorded at the weather station, rainforest habitats generally supply ample moisture year-round. Growers indicate that the plant is healthiest if given frequent waterings, particularly if temperatures are warm.

GROWING MEDIA: A fertile, terrestrial peat mix with good drainage. Repotting is best done in the spring, just as new growth is evident.

MISCELLANEOUS NOTES: *P. pictus* is sometimes considered a doubtful species.

Plant and Flower Information

PLANT SIZE AND TYPE: A 60 in. (150 cm) sympodial terrestrial.

PSEUDOBULB: 16–24 in. (40–61 cm) long. The thin, elongated stems are slightly swollen at the base.

LEAVES: 3–5 per growth. The leaves are 12–28 in. (30–71 cm) long, broad, and pleated, occurring near the apex of the stem.

INFLORESCENCE: 20–36 in. (51–91 cm) long. The 1 or 2 spikes emerge from the axils of the lower leaves.

FLOWERS: 4–20 per inflorescence. The blossoms, 2 in. (5 cm) across, are yellow on the outside and brick-red with yellow stripes on the inside. The dorsal sepal projects forward, while the petals and lateral sepals are reflexed at the tips. The ruffled lip is yellow, with numerous lines of red dots. There is an extensive area of white hairs near the apex.

HYBRIDIZING NOTES: N/A.

REFERENCES: 131.

PHOTOS/DRAWINGS: 131.

Phaius platychilus. See *P. flavus.* REFERENCES: 168.

Phaius pulchellus Kraenzlin

AKA: N/A.

ORIGIN/HABITAT: Endemic to Madagascar, it grows in shady, humid forests at 2296–4920 ft. (700–1500 m).

CLIMATE: Station # 67015, Ambilobe, Malagasy, Lat. 13.1°S, Long. 49.1°E, at 95 ft. (29 m). Temperatures are calculated for an elevation of 3500 ft. (1067 m), resulting in probable extremes of 89°F (31.7°C) and 45°F (7.2°C).

N/HEMISPHERE	JAN	FEB	MAR	APR	MAY	JUN	JUL	AUG	SEP	OCT	NOV	DEC
°F AVG MAX	77	78	80	82	83	81	78	78	80	80	80	78
°F AVG MIN	53	54	56	60	62	62	63	63	63	62	59	55
DIURNAL RANGE	24	24	24	22	21	19	15	15	17	18	21	23
RAIN/INCHES	0.4	0.5	0.4	1.3	4.1	11.2	19.6	18.7	11.7	4.2	0.7	0.6
HUMIDITY/%	N/A											
BLOOM SEASON		*		*		*		*				
DAYS CLR	N/A											
RAIN/MM	10	13	10	33	104	284	498	475	297	107	18	15
°C AVG MAX	24.9	25.4	26.5	27.6	28.2	27.1	25.4	25.4	26.5	26.5	26.5	25.4
°C AVG MIN	11.5	12.1	13.2	15.4	16.5	16.5	17.1	17.1	17.1	16.5	14.9	12.6
DIURNAL RANGE	13.4	13.3	13.3	12.2	11.7	10.6	8.3	8.3	9.4	10.0	11.6	12.8
S/HEMISPHERE	JUL	AUG	SEP	OCT	NOV	DEC	JAN	FEB	MAR	APR	MAY	JUN

Cultural Recommendations

LIGHT: 1800–2400 fc or less. Diffused or barely dappled light is suggested. Direct sunlight should be avoided, as the plant prefers shady, humid forests.

TEMPERATURES: Summer days average 78–83°F (25–28°C), and nights average 62–63°F (17°C), with a diurnal range of 15–21°F (8–12°C).

HUMIDITY: 75–85%. Although records are not available, the habitat is described as humid.

WATER: Ample moisture is needed in the active growing season. The medium should be wet, but not soggy. The rainfall pattern is wet/dry.

FERTILIZER: ½ strength, applied weekly when plants are actively growing.

REST PERIOD: Winter days average 77–80 °F (25–27 °C), and for 3 months nights average 53–56 °F (12–13 °C), with a diurnal range of 22–24 °F (12–13 °C). The dry season lasts through winter, and habitat information does not indicate whether plants have other sources of water. Water should be restricted to occasional misting, or to a watering every 3–4 weeks with occasional misting between waterings. Fertilizer should be eliminated during this period.

GROWING MEDIA: A fertile terrestrial mix with good drainage. Repotting is best done in early spring, just as new roots begin to grow.

MISCELLANEOUS NOTES: Spring flowering is reported in cultivation, but in the plant's natural habitat, blooming occurs in Jun.–Sep. (Dec.–Mar.), which corresponds with the rainy season.

Plant and Flower Information

PLANT SIZE AND TYPE: A 16–32 in. (41–82 cm) sympodial terrestrial.

PSEUDOBULB: Small and close together, the pseudobulbs have thick white roots.

LEAVES: 3–4 per growth. The leaves are 5–12 in. (13–30 cm) long, narrowly lanceolate, and wavy at the margins.

INFLORESCENCE: 32 in. (82 cm) long. The spikes arise laterally from the base of the pseudobulb.

FLOWERS: 12–15. The blossoms open sequentially, but many are open at a time. The flowers are 2–3 in. (5–8 cm) across, with greenish-to-pink sepals and petals. The white lip is marked with rose or reddish violet. Blossoms vary in size and color, and several varieties have been named.

HYBRIDIZING NOTES: N/A.

REFERENCES: 21, 35.

PHOTOS/DRAWINGS: 21, 35.

Phaius pulcher (Humbert and H. Perrier de la Bathie) Summerhayes

AKA: *Gastorchis pulchra.*

ORIGIN/HABITAT: Endemic to Madagascar, it grows in shady, humid forests at 2624–5576 ft. (800–1700 m), which normally implies adaptability. The plant is found in only 2 locations on the island: at the warmer, northern location it grows at higher elevations, and at the cooler, southern end it is found at lower elevations. The climate information given here represents the southern location, and the records are adjusted to the median elevation for that area.

CLIMATE: Station # 67197, Ft. Dauphin, Malagasy, Lat. 25.0 °S, Long. 47.0 °E, at 144 ft. (44 m). Temperatures are calculated for an elevation of 2952 ft. (900 m), resulting in probable extremes of 85 °F (29.4 °C) and 40 °F (4.4 °C).

N/HEMISPHERE	JAN	FEB	MAR	APR	MAY	JUN	JUL	AUG	SEP	OCT	NOV	DEC
°F AVG MAX	65	65	67	70	72	74	75	75	73	72	69	66
°F AVG MIN	52	52	54	56	59	61	63	63	62	60	56	53
DIURNAL RANGE	13	13	13	14	13	13	12	12	11	12	13	13
RAIN/INCHES	3.9	3.4	1.9	2.8	3.3	5.1	7.7	7.9	9.0	4.3	4.9	6.1
HUMIDITY/%	80	79	78	79	80	80	82	81	83	81	80	80
BLOOM SEASON	N/A											
DAYS CLR @ 3PM	15	13	16	16	7	8	7	7	7	12	11	9
RAIN/MM	99	86	48	71	84	130	196	201	229	109	124	155
°C AVG MAX	18.2	18.2	19.3	21.0	22.1	23.2	23.7	23.7	22.6	22.1	20.4	18.7
°C AVG MIN	11.0	11.0	12.1	13.2	14.9	16.0	17.1	17.1	16.5	15.4	13.2	11.5
DIURNAL RANGE	7.2	7.2	7.2	7.8	7.2	7.2	6.6	6.6	6.1	6.7	7.2	7.2
S/HEMISPHERE	JUL	AUG	SEP	OCT	NOV	DEC	JAN	FEB	MAR	APR	MAY	JUN

Cultural Recommendations

LIGHT: 1200–1800 fc. Diffused light is preferred.

TEMPERATURES: Summer days average 70–75 °F (21–24 °C), and nights average 56–63 °F (13–17 °C), with a diurnal range of 11–14 °F (6–8 °C).

HUMIDITY: 80% throughout the year.

WATER: Ample moisture is needed during periods of active growth. The rainfall pattern is wet/drier. Humidity levels in the habitat indicate that fog and dew provide some moisture during the drier period.

FERTILIZER: ½ strength, applied weekly when plants are actively growing.

REST PERIOD: Winter days average 65–70 °F (18–21 °C), and for 5 months nights average 52–56 °F (11–13 °C). Highs and lows decline simultaneously, maintaining a uniform diurnal range. The rainfall pattern indicates that water should be reduced in winter, with a dry period of 1–2 months occurring in early spring. For 2–3 months, fertilizer may be reduced or eliminated, and light increased.

GROWING MEDIA: A fertile terrestrial mix with high humus and good drainage.

MISCELLANEOUS NOTES: N/A.

Plant and Flower Information

PLANT SIZE AND TYPE: A large sympodial terrestrial.

PSEUDOBULB: Small. The pseudobulbs are spaced about 1.5 in. (4 cm) apart on the rhizome.

LEAVES: 3–4 per growth. The leaves are 12–24 in. (30–61 cm) long and very narrow, particularly on var. *perrieri*.

INFLORESCENCE: 24–48 in. (61–122 cm) long. Flowers emerge near the apex of the spikes, which arise from nodes on the side of the pseudobulb.

FLOWERS: 6–8. The blossoms are approximately 1.5 in. (4 cm) across. Var. *perrieri* may have up to 15 smaller flowers. The sepals and petals are white, while the lip may be white or rose to violet with white margins.

HYBRIDIZING NOTES: N/A.

REFERENCES: 21.

PHOTOS/DRAWINGS: 21.

Phaius ramosii Ames.

Originally described as *Calanthe ramosii*, it was collected in Dec. (Jun.) 1915 at Zambales, Philippines. Additional habitat information was not recorded, and the plant is unlikely to be available for cultivation. REFERENCES: 203.

Phaius robertsii von Mueller

AKA: *P. monticola*.

ORIGIN/HABITAT: Endemic to the humid forests of New Caledonia. It is usually found between 295–984 ft. (90–300 m), but one collection was recorded at 4592 ft. (1400 m).

CLIMATE: Station # 91592, Noumea, New Caledonia, Lat. 22.3°S, Long. 166.5°E, at 246 ft. (75 m). Temperatures are calculated for an elevation of 670 ft. (204 m), resulting in probable extremes of 98°F (36.7°C) and 51°F (10.6°C).

N/HEMISPHERE	JAN	FEB	MAR	APR	MAY	JUN	JUL	AUG	SEP	OCT	NOV	DEC
°F AVG MAX	75	75	77	79	82	85	85	84	84	82	78	76
°F AVG MIN	61	60	62	64	67	69	72	71	71	69	65	63
DIURNAL RANGE	14	15	15	15	15	16	14	12	13	13	13	13
RAIN/INCHES	3.6	2.6	2.5	2.0	2.4	2.6	3.7	5.1	5.7	5.2	4.4	3.7
HUMIDITY/%	73	70	69	67	68	69	71	74	75	76	73	73
BLOOM SEASON									*	*	*	*
DAYS CLR @ 11AM	7	9	9	15	12	10	7	6	7	7	7	7
DAYS CLR @ 5PM	7	11	6	11	7	6	5	4	4	5	3	7
RAIN/MM	91	66	64	51	61	66	94	130	145	132	112	94
°C AVG MAX	23.7	23.7	24.8	25.9	27.6	29.2	29.2	28.7	28.7	27.6	25.3	24.2
°C AVG MIN	15.9	15.3	16.4	17.6	19.2	20.3	21.4	22.0	21.4	20.3	18.1	17.0
DIURNAL RANGE	7.8	8.4	8.4	8.3	8.4	8.9	7.8	6.7	7.3	7.3	7.2	7.2
S/HEMISPHERE	JUL	AUG	SEP	OCT	NOV	DEC	JAN	FEB	MAR	APR	MAY	JUN

Cultural Recommendations

LIGHT: 1000–1500 fc.

TEMPERATURES: Summer days average 82–85°F (28–29°C), and nights average 67–72°F (19–22°C), with a diurnal range of 12–16°F (7–9°C).

HUMIDITY: 70–75%.

WATER: The medium should be kept moist. The rainfall pattern is moderately wet year-round, with even greater amounts in the mountains.

FERTILIZER: ½ strength, applied weekly when plants are actively growing.

REST PERIOD: Winter days average 75–78°F (24–27°C), and nights average 60–65°F (15–18°C), with a diurnal range of 13–15°F (7–8°C). High and low temperatures decline simultaneously, resulting in little change in the diurnal range. Plants cannot tolerate drying out, but in cultivation water should be reduced, particularly if temperatures are somewhat low. The higher number of clear days in the habitat indicates increased light.

GROWING MEDIA: A fertile terrestrial mix with good drainage.

MISCELLANEOUS NOTES: Sep.–Dec. (Mar.–Jun.) is the normal bloom period, but flowering may occur as early as Jun. (Dec.), suggesting that flowering may be initiated by increased rainfall. The high-elevation collection indicates that *P. robertsii* may tolerate cooler average temperatures.

Plant and Flower Information

PLANT SIZE AND TYPE: A sympodial terrestrial. No measurements were located.

PSEUDOBULB: Small, arising from a short rhizome.

LEAVES: 2 per growth. The leaves are plicate, ovate, and sharply pointed.

INFLORESCENCE: Tall and erect to spreading. The spike emerges from between the leaf bracts near the base of the growth.

FLOWERS: 2–6. The blossoms appear sequentially and do not open fully. The round lip is white marked with rose, clawed at the apex, ruffled near the front margin, and densely pubescent.

HYBRIDIZING NOTES: N/A.

REFERENCES: 107.

PHOTOS/DRAWINGS: 107.

Phaius roeblingii. See *P. tankervilleae*. REFERENCES: 122.

Phaius rosellus. Now considered a synonym of *Galeandra*. REFERENCES: 122.

Phaius roseus. See *P. mishmensis*. REFERENCES: 122, 168.

Phaius rumphii. Now considered a synonym of *Spathoglottis plicata*. REFERENCES: 122.

Phaius schlechteri. See *P. humblotii*. REFERENCES: 21, 122.

Phaius simulans Rolfe. Often considered conspecific with *P. tuberculosus*. However, when J. Bosser reviewed the genus in *Revision du genre* Phaius *Loureiro* (1971), he wrote, "It is interesting to see how distinct the two species are in habit and yet, how closely they resemble each other in the shape, color, and markings of the flowers."

P. simulans is described as easily identifiable when not in flower. It is epiphytic, with widely spaced growths on a climbing, branching rhizome, and is endemic to the forests of Didy in central Madagascar, where it grows on moss-covered tree trunks. No elevation was recorded. This species is not currently available for cultivation. REFERENCES: 21, 35.

Phaius sinensis Rolfe. Found in Swatow District in eastern Kwangtung, China. Information on habitat elevation is insufficient to allow the selection of weather records. The plant is unlikely to be available for cultivation. REFERENCES: 122.

Phaius somai. See *P. flavus*. REFERENCES: 168.

Phaius stenocentron Schlechter. This species originated on Sulawesi (Celebes) Island, Indonesia. Habitat information is unavailable. The plant is not mentioned in current literature and is unlikely to be available for cultivation. REFERENCES: 122.

Phaius steppicola Hand.-Mazz. This species originated in Kweichau (Guidschou), China. The habitat was described as rocky and subtropical, but information on elevation was insufficient to allow the selection of climate data. The plant is not mentioned in current literature and is unlikely to be available for cultivation. REFERENCES: 122.

Phaius stuppeus. See *P. tankervilleae*. REFERENCES: 122.

Phaius subtrilobus Ames and Schweinfurth

AKA: N/A.

ORIGIN/HABITAT: Mt. Kinabalu, North Borneo, at approximately 5000 ft. (1524 m).

CLIMATE: Station # 49613, Tambunan, North Borneo (Sabah), Lat. 5.7°N, Long. 116.4°E, at 1200 ft. (366 m). Temperatures are calculated for an elevation of 5000 ft. (1524 m), resulting in probable extremes of 86°F (30.0°C) and 42°F (5.6°C).

N/HEMISPHERE	JAN	FEB	MAR	APR	MAY	JUN	JUL	AUG	SEP	OCT	NOV	DEC
°F AVG MAX	73	74	76	77	77	76	76	76	76	75	74	73
°F AVG MIN	54	52	53	54	55	54	53	53	54	54	54	55
DIURNAL RANGE	19	22	23	23	22	22	23	23	22	21	20	18
RAIN/INCHES	5.8	3.7	5.8	7.5	8.2	7.3	5.1	4.9	6.4	7.0	6.8	6.0
HUMIDITY/%	N/A											
BLOOM SEASON	*	*										
DAYS CLR	N/A											
RAIN/MM	147	94	147	190	208	185	130	124	163	178	173	152
°C AVG MAX	23.0	23.6	24.7	25.3	25.3	24.7	24.7	24.7	24.7	24.1	23.6	23.0
°C AVG MIN	12.5	11.4	11.9	12.5	13.0	12.5	11.9	11.9	12.5	12.5	12.5	13.0
DIURNAL RANGE	10.5	12.2	12.8	12.8	12.3	12.2	12.8	12.8	12.2	11.6	11.1	10.0
S/HEMISPHERE	JUL	AUG	SEP	OCT	NOV	DEC	JAN	FEB	MAR	APR	MAY	JUN

Cultural Recommendations

LIGHT: 1800–2400 fc is a reasonable starting point, since habitat details and sky-cover data are lacking. Plants should be watched carefully, and light modified as the condition of the leaves indicates.

TEMPERATURES: Summer days average 76–77°F (25°C), and nights average 53–55°F (12–13°C), with a diurnal range of 22–23°F (12–13°C). These plants probably would not tolerate summer heat. Year-round average highs fluctuate only 4 °F (2 °C), and lows vary even less.

HUMIDITY: 80–85%. Though weather records are incomplete, the steady, year-round rainfall would result in high average humidity.

WATER: Ample moisture is needed in the active growing season, and the medium should not be allowed to dry out. The rainfall pattern is wet year-round.

FERTILIZER: ½ strength, applied weekly when plants are actively growing.

REST PERIOD: Growing conditions should be maintained year-round. The slight variation in average temperatures occurs naturally in cultivation.

GROWING MEDIA: A fertile terrestrial mix with good drainage. Repotting is best done after flowering or when new root growth is evident.

MISCELLANEOUS NOTES: N/A.

Plant and Flower Information

PLANT SIZE AND TYPE: A stout, erect sympodial terrestrial.

PSEUDOBULB: N/A.

LEAVES: 3–4 per growth. The leaves are 14–20 in. (36–51 cm) long.

INFLORESCENCE: 12–20 in. (30–51 cm) long, arising from the base of the pseudobulb. The spike is stout, suberect, slightly zigzag, and tapering at the tip.

FLOWERS: 4–10. The flowers are 3 in. (7.5 cm) across. The sepals and petals are coppery red and spreading. The shiny lip is yellowish white, ruffled, and marked with deep yellow-orange in the throat.

HYBRIDIZING NOTES: N/A.

REFERENCES: 2.

PHOTOS/DRAWINGS: 63.

Phaius tahitensis Schlechter.

This species was originally described as *Calanthe grandiflora*. Insufficient information is available to allow the selection of weather data. The plant is unlikely to be available for cultivation. REFERENCES: 122.

Phaius tankervilleae Blume

AKA: *P. tancarvilliae* is apparently the correct spelling of the botanical name, but the International Orchid Commission recognizes the spelling *tankervillea*, which is still in common use by taxonomists. Other spellings used over the years include *tancervilleae*, *tankervillae*, *tankervillia*, *tankervilliae*, and *tankervillieae*. The International Orchid Commission continues to use the synonym *P. grandifolius* for registering hybrids.

Dr. Seidenfaden lists the following synonyms: *Bletia tankervilleae*, *Calanthe bachmaensis*, *C. speciosa* (non Lindl.), *Limodorum incarvillei*, *L. tankervilleae*, *Pachyne spectabilis*, *Phaius bicolor*, *P. blumei*, *P. blumei* var. *assamicus*, *P. blumei* var. *pulcher*, *P. carronii*, *P. grandiflorus*, *P. grandifolius*, *P. incarvillae*, *P. incarvillae* var. *speciosa*, *P. leucophoeus*, *P. longicornu*, *P. tankervillieae*, *P. tankervillieae* var. *superbus*, *P. tankervillieae* f. *veronicae*, *P. wallichii*, *P. wallichii* var. *assamicus*, and *Tankervillia cantonensis*. *Index Kewensis* lists *Phaius mannii* and *P. roeblingii* as synonyms for *P. wallichii*. Other authors list *P. australis*, *P. bernaysii*, and *P. tenuis*, some of which do not even appear in *Index Kewensis*.

ORIGIN/HABITAT: Tropical and subtropical regions in Asia, the Pacific islands, Australia, and Africa. This wide-ranging, variable species is also found at high elevations in nearly temperate weather conditions. It grows in open, grassy fields, in moist, open deciduous forests, and in swampy areas of shady, evergreen forests. It has naturalized at higher elevations in Hawaii and the Caribbean islands.

CLIMATE: Northeast Thailand, Zone 2, is typical of many of the natural habitats. All stations in the Korat Plateau region are averaged, giving an elevation of 508 ft. (155 m). Temperatures are calculated for an elevation of 2460 ft. (750 m), resulting in probable extremes of 106 °F (41.1 °C) and 32 °F (0.0 °C).

N/HEMISPHERE	JAN	FEB	MAR	APR	MAY	JUN	JUL	AUG	SEP	OCT	NOV	DEC
°F AVG MAX	81	84	89	91	88	85	84	84	83	82	81	80
°F AVG MIN	53	59	65	69	70	70	69	69	68	65	60	55
DIURNAL RANGE	28	25	24	22	18	15	15	15	15	17	21	25
RAIN/INCHES	0.2	0.7	1.6	3.2	7.8	8.2	8.8	10.0	10.8	3.6	0.6	0.2
HUMIDITY/%	62	62	62	63	73	77	78	80	82	76	70	66
BLOOM SEASON		**	***	**								
DAYS CLR @ 7AM	8	6	7	7	3	2	2	1	1	8	10	9
DAYS CLR @ 1PM	17	12	10	5	1	0	0	0	1	4	7	12
RAIN/MM	5	18	41	81	198	208	224	254	274	91	15	5
°C AVG MAX	27.0	28.6	31.4	32.5	30.9	29.2	28.6	28.6	28.1	27.5	27.0	26.4
°C AVG MIN	11.4	14.8	18.1	20.3	20.9	20.9	20.3	20.3	19.8	18.1	15.3	12.5
DIURNAL RANGE	15.6	13.8	13.3	12.2	10.0	8.3	8.3	8.3	8.3	9.4	11.7	13.9
S/HEMISPHERE	JUL	AUG	SEP	OCT	NOV	DEC	JAN	FEB	MAR	APR	MAY	JUN

Cultural Recommendations

LIGHT: 3000–5000 fc. Diffused or dappled light is recommended.

TEMPERATURES: Summer days average 83–91 °F (28–33 °C), and nights average 68–70 °F (20–21 °C), with a diurnal range of 15–22 °F (8–12 °C).

HUMIDITY: 70–80% during the summer.

WATER: Ample moisture is needed in the active growing season. The medium should be wet, but not soggy. The rainfall pattern is seasonally wet/dry.

FERTILIZER: ½ strength, applied weekly when plants are actively growing.

REST PERIOD: Winter days average 80–84 °F (26–29 °C), and nights average 53–60 °F (11–15 °C), with a diurnal range of 24–28 °F (13–16 °C). In some habitats, winter lows may average just above freezing, with extremes below freezing. In cultivation, *P. tankervilleae* tolerates cool days with nights averaging 40 °F (5 °C). A cool, dry rest is required to induce flowering. Air-conditioning is necessary to provide seasonal fluctuation when the plants are cultivated in a uniformly warm climate. Water and fertilizer must be reduced; the cooler the rest, the less moisture the plants can tolerate. In all habitats, moisture is low when temperatures are low and increases as average temperatures increase.

GROWING MEDIA: A fertile terrestrial mix with good drainage. Although plants will flower in small pots, large containers provide stability and room for the extensive root system. Repotting is best done in early spring.

MISCELLANEOUS NOTES: *P. tankervilleae* is very adaptable, but winter cooling must be provided. The climate shown in the table is a reasonable average, but conditions vary widely.

Flowering time may be controlled by maintaining cool conditions and low light. Research has shown the species to be somewhat photoperiodic, with the best blooms occurring when plants receive either 10.5 or 13.5 hours of light each day.

Plant and Flower Information

PLANT SIZE AND TYPE: A variably sized, 24–80 in. (60–200 cm) sympodial terrestrial.

PSEUDOBULB: 1–3 in. (3–8 cm) long. Pseudobulbs are ovate, thick, green, and tightly clustered.

LEAVES: 2–4 per growth. The leaves are 12–40 in. (30–102 cm) long, elliptic-lanceolate, evergreen, and plicate.

INFLORESCENCE: 24–48 in. (61–122 cm) long. The spike arises from the base of the pseudobulb.

FLOWERS: 10–20. The fragrant blossoms are 4–5 in. (10–13 cm) across; several are open at a time. Variably colored, they are reddish, purplish, or yellowish brown on the front and buff, greenish, or rose-pink on the back. White forms are known. The crisped, trumpet-shaped lip has recurved margins marked with gold, is whitish outside, and is wine to purple inside. Flowers last 17–18 days, but Java plants reportedly have self-pollinating flowers, which are short-lived.

HYBRIDIZING NOTES: Chromosome counts are 2n = 48 and 2n = 50.

REFERENCES: 6, 9, 14, 20, 31, 34, 36, 112, 118, 120, 126, 131, 132, 139, 148, 152, 153, 157, 167, 168, 174, 175, 181, 203.

PHOTOS/DRAWINGS: *14, 20, 24, 27, 31,* 34, 118, 120, 126, *132, 139, 152,* 153, 168, *174,* 175.

Phaius tenuis Rchb.f. This species was said to originate in Salak, Java. However, J. J. Smith considered it possible that *P. tenuis* was the same as *P. wallichii* (or *P. tankervilleae,* as the 2 species are now considered conspecific). *P. tenuis* is not mentioned in current literature. REFERENCES: 122, 175.

Phaius tetragonus Rchb.f. This plant was described as originating in Madagascar, but it was not included in J. Bosser's 1971 review of the *Phaius* of Madagascar. REFERENCES: 122, 164.

Phaius trichoneurus Schlechter

AKA: N/A.

ORIGIN/HABITAT: Endemic to central Sulawesi (Celebes) Island, Indonesia. The plant was found growing in a garden near Dongalla.

CLIMATE: Station # 97014, Manado, Indonesia, Lat. 1.5 °N, Long. 124.9 °E, at 264 ft. (80 m). The record high is 97 °F (36.1 °C), and the record low is 65 °F (18.3 °C).

N/HEMISPHERE	JAN	FEB	MAR	APR	MAY	JUN	JUL	AUG	SEP	OCT	NOV	DEC
˚F AVG MAX	85	85	85	86	87	87	87	89	89	89	87	86
˚F AVG MIN	73	73	73	73	74	73	73	73	73	72	73	74
DIURNAL RANGE	12	12	12	13	13	14	14	16	16	17	14	12
RAIN/INCHES	18.6	13.8	12.2	8.0	6.4	6.5	4.8	4.0	3.4	4.9	8.9	14.7
HUMIDITY/%	84	83	83	83	81	80	75	72	75	77	82	83
BLOOM SEASON	N/A											
DAYS CLR @ 8AM	4	3	6	11	11	12	12	12	14	17	12	8
DAYS CLR @ 2PM	1	1	1	2	1	3	3	4	4	4	1	1
RAIN/MM	472	351	310	203	163	165	122	102	86	124	226	373
˚C AVG MAX	29.4	29.4	29.4	30.0	30.6	30.6	30.6	31.7	31.7	31.7	30.6	30.0
˚C AVG MIN	22.8	22.8	22.8	22.8	23.3	22.8	22.8	22.8	22.8	22.2	22.8	23.3
DIURNAL RANGE	6.6	6.6	6.6	7.2	7.3	7.8	7.8	8.9	8.9	9.5	7.8	6.7
S/HEMISPHERE	JUL	AUG	SEP	OCT	NOV	DEC	JAN	FEB	MAR	APR	MAY	JUN

Cultural Recommendations

LIGHT: 2400–4000 fc is suggested. In the habitat, summer skies are frequently clear, particularly in the mornings.

TEMPERATURES: Summer days average 87–89 ˚F (31–32 ˚C), and nights average 73–74 ˚F (23 ˚C), with a diurnal range of 14–16 ˚F (8–9 ˚C).

HUMIDITY: 72–84%.

WATER: Plants should be kept moist while actively growing. The rainfall pattern is wet/less wet, with the driest weather occurring in late summer when temperatures are warm.

FERTILIZER: ½ strength, applied weekly when plants are actively growing.

REST PERIOD: Winter days average 85–86 ˚F (30 ˚C), and nights average 72–74 ˚F (22–23 ˚C), with a winter diurnal range of 12–14 ˚F (7–8 ˚C). In the habitat, the average highs, lows, and diurnal range fluctuate only a few degrees during the year. The plants may rest during the drier period occurring in late summer which coincides with the period of highest diurnal range.

GROWING MEDIA: A fertile terrestrial mix with good drainage.

MISCELLANEOUS NOTES: N/A.

Plant and Flower Information

PLANT SIZE AND TYPE: A 48 in. (122 cm), erect terrestrial.

PSEUDOBULB: N/A.

LEAVES: Number unknown. The leaves are 32–44 in. (80–110 cm) long, erect to arching, lanceolate, and pointed at the apex.

INFLORESCENCE: 48 in. (122 cm) long, the spike is somewhat laxly flowered near the apex.

FLOWERS: 8–10. The flowers are 3.0–3.2 in. (8 cm) across. The sepals and petals are spreading, oblong-lanceolate, and pointed at the apex. The lip is decorated with 3 raised keels.

HYBRIDIZING NOTES: N/A.

REFERENCES: 163.

PHOTOS/DRAWINGS: N/A.

Phaius tuberculatus. See *P. tuberculosus*. REFERENCES: 122.

Phaius tuberculosus Blume

AKA: *P. tuberculatus. P. simulans* is sometimes considered conspecific.

ORIGIN/HABITAT: Endemic to Madagascar in eastern forests at 656–2952 ft. (200–900 m).

CLIMATE: Station # 67095, Tamatave, Malagasy, Lat. 18.1 ˚S, Long. 49.4 ˚E, at 16 ft. (5 m). Temperatures are calculated for an elevation of 1750 ft. (533 m), resulting in probable extremes of 92 ˚F (33.3 ˚C) and 50 ˚F (10.0 ˚C).

N/HEMISPHERE	JAN	FEB	MAR	APR	MAY	JUN	JUL	AUG	SEP	OCT	NOV	DEC
˚F AVG MAX	69	70	72	75	78	79	80	80	79	77	74	71
˚F AVG MIN	59	58	59	61	64	67	68	68	67	66	63	60
DIURNAL RANGE	10	12	13	14	14	12	12	12	12	11	11	11
RAIN/INCHES	11.9	8.0	5.2	3.9	4.6	10.3	14.4	14.8	17.8	15.7	10.4	11.1
HUMIDITY/%	85	84	82	81	82	83	84	84	86	85	85	85
BLOOM SEASON	*	**	*	*								*
DAYS CLR @ 3AM	10	10	9	10	8	10	8	10	6	9	13	10
DAYS CLR @ 3PM	7	9	13	13	12	10	6	7	4	8	12	9
RAIN/MM	302	203	132	99	117	262	366	376	452	399	264	282
˚C AVG MAX	20.7	21.3	22.4	24.0	25.7	26.3	26.8	26.8	26.3	25.2	23.5	21.8
˚C AVG MIN	15.2	14.6	15.2	16.3	17.9	19.6	20.2	20.2	19.6	19.0	17.4	15.7
DIURNAL RANGE	5.5	6.7	7.2	7.7	7.8	6.7	6.6	6.6	6.7	6.2	6.1	6.1
S/HEMISPHERE	JUL	AUG	SEP	OCT	NOV	DEC	JAN	FEB	MAR	APR	MAY	JUN

Cultural Recommendations

LIGHT: 1200–1800 fc. Low, diffused light is recommended. Growers report that plants do best in a shady corner with *Phalaenopsis*.

TEMPERATURES: Summer days average 78–80 ˚F (26–27 ˚C), and nights average 64–68 ˚F (18–20 ˚C), with a 12–14 ˚F (7–8 ˚C) diurnal range, which varies little through the year. High and low temperatures rise and fall simultaneously.

HUMIDITY: 80–85%.

WATER: Ample moisture is needed year-round. The medium should be wet, but not soggy. The rainfall pattern is wet/wetter. Adequate air movement is critical for this plant.

FERTILIZER: ½ strength, applied weekly when plants are actively growing.

REST PERIOD: Winter days average 69–72 °F (21–22 °C), and nights average 58–61 °F (14–16 °C), with a diurnal range of 10–13 °F (6–7 °C). Water and fertilizer may be reduced slightly for 2–3 months in late winter and early spring, but the medium should never be allowed to dry out.

GROWING MEDIA: A moss-based terrestrial mix with charcoal added for good drainage. Repotting is best done immediately after flowering.

MISCELLANEOUS NOTES: *P. tuberculosus* is reportedly difficult to maintain, as it is prone to infestations of red spider, thrips, and green fly. It may be less susceptible if conditions are correct for the species.

Plant and Flower Information

PLANT SIZE AND TYPE: A 12–24 in. (30–60 cm) sympodial terrestrial.

PSEUDOBULB: 1.0–2.5 in. (3–6 cm) long. New growths arise from a short, ascending rhizome.

LEAVES: 5–6 per growth. The variably sized leaves are 6–24 in. (15–61 cm) long, oblong, plicate, suberect to spreading, and paler on the underside.

INFLORESCENCE: 16–26 in. (41–66 cm) long.

FLOWERS: 6–8. The showy blossoms are 2.5–3.0 in. (6–8 cm) across. The sepals and petals are white with rosy-purple spots, and the ruffled lip is ornamented with an orange-yellow crest. Below the callus is a dense tuft of sulphur-yellow hairs. Each flower normally lasts 15–20 days. This species is distinguished from others by the white bracts, sepals, and petals, and by the yellow sidelobes which are heavily spotted with red or orange-brown.

HYBRIDIZING NOTES: Chromosome counts are n = 23 and 2n = 50.

REFERENCES: 14, 21, 35, 205, 206, 211.

PHOTOS/DRAWINGS: 21, 205, 206, 211.

Phaius undulatomarginata. See *P. flavus*. REFERENCES: 168.

Phaius undulatomarginatus. See *P. flavus*. REFERENCES: 122.

Phaius veratrifolius Lindley. Described as originating in the Himalayas, this plant is not mentioned in current literature and is unavailable for cultivation. REFERENCES: 122.

Phaius wallichii. See *P. tankervilleae*. REFERENCES: 168.

Phaius woodfordii (woodfortii). See *P. flavus*. REFERENCES: 122, 168.

Phaius zollingeri. See *P. amboinensis*. REFERENCES: 122.

4
Phalaenopsis
General Information

SUBFAMILY: Vandoidea.

TRIBE: *Vandeae*.

SUBTRIBE: *Sarcanthinea*.

GENUS: *Phalaenopsis* Blume.

AKA: Species in this genus have also been known as *Polychilus, Polystylus, Stauritis, Stauroglottis,* and *Synadena*.

SPECIES: This genus consists of approximately 40 species. Dr. Herman Sweet's book *The Genus* Phalaenopsis (1980) was our authority for valid species and synonyms, except for species described since his work was published.

ORIGIN/HABITAT: The natural habitat includes most of the South Pacific islands and extends west to India, south to Australia, and north to Taiwan.

CLIMATE: Tropical to subtropical climates are normal throughout the range.

Cultural Recommendations

LIGHT: Species described as "easy to grow" or those with the widest distribution range are most likely to adapt to an east-facing window with light diffused by a sheer curtain. No shadow should be seen when a hand is moved across the leaves, and leaves should feel cool to the touch, especially during periods of high light.

For most *Phalaenopsis* species and hybrids, the acceptable light level is 1000–1200 fc for at least 6 hours a day. Light may be lowered to this level in most temperate-zone greenhouses by using 85–90% shade cloth during the summer, by placing plants under a greenhouse bench, or by placing plants about 12 in. (30 cm) below fluorescent lights.

Some growers report success with light as low as 600 fc, while others indicate that plants do not bloom well with only a northern exposure. However, a northern exposure with good reflected light is adequate for some species.

The maximum light most *Phalaenopsis* can tolerate is 1500 fc for 14 hours a day. In most midlatitude greenhouses, 70–75% shade cloth reduces summer light to this level. Most species do poorly if grown year-round at these higher levels, but many need a period of higher light to initiate blooming. Many *Phalaenopsis* can tolerate higher light in winter when not actively growing. Plant stress due to excess light may be reduced by keeping temperatures at the low end of the recommended range and increasing humidity.

New leaves are particularly susceptible to leaf-burn from excess light, and severe sunburn may kill *Phalaenopsis*. Light levels should be watched carefully during seasonal shifts in light patterns. Hanging plants high in the greenhouse or placing them near south-facing glass can be disastrous.

The schedule for artificial lights included in Chapter 1 is satisfactory for *Phalaenopsis* and also meets the needs of many other orchids.

TEMPERATURES: Most species are healthiest if temperatures are not allowed to fall below 62–65 °F (17–18 °C). However, equatorial species will be healthier if lows are 68 °F (20 °C) or warmer.

Since different species have somewhat different temperature requirements, the individual climate tables should be consulted before implementing any regime. Temperatures outside the recommended range are conducive to stress and disease.

Highs of 70–85 °F (21–30 °C) are nearly ideal; most species will tolerate short periods at 90–95 °F (32–35 °C). Plants exposed to excess heat for too long, however, may not bloom. High humidity and good air circulation are critically important in a hot environment.

HUMIDITY: Humidity averaging 60–70% is adequate for most potted *Phalaenopsis*. However, 80% is preferred if plants are mounted, and many Malayan and Indonesian species prefer the higher levels even when potted.

WATER: The condition of root-tips indicates whether water is sufficient: green root-tips indicate adequate moisture levels, while white root-tips indicate a need for more water. *Phalaenopsis* roots are the plant's only means of water storage and should never be allowed to become desiccated, even during dry periods.

Allowing water to stand on the leaves may lead to crown rot. Watering early in the morning allows moisture to evaporate completely before night, and tipping pots at a 30–45° angle improves drainage.

Water temperature is important; 62°F(17°C) is a minimum water temperature for most species and many hybrids. However, the warmest-growing types should be given 70°F (21°C)water, as they are also the plants most likely to be found growing in limestone areas. Notes regarding the use of limestone are included under "Growing Media" in the following pages.

Cold water may cause tissue collapse, adversely affecting flowers and leaves. Symptoms to watch for are listed under "Plant and Flower Information" in the next few pages.

FERTILIZER: Some growers recommend a balanced (20–20–20) fertilizer. The balanced formula seems to slow the breakdown of bark, and *Phalaenopsis* receive enough nitrogen for growth. However, other growers suggest using a formula with higher nitrogen (30–10–10) at least monthly if plants are potted in fir bark.

Recommendations range from fertilizing monthly to fertilizing with every other watering depending on the strength of the fertilizer mixture. Growers report good results using frequent applications of very dilute solutions (0.1 tsp. per gal.; 0.1 tsp. per 3.8 liters.)

Periodic foliar feeding with dilute fish emulsion is beneficial, especially if a plant is producing keikis, or young plants. A dilute solution of a balanced chemical fertilizer can also be used as a foliar spray.

Seedlings bloom more quickly if a high-phosphate fertilizer such as 10–52–10 is applied periodically.

REST PERIOD: All environmental changes should be introduced gradually, and plants should be monitored carefully for indications of stress. The following cool-rest guide should be used only when the average winter lows on the climate table indicate the need for such a rest. The minimum rest period recommended is 2–5 weeks, with lows averaging 65°F (18°C)and highs averaging below 80°F (26–27°C).

Cool-Rest Guide

Bob Gordon recommends the following cool-rest regime in his book *Culture of the* Phalaenopsis *Orchid* (1985).

Night temperatures should be reduced to 55–62°F (13–17°C) in Oct.(Apr.) but should never fall below 52°F (11°C), and drafts should be avoided. Maximum daytime temperatures should be below 80°F (27°C) for about 4 weeks. The normal fertilizing schedule is continued for 3 weeks then withheld during the last week, but the pots should be flushed.

As temperatures are lowered, light levels should be raised to 1300–1500 fc and air circulation increased.

Since *Phalaenopsis* are prone to disease when cool, water should evaporate from the crown before night. As temperatures are gradually returned to normal, a magnesium sulfate (Epsom salts) solution is applied at the rate of ¼ lb. per 5 gal. (550 g per 19 liters) for the next 3–4 weeks. The pots are then flushed for 1 week.

Higher light is continued until Jan. (Jul.), then light is reduced to 800–1200 fc when the regular winter schedule of feeding with a high-phosphate fertilizer is resumed. In Jan. (Jul.) most spikes reach about half their mature length and normal fertilizing is reinstated. Blooming occurs 120–130 days after the rest is initiated.

Caution: The preceding guide should *not* be used to initiate blooms in warmer-growing species. Equatorial species need no cool rest and may be seriously injured or killed if allowed to dry out or if exposed to near-record lows for their native habitats. Also, some species are not healthy with continuous lows of 65°F (18°C). Bloom initiators are discussed further under the heading "Miscellaneous Notes."

GROWING MEDIA: ½–⅝ in. (12–16 mm) fir bark is the most commonly used medium. Note that although some warm-growing species grow on limestone cliffs, limestone should not be added to the growing medium unless water of 70°F (21°C) is always used. Lime is one of the few minerals that dissolve more readily in water cooler than 70°F (21°C), and it dissolves so rapidly in cooler water that toxic levels may be created.

Shallow pots with additional holes punched for increased drainage and air circulation are best for *Phalaenopsis*. Specific suggestions for increasing drainage are included in Chapter 1.

Phalaenopsis roots are nearly always thick and fleshy and continue to elongate and branch with maturity. They are the plant's only means of water storage, enabling it to survive adverse conditions. The roots should be trimmed only if they are damaged or deteriorated.

Keikis, young plants that sometimes develop at unbloomed nodes on old flower spikes, bloom most rapidly if separated from the mother plant and potted when 3 or 4 roots are ½–¾ in. (13–18 mm) long.

MISCELLANEOUS NOTES: The factors which induce flowering in species not needing a rest period are often unknown, but initiators may include fluctuations in rainfall patterns, light levels, or day/night temperature ranges. Varying the diurnal temperature range, rather than exposing the plant to stressfully low temperatures, may be an effective technique that will not put the plant at risk.

Phalaenopsis are not normally photoperiodic, but reports indicate that seasonal light fluctuations initiate flowering in *P. amabilis* and *P. schillerana*, parents of many of today's broad-petaled, early-spring–blooming hybrids. Whenever possible, flowers should be initiated in these hybrids by varying the day length while maintaining temperature averages appropriate for the parent species.

The importance of good air circulation cannot be emphasized too strongly. It helps the plant resist disease, reduces the risk of sunburn by keeping leaf temperature cool, and tempers damage from excessive light, heat, or humidity. If their requirements can be met, *Phalaenopsis* do well when summered outside.

Plant and Flower Information

PLANT SIZE AND TYPE: All *Phalaenopsis* are monopodial, and most are epiphytic. Notes regarding individual growth habits are included for each species.

LEAVES: Most *Phalaenopsis* leaves are rich green, firm, and succulent. However, some species have limp, notched, wavy, recurved, grey-green, or purplish leaves. Normal leaves are described for each species.

In addition to the general leaf symptoms of cultural and disease problems described in Chapter 1 and in Appendix A, the following symptoms indicate the problems most likely to occur with *Phalaenopsis*.

Clear or watery yellow spots on the leaves may be caused by a bacterial infection.

Crinkled leaves, if not normal to the species, may be caused by insufficient water.

Curled margins on new leaves are caused by low humidity during early leaf growth.

Dull, wrinkled leaves indicate too dry an atmosphere.

Inadequate leaf production is usually the result of insufficient nitrogen or phosphorous.

Pale, medium-brown discoloration in the center of the plant or at the base of the leaves indicates crown rot. The disease occurs when water is allowed to stand in the crown overnight, particularly when temperatures are too cool and when air circulation is inadequate. While the disease is normally fatal, Bob Gordon's book *Culture of the* Phalaenopsis *Orchid* (1985) suggests a technique that sometimes induces a keiki to form before the plant dies.

Pitting on new foliage indicates tissue collapse caused by exposure to cold water or cold temperatures. Using water warmed to the prevailing air temperature will prevent temperature shock.

Red coloration on the surface of new leaves is apparently caused by an unidentified fungus. Often the plant will respond to treatment with a systemic fungicide such as Benlate.

Reddish or discolored bottom leaves are probably dying back as new leaves are formed. Usually a mature plant has 3–6 leaves, replacing 1 or 2 each year.

A round, discolored area on the top of a curved leaf surface is nearly always sunburn. Leaves should feel cool to the touch, and temperatures should never exceed the growing temperature by more than 25 °F (14 °C). In fact, some species cannot tolerate that much heating.

Leaf loss in evergreen *Phalaenopsis* is an indication of stress. But plants that lose all their leaves can recover. Plants should be soaked for several hours in Natriphene, repotted in sphagnum, and given an environment ideal for the species. Enclosing them in a plastic bag prevents additional contamination and maintains humidity. While this method is not always successful, plants may eventually produce new leaves or a keiki.

INFLORESCENCE: *Phalaenopsis* flower spikes emerge from the leaf axils. Many species have evergreen inflorescences which normally should not be removed. Flower spikes which do not die back will continue to elongate and will often branch as the plant matures, producing more and larger flowers. If they become too long or unattractive, they may be cut just above the lowest node to initiate new growth.

It is important to maintain appropriate heat and moisture levels. If a plant is allowed to bloom when conditions are stressfully hot or dry, it may become so severely dehydrated that the damage is irreversible.

The following flower-spike symptoms provide clues to cultural problems.

Crooked or discolored flower stems may be infected with a virus. Plants should be destroyed or isolated until the problem can be diagnosed.

Limp spikes that need staking may indicate inadequate light if this characteristic is abnormal for the species.

Short flower spikes on the broad-petaled varieties are usually caused by too much light.

Spikes which damp-off, wither, or turn brown at the tip have usually been watered with cold water, causing plant tissue to collapse.

FLOWERS: Blossoms often last 2–5 months, but water on the flowers will spoil them much sooner.

On broad-petaled species, blossoms of maximum size and number will be achieved the next season if, after the flowers fade, the old spike is removed. Cuts should be made below the lowest vegetative node, thereby preventing the formation of additional blossoms.

Phalaenopsis with broad-petaled flowers may be forced into extended blooming by the following technique. After the flowers fade, remove the inflorescence by cutting it just below the first node that produced a blossom, leaving the lower vegetative buds. Plants will frequently grow a new branch or keiki from latent vegetative buds. Succeeding flowers will decline in size and number with each forced branching, and unless the plant is very strong and healthy, it may not bloom the following season.

The following flower problems provide clues to cultural problems.

Flowers that do not open fully may be due to low humidity, resulting in excessively thick nectar that actually glues sepals and petals together. Some growers suggest syringing the flower to dissolve the nectar.

No blossoms may result from inadequate light, insufficient rest, or the absence of another cultural element necessary to initiate flowering. If the plant has bloomed for many years, the problem may simply be old age.

Poor flower form, if not caused by genetic faults, may be induced by exposure to cold, which can severely retard flower development.

Small or short-lived blossoms may be caused by too much light, exposure to hot or cold temperatures, inadequate fertilizer, or trauma while growing. Smaller or fewer flowers may occur when a rest period is not enforced.

Keikis, frequently formed by plants in poor health, may also result from inadequate light, deteriorated potting medium, or inadequate water or fertilizer.

HYBRIDIZING NOTES: The normal chromosome count for all *Phalaenopsis* is $2n = 38$. Rare individual plants may be tetraploid with twice that number.

Phalaenopsis seeds normally mature sufficiently to be viable for use in green pod culture about 85 days after pollination. In 110–120 days, the seeds are fully mature and the fruits open. Changes in the capsule appearance may indicate that seeds should be sown immediately; otherwise they will become contaminated when the fruits open and will require sterilization before sowing. Some hybrid seeds are viable in 70–80 days. Hybrids often bloom in 2 years.

REFERENCES: 18, 20, 25, 48, 75, 78, 82, 84, 113, 118, 136, 148, 177, 195, 197, 201, 205, 206, 210.

PHOTOS/DRAWINGS: See species listings.

Species Culture

Phalaenopsis acutifolia. See *P. sumatrana*. REFERENCES: 195.

Phalaenopsis alboviolacea. Now considered a synonym of *Kingidium deliciosum*. REFERENCES: 195.

Phalaenopsis alcicornis. See *P. sanderana*. REFERENCES: 195.

Phalaenopsis amabilis (Linnaeus) Blume

AKA: *P. celebica, P. gloriosa, P. grandiflora, P. hombronii, P. pleihary, P. rimestadiana, P. rosenstromii. P. aphrodite* hybrids are registered under *P. amabilis* by the International Orchid Commission; plants of the 2 species are easily confused and often mislabeled. *P. aphrodite* is known to hybridize naturally with *P. equestris*, producing *P. × intermedia*.

ORIGIN/HABITAT: Queensland, Australia, through Indonesia, to the Philippines. In this extended range, plants may grow high in tall trees in dense forests or on tree branches sometimes so close to the ocean that the plants are washed by salt spray.

CLIMATE: Southern Java, Zone 4, Lat. 8.0°S, Long. 110.5°E. The elevation averages 1060 ft. (323 m), and the record temperatures average 95°F (35.0°C) and 52°F (11.1°C).

N/HEMISPHERE	JAN	FEB	MAR	APR	MAY	JUN	JUL	AUG	SEP	OCT	NOV	DEC
°F AVG MAX	84	85	86	86	84	83	83	82	83	85	84	84
°F AVG MIN	66	66	68	69	69	70	70	70	70	70	69	67
DIURNAL RANGE	18	19	18	17	15	13	13	12	13	15	15	17
RAIN/INCHES	1.9	1.5	1.5	4.8	8.2	12.0	13.2	11.7	12.0	7.9	5.3	3.2
HUMIDITY/%	76	73	70	73	77	81	82	81	81	79	77	72
BLOOM SEASON	**	**	**	**	***	***	***	*	*	*	*	*
DAYS CLR @7AM	6	7	7	6	4	1	1	1	3	4	5	8
DAYS CLR @1PM	4	5	3	2	1	0	0	1	1	1	2	4
RAIN/MM	48	38	38	122	208	305	335	297	305	201	135	81
°C AVG MAX	28.9	29.4	30.0	30.0	28.9	28.3	28.3	27.8	28.3	29.4	28.9	28.9
°C AVG MIN	18.9	18.9	20.0	20.6	20.6	21.1	21.1	21.1	21.1	21.1	20.6	19.4
DIURNAL RANGE	10.0	10.5	10.0	9.4	8.3	7.2	7.2	6.7	7.2	8.3	8.3	9.5
S/HEMISPHERE	JUL	AUG	SEP	OCT	NOV	DEC	JAN	FEB	MAR	APR	MAY	JUN

Cultural Recommendations

LIGHT: 1200–1500 fc. Plants tolerate morning sun. Although clear days in the habitat are rare, light can be bright with a thin overcast.

TEMPERATURES: Summer days average 82–86°F (28–30°C), and nights average 69–70°F (21°C), with a diurnal range of 12–15°F (7–8°C).

HUMIDITY: 70–80%. Plants are healthier with good air circulation.

WATER: While plants will survive some drying, they grow faster and are more floriferous if kept moist and evergreen. All habitats are deluged by rain for about 6 months.

FERTILIZER: ¼–½ strength, applied weekly to biweekly during the growing season.

REST PERIOD: Warmer winter days average 84–86°F (29–30°C), but nights are cooler averaging 66–69°F (19–21°C), with an increased diurnal range of 18–19°F (10–11°C). Water and fertilizer should be reduced for 2–3 months. The plants should not dry out, since the high average humidity in their native habitat indicates that moisture is available from frequent dew, fog, or mist, which is absorbed and stored in the extremely long roots.

GROWING MEDIA: ½–⅝ in. (12–16 mm) fir bark. Repotting is best done immediately after blooming.

MISCELLANEOUS NOTES: *P. amabilis* is easy, adaptable, and robust in cultivation. Flowering is induced by shorter days and night temperatures averaging about 65°F (18°C) for 2–5 weeks.

Plant and Flower Information

PLANT SIZE AND TYPE: A monopodial epiphyte that is wider than it is tall.

LEAVES: 3–5 per plant. The leaves are 4–18 in. (10–46 cm) long and glossy dark green with purplish tones on the underside, thin textured, and pendulous. The leaves are sometimes deciduous, in habitats with an extended dry season; but in cultivation, plants are healthiest when the foliage is evergreen.

INFLORESCENCE: 24–36 in. (61–91 cm) long. Plants often produce 2 spikes, which are arching, branching, and tinged with purple.

FLOWERS: Many, often 15 per branch. Mature plants may have 70–80 fragrant blossoms. Plants often produce 2 inflorescences, and the flowers on each spike open simultaneously and may last 6 months.

The blossoms are 3.0–3.5 in. (8–9 cm) across, and on rare plants they may be as large as 5 in. (13 cm). They are broad-petaled, showy, milky white, and often flushed with pink on the back. Lip margins are spotted with yellow and red. Slender, crumpled, recurved antennae about 1 in. (3 cm) long project from the apex of the lip. Flower size and color are variable.

HYBRIDIZING NOTES: *P. amabilis* is a primary parent of many modern hybrids. Seeds mature in 75–80 days when crossed with *P. stuartiana*.

REFERENCES: 2, 14, 24, 112, 118, 130, 139, 148, 164, 181, 195, 205, 211.

PHOTOS/DRAWINGS: *14*, 24, *62*, 118, *130, 139, 141*, 164, 181, *184, 186, 195*, 203, 205, 206.

Phalaenopsis ambigua. See *P. aphrodite*. REFERENCES: 195.

Phalaenopsis amboinensis J. J. Smith

AKA: *P. hombronii, P. psilantha*.

ORIGIN/HABITAT: Ambon Island, in the Toli Toli district of Ceram, near Djangdjang, Sulawesi (Celebes) Island, Indonesia.

CLIMATE: Station # 97014, Manado, Indonesia, Lat. 1.5°N, Long. 124.9°E, at 262 ft. (80 m). The record high is 97°F (36.1°C), and the record low is 65°F (18.3°C).

N/HEMISPHERE	JAN	FEB	MAR	APR	MAY	JUN	JUL	AUG	SEP	OCT	NOV	DEC
°F AVG MAX	85	85	85	86	87	87	87	89	89	89	87	86
°F AVG MIN	73	73	73	73	74	73	73	73	73	72	73	74
DIURNAL RANGE	12	12	12	13	13	14	14	16	16	17	14	12
RAIN/INCHES	18.6	13.8	12.2	8.0	6.4	6.5	4.8	4.0	3.4	4.9	8.9	14.7
HUMIDITY/%	84	83	83	83	81	80	75	72	75	77	82	83
BLOOM SEASON	*	*	*	*	*	*	*	*	*	*	*	*
DAYS CLR @ 8AM	4	3	6	11	11	12	12	12	14	17	12	8
DAYS CLR @ 2PM	1	1	1	2	1	3	3	4	4	4	1	1
RAIN/MM	472	351	310	203	163	165	122	102	86	124	226	373
°C AVG MAX	29.4	29.4	29.4	30.0	30.6	30.6	30.6	31.7	31.7	31.7	30.6	30.0
°C AVG MIN	22.8	22.8	22.8	22.8	23.3	22.8	22.8	22.8	22.8	22.2	22.8	23.3
DIURNAL RANGE	6.6	6.6	6.6	7.2	7.3	7.8	7.8	8.9	8.9	9.5	7.8	6.7
S/HEMISPHERE	JUL	AUG	SEP	OCT	NOV	DEC	JAN	FEB	MAR	APR	MAY	JUN

Cultural Recommendations

LIGHT: 1000–1200 fc. Morning light is preferred. The habitat is frequently clear in the morning and usually cloudy in the afternoon.

TEMPERATURES: Summer days average 87–89°F (31–32°C), and nights average 72–74°F (22–23°C), varying only 2°F (1°C) during the year, with a diurnal range of 14–17°F (8–9°C). The daily diurnal range exceeds the seasonal variation in this habitat.

HUMIDITY: 75–85%.

WATER: Plants should be kept very moist during the growing season. Warm water, about 70°F (21°C), is highly recommended. The rainfall pattern is wet/wetter, with the driest period occurring in late summer. Weather stations at all elevations in the region report 6 months of extremely wet conditions. The onset of the dominant rainy season is variable, determined by local terrain and monsoonal influences.

FERTILIZER: ¼–½ strength, applied weekly to biweekly during the growing season.

REST PERIOD: Winter days average 85–86°F (29–30°C), and nights average 72–74°F (22–23°C), with a narrower diurnal range of 12–13°F (7°C). Water should be reduced only if temperatures are somewhat cool, and fertilizer should be decreased when plants are not actively growing.

GROWING MEDIA: ½–⅝ (12–16 mm) fir bark with moisture-retentive additives, or sphagnum moss with perlite or charcoal added for drainage. Plants are best repotted after blooming or when root growth starts.

MISCELLANEOUS NOTES: Reportedly more demanding than some species, *P. amboinensis* should be kept uniformly warm and moist.

Plant and Flower Information

PLANT SIZE AND TYPE: A moderately sized monopodial epiphyte.

LEAVES: 3–5 per plant. The leaves are 10 in. (25 cm) long and elliptic to oblong.

INFLORESCENCE: 6–9 in. (15–23 cm) long, the spikes are usually arching to pendent. *P. amboinensis* produces a new evergreen spike each year, and the older spikes elongate and sometimes branch after the first year.

FLOWERS: Few, with individual blossoms opening 1 or 2 at a time on each spike. However, since each inflorescence continues to produce blooms for about 5 years, the plants can have a number of flowers. Individual blossoms are 2–3 in. (5–8 cm) across. The sepals and petals are slightly cupped and pointed at the apex, but they are usually broad enough to overlap at the base. The flowers are off-white, pale lemon-yellow, or orange-yellow and are marked with red-brown bars. The lip is small.

HYBRIDIZING NOTES: As a parent, *P. amboinensis* contributes heavy flower substance and strong color and helps to eliminate wavy petals. Inflorescences may be weak, and the star-shaped flowers tend to be poorly arranged. When crossed with *P. lueddemanniana*, hybrids are consistently white with yellow or green at the tips of the segments. When crossed with pink *Phalaenopsis*, the progeny are pink. Hybridizers had expected spotting and richer color, but it did not appear in the first-generation crosses.

REFERENCES: 81, 83, 111, 134, 148, 170, 176, 190, 195, 210.

PHOTOS/DRAWINGS: *12, 52, 68, 81, 83, 85,* 99, *103, 111, 134, 170,* 176, *189,* 195, 210, *213.*

Phalaenopsis amethystina. Now considered a synonym of *Kingidium deliciosum.* REFERENCES: 195.

Phalaenopsis antennifera. Now considered a synonym of *Doritis pulcherrima.* REFERENCES: 195.

Phalaenopsis aphrodite Rchb.f.

AKA: *P. amabilis,* with which it is easily confused, is still the name used for hybrid registration purposes. Over the years plants have been known as *P. amabilis* var. *ambigua,* var. *aphrodite,* var. *dayana,* var. *erubescens,* var. *longifolia,* and var. *rotundifolia.* Other synonyms include *P. ambigua, P. babuyana, P. erubescens, P. formosa, P. formosana,* and *P. formosum.*

ORIGIN/HABITAT: Taiwan to the Philippines. Found in primary and secondary forests, between sea level and 1000 ft. (305 m).

CLIMATE: Station # 98135, Basco, Philippines, Lat. 20.5°N, Long. 122.0°E, at 36 ft. (11 m). The record high is 98°F (36.7°C), and the record low is 53°F (11.7°C).

N/HEMISPHERE	JAN	FEB	MAR	APR	MAY	JUN	JUL	AUG	SEP	OCT	NOV	DEC
°F AVG MAX	76	78	81	84	88	88	88	88	87	84	81	78
°F AVG MIN	67	69	71	75	77	78	78	77	76	75	73	70
DIURNAL RANGE	9	9	10	9	11	10	10	11	11	9	8	8
RAIN/INCHES	7.9	5.9	4.9	3.8	5.0	11.8	10.3	16.2	14.6	11.8	11.6	11.0
HUMIDITY/%	82	81	81	82	82	84	83	84	84	81	81	81
BLOOM SEASON	**	**	**	*								*
DAYS CLR @ 8AM	1	1	3	2	2	1	1	1	2	1	1	1
DAYS CLR @ 2PM	1	2	3	2	2	0	1	0	1	1	1	1
RAIN/MM	201	150	124	97	127	300	262	411	371	300	295	279
°C AVG MAX	24.4	25.6	27.2	28.9	31.1	31.1	31.1	31.1	30.6	28.9	27.2	25.6
°C AVG MIN	19.4	20.6	21.7	23.9	25.0	25.6	25.6	25.0	24.4	23.9	22.8	21.1
DIURNAL RANGE	5.0	5.0	5.5	5.0	6.1	5.5	5.5	6.1	6.2	5.0	4.4	4.5
S/HEMISPHERE	JUL	AUG	SEP	OCT	NOV	DEC	JAN	FEB	MAR	APR	MAY	JUN

Cultural Recommendations

LIGHT: 1000–1200 fc. The habitat is usually overcast.

TEMPERATURES: Summer days average 84–88°F (29–31°C), and nights average 75–78°F (22–26°C), with a diurnal range of 9–11°F (5–6°C).

HUMIDITY: Near 80–85% year-round.

WATER: Plants must be kept moist. Warm water, about 70°F (21°C), is highly recommended. The rainfall pattern is wet/wetter, with a slightly drier period of 1–2 months in spring.

FERTILIZER: ¼–½ strength, applied weekly to biweekly during the growing season.

REST PERIOD: Winter days average 76–81°F (24–27°C), and nights average 67–73°F (19–23°C), with a diurnal range of 8–10°F (4–6°C). *P. aphrodite* may adjust to cooler winters but is healthiest in a warmer environment. One grower reports that his plants survive winter lows of 35°F (1.7°C), providing they are kept dry at temperatures of 45°F (7°C) or below. Water and fertilizer should be reduced slightly for 1–2 months when the plant has finished blooming.

GROWING MEDIA: ½–⅝ in. (12–16 mm) fir bark with moisture-retentive additives, or sphagnum moss with perlite or charcoal added for drainage. Plants are best repotted after flowering.

MISCELLANEOUS NOTES: *P. aphrodite* is adaptable in cultivation.

Plant and Flower Information

PLANT SIZE AND TYPE: A moderately sized to large monopodial epiphyte.

LEAVES: 3–5 per plant. The leaves are 8–15 in. (20–38 cm) long; the top surface is uniformly dark green, while the underside is tinged with purple.

INFLORESCENCE: Much longer than the leaves and occasionally branching. The spikes, usually 2, are loosely flowered and drooping.

FLOWERS: Many. The blossoms are 2.5–3.5 in. (6–9 cm) across. They are delicately textured with a showy, broad-petaled form. Sepals and petals are white with a creamy or greenish suffusion. The lip is also white and is marked with red and yellow. Long, crumpled, filamentlike appendages project from the apex.

HYBRIDIZING NOTES: N/A.

REFERENCES: 112, 141, 148, 174, 184, 186, 195, 203, 205, 210.

PHOTOS/DRAWINGS: 141, *184,* 186, 195, 205, *210.*

Phalaenopsis appendiculata C. E. Carr

AKA: N/A.

ORIGIN/HABITAT: Found only near Tembeling in Pahang State, Malaya, on small trees in forested lowlands. Only 2 collections are presently recorded.

CLIMATE: Station # 48657, in Kuantan, Malaya, Lat. 3.8°N, Long. 103.2°E, at 58 ft. (18 m). The record high is 98°F (36.7°C), and the record low is 61°F (16.1°C).

N/HEMISPHERE	JAN	FEB	MAR	APR	MAY	JUN	JUL	AUG	SEP	OCT	NOV	DEC
°F AVG MAX	83	85	88	89	90	90	89	89	89	88	86	84
°F AVG MIN	71	71	71	72	73	72	72	72	72	72	72	71
DIURNAL RANGE	12	14	17	17	17	18	17	17	17	16	14	13
RAIN/INCHES	16.4	7.5	10.6	8.3	7.8	7.3	7.4	7.8	8.4	10.6	11.1	20.9
HUMIDITY/%	88	88	87	86	87	86	86	86	86	87	90	90
BLOOM SEASON	N/A											
DAYS CLR @ 7AM	1	1	2	1	1	1	1	0	0	0	0	1
DAYS CLR @ 1PM	0	0	0	0	0	0	0	0	0	0	0	0
RAIN/MM	417	190	269	211	198	185	188	198	213	269	282	531
°C AVG MAX	28.3	29.4	31.1	31.7	32.2	32.2	31.7	31.7	31.7	31.1	30.0	28.9
°C AVG MIN	21.7	21.7	21.7	22.2	22.8	22.2	22.2	22.2	22.2	22.2	22.2	21.7
DIURNAL RANGE	6.6	7.7	9.4	9.5	9.4	10.0	9.5	9.5	9.5	8.9	7.8	7.2
S/HEMISPHERE	JUL	AUG	SEP	OCT	NOV	DEC	JAN	FEB	MAR	APR	MAY	JUN

Cultural Recommendations

LIGHT: 800–1200 fc. Low light is indicated, as clear weather is rare in the plant's habitat.

TEMPERATURES: Days average 88–90°F (31–32°C), and nights average 72–73°F (22–23°C), with a summer diurnal range of 17–18°F (9–10°C).

HUMIDITY: Above 85% if possible.

WATER: Plants should be kept very moist. Warm water, about 70°F (21°C), is highly recommended. Heavy rainfall occurs every month of the year.

FERTILIZER: ¼–½ strength, applied weekly to biweekly during the growing season.

REST PERIOD: Winter days are cooler, averaging 83–85°F (28–29°C), and nights average 71–72°F (22°C), resulting in a lower diurnal range of 12–14°F (7–8°C). Although rainfall is highest in winter, increasing water during the rest period is not desirable as temperatures in cultivation are likely to be somewhat low.

GROWING MEDIA: ½–⅝ in. (12–16 mm) fir bark with moisture-retentive additives, or sphagnum moss with perlite or charcoal added for drainage. Plants are best repotted after blooming or as new root growth starts.

MISCELLANEOUS NOTES: N/A.

Plant and Flower Information

PLANT SIZE AND TYPE: A small monopodial epiphyte.

LEAVES: 2–4 per plant. The leaves are 3 in. (8 cm) long and elliptic.

INFLORESCENCE: Shorter than the leaves. Plants produce 2 suberect inflorescences per year.

FLOWERS: Few. The small flowers are 0.5 in. (1 cm) across, open in succession, and last 8–10 days. They are delicately textured, with a round-petaled form. Sepals and petals are white with purple markings, and the white lip is marked with pale violet and pale yellow. Long white filaments project from the apex of the lip.

HYBRIDIZING NOTES: The purple markings appear to be dominant.

REFERENCES: 118, 195.

PHOTOS/DRAWINGS: 195.

Phalaenopsis babuyana. See *P. aphrodite*. REFERENCES: 195.

Phalaenopsis barrii. See *P. speciosa*. REFERENCES: 195.

Phalaenopsis bella. Now considered a synonym of *Kingidium deliciosum*. REFERENCES: 195.

Phalaenopsis boxallii. See *P. mannii*. REFERENCES: 195.

Phalaenopsis buyssoniana. Now considered a synonym of *Doritis pulcherrima*. REFERENCES: 195.

Phalaenopsis celebensis Sweet

AKA: N/A.

ORIGIN/HABITAT: Sulawesi (Celebes) Island, Indonesia. No precise location or elevation was recorded.

CLIMATE: Station # 97014, Manado, Indonesia, Lat. 1.5°N, Long. 124.9°E, at 264 ft. (80 m). The record high is 97°F (36.1°C), and the record low is 65°F (18.3°C). Since precise habitat information is unavailable, the following data should be used with caution.

N/HEMISPHERE	JAN	FEB	MAR	APR	MAY	JUN	JUL	AUG	SEP	OCT	NOV	DEC
°F AVG MAX	85	85	85	86	87	87	87	89	89	89	87	86
°F AVG MIN	73	73	73	73	74	73	73	73	73	72	73	74
DIURNAL RANGE	12	12	12	13	13	14	14	16	16	17	14	12
RAIN/INCHES	18.6	13.8	12.2	8.0	6.4	6.5	4.8	4.0	3.4	4.9	8.9	14.7
HUMIDITY/%	84	83	83	83	81	80	75	72	75	77	82	83
BLOOM SEASON							*	*			*	*
DAYS CLR @ 8AM	4	3	6	11	11	12	12	12	14	17	12	8
DAYS CLR @ 2PM	1	1	1	2	1	3	3	4	4	4	1	1
RAIN/MM	472	351	310	203	163	165	122	102	86	124	226	373
°C AVG MAX	29.4	29.4	29.4	30.0	30.6	30.6	30.6	31.7	31.7	31.7	30.6	30.0
°C AVG MIN	22.8	22.8	22.8	22.8	23.3	22.8	22.8	22.8	22.8	22.2	22.8	23.3
DIURNAL RANGE	6.6	6.6	6.6	7.2	7.3	7.8	7.8	8.9	8.9	9.5	7.8	6.7
S/HEMISPHERE	JUL	AUG	SEP	OCT	NOV	DEC	JAN	FEB	MAR	APR	MAY	JUN

Cultural Recommendations

LIGHT: 1000–1200 fc. Morning light is preferable as the habitat is typically cloudy in the afternoon.

TEMPERATURES: Warm and uniform. Days average 86–89°F (30–32°C), and nights average 72–74°F (22–23°C), with a summer diurnal range of 13–17°F (7–9°C). Night temperatures vary by only 2°F (1°C) throughout the year, and the record low is 65°F (18.3°C), less than 10°F (6°C) below the averages. The diurnal range is greater than the seasonal variation.

HUMIDITY: 80% during the growing season.

WATER: Plants should be kept moist. Warm water, about 70°F (21°C), is highly recommended. Ample water should be provided for 6 months, then water should be reduced slightly for 6 months. The rainfall pattern is wet/wetter.

FERTILIZER: ¼–½ strength, applied weekly to biweekly during the growing season.

REST PERIOD: Winter days should average 85–86°F (29–30°C), and nights average 72–74°F (22–23°C), with a low diurnal range of 12–14°F (7–8°C). In the plant's native habitat, the heaviest rainfall occurs in winter; but if the plant is kept moist, watering need not be increased. Cultivation temperatures may be somewhat low, and additional water could result in root rot. Light may be increased slightly during the fall months, and fertilizer should be reduced when plants are not actively growing.

GROWING MEDIA: ½–⅝ in. (12–16 mm) fir bark with moisture-retentive additives, or sphagnum moss with perlite or charcoal added for drainage. Repotting is best done in spring when new root growth begins.

MISCELLANEOUS NOTES: N/A.

Plant and Flower Information

PLANT SIZE AND TYPE: A small monopodial epiphyte.

LEAVES: 3–5 per plant. The ovate-oblong leaves are 6–7 in. (15–18 cm) long and green with silvery white marmorations.

INFLORESCENCE: 16 in. (41 cm) long. The densely flowered, dark purplish-green spikes are usually arching, but may be pendent.

FLOWERS: Many. The blossoms are 0.8 in. (2 cm) across and open a few at a time, starting at the base of the inflorescence. They are showy, star-shaped, and snow-white, with bright orange or lilac markings on the lip. Petals are somewhat incurved.

HYBRIDIZING NOTES: N/A.

REFERENCES: 62, 195.

PHOTOS/DRAWINGS: 195.

Phalaenopsis celebica. See *P. amabilis.* REFERENCES: 195.

Phalaenopsis cochlearis Holttum

AKA: N/A.

ORIGIN/HABITAT: Discovered in 1964 in Sarawak at 1500–2000 ft. (457–610 m) in limestone areas. It is also found on limestone cliffs at Bau, Borneo.

CLIMATE: Station #96413, Kuching, Sarawak, Lat. 1.5°N, Long. 110.3°E, at 85 ft. (26 m). Temperatures are calculated for an elevation of 1750 ft. (533 m), resulting in probable extremes of 92°F (33.3°C) and 59°F (15.0°C).

N/HEMISPHERE	JAN	FEB	MAR	APR	MAY	JUN	JUL	AUG	SEP	OCT	NOV	DEC
°F AVG MAX	83	83	84	85	86	86	86	87	85	85	85	83
°F AVG MIN	67	67	67	67	67	68	67	67	67	67	67	67
DIURNAL RANGE	16	16	17	18	19	18	19	20	18	18	18	16
RAIN/INCHES	27.1	19.7	14.2	9.7	9.0	8.5	6.9	8.8	9.5	12.6	13.1	20.1
HUMIDITY/%	89	88	86	85	85	83	82	83	84	85	87	88
BLOOM SEASON				*	*		*	*				
DAYS CLR @ 7AM	1	0	1	2	3	2	4	1	2	1	1	1
DAYS CLR @ 1PM	0	0	0	0	0	1	1	1	0	0	0	0
RAIN/MM	688	500	361	246	229	216	175	224	241	320	333	511
°C AVG MAX	28.1	28.1	28.6	29.2	29.7	29.7	29.7	30.3	29.2	29.2	29.2	28.1
°C AVG MIN	19.2	19.2	19.2	19.2	19.2	19.7	19.2	19.2	19.2	19.2	19.2	19.2
DIURNAL RANGE	8.9	8.9	9.4	10.0	10.5	10.0	10.5	11.1	10.0	10.0	10.0	8.9
S/HEMISPHERE	JUL	AUG	SEP	OCT	NOV	DEC	JAN	FEB	MAR	APR	MAY	JUN

Cultural Recommendations

LIGHT: 800–1200 fc.

TEMPERATURES: Days average 85–87°F (29–30°C) and fluctuate only 4°F (2°C) during the year. The average lows of 67–68°F (19°C) are so uniform that the data look erroneous, but the averages fluctuate only 1°F (0.6°C) during the year. The summer diurnal range is 18–20°F (10–11°C).

HUMIDITY: 80–85%. High humidity and excellent air circulation are particularly important.

WATER: Plants should be kept very moist year-round. Warm water, about 70°F (21°C), is suggested.

FERTILIZER: ¼–½ strength, applied weekly to biweekly during the growing season.

REST PERIOD: Winter days average 83–85°F (28–29°C), and nights average 67–68°F (19°C), with a reduced diurnal range of 16–18°F (9–10°C) resulting from cooler days, not cooler nights. The record low temperature is only 10°F (5.5°C) below the average lows, indicating an intolerance to wide temperature fluctuations. Moisture and humidity levels should be maintained. Light is slightly lower in winter.

GROWING MEDIA: ½–⅝ in. (12–16 mm) fir bark with moisture-retentive additives, or sphagnum moss with perlite or charcoal added for drainage. Small bits of limestone may be added to the medium. Limestone is reported to be beneficial to the plant, but only when warm, 70°F (21°C) water is used. Repotting may be done after flowering or while roots are actively growing. The copious, flattened roots should not be trimmed when repotting, as they continue to elongate and branch with age.

MISCELLANEOUS NOTES: N/A.

Plant and Flower Information

PLANT SIZE AND TYPE: A moderately sized monopodial lithophyte.

LEAVES: Number unknown. The leaves are 8–9 in. (20–23 cm) long. The foliage is thin, recurved, and oblong-ovate, with raised veins on each side of the midline.

INFLORESCENCE: 12–20 in. (30–51 cm). Spikes are usually suberect and branched.

FLOWERS: Only a few per branch, but many per plant. Blossoms are 1.5–2.0 in. (4–5 cm) across and delicately textured, with a spreading, star-shaped form. Sepals and petals are creamy yellow, marked with rusty bars at the base. The lip is a deeper golden-yellow with rust-colored stripes and is ridged like a snail shell.

HYBRIDIZING NOTES: When used in hybridizing, *P. cochlearis* contributes good substance and star-shaped flowers, but color in the progeny is poor and tends to be washed-out.

REFERENCES: 30, 83, 148, 193, 195.

PHOTOS/DRAWINGS: *30, 83, 193, 195.*

Phalaenopsis corningiana Rchb.f.

AKA: *P. cumingiana, P. sumatrana* var. *sanguinea.*

ORIGIN/HABITAT: Borneo, on limestone cliffs at 1500–2000 ft. (457–610 m). Plants are usually found near waterfalls on huge, mossy trees 10–20 ft. (3–6 m) above the ground. They die quickly if moved to the lowlands.

CLIMATE: Station #96583, Pontianak, Borneo, Lat. 0.0°N, Long. 109.3°E, at 13 ft. (4 m). Temperatures are calculated for an elevation of 1800 ft. (549 m), resulting in probable extremes of 90°F (32.2°C) and 62°F (16.7°C).

N/HEMISPHERE	JAN	FEB	MAR	APR	MAY	JUN	JUL	AUG	SEP	OCT	NOV	DEC
°F AVG MAX	81	83	83	83	84	84	83	84	84	83	82	81
°F AVG MIN	68	70	69	69	69	69	68	68	69	69	69	68
DIURNAL RANGE	13	13	14	14	15	15	15	16	15	14	13	13
RAIN/INCHES	10.8	8.2	9.5	10.9	11.1	8.7	6.5	8.0	9.0	14.4	15.3	12.7
HUMIDITY/%	85	85	84	84	82	81	79	82	83	87	86	87
BLOOM SEASON				*	**	*	*	*				
DAYS CLR @ 7AM	1	1	1	3	2	4	5	1	2	1	1	2
DAYS CLR @ 1PM	0	0	1	0	0	0	1	1	1	0	1	0
RAIN/MM	274	208	241	277	282	221	165	203	229	366	389	323
°C AVG MAX	27.3	28.4	28.4	28.4	28.9	28.9	28.4	28.9	28.9	28.4	27.8	27.3
°C AVG MIN	20.1	21.2	20.6	20.6	20.6	20.6	20.1	20.1	20.6	20.6	20.6	20.1
DIURNAL RANGE	7.2	7.2	7.8	7.8	8.3	8.3	8.3	8.8	8.3	7.8	7.2	7.2
S/HEMISPHERE	JUL	AUG	SEP	OCT	NOV	DEC	JAN	FEB	MAR	APR	MAY	JUN

Cultural Recommendations

LIGHT: 800–1200 fc. Morning light is preferable, since the habitat is usually cloudy in the afternoon.

TEMPERATURES: Summer days average 83–84°F (28–29°C), and nights average 68-69°F (20–21°C), with a diurnal range of 15-16°F (8–9°C). Nights should not exceed 70°F (21°C), as plants die quickly if moved to warmer climates. The record high is 90°F (32°C), just a few degrees above the average highs. Diurnal range varies by only 3°F (1.6°C) throughout the year.

HUMIDITY: 80–85%.

WATER: Plants should be kept moist. Warm water, about 70°F (21°C), is highly recommended. *P. corningiana* is unusually sensitive to cold water, which causes bud blast and cellular damage.

FERTILIZER: ¼–½ strength, applied weekly to biweekly during the growing season.

REST PERIOD: Winter days average 81–83 °F (27–28 °C), and nights average 68–70 °F (20–21 °C), with a diurnal range of 13–14 °F (7–8 °C). Moisture and humidity levels should remain constant. In the habitat, a period of heavy rainfall occurs in winter, but water should not be increased in cultivation since temperatures are likely to be somewhat low.

GROWING MEDIA: ½–⅝ in. (12–16 mm) fir bark, with moisture-retentive additives, or sphagnum moss with perlite or charcoal added for drainage. Small amounts of limestone may be added to the medium if 70 °F (21 °C) water is used. Repotting is best done either after flowering or in early spring.

MISCELLANEOUS NOTES: *P. corningiana* is considered difficult in cultivation. Seasonal temperatures should be watched carefully, and a low diurnal range should be maintained. The reported susceptibility to rot is probably due to continuous stress from temperatures outside the plant's tolerance range. Setting the pots at an angle will improve drainage from the surface of the leaves and help prevent crown rot.

Plant and Flower Information

PLANT SIZE AND TYPE: A moderately sized monopodial epiphyte or lithophyte.

LEAVES: Number unknown. The leaves are 6–12 in. (15–30 cm) long. The foliage is oblong to elliptic, narrow, fleshy, and drooping. Leaves may be dark to bright green.

INFLORESCENCE: Length unknown. The zigzag spikes are shorter than the leaves.

FLOWERS: 1–3. The blossoms are 2.0–2.5 in. (5–6 cm) across, open sequentially, and are roughly star-shaped. The shiny, fleshy sepals and petals are various shades of white, yellow, gold, or green. They have red to purple-brown markings except at the margins. The lip is white and violet with yellow markings, with the violet sometimes extending to the sepals and petals.

HYBRIDIZING NOTES: Although this plant contributes a strong red influence when used in hybridizing, progeny tend to produce only a few star-shaped flowers.

REFERENCES: 19, 64, 66, 73, 77, 195, 211.

PHOTOS/DRAWINGS: *19, 64, 66, 71, 73, 195.*

Phalaenopsis cornu-cervi (Breda) Blume and Rchb.f.

AKA: *P. devriesiana.*

ORIGIN/HABITAT: Widespread in Thailand. In Burma the species grows at low elevations on swampy islands at the mouth of the Irrawaddy River. Here it prefers the dense, humid shade of mango trees protected from drying winds, but it is exposed to full sun during the dormant period. Dew is the primary source of moisture during the dry season. In India it grows in the jungle with *Dendrobium aggregatum*. In Indonesia it is found on trees on limestone hills, often intermixed with *P. maculata*. It grows near *P. violacea* in Malaya but prefers exposed locations with at least a short rest.

CLIMATE: Station # 48450, Kanchanaburi, Thailand, Lat. 14.0 °N, Long. 99.5 °E, at 92 ft. (28 m), is near the geographical center of the plant's range. Temperatures are calculated for an elevation of 800 ft. (244 m), resulting in probable extremes of 107 °F (41.7 °C) and 40 °F (4.4 °C).

N/HEMISPHERE	JAN	FEB	MAR	APR	MAY	JUN	JUL	AUG	SEP	OCT	NOV	DEC
°F AVG MAX	89	94	98	98	94	91	90	89	89	87	86	86
°F AVG MIN	61	67	71	75	75	74	73	73	72	71	67	61
DIURNAL RANGE	28	27	27	23	19	17	17	16	17	16	19	25
RAIN/INCHES	0.1	0.6	1.2	2.8	5.1	3.5	4.4	3.8	7.5	7.1	2.5	0.2
HUMIDITY/%	61	61	58	58	72	74	73	75	79	80	75	67
BLOOM SEASON					*	**	**	***	**	**	*	
DAYS CLR @ 7AM	8	4	3	6	3	1	1	0	0	2	4	6
DAYS CLR @ 1PM	13	6	5	5	1	0	0	0	1	2	3	7
RAIN/MM	3	15	30	71	130	89	112	97	190	180	64	5
°C AVG MAX	31.5	34.3	36.5	36.5	34.3	32.6	32.0	31.5	31.5	30.4	29.8	29.8
°C AVG MIN	15.9	19.3	21.5	23.7	23.7	23.1	22.6	22.6	22.0	21.5	19.3	15.9
DIURNAL RANGE	15.6	15.0	15.0	12.8	10.6	9.5	9.4	8.9	9.5	8.9	10.5	13.9
S/HEMISPHERE	JUL	AUG	SEP	OCT	NOV	DEC	JAN	FEB	MAR	APR	MAY	JUN

Cultural Recommendations

LIGHT: 1200–1500 fc. Plants grow luxuriously in deep shade but reportedly produce more blooms when light is high enough to turn the leaves yellowish.

TEMPERATURES: Summer days average 89–98 °F (32–37 °C), and nights average 72–75 °F (22–24 °C), with a diurnal range of 16–23 °F (9–13 °C). This plant tolerates summer heat.

HUMIDITY: 70–80%, which is lower than for most species.

WATER: Plants need moderate watering during the growing season. The rainfall pattern is wet/dry, and even during the wet period, rainfall is relatively low.

FERTILIZER: ¼–½ strength, applied weekly to biweekly during the growing season.

REST PERIOD: Winter days average 86–98 °F (30–37 °C), and nights average 61–67 °F (16–19 °C), with a winter diurnal range of 25–28 °F (14–16 °C). In cultivation, light should gradually be increased to 1500 fc. During the 3–4 dry winter months, dew is the primary source of moisture, indicating that water should be restricted to occasional misting. Average humidity should be reduced to 55–60%. Unlike most *Phalaenopsis*, this species regularly survives temperatures of 45 °F (7 °C) when it is dry.

GROWING MEDIA: Recommended media include tree fern, coconut husk, a mix of tree fern and charcoal, or ½–⅝ in. (12–16 mm) fir bark with perlite and sphagnum added. Repotting is best done in spring.

MISCELLANEOUS NOTES: *P. cornu-cervi* is wide-ranging and adaptable.

Plant and Flower Information

PLANT SIZE AND TYPE: A small to moderately sized monopodial epiphyte that may be quite robust.

LEAVES: 3–5 per plant. The leaves are 5–9 in. (13–23 cm) long, unusually narrow, glossy, yellowish, and leathery.

INFLORESCENCE: Usually several. The spikes are 4–18 in. (10–46 cm) long. They are evergreen, flat, and suberect and will elongate, branch, and bloom for years. An additional inflorescence is produced each year. Some growers feel that floral displays are improved if spikes are cut just above the lowest nodes before the plant rests.

FLOWERS: 6–12 per inflorescence. The blossoms are 1.5–2.0 in. (4–5 cm) across and open over several months, with 3–5 open at a time. Each flower lasts about 2 weeks. The blooms are waxy, star-shaped, and dull yellow-green variably marked with chestnut-brown. The lip is white.

HYBRIDIZING NOTES: N/A.

REFERENCES: 14, 83, 112, 118, 126, 130, 148, 155, 174, 191, 195, 197, 205, 211.

PHOTOS/DRAWINGS: 12, 14, 52, 83, 126, 148, 155, 191, 195, 197, 214.

Phalaenopsis cruciata. See *P. maculata*. REFERENCES: 195.

Phalaenopsis cumingiana. See *P. corningiana*. REFERENCES: 195.

Phalaenopsis curnowiana. See *P. schillerana*. REFERENCES: 195.

Phalaenopsis decumbens. See *P. parishii*. REFERENCES: 195.

Phalaenopsis decumbens var. *lobbii.* See *P. lobbii*. REFERENCES: 195.

Phalaenopsis deliciosa. Now considered a synonym of *Kingidium deliciosum*. REFERENCES: 195.

Phalaenopsis denevei. Now considered a synonym of *Paraphalaenopsis denevei*. REFERENCES: 195.

Phalaenopsis denisiana. See *P. fuscata*. REFERENCES: 195.

Phalaenopsis denticulata. See *P. pallens*. REFERENCES: 195.

Phalaenopsis devriesiana. See *P. cornu-cervi*. REFERENCES: 195.

Phalaenopsis equestris (Schauer) Rchb.f.

AKA: *P. riteiwanensis* and *P. rosea* are recognized synonyms. *P. equestris* is known to cross with *P. amabilis*, producing the natural hybrid *P. × intermedia*, and with *P. schillerana*, producing the natural hybrid *P. × veitchiana*.

ORIGIN/HABITAT: Luzon Island, Philippines, to Taiwan at 0–990 ft. (0–300 m), near streams in hot valleys.

CLIMATE: Station # 98427, Manila, Philippines, Lat. 14.5 °N, Long 121.0 °E, at 85 ft. (26 m). Temperatures are calculated for 800 ft. (244 m), resulting in probable extremes of 99 °F (37.2 °C) and 56 °F (13.3 °C).

N/HEMISPHERE	JAN	FEB	MAR	APR	MAY	JUN	JUL	AUG	SEP	OCT	NOV	DEC
°F AVG MAX	84	86	89	91	91	89	86	85	86	86	85	84
°F AVG MIN	67	67	69	71	73	73	73	73	73	72	70	68
DIURNAL RANGE	17	19	20	20	18	16	13	12	13	14	15	16
RAIN/INCHES	0.9	0.5	0.7	1.3	5.1	10.0	17.0	16.6	14.0	7.6	5.7	2.6
HUMIDITY/%	77	73	70	68	71	81	84	86	87	84	82	89
BLOOM SEASON	*	**	**	**	*	*	*	*	**	**	**	*
DAYS CLR @ 8AM	6	9	14	14	10	3	2	1	1	6	7	6
DAYS CLR @ 2PM	3	6	10	10	8	2	1	1	0	2	2	3
RAIN/MM	23	13	18	33	130	254	432	422	356	193	145	66
°C AVG MAX	28.7	29.8	31.4	32.6	32.6	31.4	29.8	29.2	29.8	29.8	29.2	28.7
°C AVG MIN	19.2	19.2	20.3	21.4	22.6	22.6	22.6	22.6	22.6	22.0	20.9	19.8
DIURNAL RANGE	9.5	10.6	11.1	11.2	10.0	8.8	7.2	6.6	7.2	7.8	8.3	8.9
S/HEMISPHERE	JUL	AUG	SEP	OCT	NOV	DEC	JAN	FEB	MAR	APR	MAY	JUN

Cultural Recommendations

LIGHT: 1000–1200 fc during the summer.

TEMPERATURES: Summer days average 85–91°F (29–33°C), and nights average 71–73°F (21–23°C), with a diurnal range of 12–18°F (7-10°C).

HUMIDITY: 80% or more in summer.

WATER: Plants should be kept moist during the growing season. The rainfall pattern is wet/dry.

FERTILIZER: ¼–½ strength, applied weekly to biweekly during the growing season.

REST PERIOD: Winter days average 84–89°F (29–31°C), and nights average 67–71°F (19-21°C), with a diurnal range of 17–20°F (9–11°C). For 3–4 months, humidity should be lowered to 70–75%, water limited to occasional light mistings, fertilizer reduced, and light increased to 1200–1500 fc.

GROWING MEDIA: ½–⅝ in. (12–16 mm) fir bark. Plants are best repotted immediately after blooming or as new roots begin to grow.

MISCELLANEOUS NOTES: *P. equestris* is adaptable and easy to grow. Keikis are frequently produced on inflorescences, and side-growths often arise from the roots and bloom simultaneously with the mother plant. Roots and flower spikes should not be cut annually, as both continue to grow and branch with age.

Plant and Flower Information

PLANT SIZE AND TYPE: A moderately sized monopodial epiphyte.

LEAVES: 3–5 per plant. The leaves are 6–8 in. (15–20 cm) long, bright green, fleshy, drooping, and oblong.

INFLORESCENCE: Up to 14 on mature plants. The spikes are 12–18 in. (30–46 cm) long. Several new evergreen inflorescences are produced each year. The spikes are purplish, stiff, zigzag, and suberect. They may be simple or branching, and they continue to bloom for years.

FLOWERS: 10–15 per inflorescence. The blossoms open 2–3 at a time over a period of months. The long-lasting blooms are 1.0–1.5 in. (2.5–3.8 cm) across; their size is variable and increases as spikes elongate. The delicate flowers, with sepals flaring back, are variably colored. The blossoms are usually white, variably flushed with pink, and may be marked with purple, orange, or pink. The lip is rose with yellow sidelobes.

HYBRIDIZING NOTES: Used in red hybrids, *P. equestris* contributes a pink lip and branching spikes. Candy-striping is a latent characteristic. The flowers of the progeny are small and spacing poor. This plant is best used as the pollen parent.

REFERENCES: 2, 11, 14, 28, 42, 112, 120, 128, 143, 148, 149, 192, 195, 203, 204, 210, 211.

PHOTOS/DRAWINGS: *11, 42,* 120, *143,* 149, *192, 195, 203, 210.*

Phalaenopsis erubescens. See *P. aphrodite.* REFERENCES: 195.

Phalaenopsis esmeralda. Now considered a synonym for *Doritis pulcherrima.* REFERENCES: 195.

Phalaenopsis fasciata Rchb.f.

AKA: Dr. Sweet reports that *P. fasciata* is easily confused with *P. lueddemanniana* var. *ochracea,* and that photographs are sometimes mislabeled. He also indicates that *P. fasciata* is sometimes erroneously called *P. lueddemanniana* var. *fasciata,* although he was unable to locate this combination of names. Although *P. fasciata* is recognized as a separate species, the International Orchid Commission uses *P. lueddemanniana* for hybrid registration purposes.

ORIGIN/HABITAT: The Philippines, generally near rivers at elevations of 0–1500 ft. (0–457 m).

CLIMATE: Station # 98645, Cebu, Philippines, Lat. 10.3°N, Long. 123.9°E, at 97 ft. (30 m). The record high is 96°F (35.6°C), and the record low is 64°F (17.8°C).

HEMISPHERE	JAN	FEB	MAR	APR	MAY	JUN	JUL	AUG	SEP	OCT	NOV	DEC
°F AVG MAX	86	87	89	91	91	89	88	88	88	88	88	87
°F AVG MIN	73	73	74	75	76	76	75	75	75	75	74	73
DIURNAL RANGE	13	14	15	16	15	13	13	13	13	13	14	14
RAIN/INCHES	4.2	2.9	2.0	1.7	4.5	6.4	7.3	5.6	6.9	7.7	6.4	5.0
HUMIDITY/%	76	74	73	70	73	77	79	79	79	81	79	77
BLOOM SEASON				*	*	*	*	*	*	*	*	*
DAYS CLR @ 8AM	4	4	6	3	1	1	2	1	1	2	3	3
DAYS CLR @ 2PM	2	3	5	5	3	2	1	0	1	1	2	2
RAIN/MM	107	74	51	43	114	163	185	142	175	196	163	127
°C AVG MAX	30.0	30.6	31.7	32.8	32.8	31.7	31.1	31.1	31.1	31.1	31.1	30.6
°C AVG MIN	22.8	22.8	23.3	23.9	24.4	24.4	23.9	23.9	23.9	23.9	23.3	22.8
DIURNAL RANGE	7.2	7.8	8.4	8.9	8.4	7.3	7.2	7.2	7.2	7.2	7.8	7.8
S/HEMISPHERE	JUL	AUG	SEP	OCT	NOV	DEC	JAN	FEB	MAR	APR	MAY	JUN

Cultural Recommendations

LIGHT: 1000–1200 fc.

TEMPERATURES: Summer days near sea level average 88–91 °F (31–33 °C), and nights average 75–76 °F (24 °C), with a diurnal range of 13–16 °F (7–9 °C). At 1500 ft. (457 m), days would average closer to 80 °F (27 °C), with nights about 70 °F (21 °C); the diurnal range would change very little. Plants should be adaptable within this range.

HUMIDITY: 70–80% year-round.

WATER: Plants should be kept moist. The rainfall pattern is wet/relatively dry. Warm water is recommended.

FERTILIZER: ¼–½ strength, applied weekly to biweekly during the growing season.

REST PERIOD: Winter days average 86–88 °F (30–31 °C), and nights average 73–75 °F (23–24 °C), with a diurnal range of 13–15 °F (7-8 °C). Water and fertilizer should be reduced and light increased slightly for 2–3 months in winter. The extreme low near sea level is 64 °F (18 °C) and would be about 58 °F (14 °C) at higher elevations, but extremes should be avoided.

GROWING MEDIA: ½–⅝ in. (12–16 mm) fir bark with moisture-retentive additives, or sphagnum moss with perlite or charcoal. Repotting is best done in early spring rather than after fall blooming.

MISCELLANEOUS NOTES: N/A.

Plant and Flower Information

PLANT SIZE AND TYPE: A moderately sized monopodial epiphyte.

LEAVES: 3–5 per plant. The leaves are 6–8 in. (15–20 cm) long and elliptic to obovate in shape.

INFLORESCENCE: The evergreen spikes are suberect to arching, somewhat zigzag, and may continue to produce flowers for 5 years.

FLOWERS: Few to several. The blossoms are 2 in. (5 cm) across and fleshy, with a waxy texture and starlike form. Sepals and petals are pale to deep yellow, often with a greenish hue, and are marked with bars of pale-to-dark cinnamon. The apex of the orange-yellow lip is bright purple or magenta. Lip sidelobes are yellow, speckled with red dots.

HYBRIDIZING NOTES: *P. fasciata* is frequently used in breeding yellow hybrids. As a parent, it tends to contribute smaller, star-shaped flowers with heavy substance, rich color, and attractive tesselations.

REFERENCES: 13, 14, 81, 83, 140, 195, 203.

PHOTOS/DRAWINGS: *13, 14, 81, 83,* 140, *195.*

Phalaenopsis fimbriata J. J. Smith

AKA: N/A.

ORIGIN/HABITAT: East central Java, Sarawak, and Sumatra. It grows on Mt. Kinabalu and in mountain passes at 2600–4300 ft. (792–1311 m). The plant usually grows in fairly bright light, either in trees in dappled sun or in moss on limestone bluffs. The bluffs face south or east, and the plants are exposed to bright reflected light. Although *P. fimbriata* is sometimes found growing with *P. viridis*, it dies quickly when moved to warmer, lower elevations.

CLIMATE: Station # 96755, Bogor, Indonesia, Lat. 6.5°S, Long. 106.8°E, at 558 ft. (170 m). Temperatures are calculated for an elevation of 2590 ft. (789 m), resulting in probable extremes of 89 °F (31.7 °C) and 59 °F (15.0 °C).

N/HEMISPHERE	JAN	FEB	MAR	APR	MAY	JUN	JUL	AUG	SEP	OCT	NOV	DEC
°F AVG MAX	79	80	81	81	80	78	77	77	78	79	80	79
°F AVG MIN	66	66	66	67	67	67	67	67	67	68	68	67
DIURNAL RANGE	13	14	15	14	13	11	10	10	11	11	12	12
RAIN/INCHES	2.1	1.0	0.5	5.0	8.1	18.8	23.7	20.2	14.4	12.0	11.9	3.4
HUMIDITY/%	72	68	65	66	74	79	84	84	81	79	77	75
BLOOM SEASON			*	*	*							
DAYS CLR @ 7AM	14	14	14	11	5	3	1	2	4	6	10	12
DAYS CLR @ 1PM	9	10	8	5	1	1	0	0	1	1	3	7
RAIN/MM	53	25	13	127	206	478	602	513	366	305	302	86
°C AVG MAX	26.3	26.8	27.4	27.4	26.8	25.7	25.2	25.2	25.7	26.3	26.8	26.3
°C AVG MIN	19.1	19.1	19.1	19.6	19.6	19.6	19.6	19.6	19.6	20.2	20.2	19.6
DIURNAL RANGE	7.2	7.7	8.3	7.8	7.2	6.1	5.6	5.6	6.1	6.1	6.6	6.7
S/HEMISPHERE	JUL	AUG	SEP	OCT	NOV	DEC	JAN	FEB	MAR	APR	MAY	JUN

Cultural Recommendations

LIGHT: 1200–1400 fc, which is higher than for most *Phalaenopsis*. This species tolerates dappled sun, providing that temperatures are below 80 °F (27 °C) during the day and air circulation is excellent.

TEMPERATURES: Days average 79–81°F (26–27°C), and nights average 66–68°F (19–20°C) throughout the year, with a low summer diurnal range of 10–11°F (6°C). Uniform temperatures are critical for plant health. The plant cannot survive continuous exposure to hot summer days. These temperatures represent the warm end of the spectrum in the plant's natural habitat, and the averages should not be exceeded in cultivation.

HUMIDITY: 75–80%. Excellent air circulation is particularly important for this species.

WATER: Plants are healthiest if they are saturated with water then allowed to dry rapidly even during the wet season. Warm water, about 65°F (18°C), is highly recommended. The rainfall pattern is wet/dry, with a dry season of 2–3 months.

FERTILIZER: ¼–½ strength, applied weekly to biweekly during the growing season.

REST PERIOD: Winter days average 79–81°F (26–27°C), and nights average 66–67°F (7–8°C), with a diurnal range of 12–15°F (7–8°C). Temperatures should be maintained as closely as possible. For about 2 months in winter, light may be increased to 1500 fc. Average humidity should be lowered to about 65% and watering limited to occasional misting. Fertilizer should be reduced when plants are not actively growing.

GROWING MEDIA: Volcanic rock about ½ in. (13 mm) in diameter. Rapid drying following frequent deluges of water duplicates the daily wet/dry pattern in the plant's natural environment. Repotting is best done immediately after flowering, but it may be done anytime roots are actively growing.

MISCELLANEOUS NOTES: In the plant's natural habitat, blooming occurs in early Apr. (Oct.) at the end of the dry cycle. Flower spikes are probably initiated by the rest period. (If initiating blooms is a problem, see the suggestion under "Miscellaneous Notes" for *P. viridis.*)

Plant and Flower Information

PLANT SIZE AND TYPE: A small to medium-sized monopodial epiphyte or lithophyte.

LEAVES: 3–5 per plant. The leaves are 6–9 in. (15–23 cm) long, oblong to elliptic, wavy margined, and arching.

INFLORESCENCE: 10 in. (25 cm) long. Plants often produce 2 flower spikes per year. The spikes are laxly flowered and recurved.

FLOWERS: Many. The blossoms are 1.0–1.5 in. (2.5–3.8 cm) across and open simultaneously. The pointed sepals and petals are fleshy and may be white or pale apple-green with magenta markings. The lip is white with yellow and red-purple markings and a densely fringed midlobe.

HYBRIDIZING NOTES: *P. fimbriata* is often used to obtain green hybrids.

REFERENCES: 14, 30, 68, 148, 183, 195.

PHOTOS/DRAWINGS: *14, 30, 68, 99, 183, 195.*

Phalaenopsis foerstermanii. See *P. pallens.* REFERENCES: 195.

Phalaenopsis forbesii. See *P. viridis.* REFERENCES: 195.

Phalaenopsis formosa, formosana, formosum. See *P. aphrodite.* REFERENCES: 195.

Phalaenopsis fugax. Now considered a synonym of *Sarcochilus pallidus.* REFERENCES: 195.

Phalaenopsis fuscata Rchb.f.

AKA: *P. denisiana.*

ORIGIN/HABITAT: Thailand to Borneo and the Philippines. It is commonly found at 0–1500 ft. (0–457 m) on trees near streams in shady forests. This plant hybridizes naturally with *P. sumatrana.*

CLIMATE: Station # 48657, Kuantan, Malaya, Lat. 3.8°N, Long. 103.2°E, at 58 ft. (18 m). The record high is 98°F (36.7°C), and the record low is 61°F (16.1°C).

N/HEMISPHERE	JAN	FEB	MAR	APR	MAY	JUN	JUL	AUG	SEP	OCT	NOV	DEC
°F AVG MAX	83	85	88	89	90	90	89	89	89	88	86	84
°F AVG MIN	71	71	71	72	73	72	72	72	72	72	72	71
DIURNAL RANGE	12	14	17	17	17	18	17	17	17	16	14	13
RAIN/INCHES	16.4	7.5	10.6	8.3	7.8	7.3	7.4	7.8	8.4	10.6	11.1	20.9
HUMIDITY/%	88	88	87	86	87	86	86	86	86	87	90	90
BLOOM SEASON				*	*	**	*	*				
DAYS CLR @ 7AM	1	1	2	1	1	1	1	0	0	0	0	1
DAYS CLR @ 1PM	0	0	0	0	0	0	0	0	0	0	0	0
RAIN/MM	417	190	269	211	198	185	188	198	213	269	282	531
°C AVG MAX	28.3	29.4	31.1	31.7	32.2	32.2	31.7	31.7	31.7	31.1	30.0	28.9
°C AVG MIN	21.7	21.7	21.7	22.2	22.8	22.2	22.2	22.2	22.2	22.2	22.2	21.7
DIURNAL RANGE	6.6	7.7	9.4	9.5	9.4	10.0	9.5	9.5	9.5	8.9	7.8	7.2
S/HEMISPHERE	JUL	AUG	SEP	OCT	NOV	DEC	JAN	FEB	MAR	APR	MAY	JUN

Cultural Recommendations

LIGHT: 1000–1200 fc.

TEMPERATURES: Days average 89–90 °F (32 °C), and nights average 71–73 °F (22–23 °C), with a summer diurnal range of 17–18 °F (9–10 °C).

HUMIDITY: 85–90%. High humidity and good air circulation are particularly important for this species.

WATER: Plants should be kept very moist. Warm water, 70 °F (21 °C), is highly recommended. The rainfall pattern is wet/wetter.

FERTILIZER: ¼–½ strength, applied weekly to biweekly during the growing season.

REST PERIOD: Days average 83–86 °F (28–30 °C), and nights average 71–73 °F (22–23 °C), with a winter diurnal range of 12–14 °F (7–8 °C). The lower diurnal range results from cooler winter days, not cooler winter nights. Although rainfall in the habitat is greater in winter and plants need to be kept very moist, water should not be increased since cultivation temperatures are likely to be somewhat low. Overly wet conditions are conducive to disease. Fertilizer should be reduced, and light should remain low.

GROWING MEDIA: ½–⅝ in. (12–16 mm) fir bark. Repotting is best done after blooming or while roots are actively growing.

MISCELLANEOUS NOTES: N/A.

Plant and Flower Information

PLANT SIZE AND TYPE: A large monopodial epiphyte.

LEAVES: 3–5 per plant. The leaves are 12 in. (30 cm) long, thin textured, obovate to oblong, spreading, and slightly twisted at the base.

INFLORESCENCE: 12–18 in. (30–46 cm) long. The spikes, usually several each year, are arching to suberect and may branch. Flowers face in all directions.

FLOWERS: 1–3 per inflorescence, usually about 12 per plant. Blossoms are 1.25 in. (3 cm) across with a fleshy texture. Sepals and petals are rounded at the tips and somewhat recurved along the side margins. Pale yellow-green, they are usually blotched with chocolate-brown at the base but may sometimes be concolor yellow. The red lip is cupped and juts forward.

HYBRIDIZING NOTES: As a parent, *P. fuscata* produces fine, intensely colored hybrids with a red lip and heavy flower substance. It also transmits the tendency to be few-flowered and to have twisted, recurved petals. Beyond primary hybrids, it is a reluctant breeder.

REFERENCES: 112, 118, 130, 193, 195, 203.

PHOTOS/DRAWINGS: *68, 86,* 118, *193, 195.*

Phalaenopsis fuscata × *hurstleri.* See *P. kunstleri.*
REFERENCES: 195.

Phalaenopsis × *gersenii* (Teijsm. and Binn.) Rolfe.
A natural hybrid between *P. sumatrana* and *P. violacea.* REFERENCES: 195.

Phalaenopsis gibbosa Sweet

AKA: N/A.

ORIGIN/HABITAT: Laos and North and South Vietnam. In South Vietnam it grows in open forests between Saigon and Da Lat.

CLIMATE: Stations # 48881 and 48900, Saigon and Da Lat, South Vietnam, Lat. 10.5 °N, Long. 107.1 °E, at 1595 ft. (486 m). Longitude, latitude, and elevation are midpoint, while weather records from the 2 stations are averaged. The average extremes are 99 °F (37.2 °C) and 50 °F (10.0 °C).

N/HEMISPHERE	JAN	FEB	MAR	APR	MAY	JUN	JUL	AUG	SEP	OCT	NOV	DEC
°F AVG MAX	85	87	89	90	88	85	85	85	84	84	83	83
°F AVG MIN	63	64	67	70	71	70	70	70	70	69	68	65
DIURNAL RANGE	22	23	22	20	17	15	15	15	14	15	15	18
RAIN/INCHES	0.4	0.5	1.0	3.3	8.9	9.3	9.7	9.5	11.5	9.9	3.6	1.7
HUMIDITY/%	69	67	67	71	78	81	82	83	84	83	78	75
BLOOM SEASON			*									
DAYS CLR @ 7AM	9	9	10	7	4	3	2	1	1	3	5	7
DAYS CLR @ 1PM	6	6	7	2	0	0	0	0	0	0	2	3
RAIN/MM	10	13	25	84	226	236	246	241	292	251	91	43
°C AVG MAX	29.4	30.6	31.7	32.2	31.1	29.4	29.4	29.4	28.9	28.9	28.3	28.3
°C AVG MIN	17.2	17.8	19.4	21.1	21.7	21.1	21.1	21.1	21.1	20.6	20.0	18.3
DIURNAL RANGE	12.2	12.8	12.3	11.1	9.4	8.3	8.3	8.3	7.8	8.3	8.3	10.0
S/HEMISPHERE	JUL	AUG	SEP	OCT	NOV	DEC	JAN	FEB	MAR	APR	MAY	JUN

Cultural Recommendations

LIGHT: 1200 fc.

TEMPERATURES: Days average 85–90 °F (29-32 °C), and nights average 70–71 °F (21–22 °C), with a summer diurnal range of 14–17 °F (8–9 °C).

HUMIDITY: 80%.

WATER: Plants should be kept moist during the growing season. The rainfall pattern is wet/dry, but the consistent humidity levels in the habitat indicate that some moisture is always available in the form of dew, fog, or mist.

FERTILIZER: ¼–½ strength, applied weekly to biweekly during the growing season.

REST PERIOD: Winter days average 83–87 °F (23–31 °C), and nights average 63–68 °F (17–20 °C), with a diurnal range of 20–23 °F (11–13 °C). The increased diurnal range results from cooler nights. A cool, dry rest of 3–4 months should be provided in winter. When temperatures are cool, humidity should be decreased to 65–75%, and water reduced to light watering every 2–3 weeks with occasional mistings in between. Plants should not become dehydrated. During the winter rest, fertilizer should be reduced or eliminated until active growth resumes, and light may be increased.

GROWING MEDIA: ½–⅝ in. (12–16 mm) fir bark. Plants are best repotted after flowering.

MISCELLANEOUS NOTES: The bloom season shown in the climate table is based on collection records.

Plant and Flower Information

PLANT SIZE AND TYPE: A small monopodial epiphyte.

LEAVES: Number unknown. The elliptic leaves are 5 in. (13 cm) long and cupped near the base.

INFLORESCENCE: 6 in. (15 cm) long. The spikes are somewhat zigzag.

FLOWERS: 8 per season. The small, star-shaped blossoms are 0.5 in. (1.2 cm) across and are cream to white. The sepals are larger than the petals, and both are somewhat pointed. The lip is triangular.

HYBRIDIZING NOTES: N/A.

REFERENCES: 195.

PHOTOS/DRAWINGS: *195.*

Phalaenopsis gigantea J. J. Smith

AKA: N/A.

ORIGIN/HABITAT: Sabah (Merutai and Tiger Mountain areas) in northern Borneo, where it is rare or extinct. It is also found on the west side of the Crocker Mountain range in Sarawak and West Kalimantan. It was recently found in primeval forest areas of Java and is reportedly easy to cultivate at an elevation of 500 ft. (152 m).

CLIMATE: Station #96583, Pontianak, Borneo, Lat. 0.0 °N, Long. 109.3 °E, at 13 ft. (4 m). Temperatures are calculated for an elevation of 500 ft. (152 m), resulting in probable extremes of 94 °F (34.4 °C) and 66 °F (18.9 °C).

N/HEMISPHERE	JAN	FEB	MAR	APR	MAY	JUN	JUL	AUG	SEP	OCT	NOV	DEC
°F AVG MAX	85	87	87	87	88	88	87	88	88	87	86	85
°F AVG MIN	72	74	73	73	73	73	72	72	73	73	73	72
DIURNAL RANGE	13	13	14	14	15	15	15	16	15	14	13	13
RAIN/INCHES	10.8	8.2	9.5	10.9	11.1	8.7	6.5	8.0	9.0	14.4	15.3	12.7
HUMIDITY/%	85	85	84	84	82	81	79	82	83	87	86	87
BLOOM SEASON	*	*	*	*	*		*	**	***	***	*	*
DAYS CLR @ 7AM	1	1	1	3	2	4	5	1	2	1	1	2
DAYS CLR @ 1PM	0	0	1	0	0	0	1	1	1	0	1	0
RAIN/MM	274	208	241	277	282	221	165	203	229	366	389	323
°C AVG MAX	29.7	30.8	30.8	30.8	31.3	31.3	30.8	31.3	31.3	30.8	30.2	29.7
°C AVG MIN	22.4	23.6	23.0	23.0	23.0	23.0	22.4	22.4	23.0	23.0	23.0	22.4
DIURNAL RANGE	7.3	7.2	7.8	7.8	8.3	8.3	8.4	8.9	8.3	7.8	7.2	7.3
S/HEMISPHERE	JUL	AUG	SEP	OCT	NOV	DEC	JAN	FEB	MAR	APR	MAY	JUN

Cultural Recommendations

LIGHT: 800–1000 fc. A very shady environment is recommended.

TEMPERATURES: Days average 85–88 °F (30–31 °C), and nights average 72–74 °F (22–24 °C), with a diurnal range of 13–16 °F (7–9 °C). Growers report that plants are healthier in cultivation if uniform but slightly cooler conditions are maintained. They recommend that high temperatures average 80–83 °F (27–28 °C), with lows near 70–73 °F (21–23 °C). *P. gigantea* will not grow in Singapore, where temperatures are a few degrees warmer. It grows but will not bloom in Bogor, Java, where highs are about 3 °F (1 °C) above those shown in the climate table.

HUMIDITY: 70–75%. Humidity is higher in the habitat, but in cultivation, higher levels may increase the potential for disease.

WATER: Plants should receive year-round moisture. Warm water, about 70 °F (21 °C), is highly recommended. Extremely prone to rot, the plant should be watered early in the day and allowed to dry quickly. Constant air movement through the long leaves is highly recommended.

FERTILIZER: Foliar feeding with a very weak fish fertilizer (0.1 tsp. per gal.; 0.1 tsp. per 3.8 liters) is highly recommended. When the plant is growing in bark, ¼–½ strength solution may be applied once a week in summer.

REST PERIOD: Winter days average 85–87 °F (30–31 °C), and nights average 72–74 °F (7–8 °C), with a diurnal range of 13 °F (7 °C). Conditions are very uniform year-round, with a slightly lower diurnal range in winter. The plants should not be subjected to wide temperature fluctuations.

GROWING MEDIA: Growers using live sphagnum moss report success with regular foliar feedings of very dilute fish fertilizer. Chemical fertilizer should not be applied directly to this medium as it will kill the moss. Repotting is best done just as roots resume growth.

MISCELLANEOUS NOTES: *P. gigantea* is extremely slow growing and susceptible to disease. Tipping pots at an angle of 30-45° insures good drainage. This is a very demanding plant with strict cultural requirements.

Plant and Flower Information

PLANT SIZE AND TYPE: A very large monopodial epiphyte.

LEAVES: 5–6 per plant. In nature, the leaves are 22–36 in. (56–91 cm) long and are leathery and shiny.

INFLORESCENCE: 1 or more. The pendent spikes are 6–15 in. (15–38 cm) long and usually branch once or twice.

FLOWERS: 20–30. A single inflorescence may have nearly 100 flowers. The fragrant blossoms open simultaneously. They are 1.50–2.75 in. (3.8–7.0 cm) across, star-shaped, and fleshy. Flowers may be greenish white to yellow, with closely spaced brown or maroon spots. The white lip is marked with bright reddish purple.

HYBRIDIZING NOTES: This plant is difficult to breed and takes 8–12 years to bloom. As a parent, it contributes heavy substance and good form and enhances reds. Hybrids often have as many as 25 flowers, each 2 in. (5 cm) across.

REFERENCES: 14, 75, 77, 83, 130, 148, 189, 195, 219.

PHOTOS/DRAWINGS: *14, 54, 75, 83, 130, 189, 195, 199, 219.*

Phalaenopsis gloriosa. See *P. amabilis.* REFERENCES: 195.

Phalaenopsis grandiflora. See *P. amabilis.* REFERENCES: 195.

Phalaenopsis hainanensis. See *P. stobartiana.* REFERENCES: 195.

Phalaenopsis hebe. Now considered a synonym of *Kingidium deliciosum.* REFERENCES: 195.

Phalaenopsis hieroglyphica (Rchb.f.) Sweet

AKA: Originally considered a variety of *P. lueddemanniana*, it has been called var. *hieroglyphica*, var. *palawanensis*, and var. *surigadensis.*

ORIGIN/HABITAT: Endemic to Luzon, Polillo, Palawan, and Mindanao in the Philippines; elevations were not reported. The climate is for near sea level. Higher elevations follow the same pattern but are a few degrees cooler.

CLIMATE: Station # 98653, Surigao, Philippines, Lat. 9.8°N, Long. 125.5°E, at 72 ft. (22 m). The record high is 99°F (37.2°C), and the record low is 65°F (18.3°C).

N/HEMISPHERE	JAN	FEB	MAR	APR	MAY	JUN	JUL	AUG	SEP	OCT	NOV	DEC
°F AVG MAX	83	84	85	87	89	89	89	89	89	88	86	84
°F AVG MIN	72	72	73	73	74	74	74	75	75	74	74	73
DIURNAL RANGE	11	12	12	14	15	15	15	14	14	14	12	11
RAIN/INCHES	21.4	14.8	19.9	10.0	6.2	4.9	7.0	5.1	6.6	10.7	16.8	24.4
HUMIDITY/%	91	90	88	85	85	82	83	82	83	84	88	89
BLOOM SEASON						*	*	*	**	**	*	*
DAYS CLR @ 8AM	1	1	2	4	2	3	2	2	1	2	1	1
DAYS CLR @ 2PM	1	2	2	6	3	1	2	1	2	3	1	1
RAIN/MM	544	376	505	254	157	124	178	130	168	272	427	620
°C AVG MAX	28.3	28.9	29.4	30.6	31.7	31.7	31.7	31.7	31.7	31.1	30.0	28.9
°C AVG MIN	22.2	22.2	22.8	22.8	23.3	23.3	23.3	23.9	23.9	23.3	23.3	22.8
DIURNAL RANGE	6.1	6.7	6.6	7.8	8.4	8.4	8.4	7.8	7.8	7.8	6.7	6.1
S/HEMISPHERE	JUL	AUG	SEP	OCT	NOV	DEC	JAN	FEB	MAR	APR	MAY	JUN

Cultural Recommendations

LIGHT: 1000–1200 fc.

TEMPERATURES: Summer days average 87–89°F (31–32°C), and nights average 73–75°F (23–24°C), with a diurnal range of 14–15°F (8°C). The widest diurnal range occurs in summer and results from warmer days.

HUMIDITY: 80–90%. The relative humidity is unusually high.

WATER: Plants should be kept moist. Warm water, about 70°F (21°C), is highly recommended. The rainfall pattern is wet/wetter.

FERTILIZER: ¼–½ strength, applied weekly to biweekly during the growing season.

REST PERIOD: Days average 83–85°F (28–29°C), while nights average 72–73°F (22–23°C), resulting in a lower winter diurnal range of 11–12°F (6–7°C). Humidity and rainfall are highest in winter, but water should not be increased in cultivation, as temperatures are likely to be somewhat low.

GROWING MEDIA: *P. hieroglyphica* has a pendent, suberect growth habit and performs best when mounted on a slab, provided that high humidity levels can be maintained. In cultivation, plants are healthiest if never allowed to completely dry. When potting is necessary, fir bark is normally used to retain moisture. Including small amounts of limestone may be helpful, provided that warm water is used when watering. The plant is suberect when potted. Plants are best repotted in early spring when roots are beginning to grow, rather than after blooming.

MISCELLANEOUS NOTES: Flowering appears to be triggered by increased day length.

Plant and Flower Information

PLANT SIZE AND TYPE: A large, normally pendent monopodial epiphyte.

LEAVES: Number is highly variable. The leaves are 12 in. (30 cm) long, oblong, and leathery.

INFLORESCENCE: 12 in. (30 cm) long. The one or more spikes may be suberect or arching, simple or branching.

FLOWERS: Many. The star-shaped blossoms are 2.0–2.5 in. (5.0–6.4 cm) across, with a firm texture. The pointed sepals and petals may overlap at the base. They are white to cream, often flushed with green at the tips and marked with red or cinnamon figures or blotches. The lip is white with a pink flush and a yellow callus.

HYBRIDIZING NOTES: *P. hieroglyphica* is used in breeding red hybrids.

REFERENCES: 14, 83, 140, 183, 195, 203.

PHOTOS/DRAWINGS: *14, 83, 140, 183, 195.*

Phalaenopsis hombronii. See *P. amabilis.* REFERENCES: 195.

Phalaenopsis imperati. See *P. speciosa.* REFERENCES: 195.

Phalaenopsis inscriptiosinensis Fowlie

AKA: N/A.

ORIGIN/HABITAT: Central Sumatra above and east of Pakanbaru, on forest trees below 3000 ft. (914 m).

CLIMATE: Indonesia, Zone 2 (Eastern Sumatra), Lat. 0.0°N, Long. 102.0°E. The average elevation for the zone is 114 ft. (35 m), while the habitat elevation is approximately 2500 ft. (762 m). Temperatures are

calculated for the habitat elevation, resulting in probable extremes of 91°F (32.8°C) and 52°F (11.1°C).

N/HEMISPHERE	JAN	FEB	MAR	APR	MAY	JUN	JUL	AUG	SEP	OCT	NOV	DEC
°F AVG MAX	77	78	79	79	80	79	79	79	79	79	78	77
°F AVG MIN	65	65	65	66	66	66	66	66	65	65	65	65
DIURNAL RANGE	12	13	14	13	14	13	13	13	14	14	13	12
RAIN/INCHES	9.5	7.8	8.5	9.0	8.2	5.9	6.2	6.0	6.6	9.0	10.8	11.9
HUMIDITY/%	82	82	81	81	82	80	79	77	76	80	83	84
BLOOM SEASON	N/A											
DAYS CLR @ 7AM	2	2	3	3	4	4	5	3	3	2	2	2
DAYS CLR @ 1PM	1	1	1	1	1	1	2	2	2	1	0	0
RAIN/MM	241	198	216	229	208	150	157	152	168	229	274	302
°C AVG MAX	25.1	25.6	26.2	26.2	26.7	26.2	26.2	26.2	26.2	26.2	25.6	25.1
°C AVG MIN	18.4	18.4	18.4	19.0	19.0	19.0	19.0	19.0	18.4	18.4	18.4	18.4
DIURNAL RANGE	6.7	7.2	7.8	7.2	7.7	7.2	7.2	7.2	7.8	7.8	7.2	6.7
S/HEMISPHERE	JUL	AUG	SEP	OCT	NOV	DEC	JAN	FEB	MAR	APR	MAY	JUN

Cultural Recommendations

LIGHT: 1000–1200 fc.

TEMPERATURES: Summer days average 79–80°F (26–27°C), and nights average 65–66°F (18–19°C), with a diurnal range of 13–14°F (7–8°C). With a record high of 91°F (32.8°C), it appears that this plant does not tolerate high temperatures or wide daily or seasonal temperature fluctuations.

HUMIDITY: 75–85%.

WATER: Plants should be kept moist year-round. The rainfall pattern is wet/wetter.

FERTILIZER: ¼–½ strength, applied weekly to biweekly during the growing season.

REST PERIOD: Days average 77–79°F (25–26°C), and nights average 65°F (18°C), with a diurnal range of 12–13°F (7°C). Winter temperatures vary only slightly from summer conditions, but days are slightly cooler and the diurnal range is slightly lower. Light should not be increased. Plants need to be kept moist throughout the year, but fertilizer should be reduced to an application every 2–3 weeks until the plant resumes active growth.

GROWING MEDIA: ½–⅝ in. (12–16 mm) fir bark. Repotting is best done while roots are actively growing.

MISCELLANEOUS NOTES: N/A.

Plant and Flower Information

PLANT SIZE AND TYPE: A small monopodial epiphyte.

LEAVES: 3–5 per plant. The leaves are 3–6 in. (8–15 cm) long, elliptic-oblong, and frequently wavy.

INFLORESCENCE: 3–5 per plant. The spikes are 3.0–4.5 in. (8–11 cm) long.

FLOWERS: 2–5. The star-shaped flowers open sequentially and are 1.2–1.4 in. (3.0–3.6 cm) across. Sepals and petals are pale yellow marked with transverse cinnamon bands and markings.

HYBRIDIZING NOTES: N/A.

REFERENCES: 66, 70.

PHOTOS/DRAWINGS: 66, 70.

Phalaenopsis × intermedia Lindley. A natural hybrid between *P. equestris* and *P. amabilis*. REFERENCES: 195.

Phalaenopsis javanica J. J. Smith

AKA: *P. latisepala*.

ORIGIN/HABITAT: The south coast of Java, between Garut (Garoet), which is located at 2300 ft. (701 m), and Pelabuhan Bay (Wijnkoops-Baai), located at sea level. No elevation is given for the plant habitat, but apparently it is cultivated at Bogor in the Botanical Garden at 558 ft. (170 m).

CLIMATE: Station # 96755, Bogor, Java, Lat. 6.5°S, Long. 106.8°E, at 558 ft. (170 m). The record high is 96°F (35.6°C), and the record low is 66°F (18.9°C).

N/HEMISPHERE	JAN	FEB	MAR	APR	MAY	JUN	JUL	AUG	SEP	OCT	NOV	DEC
°F AVG MAX	86	87	88	88	87	85	84	84	85	86	87	86
°F AVG MIN	73	73	73	74	74	74	74	74	74	75	75	74
DIURNAL RANGE	13	14	15	14	13	11	10	10	11	11	12	12
RAIN/INCHES	2.1	1.0	0.5	5.0	8.1	18.8	23.7	20.2	14.4	12.0	11.9	3.4
HUMIDITY/%	72	68	65	66	74	79	84	84	81	79	77	75
BLOOM SEASON	*			*	*					*		
DAYS CLR @ 7AM	14	14	14	11	5	3	1	2	4	6	10	12
DAYS CLR @ 1PM	9	10	8	5	1	1	0	0	1	1	3	7
RAIN/MM	53	25	13	127	206	478	602	513	366	305	302	86
°C AVG MAX	30.0	30.6	31.1	31.1	30.6	29.4	28.9	28.9	29.4	30.0	30.6	30.0
°C AVG MIN	22.8	22.8	22.8	23.3	23.3	23.3	23.3	23.3	23.3	23.9	23.9	23.3
DIURNAL RANGE	7.2	7.8	8.3	7.8	7.3	6.1	5.6	5.6	6.1	6.1	6.7	6.7
S/HEMISPHERE	JUL	AUG	SEP	OCT	NOV	DEC	JAN	FEB	MAR	APR	MAY	JUN

Cultural Recommendations

LIGHT: 1000–1200 fc.

TEMPERATURES: Days average 84–88°F (29–31°C), with averages varying only 4°F (2°C) throughout the year, while nights average 73–75°F (23–24°C) and fluctuate even less. The summer diurnal range is 10-12°F (6–7°C). However, this species also grows at higher elevations, so the average temperatures may be gradually lowered as much as 6°F (3°C) if a plant is not doing well in cultivation. At the latitude of the habitat, temperatures at higher elevations are cooler but still uniform, and the diurnal range would be similar.

HUMIDITY: 80% during the growing season.

WATER: Plants should not be allowed to dry completely. The rainfall pattern is wet/dry, but the dry period is quite short. Warm water, 70°F (21°C), is recommended for watering.

FERTILIZER: ¼–½ strength, applied weekly to biweekly during the growing season.

REST PERIOD: Growing temperatures should be maintained year-round. Despite the uniform temperatures, plants need a winter rest of 2–3 months. Humidity should be reduced to 60–65%, water restricted to light misting every few days, and fertilizer limited to biweekly or monthly applications. Light may be increased slightly for 1–2 months. Constant temperatures are important since the record low is a warm 66°F (19°C). Minor fluctuations in average highs and lows result in an increase in the diurnal range to 12–15°F (7–8°C).

GROWING MEDIA: ½–⅝ in. (12–16 mm) fir bark. Adding small amounts of limestone may be helpful, but only if warm water is used when watering and if a minimum growing temperature of 70°F (21°C) is maintained. Plants are best repotted after flowering or while roots are actively growing.

MISCELLANEOUS NOTES: Flower initiators are unknown. See "Miscellaneous Notes" for *P. viridis* for a discussion of possible bloom initiators.

Plant and Flower Information

PLANT SIZE AND TYPE: A moderately sized monopodial epiphyte.

LEAVES: 3–5 per plant. The shiny, fleshy leaves are 9 in. (23 cm) long and oblong to elliptic.

INFLORESCENCE: The single spike is 8–10 in. (20–25 cm) long and somewhat zigzag. It is usually simple but may branch.

FLOWERS: Few. The plant blooms sporadically, and the flowers open simultaneously. The blossoms are 1 in. (2.5 cm) across, violet-scented, and fleshy, with a spreading, somewhat cupped form. The overlapping sepals and petals are white, greenish yellow, or yellow and are marked with longitudinal stripes which are actually lines of small spots. The lip is purple, yellow, and white.

HYBRIDIZING NOTES: N/A.

REFERENCES: 195, 209.

PHOTOS/DRAWINGS: *195, 209.*

Phalaenopsis kimballiana. See *P. reichenbachiana.*
REFERENCES: 195.

Phalaenopsis kunstleri Hooker f.

AKA: *P. fuscata* var. *hurstleri.*

ORIGIN/HABITAT: The Malay Peninsula in Perak State, near Ipoh and Tapah, and in Johore State and the Chin Hills near Falam, Burma. The habitats given are about 1400 miles (2200 km) apart, and no collections have been reported between the two locations. The climates are dramatically different. Falam has very cool, dry winters, while the Malay climate has little seasonal variation. Ipoh data are provided in the climate table. Habitat elevation is not available, but Ipoh is located in a river valley surrounded on 3 sides by mountains, the highest over 6000 ft. (1829 m). Plants may be collected at high elevations where temperatures are cooler than those given in the table. In the tropics, temperatures at higher elevations are cooler but remain uniform.

CLIMATE: Station # 48625, Ipoh, Malaya, Lat. 4.6°N, Long. 101.1°E, at 123 ft. (37 m). The record high is 99°F (37.2°C), and the record low is 64°F (17.8°C).

N/HEMISPHERE	JAN	FEB	MAR	APR	MAY	JUN	JUL	AUG	SEP	OCT	NOV	DEC
°F AVG MAX	90	92	93	92	92	92	91	91	90	89	89	89
°F AVG MIN	72	72	73	73	74	73	72	72	73	72	72	72
DIURNAL RANGE	18	20	20	19	18	19	19	19	17	17	17	17
RAIN/INCHES	7.9	3.1	7.6	8.4	6.2	3.6	7.2	6.9	8.8	11.0	13.0	8.9
HUMIDITY/%	76	74	76	78	78	75	76	77	79	82	82	81
BLOOM SEASON			*	*		**						
DAYS CLR @ 7AM	3	3	3	1	1	2	1	1	0	0	1	2
DAYS CLR @ 1PM	2	2	2	1	1	1	1	1	0	0	0	2
RAIN/MM	201	79	193	213	157	91	183	175	224	279	330	226
°C AVG MAX	32.2	33.3	33.9	33.3	33.3	33.3	32.8	32.8	32.2	31.7	31.7	31.7
°C AVG MIN	22.2	22.2	22.8	22.8	23.3	22.8	22.2	22.2	22.8	22.2	22.2	22.2
DIURNAL RANGE	10.0	11.1	11.1	10.5	10.0	10.5	10.6	10.6	9.4	9.5	9.5	9.5
S/HEMISPHERE	JUL	AUG	SEP	OCT	NOV	DEC	JAN	FEB	MAR	APR	MAY	JUN

Cultural Recommendations

LIGHT: 1000–1200 fc.

TEMPERATURES: Days average 89–93°F (32–34°C), fluctuating only 4°F (2°C) through the year; while the average lows of 72–74°F (22–23°C) vary only 2°F (1°C). The diurnal range is 17–20°F (9–11°C).

HUMIDITY: 75% or higher year-round.

WATER: Plants should be kept moist. The rainfall pattern is wet/wetter.

FERTILIZER: ¼–½ strength, applied weekly to biweekly during the growing season.

REST PERIOD: None. However, the 2 reported collecting sites have very different climates. If a plant is not blooming or thriving in warm, uniform conditions, a cooler, drier rest should be gradually introduced.

GROWING MEDIA: ½–⅝ in. (12–16 mm) fir bark. Repotting is best done while roots are actively growing or after flowering.

MISCELLANEOUS NOTES: N/A.

Plant and Flower Information

PLANT SIZE AND TYPE: A small to moderately sized monopodial epiphyte.

LEAVES: 2–4 per plant. The shiny leaves are 4–9 in. (10–23 cm) long, obovate, fleshy, and pendent.

INFLORESCENCE: Several. The spikes are 16 in. (41 cm) long, arching to suberect, and usually branching.

FLOWERS: Several at a time. The blossoms are 1.5 in. (4 cm) across and open sequentially. The star-shaped flowers have a fleshy texture and a full, spreading form. The sepals and petals are yellow to greenish yellow with large brown or cinnamon spots. The cupped lip is marked with cinnamon stripes.

HYBRIDIZING NOTES: *P. kunstleri* is reported to hybridize naturally with *P. sumatrana.*

REFERENCES: 30, 81, 83, 193, 195.

PHOTOS/DRAWINGS: *30, 52, 83, 195.*

Phalaenopsis lamelligera Sweet. It reportedly originated in Borneo, but additional habitat information is unavailable. The only known collection is the type specimen. REFERENCES: 195.

Phalaenopsis latisepala. See *P. javanica.* REFERENCES: 195.

Phalaenopsis laycockii. Now considered a synonym of *Paraphalaenopsis laycockii.* REFERENCES: 195.

Phalaenopsis × *leucorrhoda* Rchb.f. A highly variable natural hybrid between *P. aphrodite* and *P. schillerana.* The parents' habitats are several hundred

miles apart at different elevations, suggesting that it may be a separate species. However, plants have reportedly been reproduced in cultivation by hybridizing the 2 parents. REFERENCES: 195, 203. PHOTOS/DRAWINGS: 65.

Phalaenopsis lindenii Lohreiro

AKA: N/A.

ORIGIN/HABITAT: Benguet and Baguio in northern Luzon, Philippines, at 5000 ft. (1524 m) or higher.

CLIMATE: Station # 98328, Baguio, Philippines, Lat. 16.4°N, Long. 120.6°E, at 4962 ft. (1512 m). The record high is 84°F (28.9°C), and the record low is 46°F (7.8°C).

N/HEMISPHERE	JAN	FEB	MAR	APR	MAY	JUN	JUL	AUG	SEP	OCT	NOV	DEC
°F AVG MAX	72	73	76	77	76	75	71	71	71	73	74	74
°F AVG MIN	55	56	58	60	61	61	60	60	60	60	59	57
DIURNAL RANGE	17	17	18	17	15	14	11	11	11	13	15	17
RAIN/INCHES	0.9	0.9	1.7	4.3	15.8	17.2	42.3	45.7	28.1	15.0	4.9	2.0
HUMIDITY/%	83	83	83	85	89	90	93	93	92	89	86	84
BLOOM SEASON	*				*	*	*	**	**	**	**	*
DAYS CLR	N/A											
RAIN/MM	23	23	43	109	401	437	1074	1161	714	381	124	51
°C AVG MAX	22.2	22.8	24.4	25.0	24.4	23.9	21.7	21.7	21.7	22.8	23.3	23.3
°C AVG MIN	12.8	13.3	14.4	15.6	16.1	16.1	15.6	15.6	15.6	15.6	15.0	13.9
DIURNAL RANGE	9.4	9.5	10.0	9.4	8.3	7.8	6.1	6.1	6.1	7.2	8.3	9.4
S/HEMISPHERE	JUL	AUG	SEP	OCT	NOV	DEC	JAN	FEB	MAR	APR	MAY	JUN

Cultural Recommendations

LIGHT: 1000–1200 fc.

TEMPERATURES: The very moderate summer days average 71–76°F (22–24°C), and nights average 60–61°F (16°C), with a diurnal range of 11–15°F (6–8°C). The plant, which is not heat tolerant, is usually grown at too warm a temperature in cultivation and is consequently considered difficult to grow.

HUMIDITY: 80–90%.

WATER: Plants should be kept moist while actively growing, since habitat rainfall during the growing season is very high. The rainfall pattern is wet/dry.

FERTILIZER: ¼–½ strength, applied weekly to biweekly during the growing season.

REST PERIOD: A 2-month rest is indicated. Winter days average 72–76°F (22–24°C), and nights average 55–59°F (13–15°C), with a diurnal range of 17–18°F (9–10°C). Water should be limited to a light watering every 2–3 weeks with occasional mistings in between, providing humidity is high. The medium should never be allowed to dry completely. The constant high humidity in the habitat indicates that moisture is normally available from fog, dew, or mist. Fertilizer should be reduced or eliminated until new growth resumes.

GROWING MEDIA: ½–⅝ in. (12–16 mm) fir bark. Plants are best repotted after blooming or while roots are actively growing.

MISCELLANEOUS NOTES: *P. lindenii* is considered difficult to cultivate by most growers. As temperatures in the climate table indicate, careful attention should be paid to maintaining cool temperatures and providing a cooler, drier rest.

Flowers open in autumn. Bloom initiators are unknown.

Plant and Flower Information

PLANT SIZE AND TYPE: A moderately sized, pendent, monopodial epiphyte.

LEAVES: 3–5 per plant. The oblong-lanceolate leaves are 10 in. (25 cm) long and green with silvery white markings.

INFLORESCENCE: The spikes are long and slender. They are normally simple but occasionally branching.

FLOWERS: Many. The blossoms are 1.0–1.5 in. (2.5–3.8 cm) and open simultaneously. Pretty and delicate, they may be white, various shades of pink, or flushed with pale rose. Sepals and petals are marked with a few rose-colored dots at the base. The unusually large amethyst lip has white sidelobes and may have 5–7 radiating, darker rose, peppermint stripes. Occasionally all segments are candy-striped.

HYBRIDIZING NOTES: *P. lindenii* is used to breed red and peppermint-striped hybrids. As a parent, it tends to increase the number of flowers and contributes branching stems and a beautifully mottled lip.

REFERENCES: 14, 62, 65, 79, 81, 135, 143, 148, 192, 195.

PHOTOS/DRAWINGS: *14, 65, 79, 135, 143, 192, 195.*

Phalaenopsis listeri. See *P. lobbii.* REFERENCES: 195.

Phalaenopsis lobbii Sweet

AKA: *P. decumbens* var. *lobbii, P. listeri, P. parishii* var. *lobbii.*

ORIGIN/HABITAT: Eastern Himalayas in Bhutan as well as the Indian states of Assam and Sikkim in foothills at 1200–1500 ft. (366–457 m). The plants also grow in the Khasia hills, near Darjeeling, and near Nampakon in Burma. *P. lobbii* occur on especially rough-barked trees with decaying material filling the deep fissures where the roots grow.

CLIMATE: Station #42398, Baghdogra, India, Lat. 26.7°N, Long. 88.3°E, at 412 ft. (126 m). Temperatures are calculated for an elevation of 1300 ft. (396 m), resulting in probable extremes of 101°F (38.3°C) and 33°F (0.6°C).

N/HEMISPHERE	JAN	FEB	MAR	APR	MAY	JUN	JUL	AUG	SEP	OCT	NOV	DEC
°F AVG MAX	71	74	82	87	87	86	86	86	85	84	79	74
°F AVG MIN	47	51	57	65	70	73	74	74	73	67	57	50
DIURNAL RANGE	24	23	25	22	17	13	12	12	12	17	22	24
RAIN/INCHES	0.3	0.7	1.3	3.7	11.8	25.9	32.2	25.3	21.2	5.6	0.5	0.2
HUMIDITY/%	73	68	57	58	74	84	86	85	85	79	75	76
BLOOM SEASON	*	*	**									
DAYS CLR @ 6AM	21	18	15	11	5	0	1	1	4	13	23	19
DAYS CLR @ 12PM	23	16	16	11	2	2	0	1	2	10	21	18
RAIN/MM	8	18	33	94	300	658	818	643	538	142	13	5
°C AVG MAX	21.7	23.4	27.8	30.6	30.6	30.0	30.0	30.0	29.5	28.9	26.1	23.4
°C AVG MIN	8.4	10.6	13.9	18.4	21.1	22.8	23.4	23.4	22.8	19.5	13.9	10.0
DIURNAL RANGE	13.3	12.8	13.9	12.2	9.5	7.2	6.6	6.6	6.7	9.4	12.2	13.4
S/HEMISPHERE	JUL	AUG	SEP	OCT	NOV	DEC	JAN	FEB	MAR	APR	MAY	JUN

Cultural Recommendations

LIGHT: 1200–1500 fc. Plants are more tolerant of higher light than most *Phalaenopsis* species.

TEMPERATURES: Summer days average 85–87°F (30–31°C), and nights average 70–74°F (21–23°C), with a diurnal range of 12–17°F (7–9°C). The plants are unusually tolerant of temperature extremes.

HUMIDITY: 75–85% during the summer.

WATER: Plants should be kept moist during the growing season. The rainfall pattern is wet/dry.

FERTILIZER: ¼–½ strength, applied weekly during the growing season. *P. lobbii* is healthiest if given frequent feedings during the short growing season.

REST PERIOD: Winter days average 71–82°F (22–28°C), and nights average 47–57°F (8–14°C), with a diurnal range of 22–25°F (12–14°C). Night temperatures frequently approach 40°F (4°C) during the dry winter and early spring, when humidity falls below 60%. A 2–4 month cool, drier rest with increased light is necessary for blooming and plant survival. Water should be reduced to occasional misting, but humidity should be sufficiently high to prevent dehydration of the leaves. Fertilizer should be eliminated during the dry period. As temperatures cool, the plants require less moisture.

In the habitat, the period of low rainfall is extremely long, but except for 2 months, the humidity levels indicate frequent fog and morning dew. In addition, the decaying material around the roots in the plant's natural habitat helps collect and hold additional moisture during the dry season and increases nutrient levels during the growth period.

GROWING MEDIA: ½–⅝ in. (12–16 mm) fir bark. Repotting is best done in early spring, immediately after flowering. Unless the roots are damaged, they should not be trimmed when repotting. In nature, they grow to great lengths over the host tree, continuing to elongate and branch with age. Plants also grow well when slabbed on cork or tree fern, providing that high humidity is maintained.

MISCELLANEOUS NOTES: N/A.

Plant and Flower Information

PLANT SIZE AND TYPE: A small monopodial epiphyte.

LEAVES: 1–2 per plant, occasionally more. The leaves are 4–5 in. (10–13 cm) long and elliptical. They may be deciduous in nature.

INFLORESCENCE: 4 in. (10 cm) long. Healthy plants may produce more than one spike. Inflorescences are usually slender and suberect.

FLOWERS: 4–5 per inflorescence. The blooms develop sequentially. Each lasts about a month if kept cool, so several are open at a time. The blossoms are 1.0 in. (2.5 cm) or less across, fleshy, creamy white, and star-shaped. The semicircular lip is white, marked with 2 wide, vertical brown bands.

HYBRIDIZING NOTES: N/A.

REFERENCES: 150, 156, 157, 194, 195.

PHOTOS/DRAWINGS: *150, 156,* 157, 194, *195.*

Phalaenopsis lowii Rchb.f.

AKA: *P. proboscidioides.*

ORIGIN/HABITAT: Borneo, and near Moulmein, Burma (Tenasserim Mountains), in the deltas of the Gyne, Salween, and Ataran Rivers, which are seasonally flooded. *P. lowii* usually grows on bare limestone rocks where it receives full morning sun but is shaded in the afternoon. It also grows on the branches of small bushes which have rooted in rock crevices. Tuberous begonias also grow in this moist, warm area.

CLIMATE: Station # 48103, Moulmein, Burma, Lat. 16.4°N, Long. 97.7°E, at 150 ft. (46 m). The record high is 103°F (39.4°C), and the record low is 52°F (11.1°C).

N/HEMISPHERE	JAN	FEB	MAR	APR	MAY	JUN	JUL	AUG	SEP	OCT	NOV	DEC
°F AVG MAX	89	92	94	95	89	85	83	83	85	88	89	87
°F AVG MIN	66	68	73	76	76	75	75	75	75	75	73	68
DIURNAL RANGE	23	24	21	19	13	10	8	8	10	13	16	19
RAIN/INCHES	0.3	0.2	0.4	3.0	20.3	35.6	46.3	43.4	28.1	8.5	2.1	0.1
HUMIDITY/%	66	68	68	70	81	91	92	93	91	81	75	64
BLOOM SEASON									*	*		
DAYS CLR @ 7AM	12	7	5	6	1	0	0	0	0	3	7	12
DAYS CLR @ 1PM	20	13	10	8	3	0	0	0	0	4	12	17
RAIN/MM	8	5	10	76	516	904	1176	1102	714	216	53	3
°C AVG MAX	31.7	33.3	34.4	35.0	31.7	29.4	28.3	28.3	29.4	31.1	31.7	30.6
°C AVG MIN	18.9	20.0	22.8	24.4	24.4	23.9	23.9	23.9	23.9	23.9	22.8	20.0
DIURNAL RANGE	12.8	13.3	11.6	10.6	7.3	5.5	4.4	4.4	5.5	7.2	8.9	10.6
S/HEMISPHERE	JUL	AUG	SEP	OCT	NOV	DEC	JAN	FEB	MAR	APR	MAY	JUN

Cultural Recommendations

LIGHT: 1000–1500 fc.

TEMPERATURES: Summer days average 83–89°F (28–32°C), and nights average 75–76°F (24°C), with a narrow diurnal range of 8–13°F (4–7°C). *P. lowii* is heat tolerant with the highest temperatures often coinciding with the lowest humidity levels.

HUMIDITY: 80% or more while actively growing.

WATER: Plants should be kept moist during the summer. In its habitat, *P. lowii* receives nearly continuous water for 5 months during the rainy season. Good air circulation and excellent drainage are particularly important.

FERTILIZER: ¼–½ strength, applied weekly to biweekly during the growing season.

REST PERIOD: Winter days average 87–95°F (31–35°C), and nights average 66–73°F (19–23°C), resulting in a diurnal range of 19–24°F (10–13°C). The wider winter diurnal range results from both warmer days and cooler nights. A 3–4 month cool, dry rest with periodic misting is indicated by the habitat climate, but growers report that a 1-month rest may be sufficient. Humidity should be reduced to 60–65%, water limited to occasional mistings, fertilizer omitted, and light increased during the rest period.

This species will not grow in Singapore where temperature variation is slight. While it can survive a long, dry dormancy, the leaves may be deciduous under these conditions, which are not recommended in cultivation. The plants are healthier and bloom more freely when leaves are evergreen.

GROWING MEDIA: ½–⅝ in. (12–16 mm) fir bark. Repotting is best done in spring while the fibrous roots are actively growing.

MISCELLANEOUS NOTES: N/A.

Plant and Flower Information

PLANT SIZE AND TYPE: A short, very small monopodial epiphyte or lithophyte.

LEAVES: 1–5 per plant. The leaves are 2–4 in. (5–10 cm) long, lanceolate or ovate, and bright green with purple speckles on the underside.

INFLORESCENCE: 10–15 in. (25–38 cm) long. The plants produce 1 or more spikes which are loosely flowered, erect or pendent, purplish green, and usually simple though sometimes branching. Evergreen leaves result in a stronger, more erect inflorescence.

FLOWERS: 4–5, though healthy, mature plants may develop up to 20. The blossoms are 1.5–2.0 in. (4–5 cm) across, which is very large relative to plant size. They are showy, star-shaped, and delicately textured. The sepals and broad petals are white flushed with pink to purple near the base. The rich purple lip is marked with yellow.

HYBRIDIZING NOTES: N/A.

REFERENCES: 14, 112, 148, 195, 205, 206, 211.

PHOTOS/DRAWINGS: *195*, 205.

Phalaenopsis lueddemanniana Rchb.f.

AKA: *P. ochracea* is a synonym of *P. lueddemanniana* var. *ochracea*. Dr. Sweet indicates that the species *P. pallens*, *P. pulchra*, and *P. reichenbachiana* have erroneously been called *P. lueddemanniana* var. *ochracea*. It should also be noted that the International Orchid Commission registers the hybrids of *P. fasciata*, *P. pallens*, *P. pulchra*, and *P. reichenbachiana* as hybrids of *P. lueddemanniana*.

ORIGIN/HABITAT: Manila, Philippines, where it is abundant at 90–200 ft. (27–61 m).

CLIMATE: Station # 98427, Manila, Philippines, Lat. 14.5°N, Long. 121.0°E, at 74 ft. (23 m). The record high is 101°F (38.3°C), and the record low is 58°F (14.4°C).

N/HEMISPHERE	JAN	FEB	MAR	APR	MAY	JUN	JUL	AUG	SEP	OCT	NOV	DEC
°F AVG MAX	86	88	91	93	93	91	88	87	88	88	87	86
°F AVG MIN	69	69	71	73	75	75	75	75	75	74	72	70
DIURNAL RANGE	17	19	20	20	18	16	13	12	13	14	15	16
RAIN/INCHES	0.9	0.5	0.7	1.3	5.1	10.0	17.0	16.6	14.0	7.6	5.7	2.6
HUMIDITY/%	77	73	70	68	71	81	84	86	87	84	82	89
BLOOM SEASON	*	*	**	**	***	**	*	*	*	*	*	*
DAYS CLR @ 8AM	6	9	14	14	10	3	2	1	1	6	7	6
DAYS CLR @ 2PM	3	6	10	10	8	2	1	1	0	2	2	3
RAIN/MM	23	13	18	33	130	254	432	422	356	193	145	66
°C AVG MAX	30.0	31.1	32.8	33.9	33.9	32.8	31.1	30.6	31.1	31.1	30.6	30.0
°C AVG MIN	20.6	20.6	21.7	22.8	23.9	23.9	23.9	23.9	23.9	23.3	22.2	21.1
DIURNAL RANGE	9.4	10.5	11.1	11.1	10.0	8.9	7.2	6.7	7.2	7.8	8.4	8.9
S/HEMISPHERE	JUL	AUG	SEP	OCT	NOV	DEC	JAN	FEB	MAR	APR	MAY	JUN

Cultural Recommendations

LIGHT: 1000–1200 fc.

TEMPERATURES: Days average 87–93°F (31–34°C), and nights average 74–75°F (23–24°C), with a summer diurnal range of 12–18°F (7–10°C). Plants are fairly heat tolerant, providing that humidity is high and air circulation is excellent.

HUMIDITY: 80%.

WATER: Plants should be kept moist during the growing season. The rainfall pattern is wet/dry.

FERTILIZER: ¼–½ strength, applied weekly to biweekly during the growing season.

REST PERIOD: Winter days average 86–91°F (30–33°C), and nights average 69–72°F (21–22°C), with a diurnal range of 16–20°F (9–11°C). Light may be increased for about 2 months. Humidity should be reduced to 70–80%. For 3–4 months, water should be limited to light waterings at 2–3 week intervals or to occasional mistings, but plants should not be allowed to dry out. Fertilizer should be eliminated when plants are not actively growing.

GROWING MEDIA: ½–⅝ in. (12–16 mm) fir bark. Repotting is best done after blooming or while roots are actively growing.

MISCELLANEOUS NOTES: *P. lueddemanniana* is an adaptable plant. It blooms sporadically for no apparent reason; bloom initiators are unknown. It grows in the uniformly warm Singapore climate but seldom flowers, perhaps indicating that blooms are triggered by increased diurnal range, lower temperatures, or a sudden daytime temperature drop. (See the discussion under *P. viridis*, "Miscellaneous Notes.")

If a plant is doing poorly in the environment described here, it may actually be *P. pulchra*, which needs a very different climate. Conditions could gradually be changed to those appropriate for *P. pulchra*.

Keikis often form on the inflorescence.

Plant and Flower Information

PLANT SIZE AND TYPE: A monopodial epiphyte that is usually moderately sized but is highly variable depending upon maturity and growing conditions.

LEAVES: 3–5 per plant. The bright, yellow-green leaves are 6–12 in. (15–30 cm) long, narrow, oblong, fleshy, and either spreading or drooping.

INFLORESCENCE: 4–12 in. (10–30 cm) long. The spikes are thick, branching, and suberect. They often grow for a year or more without blooming then suddenly flower along their entire length and remain in bloom for months.

FLOWERS: 4–5 per inflorescence. The blossoms are 2.0–2.5 in. (5–6 cm) across, highly fragrant, waxy, fleshy, and star-shaped and last about 2 months. The species is variable, and the sepals and petals may be rose-purple to white, often marked with bars or speckles. The lip is violet and orange.

HYBRIDIZING NOTES: *P. lueddemanniana* is used for reds, semialbas, and latent candy-stripes. As a parent, it intensifies color and improves flower substance. The lip color and shape are dominant characteristics, while the spotting is highly variable. After pollination, flowers turn green and stay fleshy while the pod develops.

HYBRIDIZING NOTES: N/A.

REFERENCES: 2, 14, 83, 112, 116, 140, 148, 149, 174, 195, 203, 205, 206, 210, 211.

PHOTOS/DRAWINGS: *14*, *83*, *140*, 149, 174, *195*, 205, *210*, 211.

Phalaenopsis lueddemanniana var. *pallens.*
See *P. pallens*. REFERENCES: 195.

Phalaenopsis lueddemanniana var. *pulchra.*
See *P. pulchra*. REFERENCES: 195.

Phalaenopsis luteola. See *P. pantherina*. REFERENCES: 195.

Phalaenopsis maculata Rchb.f.

AKA: *P. cruciata, P. musicola.*

ORIGIN/HABITAT: Sarawak, Borneo, where it is found on limestone hills at 800–3000 ft. (244–914 m). It grows in the shade on moist, almost bare rocks or at the base of moss-covered trees.

CLIMATE: Station #96413, Kuching, Sarawak, Lat. 1.5°N, Long. 110.3°E, at 85 ft. (26 m). Temperatures are calculated for an elevation of 1750 ft. (533 m), resulting in probable extremes of 92°F (33.3°C) and 59°F (15.0°C).

N/HEMISPHERE	JAN	FEB	MAR	APR	MAY	JUN	JUL	AUG	SEP	OCT	NOV	DEC
°F AVG MAX	83	83	84	85	86	86	86	87	85	85	85	83
°F AVG MIN	67	67	67	67	67	68	67	67	67	67	67	67
DIURNAL RANGE	16	16	17	18	19	18	19	20	18	18	18	16
RAIN/INCHES	27.1	19.7	14.2	9.7	9.0	8.5	6.9	8.8	9.5	12.6	13.1	20.1
HUMIDITY/%	89	88	86	85	85	83	82	83	84	85	87	88
BLOOM SEASON								*	*			
DAYS CLR @ 7AM	1	0	1	2	3	2	4	1	2	1	1	1
DAYS CLR @ 1PM	0	0	0	0	0	1	1	1	0	0	0	0
RAIN/MM	688	500	361	246	229	216	175	224	241	320	333	511
°C AVG MAX	28.1	28.1	28.6	29.2	29.7	29.7	29.7	30.3	29.2	29.2	29.2	28.1
°C AVG MIN	19.2	19.2	19.2	19.2	19.2	19.7	19.2	19.2	19.2	19.2	19.2	19.2
DIURNAL RANGE	8.9	8.9	9.4	10.0	10.5	10.0	10.5	11.1	10.0	10.0	10.0	8.9
S/HEMISPHERE	JUL	AUG	SEP	OCT	NOV	DEC	JAN	FEB	MAR	APR	MAY	JUN

Cultural Recommendations

LIGHT: 1000–1200 fc.

TEMPERATURES: Summer highs average 85–87°F (29–30°C), and nights average 67–68°F (19–20°C), with a diurnal range of 18–20°F (10–11°C). This habitat has essentially no seasonal temperature fluctuations; the average high temperatures fluctuate only 4°F (2°C), and the average lows vary only 1°F (0.6°C) throughout the year.

HUMIDITY: Above 85% most of the year.

WATER: Plants should be kept moist year-round.

FERTILIZER: ¼–½ strength, applied weekly to biweekly during the growing season.

REST PERIOD: Winter days are slightly cooler at 83–85°F (28–29°C), but night temperatures remain constant, resulting in a slightly lower diurnal range of 16–18°F (9–10°C). Plants should be kept moist, but fertilizer should be reduced when they are not actively growing.

GROWING MEDIA: ½–⅝ in. (12–16 mm) fir bark. Growers report that adding limestone to the medium improves plant growth, but only if warm water is used when watering. When maintaining constant moisture is a problem, a recommended medium is a mixture of sphagnum with large perlite, oyster shell, or charcoal added for drainage. Plants are best repotted in early spring as new roots begin to grow.

MISCELLANEOUS NOTES: N/A.

Plant and Flower Information

PLANT SIZE AND TYPE: A very small monopodial lithophyte or epiphyte. This species is one of the smallest of the genus.

LEAVES: 3–5 per plant. The leaves are 2–4 in. (5–10 cm) long, elliptic to oblong, and fleshy.

INFLORESCENCE: 2–4 in. (5–10 cm) long. Plants usually produce 2 spikes per year. They are ascending and non-branching, and the flowers are arranged in 2 parallel rows.

FLOWERS: Few. The small, 0.5–0.75 in. (1–2 cm) blossoms are fairly large in relation to plant size. The blooms are star-shaped and delicately textured with slightly cupped, creamy white sepals and petals sometimes suffused with green. Markings are red-brown except at the margins, so that each segment appears picoteed, or outlined. The lip is marked with bright red to red-brown spots.

HYBRIDIZING NOTES: N/A.

REFERENCES: 69, 130, 148, 187, 195, 205.

PHOTOS/DRAWINGS: *69, 130, 187, 195.*

Phalaenopsis mannii Rchb.f.

AKA: *P. boxallii.*

ORIGIN/HABITAT: India and Vietnam at 1500 ft. (457 m). It usually grows near forest streams or marshes which, together with dense undergrowth, result in high humidity year-round, despite dry conditions in adjacent areas. The plants grow 10–15 ft. (3–5 m) above the very dark forest floor on rough-barked trees.

CLIMATE: Station #42398, Baghdogra, India (Darjeeling), Lat. 26.7°N, Long. 88.3°E, at 412 ft. (126 m). Temperatures are calculated for an elevation of 1500 ft. (457 m), resulting in probable extremes of 100°F (37.8°C) and 32°F (0.0°C).

N/HEMISPHERE	JAN	FEB	MAR	APR	MAY	JUN	JUL	AUG	SEP	OCT	NOV	DEC
°F AVG MAX	70	73	81	86	86	85	85	85	84	83	78	73
°F AVG MIN	46	50	56	64	69	72	73	73	72	66	56	49
DIURNAL RANGE	24	23	25	22	17	13	12	12	12	17	22	24
RAIN/INCHES	0.3	0.7	1.3	3.7	11.8	25.9	32.2	25.3	21.2	5.6	0.5	0.2
HUMIDITY/%	73	68	57	58	74	84	86	85	85	79	75	76
BLOOM SEASON	*	*	**	**	**	*	*	*				
DAYS CLR @ 6AM	21	18	15	11	5	0	1	1	4	13	23	19
DAYS CLR @ 12PM	23	16	16	11	2	2	0	1	2	10	21	18
RAIN/MM	8	18	33	94	300	658	818	643	538	142	13	5
°C AVG MAX	21.3	23.0	27.4	30.2	30.2	29.7	29.7	29.7	29.1	28.6	25.8	23.0
°C AVG MIN	8.0	10.2	13.6	18.0	20.8	22.4	23.0	23.0	22.4	19.1	13.6	9.7
DIURNAL RANGE	13.3	12.8	13.8	12.2	9.4	7.3	6.7	6.7	6.7	9.5	12.2	13.3
S/HEMISPHERE	JUL	AUG	SEP	OCT	NOV	DEC	JAN	FEB	MAR	APR	MAY	JUN

Cultural Recommendations

LIGHT: 800–1000 fc. This species needs very low light.

TEMPERATURES: Summer days average 84–86°F (29–30°C), and nights average 69–73°F (21–23°C), with a diurnal range of 12–17°F (7–9°C).

HUMIDITY: 85–90% is recommended, which is higher than the levels recorded at the nearest weather station. The microclimate near streams and marshes indicates that the plant needs high relative humidity.

WATER: Plants should be kept moist during the growing season. The rainfall pattern is wet/dry.

FERTILIZER: ¼–½ strength, applied weekly during the fairly short growing period.

REST PERIOD: Winter days average 70–81°F (21–27°C), and nights average 46–56°F (8–14°C), with a winter diurnal range of 22–25°F (12–14°C). The climate indicates that a 3–5 month cool, dry rest should be provided. Fertilizer should be eliminated when the plants are not actively growing. Light may be increased for about 3 months since winter skies are normally clear. In the habitat, temperatures occasionally drop to near freezing, but the microclimate may protect the plant from the extremes, which should be avoided in cultivation. Although winter rainfall is quite low, the high humidity and cool temperatures result in large deposits of dew, which the extremely long roots absorb. These conditions may be simulated in cultivation by misting daily early in the morning and giving a light watering every 2–3 weeks.

GROWING MEDIA: The plants should be slabbed if possible, since they are pendent. ½–⅝ in. (12–16 mm) fir bark is the most common medium used for potted plants, which can also be successfully grown in charcoal covered with sphagnum. Plants are best repotted immediately after flowering, while the roots are actively growing. Roots continue to elongate with age, often extending 10–12 ft. (3–4 m) over the tree trunk.

MISCELLANEOUS NOTES: Blooming is initiated by the rest period, and the flowers open in early spring.

Plant and Flower Information

PLANT SIZE AND TYPE: A moderately sized monopodial epiphyte with a pendent growth habit.

LEAVES: 2–3 per plant. The leaves are 6–18 in. (15–46 cm) long, glossy green, soft or rigid, and marked with violet.

INFLORESCENCE: 18 in. (46 cm) long, depending on plant size. The spikes, up to 5 a year, are normally simple, pendulous, and loosely flowered.

FLOWERS: 10–15 per branch. The fragrant flowers are 1–2 in. (2.5–5.0 cm) across, open in succession, and last 3 months. They are waxy, spreading, star-shaped, and slightly reflexed. The yellow-to-bronze sepals and petals are usually marked with reddish blotches but may be pure yellow, while the anchor-shaped lip is white and purple with short claws.

HYBRIDIZING NOTES: Used in yellow hybrids, *P. mannii* contributes many small flowers which may twist. The lip shape tends to be dominant for several generations.

REFERENCES: 14, 20, 83, 112, 148, 155, 156, 157, 174, 191, 205, 210, 211.

PHOTOS/DRAWINGS: 14, 20, 83, *155, 156, 157,* 174, *191, 195,* 210, 211, *213.*

Phalaenopsis mariae Burbidge ex Warner and Williams

AKA: N/A.

ORIGIN/HABITAT: Borneo to the Philippines. Common on Sulu (Jolo) Island, this species is also found in the southeast coastal hills of Mindanao Island at approximately 2000 ft. (610 m), where it grows on tree trunks and branches always in dense shade.

CLIMATE: Station # 98830, Jolo Bay, Philippines, Lat. 6.1°N, Long. 121.0°E, at 43 ft. (13 m). Temperatures are calculated for an elevation of 2000 ft. (610 m), resulting in probable extremes of 90°F (32.2°C) and 57°F (13.9°C).

Phalaenopsis mariae

N/HEMISPHERE	JAN	FEB	MAR	APR	MAY	JUN	JUL	AUG	SEP	OCT	NOV	DEC
°F AVG MAX	80	80	81	82	83	83	82	83	83	82	81	81
°F AVG MIN	66	66	66	66	66	67	66	67	67	66	66	67
DIURNAL RANGE	14	14	15	16	17	16	16	16	16	16	15	14
RAIN/INCHES	4.8	4.1	4.2	5.4	7.5	8.5	6.3	6.8	7.1	8.9	7.9	6.7
HUMIDITY/%	87	87	87	87	87	87	86	85	86	88	88	88
BLOOM SEASON	*	*	*	*	*	*	**	*	*	*	*	
DAYS CLR @ 8AM	3	2	2	3	3	2	2	2	2	3	2	1
DAYS CLR @ 2PM	1	1	1	0	1	0	0	0	1	1	0	0
RAIN/MM	122	104	107	137	190	216	160	173	180	226	201	170
°C AVG MAX	26.4	26.4	27.0	27.5	28.1	28.1	27.5	28.1	28.1	27.5	27.0	27.0
°C AVG MIN	18.6	18.6	18.6	18.6	18.6	19.2	18.6	19.2	19.2	18.6	18.6	19.2
DIURNAL RANGE	7.8	7.8	8.4	8.9	9.5	8.9	8.9	8.9	8.9	8.9	8.4	7.8
S/HEMISPHERE	JUL	AUG	SEP	OCT	NOV	DEC	JAN	FEB	MAR	APR	MAY	JUN

Cultural Recommendations

LIGHT: 800–1000 fc. The plants are found in dense shade in an environment where skies are predominantly overcast, a combination which may make low light extremely important.

TEMPERATURES: Summer days average 82–83°F (28°C), and nights average 66–67°F (19°C), with a diurnal range of 16–17°F (9°C).

HUMIDITY: 80–85% year-round.

WATER: Plants should be kept moist throughout the year. Warm water, about 70°F (21°C), is highly recommended.

FERTILIZER: ¼–½ strength, applied weekly to biweekly during the growing season.

REST PERIOD: Winter days are slightly cooler and average 80–81°F (26–27°C), while nights should be uniform year-round, resulting in a slightly lower diurnal range of 14–15°F (8°C). Humidity, water, and light levels remain constant, but fertilizer should be reduced when plants are not actively growing.

GROWING MEDIA: ½–⅝ in. (12–16 mm) fir bark, or sphagnum mixed with large perlite or charcoal. Repotting is best done when roots are actively growing.

MISCELLANEOUS NOTES: This plant very seldom produces keikis on the flower spike.

Plant and Flower Information

PLANT SIZE AND TYPE: A moderately sized monopodial epiphyte.

LEAVES: 3–5 per plant. The leaves are 6–12 in. (15–30 cm) long, oblong in shape, fleshy, glossy green, and twisted at the base.

INFLORESCENCE: 8–14 in. (20–36 cm) long, depending on plant size. The pendulous, evergreen spikes branch and continue to produce widely spaced flowers for years. Plants usually have several inflorescences, since 1–2 new spikes arise yearly.

FLOWERS: Few to as many as 145, depending on plant maturity. The handsome, star-shaped blossoms are 1.5–2.0 in. (4–5 cm) across, have a slight fragrance, and open simultaneously. The white-to-cream sepals and petals are marked with large maroon or chestnut spots, while the lip is stained with purple and edged with white.

HYBRIDIZING NOTES: *P. mariae* contributes floriferousness and red color to its progeny, although the red color fades more rapidly than that contributed by *P. sumatrana* or *P. lueddemanniana*.

Hybridizers may choose from 3 known forms: from Sulu, white flowers marked with red bars; from Mindanao, white flowers marked with green tips; and from Luzon, yellow flowers marked with red bars.

REFERENCES: 14, 104, 112, 140, 148, 187, 195, 203, 205, 210, 211.

PHOTOS/DRAWINGS: 14, 104, *140*, *187*, *195*, *210*, 211.

Phalaenopsis mastersii. Now considered a synonym of *Doritis*. REFERENCES: 195.

Phalaenopsis micholitzii Rolfe

AKA: N/A.

ORIGIN/HABITAT: Mindanao, Philippines, at 0–1500 ft. (0–457 m). It has been collected only a few times and may not be available for cultivation.

CLIMATE: The collectors provided insufficient information on the habitat to allow the selection of records for a specific weather station. However, all stations near sea level report average high temperatures of 85–95°F (29–35°C), with average low temperatures of 72–74°F (22–23°C). Temperatures at higher elevations would remain uniform but average a few degrees lower. The rainfall pattern is wet/wetter.

Cultural Recommendations

LIGHT: 800–1200 fc.

TEMPERATURES: Days average 85–95°F (29–35°C), and nights average 72–74°F (22–23°C), with a probable diurnal range of 10–23°F (6–13°C).

HUMIDITY: 80–85% is common year-round at all reporting stations.

WATER: Plants should be kept moist year-round. Warm water, about 70 °F (21 °C), is recommended.

FERTILIZER: ¼–½ strength, applied weekly to biweekly during the growing season.

REST PERIOD: Plants should be kept moist and growing conditions maintained year-round. Any winter temperature fluctuation would be minor. Slightly higher winter light might be beneficial.

GROWING MEDIA: ½–⅝ in. (12–16 mm) fir bark with moisture-retentive additives, or sphagnum moss with perlite or charcoal added for drainage. Repotting is best done while roots are actively growing.

MISCELLANEOUS NOTES: N/A.

Plant and Flower Information

PLANT SIZE AND TYPE: A monopodial epiphyte.

LEAVES: Number unknown.

INFLORESCENCE: 2 in. (5 cm) long. Usually several spikes are produced each year. They tend to be short and may be erect or arching.

FLOWERS: 3–5 per inflorescence. The star-shaped blossoms are 2.5–3.0 in. (6–8 cm) across. They are spreading, delicately textured, and open in succession. The sepals and petals are creamy white to greenish yellow and tend to be lighter in the center. The collections were concolor with an orange-yellow callus on the lip.

HYBRIDIZING NOTES: *P. micholitzii* is reportedly difficult to breed.

REFERENCES: 143, 148, 183, 195, 203.

PHOTOS/DRAWINGS: *99, 143, 148, 183, 195.*

Phalaenopsis modesta J. J. Smith

AKA: N/A.

ORIGIN/HABITAT: Borneo, including Sabah, West Kotah, Mt. Kinabalu, and Tawau in the province of Elphiastone. It also grows in the Crocker Mountain range on trees near streams at 1200 ft. (366 m).

CLIMATE: Station # 49609, Tawau, North Borneo, Lat. 4.3 °N, Long. 117.9 °E, at 58 ft. (18 m). Temperatures are calculated for an elevation of 1200 ft. (366 m), giving probable extremes of 93 °F (33.9 °C) and 57 °F (13.9 °C).

N/HEMISPHERE	JAN	FEB	MAR	APR	MAY	JUN	JUL	AUG	SEP	OCT	NOV	DEC
°F AVG MAX	85	85	85	86	85	84	85	84	85	86	85	85
°F AVG MIN	67	67	67	68	67	67	67	67	67	67	67	67
DIURNAL RANGE	18	18	18	18	18	17	18	17	18	19	18	18
RAIN/INCHES	4.8	3.8	3.9	5.0	7.0	7.4	7.7	7.6	6.0	5.8	6.7	6.2
HUMIDITY/%	N/A											
BLOOM SEASON	N/A											
DAYS CLR	N/A											
RAIN/MM	122	97	99	127	178	188	196	193	152	147	170	157
°C AVG MAX	29.6	29.6	29.6	30.1	29.6	29.0	29.6	29.0	29.6	30.1	29.6	29.6
°C AVG MIN	19.6	19.6	19.6	20.1	19.6	19.6	19.6	19.6	19.6	19.6	19.6	19.6
DIURNAL RANGE	10.0	10.0	10.0	10.0	10.0	9.4	10.0	9.4	10.0	10.5	10.0	10.0
S/HEMISPHERE	JUL	AUG	SEP	OCT	NOV	DEC	JAN	FEB	MAR	APR	MAY	JUN

Cultural Recommendations

LIGHT: 1000–1200 fc.

TEMPERATURES: Summer days average 84–86 °F (29–30 °C), and nights consistently average 67–68 °F (20 °C), with a diurnal range of 17–18 °F (9–10 °C) which varies less than 2 °F (1 °C) year-round. The probable extremes are just 10 °F (6 °C) above and below average high and low temperatures, indicating an intolerance to wide temperature fluctuations.

HUMIDITY: 70–85%.

WATER: Plants should be moist year-round. Warm water, about 65 °F (18 °C), might be beneficial. The rainfall pattern is wet/wetter.

FERTILIZER: ¼–½ strength, applied weekly to biweekly during the growing season.

REST PERIOD: Growing conditions should be maintained throughout the year.

GROWING MEDIA: ½–⅝ in. (12–16 mm) fir bark, or a mixture of sphagnum and large perlite or charcoal. Adding charcoal to the medium is reported to promote plant health. Plants are best repotted after flowering or while roots are actively growing.

MISCELLANEOUS NOTES: N/A.

Plant and Flower Information

PLANT SIZE AND TYPE: A small monopodial epiphyte.

LEAVES: Number unknown. The leaves are small, usually 4.5–6.0 in. (11–15 cm) long.

INFLORESCENCE: Shorter than the leaves. The spikes are slender and arching.

FLOWERS: Few. The star-shaped blossoms are 1.0–1.5 in. (2.5–3.8 cm) across and spreading, with a delicate texture and a "strong, magnificent" fragrance. The narrow sepals and broad petals are white to pale rose. They are marked on the basal half with fine purple bars or stripes. The markings become greenish with age. The white lip sometimes has purple at the apex of the midlobe. The sidelobes are white, yellow, and purple.

HYBRIDIZING NOTES: *P. modesta* sometimes transmits its strong fragrance to hybrids.

REFERENCES: 61, 130, 176, 195.

PHOTOS/DRAWINGS: *52, 61, 77, 130, 176, 195.*

Phalaenopsis musicola. See *P. maculata.* REFERENCES: 195.

Phalaenopsis mysorensis Saldanha

AKA: N/A.

ORIGIN/HABITAT: Endemic to the Vanapur-Banagore region near Hassan in southern India.

CLIMATE: Station # 43296, Bangalore-Hindustan, India, Lat. 13.0°N, Long. 77.7°E, at 2937 ft. (895 m). The record high is 102°F (38.9°C), and the record low is 46°F (7.8°C).

N/HEMISPHERE	JAN	FEB	MAR	APR	MAY	JUN	JUL	AUG	SEP	OCT	NOV	DEC
°F AVG MAX	80	86	90	93	91	84	81	81	82	82	79	78
°F AVG MIN	57	60	65	69	69	67	66	66	65	65	62	58
DIURNAL RANGE	23	26	25	24	22	17	15	15	17	17	17	20
RAIN/INCHES	0.2	0.3	0.4	1.6	4.2	2.9	3.8	5.0	6.7	5.9	2.7	0.4
HUMIDITY/%	64	57	55	59	63	73	80	79	79	79	81	74
BLOOM SEASON												**
DAYS CLR @ 11AM	11	14	18	10	4	1	0	0	0	0	9	9
DAYS CLR @ 5PM	14	13	13	3	1	0	0	0	1	1	5	8
RAIN/MM	5	8	10	41	107	74	97	127	170	150	69	10
°C AVG MAX	26.7	30.0	32.2	33.9	32.8	28.9	27.2	27.2	27.8	27.8	26.1	25.6
°C AVG MIN	13.9	15.6	18.3	20.6	20.6	19.4	18.9	18.9	18.3	18.3	16.7	14.4
DIURNAL RANGE	12.8	14.4	13.9	13.3	12.2	9.5	8.3	8.3	9.5	9.5	9.4	11.2
S/HEMISPHERE	JUL	AUG	SEP	OCT	NOV	DEC	JAN	FEB	MAR	APR	MAY	JUN

Cultural Recommendations

LIGHT: 1000–1200 fc.

TEMPERATURES: Summer days average 81–93°F (27–34°C), and nights average 65–69°F (18–21°C), with a diurnal range of 15–24°F (8–13°C). The record high for this station is 102°F (39°C), indicating that plants should be heat tolerant if moderate humidity and good air movement are provided.

HUMIDITY: 70–80% during the growing season.

WATER: Plants should be kept moist while actively growing. The rainfall pattern is wet/dry.

FERTILIZER: ¼–½ strength. To produce the best flowering, fertilizer should be applied weekly during the relatively short growing season.

REST PERIOD: A cool, dry rest of 2–3 months is important. Winter days average 78–90°F (26–32°C), and nights average 57–60°F (14–16°C), with a diurnal range of 20–26°F (11–14°C). The record low for this station indicates that the plants should be able to tolerate occasional periods of cooler winter temperatures. Water and humidity should be reduced. In the microclimate, dew will form occasionally, but the decline in relative humidity to 55–65% indicates that the region is surprisingly dry. Light may be increased to correspond with the increased number of clear days in the habitat. Fertilizer should be eliminated until new growth begins.

GROWING MEDIA: ½–⅝ in. (12–16 mm) fir bark. Plants are best repotted in early spring when new root growth begins. It is best not to wait until after blooming to repot.

MISCELLANEOUS NOTES: Blooming is apparently initiated during the rapid growth phase, with flowers opening in late autumn at the end of the rainy season. This plant is not known to be in cultivation.

Plant and Flower Information

PLANT SIZE AND TYPE: A small, very short monopodial epiphyte.

LEAVES: 2 per plant, rarely 3 or more. The leaves are 3.5–4.5 in. (9–11 cm) long.

INFLORESCENCE: 3 in. (8 cm) long, usually shorter than the leaves.

FLOWERS: 2–8. The blossoms are 0.5 in. (1.3 cm) across, which is tiny even in relation to the small plant size. Sepals and petals are white with yellow on the lip. Plants have been collected in Dec. (Jun.) and also in Apr.–May (Oct.–Nov.), which may indicate extended or multiple blooming or may indicate adaptation to different rainfall patterns.

HYBRIDIZING NOTES: N/A.

REFERENCES: 157, 195.

PHOTOS/DRAWINGS: *195.*

Phalaenopsis ochracea. See *P. lueddemanniana.* REFERENCES: 195.

Phalaenopsis pallens (Lindley) Rchb.f.

AKA: *P. denticulata, P. foerstermanii, P. lueddemanniana* var. *pallens, P. mariae* var. *alba.* Although *P. pallens* is now considered a botanically separate species, the

International Orchid Commission uses *P. lueddemanniana* for hybrid registration purposes.

ORIGIN/HABITAT: Endemic to the Philippines. It has been collected near Manila and near Puerto Princesa on Palawan Island at 0–1500 ft. (0–457 m).

CLIMATE: Station # 98618, Puerto Princesa, Philippines, Lat. 9.7°N, Long. 118.8°E, at 20 ft. (6 m) elevation. The record high is 96°F (35.6°C), and the record low is 65°F (18.3°C).

N/HEMISPHERE	JAN	FEB	MAR	APR	MAY	JUN	JUL	AUG	SEP	OCT	NOV	DEC
°F AVG MAX	87	88	89	91	90	88	87	87	87	88	88	87
°F AVG MIN	73	73	74	75	76	75	74	74	74	74	74	74
DIURNAL RANGE	14	15	15	16	14	13	13	13	13	14	14	13
RAIN/INCHES	1.4	1.0	2.2	1.5	5.7	6.7	7.3	7.8	7.8	7.6	7.5	5.2
HUMIDITY/%	84	82	82	81	84	87	87	88	87	87	87	86
BLOOM SEASON	*	*	**	*					*	*	**	**
DAYS CLR @ 8AM	8	6	11	10	6	4	4	3	4	6	6	6
DAYS CLR @ 2PM	5	4	6	8	4	1	1	1	1	2	2	3
RAIN/MM	35	25	56	38	146	170	185	199	197	192	190	133
°C AVG MAX	30.6	31.1	31.7	32.8	32.2	31.1	30.6	30.6	30.6	31.1	31.1	30.6
°C AVG MIN	22.8	22.8	23.3	23.9	24.4	23.9	23.3	23.3	23.3	23.3	23.3	23.3
DIURNAL RANGE	7.8	8.3	8.4	8.9	7.8	7.2	7.3	7.3	7.3	7.8	7.8	7.3
S/HEMISPHERE	JUL	AUG	SEP	OCT	NOV	DEC	JAN	FEB	MAR	APR	MAY	JUN

Cultural Recommendations

LIGHT: 1000–1200 fc.

TEMPERATURES: Days average 87–91°F (31–33°C), and nights average 73–76°F (23–24°C) throughout the year, with a summer diurnal range of 13–14°F (7–8°C). The diurnal range is lowest during the summer, when overcast skies prevent daytime heating.

HUMIDITY: 80–85%.

WATER: Plants should be kept moist. Warm water, about 70°F (21°C), is highly recommended. The rainfall pattern is wet/dry.

FERTILIZER: ¼–½ strength, applied weekly to biweekly during the growing season.

REST PERIOD: Winter days average 87–89°F (31–32°C), and nights average 73–75°F (23°C), with a diurnal range of 14–16°F (8-9°C). Water should be restricted to a light watering every 2–3 weeks with occasional mistings in between. Plants should not be allowed to dry out since blooming occurs during this season. Fertilizer should be eliminated and light increased.

GROWING MEDIA: ½–⅝ in. (12–16 mm) fir bark with moisture-retentive additives, or sphagnum moss with perlite or charcoal added for drainage. Adding charcoal seems to improve plant health, and small amounts of limestone may also be helpful, but only

if warm water, about 70°F (21°C), is used in watering. Repotting is best done immediately after flowering, while roots are actively growing.

MISCELLANEOUS NOTES: Bloom initiators are unknown.

Plant and Flower Information

PLANT SIZE AND TYPE: A dwarf monopodial epiphyte.

LEAVES: 3–5 per plant. The leaves are 5–7 in. (13–18 cm) long.

INFLORESCENCE: 5–7 in. (13–18 cm) long. The spikes, usually 2 per year, rarely exceed the length of the leaves.

FLOWERS: One, to few per inflorescence. The star-shaped blossoms are 1.5–2.0 in. (4-5 cm) across. Sepals and petals are white to pale yellow-green marked with darker lines, but colors fade to nearly white in the center. The white lip is marked with yellow.

HYBRIDIZING NOTES: N/A.

REFERENCES: 14, 83, 140, 149, 195, 203.

PHOTOS/DRAWINGS: *14, 83, 140, 195.*

Phalaenopsis pantherina Rchb.f.

AKA: *P. luteola.*

ORIGIN/HABITAT: Indonesia, including the Kalimantan district of Borneo, Sarawak, and Labuan Island off the coast of Sabah. It grows on moss-covered rocks near rushing streams, which suggests a high elevation with uniform temperatures somewhat cooler than those given in the climate table.

CLIMATE: Station # 96465, Labuan, North Borneo, Lat. 5.3°N, Long. 115.2°E, at 98 ft. (30 m). The record high is 99°F (37.2°C), and the record low is 59°F (15.0°C).

N/HEMISPHERE	JAN	FEB	MAR	APR	MAY	JUN	JUL	AUG	SEP	OCT	NOV	DEC
°F AVG MAX	86	86	87	89	89	88	88	88	87	87	87	86
°F AVG MIN	76	76	76	76	76	76	77	76	76	76	76	76
DIURNAL RANGE	10	10	11	13	13	12	11	12	11	11	11	10
RAIN/INCHES	4.4	4.6	5.9	11.7	13.6	13.8	12.5	11.7	16.4	18.3	16.5	11.2
HUMIDITY/%	83	84	83	82	82	82	82	79	80	81	81	82
BLOOM SEASON						*	**					
DAYS CLR @ 8AM	1	3	3	4	3	0	1	2	1	2	1	2
DAYS CLR @ 2PM	3	5	5	5	2	2	4	3	1	3	1	1
RAIN/MM	112	117	150	297	345	351	318	297	417	465	419	284
°C AVG MAX	30.0	30.0	30.6	31.7	31.7	31.1	31.1	31.1	30.6	30.6	30.6	30.0
°C AVG MIN	24.4	24.4	24.4	24.4	24.4	24.4	25.0	24.4	24.4	24.4	24.4	24.4
DIURNAL RANGE	5.6	5.6	6.2	7.3	7.3	6.7	6.1	6.7	6.2	6.2	6.2	5.6
S/HEMISPHERE	JUL	AUG	SEP	OCT	NOV	DEC	JAN	FEB	MAR	APR	MAY	JUN

Cultural Recommendations

LIGHT: 1000–1200 fc.

TEMPERATURES: Days average 86–89 °F (30–32 °C), while nights consistently average 76–77 °F (24–25 °C), resulting in a year-round diurnal range of 10–13 °F (6–7 °C). If plants grow at higher elevations, habitat temperatures may be a little cooler than indicated, but they would also remain constant throughout the year.

HUMIDITY: 80–85% year-round.

WATER: Plants should be kept moist. Warm water, about 70 °F (21 °C), is highly recommended. The rainfall pattern is wet/wetter.

FERTILIZER: ¼–½ strength, applied weekly to biweekly during the growing season.

REST PERIOD: Growing temperatures should be maintained, but the diurnal range should decrease slightly to 10–11 °F (6 °C). Water and fertilizer should be reduced slightly, particularly if cultivation temperatures are somewhat cool; but plants will not tolerate dehydration. In the habitat, the number of clear days increases in winter, indicating a possible increase in light levels.

GROWING MEDIA: ½–⅝ in. (12–16 mm) fir bark. The addition of small amounts of limestone may be helpful if warm water, 70 °F (21 °C), is also used. Repotting is best done immediately after flowering.

MISCELLANEOUS NOTES: N/A.

Plant and Flower Information

PLANT SIZE AND TYPE: A monopodial lithophyte.

LEAVES: Number and size were not reported, but the leaves were described as glossy.

INFLORESCENCE: 4 in. (10 cm) long and flattened.

FLOWERS: Few. The spreading blossoms are 2.0–2.5 in. (5–6 cm) across, star-shaped, and waxy. Sepals and petals are yellow, with red spots arranged in lines giving a striped appearance to the bottom half of the lower sepals.

HYBRIDIZING NOTES: N/A.

REFERENCES: 195.

PHOTOS/DRAWINGS: *195.*

Phalaenopsis parishii Rchb.f.

AKA: *P. decumbens.*

ORIGIN/HABITAT: Eastern Himalayas; Assam, India; Moulmein, Burma. It is found on moss-covered tree branches overhanging streams, where hot, moist conditions prevail during the growing season.

CLIMATE: Station # 48103, Moulmein, Burma, Lat. 16.4 °N, Long. 97.7 °E, at 150 ft. (46 m). The record high is 103 °F (39.4 °C), and the record low is 52 °F (11.1 °C).

N/HEMISPHERE	JAN	FEB	MAR	APR	MAY	JUN	JUL	AUG	SEP	OCT	NOV	DEC
°F AVG MAX	89	92	94	95	89	85	83	83	85	88	89	87
°F AVG MIN	66	68	73	76	76	75	75	75	75	75	73	68
DIURNAL RANGE	23	24	21	19	13	10	8	8	10	13	16	19
RAIN/INCHES	0.3	0.2	0.4	3.0	20.3	35.6	46.3	43.4	28.1	8.5	2.1	0.1
HUMIDITY/%	66	68	68	70	81	91	92	93	91	81	75	64
BLOOM SEASON	*	*	*	*	*	*	*					
DAYS CLR @ 7AM	12	7	5	6	1	0	0	0	0	3	7	12
DAYS CLR @ 1PM	20	13	10	8	3	0	0	0	0	4	12	17
RAIN/MM	8	5	10	76	516	904	1176	1102	714	216	53	3
°C AVG MAX	31.7	33.3	34.4	35.0	31.7	29.4	28.3	28.3	29.4	31.1	31.7	30.6
°C AVG MIN	18.9	20.0	22.8	24.4	24.4	23.9	23.9	23.9	23.9	23.9	22.8	20.0
DIURNAL RANGE	12.8	13.3	11.6	10.6	7.3	5.5	4.4	4.4	5.5	7.2	8.9	10.6
S/HEMISPHERE	JUL	AUG	SEP	OCT	NOV	DEC	JAN	FEB	MAR	APR	MAY	JUN

Cultural Recommendations

LIGHT: 1500 fc. In cultivation, plants prefer dappled light rather than deep shade.

TEMPERATURES: Summer days average 83–89 °F (28–32 °C), and nights average 75–76 °F (24 °C), with a diurnal range of 8–13 °F (4–7 °C). The plants should be able to tolerate high temperatures since the warmest weather occurs during clear, dry periods.

HUMIDITY: 80–90% during the growing season.

WATER: Plants should be kept moist in summer. Warm water is highly recommended. The rainfall pattern is wet/dry.

FERTILIZER: ¼–½ strength, applied weekly to biweekly during the growing season.

REST PERIOD: A 3–4 month rest is indicated. Winter days average 87–95 °F (31–35 °C), and nights average 66–73 °F (19–23 °C), with a diurnal range of 16–24 °F (9–13 °C). The increased diurnal range results from both warmer days and cooler nights. Increased light might be beneficial. Fertilizer should be reduced or eliminated. Water should be limited to occasional light misting, but the plants should not be allowed to wither. Blooming occurs during the dry winter.

GROWING MEDIA: Tree-fern slabs are recommended if high humidity can be maintained, but fir bark or a mixed tree-fern medium may also be used. Plants are best repotted in the spring after flowering, while the roots are actively growing.

MISCELLANEOUS NOTES: The plant survives localized dry periods by losing its leaves, and if seasonal rains are late, it often blooms before producing new leaves. The leaves are evergreen in damper areas and in cultivation.

Plant and Flower Information

PLANT SIZE AND TYPE: A small to very small monopodial epiphyte with extremely long, flat roots.

LEAVES: 3–5 per plant. The dark green leaves are 2–6 in. (5–15 cm) long, oval, arching, and fleshy. They will become leathery or may even be deciduous if water levels are inadequate.

INFLORESCENCE: 3–4 in. (8–10 cm) long. The arching spikes are zigzag and densely flowered. Plants may produce up to 5 per year.

FLOWERS: 4–10 per inflorescence. The small blooms are 0.8 in. (2 cm) across, yet they are large relative to overall plant size. The blossoms open simultaneously and last about a month. The flowers are star-shaped, and sepals have a tendency to recurve. Sepals and petals may be white or yellow. The lip has violet to magenta-red markings, and 4 filamentlike appendages project from the apex of the lip. The sidelobes are yellow with purple spotting.

HYBRIDIZING NOTES: *P. parishii* is a reluctant breeder.

REFERENCES: 20, 112, 155, 157, 174, 195, 205, 211, 218.

PHOTOS/DRAWINGS: 20, *155*, 174, *195*, *218*.

Phalaenopsis parishii **var.** *lobbii.* See *P. lobbii.*
REFERENCES: 195.

Phalaenopsis philippinense Golamco ex Fowlie and Tang

AKA: Once considered a primary hybrid between *P. aphrodite* and *P. schillerana.*

ORIGIN/HABITAT: Endemic to the Philippines, it originates on Luzon Island in the provinces of Nueva Vizcaya, Quirino, Isabela, and northern Aurora. It is found in the Sierra Madre rainforests, where it grows in the shade on tall trees, usually near streams. Habitat elevation was not recorded by the collectors.

CLIMATE: Station # 98336, Casiguran, Philippines, Lat. 16.3°N, Long. 122.1°E, at 13 ft. (4 m). The record high is 98°F (36.7°C), and the record low is 57°F (13.9°C).

N/HEMISPHERE	JAN	FEB	MAR	APR	MAY	JUN	JUL	AUG	SEP	OCT	NOV	DEC
°F AVG MAX	82	83	85	88	90	91	90	90	90	88	86	84
°F AVG MIN	67	67	68	70	72	73	73	73	72	71	70	68
DIURNAL RANGE	15	16	17	18	18	18	17	17	18	17	16	16
RAIN/INCHES	9.4	8.6	10.4	6.5	9.2	9.7	8.3	9.9	12.0	14.2	24.2	19.5
HUMIDITY/%	89	89	87	86	85	85	86	87	89	85	88	87
BLOOM SEASON	*	*	*	*	*	*	*	*	*	*	*	*
DAYS CLR @ 8AM	7	8	12	14	14	8	7	6	8	11	9	8
DAYS CLR @ 2PM	5	6	10	12	11	6	4	4	3	4	7	5
RAIN/MM	240	217	264	164	234	247	212	251	305	360	614	496
°C AVG MAX	27.8	28.3	29.4	31.1	32.2	32.8	32.2	32.2	32.2	31.1	30.0	28.9
°C AVG MIN	19.4	19.4	20.0	21.1	22.2	22.8	22.8	22.8	22.2	21.7	21.1	20.0
DIURNAL RANGE	8.4	8.9	9.4	10.0	10.0	10.0	9.4	9.4	10.0	9.4	8.9	8.9
S/HEMISPHERE	JUL	AUG	SEP	OCT	NOV	DEC	JAN	FEB	MAR	APR	MAY	JUN

Cultural Recommendations

LIGHT: 1000–1200 fc. The coastal climate, with frequent clear skies, suggests higher light, but the plants grow in shady places.

TEMPERATURES: Summer days average 88–91°F (31–33°C), and nights average 70–73°F (21–23°C), with a diurnal range of 17–18°F (9–10°C).

HUMIDITY: 85–90%. The general humidity is high, and microclimates near streams have moisture levels that are higher still.

WATER: Plants should be kept moist year-round. The rainfall pattern is wet/wetter.

FERTILIZER: ¼–½ strength, applied weekly to biweekly during the growing season.

REST PERIOD: A gentle rest is indicated. Winter days average 82–86°F (28–31°C), and nights average 67–70°F (19–21°C). In the habitat, high and low temperatures decline simultaneously, resulting in little seasonal fluctuation in the diurnal range. Plants should be kept moist and light increased during the rest period.

GROWING MEDIA: Slabbing accommodates the pendent growth habit. For potted plants, recommended media include ½–⅝ in. (12–16 mm) fir bark with moisture-retaining additives, or sphagnum moss with perlite or charcoal added. Repotting is best done while roots are actively growing.

MISCELLANEOUS NOTES: This plant is said to bloom "at any time" in the wild, which may indicate that it is free-flowering. Also see the discussion of possible bloom initiators under *P. viridis*, "Miscellaneous Notes."

Plant and Flower Information

PLANT SIZE AND TYPE: A moderately sized to large, pendent monopodial epiphyte.

LEAVES: 3–7 per plant. The oblong leaves are 10–14 in. (25–36 cm) long, fleshy, and dark green, with silvery grey marmorations on the upper surface and a purplish underside.

INFLORESCENCE: 24–48 in. (61–122 cm) long. The spikes are slender, zigzag, and arching, with nicely spaced flowers. After the flowers fade, a new spike may develop and bloom within a few weeks.

FLOWERS: 3–30 per inflorescence. Mature plants may produce more than 100 blossoms, which open simultaneously. The flowers are 2.5–3.5 in. (6–9 cm) across, full, flat, delicately textured, and broad-petaled. They are pink initially but turn bluish white with age. The lateral sepals are dotted with red at the base. The white lip is anchor-shaped, with bright yellow or green and red on the sidelobes.

HYBRIDIZING NOTES: N/A.

REFERENCES: 199.

PHOTOS/DRAWINGS: *199.*

Phalaenopsis pleihary. See *P. amabilis.* REFERENCES: 195.

Phalaenopsis proboscidioides. See *P. lowii.* REFERENCES: 195.

Phalaenopsis psilantha. See *P. amboinensis.* REFERENCES: 195.

Phalaenopsis pulcherrima. Now considered a synonym of *Doritis pulcherrima.* REFERENCES: 195.

Phalaenopsis pulchra (Rchb.f.) Sweet

AKA: *P. lueddemanniana* var. *pulchra.* Although *P. pulchra* is now considered a botanically separate species, the International Orchid Commission uses *P. lueddemanniana* for hybrid registration purposes.

ORIGIN/HABITAT: Luzon, Philippines, near Balete Pass. It is found on eastern mountain slopes at 4500 ft. (1372 m).

CLIMATE: Station # 98336, Casiguran, Philippines, Lat. 16.3°N, Long. 122.1°E, at 13 ft. (4 m). Temperatures are calculated for an elevation of 4920 ft. (1500 m), resulting in probable extremes of 83°F (28.3°C) and 42°F (5.6°C).

N/HEMISPHERE	JAN	FEB	MAR	APR	MAY	JUN	JUL	AUG	SEP	OCT	NOV	DEC
°F AVG MAX	67	68	70	73	75	76	75	75	75	73	71	69
°F AVG MIN	52	52	53	55	57	58	58	58	57	56	55	53
DIURNAL RANGE	15	16	17	18	18	18	17	17	18	17	16	16
RAIN/INCHES	9.4	8.6	10.4	6.5	9.2	9.7	8.3	9.9	12.0	14.2	24.2	19.5
HUMIDITY/%	89	89	87	86	85	85	86	87	89	85	88	87
BLOOM SEASON					*	*	*	*	*			
DAYS CLR @ 8AM	7	8	12	14	14	8	7	6	8	11	9	8
DAYS CLR @ 2PM	5	6	10	12	11	6	4	4	3	4	7	5
RAIN/MM	240	217	264	164	234	247	212	251	305	360	614	496
°C AVG MAX	19.4	20.0	21.1	22.8	23.9	24.4	23.9	23.9	23.9	22.8	21.6	20.5
°C AVG MIN	11.1	11.1	11.6	12.8	13.9	14.4	14.4	14.4	13.9	13.3	12.8	11.6
DIURNAL RANGE	8.3	8.9	9.5	10.0	10.0	10.0	9.5	9.5	10.0	9.5	8.8	8.9
S/HEMISPHERE	JUL	AUG	SEP	OCT	NOV	DEC	JAN	FEB	MAR	APR	MAY	JUN

Cultural Recommendations

LIGHT: 1000–1200 fc. Morning light is preferred.

TEMPERATURES: Summer days average 75–76°F (24°C), and nights average a cool 57–58°F (14°C), with a diurnal range of 17–18°F (9–10°C). This plant is unlikely to be heat tolerant, with a probable extreme high of only 83°F (28°C).

HUMIDITY: 80–90%.

WATER: Plants should be kept moist year-round. The rainfall pattern is wet/wetter, and rainfall amounts in the habitat are probably greater than the climate table indicates.

Growers report that the plants are sensitive to cold water, but the climate of the habitat indicates that this should not be the case. However, if a plant is already stressed from temperatures that are too warm, it could be extremely sensitive to the difference between water and air temperatures. The risk of shock can be reduced by matching water and air temperatures.

FERTILIZER: ¼–½ strength, applied weekly to biweekly during the growing season.

REST PERIOD: Winter days average 67–73°F (19–23°C), and nights average 52–55°F (11–13°C), with a diurnal range of 15–17°F (8–9°C). Light in the habitat may be slightly higher in winter. Plants should be kept moist, but fertilizer may be reduced when they are not actively growing.

GROWING MEDIA: ½–⅝ in. (12–16 mm) fir bark with moisture-retentive additives, or sphagnum moss with perlite or charcoal added for drainage. Plants are best repotted while roots are actively growing.

MISCELLANEOUS NOTES: This species is considered very difficult to maintain in cultivation, probably due to its lack of heat tolerance. Temperatures in the habitat are unusually cool for a *Phalaenopsis*, and the plants are difficult to grow in warm conditions.

P. *pulcra* is often mislabeled and cultivated as *P. lueddemanniana*, which is most unfortunate, since the growing climates for the 2 species are quite different. If a plant does not thrive, it may have been mislabeled, and its environment should gradually be modified to that suggested for *P. lueddemanniana*.

Plant and Flower Information

PLANT SIZE AND TYPE: A moderately sized monopodial epiphyte.

LEAVES: 3–5 per plant. The leaves are 6–12 in. (15–30 cm) long, oval to oblong, fleshy, and light green.

INFLORESCENCE: 4–10 in. (10–25 cm) long. The spikes, often more than one, are arching and laxly flowered.

FLOWERS: Few per inflorescence. The blossoms are 2.0–2.5 in. (5–6 cm) across, fragrant, fleshy, waxy, open, and star-shaped. The sepals and petals are magenta to purple on the front, with faint cross-barring, and white on the back. The lip is marked with yellow on the sidelobes.

HYBRIDIZING NOTES: N/A.

REFERENCES: 14, 81, 140, 149, 195, 203.

PHOTOS/DRAWINGS: *14, 81, 140, 149, 195.*

Phalaenopsis regnierana. Now considered a synonym of *Doritis regnierana*. REFERENCES: 195.

Phalaenopsis reichenbachiana Rchb.f. and Sander. *P. kimballiana* is a synonym. Dr. Sweet considers *P. reichenbachiana* a separate species, but the International Orchid Commission uses the name *P. lueddemanniana* for hybrid registration purposes. Reported to originate in Mindanao, Philippines, the plant apparently grows in light shade, but no elevation or additional habitat details were recorded. The plant is similar in appearance to *P. fasciata*, but the lip is unique. The species is very rare and unlikely to be available for cultivation. Habitat information is insuf-

ficient for the selection of climate data. REFERENCES: 195, 203, 211.

Phalaenopsis rimestadiana. See *P. amabilis*. REFERENCES: 195.

Phalaenopsis riteiwanensis. See *P. equestris*. REFERENCES: 195.

Phalaenopsis robinsonii J. J. Smith. Collected only once in 1913 on Ambon Island. The flowers were said to be white with lilac markings. The plant is unlikely to be available for cultivation, and habitat information insufficient for the selection of climate data. REFERENCES: 195.

Phalaenopsis rosea. See *P. equestris*. REFERENCES: 195.

Phalaenopsis rosenstromii. See *P. amabilis*. REFERENCES: 195.

Phalaenopsis ruckerana. Now considered a synonym of *Sarcochilus pallidus*. REFERENCES: 195.

Phalaenopsis ruckeri. Now considered a synonym of *Sarcochilus pallidus*. REFERENCES: 195.

Phalaenopsis sanderana Rchb.f.

AKA: Frequently spelled *P. sanderiana*. We have followed the spelling Dr. Sweet considers correct. This plant has also been known as *P. amabilis* var. *aphrodite* subvar. *sanderana*, *P. aphrodite* var. *sanderana*, and *P. amabilis* var. *sanderana*. It was once considered a natural hybrid between *P. schillerana* and *P. amabilis* var. *aphrodite*. *P. alcicornis* is a synonym for *P. sanderana* var. *alba*.

ORIGIN/HABITAT: The south side of Mindanao Island, Philippines, in the provinces of Davao and Amboango, and Igat, Balut, and Saragani Islands, at 0–1500 ft. (0–457 m).

CLIMATE: Station # 98754, Davao, Philippines, Lat. 7.1°N, Long. 125.6°E, at 88 ft. (27 m). Temperatures are calculated for an elevation of 800 ft. (244 m), resulting in probable extremes of 95°F (35.0°C) and 63°F (17.2°C).

Phalaenopsis sanderana

N/HEMISPHERE	JAN	FEB	MAR	APR	MAY	JUN	JUL	AUG	SEP	OCT	NOV	DEC
°F AVG MAX	85	86	88	89	88	86	86	86	86	87	87	86
°F AVG MIN	70	70	70	71	72	71	71	71	71	71	71	70
DIURNAL RANGE	15	16	18	18	16	15	15	15	15	16	16	16
RAIN/INCHES	4.8	4.5	5.2	5.8	9.2	9.1	6.5	6.5	6.7	7.9	5.3	6.1
HUMIDITY/%	81	82	78	79	82	83	84	83	83	82	82	82
BLOOM SEASON	*	*	*	*	**	*	*	*	*	*	*	*
DAYS CLR @ 8AM	5	7	9	9	6	4	5	4	5	7	6	6
DAYS CLR @ 2PM	3	1	3	4	2	2	3	2	2	2	2	2
RAIN/MM	122	114	132	147	234	231	165	165	170	201	135	155
°C AVG MAX	29.3	29.8	30.9	31.5	30.9	29.8	29.8	29.8	29.8	30.4	30.4	29.8
°C AVG MIN	20.9	20.9	20.9	21.5	22.0	21.5	21.5	21.5	21.5	21.5	21.5	20.9
DIURNAL RANGE	8.4	8.9	10.0	10.0	8.9	8.3	8.3	8.3	8.3	8.9	8.9	8.9
S/HEMISPHERE	JUL	AUG	SEP	OCT	NOV	DEC	JAN	FEB	MAR	APR	MAY	JUN

Cultural Recommendations

LIGHT: 1000–1200 fc.

TEMPERATURES: Days average 85–89°F (29–32°C), fluctuating only 4°F (2.2°C), and nights average 70–72°F (21–22°C), with a 2°F (1.1°C) seasonal variation. The diurnal range is 15–18°F (8–9°C). This habitat has extremely uniform conditions.

HUMIDITY: 80% year-round.

WATER: Plants should be kept moist throughout the year. Warm water, about 70°F (21°C), is highly recommended. The rainfall pattern is wet year-round.

FERTILIZER: ¼–½ strength, applied weekly to biweekly during the growing season.

REST PERIOD: Growing conditions should be maintained year-round. Days are slightly warmer for 2 months in winter. In the habitat, nighttime lows occasionally drop below 70°F (21°C), but the probable extreme low of 63°F (17°C) should be avoided.

GROWING MEDIA: ½–⅝ in. (12–16 mm) fir bark with moisture-retentive additives, or sphagnum moss with perlite or charcoal added for drainage. Plants may be repotted after flowering or while roots are actively growing.

MISCELLANEOUS NOTES: P. sanderana is adaptable and easily cultivated.

Plant and Flower Information

PLANT SIZE AND TYPE: A moderately sized monopodial epiphyte.

LEAVES: 3–5 per plant. The leaves are 10 in. (25 cm) long, elliptic-oblong, fleshy, and dark green, often with a silvery "bloom" and a purple-brown suffusion.

INFLORESCENCE: 30 in. (76 cm) long. The spikes, usually 2 per year, are purplish and rarely branch.

FLOWERS: Few per inflorescence. The blossoms are 2.75–3.25 in. (7–8 cm) across, round-petaled, and delicately textured. The highly variable color ranges from white to pinkish white or even rose-purple. Markings on the white lip may be cinnamon, yellow, or purple. A pair of long, filamentlike appendages project from the apex of the lip.

HYBRIDIZING NOTES: P. sanderana is a significant parent in the development of modern pink, lavender, and red hybrids. It contributes long, arching flower stems and improves flower form.

REFERENCES: 58, 62, 79, 142, 186, 195, 203, 205, 206, 210, 211.

PHOTOS/DRAWINGS: 58, 62, 79, 134, 142, 144, 186, 195, 210.

Phalaenopsis schillerana Rchb.f.

AKA: Frequently spelled P. schilleriana. We have followed the spelling used by Dr. Sweet. Synonyms include P. curnowiana, P. schillerana var. stuartiana and var. vestalis, and P. vestalis. P. schillerana is known to hybridize with P. aphrodite, producing the natural hybrid P. × leucorrhoda, and with P. equestris, producing the natural hybrid P. × veitchiana.

ORIGIN/HABITAT: The Philippines, on Luzon Island south of Quezon City, and on the eastern shores of adjacent islands. It is found at 0–1500 ft. (0–457 m) growing high on tree trunks and on high branches.

CLIMATE: Station # 98427, Manila, Philippines, Lat. 14.5°N, Long. 121.0°E, at 74 ft. (23 m). Temperatures are calculated for an elevation of 800 ft. (244 m), resulting in probable extremes of 99°F (37.2°C) and 56°F (13.3°C).

N/HEMISPHERE	JAN	FEB	MAR	APR	MAY	JUN	JUL	AUG	SEP	OCT	NOV	DEC
°F AVG MAX	84	86	89	91	91	89	86	85	86	86	85	84
°F AVG MIN	67	67	69	71	73	73	73	73	73	72	70	68
DIURNAL RANGE	17	19	20	20	18	16	13	12	13	14	15	16
RAIN/INCHES	0.9	0.5	0.7	1.3	5.1	10.0	17.0	16.6	14.0	7.6	5.7	2.6
HUMIDITY/%	77	73	70	68	71	81	84	86	87	84	82	89
BLOOM SEASON	**	***	**	*	*	*	*	*		*	*	*
DAYS CLR @ 8AM	6	9	14	14	10	3	2	1	1	6	7	6
DAYS CLR @ 2PM	3	6	10	10	8	2	1	1	0	2	2	3
RAIN/MM	23	13	18	33	130	254	432	422	356	193	145	66
°C AVG MAX	28.7	29.8	31.4	32.6	32.6	31.4	29.8	29.2	29.8	29.8	29.2	28.7
°C AVG MIN	19.2	19.2	20.3	21.4	22.6	22.6	22.6	22.6	22.6	22.0	20.9	19.8
DIURNAL RANGE	9.5	10.6	11.1	11.2	10.0	8.8	7.2	6.6	7.2	7.8	8.3	8.9
S/HEMISPHERE	JUL	AUG	SEP	OCT	NOV	DEC	JAN	FEB	MAR	APR	MAY	JUN

Cultural Recommendations

LIGHT: 1000–1200 fc. Morning light is preferred.

TEMPERATURES: Summer days average 84–91 °F (29–33 °C), and nights average 71–73 °F (21–23 °C), with a diurnal range of 12–16 °F (7–9 °C).

HUMIDITY: 80% during warm weather.

WATER: Plants should be kept moist during the growing season. The rainfall pattern is wet/dry.

FERTILIZER: ¼–½ strength, applied weekly to biweekly during the growing season.

REST PERIOD: Winter days average 84–89 °F (29–31 °C), and nights average 67–71 °F (19–21 °C), resulting in an increased diurnal range of 15–20 °F (8–11 °C). Light may be increased, since clear days in the habitat are more frequent in winter. Fertilizer should be eliminated when the plants are not actively growing.

Climate records indicate a winter dry period of 2–3 months. In the habitat, winter humidity is lower but still high enough to indicate frequent fog and low clouds. Leaves should not be allowed to desiccate. Fertilizer should be reduced or eliminated, and water should be limited to occasional misting. Blooming occurs during the cooler, drier period with higher light.

GROWING MEDIA: ½–⅝ in. (12–16 mm) fir bark. Plants are best repotted after flowering, while the flat, rough-textured roots are actively growing.

MISCELLANEOUS NOTES: *P. schillerana* is an adaptable species which is easily cultivated. It will not grow or flower in the coastal lowlands of Malaya but grows in the slightly cooler temperatures found at elevations of 1000–2000 ft. (305–610 m). Distinct seasonal temperature fluctuations or a wider diurnal range are necessary, since the plant does not survive constant warm temperatures.

Plant and Flower Information

PLANT SIZE AND TYPE: A moderately sized to large monopodial epiphyte.

LEAVES: 3–5 per plant. The leaves are 6–18 in. (15–46 cm) long, dull, dark green mottled with greyish white, and marked with purple on the underside.

INFLORESCENCE: 36 in. (91 cm) long. Plants may produce 2–3 spikes per year. The inflorescences are erect and branching and droop at the apex. Flowers are arranged in 2 rows along each branch.

FLOWERS: Many. It is not unusual for a plant to have 100 flowers, and one plant had 733, with 400 blossoms on a single spike. The blooms are 3.0–3.5 in. (8–9 cm) across, often smaller if very numerous. They are fragrant and last several weeks. Wide-petaled and delicately textured, the sepals and petals may be white, pale rose, lilac-pink, or deep rose-purple with white at the edges. The white lip is anchor-shaped, and the magenta sidelobes have carmine dots. The flowers are variable in color and form.

HYBRIDIZING NOTES: Used in many pink hybrids, *P. schillerana* contributes branching, fair-to-heavy flower substance, large flower size, and floriferousness.

REFERENCES: 2, 11, 14, 51, 62, 111, 112, 116, 142, 148, 186, 195, 203, 206, 210, 211.

PHOTOS/DRAWINGS: *11, 14, 26, 62, 111, 142, 144, 186, 195, 210,* 211.

Phalaenopsis serpentilingua. Now considered a synonym of *Paraphalaenopsis serpentilingua.* REFERENCES: 195.

Phalaenopsis simonsei. Now considered a synonym of *Paraphalaenopsis serpentilingua.* REFERENCES: 195.

Phalaenopsis speciosa Rchb.f.

AKA: *P. imperati, P. speciosa* var. *maculata, P. tetraspis. P. barrii* is a synonym for *P. speciosa* var. *tetraspis.*

ORIGIN/HABITAT: Endemic to Nicobar Island, it grew on mangroves in muddy swamps. Plants hung from large branches just a few feet above freshwater creeks, fully exposed. The localized population was decimated by overcollecting, and all records are historical. Dr. Sweet was unable to locate any specimens in cultivation, and the plant may be extinct.

CLIMATE: Station # 43367, Car Nicobar, Nicobar, Lat. 9.0 °N, Long. 92.9 °E, at 47 ft. (14 m). The record high is 95 °F (35.0 °C), and the record low is 66 °F (18.9 °C).

N/HEMISPHERE	JAN	FEB	MAR	APR	MAY	JUN	JUL	AUG	SEP	OCT	NOV	DEC
°F AVG MAX	86	87	89	90	87	86	86	86	86	85	85	85
°F AVG MIN	77	77	77	77	77	78	77	77	76	75	76	77
DIURNAL RANGE	9	10	12	13	10	8	9	9	10	10	9	8
RAIN/INCHES	3.9	1.2	2.1	3.5	12.5	12.4	9.3	10.2	12.9	11.6	11.4	7.8
HUMIDITY/%	78	77	78	81	89	88	88	89	90	92	88	81
BLOOM SEASON						*	*	*	*	*	*	
DAYS CLR	N/A											
RAIN/MM	99	30	53	89	318	315	236	259	328	295	290	198
°C AVG MAX	30.0	30.6	31.7	32.2	30.6	30.0	30.0	30.0	30.0	29.4	29.4	29.4
°C AVG MIN	25.0	25.0	25.0	25.0	25.0	25.6	25.0	25.0	24.4	23.9	24.4	25.0
DIURNAL RANGE	5.0	5.6	6.7	7.2	5.6	4.4	5.0	5.0	5.6	5.5	5.0	4.4
S/HEMISPHERE	JUL	AUG	SEP	OCT	NOV	DEC	JAN	FEB	MAR	APR	MAY	JUN

Cultural Recommendations

LIGHT: 1000–1200 fc.

TEMPERATURES: Summer days average 85–90°F (29–32°C), and nights average 75–78°F (24–26°C), with a diurnal range of 8–13°F (4–7°C). The average highs vary only 5°F (2.8°C), and average lows fluctuate only 3°F (1.7°C) throughout the year.

HUMIDITY: 80–90%.

WATER: Plants would require constant moisture, and warm water, 70°F (21°C), could be very important. The rainfall pattern is wet/dry. The late-winter dry period is very brief.

FERTILIZER: ¼–½ strength, applied weekly to biweekly during the growing season.

REST PERIOD: In cultivation, water, humidity, and fertilizer would probably need to be reduced for 2–3 months. Average daytime temperatures in winter could be raised slightly to produce a small increase in diurnal range.

GROWING MEDIA: ½–⅝ in. (12–16 mm) fir bark would probably be a good choice. Repotting would best be done when roots begin actively growing.

MISCELLANEOUS NOTES: Since *P. speciosa* grew in such a limited area, any plants that may be rediscovered could prove difficult to cultivate for an extended period.

Plant and Flower Information

PLANT SIZE AND TYPE: A moderately sized monopodial epiphyte.

LEAVES: Usually 3 per plant. The leaves, which were 6–12 in. (15–30 cm) long, were bright yellow-green and somewhat recurved.

INFLORESCENCE: 6 ft. (2 m) long. The spikes, often more than one, were drooping and usually branched when mature.

FLOWERS: 9–12. The blooms, which opened sequentially, were 2 in. (5 cm) across and so fragrant they would scent an entire greenhouse. Flowers were described as handsome and star-shaped, with highly variable color, most commonly amethyst-purple with pale margins. No 2 plants produced flowers which were quite the same, and even blossoms on the same inflorescence often differed from one another.

HYBRIDIZING NOTES: N/A.

REFERENCES: 20, 112, 183, 185, 195, 205, 211.

PHOTOS/DRAWINGS: 20, *183*, *185*, *195*, 211.

Phalaenopsis stobartiana Rchb.f.

AKA: *P. hainanensis.* This species was once considered a variety of *P. wightii*.

ORIGIN/HABITAT: China, in the Pai Sha District. It is also found in the Patkai Mountain range in Burma, near the Indian border. The plant prefers warm, dense forests at about 300 ft. (91 m), where it grows on large tree branches overhanging streams, a very small ecological niche. The following climate information may be used as a starting point, but the recorded extremes may not apply.

CLIMATE: Station # 48008, Myitkyina, Burma, Lat. 25.4°N, Long. 97.4°E, at 472 ft. (144 m). The record high is 110°F (43.3°C), and the record low is 40°F (4.4°C).

N/HEMISPHERE	JAN	FEB	MAR	APR	MAY	JUN	JUL	AUG	SEP	OCT	NOV	DEC
°F AVG MAX	75	78	86	90	91	88	87	87	88	86	81	76
°F AVG MIN	50	55	61	68	72	75	76	76	75	70	61	52
DIURNAL RANGE	25	23	25	22	19	13	11	11	13	16	20	24
RAIN/INCHES	0.4	0.9	0.9	1.8	6.3	18.9	18.8	17.1	10.1	7.2	1.5	0.5
HUMIDITY/%	75	72	66	62	70	83	86	88	84	86	82	80
BLOOM SEASON							**					
DAYS CLR @ 6AM	17	14	13	9	5	2	0	1	2	7	13	14
DAYS CLR @ 12PM	23	18	17	11	6	2	0	1	4	9	20	22
DAYS CLR @ 6PM	22	15	16	11	6	2	1	2	5	11	19	25
RAIN/MM	10	23	23	46	160	480	478	434	257	183	38	13
°C AVG MAX	23.9	25.6	30.0	32.2	32.8	31.1	30.6	30.6	31.1	30.0	27.2	24.4
°C AVG MIN	10.0	12.8	16.1	20.0	22.2	23.9	24.4	24.4	23.9	21.1	16.1	11.1
DIURNAL RANGE	13.9	12.8	13.9	12.2	10.6	7.2	6.2	6.2	7.2	8.9	11.1	13.3
S/HEMISPHERE	JUL	AUG	SEP	OCT	NOV	DEC	JAN	FEB	MAR	APR	MAY	JUN

Cultural Recommendations

LIGHT: 800–1200 fc.

TEMPERATURES: Summer days average 86–91°F (30–33°C), and nights average 70–76°F (21–24°C), with a diurnal range of 11–19°F (6–11°C). The record high of 110°F (43°C) indicates that this species may tolerate hot summer weather.

HUMIDITY: 70–80%.

WATER: Plants should be kept moist during the growing season. The rainfall pattern is wet/dry, but humidity is high throughout the year, indicating that moisture is available in the form of dew, mist, and fog.

FERTILIZER: ¼–½ strength. It should be applied at least weekly during the growing season. The relatively short growing season suggests fairly rapid growth, so frequent applications could be beneficial.

REST PERIOD: For 2–4 months in winter, days average 75–86°F (24–30°C), and nights average 50–61°F (10–16°C), with an increased diurnal range of 20–25°F (11–14°C). Light levels could be increased to simulate the nearly continuous clear weather in winter. Plants may be misted or lightly watered occasionally, but they will not tolerate excess water when cool. Early morning misting simulates the nightly dew in the habitat and helps maintain humidity. Fertilizer may be eliminated.

GROWING MEDIA: ½–⅝ in. (12–16 mm) fir bark. Plants are best repotted as new growth begins, immediately after the rest period.

MISCELLANEOUS NOTES: Summer flowering is probably initiated by warmer spring temperatures and increased moisture.

Plant and Flower Information

PLANT SIZE AND TYPE: A small monopodial epiphyte consisting mostly of roots.

LEAVES: Number unknown. The leaves are usually 4 in. (10 cm) long but often smaller. In nature, the leaves are usually deciduous and often absent during the flowering period. Plant health improves and blooming increases if conditions in cultivation are sufficiently moderate to keep the leaves evergreen.

INFLORESCENCE: 8 in. (20 cm) long. The spikes are generally arching to pendent. Though most often simple, they may branch once.

FLOWERS: Few to many. The blossoms are 1.0–1.5 in. (2.5–3.8 cm) across, which is very large in relation to plant size. The flowers are star-shaped, delicately textured, and normally apple-green changing to yellow-green with age. The lip is marked with bright amethyst.

HYBRIDIZING NOTES: N/A.

REFERENCES: 195.

PHOTOS/DRAWINGS: *195.*

Phalaenopsis stuartiana Rchb.f.

AKA: *P. schillerana* var. *alba*, var. *stuartiana*, and var. *vestalis*.

ORIGIN/HABITAT: In the Philippines, it grows on north and northeast Mindanao Island near Lake Maynit, in Agusan and Surigao Provinces, and in the Talacogon and Agusan Valleys. It is usually found near water, often close enough to the ocean to be sprayed with salt water, though elevations cover the range 0–1500 ft. (0–457 m).

CLIMATE: Station # 98653, Surigao, Philippines, Lat. 9.8°N, Long. 125.5°E, at 72 ft. (22 m). Temperatures are calculated for an elevation of 800 ft. (244 m), resulting in probable extremes of 97°F (36.1°C) and 63°F (17.2°C).

N/HEMISPHERE	JAN	FEB	MAR	APR	MAY	JUN	JUL	AUG	SEP	OCT	NOV	DEC
°F AVG MAX	81	82	83	85	87	87	87	87	87	87	84	82
°F AVG MIN	70	70	71	71	72	72	72	73	73	72	72	71
DIURNAL RANGE	11	12	12	14	15	15	15	14	14	14	12	11
RAIN/INCHES	21.4	14.8	19.9	10.0	6.2	4.9	7.0	5.1	6.6	10.7	16.8	24.4
HUMIDITY/%	91	90	88	85	85	82	83	82	83	84	88	89
BLOOM SEASON	*	**	**	*	*		*	*	*		*	*
DAYS CLR @ 8AM	1	1	2	4	2	3	2	2	1	2	1	1
DAYS CLR @ 2PM	1	2	2	6	3	1	2	1	2	3	1	1
RAIN/MM	544	376	505	254	157	124	178	130	168	272	427	620
°C AVG MAX	27.0	27.6	28.1	29.2	30.3	30.3	30.3	30.3	30.3	29.8	28.7	27.6
°C AVG MIN	20.9	20.9	21.4	21.4	22.0	22.0	22.0	22.6	22.6	22.0	22.0	21.4
DIURNAL RANGE	6.1	6.7	6.7	7.8	8.3	8.3	8.3	7.7	7.7	7.8	6.7	6.2
S/HEMISPHERE	JUL	AUG	SEP	OCT	NOV	DEC	JAN	FEB	MAR	APR	MAY	JUN

Cultural Recommendations

LIGHT: 1000–1200 fc.

TEMPERATURES: Summer days average 85–87°F (29–30°C), and nights average 71–73°F (21–23°C), with a diurnal range of 14–15°F (8°C).

HUMIDITY: 80–90% year-round.

WATER: Plants should be kept constantly moist, and warm water is recommended. The rainfall pattern is wet/wetter.

FERTILIZER: ¼–½ strength, applied weekly to biweekly during the growing season.

REST PERIOD: Winter days are cooler, averaging 81–85 °F (27–29 °C), while nights average 70–72 °F (21–22 °C), resulting in a slightly decreased diurnal range of 11–14 °F (6–8 °C). The record low is only 62 °F (17 °C), and extremes should normally be avoided. However, local aspects of the microclimate where *P. stuartiana* is found may result in lower temperatures than those indicated; or the species may be somewhat adaptable to cooler winter temperatures, since plants are known to grow and bloom for years in cultivation with winter temperatures of 60–65 °F (16–18 °C). Plants should be kept moist. The heaviest rainfall occurs in winter, but in cultivation watering probably should not be increased. Light in the habitat is slightly lower in winter.

GROWING MEDIA: ½–⅝ in. (12–16 mm) fir bark with moisture-retentive additives, or sphagnum moss with perlite or charcoal added for drainage. Plants are best repotted after blooming, while roots are actively growing.

MISCELLANEOUS NOTES: *P. stuartiana* is generally considered easy to cultivate when growing conditions are appropriate. It is difficult to grow in Singapore, which is only slightly warmer, but with extra care it will grow and bloom in warmer climates. Mature plants will occasionally grow keikis on undisturbed roots that have become permanently attached to a slab or a greenhouse bench.

Plant and Flower Information

PLANT SIZE AND TYPE: A moderately sized to large monopodial epiphyte.

LEAVES: 3–5 per plant. The leaves are 12–18 in. (30–46 cm) long and flaccid. Silvery grey on top, they are magenta on the underside.

INFLORESCENCE: 24 in. (61 cm) long. The plants usually produce 2 or more spikes per year. The inflorescences are purplish, arching, and branching.

FLOWERS: Many, sometimes hundreds. The flowers are usually 2–4 in. (5–10 cm) across but are variable in size, since the size declines as the number of flowers increases. Slightly fragrant and long-lasting, they have wide petals with a delicate substance. The blossoms are white to cream with a sulfur-yellow lip. The lower half of the sepals and horned lip are speckled with purple. One specimen plant had 650 blossoms on 10 inflorescences.

HYBRIDIZING NOTES: *P. stuartiana* is used in pink hybrids to contribute floriferousness, fine form, attractive spacing, spotting, long flower stems, and a beautifully patterned lip. The delicate substance is recessive and can be improved.

REFERENCES: 2, 11, 14, 62, 74, 81, 112, 142, 148, 174, 186, 195, 203, 205, 206, 210, 211.

PHOTOS/DRAWINGS: *11, 14, 28, 62, 74, 88, 142, 186, 195, 210.*

Phalaenopsis sumatrana Korth and Rchb.f.

AKA: *P. acutifolia, P. zebrina. P. sumatrana* var. *sanguinea* is now known as *P. corningiana. P. sumatrana* is known to cross-pollinate with *P. violacea,* producing the natural hybrid *P.* × *gersenii.*

ORIGIN/HABITAT: Malaysia, Java, Borneo, Thailand, and Sumatra. It grows on trees and in shady nooks near streams, and it thrives in the warm climate of Singapore.

CLIMATE: Station # 48674, Mersing, Malaya, Lat. 2.5 °N, Long. 103.8 °E, at 151 ft. (46 m). The record high is 99 °F (37.2 °C), and the record low is 68 °F (20.0 °C).

N/HEMISPHERE	JAN	FEB	MAR	APR	MAY	JUN	JUL	AUG	SEP	OCT	NOV	DEC
°F AVG MAX	82	83	86	89	90	89	88	87	87	87	86	82
°F AVG MIN	74	74	74	73	73	72	72	72	72	72	72	73
DIURNAL RANGE	8	9	12	16	17	17	16	15	15	15	14	9
RAIN/INCHES	14.4	6.3	6.1	4.6	7.1	5.1	5.6	6.7	9.3	9.9	13.4	24.3
HUMIDITY/%	82	82	81	82	83	83	84	84	84	84	85	86
BLOOM SEASON		*	*	*	**	*	*	*	*	*	*	
DAYS CLR @ 7AM	0	0	1	3	2	2	3	2	1	0	1	1
DAYS CLR @ 1PM	0	0	1	2	1	1	1	0	1	0	0	0
RAIN/MM	366	160	155	117	180	130	142	170	236	251	340	617
°C AVG MAX	27.8	28.3	30.0	31.7	32.2	31.7	31.1	30.6	30.6	30.6	30.0	27.8
°C AVG MIN	23.3	23.3	23.3	22.8	22.8	22.2	22.2	22.2	22.2	22.2	22.2	22.8
DIURNAL RANGE	4.5	5.0	6.7	8.9	9.4	9.5	8.9	8.4	8.4	8.4	7.8	5.0
S/HEMISPHERE	JUL	AUG	SEP	OCT	NOV	DEC	JAN	FEB	MAR	APR	MAY	JUN

Cultural Recommendations

LIGHT: 800–1000 fc. *P. sumatrana* does not tolerate direct sun.

TEMPERATURES: Summer days average 87–90 °F (31–32 °C), and nights average 72–73 °F (22–23 °C), with a diurnal range of 15–17 °F (8–9 °C). The diurnal range is greatest in the summer, the result of warmer days rather than cooler nights.

HUMIDITY: 80% year-round.

WATER: Plants should be kept moist year-round. Warm water is highly recommended. The rainfall pattern is wet/wetter.

FERTILIZER: ¼–½ strength, applied weekly to biweekly during the growing season.

REST PERIOD: Winter days average 82–86 °F (28–30 °C), and nights average 73–74 °F (23 °C). Lows vary only 2 °F (1 °C) throughout the year. The winter diurnal range of 8–12 °F (4–7 °C) is narrower. Plants should be kept moist but fertilizer reduced when plants are not actively growing. Light should not be increased.

GROWING MEDIA: ½–⅝ in. (12–16 mm) fir bark with moisture-retentive additives, or sphagnum moss with perlite or charcoal added for drainage. Repotting is best done while plants are actively growing.

MISCELLANEOUS NOTES: *P. sumatrana* is a robust grower. Flowering is reportedly induced by seasonal variations in light levels.

Plant and Flower Information

PLANT SIZE AND TYPE: A large monopodial epiphyte.

LEAVES: 3–5 per plant. The leaves are 6–12 in. (15–30 cm) in nature but may be smaller in cultivation. They are bright green, fleshy, oblong, and pendent.

INFLORESCENCE: 12 in. (30 cm) long. The spikes, usually 2, are erect to arching. The well-spaced flowers face in all directions.

FLOWERS: 5–10. The blossoms are 2.5–3.0 in. (6.0–7.6 cm) across, spreading, star-shaped, and cream, white, or yellow with purplish markings. The lip is edged with brown and has purple stripes on the midlobe. Flower size, color, and markings are variable.

HYBRIDIZING NOTES: As a parent, *P. sumatrana* contributes peppermint stripes (a latent characteristic), enhances reds, and increases the number of star-shaped flowers.

REFERENCES: 2, 14, 19, 29, 64, 66, 71, 81, 105, 112, 118, 130, 134, 148, 190, 195, 205, 211.

PHOTOS/DRAWINGS: *19, 29, 64, 65, 66, 71, 99,* 105, 134, *190, 195.*

Phalaenopsis tetraspis. See *P. speciosa.* REFERENCES: 195.

Phalaenopsis × thorntonii. Now considered a synonym of *Paraphalaenopsis × thorntonii.* REFERENCES: 195.

Phalaenopsis × veitchiana Rchb.f. A natural hybrid between *P. equestris* and *P. schillerana.* REFERENCES: 195.

Phalaenopsis venosa Shim and Fowlie

AKA: N/A.

ORIGIN/HABITAT: Central Sulawesi (Celebes) Island, Indonesia, Lat. 1.5 °S, Long. 120.5 °E. It is found growing on trees at approximately 3000 ft. (914 m). No weather records are available for the central part of the island. The following climate is for northern Sulawesi, so rainfall and sky-cover data are rough approximations only.

CLIMATE: Station # 97014, Manado, Sulawesi, Lat. 1.5 °N, Long. 124.9 °E, at 264 ft. (80 m). Temperatures are calculated for an elevation of 3000 ft. (914 m), resulting in probable extremes of 88 °F (31.1 °C) and 56 °F (13.3 °C).

N/HEMISPHERE	JAN	FEB	MAR	APR	MAY	JUN	JUL	AUG	SEP	OCT	NOV	DEC
°F AVG MAX	76	76	76	77	78	78	78	80	80	80	78	77
°F AVG MIN	64	64	64	64	65	64	64	64	64	63	64	65
DIURNAL RANGE	12	12	12	13	13	14	14	16	16	17	14	12
RAIN/INCHES	18.6	13.8	12.2	8.0	6.4	6.5	4.8	4.0	3.4	4.9	8.9	14.7
HUMIDITY/%	84	83	83	83	81	80	75	72	75	77	82	83
BLOOM SEASON								*	*	**	*	
DAYS CLR @ 8AM	4	3	6	11	11	12	12	12	14	17	12	8
DAYS CLR @ 2PM	1	1	1	2	1	3	3	4	4	4	1	1
RAIN/MM	472	351	310	203	163	165	122	102	86	124	226	373
°C AVG MAX	24.4	24.4	24.4	25.0	25.5	25.5	25.5	26.7	26.7	26.7	25.5	25.0
°C AVG MIN	17.8	17.8	17.8	17.8	18.3	17.8	17.8	17.8	17.8	17.2	17.8	18.3
DIURNAL RANGE	6.6	6.6	6.6	7.2	7.2	7.7	7.7	8.9	8.9	9.5	7.7	6.7
S/HEMISPHERE	JUL	AUG	SEP	OCT	NOV	DEC	JAN	FEB	MAR	APR	MAY	JUN

Cultural Recommendations

LIGHT: 800–1200 fc. Morning light is preferred as the habitat is usually overcast in the afternoon.

TEMPERATURES: Summer days average 78–80 °F (26–27 °C), and nights average 64–65 °F (18 °C), with a diurnal range of 14–17 °F (8–9 °C). The plant is not heat tolerant and could be difficult to cultivate in hot climates. Weather in this habitat is moderate year-round, and the record high is only a few degrees above the average high.

HUMIDITY: 75–85%.

WATER: Plants should be kept moist year-round. The rainfall pattern is wet/wetter.

FERTILIZER: ¼–½ strength, applied weekly to biweekly during the growing season.

REST PERIOD: Winter days average 76–78°F (24–25°C), and nights average 63–65°F (17–18°C), with a diurnal range of 12–17°F (7–9°C). Plants should be kept moist. In the habitat, rainfall is heaviest in winter; but increasing water could be detrimental in cultivation, particularly if temperatures are too cool. Weather in this habitat is moderate year-round, and the record low is just a few degrees below the average low.

GROWING MEDIA: ½–⅝ in. (12–16 mm) fir bark with moisture-retentive additives, or sphagnum moss with perlite or charcoal added for drainage. Plants are best repotted in spring rather than after flowering.

MISCELLANEOUS NOTES: *P. venosa* is frequently cultivated as *P. psilantha* due to an error in identification when the plants were introduced.

Plant and Flower Information

PLANT SIZE AND TYPE: A moderately sized monopodial epiphyte.

LEAVES: 3–5 per plant. The variable leaves are 4-10 in. (10–25 cm) long, elliptic, slightly wavy, and strongly recurved.

INFLORESCENCE: 5–7 in. (13–18 cm) long. The spikes are erect, simple, and loosely flowered.

FLOWERS: 3–5 per plant. The blossoms, which are 1.5–2.0 in. (4–5 cm) across, open in succession; often several are open at a time. The heavy textured, spreading, star-shaped sepals and petals are white on the backside and yellow to beige on the front. Red blotches overlie the yellow and sometimes merge to make the sepals and petals appear entirely red except for yellowish margins and white centers. The white lip is flushed with pink.

HYBRIDIZING NOTES: *P. venosa* is used to breed for red hybrids.

REFERENCES: 170, 176.

PHOTOS/DRAWINGS: *99, 170, 176.*

Phalaenopsis vestalis. See *P. schillerana.* REFERENCES: 195.

Phalaenopsis violacea Witte

AKA: N/A

ORIGIN/HABITAT: Borneo, Sumatra, and Malaya. It usually grows on shady trees near lowland rivers, sometimes with *P. sumatrana.*

CLIMATE: Station # 48674, Mersing, Malaya, Lat. 2.5°N, Long. 103.8°E, at 151 ft. (46 m). The record high is 99°F (37.2°C), and the record low is 68°F (20.0°C).

N/HEMISPHERE	JAN	FEB	MAR	APR	MAY	JUN	JUL	AUG	SEP	OCT	NOV	DEC
°F AVG MAX	82	83	86	89	90	89	88	87	87	87	86	82
°F AVG MIN	74	74	74	73	73	72	72	72	72	72	72	73
DIURNAL RANGE	8	9	12	16	17	17	16	15	15	15	14	9
RAIN/INCHES	14.4	6.3	6.1	4.6	7.1	5.1	5.6	6.7	9.3	9.9	13.4	24.3
HUMIDITY/%	82	82	81	82	83	83	84	84	84	84	85	86
BLOOM SEASON					*	*	*	**	**	**	*	
DAYS CLR @ 7AM	0	0	1	3	2	2	3	2	1	0	1	1
DAYS CLR @ 1PM	0	0	1	2	1	1	1	0	1	0	0	0
RAIN/MM	366	160	155	117	180	130	142	170	236	251	340	617
°C AVG MAX	27.8	28.3	30.0	31.7	32.2	31.7	31.1	30.6	30.6	30.6	30.0	27.8
°C AVG MIN	23.3	23.3	23.3	22.8	22.8	22.2	22.2	22.2	22.2	22.2	22.2	22.8
DIURNAL RANGE	4.5	5.0	6.7	8.9	9.4	9.5	8.9	8.4	8.4	8.4	7.8	5.0
S/HEMISPHERE	JUL	AUG	SEP	OCT	NOV	DEC	JAN	FEB	MAR	APR	MAY	JUN

Cultural Recommendations

LIGHT: 1000–1200 fc. Direct sun should be avoided.

TEMPERATURES: Summer days average 87–90°F (31–32°C), and nights average 72–73°F (22–23°C), with a diurnal range of 15–17°F (8–9°C).

HUMIDITY: 80–85%.

WATER: Plants should be kept moist. Warm water is highly recommended. The rainfall pattern is wet/very wet.

FERTILIZER: ¼–½ strength, applied weekly to biweekly during the growing season.

REST PERIOD: A 3-month gentle winter is indicated. Days average 82–86°F (28–30°C), and nights average 73–74°F (23°C), with a diurnal range of 8–12°F (4–7°C). Winters are very wet, but excess moisture is harmful in cultivation, particularly if temperatures are somewhat cool. In the habitat, clear days are rare in winter, but at 2.5° north of the equator, seasonal light variations are minor.

GROWING MEDIA: Plants may be mounted on a coconut husk or tree-fern slab if high humidity can be maintained. For potted plants, ½–⅝ in. (12–16 mm) fir bark or sphagnum moss with perlite or charcoal added for drainage are suggested media. Plants are best repotted in early spring.

MISCELLANEOUS NOTES: *P. violacea* requires a warm, humid environment but is somewhat adaptable to gradual changes.

Plant and Flower Information

PLANT SIZE AND TYPE: A moderately sized monopodial epiphyte.

LEAVES: 3–5 per plant. The leaves are 6–12 in. (15–30 cm) long, shiny, fleshy, and ovoid. They are pale to dark green depending on the light and may be leathery with inadequate water or in high light.

INFLORESCENCE: Variable in length. The spikes, usually 2, are zigzag, horizontal, non-branching, and evergreen. They continue to produce flowers for years. Plants may bloom more than once a year.

FLOWERS: 1–5 per inflorescence. The blossoms are 2–3 in. (5.0–7.6 cm) across depending on the variety and open in succession, with rarely more than 2 open at a time. The flowers are fragrant, star-shaped, and waxy. Normally they are creamy green with violet flecks, though in rare cases they are white. The lip is magenta.

HYBRIDIZING NOTES: As a parent, *P. violacea* improves color and flower substance but decreases the size and number of flowers and inflorescence length. It is used for reds and for peppermint stripes (a latent characteristic). This plant is always best as a pod parent.

Two races of *P. violacea* are recognized. Plants from Sumatra-Malaya are smaller, with leaves 6–9 in. (15–23 cm) long and flowers only 2 in. (5 cm) across but more highly colored. This plant breeds easily. Plants from Borneo have leaves up to 12 in. (30 cm) long and flowers up to 3 in. (7.6 cm) across. The Borneo race is a most reluctant breeder. When crosses are successful, however, it produces better hybrids than the Sumatra-Malaya form. Hybrid colors tend to fade unless diploid clones are used.

REFERENCES: 2, 14, 22, 42, 73, 79, 80, 105, 111, 112, 118, 148, 188, 195, 205, 206, 210, 211.

PHOTOS/DRAWINGS: *14, 42, 73, 79,* 105, 118, *188, 195,* 205, *210,* 211.

Phalaenopsis viridis J. J. Smith

AKA: *P. forbesii.*

ORIGIN/HABITAT: Sumatra. It is found at 2600 ft. (792 m), usually on limestone rocks or low on tree trunks in dark nooks, sometimes with *P. fimbriata*. Unlike *P. fimbriata*, it dies quickly at higher elevations but grows well in lower, warmer climates.

CLIMATE: Station # 96035, Medan, Indonesia, Lat. 3.6°N, Long. 98.7°E, at 87 ft. (27 m). Temperatures are calculated for an elevation of 1300 ft. (396 m), resulting in probable extremes of 95°F (35.0°C) and 56°F (13.3°C).

N/HEMISPHERE	JAN	FEB	MAR	APR	MAY	JUN	JUL	AUG	SEP	OCT	NOV	DEC
°F AVG MAX	81	83	84	85	85	85	85	85	84	82	82	81
°F AVG MIN	67	67	68	69	69	68	68	68	68	68	68	68
DIURNAL RANGE	14	16	16	16	16	17	17	17	16	14	14	13
RAIN/INCHES	5.4	3.6	4.1	5.2	6.9	5.2	5.3	7.0	8.3	10.2	9.7	9.0
HUMIDITY/%	80	79	78	78	79	78	79	79	81	83	83	82
BLOOM SEASON				*								
DAYS CLR @ 7AM	4	2	2	2	2	2	2	0	0	0	1	1
DAYS CLR @ 1PM	0	1	0	0	1	0	2	1	0	0	0	0
RAIN/MM	137	91	104	132	175	132	135	178	211	259	246	229
°C AVG MAX	27.2	28.3	28.9	29.4	29.4	29.4	29.4	29.4	28.9	27.8	27.8	27.2
°C AVG MIN	19.4	19.4	20.0	20.6	20.6	20.0	20.0	20.0	20.0	20.0	20.0	20.0
DIURNAL RANGE	7.8	8.9	8.9	8.8	8.8	9.4	9.4	9.4	8.9	7.8	7.8	7.2
S/HEMISPHERE	JUL	AUG	SEP	OCT	NOV	DEC	JAN	FEB	MAR	APR	MAY	JUN

Cultural Recommendations

LIGHT: 800–1000 fc. Plants prefer a dark nook.

TEMPERATURES: Days average 84–85°F (29°C), and nights average 67–69°F (19–21°C), with a summer diurnal range of 16–17°F (9°C). Average lows vary only 2°F (1°C) year-round.

HUMIDITY: 75-80%.

WATER: Plants should be kept moist all year. Warm water is highly recommended. The rainfall pattern is wet/wetter.

FERTILIZER: ¼–½ strength, applied weekly to biweekly during the growing season.

REST PERIOD: Winter days average 81–84°F (27–29°C), and nights average 67–68°F (19–20°C), with a diurnal range of 13–16°F (7–9°C). In the habitat, the cloud cover is reduced for about 3 months, resulting in somewhat higher winter light levels. Humidity levels should be high, and the plants should be kept moist throughout the year.

GROWING MEDIA: ½–⅝ in. (12–16 mm) fir bark or sphagnum moss with perlite or charcoal added. Limestone may be added if warm water is used. Repotting may be done anytime growth is evident.

MISCELLANEOUS NOTES: Reports indicate that the plant's erratic flowering is not initiated by rain cycles, light patterns, or cooler nights during the rest period. The situation is similar for species in other genera originating in this area. The following technique is effective for them and may work with *P. viridis* when flowering is a problem.

The plants are subjected to a sudden daytime cooling of about 10 °F (5.6 °C), such as the temperature drop associated with a cool summer shower or with misting in a warm greenhouse. Temperature drops are most dramatic in the warmest weather, when humidity is lowest and the cooling effects of rapid evaporation are greatest. In other species, the flowers emerge a given number of days following this stimulus if the plants have sufficient energy to produce blooms. There is no assurance that this method will initiate flowering in *P. viridis*, but experimenting with it will not harm the plant.

Plant and Flower Information

PLANT SIZE AND TYPE: A moderately sized monopodial epiphyte or lithophyte.

LEAVES: 3–5 per plant. The leaves are 12 in. (30 cm) long, ovate, flat, shiny, and somewhat leathery.

INFLORESCENCE: 16 in. (41 cm). The 1 or 2 loosely flowered spikes are usually simple but may branch.

FLOWERS: Usually about 7 are open at one time. The blooms are 1.5 in. (4 cm) across, fleshy, spreading, and star-shaped. The sepals and petals have somewhat incurved margins and are greenish yellow marked with reddish brown blotches. The lip and column are white with violet stripes and a yellow callus.

HYBRIDIZING NOTES: N/A.

REFERENCES: 30, 68, 174, 193, 195, 208.

PHOTOS/DRAWINGS: *30, 68, 193, 195, 208.*

Phalaenopsis wightii. Now considered a synonym of *Kingidium deliciosum.* REFERENCES: 195.

Phalaenopsis wightii var. *stobartiana.* See *P. stobartiana.* REFERENCES: 195.

Phalaenopsis wilsonii Rolfe

AKA: N/A.

ORIGIN/HABITAT: Szechuan and Yunnan Provinces of western China, eastern Tibet, and the Likiang snow range and Yangtze watershed at 4920–7052 ft. (1500–2150 m).

CLIMATE: Station # 56739, Teng-Chung, China, Lat. 25.1 °N, Long. 98.5 °E, at 5340 ft. (1628 m). The record high is 84 °F (28.9 °C), and the record low is 25 °F (-3.9 °C).

N/HEMISPHERE	JAN	FEB	MAR	APR	MAY	JUN	JUL	AUG	SEP	OCT	NOV	DEC
°F AVG MAX	63	64	73	75	75	73	75	76	77	72	68	64
°F AVG MIN	32	35	41	49	55	63	64	63	57	53	40	35
DIURNAL RANGE	31	29	32	26	20	10	11	13	20	19	28	29
RAIN/INCHES	0.5	1.6	1.4	2.7	5.1	9.3	12.3	11.1	6.4	6.2	1.6	0.9
HUMIDITY/%	68	64	61	68	78	88	89	87	84	84	75	73
BLOOM SEASON			*									
DAYS CLR @ 7AM	23	17	22	12	5	1	0	1	3	8	22	22
DAYS CLR @ 1PM	20	9	15	6	3	2	0	1	1	7	17	21
RAIN/MM	13	41	36	69	130	236	312	282	163	157	41	23
°C AVG MAX	17.2	17.8	22.8	23.9	23.9	22.8	23.9	24.4	25.0	22.2	20.0	17.8
°C AVG MIN	0.0	1.7	5.0	9.4	12.8	17.2	17.8	17.2	13.9	11.7	4.4	1.7
DIURNAL RANGE	17.2	16.1	17.8	14.5	11.1	5.6	6.1	7.2	11.1	10.5	15.6	16.1
S/HEMISPHERE	JUL	AUG	SEP	OCT	NOV	DEC	JAN	FEB	MAR	APR	MAY	JUN

Cultural Recommendations

LIGHT: 800–1200 fc. Skies are generally overcast during the summer growing season.

TEMPERATURES: Summer days average 73–77 °F (23–25 °C), while nights average 57–63 °F (14–17 °C), with a diurnal range of 10–20 °F (6–11 °C). With a record high of 84 °F (29 °C) in its natural habitat, *P. wilsonii* is probably intolerant of hot summer weather.

HUMIDITY: 80–90% during summer.

WATER: Plants should be kept moist during the growing season. The rainfall pattern is wet/dry.

FERTILIZER: ¼–½ strength, applied weekly to biweekly during the growing season.

REST PERIOD: Winter days average 63–64 °F (17–18 °C), while nights average 32–35 °F (0–2 °C), and the diurnal range increases to 29–32 °F (16–18 °C). In cultivation, for 2–3 months during winter, water should be restricted to occasional misting, fertilizer withheld, and humidity decreased to 60–70%. The number of clear days indicates increased light levels. Since the leaves are not always deciduous in nature, conditions during the rest should be sufficiently moderate to keep the leaves evergreen, which should improve plant health and increase blooming in cultivation.

GROWING MEDIA: ½–⅝ in. (12–16 mm) fir bark with moisture-retentive additives, or sphagnum moss with perlite or charcoal added for drainage. Plants are best repotted after blooming or when root growth starts.

MISCELLANEOUS NOTES: N/A.

Plant and Flower Information

PLANT SIZE AND TYPE: A small monopodial epiphyte.

LEAVES: Number unknown. The tiny leaves are only 1 in. (2.5 cm) long. They are usually deciduous and absent at flowering. In cultivation, plants may be healthier if the leaves are kept evergreen.

INFLORESCENCE: Length is highly variable. The zigzag spikes may be arching or pendent.

FLOWERS: 1–3 per inflorescence. The blooms are 1.5 in. (4 cm) across, which is very large relative to leaf size. The flowers are fragrant, delicately textured, and star-shaped. The sepals and petals are pink to white with a purplish suffusion, while the lip is rose to deep magenta. The species is apparently variable.

HYBRIDIZING NOTES: N/A.

REFERENCES: 195.

PHOTOS/DRAWINGS: *195*.

Phalaenopsis zebrina. See *P. sumatrana*. REFERENCES: 195.

5
Pholidota
General Information

SUBFAMILY: Epidendroideae.

TRIBE: *Coelogyneae.*

SUBTRIBE: *Coelogyninae.*

GENUS: *Pholidota* Lindley.

AKA: Popularly known as the "rattlesnake orchid" due to the arrangement of the often persistent floral bracts. Many *Pholidota* species were originally classified as *Coelogyne.* Other names that have been applied to this genus include *Acanthoglossum, Camelostalix, Chelonanthera, Crinonia,* and *Ptilocnema.*

SPECIES: Previous estimates of the number of species ranged from 30–55, but Dr. E. F. De Vogel found 29 valid species in his 1988 review of the genus, *Orchid Monographs,* Vol. 3, *Revisions in* Coelogyninae (Orchidaceae) III: *The Genus* Pholidota. We have followed Dr. De Vogel's listing of valid species.

ORIGIN/HABITAT: The natural habitat of this widespread genus includes India, Malaysia, Indonesia, Australia, Polynesia, the Philippines, and China.

CLIMATE: Tropical to subtropical climates are normal throughout the range; but for some high-elevation species, growing temperatures approximate those found in temperate zones.

Cultural Recommendations

LIGHT: Variable. Diffused light is most often required. However, species may grow either in dense forests or on exposed lava flows. Species with somewhat soft leaves may be very subject to sunburn in direct sun.

TEMPERATURES: Variable, but generally warm during the growing season.

HUMIDITY: High summer humidity usually predominates in the natural habitats.

WATER: Variable, but the habitats are most often wet when the plants are actively growing. *Pholidota* should be kept quite moist but never allowed to become soggy. Water should be applied directly at the roots, as new growths are funnel-shaped and may be very susceptible to disease if water is allowed to stand in them.

FERTILIZER: ¼–½ the recommended strength. A balanced fertilizer may be applied weekly to biweekly while the plants are actively growing. *Pholidota* generally respond well to regular applications of nutrients.

REST PERIOD: Requirements are highly variable. Low-elevation equatorial species have essentially no variation in their environment, so growing conditions should be maintained year-round. However, some species originate at fairly high altitudes and will tolerate a dry, very severe rest including a wide diurnal range and temperatures near freezing. For these species, the winter dormant period is frequently necessary to initiate blooms. Cultural conditions should be dry when temperatures are cold, as excess moisture may seriously damage the plants. The native climate for each species should be studied before any winter rest period regime is implemented.

GROWING MEDIA: *Pholidota* may be slabbed on cork, tree fern, or coconut husk, and slabbing is preferred for species with climbing rhizomes. Plants may also be potted or placed in baskets. Containers may be filled with a 4–2–2 mixture of shredded tree-fern, charcoal, and sphagnum moss. Fine or medium bark may be used in place of tree fern, but most species do better in the latter because it retains substantial amounts of moisture.

Plants should not be repotted more often than necessary, as some require several years of recovery before they are sufficiently reestablished to bloom.

MISCELLANEOUS NOTES: Dividing is best done in the spring when new roots are beginning to grow. Since some species are very slow to recover, divisions should be as large as possible, consisting of at least 3 or 4 pseudobulbs.

Several *Pholidota* species are survivors, adapting to the incursion of civilization; consequently they are quite easy to cultivate.

Plant and Flower Information

PLANT SIZE AND TYPE: Notes regarding individual growth habits are included for each species. Most are creeping or pendulous sympodial epiphytes, but others are lithophytes or terrestrials. Growers have found it beneficial to treat the terrestrials as epiphytes in cultivation.

PSEUDOBULB: The pseudobulbs may be clustered or widely spaced.

LEAVES: Normally 1 or 2 per growth. Tropical species are usually evergreen, while those from cooler climates are frequently deciduous.

Brown leaf tips nearly always indicate inadequate moisture or tissue burn from salt buildup rather than a disease.

INFLORESCENCE: The relatively long spikes are never branching and are usually arching to pendulous with racemes of flowers on the apical portion. Inflorescences normally emerge from the apex of the pseudobulb according to one of the following growth patterns:

Heteranthous: The inflorescence is an independent growth.

Hysteranthous: Inflorescences emerge after the newest growth is fully mature.

Proteranthous: Flowering occurs prior to the vegetative growth.

Synanthous: Inflorescences emerge before or at the same time as the vegetative growth.

FLOWERS: Most species have numerous small flowers. The blossoms are usually arranged in 2 densely flowered, distichous rows, though occasionally all the flowers of a species are arranged on one side of the spike. Some species have fewer, larger, more widely spaced flowers. The flowers may open simultaneously, but they generally open sequentially, starting from either the base or the middle of the raceme.

HYBRIDIZING NOTES: Few chromosome counts have been done for *Pholidota* species.

REFERENCES: 37, 113.

PHOTOS/DRAWINGS: See species listings.

Species Culture

Pholidota advena Hooker f. Not recently collected, it reportedly originated in Burma and Southeast Asia, but no details regarding the habitat are known. It is not presently available for cultivation. REFERENCES: 37.

Pholidota aidiolepis Seidenfaden and De Vogel

AKA: N/A.

ORIGIN/HABITAT: Endemic to southwest Thailand. Only one collection has been made to date, from a mountain peak west of Nakhon, at 4400 ft. (1341 m).

CLIMATE: Station # 48552, Nakhon Si Thammarat, Thailand, Lat. 8.4°N, Long. 100.0°E, at 24 ft. (7 m). Temperatures are calculated for an elevation of 4428 ft. (1350 m), resulting in probable extremes of 89°F (31.7°C) and 48°F (8.9°C).

N/HEMISPHERE	JAN	FEB	MAR	APR	MAY	JUN	JUL	AUG	SEP	OCT	NOV	DEC
°F AVG MAX	71	73	75	77	77	77	76	76	76	73	71	70
°F AVG MIN	57	56	57	58	60	59	58	58	58	58	58	57
DIURNAL RANGE	14	17	18	19	17	18	18	18	18	15	13	13
RAIN/INCHES	8.1	3.3	4.1	5.7	7.2	4.4	3.9	4.7	6.1	13.1	23.7	18.5
HUMIDITY/%	78	76	72	73	76	71	73	74	76	80	83	82
BLOOM SEASON	N/A											
DAYS CLR @ 7AM	4	3	4	4	1	1	2	1	1	1	2	3
DAYS CLR @ 1PM	1	3	4	4	1	1	2	1	1	0	1	1
RAIN/MM	206	84	104	145	183	112	99	119	155	333	602	470
°C AVG MAX	21.9	23.0	24.1	25.3	25.3	25.3	24.7	24.7	24.7	23.0	21.9	21.4
°C AVG MIN	14.1	13.6	14.1	14.7	15.8	15.3	14.7	14.7	14.7	14.7	14.7	14.1
DIURNAL RANGE	7.8	9.4	10.0	10.6	9.5	10.0	10.0	10.0	10.0	8.3	7.2	7.3
S/HEMISPHERE	JUL	AUG	SEP	OCT	NOV	DEC	JAN	FEB	MAR	APR	MAY	JUN

Cultural Recommendations

LIGHT: 1800–3600 fc. Low, diffused or dappled light is suggested as a starting point, since specific habitat information is lacking. Direct sunlight should probably be avoided, and plants should be watched for any sign of stress.

TEMPERATURES: Days average 75–77°F (24–25°C), and nights average 58–60°F (15–16°C), with a diurnal range of 17–19°F (9–11°C). The lows vary only 4°F (2°C) through the year. The probable extreme high of 89°F (32°C) indicates a general intolerance of hot summer weather.

HUMIDITY: 70–80%.

WATER: Plants should be kept constantly moist, but not soggy. Air circulation could be critically important for this species. The rainfall pattern is wet/wetter.

FERTILIZER: ¼–½ the recommended strength. A balanced fertilizer may be applied weekly during periods of active growth.

REST PERIOD: Days average 70–75°F (21–24°C), and nights average 56–58°F (14–15°C), with a reduced diurnal range of 13–18°F (7–10°C) during winter. While temperatures can be reduced slightly, the probable extreme low is just 10°F (6°C) below winter averages, indicating an intolerance of temperature extremes. In general, growing conditions should be maintained with a very gentle, 1–2 month rest.

GROWING MEDIA: Mounting on a tree-fern slab will accommodate the plant's pendulous growth habit. Repotting is probably best done when roots are actively growing in early spring.

MISCELLANEOUS NOTES: The plant is unlikely to be available for cultivation.

Plant and Flower Information

PLANT SIZE AND TYPE: A 7 in. (18 cm) pendulous sympodial epiphyte.

PSEUDOBULB: 0.75 in. (1.7 cm) long. The closely spaced pseudobulbs are slender and conical.

LEAVES: 2, rarely 3, per growth. The leaves are 3–4 in. (8–10 cm) long and leathery. They may be linear or narrowly lanceolate.

INFLORESCENCE: 4–6 in. (10–15 cm) long. The spikes may precede or emerge with the new growth.

FLOWERS: 10–18. The tiny, widely spaced, distichous, white flowers are ¼ in. (0.6 cm) across and nearly hidden by the persistent floral bracts.

HYBRIDIZING NOTES: N/A.

REFERENCES: 37.

PHOTOS/DRAWINGS: 37.

Pholidota annamensis. See *P. chinensis.* REFERENCES: 37.

Pholidota articulata Lindley

AKA: The numerous synonyms include *P. decurva, P. griffithii, P. khasiyana, P. lugardii, P. minahassae, P. obovata, P. repens.*

ORIGIN/HABITAT: Southeast Asia. The wide-ranging plants are usually found at 2000–3000 ft. (610–914 m), but elevations range from 980–6500 ft. (299–1981 m).

CLIMATE: Station # 48552, Nakhon Si Thammarat, Thailand, Lat. 8.4°N, Long. 100.0°E, at 23 ft. (7 m). Temperatures are calculated for 3600 ft. (1097 m), which is the plant elevation in this area of Thailand. The resulting probable extremes are 92°F (33.3°C) and 51°F (10.6°C).

N/HEMISPHERE	JAN	FEB	MAR	APR	MAY	JUN	JUL	AUG	SEP	OCT	NOV	DEC
°F AVG MAX	74	76	78	80	80	80	79	79	79	76	74	73
°F AVG MIN	60	59	60	61	63	62	61	61	61	61	61	60
DIURNAL RANGE	14	17	18	19	17	18	18	18	18	15	13	13
RAIN/INCHES	8.1	3.3	4.1	5.7	7.2	4.4	3.9	4.7	6.1	13.1	23.7	18.5
HUMIDITY/%	78	76	72	73	76	71	73	74	76	80	83	82
BLOOM SEASON				*	**	**	*	*	*			
DAYS CLR @ 7AM	4	3	4	4	1	1	2	1	1	1	2	3
DAYS CLR @ 1PM	1	3	4	4	1	1	2	1	1	0	1	1
RAIN/MM	206	84	104	145	183	112	99	119	155	333	602	470
°C AVG MAX	23.4	24.6	25.7	26.8	26.8	26.8	26.2	26.2	26.2	24.6	23.4	22.9
°C AVG MIN	15.7	15.1	15.7	16.2	17.3	16.8	16.2	16.2	16.2	16.2	16.2	15.7
DIURNAL RANGE	7.7	9.5	10.0	10.6	9.5	10.0	10.0	10.0	10.0	8.4	7.2	7.2
S/HEMISPHERE	JUL	AUG	SEP	OCT	NOV	DEC	JAN	FEB	MAR	APR	MAY	JUN

Cultural Recommendations

LIGHT: 1800–2600 fc. Low, diffused or dappled light is recommended. Direct sunlight should be avoided, since clear days are rare in the habitat.

TEMPERATURES: Days average 79–80°F (26–27°C), and nights average 61–63°F (16–17°C), with a summer diurnal range of 17–19°F (9–11°C). The average low temperature fluctuates only 4°F (2°C), and the probable extreme low is just 12°F (7°C) below the averages.

HUMIDITY: 75–80%.

WATER: If plants are slabbed, daily misting is suggested in summer. The rainfall pattern is wet/wetter.

FERTILIZER: ¼–½ strength, applied weekly during periods of active growth.

REST PERIOD: Days average 73–76°F (23–25°C), and nights average 59–60°F (15–16°C), with a lower winter diurnal range of 13–14°F (7–8°C). Water may be reduced, particularly if temperatures are somewhat low; but plants should not become desiccated. Fertilizer should be reduced when plants are not actively growing.

GROWING MEDIA: It is preferable to mount the plant on cork or tree fern, as it will climb regardless of attempts to contain it in a pot. Roots should be disturbed as seldom as possible, but when reslabbing is necessary, it is best done in early spring when new roots are growing.

MISCELLANEOUS NOTES: Time of flowering differs in the plant's various habitats, apparently depending on the timing of the wettest season.

Plant and Flower Information

PLANT SIZE AND TYPE: A 10–20 in. (25–51 cm) climbing, sympodial epiphyte that becomes pendulous as it matures.

113

PSEUDOBULB: 1.5–4.0 in. (4–10 cm) long. Each slender, cylindrical new pseudobulb arises from the apex of the preceding one.

LEAVES: 2–3 per growth. The leaves are 3–5 in. (8–13 cm) long and leathery. They may be linear-lanceolate or ovate.

INFLORESCENCE: 6–11 in. (15–28 cm) long. The spike, which is slender, drooping, and zigzag, emerges when the new leaves are at various stages of development.

FLOWERS: 12–16. The small flowers are 0.5 in. (1.2 cm) across, distichous, and highly variable. They may open fully or only partially. Translucent or opaque, they are pinkish, dull tan, cream, or greenish white in color. The lip is usually darker than the sepals and petals. The fragrance is described as musk- or chocolate-scented.

HYBRIDIZING NOTES: Chromosome counts are n = 20 + 1 - 3B, 2n = 40, and, for var. *griffithii*, n = 20.

REFERENCES: 9, 20, 32, 36, 112, 118, 157, 175.

PHOTOS/DRAWINGS: 9, 20, 32, 36, 37, 175.

Pholidota assamica. See *P. imbricata*. REFERENCES: 37.

Pholidota beccarii. See *P. imbricata*. REFERENCES: 37.

Pholidota bismarckiensis. See *P. carnea*. REFERENCES: 37.

Pholidota bracteata. This name has been used for both *P. imbricata* and *P. pallida*. REFERENCES: 37.

Pholidota caduca. See *P. gibbosa*. REFERENCES: 37.

Pholidota calceata. See *P. pallida*. REFERENCES: 37.

Pholidota camelostalix Rchb.f.

AKA: N/A.

ORIGIN/HABITAT: Sumatra and Java at 2600–6500 ft. (792–1981 m). Var. *grandiflora* is most likely to be available for cultivation. It is found in deep shade in the lower mountain forests, while smaller-flowered varieties are usually found at higher elevations in higher light.

CLIMATE: Station # 96755, Bogor, Indonesia, Lat. 6.5°S, Long. 106.8°E, at 558 ft. (170 m). Temperatures are calculated for an elevation of 3598 ft. (1097 m), resulting in probable extremes of 85°F (29.4°C) and 56°F (13.3°C).

N/HEMISPHERE	JAN	FEB	MAR	APR	MAY	JUN	JUL	AUG	SEP	OCT	NOV	DEC
°F AVG MAX	76	77	78	78	77	75	74	74	75	76	77	76
°F AVG MIN	63	63	63	64	64	64	64	64	64	65	65	64
DIURNAL RANGE	13	14	15	14	13	11	10	10	11	11	12	12
RAIN/INCHES	2.1	1.0	0.5	5.0	8.1	18.8	23.7	20.2	14.4	12.0	11.9	3.4
HUMIDITY/%	72	68	65	66	74	79	84	84	81	79	77	75
BLOOM SEASON						*	*	*	*	*		
DAYS CLR @ 7AM	14	14	14	11	5	3	1	2	4	6	10	12
DAYS CLR @ 1PM	9	10	8	5	1	1	0	0	1	1	3	7
RAIN/MM	53	25	13	127	206	478	602	513	366	305	302	86
°C AVG MAX	24.4	25.0	25.5	25.5	25.0	23.9	23.3	23.3	23.9	24.4	25.0	24.4
°C AVG MIN	17.2	17.2	17.2	17.8	17.8	17.8	17.8	17.8	17.8	18.3	18.3	17.8
DIURNAL RANGE	7.2	7.8	8.3	7.7	7.2	6.1	5.5	5.5	6.1	6.1	6.7	6.6
S/HEMISPHERE	JUL	AUG	SEP	OCT	NOV	DEC	JAN	FEB	MAR	APR	MAY	JUN

Cultural Recommendations

LIGHT: 1000 fc. Low light to deep shade is preferred; direct sunlight should be avoided.

TEMPERATURES: Days average 74–78°F (24–26°C), and nights average 63–65°F (17–18°C), with a summer diurnal range of 10–13°F (6–7°C). Night temperatures vary only 2°F (1°C) year-round, and average daytime temperatures fluctuate only 4°F (2.2°C). The probable extreme high is only about 10°F (5.6°C) above the average highs.

HUMIDITY: 75–85%.

WATER: Constant moisture should be available from late spring through autumn. The rainfall pattern is wet/dry.

FERTILIZER: ¼–½ strength, applied weekly during periods of active growth.

REST PERIOD: Winter days average 76–78°F (24–26°C), which is slightly warmer than in summer, while nights average 63–64°F (17–18°C), slightly cooler than in summer. This results in an increased diurnal range of 13-15°F (7–8°C). However, in the habitat, the probable extreme low is only 7–8°F (4–5°C) below the average winter lows. Light may be slightly increased to simulate the increase in clear days. Water should be reduced, but the high winter humidity levels in the habitat indicate frequent dew, mist, fog, and low clouds. Fertilizer should be reduced or eliminated when the plants are not actively growing.

GROWING MEDIA: A shredded tree-fern mix. Repotting is best done in early spring when new root growth is evident.

MISCELLANEOUS NOTES: The bloom season is variable and appears to depend on the timing of the rainy season.

Plant and Flower Information

PLANT SIZE AND TYPE: A 12 in. (30 cm) sympodial epiphyte or lithophyte.

PSEUDOBULB: 2.5–4.5 in. (6–11 cm) long. The pseudobulbs are curved and densely clustered.

LEAVES: 2 per growth. The leaves are 10–12 in. (25–30 cm) long, pointed at the apex, and prominently veined.

INFLORESCENCE: 10–28 in. (25-70 cm) long. The spike is zigzag and quite stiff, arising from between the leaves at the apex of the pseudobulb after it is fully mature. Initially upright, the spike becomes sharply pendulous.

FLOWERS: 25–70. The tiny blossoms are 0.5 in. (1.3 cm) across. Fleshy and somewhat hidden by the persistent floral bracts, the wide-opening flowers have no fragrance. They are usually greenish to brownish, with a bright red or orange anther.

HYBRIDIZING NOTES: N/A.

REFERENCES: 32, 175.

PHOTOS/DRAWINGS: 32, *37*, 175.

Pholidota cantonensis Rolfe

AKA: *P. uraniensis.*

ORIGIN/HABITAT: Taiwan. It is found throughout the island on trees and bare rocks in shade, semishade, or full sun at 650–6500 ft. (198–1981 m). Plants are also found in Hong Kong, where they grow on shady rock-faces at 1000 ft. (328 m), and in several provinces of China.

CLIMATE: Station # 45007, Hong Kong, Lat. 22.3°N, Long. 114.2°E, at 15 ft. (5 m). Temperatures are calculated for an elevation of 1000 ft. (328 m), resulting in probable extremes of 94°F (34.4°C) and 29°F (-1.7°C).

N/HEMISPHERE	JAN	FEB	MAR	APR	MAY	JUN	JUL	AUG	SEP	OCT	NOV	DEC
°F AVG MAX	61	60	64	73	79	82	84	84	82	78	71	65
°F AVG MIN	53	52	57	64	71	75	75	75	74	70	62	56
DIURNAL RANGE	8	8	7	9	8	7	9	9	8	8	9	9
RAIN/INCHES	1.3	1.8	2.9	5.4	11.5	15.5	15.0	14.2	10.1	4.5	1.7	1.2
HUMIDITY/%	72	78	79	82	83	82	82	82	78	69	67	69
BLOOM SEASON			*	*	*							
DAYS CLR @ 8AM	7	3	2	2	2	1	1	3	4	9	8	8
DAYS CLR @ 2PM	10	5	4	2	2	1	2	2	4	11	10	11
RAIN/MM	33	46	74	137	292	394	381	361	257	114	43	30
°C AVG MAX	16.0	15.4	17.6	22.6	26.0	27.6	28.7	28.7	27.6	25.4	21.5	18.2
°C AVG MIN	11.5	11.0	13.7	17.6	21.5	23.7	23.7	23.7	23.2	21.0	16.5	13.2
DIURNAL RANGE	4.5	4.4	3.9	5.0	4.5	3.9	5.0	5.0	4.4	4.4	5.0	5.0
S/HEMISPHERE	JUL	AUG	SEP	OCT	NOV	DEC	JAN	FEB	MAR	APR	MAY	JUN

Cultural Recommendations

LIGHT: 1200–2000 fc. Light should be diffused or dappled, and direct sunlight should be avoided, particularly when temperatures are high.

TEMPERATURES: Summer days average 78–84°F (25–29°C), and nights average 70–75°F (21–24°C), with a diurnal range of 7–9°F (4-5°C). The warmest weather coincides with the period of heaviest rainfall. The climate information given for Hong Kong probably represents the warmest end of the plant's range.

HUMIDITY: 80%.

WATER: Plants should be kept constantly moist during the growing season. The rainfall pattern is wet/dry.

FERTILIZER: ¼–½ strength, applied weekly during periods of active growth.

REST PERIOD: Winter days average 60–65°F (15–18°C), and nights average 52–57°F (11–14°C), with a diurnal range of 7–9°F (4–5°C). Day and night temperatures decline simultaneously, resulting in a consistent average diurnal range. Unless the plants are exceptionally protected by the microclimate, they are occasionally subjected to outbreaks of cold air which cause temperatures to drop dramatically, resulting in the below-freezing record low of 29°F (-1.8°C). During the rest, water should be reduced to infrequent waterings with occasional light mistings for 2–4 months, humidity reduced slightly, light increased somewhat, and fertilizer reduced or eliminated.

GROWING MEDIA: Mounting on cork or tree fern accommodates the plant's creeping growth habit. Remounting should be done as seldom as possible, and only when new roots are actively growing.

MISCELLANEOUS NOTES: Cultivation bloom records are not available, but blooming apparently occurs throughout the year, as collections have been made every month except Dec. (Jun.).

Plant and Flower Information

PLANT SIZE AND TYPE: A 3–10 in. (6–25 cm) creeping, sympodial epiphyte or lithophyte.

PSEUDOBULB: 0.5–1.0 in. (1.3–2.5 cm) long. Ovoid, tapering at the apex, and widely spaced, the pseudobulbs are shiny and wrinkled when dry. New growths emerge from the apex of the sheath-covered, branching, ascending rhizome.

LEAVES: 2 per growth. The leaves are 4–10 in. (10–25 cm) long, linear-lanceolate, rich green, and somewhat shiny. The foliage persists for a long time.

INFLORESCENCE: 2–3 in. (5–8 cm) long. Arching, slightly zigzag, and laxly flowered, the spike emerges from the apex of the rhizome before the new vegetative growth.

FLOWERS: 10–20. The small, attractive blossoms are ¼ in. (0.6 cm) across. Alternating and held in 2 ranks, they may be spreading to nearly closed. The thin-textured sepals and petals are whitish to cream, while the lip is golden yellow with a pink anther. Flowers open sequentially, starting near the base.

HYBRIDIZING NOTES: N/A.

REFERENCES: 24, 37, 120, 132, 181.

PHOTOS/DRAWINGS: 37.

Pholidota carnea Lindley

AKA: *P. bismarckiensis, P. celebica, P. elizabethiana, P. micrantha, P. parviflora, P. torricellensis.*

ORIGIN/HABITAT: New Guinea to the Philippines, throughout Indonesia, Burma, and Thailand. In Malaya, it grows in rather exposed places above 4900 ft. (1494 m).

CLIMATE: Station # 48625, Ipoh, Malaya, Lat. 4.6°N, Long. 101.1°E, at 123 ft. (37 m). Temperatures are calculated for an elevation of 4920 ft. (1500 m), resulting in probable extremes of 83°F (28.3°C) and 48°F (8.9°C).

N/HEMISPHERE	JAN	FEB	MAR	APR	MAY	JUN	JUL	AUG	SEP	OCT	NOV	DEC
°F AVG MAX	74	76	77	76	76	76	75	75	74	73	73	73
°F AVG MIN	56	56	57	57	58	57	56	56	57	56	56	56
DIURNAL RANGE	18	20	20	19	18	19	19	19	17	17	17	17
RAIN/INCHES	7.9	3.1	7.6	8.4	6.2	3.6	7.2	6.9	8.8	11.0	13.0	8.9
HUMIDITY/%	76	74	76	78	78	75	76	77	79	82	82	81
BLOOM SEASON	*	**	*	*								**
DAYS CLR @ 7AM	3	3	3	1	1	2	1	1	0	0	1	2
DAYS CLR @ 1PM	2	2	2	1	1	1	1	1	0	0	0	2
RAIN/MM	201	79	193	213	157	91	183	175	224	279	330	226
°C AVG MAX	23.4	24.5	25.1	24.5	24.5	24.5	24.0	24.0	23.4	22.9	22.9	22.9
°C AVG MIN	13.4	13.4	14.0	14.0	14.5	14.0	13.4	13.4	14.0	13.4	13.4	13.4
DIURNAL RANGE	10.0	11.1	11.1	10.5	10.0	10.5	10.6	10.6	9.4	9.5	9.5	9.5
S/HEMISPHERE	JUL	AUG	SEP	OCT	NOV	DEC	JAN	FEB	MAR	APR	MAY	JUN

Cultural Recommendations

LIGHT: 1500–2400 fc. Light should be diffused or dappled, and direct sunlight should be avoided. Clear days are quite rare in the habitat.

TEMPERATURES: Days average 75–77°F (24–25°C), and nights average 56–58°F (13–15°C), with a year-round diurnal range of 17–20°F (9–11°C). The extreme high does not exceed the warmest average by more than 6°F (3°C), indicating a possible sensitivity to wide temperature fluctuations.

HUMIDITY: 75–80% year-round.

WATER: Plants should be kept moist. The rainfall pattern is wet/wetter.

FERTILIZER: ¼–½ strength, applied weekly during periods of active growth.

REST PERIOD: Growing conditions should be maintained year-round. In the habitat, the average low varies only 2°F (1°C), and the extreme low is just 8°F (4°C) below the coolest average winter low. *P. carnea* will be healthiest with uniform temperatures. Plants should not be allowed to dry out. Despite higher winter rainfall in the habitat, watering probably should not be increased in cultivation, particularly when temperatures are cool. Fertilizer may be reduced or eliminated when plants are not actively growing.

GROWING MEDIA: Mounting on tree fern or cork accommodates the plant's creeping growth habit. Remounting, which should be done infrequently, is best done when roots begin active growth, since the plant recovers slowly when disturbed.

MISCELLANEOUS NOTES: The climate table shows cultivation bloom records, but blooming occurs in the same season in the plant's natural habitat. Var. *carnea* reportedly blooms anytime during the year; var. *par-*

viflora and var. *pumila* usually bloom in Jun.–Aug. (Dec.–Feb.). The 3 varieties differ primarily in technical details of the lips; however, var. *parviflora* is likely to be the most attractive plant in cultivation. Warmer-growing plants from lower elevations tend to have longer internodes and a more pendent growth habit.

Plant and Flower Information

PLANT SIZE AND TYPE: A 6–20 in. (15–51 cm), variably sized, creeping, sympodial epiphyte.

PSEUDOBULB: 1.5 in. (4 cm) long. The ovoid pseudobulbs, which tend to lie against the branching rhizome, may be either densely crowded or spaced up to 2 in. (5 cm) apart.

LEAVES: 2 per growth. Ranging in size from 2–25 in. (5–65 cm), the narrow, leathery leaves are usually uniformly green but may be tinged with red.

INFLORESCENCE: Inflorescence length is highly variable, but the spike is usually longer than the leaves. Thick, erect to down-curving, and laxly flowered, the spikes emerge prior to the new vegetative growth or with the new leaves.

FLOWERS: 15 or more. The tiny flowers are ¼ in. (0.6 cm) across. Arranged in 2 rows, the blossoms are variable in size and color and may be pinkish, brick-red, maroon, brown, or creamy white.

HYBRIDIZING NOTES: N/A.

REFERENCES: 2, 3, 32, 112, 118, 164, 175, 203.

PHOTOS/DRAWINGS: 32, *37*, 118, 164, 175.

Pholidota celebica. See *P. carnea.* REFERENCES: 37.

Pholidota chinensis Lindley

AKA: *Coelogyne pholas, Pholidota annamensis, P. corniculata, P. laucheana, P. pyrranthela.*

ORIGIN/HABITAT: Da Nang, Vietnam, the southern provinces of China, and Hong Kong. The plant usually grows on damp rocks near streams in shady as well as open places.

CLIMATE: Station # 48855, Da Nang, Vietnam, Lat. 16.0°N, Long. 108.2°E, at 33 ft. (10 m). Temperatures are calculated for an elevation of 1000 ft. (328 m), resulting in probable extremes of 102°F (38.9°C) and 47°F (8.3°C).

N/HEMISPHERE	JAN	FEB	MAR	APR	MAY	JUN	JUL	AUG	SEP	OCT	NOV	DEC
°F AVG MAX	73	76	79	84	88	91	90	90	86	81	78	74
°F AVG MIN	63	64	67	71	73	75	74	74	72	70	68	64
DIURNAL RANGE	10	12	12	13	15	16	16	16	14	11	10	10
RAIN/INCHES	4.5	1.6	1.0	1.2	2.4	2.9	3.0	4.6	15.3	22.4	15.2	8.8
HUMIDITY/%	85	84	84	82	79	76	75	77	82	85	85	85
BLOOM SEASON	*	*	**	***	***							
DAYS CLR @ 7AM	3	3	5	6	5	4	4	4	3	4	3	2
DAYS CLR @ 1PM	4	7	12	11	6	2	4	3	2	3	2	2
RAIN/MM	114	41	25	30	61	74	76	117	389	569	386	224
°C AVG MAX	22.7	24.3	26.0	28.8	31.0	32.7	32.1	32.1	29.9	27.1	25.4	23.2
°C AVG MIN	17.1	17.7	19.3	21.6	22.7	23.8	23.2	23.2	22.1	21.0	19.9	17.7
DIURNAL RANGE	5.6	6.6	6.7	7.2	8.3	8.9	8.9	8.9	7.8	6.1	5.5	5.5
S/HEMISPHERE	JUL	AUG	SEP	OCT	NOV	DEC	JAN	FEB	MAR	APR	MAY	JUN

Cultural Recommendations

LIGHT: 1800–3000 fc. Light should be diffused or dappled, and direct sunlight avoided.

TEMPERATURES: Summer days average 84–90°F (29-32°C), and nights average 71–75°F (22–24°C), with a diurnal range of 13–16°F (7-9°C). Cool to intermediate growing conditions are commonly recommended, but the climate indicates that warm to very warm conditions during summer may be less stressful and more conducive to plant health.

HUMIDITY: 75%.

WATER: Plants should be kept very moist in late summer. The rainfall pattern is wet/dry, but the plants grow in areas where moisture is constantly available to the roots.

FERTILIZER: ¼–½ strength, applied weekly during periods of active growth.

REST PERIOD: Days average 73–79°F (23–26°C), and nights average 63–68°F (17–20°C), with a diurnal range of 10–12°F (6–7°C). Day and night temperatures decline simultaneously, resulting in a slightly lower winter diurnal range. Light may be increased somewhat to correspond with the increased number of clear days. Water may be reduced for 2–3 months, but the plants should not be allowed to dry out. In the moist habitat, water from dew, mist, and fog is continually available to the roots, even during the dry period. Fertilizer should be reduced when plants are not actively growing.

GROWING MEDIA: Mounting on tree fern or cork accommodates the creeping growth habit. Remounting should be done infrequently and is best done when roots begin active growth, since the plant recovers slowly when disturbed.

MISCELLANEOUS NOTES: The roots are unusually long and probably will not stay confined to a pot.

Plant and Flower Information

PLANT SIZE AND TYPE: A 4–12 in. (10–30 cm) creeping, sympodial epiphyte.

PSEUDOBULB: 1.2 in. (3 cm) long. The pseudobulbs are often curved, taper near the tip, and are spaced 0.5–1.0 in. (1–3 cm) apart on the rhizome. Plants usually have few back-bulbs since pseudobulbs wither quickly.

LEAVES: 2 per growth. The leaves are 4–10 in. (10–25 cm) long and become deciduous after new leaves have formed. Leaf shape may be elliptic or lanceolate.

INFLORESCENCE: 6 in. (10 cm) long. The arching to pendulous spikes emerge from the apex of the new growth prior to or with the new, undeveloped leaves.

FLOWERS: 6–10. The blossoms may reach 0.75 in. (2 cm) across, which is large for *Pholidota*. The sepals and narrow petals are wide-spreading, translucent, and may be white, yellow-green, or honey-colored. The opaque lip is a deeper shade of yellow. The flowers are sometimes fragrant.

HYBRIDIZING NOTES: Fruits are well developed by Oct. (Apr.).

REFERENCES: 37, 120, 148, 210.

PHOTOS/DRAWINGS: 37, 120, 210.

Pholidota clemensii Ames

AKA: *P. dentiloba*. The plant is often considered a small form of *P. ventricosa*.

ORIGIN/HABITAT: Borneo. It is found in open areas at high elevations of 4200-7700 ft. (1280-2347 m).

CLIMATE: Station # 49613, Tambunan, North Borneo, Lat. 5.7°N, Long. 116.4°E, at 1200 ft. (366 m). Temperatures are calculated for an elevation of 5904 ft. (1800 m), resulting in probable extremes of 82°F (27.8°C) and 38°F (3.3°C).

N/HEMISPHERE	JAN	FEB	MAR	APR	MAY	JUN	JUL	AUG	SEP	OCT	NOV	DEC
°F AVG MAX	70	71	73	74	74	73	73	73	73	72	71	70
°F AVG MIN	51	49	50	51	52	51	50	50	51	51	51	52
DIURNAL RANGE	19	22	23	23	22	22	23	23	22	21	20	18
RAIN/INCHES	5.8	3.7	5.8	7.5	8.2	7.3	5.1	4.9	6.4	7.0	6.8	6.0
HUMIDITY/%	N/A											
BLOOM SEASON	*	*	*	*	*	*	*				*	**
DAYS CLR	N/A											
RAIN/MM	147	94	147	190	208	185	130	124	163	178	173	152
°C AVG MAX	21.4	21.9	23.1	23.6	23.6	23.1	23.1	23.1	23.1	22.5	21.9	21.4
°C AVG MIN	10.8	9.7	10.3	10.8	11.4	10.8	10.3	10.3	10.8	10.8	10.8	11.4
DIURNAL RANGE	10.6	12.2	12.8	12.8	12.2	12.3	12.8	12.8	12.3	11.7	11.1	10.0
S/HEMISPHERE	JUL	AUG	SEP	OCT	NOV	DEC	JAN	FEB	MAR	APR	MAY	JUN

Cultural Recommendations

LIGHT: 2400 fc. Diffused light or dappled shade is suggested.

TEMPERATURES: Summer days average 73–74°F (23–24°C), and nights average 50–52°F (10–11°C), with a diurnal range of 22–23°F (12–13°C). The plants are unlikely to tolerate consistently warm conditions.

HUMIDITY: 75–80%.

WATER: Plants should be kept constantly moist. The rainfall pattern is wet year-round.

FERTILIZER: ¼–½ strength, applied weekly during periods of active growth.

REST PERIOD: In the habitat, average conditions are very consistent, except that winter days are slightly cooler, resulting in a somewhat narrower diurnal range. The extreme low indicates that *P. clemensii* is subject to periodic outbreaks of cold air.

GROWING MEDIA: A moisture-retaining medium of shredded tree-fern or bark is suggested, or plants may be mounted on a tree-fern slab. Repotting should be avoided. When repotting is necessary, it is best done immediately after flowering, when new roots are actively growing.

MISCELLANEOUS NOTES: *P. clemensii* could be very difficult to maintain in cultivation. The constant, steady rain, uniformly cool temperatures, and limited habitat indicate a demanding plant.

Plant and Flower Information

PLANT SIZE AND TYPE: A 14–27 in. (36–69 cm) sympodial epiphyte or terrestrial.

PSEUDOBULB: 1.2–2.5 in. (3–6 cm) long.

LEAVES: 1 per growth. The single leaf is 6–16 in. (15–41 cm) long, dark green, lanceolate, and plicate.

INFLORESCENCE: 8 in. (20 cm) long. The spike is rigidly

erect. Normally it emerges prior to the vegetative growth, but it may occasionally appear with the partially developed leaves. The attractive spikes produce flowers on the apical half.

FLOWERS: 18–25. The small, slightly fragrant blossoms are 0.5–1.0 in. (1.3–2.5 cm) across. White or sometimes pinkish in color, they become yellow with age. The floral bracts are pink and usually fall as the flowers open.

HYBRIDIZING NOTES: N/A.

REFERENCES: 2, 37.

PHOTOS/DRAWINGS: *37.*

Pholidota clypeata. See *P. gibbosa.* REFERENCES: 37.

Pholidota conchoidea. See *P. imbricata.* REFERENCES: 37.

Pholidota convallariae Hooker f.

AKA: *P. fragrans.*

ORIGIN/HABITAT: India, Burma, Thailand, Vietnam, and Java. It is usually found above 3280 ft. (1000 m) both in primary forests and on open lava beds.

CLIMATE: Station # 48375, Ban Mae Sot, Thailand, Lat. 16.7°N, Long. 98.5°E, at 742 ft. (226 m). Temperatures are calculated for an elevation of 3280 ft. (1000 m), resulting in probable extremes of 98°F (36.7°C) and 31°F (-0.6°C).

N/HEMISPHERE	JAN	FEB	MAR	APR	MAY	JUN	JUL	AUG	SEP	OCT	NOV	DEC
°F AVG MAX	81	85	89	91	86	79	77	77	80	82	81	79
°F AVG MIN	50	53	59	65	67	67	66	67	66	64	59	52
DIURNAL RANGE	31	32	30	26	19	12	11	10	14	18	22	27
RAIN/INCHES	0.2	0.2	0.2	1.5	5.7	8.8	13.6	16.0	7.8	4.1	0.7	0.1
HUMIDITY/%	67	64	58	63	75	84	86	87	85	81	76	74
BLOOM SEASON		*	*	*	*				*	*	*	*
DAYS CLR @ 7AM	2	1	2	5	1	0	0	0	0	2	2	2
DAYS CLR @ 1PM	20	19	17	10	1	0	0	0	0	2	7	13
RAIN/MM	5	5	5	38	145	224	345	406	198	104	18	3
°C AVG MAX	27.0	29.2	31.5	32.6	29.8	25.9	24.8	24.8	26.5	27.6	27.0	25.9
°C AVG MIN	9.8	11.5	14.8	18.1	19.2	19.2	18.7	19.2	18.7	17.6	14.8	10.9
DIURNAL RANGE	17.2	17.7	16.7	14.5	10.6	6.7	6.1	5.6	7.8	10.0	12.2	15.0
S/HEMISPHERE	JUL	AUG	SEP	OCT	NOV	DEC	JAN	FEB	MAR	APR	MAY	JUN

Cultural Recommendations

LIGHT: 1800–2400 fc. Diffused light is recommended. In nature, even plants growing in open areas are exposed to low light levels, since clear days in summer are rare.

TEMPERATURES: Summer days average 77–86°F (25–30°C), and nights average 64–67°F (18–19°C), with a seasonal diurnal range of 10–14°F (6–11°C).

HUMIDITY: 75–85%.

WATER: Plants need constant moisture during the summer, when daily mistings could be beneficial. The rainfall pattern is wet/dry.

FERTILIZER: ¼–½ strength, applied weekly during periods of active growth.

REST PERIOD: Winter days average 79–85°F (26–29°C), and nights average 50–53°F (10–12°C), with a diurnal range of 27–32°F (12–18°C). The dramatic increase in the diurnal range is the result of warmer days and cooler nights during clear winter weather. Light should be increased to correspond with the dramatic increase in clear afternoons. Water should be reduced, but plants should not be allowed to dry out, since in the habitat, some moisture is continuously available from dew, fog, and morning mist. Fertilizer should be reduced or eliminated anytime the plants are not actively growing. The probable extremes indicate that plants might survive short exposures to freezing temperatures. The plant is most likely to survive if it is dry during the cold period.

GROWING MEDIA: Baskets filled with a 2–2–4 mixture of moss, tree fern, and charcoal are used successfully. Plants may be mounted if the environment is moist and humid. Repotting is best avoided except in early spring when the roots are actively growing.

MISCELLANEOUS NOTES: The roots are branching and unusually long. Plants in Thailand reportedly bloom during the 2 periods shown in the table. Cultivation bloom records indicate that heaviest blooming occurs in Mar. (Sep.), Jun. (Dec.), and Oct. (Apr.). Bloom initiators have not been identified.

Plant and Flower Information

PLANT SIZE AND TYPE: A 5–10 in. (13–25 cm) sympodial epiphyte or lithophyte.

PSEUDOBULB: 1.2–2.5 in. (3–6 cm) long. The pseudobulbs are flask-shaped and densely crowded on a creeping rhizome.

LEAVES: 2 per growth. The leaves are 4–8 in. (10–20 cm) long.

INFLORESCENCE: 2–4 in. (5–10 cm) long. The flower spikes are zigzag, stout, and usually erect. They may emerge with the new vegetative growth or just prior to it.

FLOWERS: 18–28. The tiny, fragrant blossoms are ¼ in. (0.6 cm) across. White with a heavy substance, they are reminiscent of lily-of-the-valley.

HYBRIDIZING NOTES: N/A.

REFERENCES: 14, 20, 32, 37, 157.

PHOTOS/DRAWINGS: 32, 37.

Pholidota corniculata. See *P. chinensis.* REFERENCES: 37.

Pholidota crotalina. See *P. imbricata.* REFERENCES: 37.

Pholidota decurva. See *P. articulata.* REFERENCES: 37.

Pholidota dentiloba. See *P. clemensii.* REFERENCES: 37.

Pholidota elizabethiana. See *P. carnea.* REFERENCES: 37.

Pholidota elmeri. Now considered a synonym of *Thecostele alata.* REFERENCES: 37.

Pholidota fragrans. See *P. convallariae.* REFERENCES: 37.

Pholidota gibbosa (Blume) de Vriese

AKA: *P. caduca, P. clypeata.*

ORIGIN/HABITAT: Sumatra and Borneo. In Malaya, it is found in primary highland forests; in western Java, it is found in the wetter southern hills at elevations of 5000-16,000 ft. (1524-4877 m). It grows on trees, on bare rock, and, infrequently, in loam-filled rock crevices.

CLIMATE: Station # 96781, Banung, Indonesia, Lat. 6.9°S, Long. 107.6°E, at 2427 ft. (740 m). Temperatures are calculated for an elevation of 4920 ft. (1500 m), resulting in probable extremes of 85°F (29.4°C) and 44°F (6.7°C).

N/HEMISPHERE	JAN	FEB	MAR	APR	MAY	JUN	JUL	AUG	SEP	OCT	NOV	DEC
°F AVG MAX	74	75	76	76	74	73	73	72	73	74	74	74
°F AVG MIN	55	55	56	57	58	59	59	59	59	59	58	56
DIURNAL RANGE	19	20	20	19	16	14	14	13	14	15	16	18
RAIN/INCHES	2.7	2.2	2.0	6.0	7.9	8.5	9.5	10.0	9.4	5.6	4.6	4.0
HUMIDITY/%	70	66	62	65	73	77	79	78	78	78	75	72
BLOOM SEASON	*	*	*								*	*
DAYS CLR @ 7AM	9	10	12	9	4	1	1	1	2	4	5	8
DAYS CLR @ 1PM	8	8	7	2	1	0	0	1	1	1	3	6
RAIN/MM	69	56	51	152	201	216	241	254	239	142	117	102
°C AVG MAX	23.1	23.6	24.2	24.2	23.1	22.5	22.5	22.0	22.5	23.1	23.1	23.1
°C AVG MIN	12.5	12.5	13.1	13.6	14.2	14.7	14.7	14.7	14.7	14.7	14.2	13.1
DIURNAL RANGE	10.6	11.1	11.1	10.6	8.9	7.8	7.8	7.3	7.8	8.4	8.9	10.0
S/HEMISPHERE	JUL	AUG	SEP	OCT	NOV	DEC	JAN	FEB	MAR	APR	MAY	JUN

Cultural Recommendations

LIGHT: 1800–3000 fc. Diffused light is preferred, since clear days are very rare in the habitat. Plants are normally found on forest trees, but they may also grow fully exposed to available light.

TEMPERATURES: Summer days average 72–74°F (22–23°C), and nights average 58–59°F (14–15°C), with a diurnal range of 13–16°F (7–9°C). The diurnal range is lowest in the summer months, when overcast skies prevent warming. Plants are unlikely to tolerate hot summer weather.

The climate above represents the warmest portion of the plant's range. If temperatures are calculated for 10,000 ft. (3048 m), the midrange in the plant's habitat, the lows are consistently 38–42°F (3–6°C).

HUMIDITY: 70–80%.

WATER: Plants should be constantly moist during the active growing season. The rainfall pattern is wet/wetter.

FERTILIZER: ¼–½ strength, applied weekly during periods of active growth.

REST PERIOD: Winter days average 74–76°F (23–24°C), and nights average 55–58°F (13–14°C), with an increased diurnal range of 18–20°F (10–11°C). The increase in the diurnal range is the result of both warmer days and cooler nights. For 2–3 months, water, humidity, and fertilizer should be reduced, and light should be increased.

GROWING MEDIA: Plants should be mounted on tree fern or cork, which accommodate their climbing growth habit. Remounting should be done infrequently and only when roots are actively growing.

MISCELLANEOUS NOTES: Collectors report that the plant is free-flowering, particularly in the drier season, and note that this is unusual. Perhaps the collectors' analysis emphasizes the wrong climatic element. Weather records indicate that this period coincides with higher light, warmer days, and wider diurnal variation, any of which, alone or in combination, could initiate blooming.

Plant and Flower Information

PLANT SIZE AND TYPE: Pendulous, multiple growths normally hang down 12–24 in. (30–60 cm), rarely to 40 in. (100 cm). Plants may grow as sympodial epiphytes, lithophytes, or semiterrestrials in loam-filled rock crevices.

PSEUDOBULB: 3 in. (7.5 cm) long. Ovoid, angular, and slender, the widely spaced pseudobulbs are 3–4 in. (7.5–10 cm) apart on a climbing, creeping, sometimes branching rhizome.

LEAVES: 2 per growth. The leaves are 8–12 in. (20–30 cm) long, rigid, and leathery.

INFLORESCENCE: 12 in. (30 cm) long. The spike is white, wiry, and zigzag. Emerging when the leaves are half grown, the inflorescence is initially erect but becomes pendulous. The flowers are arranged in 2 precise rows.

FLOWERS: 25 to many. The blossoms are ½ in. (1.3 cm) across, wide-opening, and variable in color. The sepals and petals are translucent and may be whitish, pinkish, greenish, or white with yellow at the tips. The lip is pale pink. The persistent floral bracts are pinkish to greenish brown.

HYBRIDIZING NOTES: N/A.

REFERENCES: 2, 32, 37, 112, 175.

PHOTOS/DRAWINGS: 32, *37*, 175.

Pholidota globosa (Blume) Lindley

AKA: N/A.

ORIGIN/HABITAT: A high mountain plant from Java, it usually grows on trees but is sometimes found in moss cushions or on rocks in old lava flows. It is most often found at 5000–8000 ft. (1524–2438 m) but can grow at still higher elevations in both very shady and completely exposed locations.

CLIMATE: Station # 96755, Bogor, Indonesia, Lat. 6.5°S, Long. 106.8°E, at 558 ft. (170 m). Temperatures are calculated for an elevation of 5000 ft. (1524 m), resulting in probable extremes of 81°F (27.2°C) and 51°F (10.6°C).

N/HEMISPHERE	JAN	FEB	MAR	APR	MAY	JUN	JUL	AUG	SEP	OCT	NOV	DEC
°F AVG MAX	71	72	73	73	72	70	69	69	70	71	72	71
°F AVG MIN	58	58	58	59	59	59	59	59	59	60	60	59
DIURNAL RANGE	13	14	15	14	13	11	10	10	11	11	12	12
RAIN/INCHES	2.1	1.0	0.5	5.0	8.1	18.8	23.7	20.2	14.4	12.0	11.9	3.4
HUMIDITY/%	72	68	65	66	74	79	84	84	81	79	77	75
BLOOM SEASON	*	*	*	*					*	*	*	
DAYS CLR @ 7AM	14	14	14	11	5	3	1	2	4	6	10	12
DAYS CLR @ 1PM	9	10	8	5	1	1	0	0	1	1	3	7
RAIN/MM	53	25	13	127	206	478	602	513	366	305	302	86
°C AVG MAX	21.9	22.4	23.0	23.0	22.4	21.3	20.7	20.7	21.3	21.9	22.4	21.9
°C AVG MIN	14.6	14.6	14.6	15.2	15.2	15.2	15.2	15.2	15.2	15.7	15.7	15.2
DIURNAL RANGE	7.3	7.8	8.4	7.8	7.2	6.1	5.5	5.5	6.1	6.2	6.7	6.7
S/HEMISPHERE	JUL	AUG	SEP	OCT	NOV	DEC	JAN	FEB	MAR	APR	MAY	JUN

Cultural Recommendations

LIGHT: 800–2000 fc. Somewhat adaptable, the plants grow in both deep shade and full sun. Clear summer days are rare, indicating that light levels below 3000 fc are probably appropriate.

TEMPERATURES: Days average 69–73°F (21–23°C), and nights average 59–60°F (15–16°C), with a summer diurnal range of 10–13°F (6–7°C). The average lows vary only 2°F (1°C) year-round. Since these averages describe the warmest of the habitats, and since the probable extreme high is 81°F (27°C), the plant is unlikely to tolerate hot summer weather. At 8000 ft. (2400 m), prevailing averages are approximately 10–15°F (6–8°C) cooler.

HUMIDITY: 75–85%.

WATER: Constant moisture should be available in summer. The rainfall pattern is wet/dry.

FERTILIZER: ¼–½ strength, applied weekly during periods of active growth.

REST PERIOD: In the habitat, average temperatures vary only a few degrees, but the slight fluctuations result in a somewhat higher diurnal range of 13–15°F (7–8°C) in winter. Water, humidity, and fertilizer should be reduced for 2–3 months, while light levels may be raised to simulate the increased number of clear days.

GROWING MEDIA: Plants may be potted in a tree-fern medium or mounted on a tree-fern slab. Repotting is best done in the spring, when new roots begin to grow.

MISCELLANEOUS NOTES: Bloom time is reported as Jan.–Apr. (Jul.–Oct.), Sep.–Nov. (Mar.–May), and "just as the rains begin." While 2 bloom periods may be indicated, the reports may simply reflect different rainy seasons in different areas.

Plant and Flower Information

PLANT SIZE AND TYPE: A 5–12 in. (13–30 cm) sympodial epiphyte or lithophyte. The plant forms a large clump.

PSEUDOBULB: 0.5–1.5 in. (1–4 cm) long. Spherical to ovoid and flat on the top, the pseudobulbs tend to alternate on opposite sides of the rhizome.

LEAVES: 2 per growth. The very narrow leaves are 2–6 in. (5–15 cm) long.

INFLORESCENCE: 8 in. (20 cm) long. The spike emerges just before or with the new leaves. Whitish and slightly zigzag, it is initially erect but becomes drooping. The flowers are arranged in 2 opposing rows.

FLOWERS: 20–40. The tiny, fragile blossoms are ¼ in. (0.6 cm) across and pinkish to cream with a red-brown anther.

HYBRIDIZING NOTES: N/A.

REFERENCES: 32, 37, 118, 175.

PHOTOS/DRAWINGS: 32, 37, 175.

Pholidota gracilis. Now considered to belong to the genus *Dendrochilum*. REFERENCES: 37.

Pholidota grandis. See *P. ventricosa.* Plants of *P. imbricata* have also been called *P. grandis.* REFERENCES: 37.

Pholidota griffithii. See *P. articulata.* REFERENCES: 37.

Pholidota guibertiae Finet. Not recently collected and unlikely to be available for cultivation. REFERENCES: 37.

Pholidota henryi. See *P. imbricata.* REFERENCES: 37.

Pholidota imbricata Hooker f.

AKA: *P. assamica, P. beccarii, P. bracteata, P. conchoidea, P. crotalina, P. grandis, P. henryi, P. loricata, P. spectabilis, P. triotos.*

P. pallida and *P. imbricata* are easily confused, and references to them are often erroneous. This is unfortunate for growers since *P. pallida* is not adaptable and requires much cooler winter temperatures. According to Dr. De Vogel, the easiest way to distinguish between the 2 species is to note that *P. imbricata* has scattered clumps of hairs on the floral bracts, giving the impression of scales or spots.

Dr. De Vogel also reports that the name *P. yunnanensis* has been applied erroneously to specimens of *P. imbricata.*

ORIGIN/HABITAT: From southern China to Australia, and from India to the Philippines. These widespread and often common plants grow both fully exposed and in shade. They may be found in trees or on limestone or lava rocks, usually at 2624–4920 ft. (800–1500 m).

CLIMATE: Station # 48327, Chiang Mai, Thailand, Lat. 18.8°N, Long. 99.0°E, at 1100 ft. (335 m). Temperatures are calculated for an elevation of 3000 ft. (914 m), resulting in probable extremes of 102°F (38.9°C) and 32°F (0.0°C).

N/HEMISPHERE	JAN	FEB	MAR	APR	MAY	JUN	JUL	AUG	SEP	OCT	NOV	DEC
°F AVG MAX	79	84	89	90	88	84	83	81	82	83	80	78
°F AVG MIN	50	51	56	64	68	68	68	69	67	65	60	51
DIURNAL RANGE	29	33	33	26	20	16	15	12	15	18	20	27
RAIN/INCHES	0.3	0.4	0.6	2.0	5.5	6.1	7.4	8.7	11.5	4.9	1.5	0.4
HUMIDITY/%	73	65	58	62	73	78	80	83	83	81	79	76
BLOOM SEASON				*	**	*			*	**	*	*
DAYS CLR @ 7AM	5	5	2	2	1	0	0	0	0	1	3	3
DAYS CLR @ 1PM	9	8	4	2	0	0	0	0	0	0	1	3
RAIN/MM	8	10	15	51	140	155	188	221	292	124	38	10
°C AVG MAX	26.0	28.7	31.5	32.1	31.0	28.7	28.2	27.1	27.6	28.2	26.5	25.4
°C AVG MIN	9.8	10.4	13.2	17.6	19.9	19.9	19.9	20.4	19.3	18.2	15.4	10.4
DIURNAL RANGE	16.2	18.3	18.3	14.5	11.1	8.8	8.3	6.7	8.3	10.0	11.1	15.0
S/HEMISPHERE	JUL	AUG	SEP	OCT	NOV	DEC	JAN	FEB	MAR	APR	MAY	JUN

Cultural Recommendations

LIGHT: 1000–3000 fc. The plants are adaptable. In the habitat, clear days are rare during the summer.

TEMPERATURES: Summer days average 81–90°F (26–32°C), and nights average 64–69°F (18–20°C), with a diurnal range of 12–26°F (7–14°C). The probable extreme high temperature indicates that the plants will tolerate consistently hot summer days.

HUMIDITY: 70-80%.

WATER: Plants should be kept moist while actively growing. The rainfall pattern is wet/dry.

FERTILIZER: ¼–½ strength, applied weekly during periods of active growth.

REST PERIOD: For 3–4 months, days average 78–89°F (25–32°C), and nights average 50–60°F (10–15°C), with an increased diurnal range of 26–33°F (14–18°C). The increase is due primarily to cooler nights, which occasionally drop to near freezing when the weather is clear and dry. Water and fertilizer should be reduced, but the plant should not be allowed to dry out, since in the habitat water is available from heavy dew, fog, and mist. Light may be increased.

GROWING MEDIA: Tree-fern slabs are satisfactory, as are hanging baskets filled with a bark or tree-fern medium. Repotting is best done in the spring when roots are actively growing.

MISCELLANEOUS NOTES: *P. imbricata* is tough and adaptable, surviving and adapting to environmental changes. Cultivation bloom records, reflected in the climate table, identify 2 pronounced blooming periods. Reports from the natural habitat indicate that blooming usually occurs May–Aug. (Nov.–Apr.).

Plant and Flower Information

PLANT SIZE AND TYPE: A 12 in. (30 cm) sympodial epiphyte or lithophyte.

PSEUDOBULB: 2–3 in. (6-8 cm) long. Hard and broadly conical, the pseudobulbs are smooth, angled, and dull grey-green, becoming wrinkled with age. They are tightly clustered, with each new pseudobulb emerging from the base of the preceding one.

LEAVES: 1 per growth. The leaf is 6–12 in. (15–30 cm) long, elliptic to lanceolate, thick, rigid, erect, and leathery. The color is variable and may be medium green, dull grey-green, or brown.

INFLORESCENCE: 12 in. (30 cm) long. Sharply drooping, the spike emerges from the apex of the new growth before the leaves or pseudobulb mature. The 2 rows of buds make it appear braided until the flowers open.

FLOWERS: 100 or more. The tiny flowers are ¼ in. (0.6 cm) across. They may be musk-scented or odorless and are nearly hidden by the persistent floral bracts. Variable in color, the sepals and petals may be greenish white, tan, or pale, fleshy pink. The lip is marked with yellow-to-orange keels.

HYBRIDIZING NOTES: N/A.

REFERENCES: 2, 9, 20, 32, 36, 37, 112, 148, 157, 162, 164, 173, 174, 175, 203.

PHOTOS/DRAWINGS: 20, 32, 36, *37*, 162, 164, *173*, 175.

Pholidota khasiyana. See *P. articulata.* REFERENCES: 37.

Pholidota kinabaluensis. Now considered a synonym of *Entomophobia kinabaluensis.* REFERENCES: 37.

Pholidota kouytcheensis. See *P. yunnanensis.* REFERENCES: 37.

Pholidota laucheana. See *P. chinensis.* REFERENCES: 37.

Pholidota leveilleana Schlechter

AKA: *P. subcalceata*, and probably *P. wenshanica.*

ORIGIN/HABITAT: Vietnam and China, at 2952–4920 ft. (900–1500 m). No additional habitat information was found.

CLIMATE: Station # 48802, Cha Pa, Vietnam, Lat. 22.3°N, Long. 103.8°E, at 5379 ft. (1640 m). The record high is 91°F (32.8°C), and the record low is 28°F (-2.2°C). Although plants are not specifically recorded from this location, which is near the border between China and Vietnam, the climate provides a reasonable starting point. At this elevation, it may represent the coolest temperatures the plants can tolerate.

N/HEMISPHERE	JAN	FEB	MAR	APR	MAY	JUN	JUL	AUG	SEP	OCT	NOV	DEC
°F AVG MAX	52	54	65	70	73	73	74	73	72	66	63	57
°F AVG MIN	41	44	52	56	61	63	64	63	61	56	51	46
DIURNAL RANGE	11	10	13	14	12	10	10	10	11	10	12	11
RAIN/INCHES	1.6	2.8	4.7	7.0	14.6	14.0	18.9	18.9	12.6	7.5	4.7	1.6
HUMIDITY/%	86	92	86	82	85	88	88	89	87	93	90	88
BLOOM SEASON			*	*	*	*						
DAYS CLR @ 7AM	7	4	6	5	1	2	1	3	5	5	9	7
DAYS CLR @ 1PM	8	3	9	7	2	1	0	0	1	1	3	7
RAIN/MM	41	71	119	178	371	356	480	480	320	190	119	41
°C AVG MAX	11.1	12.2	18.3	21.1	22.8	22.8	23.3	22.8	22.2	18.9	17.2	13.9
°C AVG MIN	5.0	6.7	11.1	13.3	16.1	17.2	17.8	17.2	16.1	13.3	10.6	7.8
DIURNAL RANGE	6.1	5.5	7.2	7.8	6.7	5.6	5.5	5.6	6.1	5.6	6.6	6.1
S/HEMISPHERE	JUL	AUG	SEP	OCT	NOV	DEC	JAN	FEB	MAR	APR	MAY	JUN

Cultural Recommendations

LIGHT: 2400 fc. Diffused light is suggested.

TEMPERATURES: Summer days average 70–74°F (21–23°C), and nights average 56–64°F (13–18°C), with a diurnal range of 10–14°F (6–8°C) throughout the year.

HUMIDITY: 85–90%.

WATER: Plants should be constantly moist while actively growing. The rainfall pattern is wet/relatively dry.

FERTILIZER: ¼–½ strength, applied weekly during periods of active growth.

REST PERIOD: For 2–3 months in winter, days average

52–57°F (11–14°C), and nights average 41–50°F (5–10°C). Little change occurs in the diurnal range, since high and low temperatures decline simultaneously. Light may be somewhat higher during the winter. Water should be reduced, but the unusually high winter humidity levels indicate frequent early morning dew, fog, and low clouds in the habitat. Fertilizer should be reduced or eliminated when plants are not actively growing.

GROWING MEDIA: Pots or baskets filled with a bark or tree-fern medium would probably be satisfactory. Repotting should be done in the spring when roots begin active growth.

MISCELLANEOUS NOTES: The bloom season shown in the climate table is based on collection records.

Plant and Flower Information

PLANT SIZE AND TYPE: A 7–16 in. (18–41 cm) sympodial terrestrial.

PSEUDOBULB: 1 in. (2.5 cm) long. Ovoid, quadrangular, and close together, the pseudobulbs emerge from an ascending rhizome.

LEAVES: 1–2 per growth. The leaves are 4–12 in. (10–30 cm) long, linear-lanceolate, and often rather stiff.

INFLORESCENCE: 5–6 in. (13–15 cm) long. Pendulous and only slightly zigzag, the spike emerges prior to or with the new leaves.

FLOWERS: 20–40. The blossoms are ¼–½ in. (0.6–1.3 cm) across. White with pale orange or carmine on the lip, the flowers remain somewhat closed, and are rather widely spaced in 2 rows.

HYBRIDIZING NOTES: N/A.

REFERENCES: 37.

PHOTOS/DRAWINGS: 37.

Pholidota longibulba Holttum

AKA: N/A.

ORIGIN/HABITAT: Pahang, Malaya, at 4264–5904 ft. (1300–1800 m) in the Cameron highlands.

CLIMATE: Station # 48657, Kuantan, Malaya, Lat. 3.8°N, Long. 103.2°E, at 58 ft. (18 m). Temperatures are calculated for an elevation of 4920 ft. (1500 m), resulting in probable extremes of 83°F (28.3°C) and 46°F (7.8°C).

N/HEMISPHERE	JAN	FEB	MAR	APR	MAY	JUN	JUL	AUG	SEP	OCT	NOV	DEC
°F AVG MAX	68	70	73	74	75	75	74	74	74	73	71	69
°F AVG MIN	56	56	56	57	58	57	57	57	57	57	57	56
DIURNAL RANGE	12	14	17	17	17	18	17	17	17	16	14	13
RAIN/INCHES	16.4	7.5	10.6	8.3	7.8	7.3	7.4	7.8	8.4	10.6	11.1	20.9
HUMIDITY/%	88	88	87	86	87	86	86	86	86	87	90	90
BLOOM SEASON	*								*	*	*	*
DAYS CLR @ 7AM	1	1	2	1	1	1	1	0	0	0	0	1
DAYS CLR @ 1PM	0	0	0	0	0	0	0	0	0	0	0	0
RAIN/MM	417	190	269	211	198	185	188	198	213	269	282	531
°C AVG MAX	20.1	21.2	22.8	23.4	23.9	23.9	23.4	23.4	23.4	22.8	21.7	20.6
°C AVG MIN	13.4	13.4	13.4	13.9	14.5	13.9	13.9	13.9	13.9	13.9	13.9	13.4
DIURNAL RANGE	6.7	7.8	9.4	9.5	9.4	10.0	9.5	9.5	9.5	8.9	7.8	7.2
S/HEMISPHERE	JUL	AUG	SEP	OCT	NOV	DEC	JAN	FEB	MAR	APR	MAY	JUN

Cultural Recommendations

LIGHT: 1200–1800 fc. Low, diffused light is suggested, as clear days in the habitat are rare.

TEMPERATURES: Summer days average 74–75°F (23–24°C), and nights average 56–58°F (13–14°C), with a diurnal range of 17–18°F (9–10°C). The lows are surprisingly uniform through the year.

HUMIDITY: 85–90%.

WATER: Plants should be kept moist, as they are probably intolerant of drying. The rainfall pattern is wet/wetter.

FERTILIZER: ¼–½ strength, applied weekly during periods of active growth.

REST PERIOD: Winter days average 68–73°F (20–23°C), but nights remain uniform. The lower, winter diurnal range is 12–14°F (7–8°C) and results from cooler days, not cooler nights. In the habitat, rainfall is higher in winter; but in cultivation, water probably should not be increased, particularly if temperatures are somewhat cool. Low light and high humidity prevail throughout the year.

GROWING MEDIA: Plants may be potted in a tree-fern medium or mounted on a tree-fern slab or coconut husk. Repotting is best done in early spring when new roots are actively growing.

MISCELLANEOUS NOTES: N/A.

Plant and Flower Information

PLANT SIZE AND TYPE: A 12–18 in. (30–47 cm) sympodial epiphyte.

PSEUDOBULB: 3.0–3.5 in. (8–9 cm) long. Ochre colored, smooth, angled, and ovoid, the pseudobulbs are spaced 0.5–1.0 in. (1.3–2.5 cm) apart on the rhizome.

LEAVES: 1 per growth. The leaf is 8–12 in. (20–30 cm) long and usually quite narrow.

INFLORESCENCE: 7–8 in. (16–21 cm) long. Nodding, wiry, and slightly zigzag, the spike arises when the new leaf is almost fully developed.

FLOWERS: 40–50. The tiny blossoms are ⅓ in. (0.8 cm) across, flesh pink, and translucent.

HYBRIDIZING NOTES: N/A.

REFERENCES: 37, 118.

PHOTOS/DRAWINGS: 37.

Pholidota longilabra De Vogel

AKA: N/A.

ORIGIN/HABITAT: Sumatra, Indonesia, at 7900–10,500 ft. (2408–3200 m), in upper mountain forests and on shrubs in more exposed locations.

CLIMATE: Station # 96163, Padang, Indonesia, Lat. 0.9°S, Long. 100.4°E, at 19 ft. (6 m). Temperatures are calculated for an elevation of 9000 ft. (2743 m), resulting in probable extremes of 64°F (17.8°C) and 38°F (3.3°C).

N/HEMISPHERE	JAN	FEB	MAR	APR	MAY	JUN	JUL	AUG	SEP	OCT	NOV	DEC
°F AVG MAX	57	57	56	56	56	56	57	57	57	57	58	57
°F AVG MIN	44	44	44	44	44	44	44	44	44	45	45	44
DIURNAL RANGE	13	13	12	12	12	12	13	13	13	12	13	13
RAIN/INCHES	10.9	13.7	6.0	19.5	20.4	18.9	13.8	10.2	12.1	14.3	12.4	12.1
HUMIDITY/%	81	82	82	84	85	84	81	81	82	83	81	81
BLOOM SEASON		*		*				*				
DAYS CLR @ 7AM	5	1	1	0	0	2	2	1	2	2	3	5
DAYS CLR @ 1PM	5	2	2	1	1	3	3	4	3	3	6	5
RAIN/MM	277	348	152	495	518	480	351	259	307	363	315	307
°C AVG MAX	14.1	14.1	13.5	13.5	13.5	13.5	14.1	14.1	14.1	14.1	14.6	14.1
°C AVG MIN	6.9	6.9	6.9	6.9	6.9	6.9	6.9	6.9	6.9	7.4	7.4	6.9
DIURNAL RANGE	7.2	7.2	6.6	6.6	6.6	6.6	7.2	7.2	7.2	6.7	7.2	7.2
S/HEMISPHERE	JUL	AUG	SEP	OCT	NOV	DEC	JAN	FEB	MAR	APR	MAY	JUN

Cultural Recommendations

LIGHT: 2000–3000 fc. Diffused light is preferred.

TEMPERATURES: The cool summer days average 56-58°F (14–15°C), and nights average 44–45°F (7°C), with a diurnal range of 12–13°F (7°C). The probable extremes vary only a few degrees from the averages, indicating that the plant probably cannot tolerate wide temperature fluctuations.

HUMIDITY: 80–85%.

WATER: Plants should be constantly moist. The rainfall pattern is wet/wetter.

FERTILIZER: ¼–½ strength, applied weekly during periods of active growth.

REST PERIOD: None. Growing conditions should be maintained year-round.

GROWING MEDIA: Plants may be potted in a tree-fern medium or mounted on a tree-fern slab or coconut husk. Repotting is best done in early spring or when roots are actively growing.

MISCELLANEOUS NOTES: *P. longilabra* could be extremely difficult to maintain in cultivation. The limited range, combined with constant moisture and cool temperatures, indicates a very specialized adaptation to its habitat.

The bloom season shown in the climate table is based on collection times.

Plant and Flower Information

PLANT SIZE AND TYPE: A 4–6 in. (10–15 cm) sympodial epiphyte or lithophyte.

PSEUDOBULB: 1.2–2.4 in. (3–6 cm) long. The pseudobulbs are curved and densely clustered.

LEAVES: 2 per growth. The leaves are 1.2–2.4 in. (3-6 cm) long and ovate-lanceolate to linear. The foliage often grows at right angles to the pseudobulb.

INFLORESCENCE: 2–5 in. (6–13 cm) long. The flower spike is an independent growth.

FLOWERS: 10–30. The tiny blossoms are ¼ in. (0.6 cm) across. They are creamy white, sometimes with an orange-red column.

HYBRIDIZING NOTES: N/A.

REFERENCES: 37.

PHOTOS/DRAWINGS: 37.

Pholidota loricata. See *P. imbricata*. REFERENCES: 37.

Pholidota lugardii. See *P. articulata*. REFERENCES: 37.

Pholidota mediocris De Vogel

AKA: N/A.

ORIGIN/HABITAT: Kalimantan Timor, Borneo, and Sarawak, Indonesia, at 4500–6500 ft. (1372–1981 m).

CLIMATE: Station # 96441, Bintulu, Sarawak, Lat. 3.2°N, Long. 113.0°E, at 10 ft. (3 m). Temperatures are calculated for an elevation of 5000 ft. (1524 m), resulting in probable extremes of 82°F (27.8°C) and 46°F (7.8°C).

N/HEMISPHERE	JAN	FEB	MAR	APR	MAY	JUN	JUL	AUG	SEP	OCT	NOV	DEC
˚F AVG MAX	70	70	71	72	72	74	72	74	71	71	72	71
˚F AVG MIN	58	58	57	58	58	58	58	58	57	57	57	58
DIURNAL RANGE	12	12	14	14	14	16	14	16	14	14	15	13
RAIN/INCHES	14.7	12.4	10.8	9.5	8.7	10.0	7.4	8.4	13.5	13.9	14.1	17.1
HUMIDITY/%	87	87	85	85	85	84	83	85	85	86	86	87
BLOOM SEASON							*		*	*		
DAYS CLR @ 8AM	0	1	1	1	3	3	2	1	0	1	1	1
DAYS CLR @ 2PM	1	0	1	3	2	2	2	1	0	1	1	1
RAIN/MM	373	315	274	241	221	254	188	213	343	353	358	434
˚C AVG MAX	20.9	20.9	21.4	22.0	22.0	23.1	22.0	23.1	21.4	21.4	22.0	21.4
˚C AVG MIN	14.2	14.2	13.6	14.2	14.2	14.2	14.2	14.2	13.6	13.6	13.6	14.2
DIURNAL RANGE	6.7	6.7	7.8	7.8	7.8	8.9	7.8	8.9	7.8	7.8	8.4	7.2
S/HEMISPHERE	JUL	AUG	SEP	OCT	NOV	DEC	JAN	FEB	MAR	APR	MAY	JUN

Cultural Recommendations

LIGHT: 1200–2000 fc. Diffused light is suggested. In the habitat, clear days are rare.

TEMPERATURES: Summer days average 72–74˚F (22–23˚C), and nights average 58˚F (14˚C), with a diurnal range of 14–16˚F (8–9˚C). The average lows vary only 1˚F (0.6˚C) throughout the year.

HUMIDITY: 85%.

WATER: Plants should be constantly moist. The rainfall pattern is wet/wetter.

FERTILIZER: ¼–½ strength, applied weekly during periods of active growth.

REST PERIOD: Winter days average 70˚F (21˚C), and nights average 58˚F (15˚C), resulting in a slightly lower diurnal range of 12–14˚F (7–8˚C). The slight seasonal variation results from cooler days rather than cooler nights.

GROWING MEDIA: Plants may be potted in a bark or tree-fern medium or mounted on a tree-fern slab or coconut husk. Repotting is best done in spring when new roots are actively growing.

MISCELLANEOUS NOTES: The bloom season shown in the climate table is based on collection records.

Plant and Flower Information

PLANT SIZE AND TYPE: A 12–18 in. (30–46 cm) sympodial epiphyte.

PSEUDOBULB: Slender, but often somewhat swollen, the pseudobulb becomes finely wrinkled with age.

LEAVES: 1 per growth. The single leaf is 12–16 in. (30–41 cm) long and linear to oblong-lanceolate.

INFLORESCENCE: 6.3–8.3 in. (16–21 cm) long. The spike emerges from the base of the pseudobulb prior to or with the new leaf.

FLOWERS: 20–30. The tiny, sweetly fragrant white blossoms are the smallest and least spectacular of the genus. The flowers at the base of the inflorescence open first.

HYBRIDIZING NOTES: N/A.

REFERENCES: 37.

PHOTOS/DRAWINGS: 37.

Pholidota membranacea. Dr. De Vogel indicates that the original description was not sufficiently complete to identify this species. REFERENCES: 37.

Pholidota micrantha. See *P. carnea*. REFERENCES: 37.

Pholidota minahassae. See *P. articulata*. REFERENCES: 37.

Pholidota missionariorum Gagnepain

AKA: *P. rupestris*.

ORIGIN/HABITAT: Bhutan and northern Yunnan, China, eastern Tibet, and Kachin, Burma, where it often grows near streams at 5500–7200 ft. (1676–2195 m).

CLIMATE: Station #57816, Kuei-yang (Guiyang), China, Lat. 26.6˚N, Long. 106.7˚E, at 3514 ft. (1071 m). Temperatures are calculated for an elevation of 5000 ft. (1524 m), resulting in probable extremes of 90˚F (32.2˚C) and 16˚F (-8.9˚C).

N/HEMISPHERE	JAN	FEB	MAR	APR	MAY	JUN	JUL	AUG	SEP	OCT	NOV	DEC
˚F AVG MAX	43	46	59	67	70	76	79	79	74	63	55	48
˚F AVG MIN	31	33	43	51	56	61	65	63	58	50	43	35
DIURNAL RANGE	12	13	16	16	14	15	14	16	16	13	12	13
RAIN/INCHES	0.8	1.1	1.6	3.6	7.6	8.4	7.8	5.3	5.0	4.1	1.9	1.0
HUMIDITY/%	74	77	71	72	77	76	77	76	73	77	78	78
BLOOM SEASON								*	*	*		
DAYS CLR @ 7AM	2	1	2	3	1	2	2	4	5	2	2	1
DAYS CLR @ 1PM	4	3	7	6	3	2	1	2	4	5	3	5
RAIN/MM	20	28	41	91	193	213	198	135	127	104	48	25
˚C AVG MAX	6.2	7.8	15.1	19.5	21.2	24.5	26.2	26.2	23.4	17.3	12.8	8.9
˚C AVG MIN	-0.6	0.6	6.2	10.6	13.4	16.2	18.4	17.3	14.5	10.1	6.2	1.7
DIURNAL RANGE	6.8	7.2	8.9	8.9	7.8	8.3	7.8	8.9	8.9	7.2	6.6	7.2
S/HEMISPHERE	JUL	AUG	SEP	OCT	NOV	DEC	JAN	FEB	MAR	APR	MAY	JUN

Cultural Recommendations

LIGHT: 2400 fc. Diffused light is recommended.

TEMPERATURES: Summer days average 70–79˚F (21–26˚C), and nights average 61–65˚F (16–18˚C), with a diurnal range of 14–16˚F (8–9˚C).

HUMIDITY: 70–78%.

WATER: Plants should be constantly moist while actively growing. The rainfall pattern is wet/dry.

FERTILIZER: ¼–½ strength, applied weekly during periods of active growth.

REST PERIOD: For 4–5 months, days average 43–59°F (6–15°C), and nights average 31–43°F (-0.6–6.0°C), with a slightly reduced winter diurnal range of 12–13°F (7°C). Day and night temperatures decline simultaneously, resulting in little variation in the diurnal range. Water may be reduced, but plants should not become dry. In the habitat, morning fog, dew, and mist provide relatively uniform year-round humidity levels, despite the low winter rainfall. Fertilizer should be reduced or eliminated.

GROWING MEDIA: Plants should probably be mounted on tree-fern or cork slabs. Repotting is best done in early spring when new roots are actively growing. Because the roots are branching, this plant should be more tolerant of reslabbing than many of the species in this genus.

MISCELLANEOUS NOTES: The cool, moist climate and limited range indicate that *P. missionariorum* would probably be extremely difficult to maintain in a warm climate or a warm-to-intermediate greenhouse.

Plant and Flower Information

PLANT SIZE AND TYPE: Normally a 3–4 in. (8–10 cm) sympodial lithophyte, the plant can also grow as an epiphyte.

PSEUDOBULB: 1 in. (2.5 cm) long. Slender and shiny, the pseudobulbs become wrinkled with age. They are spaced ½–¾ in. (1–2 cm) apart on the rhizome.

LEAVES: 2 per growth. The leaves are linear-lanceolate to ovate and 0.8–2.5 in. (2.0–6.5 cm) long.

INFLORESCENCE: 0.8–1.5 in. (2–4 cm) long. The spike arises prior to or with the newly emerging foliage.

FLOWERS: 7–13. The tiny, fragrant blossoms are ¼ in. (0.6 cm) across and may be white, greenish white, or cream.

HYBRIDIZING NOTES: The seed capsule remains on the plant until the following spring.

REFERENCES: 37.

PHOTOS/DRAWINGS: 37.

Pholidota nervosa Rchb.f.

AKA: N/A.

ORIGIN/HABITAT: Sumatra and Java, Indonesia. The only specific location reported is Salak, a mountain southwest of Bogor, Indonesia. Elevation was not recorded.

CLIMATE: Station # 96755, Bogor, Indonesia, Lat. 6.5°S, Long. 106.8°E, at 558 ft. (170 m). The record high is 96°F (35.6°C), and the record low is 66°F (18.9°C).

N/HEMISPHERE	JAN	FEB	MAR	APR	MAY	JUN	JUL	AUG	SEP	OCT	NOV	DEC
°F AVG MAX	86	87	88	88	87	85	84	84	85	86	87	86
°F AVG MIN	73	73	73	74	74	74	74	74	74	75	75	74
DIURNAL RANGE	13	14	15	14	13	11	10	10	11	11	12	12
RAIN/INCHES	2.0	1.0	0.5	5.0	8.1	18.8	23.7	20.2	14.4	12.0	11.9	3.4
HUMIDITY/%	72	68	65	66	74	79	84	84	81	79	77	75
BLOOM SEASON		*	*									
DAYS CLR @ 7AM	14	14	14	11	5	3	1	2	4	6	10	12
DAYS CLR @ 1PM	9	10	8	5	1	1	0	0	1	1	3	7
RAIN/MM	53	25	13	127	206	478	602	513	366	305	302	86
°C AVG MAX	30.0	30.6	31.1	31.1	30.6	29.4	28.9	28.9	29.4	30.0	30.6	30.0
°C AVG MIN	22.8	22.8	22.8	23.3	23.3	23.3	23.3	23.3	23.3	23.9	23.9	23.3
DIURNAL RANGE	7.2	7.8	8.3	7.8	7.3	6.1	5.6	5.6	6.1	6.1	6.7	6.7
S/HEMISPHERE	JUL	AUG	SEP	OCT	NOV	DEC	JAN	FEB	MAR	APR	MAY	JUN

Cultural Recommendations

LIGHT: 1000–2000 fc. Diffused light is suggested.

TEMPERATURES: Summer days average 84–87°F (29–31°C), and nights average 74°F (23°C), with a diurnal range of 10–13°F (6–7°C). At the latitudes of the natural habitat, the diurnal range would remain constant even at higher elevations. These temperatures should be considered as starting points, since information on plant elevation was not available.

HUMIDITY: 80–85%.

WATER: Plants should be constantly moist while actively growing. The rainfall pattern is very wet/dry.

FERTILIZER: ¼–½ strength, applied weekly during periods of active growth.

REST PERIOD: Winter days average 86–88°F (30–31°C), and nights average 73–75°F (23–24°C), with a slightly increased diurnal range of 13–15°F (7–8°C). Higher elevations are somewhat cooler, but temperatures follow a similar pattern. Increased light is indicated by the greater number of clear winter days in the habitat. Water, humidity, and fertilizer should be reduced for 2–3 months, but the plant should not be allowed to dry out, since moisture is normally available from dew and heavy fog.

GROWING MEDIA: Plants should be potted in a tree-fern

medium or mounted on tree-fern or coconut-husk slabs. Repotting is best done in the spring when new roots are actively growing.

MISCELLANEOUS NOTES: N/A.

Plant and Flower Information

PLANT SIZE AND TYPE: A 16 in. (41 cm) sympodial epiphyte.

PSEUDOBULB: Size unknown. The bulbs are ovoid and slender.

LEAVES: 2 per growth. The leaves are 9–10 in. (23–25 cm) long, linear-lanceolate, and quite stiff.

INFLORESCENCE: 6–12 in. (15–30 cm) long. Emerging prior to the new vegetative growth, the spike is erect, flattened, and somewhat zigzag. The flowers all turn to one side, facing the same direction and forming a single row.

FLOWERS: 25–40. The tiny blossoms are pale green to white, with a whitish, yellowish, or greenish lip. The sepals have black scales on the outer surface, and the floral bracts are sometimes persistent.

HYBRIDIZING NOTES: N/A.

REFERENCES: 32, 37, 175.

PHOTOS/DRAWINGS: 32, 37, 175.

Pholidota obovata. See *P. articulata.* REFERENCES: 37.

Pholidota pallida Lindley

AKA: *P. bracteata*, *P. schlechteri*, *P. tixieri*. The name *P. calceata* is often used for smaller plants.

P. pallida and *P. imbricata* are easily confused, and references to them are often erroneous, which is unfortunate for growers since *P. pallida* requires precise growing conditions, while *P. imbricata* is adaptable. According to Dr. De Vogel, the easiest way to distinguish between the 2 species is to note that *P. imbricata* has scattered clumps of hairs on the floral bracts, giving the impression of scales or spots.

ORIGIN/HABITAT: China, Burma, Nepal, India, and Laos. In Thailand, it grows near Doi Suthep at 3300–6500 ft. (1006–1981 m).

CLIMATE: Station # 42619, Silchar, India, Lat. 24.8°N, Long. 92.8°E, at 95 ft. (29 m). Temperatures are calculated for an elevation of 4000 ft. (1219 m), resulting in probable extremes of 90°F (32.2°C) and 28°F (-2.2°C).

N/HEMISPHERE	JAN	FEB	MAR	APR	MAY	JUN	JUL	AUG	SEP	OCT	NOV	DEC
°F AVG MAX	65	68	74	75	76	76	77	77	77	75	72	67
°F AVG MIN	39	43	50	56	60	63	64	64	63	59	51	42
DIURNAL RANGE	26	25	24	19	16	13	13	13	14	16	21	25
RAIN/INCHES	0.8	2.1	7.9	14.3	15.6	21.7	19.7	19.7	14.4	6.5	1.4	0.4
HUMIDITY/%	76	72	67	74	79	85	85	86	86	84	81	79
BLOOM SEASON					*	*	*	*				
DAYS CLR @ 6PM	26	22	19	13	10	2	2	3	8	16	25	27
RAIN/MM	20	53	201	363	396	551	500	500	366	165	36	10
°C AVG MAX	18.4	20.1	23.4	24.0	24.5	24.5	25.1	25.1	25.1	24.0	22.3	19.5
°C AVG MIN	4.0	6.2	10.1	13.4	15.6	17.3	17.8	17.8	17.3	15.1	10.6	5.6
DIURNAL RANGE	14.4	13.9	13.3	10.6	8.9	7.2	7.3	7.3	7.8	8.9	11.7	13.9
S/HEMISPHERE	JUL	AUG	SEP	OCT	NOV	DEC	JAN	FEB	MAR	APR	MAY	JUN

Cultural Recommendations

LIGHT: 2000–3000 fc. Diffused light is preferred.

TEMPERATURES: Summer days average 75–77°F (24–25°C), and nights average 56–64°F (13–18°C), with a diurnal range of 14–16°F (7–9°C).

HUMIDITY: 80–85%.

WATER: Plants should be constantly moist while actively growing. The rainfall pattern is wet/dry.

FERTILIZER: ¼–½ strength, applied weekly during periods of active growth.

REST PERIOD: Winter days average 65–72°F (18–22°C), and nights average 39–50°F (4–10°C), with a diurnal range of 21–26°F (12–14°C). Water should be reduced for 3–4 months, but plants should be misted occasionally, and humidity should remain above 65%. Although the rainfall pattern in the habitat is wet/dry, the high relative humidity indicates that some moisture is constantly available from early morning dew, fog, and low clouds. Light may be increased, but fertilizer should be eliminated.

GROWING MEDIA: Pots or baskets filled with a bark or tree-fern medium may be used, or the plants may be mounted on a tree-fern slab or coconut husk. Repotting is best done in early spring when new roots are actively growing.

MISCELLANEOUS NOTES: *P. pallida* is not adaptable and is considered difficult to maintain in temperate-zone greenhouses. It requires a cold winter rest.

Plant and Flower Information

PLANT SIZE AND TYPE: A 4–15 in. (10–38 cm) sympodial epiphyte or lithophyte.

PSEUDOBULB: 1.0–2.4 in. (2.5–6.0 cm) long.

LEAVES: 1 per pseudobulb. The leaf may be oblong to linear-lanceolate.

INFLORESCENCE: Length unknown. Slender and wiry, the spike emerges when the new leaf is almost entirely developed. The flowers appear randomly around the inflorescence.

FLOWERS: 15–50. The somewhat fragrant blossoms are usually ½ in. (1.3 cm) across, but size is variable. The flowers, which may be white, creamy white, or tinged with pink, open simultaneously. The floral bracts are usually white to pink, becoming pale brown with darker veins when dry.

HYBRIDIZING NOTES: Fruits are described as well developed by Oct.–Dec. (Apr.–Jun.).

REFERENCES: 14, 34, 37, 139, 157.

PHOTOS/DRAWINGS: *14, 34, 37, 139.*

Pholidota parviflora. See *P. carnea.* REFERENCES: 37.

Pholidota pectinata Ames

AKA: N/A.

ORIGIN/HABITAT: Borneo, normally growing in open, mossy, dwarf forests at 5000–8000 ft. (1524–2438 m).

CLIMATE: Station # 49613, Tambunan, North Borneo, Lat. 5.7°N, Long. 116.4°E, at 1200 ft. (366 m). Temperatures are calculated for an elevation of 6500 ft. (1981 m), resulting in probable extremes of 80°F (26.7°C) and 37°F (2.8°C).

N/HEMISPHERE	JAN	FEB	MAR	APR	MAY	JUN	JUL	AUG	SEP	OCT	NOV	DEC
°F AVG MAX	69	70	72	73	73	72	72	72	72	71	70	69
°F AVG MIN	50	48	49	50	51	50	49	49	50	50	50	51
DIURNAL RANGE	19	22	23	23	22	22	23	23	22	21	20	18
RAIN/INCHES	5.8	3.7	5.8	7.5	8.2	7.3	5.1	4.9	6.4	7.0	6.8	6.0
HUMIDITY/%	N/A											
BLOOM SEASON	*									*	*	*
DAYS CLR	N/A											
RAIN/MM	147	94	147	190	208	185	130	124	163	178	173	152
°C AVG MAX	20.3	20.8	21.9	22.5	22.5	21.9	21.9	21.9	21.9	21.4	20.8	20.3
°C AVG MIN	9.7	8.6	9.2	9.7	10.3	9.7	9.2	9.2	9.7	9.7	9.7	10.3
DIURNAL RANGE	10.6	12.2	12.7	12.8	12.2	12.2	12.7	12.7	12.2	11.7	11.1	10.0
S/HEMISPHERE	JUL	AUG	SEP	OCT	NOV	DEC	JAN	FEB	MAR	APR	MAY	JUN

Cultural Recommendations

LIGHT: 2400 fc. Diffused light is suggested. Although observed data are not available, the steady, year-round rainfall indicates a high incidence of cloud cover.

TEMPERATURES: Days average 69–73°F (20–23°C), and nights average 48-51°F (9–10°C), with a diurnal range of 19–23°F (11–13°C). Uniformly cool temperatures are required throughout the year. The plant is unlike-

ly to be adaptable, since it apparently does not grow at lower elevations.

HUMIDITY: 70–80%. Although precise data are not available, the steady, year-round rainfall, cool temperatures, and mossy habitat indicate high humidity.

WATER: Plants should be constantly moist. The rainfall pattern is wet year-round.

FERTILIZER: ¼–½ strength, applied weekly during periods of active growth.

REST PERIOD: Growing conditions vary only slightly through the year. The diurnal range is slightly lower in winter due to somewhat cooler days. Fertilizer should be decreased when plants are not actively growing.

GROWING MEDIA: Pots or baskets filled with a bark or tree-fern medium may be used, or the plants may be mounted on a tree-fern slab or coconut husk. Repotting is best done in early spring when new roots are actively growing.

MISCELLANEOUS NOTES: The bloom season shown in the climate table is based on collection records.

Plant and Flower Information

PLANT SIZE AND TYPE: An 8–20 in. (20–51 cm) sympodial terrestrial or epiphyte with a thin, wiry appearance.

PSEUDOBULB: 0.5–1.2 in. (1.3–3.0 cm) long. Erect, angular, and swollen, the pseudobulb arises from a short rhizome.

LEAVES: 1 per growth. The single leaf is 6–18 in. (15–46 cm) long and elliptic-oblong. The variability in plant size is due to variations in the leaves.

INFLORESCENCE: 8–10 in. (20–25 cm) long. Wiry and erect then arching, the shiny, light green spike emerges when the new leaf is about half developed.

FLOWERS: 10–40. The cupped, slightly fragrant blossoms are ⅓ in. (0.8 cm) across. Variably colored, they may be white, creamy, pinkish, or tan. The lip is marked with pinkish keels and has a yellow or pink blotch in front of the keels. The persistent floral bracts are pale pink or pale red.

HYBRIDIZING NOTES: N/A.

REFERENCES: 2, 37.

PHOTOS/DRAWINGS: *37.*

Pholidota pholas. See *P. chinensis.* REFERENCES: 37.

Pholidota protracta Hooker f.

AKA: N/A.

ORIGIN/HABITAT: Sikkim, Manipur, and the Khasia and Naga hills in India, at 5900-8200 ft. (1798-2499 m).

CLIMATE: Station # 42619, Silchar, India, Lat. 24.8°N, Long. 92.8°E, at 95 ft. (29 m). Temperatures are calculated for an elevation of 7216 ft. (2200 m), resulting in probable extremes of 80°F (26.7°C) and 17°F (-8.3°C).

N/HEMISPHERE	JAN	FEB	MAR	APR	MAY	JUN	JUL	AUG	SEP	OCT	NOV	DEC
°F AVG MAX	55	58	64	65	66	66	67	67	67	65	62	57
°F AVG MIN	29	33	40	46	50	53	54	54	53	49	41	32
DIURNAL RANGE	26	25	24	19	16	13	13	13	14	16	21	25
RAIN/INCHES	0.8	2.1	7.9	14.3	15.6	21.7	19.7	19.7	14.4	6.5	1.4	0.4
HUMIDITY/%	76	72	67	74	79	85	85	86	86	84	81	79
BLOOM SEASON			*		*		*		*			*
DAYS CLR @ 6PM	26	22	19	13	10	2	2	3	8	16	25	27
RAIN/MM	20	53	201	363	396	551	500	500	366	165	36	10
°C AVG MAX	12.5	14.2	17.5	18.1	18.6	18.6	19.2	19.2	19.2	18.1	16.4	13.6
°C AVG MIN	-1.9	0.3	4.2	7.5	9.8	11.4	12.0	12.0	11.4	9.2	4.8	-0.2
DIURNAL RANGE	14.4	13.9	13.3	10.6	8.8	7.2	7.2	7.2	7.8	8.9	11.6	13.8
S/HEMISPHERE	JUL	AUG	SEP	OCT	NOV	DEC	JAN	FEB	MAR	APR	MAY	JUN

Cultural Recommendations

LIGHT: 2000–3000 fc. Diffused light is preferred.

TEMPERATURES: Summer days average 65–67°F (18–19°C), and nights average 46–54°F (8–12°C), with a diurnal range of 13–16°F (7–9°C).

HUMIDITY: 80–85%.

WATER: Plants should be constantly moist while actively growing. The rainfall pattern is wet/dry.

FERTILIZER: ¼–½ strength, applied weekly during periods of active growth.

REST PERIOD: Winter days average 55–64°F (12–18°C), and nights average 29–41°F (-2–5°C), with a diurnal range of 21–26°F (12–14°C). The plants may not need below-freezing temperatures since they also grow at lower elevations, but they should certainly tolerate them, as the habitat extends to still cooler elevations. Although the rainfall pattern in the habitat is wet/dry, the high winter humidity levels indicate that some moisture is constantly available from early morning dew, fog, and low clouds. Fertilizer should be eliminated. Light is probably higher, as indicated by the increased number of clear days.

GROWING MEDIA: Plants may be grown in baskets filled with a bark or tree-fern medium or mounted on a tree-fern slab or coconut husk. Plants are best repotted in early spring.

MISCELLANEOUS NOTES: The bloom season shown in the climate table was based on collection records. Each plant may bloom several times, or these records may simply reflect different bloom seasons in different areas.

Weather in the habitat suggests that it might be very difficult to maintain *P. protracta* in cultivation.

Plant and Flower Information

PLANT SIZE AND TYPE: A 7–36 in. (18–91 cm) climbing, sympodial epiphyte.

PSEUDOBULB: 1.5–4.0 in. (4–10 cm) long. Slender and often curved, the pseudobulbs may be clustered or widely spaced on the thick rhizome.

LEAVES: 2 per growth. The leaves are 3–5 in. (8–13 cm) long and lanceolate to linear.

INFLORESCENCE: 1.5 in. (4 cm) long. The spikes, often several, emerge as independent growths directly from the rhizome.

FLOWERS: 4–10. The tiny blossoms are ¼ in. (0.6 cm) across. The flower color ranges from cream to green, and the lip is marked with 4 yellow patches. The floral bracts are persistent.

HYBRIDIZING NOTES: N/A.

REFERENCES: 9, 20, 37, 157.

PHOTOS/DRAWINGS: 9, 20, 37.

Pholidota pusilla. Now considered a synonym of *Chelonistele sulphurea*. REFERENCES: 37.

Pholidota pyrranthela. See *P. chinensis*. REFERENCES: 37.

Pholidota recurva Lindley

AKA: N/A.

ORIGIN/HABITAT: India, Nepal, Sikkim, and Bhutan, at 2300–4300 ft. (701–1310 m). In Thailand, it grows on Doi Inthanond, near Chiang Mai, at 6200 ft. (1900 m). At other locations, the elevation range is 4264-5904 ft. (1300–1800 m).

CLIMATE: Station # 48327, Chiang Mai, Thailand, Lat. 18.8°N, Long. 99.0°E, at 1100 ft. (335 m). Temperatures are calculated for an elevation of 5000 ft. (1524 m), resulting in probable extremes of 96°F (35.6°C) and 25°F (-3.9°C).

N/HEMISPHERE	JAN	FEB	MAR	APR	MAY	JUN	JUL	AUG	SEP	OCT	NOV	DEC
°F AVG MAX	72	77	82	83	81	77	76	74	75	76	73	71
°F AVG MIN	43	44	49	57	61	61	61	62	60	58	53	44
DIURNAL RANGE	29	33	33	26	20	16	15	12	15	18	20	27
RAIN/INCHES	0.3	0.4	0.6	2.0	5.5	6.1	7.4	8.7	11.5	4.9	1.5	0.4
HUMIDITY/%	73	65	58	62	73	78	80	83	83	81	79	76
BLOOM SEASON								*	*			
DAYS CLR @ 7AM	5	5	2	2	1	0	0	0	0	1	3	3
DAYS CLR @ 1PM	9	8	4	2	0	0	0	0	0	0	1	3
RAIN/MM	8	10	15	51	140	155	188	221	292	124	38	10
°C AVG MAX	22.3	25.1	27.9	28.4	27.3	25.1	24.5	23.4	24.0	24.5	22.9	21.7
°C AVG MIN	6.2	6.7	9.5	14.0	16.2	16.2	16.2	16.7	15.6	14.5	11.7	6.7
DIURNAL RANGE	16.1	18.4	18.4	14.4	11.1	8.9	8.3	6.7	8.4	10.0	11.2	15.0
S/HEMISPHERE	JUL	AUG	SEP	OCT	NOV	DEC	JAN	FEB	MAR	APR	MAY	JUN

Cultural Recommendations

LIGHT: 1800–2400 fc. Diffused light is suggested.

TEMPERATURES: Summer days average 74–83°F (23–28°C), and nights average 57–62°F (14–17°C), with a diurnal range of 12–20°F (7–11°C). The warmest temperatures occur in the spring.

HUMIDITY: 75–80%.

WATER: Plants should be constantly moist while actively growing. The rainfall pattern is wet/dry.

FERTILIZER: ¼–½ strength, applied weekly during periods of active growth.

REST PERIOD: Winter days average 71–82°F (22–28°C), and nights average 43–49°F (6–10°C), with a diurnal range of 26–33°F (14–18°C). The warmest weather occurs in the spring and coincides with, or immediately follows, the period of widest diurnal range. In cultivation, water and humidity should be reduced for 3-4 months; but plants should not be allowed to dry out, since in the habitat, moisture is available from heavy morning dew, fog, and mist, even during the dry season. Light may be increased somewhat, reflecting the increase in the number of clear days.

GROWING MEDIA: Plants are most easily managed when mounted on slabs of tree fern, cork, or coconut husk. Remounting is best done in spring when new roots begin active growth.

MISCELLANEOUS NOTES: The bloom season shown in the climate table is based on collection records.

Plant and Flower Information

PLANT SIZE AND TYPE: A 6–18 in. (15–46 cm) sympodial epiphyte.

PSEUDOBULB: 1–4 in. (2.5–10.0 cm) long. New pseudobulbs form at the apex of the older pseudobulbs. Occasionally more than one new growth will form, giving the appearance of branching. Older pseudobulbs are shiny, smooth, and angular and may be either swollen or slender.

LEAVES: 1–2 per growth. The leaves are 2–4 in. (5–10 cm) long, quite stiff, and linear-lanceolate.

INFLORESCENCE: 3–6 in. (8–15 cm) long. The spike is recurved, with all flowers facing in one direction.

FLOWERS: 25–35. The tiny flowers are ¼ in. (0.6 cm) across; they may be either wide-opening or rather closed. They are creamy white or pale brown to orange-brown.

HYBRIDIZING NOTES: N/A.

REFERENCES: 20, 37, 157.

PHOTOS/DRAWINGS: 20, 37.

Pholidota repens. See *P. articulata.* REFERENCES: 37.

Pholidota rhombophora. Now considered a synonym of *Acoridium rhombophorum.* REFERENCES: 37.

Pholidota roseans Schlechter

AKA: N/A.

ORIGIN/HABITAT: Yunnan and Guizhou Provinces of China, in mixed forests at 4100-6560 ft. (1250-2000 m).

CLIMATE: Station # 57816, Kuei-yang (Guiyang), China, Lat. 26.6°N, Long. 106.7°E, at 3514 ft. (1071 m). Temperatures are calculated for an elevation of 5000 ft. (1524 m), resulting in probable extremes of 90°F (32.2°C) and 16°F (-8.9°C).

N/HEMISPHERE	JAN	FEB	MAR	APR	MAY	JUN	JUL	AUG	SEP	OCT	NOV	DEC
°F AVG MAX	43	46	59	67	70	76	79	79	74	63	55	48
°F AVG MIN	31	33	43	51	56	61	65	63	58	50	43	35
DIURNAL RANGE	12	13	16	16	14	15	14	16	16	13	12	13
RAIN/INCHES	0.8	1.1	1.6	3.6	7.6	8.4	7.8	5.3	5.0	4.1	1.9	1.0
HUMIDITY/%	74	77	71	72	77	76	77	76	73	77	78	78
BLOOM SEASON	N/A											
DAYS CLR @ 7AM	2	1	2	3	1	2	2	4	5	2	2	1
DAYS CLR @ 1PM	4	3	7	6	3	2	1	2	4	5	3	5
RAIN/MM	20	28	41	91	193	213	198	135	127	104	48	25
°C AVG MAX	6.2	7.8	15.1	19.5	21.2	24.5	26.2	26.2	23.4	17.3	12.8	8.9
°C AVG MIN	-0.5	0.6	6.2	10.6	13.4	16.2	18.4	17.3	14.5	10.1	6.2	1.7
DIURNAL RANGE	6.7	7.2	8.9	8.9	7.8	8.3	7.8	8.9	8.9	7.2	6.6	7.2
S/HEMISPHERE	JUL	AUG	SEP	OCT	NOV	DEC	JAN	FEB	MAR	APR	MAY	JUN

Cultural Recommendations

LIGHT: 2000–3000 fc. Diffused light is suggested.

TEMPERATURES: Summer days average 67–79°F (19–26°C), and nights average 51–65°F (11–18°C), with a diurnal range of 14–16°F (8–9°C). The diurnal range is quite consistent all year, but it is slightly higher in spring and summer.

HUMIDITY: 70–78%.

WATER: Plants should be constantly moist while actively growing. The rainfall pattern is wet/dry.

FERTILIZER: ¼–½ strength, applied weekly during periods of active growth.

REST PERIOD: Winter days average 43–59°F (6–15°C), and nights average 31–43°F (-0.5–6.0°C), with a diurnal range of 12–16°F (7–9°C). The diurnal range fluctuates only slightly through the year, since highs and lows fluctuate simultaneously. Water may be reduced for 3–4 months, but plants should be misted to prevent desiccation, since in the habitat, some moisture is available from morning dew, fog, and low clouds. Humidity should remain fairly constant. Fertilizer should be eliminated.

GROWING MEDIA: Although no cultivation information is available, plants should probably be slabbed or potted in a bark or tree-fern medium. Repotting is probably best done in early spring when roots resume active growth.

MISCELLANEOUS NOTES: N/A.

Plant and Flower Information

PLANT SIZE AND TYPE: A 7–8 in. (18–20 cm) sympodial epiphyte.

PSEUDOBULB: 2.5–3.5 in. (6–9 cm) long. The pseudobulbs, which are slender and close together, become wrinkled with age.

LEAVES: 2 per growth. The leaves are 3.5–4.5 in. (9–11 cm) long and rather stiff.

INFLORESCENCE: 2 in. (5 cm) long. The spike is erect.

FLOWERS: 7–9. The blossoms are ¾ in. (2 cm) across, wide-opening, and white to pinkish white. The floral bracts are persistent, but the flowers are held well above the bracts.

HYBRIDIZING NOTES: N/A.

REFERENCES: 37.

PHOTOS/DRAWINGS: 37.

Pholidota rubra Lindley

AKA: *P. undulata.*

ORIGIN/HABITAT: Vietnam and Darjeeling, Sikkim, and the Khasia hills in India. It is usually found at 3500–6500 ft. (1067–1981 m).

CLIMATE: Station #42398, Baghdogra, India, Lat. 26.7°N, Long. 88.3°E, at 412 ft. (126 m). Temperatures are calculated for an elevation of 5000 ft. (1524 m), resulting in probable extremes of 89°F (31.7°C) and 21°F (-6.1°C).

N/HEMISPHERE	JAN	FEB	MAR	APR	MAY	JUN	JUL	AUG	SEP	OCT	NOV	DEC
°F AVG MAX	59	62	70	75	75	74	74	74	73	72	67	62
°F AVG MIN	35	39	45	53	58	61	62	62	61	55	45	38
DIURNAL RANGE	24	23	25	22	17	13	12	12	12	17	22	24
RAIN/INCHES	0.3	0.7	1.3	3.7	11.8	25.9	32.2	25.3	21.2	5.6	0.5	0.2
HUMIDITY/%	73	68	57	58	74	84	86	85	85	79	75	76
BLOOM SEASON											*	*
DAYS CLR @ 6AM	21	18	15	11	5	0	1	1	4	13	23	19
DAYS CLR @ 12PM	23	16	16	11	2	2	0	1	2	10	21	18
DAYS CLR @ 6PM	15	14	13	10	7	3	1	1	2	14	17	14
RAIN/MM	8	18	33	94	300	658	818	643	538	142	13	5
°C AVG MAX	14.9	16.6	21.0	23.8	23.8	23.3	23.3	23.3	22.7	22.1	19.4	16.6
°C AVG MIN	1.6	3.8	7.1	11.6	14.4	16.0	16.6	16.6	16.0	12.7	7.1	3.3
DIURNAL RANGE	13.3	12.8	13.9	12.2	9.4	7.3	6.7	6.7	6.7	9.4	12.3	13.3
S/HEMISPHERE	JUL	AUG	SEP	OCT	NOV	DEC	JAN	FEB	MAR	APR	MAY	JUN

Cultural Recommendations

LIGHT: 2000–3000 fc. Diffused light is suggested.

TEMPERATURES: Summer days average 73–75°F (23–24°C), and nights average 58-62°F (14–17°C), with a diurnal range of 12–17°F (7–9°C).

HUMIDITY: 75–85%.

WATER: Plants should be constantly moist while actively growing. Although the rainfall pattern is wet/dry in this area, more moisture is available at higher elevations than is recorded for the lower-elevation station.

FERTILIZER: ¼–½ strength, applied weekly during periods of active growth.

REST PERIOD: For 2–4 months in winter, days average 59–70°F (15–21°C), and nights average 35–45°F (2–7°C), with an increased diurnal range of 22–25°F (12–14°C). Water and fertilizer should be reduced, but the humidity in the habitat remains fairly high, indicating that some moisture is available to the plants from fog, dew, and mist even when rainfall is low. Light may be increased since the number of clear days in the habitat is greater in winter.

GROWING MEDIA: Pots or baskets filled with a bark or tree-fern medium are suggested. Repotting is best done in early spring when new roots resume active growth.

MISCELLANEOUS NOTES: N/A.

Plant and Flower Information

PLANT SIZE AND TYPE: A 7–10 in. (18–25 cm) sympodial epiphyte.

PSEUDOBULB: 3 in. (7–8 cm) long. The pseudobulbs taper at both ends and are usually furrowed. They may be spaced up to ¾ in. (1.8 cm) apart on the stout rhizome.

LEAVES: 2 per growth. The leaves are 5–10 in. (13–25 cm) long and usually linear-lanceolate.

INFLORESCENCE: 6–10 in. (15–25 cm) long. The arching spike is wiry and somewhat laxly flowered in 2 distichous rows. It arises from the base of the pseudobulb, either with the partially developed leaves or before the new vegetative growth appears.

FLOWERS: 30–55. The blossoms are approximately ½ in. (1 cm) across. Variable in color, they may be yellowish green, pale gold, or dull yellow. The lip may be light green, yellow, white, or pinkish brown. The floral bracts are persistent.

HYBRIDIZING NOTES: N/A.

REFERENCES: 20, 37, 157.

PHOTOS/DRAWINGS: 20, 37.

Pholidota rupestris. See *P. missionariorum.* REFERENCES: 37.

Pholidota schlechteri. See *P. pallida.* REFERENCES: 37.

Pholidota schweinfurthiana L. O. Williams

AKA: N/A.

ORIGIN/HABITAT: Borneo, including Sarawak and Sabah. Plants are usually found growing at 4250–5500 ft. (1280–1676 m), either on ridge tops or in open forests.

CLIMATE: Station # 49613, Tambunan, North Borneo, Lat. 5.7°N, Long. 116.4°E, at 1200 ft. (366 m). Temperatures are calculated for an elevation of 5379 ft. (1640 m), resulting in probable extremes of 85°F (29.4°C) and 42°F (5.6°C).

N/HEMISPHERE	JAN	FEB	MAR	APR	MAY	JUN	JUL	AUG	SEP	OCT	NOV	DEC
°F AVG MAX	73	74	76	77	77	76	76	76	76	75	74	73
°F AVG MIN	54	52	53	54	55	54	53	53	54	54	54	55
DIURNAL RANGE	19	22	23	23	22	22	23	23	22	21	20	18
RAIN/INCHES	5.8	3.7	5.8	7.5	8.2	7.3	5.1	4.9	6.4	7.0	6.8	6.0
HUMIDITY/%	N/A											
BLOOM SEASON										*	*	*
DAYS CLR	N/A											
RAIN/MM	147	94	147	190	208	185	130	124	163	178	173	152
°C AVG MAX	23.0	23.6	24.7	25.3	25.3	24.7	24.7	24.7	24.7	24.1	23.6	23.0
°C AVG MIN	12.5	11.4	11.9	12.5	13.0	12.5	11.9	11.9	12.5	12.5	12.5	13.0
DIURNAL RANGE	10.5	12.2	12.8	12.8	12.3	12.2	12.8	12.8	12.2	11.6	11.1	10.0
S/HEMISPHERE	JUL	AUG	SEP	OCT	NOV	DEC	JAN	FEB	MAR	APR	MAY	JUN

Cultural Recommendations

LIGHT: 2400 fc. Diffused light or dappled shade is suggested.

TEMPERATURES: Summer days average 76–77°F (25°C), and nights average 53–55°F (12–13°C), with a diurnal range of 22–23°F (12–13°C). The plants are unlikely to tolerate hot weather since the probable extreme high is 85°F (30°C).

HUMIDITY: 75–80%.

WATER: Plants should be kept constantly moist. The rainfall pattern is wet year-round.

FERTILIZER: ¼–½ strength, applied weekly during periods of active growth.

REST PERIOD: Growing conditions are relatively uniform throughout the year. Winter days average 73–76°F (23–25°C), and nights average 52–54°F (11–13°C), with a slightly lower diurnal range of 18–22°F (10–12°C). Plants should be kept moist, but fertilizer should be reduced when plants are not actively growing.

GROWING MEDIA: A moisture-retaining medium of shredded tree-fern is suggested, or plants may be mounted on tree-fern slabs to accommodate their climbing growth habit. Remounting, which should be done as seldom as possible, is best done when new roots are actively growing.

MISCELLANEOUS NOTES: This plant could be very difficult to maintain in cultivation. Its limited habitat, together with the constant, steady rain and uniformly cool temperatures, indicates a demanding plant.

Plant and Flower Information

PLANT SIZE AND TYPE: A 6–11 in. (15–28 cm) sympodial epiphyte.

PSEUDOBULB: 1 in. (2.5 cm) long. Slender and clustered, the pseudobulbs emerge from an ascending rhizome.

LEAVES: 1 per growth. The linear leaf is 4–10 in. (10–25 cm) long.

INFLORESCENCE: Extending 3–6 in. (7–15 cm) above the bracts, the erect spike is wiry and distinctly zigzag at the apex. It emerges when the leaf is half developed.

FLOWERS: 5–8. The small, nearly globular blossoms have white or dingy pink sepals and whitish petals. The lip is whitish and marked with bright yellow, while the column and anther are marked with orange. The persistent floral bracts are brownish to reddish.

HYBRIDIZING NOTES: N/A.

REFERENCES: 37.

PHOTOS/DRAWINGS: 37.

Pholidota sesquitorta. See *P. ventricosa.* REFERENCES: 37.

Pholidota sigmatochilus. Now considered a synonym of *Chelonistele kinabaluensis.* REFERENCES: 37.

Pholidota sororia. See *P. ventricosa.* REFERENCES: 37.

Pholidota spectabilis. See *P. imbricata.* REFERENCES: 37.

Pholidota suaveolens. Now considered a synonym of *Coelogyne suaveolens.* REFERENCES: 37.

Pholidota subcalceata. See *P. leveilleana.* REFERENCES: 37.

Pholidota sulcata J. J. Smith

AKA: N/A.

ORIGIN/HABITAT: Endemic to Borneo. The plants grow in both densely bushy and open areas at 3600–4900 ft. (1097–1494 m).

CLIMATE: Station # 96755, Bogor, Indonesia, Lat. 6.5°S, Long. 106.8°E, at 558 ft. (170 m). Temperatures are calculated for an elevation of 3500 ft. (1067 m), resulting in probable extremes of 86°F (30.0°C) and 56°F (13.3°C).

N/HEMISPHERE	JAN	FEB	MAR	APR	MAY	JUN	JUL	AUG	SEP	OCT	NOV	DEC
°F AVG MAX	76	77	78	78	77	75	74	74	75	76	77	76
°F AVG MIN	63	63	63	64	64	64	64	64	64	65	65	64
DIURNAL RANGE	13	14	15	14	13	11	10	10	11	11	12	12
RAIN/INCHES	2.1	1.0	0.5	5.0	8.1	18.8	23.7	20.2	14.4	12.0	11.9	3.4
HUMIDITY/%	72	68	65	66	74	79	84	84	81	79	77	75
BLOOM SEASON		*									*	*
DAYS CLR @ 7AM	14	14	14	11	5	3	1	2	4	6	10	12
DAYS CLR @ 1PM	9	10	8	5	1	1	0	0	1	1	3	7
RAIN/MM	53	25	13	127	206	478	602	513	366	305	302	86
°C AVG MAX	24.6	25.2	25.7	25.7	25.2	24.1	23.5	23.5	24.1	24.6	25.2	24.6
°C AVG MIN	17.4	17.4	17.4	17.9	17.9	17.9	17.9	17.9	17.9	18.5	18.5	17.9
DIURNAL RANGE	7.2	7.8	8.3	7.8	7.3	6.2	5.6	5.6	6.2	6.1	6.7	6.7
S/HEMISPHERE	JUL	AUG	SEP	OCT	NOV	DEC	JAN	FEB	MAR	APR	MAY	JUN

Cultural Recommendations

LIGHT: 2000–3000 fc. Diffused light or dappled shade is recommended.

TEMPERATURES: Summer days average 74–78°F (24–26°C), and nights average 64–65°F (18–19°C), with a diurnal range of 10-12°F (6–7°C). Night temperatures vary only 2°F (1°C) throughout the year. The lower diurnal range in summer is due to frequent overcast skies during the wet season, which prevent daytime heating.

HUMIDITY: 75–85%.

WATER: Plants should be constantly moist while actively growing. The rainfall pattern is very wet/dry.

FERTILIZER: ¼–½ strength, applied weekly during periods of active growth.

REST PERIOD: Winter days are slightly warmer, and nights are slightly cooler, resulting in a small increase in the diurnal range to 13–15°F (7–8°C). Light might be increased slightly, simulating the increased number of clear mornings in the habitat. Water and fertilizer should be reduced for 2–3 months, but plants should not be allowed to dry out.

GROWING MEDIA: A shredded tree-fern mix. Repotting is best done in early spring when new root growth is evident.

MISCELLANEOUS NOTES: The bloom season shown in the climate table is based on collection records. It may extend from Nov.–Mar. (May–Sep.).

Plant and Flower Information

PLANT SIZE AND TYPE: A 10–25 in. (25–64 cm) sympodial terrestrial which is occasionally found growing epiphytically.

PSEUDOBULB: 1.2–2.5 in. (3–6 cm) long, the pseudobulbs

may be slender or swollen. Olive-green in color, they may be tinged with red to yellowish green at the base.

LEAVES: 2 per growth. The leaves are 10–23 in. (25–58 cm) long, linear-lanceolate, and medium green.

INFLORESCENCE: 2–6 in. (5–15 cm) long. The spike is pale green, flattened, erect, and zigzag at the apex.

FLOWERS: 25–55. The small white blossoms are 0.4 in. (1 cm) across with deeply concave sepals.

HYBRIDIZING NOTES: N/A.

REFERENCES: 37.

PHOTOS/DRAWINGS: 37.

Pholidota talagensis. See *P. camelostalix.* REFERENCES: 37.

Pholidota tixieri. See *P. pallida.* REFERENCES: 37.

Pholidota torricellensis. See *P. carnea.* REFERENCES: 37.

Pholidota triloba. Now considered a synonym of *Geesinkorchis phaiostele.* REFERENCES: 37.

Pholidota triotos. See *P. imbricata.* REFERENCES: 37.

Pholidota tristis. Dr. De Vogel found no description. REFERENCES: 37.

Pholidota undulata. See *P. rubra.* REFERENCES: 37.

Pholidota uraniensis. See *P. cantonensis.* REFERENCES: 37.

Pholidota ventricosa Rchb.f.

AKA: *P. grandis, P. sesquitorta, P. sororia.* Small forms of the plant are sometimes called *P. clemensii.*

ORIGIN/HABITAT: New Guinea, Borneo, Sumatra, Java, and Malaya. While this species is wide-ranging, it is usually found at 5200 ft. (1585 m), except in the most northerly part of its habitat.

CLIMATE: Station # 48625, Ipoh, Malaya, Lat. 4.6°N, Long. 101.1°E, at 123 ft. (37 m). Temperatures are calculated for an elevation of 4920 ft. (1500 m), giving probable extremes of 83°F (28.3°C) and 48°F (8.9°C).

N/HEMISPHERE	JAN	FEB	MAR	APR	MAY	JUN	JUL	AUG	SEP	OCT	NOV	DEC
°F AVG MAX	74	76	77	76	76	76	75	75	74	73	73	73
°F AVG MIN	56	56	57	57	58	57	56	56	57	56	56	56
DIURNAL RANGE	18	20	20	19	18	19	19	19	17	17	17	17
RAIN/INCHES	7.9	3.1	7.6	8.4	6.2	3.6	7.2	6.9	8.8	11.0	13.0	8.9
HUMIDITY/%	76	74	76	78	78	75	76	77	79	82	82	81
BLOOM SEASON			*	*	*							
DAYS CLR @ 7AM	3	3	3	1	1	2	1	1	0	0	1	2
DAYS CLR @ 1PM	2	2	2	1	1	1	1	1	0	0	0	2
RAIN/MM	201	79	193	213	157	91	183	175	224	279	330	226
°C AVG MAX	23.4	24.5	25.1	24.5	24.5	24.5	24.0	24.0	23.4	22.9	22.9	22.9
°C AVG MIN	13.4	13.4	14.0	14.0	14.5	14.0	13.4	13.4	14.0	13.4	13.4	13.4
DIURNAL RANGE	10.0	11.1	11.1	10.5	10.0	10.5	10.6	10.6	9.4	9.5	9.5	9.5
S/HEMISPHERE	JUL	AUG	SEP	OCT	NOV	DEC	JAN	FEB	MAR	APR	MAY	JUN

Cultural Recommendations

LIGHT: 1500–2400 fc. Light should be diffused or dappled, and direct sun should be avoided. In the habitat, clear days are quite rare.

TEMPERATURES: Days average 73–77°F (23–25°C), and nights average 56–58°F (13–15°C), with a diurnal range of 17–20°F (9–11°C). The average temperatures vary only a few degrees through the year, and the extremes are very close to the averages, indicating an intolerance to temperature fluctuations.

HUMIDITY: 75–80%.

WATER: Plants should be kept moist. The rainfall pattern is wet/wetter.

FERTILIZER: ¼–½ strength, applied weekly during periods of active growth.

REST PERIOD: Growing conditions should be maintained year-round. Fertilizer may be reduced, but plants should not be allowed to dry out. In the habitat, rainfall is highest in winter; but in cultivation, water should not be increased.

GROWING MEDIA: Mounting the plants on tree fern or cork accommodates their creeping growth habit. They may also be potted in a bark or tree-fern mix. The medium should be changed as infrequently as possible, and then only when roots are actively growing.

MISCELLANEOUS NOTES: The bloom season shown on the climate table is based on cultivation reports and some collection records. However, collections have been made at other times, and reports from the field indicate that *P. ventricosa* blooms throughout the year, often more than once, blooming most heavily at year's end.

Plant and Flower Information

PLANT SIZE AND TYPE: A robust, 18–32 in. (46–81 cm) sympodial terrestrial or epiphyte. It is also found growing as a lithophyte on limestone.

PSEUDOBULB: 2–6 in. (5–15 cm) long. Ovoid, flattened, and ribbed, the pseudobulbs develop on one side of the creeping, rooting rhizome. The closely spaced pseudobulbs become ochre to yellowish with age.

LEAVES: 2 per growth. The leaves are 18–24 in. (46–61 cm) long, rigid and leathery, and usually lanceolate.

INFLORESCENCE: 8–18 in. (20–46 cm) long. The spikes emerge from the new growths with the immature leaves. They are very densely flowered along the upper half, and all blossoms face in the same direction.

FLOWERS: 30–80. The small, translucent blossoms are 0.4 in. (1 cm) across with wide-opening, greenish sepals and nearly white, sharply recurving petals. The lip is prominent and is opaque white or cream except deep in the throat, where it is marked with rich yellow. The fragrance is described as sweetish, and the floral bracts are deciduous.

HYBRIDIZING NOTES: N/A.

REFERENCES: 2, 32, 37, 112, 118, 164, 175, 203.

PHOTOS/DRAWINGS: 32, 37, 164, 175.

Pholidota wattii. Dr. De Vogel considers this a doubtful species. REFERENCES: 37.

Pholidota wenshanica. Dr. De Vogel believes this plant is probably conspecific with *P. leveilleana.* REFERENCES: 37.

Pholidota yunnanensis Rolfe

AKA: *P. kouytcheensis.* According to Dr. De Vogel, the name *P. yunnanensis* has been applied erroneously to specimens of *P. imbricata.*

ORIGIN/HABITAT: China, in the Yunnan and Guizhou Provinces, in mossy areas at 2460–6560 ft. (750-2000 m).

CLIMATE: Station # 57816, Kuei-yang (Guiyang), China, Lat. 26.6°N, Long. 106.7°E, at 3514 ft. (1071 m) elevation. The record high is 95°F (35.0°C), and the record low is 21°F (-6.1°C).

N/HEMISPHERE	JAN	FEB	MAR	APR	MAY	JUN	JUL	AUG	SEP	OCT	NOV	DEC
°F AVG MAX	48	51	64	72	75	81	84	84	79	68	60	53
°F AVG MIN	36	38	48	56	61	66	70	68	63	55	48	40
DIURNAL RANGE	12	13	16	16	14	15	14	16	16	13	12	13
RAIN/INCHES	0.8	1.1	1.6	3.6	7.6	8.4	7.8	5.3	5.0	4.1	1.9	1.0
HUMIDITY/%	74	77	71	72	77	76	77	76	73	77	78	78
BLOOM SEASON					*	*	*	*				
DAYS CLR @ 7AM	2	1	2	3	1	2	2	4	5	2	2	1
DAYS CLR @ 1PM	4	3	7	6	3	2	1	2	4	5	3	5
RAIN/MM	20	28	41	91	193	213	198	135	127	104	48	25
°C AVG MAX	8.9	10.6	17.8	22.2	23.9	27.2	28.9	28.9	26.1	20.0	15.6	11.7
°C AVG MIN	2.2	3.3	8.9	13.3	16.1	18.9	21.1	20.0	17.2	12.8	8.9	4.4
DIURNAL RANGE	6.7	7.3	8.9	8.9	7.8	8.3	7.8	8.9	8.9	7.2	6.7	7.3
S/HEMISPHERE	JUL	AUG	SEP	OCT	NOV	DEC	JAN	FEB	MAR	APR	MAY	JUN

Cultural Recommendations

LIGHT: 1200–2400 fc. Diffused light is recommended, since clear days in the habitat are rare.

TEMPERATURES: Summer days average 72–84°F (22–29°C), and nights average 56–70°F (13–21°C), with a diurnal range of 14–16°F (8–9°C), which is greatest in spring and summer.

HUMIDITY: 70–78%.

WATER: Plants should be kept moist while actively growing. Although the rainfall pattern is wet/dry, the high year-round humidity in the habitat indicates that some moisture is always available.

FERTILIZER: ¼–½ strength, applied weekly during periods of active growth.

REST PERIOD: For 3-4 months, winter days average 48–64°F (9–18°C), and nights average 36-48°F (2–9°C), with a diurnal range of 12–13°F (7°C). The more restricted diurnal range results from the simultaneous decline of both high and low temperatures. Water may be reduced, but plants should be misted to prevent desiccation. Despite the low winter rainfall in the habitat, moisture is available from dew, fog, or mist throughout the year. The relative consistency of year-round humidity levels indicates a high incidence of morning fog and low clouds. Fertilizer should be eliminated.

GROWING MEDIA: Mounting the plant on a slab accommodates its climbing growth habit. Remounting is best done in early spring when new roots are actively growing.

MISCELLANEOUS NOTES: The bloom season shown in the climate table is based on collection records.

Plant and Flower Information

PLANT SIZE AND TYPE: A creeping, 3.5–7.5 in. (9–19 cm) sympodial lithophyte or terrestrial. The mat-forming plants are usually found growing in moss.

PSEUDOBULB: 1–2 in. (2.5–5.0 cm) long. Shiny, slender, and long-lasting, the pseudobulbs emerge from a slender rhizome. Plants produce 1–3 roots from the base of each growth. The roots are long and branching.

LEAVES: 2 per growth. The leaves are 2–5 in. (5–13 cm) long, stiff, and linear-lanceolate.

INFLORESCENCE: 1–3 in. (2.5–8.0 cm) long. The spike is somewhat zigzag and usually emerges before the new leaves.

FLOWERS: 10–20. The tiny blossoms are ¼–½ in. (0.5–1.0 cm) across. They may be white, cream, or pinkish.

HYBRIDIZING NOTES: N/A.

REFERENCES: 37.

PHOTOS/DRAWINGS: 37.

6
Phragmipedium
General Information

SUBFAMILY: Cypripedioideae.

TRIBE: *Cypripedium.*

SUBTRIBE: *Cypripedilinae.*

GENUS: *Phragmipedium* Rolfe.

AKA: Species in this genus have been known over the years as *Cypripedium*, *Paphiopedilum*, and *Selenipedium*. The genus itself has been called *Phragmopedilum* and *Uropedium*.

SPECIES: Approximately 20. For our listing of valid species and synonyms, we have used Dr. Leslie Garay's survey in *The Genus* Phragmipedium, published in the *Orchid Digest* of July–August 1979.

As the result of recent field work, several botanists and expert growers suggest that Dr. Garay's treatment may be outdated and believe that several species listed here should be considered synonyms or reduced to varietal status. To our knowledge, however, no complete review of the genus has been published in support of these views.

ORIGIN/HABITAT: The natural habitat extends from southern Mexico through Central America and northern South America to Brazil, where *Phragmipedium* species are most often found in the mountains at 3000–5000 ft. (914–1524 m). However, some species are found near sea level, and others are found as high as 8000–10,000 ft. (2438–3048 m).

CLIMATE: Tropical to subtropical climates are normal throughout the range.

Cultural Recommendations

LIGHT: 2400–5000 fc. Most species prefer rather bright light, but they are intolerant of direct sun, and leaves must be protected from sunburn.

TEMPERATURES: Despite most species' high-elevation natural habitat, growers report that *intermediate* conditions generally produce better results in cultivation than cooler temperatures. Most *Phragmipedium* tolerate average summer highs of 85–90°F (29–32°C) and prefer average winter lows of 60°F (16°C), but many will tolerate average night temperatures of 55°F (13°C). A diurnal range of 10–20°F (6–11°C) is usually appropriate, but the climate in the particular habitat is the best guide.

HUMIDITY: 70–95%. High humidity and good air circulation are essential, particularly if the highs are near the upper limit of the plant's range.

WATER: *Phragmipedium* must be kept moist year-round, as they have no means of storing moisture. This means that plants should be watered every other day, or at least twice weekly while they are actively growing. Underwatering is generally more damaging than overwatering, but excess moisture rapidly creates cultural problems. Indications of improper watering are discussed under the plant part affected.

Several successful growers report improved growth and increased flowering when the pots are placed in a saucer of water. These growers were unable to maintain adequate moisture until water was constantly available to the plants.

FERTILIZER: Several successful growers recommend an acidic 30–10–10 fertilizer with trace minerals mixed at ½ the recommended strength. To stimulate blooming, they use a 15–30–15 fertilizer with trace minerals mixed at ½ the recommended strength. Other growers suggest that a balanced 20–20–20 fertilizer mixed at ¼–½ the recommended strength should be applied weekly to biweekly when the plants are actively growing.

Growers report improved plant growth when 2–3 drops of Superthrive (a commercial hormone and vitamin solution) are added to the fertilizer. In addition to regular fertilizing, a semiannual top dressing of steamed bone meal and blood meal reportedly gives good results. Excess fertilizer may cause dieback of the leaf tips.

REST PERIOD: Some *Phragmipedium* need uniform growing conditions year-round, while others originate in areas with distinct seasonal fluctuations.

GROWING MEDIA: In cultivation, *Phragmipedium* are most frequently grown in well-drained plastic pots. Growers report success with a variety of media that provide perfect drainage and moisture retention. An open, porous mixture requires more frequent watering but is less likely to become stagnant. It also encourages more active root growth, which results in more new growths and increased flower production.

Recommended media include the following:

A mixture of 8 parts medium-grade fir-bark, 4 parts medium-to-fine charcoal, 2 parts chopped tree-fern, and 2 parts perlite. Sphagnum moss may be added to the mixture for small plants.

A mixture of 6 parts bark, 1 part perlite, 1 part coarse peat, and 1 part charcoal.

Seedlings should be planted in a mixture of equal parts fine fir-bark, fine charcoal, chopped sphagnum, and fine perlite or pumice.

Plants may be divided, but this should be done infrequently since large clumps grow and bloom better than small divisions. For example, 4 mature growths may produce 2 new growths during the year from each front lead, while a single-growth plant may initiate only 1 new growth in 2–3 years.

Plants should be repotted when the medium breaks down, at least every 12–24 months. Unlike most orchids, *Phragmipedium* should be watered daily after repotting until they are reestablished. Growers who place the pots in a saucer of water indicate that plants should be repotted every 6–12 months, since the additional moisture rapidly breaks down the bark.

MISCELLANEOUS NOTES: When bloom initiators have been identified, they are described under this category.

New roots emerge from immature growths after the flowering season.

Plant and Flower Information

PLANT SIZE AND TYPE: Notes regarding individual growth habits are included for each species. *Phragmipedium* are normally fairly large terrestrials, but some species are epiphytic or lithophytic.

LEAVES: Generally firm-textured, the leaves appear creased along their length. Normally light green when exposed to correct light levels, the leaves turn yellowish when given too much light or dark green when given too little.

The following leaf symptoms may indicate cultural problems:

Brown or spotted leaf tips that die back usually indicate insufficient moisture, most frequently caused by

inadequate watering or by root rot. During hot, dry weather, low moisture is probably the cause. If watering is increased immediately, the deterioration can usually be stopped.

In cooler, wetter weather or when watering has been frequent, root rot resulting from deteriorated medium may be the underlying problem. Affected plants should be repotted immediately; growers should not wait for new root growth to begin. Roots are less likely to deteriorate in an open medium, but the plants must be watered more frequently.

Spotted or brown leaf tips may also be caused by excess fertilizer or salt buildup, particularly if conditions are dry. In either case, the pots should be thoroughly flushed (see Chapter 1). If salt buildup from hard water is the cause, pots should be flushed more frequently. If excess fertilizer is the suspected cause, plants should be fertilized less frequently.

Watery patches which turn black, grey, or brown, with yellow margins, are caused by bacterial rot. These may be treated by cutting out the affected area and surrounding tissue, going well beyond the edge of the infection. If the infected parts are not removed, the infection may spread rapidly, killing the infected plant and spreading the infection to other plants.

White spots and irregular dark patches are both symptoms of fungal infections. Affected plants should be treated with a commercial fungicide.

INFLORESCENCE: Flower spikes emerge from the center of the leaves. Water in the crown causes new inflorescences to rot with alarming speed. Good air movement is essential to promote rapid drying in the crown.

FLOWERS: In most *Phragmipedium* species the flowers open in succession, but in some species all the blooms open at one time. The few-flowered species tend to have long-lasting blossoms and stay in bloom for months. Flower size increases with plant maturity. Failure to flower is usually caused by inadequate light, but too much light may also limit flowering.

Growers wishing to achieve maximum petal length may be interested in the "old growers' tale" suggesting that the petals on exceptionally long-petaled varieties continue to grow until the tips touch something. The theory behind this adage is that the long petals provide insect pollinators with easy access to the flower. Other growers believe that petal length is a function of light or the genetic makeup of the plant.

HYBRIDIZING NOTES: Chromosome counts are included for many species. *Phragmipedium* hybrids have been created. Intergeneric crosses with *Paphiopedilum* have been reported, but these crosses are considered questionable since the hybrids showed the traits of only one parent, and subsequent chromosome counts failed to confirm hybridization.

REFERENCES: 90, 113, 168.

PHOTOS/DRAWINGS: See species listings.

Species Culture

Phragmipedium besseae Dodson and Kuhn

AKA: N/A.

ORIGIN/HABITAT: Recently discovered in Ecuador and in the San Martin area of Peru. In both locations, the plants grow in semishade at 3608 ft. (1100 m) on steep, east-facing, wet embankments or wet granite rocks where they are exposed to early morning sun. In Peru, they grow in close association with *P. boisseranum*, while in Ecuador, *P. besseae* grows very near colonies of *P. schlimii*.

CLIMATE: Station # 84435, Moyobamba, Peru, Lat. 6.0°S, Long. 77.0°W, at 2730 ft. (832 m). Temperatures are calculated for an elevation of 3608 ft. (1100 m). Extreme temperatures are not available.

N/HEMISPHERE	JAN	FEB	MAR	APR	MAY	JUN	JUL	AUG	SEP	OCT	NOV	DEC
°F AVG MAX	78	79	81	80	80	80	79	80	79	79	79	79
°F AVG MIN	59	60	60	61	63	62	62	63	63	63	63	61
DIURNAL RANGE	19	19	21	19	17	18	17	17	16	16	16	18
RAIN/INCHES	2.1	1.8	1.4	3.0	3.6	3.7	3.4	2.6	4.3	3.6	1.3	1.5
HUMIDITY/%	N/A											
BLOOM SEASON		**	**					*	*			
DAYS CLR	N/A											
RAIN/MM	53	46	36	76	91	94	86	66	109	91	33	38
°C AVG MAX	25.6	26.2	27.3	26.7	26.7	26.7	26.2	26.7	26.2	26.2	26.2	26.0
°C AVG MIN	15.1	15.6	15.6	16.2	17.3	16.7	16.7	17.3	17.3	17.3	17.3	16.0
DIURNAL RANGE	10.5	10.6	11.7	10.5	9.4	10.0	9.5	9.4	8.9	8.9	8.9	10.0
S/HEMISPHERE	JUL	AUG	SEP	OCT	NOV	DEC	JAN	FEB	MAR	APR	MAY	JUN

Cultural Recommendations

LIGHT: 1200–1500 fc, possibly as low as 600 fc. Light should be diffused and direct sun avoided. Growers report that this species prefers lower light than other *Phragmipedium*. At the Los Angeles State and County Arboretum, they brought a small piece to flower in the *Phalaenopsis* house under additional shade. Other growers indicate that this species is healthiest and that root growth increases dramatically when the plants are given 16 hours of light daily throughout the year.

TEMPERATURES: Summer days average 78–81°F (26-27°C), and nights average 59–63°F (15–17°C), with a diurnal range of 16–21°F (9–12°C). In this exceptionally uniform climate, the average highs and lows vary only 4–5°F (2–3°C) throughout the year.

HUMIDITY: 80–90%. Humidity records are not available, but collectors describe the habitat as very humid tropical rainforests. Successful growers report that very high humidity may be critical.

WATER: Plants should be constantly moist. While rainfall amounts are relatively low and the rainfall pattern is wet/dry, collectors report finding the plants on wet slopes that are never dry. In the habitat, they observed constant water seepage down the cliff face through lithophytic mosses and onto the roots of *P. besseae*.

FERTILIZER: ¼–½ strength solution can be applied weekly to biweekly while the plants are actively growing, unless live sphagnum is used as the potting medium. Growers indicate that *P. besseae* is a very heavy feeder, and that flower color improves when fertilizer is adequate. Manure tea is used very successfully.

REST PERIOD: Average day temperatures should be maintained in winter, but nights may average a few degrees cooler, resulting in a slight increase in the diurnal range. Water, humidity, and fertilizer may be reduced, while light levels might be raised slightly to simulate the increased number of clear days.

GROWING MEDIA: A medium that retains moisture is needed, and several successful growers report having the best results when using live sphagnum moss. Information regarding the use of live sphagnum is included in Chapter 1. The Los Angeles Arboretum plant mentioned above was grown in a plastic pot with conventional fir bark mix topped with New Zealand moss. Repotting is best done after flowering, just as new roots begin to grow.

MISCELLANEOUS NOTES: The bloom season shown in the climate table is based on cultivation records. Reports from the habitat indicate that the Ecuadorean race has no peak bloom season.

P. besseae is a difficult plant in cultivation. Growers variously speculate that the problems arise from the medium used, hard water, or chemical fertilizer.

Plant and Flower Information

PLANT SIZE AND TYPE: An 8–9 in. (22 cm) sympodial lithophyte or terrestrial.

PSEUDOBULB: None. The growths emerge from a short rhizome.

LEAVES: 4 per growth. The leaves are 6–10 in. (15–25 cm) long, dark green, and narrowly elliptical with a heavy, fleshy texture. The leaves are held almost at right angles to the stem.

INFLORESCENCE: 12–16 in. (30–41 cm) long. The plant flowers on the elongated apical portion of the stem.

FLOWERS: 1–4. The blossoms are 1.5–2.5 in. (4–6 cm) across and open in succession. The bright scarlet sepals and petals fade to yellow in the center and are broadly elliptical. The downy pouch is striped with scarlet and yellow.

HYBRIDIZING NOTES: This species is said to be difficult to propagate, but it has been hybridized.

REFERENCES: 15, 41, 49.

PHOTOS/DRAWINGS: *15, 26, 41, 49, 145, 146, 154.*

Phragmipedium boisseranum (Rchb.f.) Rolfe

AKA: *Selenipedium boisseranum.* We have followed the spelling used in Dr. Garay's review of the genus. The International Orchid Commission uses *P. bois-sieranum,* and the name is sometimes spelled *P. bois-sierianum.* The largest forms are occasionally sold as *P. cajamarcae.*

ORIGIN/HABITAT: Ecuador and Peru, at 2050–3608 ft. (625–1100 m). In the Tingo Maria area, it grows in the valleys between high ridges on southwest-facing slopes with constant water seepage. In other areas, plants are also found growing on grassy, sparsely bushy clay slopes and in rich black loam near the edge of the jungle.

CLIMATE: Station # 84534, Tingo Maria, Peru, Lat. 9.1°S, Long. 75.9°W, at 2106 ft. (642 m). The record high is 97°F (36.1°C), and the record low is 39°F (3.9°C).

N/HEMISPHERE	JAN	FEB	MAR	APR	MAY	JUN	JUL	AUG	SEP	OCT	NOV	DEC
°F AVG MAX	86	88	88	87	87	87	86	85	86	86	87	86
°F AVG MIN	63	64	64	65	65	66	66	66	66	66	65	64
DIURNAL RANGE	23	24	24	22	22	21	20	19	20	20	22	22
RAIN/INCHES	5.8	8.2	8.0	15.9	24.9	12.0	15.9	16.4	22.8	8.5	8.7	4.5
HUMIDITY/%	N/A											
BLOOM SEASON	*	*	*	*					*	*	*	*
DAYS CLR @ 7AM	2	3	3	1	1	1	0	0	0	1	1	1
DAYS CLR @ 1PM	15	12	9	3	4	4	4	1	4	2	7	12
RAIN/MM	147	208	203	404	632	305	404	417	579	216	221	114
°C AVG MAX	30.0	31.1	31.1	30.6	30.6	30.6	30.0	29.4	30.0	30.0	30.6	30.0
°C AVG MIN	17.2	17.8	17.8	18.3	18.3	18.9	18.9	18.9	18.9	18.9	18.3	17.8
DIURNAL RANGE	12.8	12.3	13.3	12.3	12.3	11.7	11.1	10.5	11.1	11.1	12.3	12.2
S/HEMISPHERE	JUL	AUG	SEP	OCT	NOV	DEC	JAN	FEB	MAR	APR	MAY	JUN

Cultural Recommendations

LIGHT: 2400 fc. Diffused light is suggested, since clear days in the habitat are very rare. Light may be gradually increased until the leaves begin to yellow.

TEMPERATURES: Days average 85–88°F (29–31°C), and nights average 63–66°F (17–19°C), with a diurnal range of 19–24°F (11–13°C). In this exceptionally uniform climate, the average highs and lows vary only 3°F (2°C). The diurnal range fluctuates only 5°F (3°C) through the year.

HUMIDITY: 80–90%. Humidity readings are not available, but the high year-round rainfall and the low number of clear days indicate high average humidity. Collectors describe the habitat as very humid tropical rainforest.

WATER: Plants should be moist throughout the year. The rainfall pattern is wet/wetter.

FERTILIZER: ¼–½ strength solution can be applied weekly to biweekly while the plants are actively growing.

REST PERIOD: Average temperatures need to be maintained, but the record low of 39°F (4°C) indicates that plants may be exposed to occasional outbreaks of cold air. Water, humidity, and fertilizer should be reduced, while winter light levels may be raised to simulate the increased number of clear days.

GROWING MEDIA: A rapidly draining, moisture-retaining medium should be used. Repotting is best done after flowering, just as new roots begin to grow.

MISCELLANEOUS NOTES: N/A.

Plant and Flower Information

PLANT SIZE AND TYPE: The large, stout, 60 in. (152 cm) plants are sympodial terrestrials.

PSEUDOBULB: None.

LEAVES: 6–8 per growth. The leaves are 25–30 in. (64–76 cm) long, leathery, uniform green, arranged distichously, and clustered near the base of the stem.

INFLORESCENCE: 25–30 in. (64–76 cm) long. The spike arises from the center of the leaves.

FLOWERS: 3–15. The blossoms measure 6 in. (15 cm) vertically. The 4-5 in. (10–13 cm) petals are twisted and ruffled and spread horizontally. The flowers are pale yellow-green to dark green with darker, emerald-green veins, and the sepals and petals are edged with white. The lateral sepals are ruffled and wavy, and the dorsal sepal is crisped at the margin.

HYBRIDIZING NOTES: Chromosome count is 2n = 18.

REFERENCES: 76, 90, 112, 165, 205.

PHOTOS/DRAWINGS: *76, 90, 178.*

Phragmipedium cajamarcae. See *P. boisseranum.*
REFERENCES: 90.

Phragmipedium caricinum (Lindley) Rolfe

AKA: *Cypripedium caricinum. Phragmipedium caricinum* was once considered conspecific with *P. pearcei,* and some plants currently in cultivation may be labeled *P. pearcei.*

ORIGIN/HABITAT: Santa Cruz, Bolivia. It is found near waterfalls at 1200–1500 ft. (366–457 m). In Peru it grows at 525–853 ft. (160–260 m) on river boulders, where the plants are often flooded during high water.

CLIMATE: Station # 85245, Santa Cruz, Bolivia, Lat. 17.8°S, Long. 63.2°W, at 1441 ft. (439 m). The record high is 105°F (40.6°C), and the record low is 36°F (2.2°C).

N/HEMISPHERE	JAN	FEB	MAR	APR	MAY	JUN	JUL	AUG	SEP	OCT	NOV	DEC
°F AVG MAX	75	81	85	85	87	88	86	87	87	81	76	74
°F AVG MIN	58	60	64	66	68	69	69	70	68	64	62	60
DIURNAL RANGE	17	21	21	19	19	19	17	17	19	17	14	14
RAIN/INCHES	1.9	0.8	2.1	3.3	3.5	4.6	5.9	3.4	3.8	3.8	2.4	2.8
HUMIDITY/%	74	65	63	65	67	72	77	78	76	75	75	76
BLOOM SEASON	*	*	*	*	*	*	*	*	*			
DAYS CLR @ 8AM	10	14	13	6	5	6	3	3	5	6	7	7
DAYS CLR @ 2PM	7	12	11	6	4	5	3	2	3	5	5	6
RAIN/MM	48	20	53	84	89	117	150	86	97	97	61	71
°C AVG MAX	23.9	27.2	29.4	29.4	30.6	31.1	30.0	30.6	30.6	27.2	24.4	23.3
°C AVG MIN	14.4	15.6	17.8	18.9	20.0	20.6	20.6	21.1	20.0	17.8	16.7	15.6
DIURNAL RANGE	9.5	11.6	11.6	10.5	10.6	10.5	9.4	9.5	10.6	9.4	7.7	7.7
S/HEMISPHERE	JUL	AUG	SEP	OCT	NOV	DEC	JAN	FEB	MAR	APR	MAY	JUN

Cultural Recommendations

LIGHT: 2400 fc. Diffused light is suggested.

TEMPERATURES: Summer days average 85–88°F (30–31°C), and nights average 64–70°F (18–21°C), with a diurnal range of 17–19°F (9–11°C).

HUMIDITY: 65–80%.

WATER: Plants should be moist while actively growing. Although the rainfall pattern is wet/dry, the microclimate near waterfalls and on river banks indicates that moisture is available year-round in the habitat.

FERTILIZER: ¼–½ strength, applied weekly to biweekly while the plants are actively growing.

REST PERIOD: For about 3 months in winter, days average 74–81°F (23–27°C), and nights average 58–62°F (14–17°C), with a more limited diurnal range of 14–17°F (8–9°C). For approximately 2 months in late winter and early spring, the diurnal range reaches its maximum spread at 21°F (12°C). This occurs when days are starting to warm but nights are still cool. Water, humidity, and fertilizer should be reduced slightly, while light levels may be raised to simulate the increased number of clear days in the habitat.

GROWING MEDIA: A rapidly draining, moisture-retaining medium. Repotting is best done after flowering, just as new roots begin to grow.

MISCELLANEOUS NOTES: *P. caricinum* is vegetatively very similar to *P. klotzscheanum.* The 2 species are difficult to differentiate when not in bloom.

Plant and Flower Information

PLANT SIZE AND TYPE: A 12–16 in. (30–41 cm) sympodial lithophyte or terrestrial.

PSEUDOBULB: The widely spaced growths arise from a creeping rhizome.

LEAVES: 4–6 per growth. The leaf fans are 11–20 in. (28–51 cm) long, deep green, linear, sedgelike, and rigidly suberect.

INFLORESCENCE: 12–24 in. (30–61 cm) long. The spikes are erect and purplish green and arise from the base.

FLOWERS: 3–7. The blossoms can measure 3–6 in. (8–15 cm) in length. Size is variable and depends somewhat on the overall size and health of the plant. Flowers are pale lime-green to whitish, with green veins and spots on the 1.5 in. (3.5 cm) slipper-shaped lip. The slightly bulbous pouch has incurved sidelobes which are spotted with dark green and purple. The petals are linear, ribbonlike, twisted, pendent, pale purple at the margins, and covered with stiff, short hairs. The dorsal sepal is lanceolate and wavy margined.

HYBRIDIZING NOTES: The chromosome count is most often 2n = 20, but one plant tested was 2n = 22.

REFERENCES: 14, 90, 112, 137, 165, 205, 220.

PHOTOS/DRAWINGS: *90, 137, 180, 205, 220.*

Phragmipedium caudatum (Lindley) Rolfe

AKA: *Cypripedium caudatum.*

ORIGIN/HABITAT: Southern Mexico to Peru. The plants normally grow at 4920–6560 ft. (1500–2000 m) but may be found as high as 8500 ft. (2591 m). The plants have been nearly exterminated in many habitats. They grow on forest trees, in shady humus soil, or on north- and west-facing cliffs (which receive high light in the Southern Hemisphere). Plants favor seepage areas.

CLIMATE: Station # 84686, Cuzco, Peru, Lat. 13.4°S, Long. 72.0°W, at 10,866 ft. (3312 m). Temperatures are calculated for an elevation of 6560 ft. (2000 m), with probable extremes of 100°F (37.8°C) and 30°F (-1.1°C).

N/HEMISPHERE	JAN	FEB	MAR	APR	MAY	JUN	JUL	AUG	SEP	OCT	NOV	DEC
°F AVG MAX	84	84	85	86	87	85	82	83	84	85	84	83
°F AVG MIN	45	48	54	57	57	58	59	59	58	54	49	47
DIURNAL RANGE	39	36	31	29	30	27	23	24	26	31	35	36
RAIN/INCHES	0.2	0.4	1.0	2.6	3.0	5.4	6.4	5.9	4.3	2.0	0.6	0.2
HUMIDITY/%	57	70	68	68	73	77	76	78	76	75	68	58
BLOOM SEASON	*	*	*	**	*	**	*	*				*
DAYS CLR @ 7AM	20	19	10	8	7	4	2	2	4	7	15	19
DAYS CLR @ 1PM	22	17	9	5	4	2	1	1	2	7	14	23
RAIN/MM	5	10	25	66	76	137	163	150	109	51	15	5
°C AVG MAX	29.0	29.0	29.6	30.1	30.7	29.6	27.9	28.4	29.0	29.6	29.0	28.4
°C AVG MIN	7.3	9.0	12.3	14.0	14.0	14.6	15.1	15.1	14.6	12.3	9.6	8.4
DIURNAL RANGE	21.7	20.0	17.3	16.1	16.7	15.0	12.8	13.3	14.4	17.3	19.4	20.0
S/HEMISPHERE	JUL	AUG	SEP	OCT	NOV	DEC	JAN	FEB	MAR	APR	MAY	JUN

Cultural Recommendations

LIGHT: 2400–3000 fc. Direct sun should be avoided.

TEMPERATURES: Summer days average 82–87°F (28–31°C), and nights average 57–59°F (14–15°C), with a wide diurnal range of 23–27°F (13–17°C). Average high temperatures are lowest during the overcast summer. Growers report that these plants are difficult to cultivate in warm tropical lowlands.

HUMIDITY: 60–80% year-round.

WATER: Constant moisture should be available. Although the rainfall pattern is wet/dry, the plants often grow in seepage areas, indicating that moisture may be available throughout the year.

FERTILIZER: ¼–½ strength solution can be applied weekly to biweekly while the plants are actively growing. Because the species usually grows in areas high in organic nutrients, an organic fertilizer is suggested.

REST PERIOD: For 3–4 months, days average 83–86°F (29–30°C), and winter nights average 45–54°F (7–12°C), with an exceptionally wide diurnal range of 35–39°F (19–22°C). Water, humidity, and fertilizer should be reduced, while light levels may be raised to simulate the increased number of clear days in the habitat.

GROWING MEDIA: A rapidly draining, moisture-retaining medium is necessary. Some growers use a mixture of chopped sphagnum and chopped tree-fern. Repotting is best done just as new roots begin to grow.

MISCELLANEOUS NOTES: Recently located plants were growing at 8500 ft. (2800 m), indicating that the average monthly temperatures could be reduced by as much as 6°F (3°C). The bloom season shown in the climate table is based on reports from the plant's native habitat, where blooming occurs during the dry season.

Plant and Flower Information

PLANT SIZE AND TYPE: A 24–30 in. (61–76 cm) sympodial epiphyte, lithophyte, or terrestrial.

PSEUDOBULB: None. The growths are closely spaced.

LEAVES: 5–7 per growth. The leaves are 24–30 in. (61–76 cm) long, bright green, leathery, and arranged in stiffly erect fans. In bright light, the leaves become yellow-green.

INFLORESCENCE: 16–24 in. (41–61 cm) long. The spikes emerge from the center of the leaf fans.

FLOWERS: 3–6. The blossoms are 4–6 in. (10–15 cm) long, the largest in the genus. The yellow petals are pendent, twisted, ribbonlike, and marked with reddish veins. They are 3–4 in. (8–10 cm) long when the flowers first open and grow as much as 2 in. (5 cm) a day from days 2–7. They may grow to 30 in. (76 cm) in length before reaching maturity. The lateral sepals, which are narrow and twisted, are yellow with green veins, and the dorsal sepal cups over the lip. The white pouch is green at the base, purplish brown at the apex, and sprinkled with rose-colored dots. The long-lasting flowers open simultaneously.

HYBRIDIZING NOTES: Chromosome count is 2n = 28.

REFERENCES: 4, 14, 43, 59, 89, 90, 112, 129, 148, 165, 174, 205, 212, 220.

PHOTOS/DRAWINGS: 4, *14*, *43*, *59*, *90*, *127*, *129*, 148, *179*, 205, *215*, 220.

Phragmipedium caudatum var. *wallisii*. See *P. wallisii*.

Phragmipedium caudatum var. *warscewiczii*. See *P. warscewiczianum*.

Phragmipedium czerwiakowianum (Rchb.f.) Rolfe. Originally described as *Selenipedium czerwiakowianum*. This species was collected once in Peru, but no habitat information was recorded. The plant is unlikely to be available for cultivation. REFERENCES: 90, 165, 172.

Phragmipedium dariense (Rchb.f.) Garay. Originally described as *Selenipedium dariense*, this species was collected once in Panama, but no habitat details were provided. The plant is not currently available. REFERENCES: 90.

Phragmipedium ecuadorense Garay

AKA: N/A.

ORIGIN/HABITAT: Banos, Ecuador, and Tarapoto, Peru. No habitat or microclimate details are available. However, Banos has an elevation of 6002 ft. (1829 m) and Tarapoto is at 4585 ft. (1398 m), fairly high on the east slopes of the Andes.

CLIMATE: Station # 84435, Moyobamba, Peru, Lat. 6.0°S, Long. 77.0°W, at 2730 ft. (832 m). Temperatures are calculated for an elevation of 5000 ft. (1524 m). Extremes are not available.

N/HEMISPHERE	JAN	FEB	MAR	APR	MAY	JUN	JUL	AUG	SEP	OCT	NOV	DEC
°F AVG MAX	74	75	77	76	76	76	75	76	75	75	75	75
°F AVG MIN	55	56	56	57	59	58	58	59	59	59	59	57
DIURNAL RANGE	19	19	21	19	17	18	17	17	16	16	16	18
RAIN/INCHES	2.1	1.8	1.4	3.0	3.6	3.7	3.4	2.6	4.3	3.6	1.3	1.5
HUMIDITY/%	N/A											
BLOOM SEASON	*	*			**	*	*	*	*			*
DAYS CLR	N/A											
RAIN/MM	53	46	36	76	91	94	86	66	109	91	33	38
°C AVG MAX	23.1	23.6	24.7	24.2	24.2	24.2	23.6	24.2	23.6	23.6	23.6	23.6
°C AVG MIN	12.5	13.1	13.1	13.6	14.7	14.2	14.2	14.7	14.7	14.7	14.7	13.6
DIURNAL RANGE	10.6	10.5	11.6	10.6	9.5	10.0	9.4	9.5	8.9	8.9	8.9	10.0
S/HEMISPHERE	JUL	AUG	SEP	OCT	NOV	DEC	JAN	FEB	MAR	APR	MAY	JUN

Cultural Recommendations

LIGHT: 1800–2500 fc. Diffused light is suggested.

TEMPERATURES: Summer days average 74–77°F (23–24°C), and nights average 57–59°F (14–15°C), with a diurnal range of 16–18°F (9–10°C).

HUMIDITY: Humidity records are not available; but this habitat is humid, and 70–80% humidity should be maintained year-round in cultivation.

WATER: Plants should be constantly moist during periods of active growth. The rainfall pattern is moderately wet/dry, and amounts are much lower than in the habitats of many *Phragmipedium*.

FERTILIZER: ¼–½ strength solution, applied weekly to biweekly while the plants are actively growing.

REST PERIOD: Winter days are slightly cooler, and nights average 55–59°F (13–15°C), with a diurnal range of 18–21°F (10–12°C). Water, humidity, and fertilizer should be reduced, while light levels may be raised slightly, simulating the increased number of clear days in the habitat.

GROWING MEDIA: A rapidly draining, moisture-retaining medium is recommended. Repotting is best done after flowering, just as new roots begin to grow.

MISCELLANEOUS NOTES: The bloom seasons May–Sep. (Nov.–Mar.) and Dec.–Feb. (Jun.–Aug.) are based on cultivation records for the Northern Hemisphere.

Plant and Flower Information

PLANT SIZE AND TYPE: An 18 in. (46 cm) sympodial terrestrial.

PSEUDOBULB: None. The growths produce stiff but flexuous roots.

LEAVES: Several per growth. The leaves are 16 in. (41 cm) long, distichous, and linear. They may be either erect or arching.

INFLORESCENCE: Length is variable. Erect and covered with sheaths, the spike emerges from the center of the leaves.

FLOWERS: Few. The greenish white flowers, which have a somewhat darker green lip, open in succession. Sparsely pubescent and pendulous, the petals are fully developed when the flowers open. At about 3 in. (7.5 cm), they are 2–3 times longer than the undulate sepals.

HYBRIDIZING NOTES: N/A.

REFERENCES: 89, 90.

PHOTOS/DRAWINGS: 89, *90, 179, 180*.

Phragmipedium hartwegii (Rchb.f.) L. O. Williams

AKA: *Cypripedium hartwegii*.

ORIGIN/HABITAT: Ecuador, along the road from Quito to Santo Domingo running from the east to the west side of the Andes at high elevations. The plants are also found near Cajamarca, Peru. Habitat details were not recorded by the collector or describer.

CLIMATE: Station # 84472, Cajamarca, Peru, Lat. 7.2°S, Long. 78.5°W, at 8418 ft. (2566 m). The record high is 79°F (26.1°C), and the record low is 28°F (-2.2°C).

N/HEMISPHERE	JAN	FEB	MAR	APR	MAY	JUN	JUL	AUG	SEP	OCT	NOV	DEC
°F AVG MAX	71	72	72	72	72	72	71	70	70	69	70	71
°F AVG MIN	39	39	42	46	44	44	46	46	46	46	41	39
DIURNAL RANGE	32	33	30	26	28	28	25	24	24	23	29	32
RAIN/INCHES	0.0	0.3	0.6	1.8	2.7	1.9	5.5	2.7	5.8	5.3	1.8	0.4
HUMIDITY/%	59	55	61	57	56	61	61	66	69	66	63	59
BLOOM SEASON					**	**	**	*	*	*	*	
DAYS CLR @ 7AM	20	21	15	10	10	13	6	2	5	6	13	20
DAYS CLR @ 1PM	11	9	4	3	4	6	2	1	1	1	4	12
RAIN/MM	0	8	15	46	69	48	140	69	147	135	46	10
°C AVG MAX	21.7	22.2	22.2	22.2	22.2	22.2	21.7	21.1	21.1	20.6	21.1	21.7
°C AVG MIN	3.9	3.9	5.6	7.8	6.7	6.7	7.8	7.8	7.8	7.8	5.0	3.9
DIURNAL RANGE	17.8	18.3	16.6	14.4	15.5	15.5	13.9	13.3	13.3	12.8	16.1	17.8
S/HEMISPHERE	JUL	AUG	SEP	OCT	NOV	DEC	JAN	FEB	MAR	APR	MAY	JUN

Cultural Recommendations

LIGHT: 3000–4000 fc. Morning light is preferred. Since skies are normally overcast by afternoon, midday light should be diffused.

TEMPERATURES: Summer days average 70–72°F (21–22°C), and nights average 44–46°F (7–8°C), with a diurnal range of 24–28°F (13–15°C). Growers report that plants grow better in somewhat warmer temperatures.

HUMIDITY: 60–70% in summer.

WATER: Plants should be constantly moist while actively growing. Although the rainfall pattern is wet/dry, the microclimate may provide more moisture than the humidity and rainfall readings indicate.

FERTILIZER: ¼–½ strength, applied weekly to biweekly while plants are actively growing.

REST PERIOD: Days average 69–72°F (21–22°C), and winter nights average 39–41°F (4-5°C), with a diurnal range of 30–33°F (17–18°C). Water, humidity, and fertilizer should be reduced, while light levels should be raised to correspond with the increased number of clear days in the habitat.

GROWING MEDIA: A rapidly draining, moisture-retaining medium is necessary. Repotting is best done after flowering, just as new roots begin to grow.

MISCELLANEOUS NOTES: N/A.

Plant and Flower Information

PLANT SIZE AND TYPE: A robust, 24–35 in. (61–90 cm) sympodial plant. Whether it is epiphytic or terrestrial was not recorded.

PSEUDOBULB: None.

LEAVES: Number unknown. The leaves are 24–32 in. (61–81 cm) long, distichous, and very leathery.

INFLORESCENCE: 24–36 in. (61–91 cm) long. Erect and green, the spike emerges from the center of the leaves.

FLOWERS: 7–9. The flowers are 5 in. (12–13 cm) long and greenish yellow with white margins and darker green veins. This species is closely related to *P. longifolium*, but the flowers are larger. The pendent, linear-lanceolate petals are lightly twisted, 3.5–4.0 in. (9–10 cm) long, and usually bordered with rose-pink, with a purplish suffusion near the tip.

HYBRIDIZING NOTES: Chromosome counts are 2n = 20 and 2n = 22.

REFERENCES: 14, 89, 90, 112, 165, 205.

PHOTOS/DRAWINGS: *14, 90*.

Phragmipedium hincksianum (Rchb.f.) Garay.

Originally described as *Cypripedium hincksianum*, this species was reportedly collected in Costa Rica and Panama. Habitat details are insufficient to select climate information, and the plant is unlikely to be available for cultivation. REFERENCES: 90, 205.

Phragmipedium kaieteurum (N. E. Brown) Garay

AKA: *Phragmopedilum kaiteurum* var. *lindleyanum, Selenipedium kaiteurum, S. kaiteurum* var. *lindleyanum.*

ORIGIN/HABITAT: Guyana and Venezuela, where it grows in the acid, black-water areas.

CLIMATE: Station # 80453, Tumeremo, Venezuela, Lat. 7.3°N, Long. 61.2°W, at 614 ft. (187 m). The record high is 101°F (38.3°C), and the record low is 58°F (14.4°C).

N/HEMISPHERE	JAN	FEB	MAR	APR	MAY	JUN	JUL	AUG	SEP	OCT	NOV	DEC
°F AVG MAX	86	87	89	90	89	87	88	90	91	91	90	87
°F AVG MIN	68	68	68	69	71	70	69	70	70	70	70	69
DIURNAL RANGE	18	19	21	21	18	17	19	20	21	21	20	18
RAIN/INCHES	3.9	3.0	2.4	3.0	6.1	7.2	6.0	4.9	3.0	2.2	2.5	4.4
HUMIDITY/%	87	85	82	81	84	88	86	84	81	81	84	86
BLOOM SEASON	N/A											
DAYS CLR @ 7AM	2	0	1	1	1	1	1	2	1	1	1	1
RAIN/MM	99	76	61	76	155	183	152	124	76	56	64	112
°C AVG MAX	30.0	30.6	31.7	32.2	31.7	30.6	31.1	32.2	32.8	32.8	32.2	30.6
°C AVG MIN	20.0	20.0	20.0	20.6	21.7	21.1	20.6	21.1	21.1	21.1	21.1	20.6
DIURNAL RANGE	10.0	10.6	11.7	11.6	10.0	9.5	10.5	11.1	11.7	11.7	11.1	10.0
S/HEMISPHERE	JUL	AUG	SEP	OCT	NOV	DEC	JAN	FEB	MAR	APR	MAY	JUN

Cultural Recommendations

LIGHT: 2400 fc. Diffused light is recommended. The habitat is usually cloudy in the mornings, and the steady rainfall suggests frequently cloudy skies.

TEMPERATURES: Summer days average 86–91°F (30–32°C), and nights average 68–71°F (20–22°C), with a diurnal range of 17–21°F (9–12°C).

HUMIDITY: 81–87%.

WATER: Plants should be constantly moist. The rainfall pattern is wet throughout the year. The pH is very low in the black-water areas of Venezuela, where even collected rainfall samples have a pH of 4–5, about the same as vinegar.

FERTILIZER: ¼–½ strength, applied weekly to biweekly while plants are actively growing.

REST PERIOD: In the habitat, conditions vary only slightly, but rainfall, average high and low temperatures, and diurnal range are all slightly lower in winter.

GROWING MEDIA: A rapidly draining, moisture-retaining medium is needed. Redwood bark may be added to the mix if the pH needs to be lowered. Repotting is best done after flowering, just as new roots begin to grow.

MISCELLANEOUS NOTES: N/A.

Plant and Flower Information

PLANT SIZE AND TYPE: A 36 in. (91 cm) sympodial lithophyte or terrestrial.

PSEUDOBULB: None.

LEAVES: 4–6 per growth. The leaves are 18–24 in. (46–61 cm) long. They are straplike, glossy, and uniformly green without yellow margins.

INFLORESCENCE: 36–48 in. (91–122 cm) long. The spike emerges from the leaf fan.

FLOWERS: 1–3. The flowers are somewhat small for the plant size. The sepals are rich green with darker veins, while the ruffled petals are marked with purple at the margins, along the veins, and at the apex of the petals. The lip is greenish yellow overlaid with reddish brown, and the edge of the pouch opening is marked with spots.

HYBRIDIZING NOTES: N/A.

REFERENCES: 90, 205.

PHOTOS/DRAWINGS: 47, *90, 179*.

Phragmipedium klotzscheanum (Rchb.f.) Rolfe

AKA: *Cypripedium klotzscheanum.*

ORIGIN/HABITAT: The border region between Venezuela, Brazil, and Guyana, at 3936–4592 ft. (1200–1400 m). The plants usually grow on shady, grassy, south-facing slopes protected from full sun. They are found in granite-rock crevices, often near waterfalls, and on sandstone tablelands near water where they are often subject to seasonal flooding. The habitat may have a pH as low as 4.5.

CLIMATE: Station # 80462, Santa Elena, Venezuela, Lat. 4.6°N, Long. 61.1°W, at 2976 ft. (907 m). Temperatures are calculated for an elevation of 4000 ft. (1219 m), resulting in probable extremes of 92°F (33.3°C) and 45°F (7.2°C).

N/HEMISPHERE	JAN	FEB	MAR	APR	MAY	JUN	JUL	AUG	SEP	OCT	NOV	DEC
°F AVG MAX	79	81	81	79	79	78	78	78	79	81	81	81
°F AVG MIN	58	58	58	60	61	60	58	60	56	58	58	58
DIURNAL RANGE	21	23	23	19	18	18	20	18	23	23	23	23
RAIN/INCHES	3.2	3.2	3.2	5.7	9.6	9.5	9.1	7.6	5.3	4.9	4.9	4.5
HUMIDITY/%	81	79	77	80	86	89	89	88	84	82	83	83
BLOOM SEASON					*	*	*	*				
DAYS CLR @ 8AM	5	7	7	6	3	1	2	3	6	4	8	3
RAIN/MM	81	81	81	145	244	241	231	193	135	124	124	114
°C AVG MAX	25.9	27.0	27.0	25.9	25.9	25.3	25.3	25.3	25.9	27.0	27.0	27.0
°C AVG MIN	14.2	14.2	14.2	15.3	15.9	15.3	14.2	15.3	13.1	14.2	14.2	14.2
DIURNAL RANGE	11.7	12.8	12.8	10.6	10.0	10.0	11.1	10.0	12.8	12.8	12.8	12.8
S/HEMISPHERE	JUL	AUG	SEP	OCT	NOV	DEC	JAN	FEB	MAR	APR	MAY	JUN

Cultural Recommendations

LIGHT: 3000–4000 fc. Diffused light is suggested.

TEMPERATURES: Days average 78–81°F (25–27°C), and nights average 56–61°F (13–16°C), with a diurnal range of 18–23°F (10–13°C) throughout the year. The average highs vary only 3°F (1.7°C), while the diurnal range and average lows fluctuate only 5°F (3°C). Reports from the habitat indicate that these temperatures may be the low end of the ideal range.

HUMIDITY: 80–90% year-round.

WATER: Plants should be constantly moist, since they are extremely sensitive to inadequate water and low humidity. The rainfall pattern is wet year-round.

FERTILIZER: ¼–½ strength, applied weekly to biweekly while the plants are actively growing. Growers suggest using an organic fertilizer for plants from this habitat.

REST PERIOD: Temperatures, water, and humidity should be maintained, although rainfall amounts are slightly lower, and the diurnal range is somewhat higher in winter.

GROWING MEDIA: A rapidly draining, moisture-retaining medium is recommended. Plants are said to be sensitive to alkaline soil or water, or to pH above 5.5. Redwood bark, added to the medium, will lower the pH. Repotting is best done just as new roots begin to grow.

MISCELLANEOUS NOTES: The bloom season shown in the climate table is based on reports from the native habitat. Cultivation records indicate that plants may bloom anytime in Jul.–Dec. (Jan.–Jun.), but flowering most often occurs in Oct.–Dec. (Apr.–Jun.). *P. klotzscheanum* is often found growing with *Sobralia stenophylla*.

Plant and Flower Information

PLANT SIZE AND TYPE: A 12 in. (30 cm) sympodial lithophyte or terrestrial.

PSEUDOBULB: None. The growths arise from a creeping rhizome.

LEAVES: 6–8 per growth. The leaves are 10 in. (25 cm) long, rigid, sedgelike, and distichous. The shiny foliage is deep green with paler undersides.

INFLORESCENCE: 12 in. (30 cm) long, erect, and pubescent, the spikes are red or maroon.

FLOWERS: 2–3. The blossoms are 2.0–2.5 in. (5–6 cm) across. The linear, twisted petals are 32 in. (81 cm) long and light brown with green and maroon veining. The sepals are pink-brown with darker veins. The lip is slipper-shaped with inrolled margins and is light green to olive-green with white on the midlobe. The flowers open sequentially.

HYBRIDIZING NOTES: N/A.

REFERENCES: 14, 44, 45, 90, 100.

PHOTOS/DRAWINGS: 44, *45, 47, 90, 100, 180.*

Phragmipedium lindenii (Lindley) Dressler and N. Williams

AKA: *Uropedium lindenii. Phragmipedium lindenii*, which has a third petal instead of a lip, was formerly considered a peloric version of *P. wallisii*, which has a normal slipper-shaped lip. It is now generally accepted that the 2 species should be kept separate because both always breed true.

ORIGIN/HABITAT: Ecuador, Colombia, and Venezuela. Plants are found in open savannas and under shrubs, tall ferns, and tall trees, or on fallen logs in cloudforests.

CLIMATE: Station # 80091, Barrancabermeja, Colombia, Lat. 7.1°N, Long. 73.8°W, at 351 ft. (107 m). Temperatures are calculated for an elevation of 5000 ft. (1524 m), resulting in probable extremes of 92°F (33.3°C) and 44°F (6.7°C).

N/HEMISPHERE	JAN	FEB	MAR	APR	MAY	JUN	JUL	AUG	SEP	OCT	NOV	DEC
°F AVG MAX	77	79	80	79	77	78	80	79	78	78	77	78
°F AVG MIN	62	62	64	63	62	62	63	62	62	61	62	65
DIURNAL RANGE	15	17	16	16	15	16	17	17	16	17	15	13
RAIN/INCHES	2.0	3.9	5.2	14.9	14.6	12.1	7.4	14.9	12.8	19.0	15.0	6.0
HUMIDITY/%	N/A											
BLOOM SEASON	*	*	**	***	***	**	**	*	*			*
DAYS CLR @ 7AM	1	1	3	2	0	0	0	0	0	0	0	0
RAIN/MM	51	99	132	378	371	307	188	378	325	483	381	152
°C AVG MAX	24.8	25.9	26.5	25.9	24.8	25.4	26.5	25.9	25.4	25.4	24.8	25.4
°C AVG MIN	16.5	16.5	17.6	17.0	16.5	16.5	17.0	16.5	16.5	15.9	16.5	18.1
DIURNAL RANGE	8.3	9.4	8.9	8.9	8.3	8.9	9.5	9.4	8.9	9.5	8.3	7.3
S/HEMISPHERE	JUL	AUG	SEP	OCT	NOV	DEC	JAN	FEB	MAR	APR	MAY	JUN

Cultural Recommendations

LIGHT: 3000–4000 fc. Diffused light is indicated. Although plants may sometimes grow in exposed areas, the skies are seldom clear, so the light is naturally diffused.

TEMPERATURES: Days average 77–80°F (25–27°C), and nights average 61–64°F (16–18°C), with a diurnal range of 13–17 °F (7–9 °C). The average highs, lows, and diurnal range vary only a few degrees throughout the year.

HUMIDITY: 75–85%. Humidity records are not available for this station, but habitat at this elevation is typically very humid.

WATER: Plants should be kept constantly moist. The rainfall pattern is wet year-round, with 2 periods of very heavy rain in spring and fall.

FERTILIZER: ¼–½ strength, applied weekly to biweekly while the plants are actively growing.

REST PERIOD: Growing temperatures should be maintained. Water, humidity, and fertilizer may be reduced somewhat. In the habitat, light levels may be slightly higher in winter.

GROWING MEDIA: A rapidly draining, moisture-retaining medium is needed, and chopped tree-fern is recommended. Repotting is best done after flowering, just as new roots begin to grow.

MISCELLANEOUS NOTES: Plants are probably adaptable, if reasonably uniform temperatures and constant moisture are maintained.

Plant and Flower Information

PLANT SIZE AND TYPE: A 12–18 in. (30–46 cm) sympodial epiphyte.

PSEUDOBULB: None. The growths emerge directly from a rhizome.

LEAVES: 7–9 per growth. The rigid leaves are 16 in. (41 cm) long.

INFLORESCENCE: 10 in. (25 cm). The spike emerges from the center of the leaf fan. Flowers are held well away from the inflorescence.

FLOWERS: 1–3. The blossoms are off-white to yellow-green with red-toned, ribbonlike petals. The petals, not fully formed when the flowers open, continue to elongate for several days. In the most common form, the lip is replaced by a third, ribbonlike petal. However, forms with a lip are found, and these plants are very similar to *P. caudatum*.

HYBRIDIZING NOTES: Chromosome count is 2n = 28. The seed capsules tend to wither without fully maturing, and the seed is sometimes not viable.

REFERENCES: 14, 43, 89, 90, 205.

PHOTOS/DRAWINGS: *14, 43, 47, 89, 90, 205.*

Phragmipedium lindleyanum (Lindley) Rolfe

AKA: *Cypripedium lindleyanum.*

ORIGIN/HABITAT: Surinam, British Guyana, and Venezuela at 2800–7000 ft. (853–2134 m). The plants usually grow in moist areas near waterfalls or seepage areas. They may be found in rock fissures, in the thin layer of soil over rocks, or in matted tree roots. Some grow in dark, rocky places with sparse vegetation on shady, south-facing slopes, while others grow in open areas with dappled light.

CLIMATE: Station # 80462, Santa Elena, Venezuela, Lat. 4.6 °N, Long. 61.1 °W, at 2976 ft. (907 m). The record high is 95 °F (35.0 °C), and the record low is 48 °F (8.9 °C). At this elevation, the climate apparently represents the warmest end of the habitat range.

N/HEMISPHERE	JAN	FEB	MAR	APR	MAY	JUN	JUL	AUG	SEP	OCT	NOV	DEC
°F AVG MAX	82	84	84	82	82	81	81	81	82	84	84	84
°F AVG MIN	61	61	61	63	64	63	61	63	59	61	61	61
DIURNAL RANGE	21	23	23	19	18	18	20	18	23	23	23	23
RAIN/INCHES	3.2	3.2	3.2	5.7	9.6	9.5	9.1	7.6	5.3	4.9	4.9	4.5
HUMIDITY/%	81	79	77	80	86	89	89	88	84	82	83	83
BLOOM SEASON	*	*	*	*	*					*	*	*
DAYS CLR @ 8AM	5	7	7	6	3	1	2	3	6	4	8	3
RAIN/MM	81	81	81	145	244	241	231	193	135	124	124	114
°C AVG MAX	27.8	28.9	28.9	27.8	27.8	27.2	27.2	27.2	27.8	28.9	28.9	28.9
°C AVG MIN	16.1	16.1	16.1	17.2	17.8	17.2	16.1	17.2	15.0	16.1	16.1	16.1
DIURNAL RANGE	11.7	12.8	12.8	10.6	10.0	10.0	11.1	10.0	12.8	12.8	12.8	12.8
S/HEMISPHERE	JUL	AUG	SEP	OCT	NOV	DEC	JAN	FEB	MAY	APR	MAY	JUN

Cultural Recommendations

LIGHT: 2400–3000 fc. Diffused light is suggested as a starting point, but light may be gradually increased until the leaves begin to yellow.

TEMPERATURES: Days average 81–84 °F (27–29 °C), and nights average 59–64 °F (15–18 °C), with a diurnal range of 18–23 °F (10–13 °C). The lowest diurnal range occurs during the heavy rains in midsummer. Collectors report that the largest plants grow in low-light, warm-water areas.

HUMIDITY: 80–90%.

WATER: Warm water is suggested. Plants should be constantly moist, since in the habitat, the rainfall pattern is wet year-round. In addition, heavy mist is frequent both mornings and evenings, and seasonal flooding may also occur.

FERTILIZER: ½ strength, applied weekly to biweekly while the plants are actively growing. Some growers report success adding steamed bone meal or fish meal to the medium. Liquid fish fertilizer or manure tea are suggested, since the plants frequently grow in algae-laden sites rich in natural amines, and organic fertilizers reportedly produce superior results.

REST PERIOD: Temperature, moisture, and humidity should be maintained. Fertilizer may be reduced when plants are not actively growing.

GROWING MEDIA: A moisture-retaining medium, such as a mixture of sand, loam, chopped tree-fern, and garden compost, has been used successfully. *P. lindleyanum* is found in the black-water regions where soil pH is very low. It might benefit from an acidic medium. Repotting is best done after flowering or as new roots begin to grow.

MISCELLANEOUS NOTES: The long bloom season extends over several months.

Plant and Flower Information

PLANT SIZE AND TYPE: A 36 in. (91 cm) sympodial plant that is normally terrestrial and rarely epiphytic.

PSEUDOBULB: None.

LEAVES: 5–6 per growth. The leaves are 18–24 in. (46–61 cm) long, straplike, and suberect. Smooth and glossy, they are dark green to grass-green, often with pale yellow margins.

INFLORESCENCE: 36–48 in. (91–122 cm) long. The erect, finely pubescent spike is green, with reddish green at the apex. It emerges from the center of the leaf fan.

FLOWERS: 6–12 in nature. The blossoms are 2.0–3.5 in. (5–9 cm) across. They open sequentially and are long-lasting. The linear sepals and slightly twisted petals are green, yellow-green, or pale olive-green, marked with purple veins, with white at the apex and margins. The lip is ochre-yellow with darker veins. All segments are fuzzy on the backside.

HYBRIDIZING NOTES: It is difficult to get viable seed when the plants are selfed.

REFERENCES: 14, 72, 90, 93, 101, 112, 205, 207.

PHOTOS/DRAWINGS: 47, *72, 90, 93, 101, 138,* 205, 207.

Phragmipedium longifolium (Warscewicz and Rchb.f.) Rolfe

AKA: *Cypripedium longifolium.*

ORIGIN/HABITAT: Mexico to Peru. In Colombia it is found at 4920-5904 ft. (1500–1800 m), always in the shade and always in wet areas. Plants usually grow either in grass just above streamside gravel bars, where they are subject to seasonal flooding, along road banks where they receive runoff, or on steep cliffs in wet mountain forests.

CLIMATE: Station # 80110, Medellín, Colombia, Lat. 6.2°N, Long. 75.6°W, at 4916 ft. (1498 m). The record high is 92°F (33.3°C), and the record low is 41°F (5.0°C).

N/HEMISPHERE	JAN	FEB	MAR	APR	MAY	JUN	JUL	AUG	SEP	OCT	NOV	DEC
°F AVG MAX	82	82	84	82	82	82	83	82	82	80	81	81
°F AVG MIN	59	60	59	60	60	58	59	60	60	60	60	61
DIURNAL RANGE	23	22	25	22	22	24	24	22	22	20	21	20
RAIN/INCHES	2.7	3.5	3.3	6.5	7.7	5.5	4.1	4.6	6.2	6.7	5.2	2.5
HUMIDITY/%	69	70	72	74	75	73	69	69	73	77	77	72
BLOOM SEASON	**	**	**	**	**	**	**	**		**	**	**
DAYS CLR @ 7AM	0	1	0	0	0	1	1	0	0	0	0	1
DAYS CLR @ 1PM	2	3	0	0	1	1	1	0	1	0	0	1
RAIN/MM	69	89	84	165	196	140	104	117	157	170	132	64
°C AVG MAX	27.8	27.8	28.9	27.8	27.8	27.8	28.3	27.8	27.8	26.7	27.2	27.2
°C AVG MIN	15.0	15.6	15.0	15.6	15.6	14.4	15.0	15.6	15.6	15.6	15.6	16.1
DIURNAL RANGE	12.8	12.2	13.9	12.2	12.2	13.4	13.3	12.2	12.2	11.1	11.6	11.1
S/HEMISPHERE	JUL	AUG	SEP	OCT	NOV	DEC	JAN	FEB	MAR	APR	MAY	JUN

Cultural Recommendations

LIGHT: 2400–3000 fc. Diffused light is suggested. In the habitat, clear days are exceedingly rare.

TEMPERATURES: Days average 80–83°F (27–28°C), and nights average 58–61°F (14–16°C), with a diurnal range of 20–25°F (11–14°C) all year.

HUMIDITY: 70–75% year-round.

WATER: Plants should be constantly moist. The rainfall pattern is wet/wetter. Evening showers with strong winds frequently occur in the mistforest zone.

FERTILIZER: ¼–½ strength, applied weekly to biweekly while plants are actively growing.

REST PERIOD: Temperatures, moisture, and diurnal range should be maintained. Fertilizer should be reduced when plants are not actively growing.

GROWING MEDIA: A moisture-retaining medium is needed. Repotting is best done after flowering, just as new roots begin to grow.

MISCELLANEOUS NOTES: N/A.

Plant and Flower Information

PLANT SIZE AND TYPE: A 24–32 in. (61–81 cm) sympodial terrestrial or lithophyte. The plant often forms a large clump.

PSEUDOBULB: None.

LEAVES: Several per growth. The bright, dark green foliage is paler on the underside. The leaves are 24–32 in. (61–81 cm) long, pointed, linear, and arranged in a distichous fan.

INFLORESCENCE: 16–24 in. (41–61 cm) long. The erect spike is pubescent at the base, emerges from the center of the leaves, and may be deep purple or green.

FLOWERS: 6–10. The blossoms are 3-5 in. (8-13 cm) vertically and up to 8 in. (20 cm) across. The pale, yellowish green flowers have darker green veins and white margins. The petals are edged with purple and have brown-purple markings near the tips. The lip margin is distinctly V-shaped. The long-lasting flowers open over an extended period.

HYBRIDIZING NOTES: Chromosome counts are 2n = 20 and 2n = 23.

REFERENCES: 14, 40, 56, 60, 89, 90, 112, 205, 212, 220.

PHOTOS/DRAWINGS: 40, *56, 60,* 89, *90, 179, 180,* 205, *220.*

Phragmipedium pearcei (Rchb.f.) Rauh and Senghas

AKA: *Selenipedium pearcei.* At one time, *Phragmipedium pearcei* was considered conspecific with *P. caricinum.*

ORIGIN/HABITAT: Ecuador and Peru, at high elevations on the eastern slopes of the Andes. It is usually found growing at water's edge or on cliffs above streams.

CLIMATE: Station # 84297, Banos, Ecuador, Lat. 1.4°S, Long. 78.4°W, at 6002 ft. (1829 m). Information on extreme temperatures, humidity, and cloud-cover is not available for this station.

N/HEMISPHERE	JAN	FEB	MAR	APR	MAY	JUN	JUL	AUG	SEP	OCT	NOV	DEC
°F AVG MAX	70	71	73	73	72	73	72	71	71	71	70	70
°F AVG MIN	51	52	52	54	55	55	54	54	55	55	54	52
DIURNAL RANGE	19	19	21	19	17	18	18	17	16	16	16	18
RAIN/INCHES	6.3	5.6	4.8	3.7	2.2	2.7	3.0	2.8	4.4	4.3	6.3	7.7
HUMIDITY/%	N/A											
BLOOM SEASON	**	**	**	**	**	**	*	*	*	*	*	*
DAYS CLR	N/A											
RAIN/MM	160	142	122	94	56	69	77	71	112	109	161	196
°C AVG MAX	21.1	21.7	22.8	22.8	22.2	22.8	22.2	21.7	21.7	21.7	21.1	21.1
°C AVG MIN	10.6	11.1	11.1	12.2	12.8	12.8	12.2	12.2	12.7	12.8	12.2	11.1
DIURNAL RANGE	10.5	10.6	11.7	10.6	9.4	10.0	10.0	9.5	9.0	8.9	8.9	10.0
S/HEMISPHERE	JUL	AUG	SEP	OCT	NOV	DEC	JAN	FEB	MAR	APR	MAY	JUN

Cultural Recommendations

LIGHT: 2400–3000 fc. Diffused light or dappled shade is indicated since clear days are probably rare due to the high rainfall.

TEMPERATURES: Days average 72–73°F (21–23°C), and nights average 54–55°F (12–13°C), with a diurnal range of 17–18°F (10°C). Growers report that plants in cultivation are less susceptible to disease when grown at somewhat warmer temperatures.

HUMIDITY: 75–85%. Although humidity data are not available for Banos, and habitat details are not available, records from other stations along the eastern slopes of the Andes indicate uniformly high humidity.

WATER: Plants should be constantly moist. The rainfall pattern is wet with a slightly drier period in late spring and early summer. In cultivation, water should not be allowed to stand in the crown. Growers emphasize this plant's susceptibility to rot when plants are in spike.

FERTILIZER: ¼–½ strength, applied weekly to biweekly while plants are actively growing.

REST PERIOD: Winter lows average 51–52°F (11°C), and the diurnal range increases to 19–21°F (11–12°C). Growers report improved plant health when the plants are grown at somewhat warmer temperatures. In cultivation, water and fertilizer should be reduced, but humidity and light should be maintained.

GROWING MEDIA: A rapidly draining, moisture-retaining medium is recommended. Repotting is best done after flowering, just as new roots begin to grow.

MISCELLANEOUS NOTES: The bloom season shown in the climate table is based on reports from the field as well as cultivation records. Flowering occurs every month. *P. pearcei* is the most commonly cultivated of several closely related species.

Plant and Flower Information

PLANT SIZE AND TYPE: A 10–12 in. (25–30 cm) sympodial terrestrial.

PSEUDOBULB: None.

LEAVES: Several per growth. The linear leaves are 9–11 in. (23–28 cm) long. They may be erect or recurved.

INFLORESCENCE: Length is variable. The purplish spikes, up to 4 per new growth, are erect.

FLOWERS: 1 per inflorescence. The blossoms are similar to those of *P. longifolium,* differing in technical details of flower structure. The strongly twisted petals are slightly contorted, pendent, and somewhat thickened at the apex. The green lip is marked with red spots and darker vertical lines. The sepals are white with greenish veins, pubescent on the edges, and pale pink at the margins.

HYBRIDIZING NOTES: Chromosome counts are 2n = 20, 2n = 21, and 2n = 22.

REFERENCES: 14, 89, 90.

PHOTOS/DRAWINGS: 89, *90*, 137, *179, 180, 216, 220.*

Phragmipedium reticulatum (Rchb.f.) Garay

AKA: *Selenipedium reticulatum.*

ORIGIN/HABITAT: Peru and Ecuador. In Ecuador it grows along the Rio Zamora, which is located at high elevations on the east side of the Andes. Additional details are not available.

CLIMATE: Station # 84139, Cuenca, Ecuador, Lat. 2.9°S, Long. 79.1°W, at 8291 ft. (2527 m). Temperatures are calculated for an elevation of 6000 ft. (1829 m), resulting in probable extremes of 88°F (31.1°C) and 37°F (2.8°C).

N/HEMISPHERE	JAN	FEB	MAR	APR	MAY	JUN	JUL	AUG	SEP	OCT	NOV	DEC
°F AVG MAX	73	74	77	78	79	79	77	78	77	77	75	74
°F AVG MIN	55	54	56	57	54	57	58	59	59	58	57	55
DIURNAL RANGE	18	20	21	21	25	22	19	19	18	19	18	19
RAIN/INCHES	0.9	1.1	1.6	3.1	1.8	2.5	2.0	1.8	3.2	4.3	4.3	1.7
HUMIDITY/%	73	75	74	76	74	74	75	76	76	77	77	75
BLOOM SEASON								*	*	*	**	
DAYS CLR @ 7AM	4	2	4	4	5	1	2	1	2	1	2	3
DAYS CLR @ 1PM	5	5	3	2	5	2	4	1	2	1	2	2
RAIN/MM	23	28	41	79	46	64	51	46	81	109	109	43
°C AVG MAX	22.5	23.1	24.8	25.3	25.9	25.9	24.8	25.3	24.8	24.8	23.6	23.1
°C AVG MIN	12.5	12.0	13.1	13.6	12.0	13.6	14.2	14.8	14.8	14.2	13.6	12.5
DIURNAL RANGE	10.0	11.1	11.7	11.7	13.9	12.3	10.6	10.5	10.0	10.6	10.0	10.6
S/HEMISPHERE	JUL	AUG	SEP	OCT	NOV	DEC	JAN	FEB	MAR	APR	MAY	JUN

Cultural Recommendations

LIGHT: 2400–4000 fc. Diffused light is suggested.

TEMPERATURES: Summer days average 77–79°F (25–26°C), and nights average 57–59°F (14–15°C), with a diurnal range of 19–22°F (11–14°C).

HUMIDITY: 73–77% year-round.

WATER: Plants should be constantly moist while actively growing. The rainfall pattern is relatively wet/dry.

FERTILIZER: ¼–½ strength, applied weekly to biweekly while the plants are actively growing.

REST PERIOD: Winter days average 73–78°F (23–25°C), and nights average 54–57°F (12–14°C), with a winter diurnal range of 18–21°F (10–12°C). Humidity should remain constant, but water and fertilizer may be reduced somewhat when the plant is not actively growing. Light levels may be raised slightly, simulating the increased number of clear days in the habitat.

GROWING MEDIA: A rapidly draining, moisture-retaining medium is recommended. Repotting is best done after flowering, just as new roots begin to grow.

MISCELLANEOUS NOTES: The roots are fleshy rather than fibrous.

Plant and Flower Information

PLANT SIZE AND TYPE: A 32 in. (81 cm) sympodial terrestrial.

PSEUDOBULB: None.

LEAVES: Several per growth. The leaves are 25–26 in. (64–66 cm) long, strap-shaped, and leathery.

INFLORESCENCE: Length unknown. The spike emerges from the center of the leaf fan.

FLOWERS: 1–2. The blossoms are 5.5–6.5 in. (14–17 cm) vertically. The sepals and petals are deep green with darker veins. The lip is grooved and shallowly bilobed in front.

HYBRIDIZING NOTES: N/A.

REFERENCES: 89, 90.

PHOTOS/DRAWINGS: 89, *90.*

Phragmipedium roezlii (Rchb.f.) Garay. Described in 1871 as *Selenipedium roezlii*, it was said to originate from Costa Rica, Panama, and Colombia. It is not mentioned in current literature and is unlikely to be available for cultivation. REFERENCES: 90.

Phragmipedium sargentianum Rolfe

AKA: *Selenipedium sargentianum.*

ORIGIN/HABITAT: Coastal mountains near Recife (Pernambuco), Brazil, at 2200-2800 ft. (671–853 m). The plants prefer to grow in the shade of trees 20–30 ft. (6-9 m) tall, in areas with permanent seepage and 24–36 in. (61–91 cm) of humus. Such areas are found at the base of east-facing granite slopes. Elsewhere, plants grow in streamside peat bogs.

CLIMATE: Station #82898, Recife, Brazil, Lat. 8.0°S, Long. 34.9°W, at 197 ft. (60 m) elevation. Temperatures are calculated for an elevation of 2500 ft. (762 m), resulting in probable extremes of 86°F (30.0°C) and 42°F (5.6°C).

N/HEMISPHERE	JAN	FEB	MAR	APR	MAY	JUN	JUL	AUG	SEP	OCT	NOV	DEC
°F AVG MAX	72	73	74	76	77	77	78	78	78	77	75	74
°F AVG MIN	63	63	65	67	68	69	69	69	68	67	66	65
DIURNAL RANGE	9	10	9	9	9	8	9	9	10	10	9	9
RAIN/INCHES	10.0	6.0	2.5	1.0	1.0	1.1	2.1	3.3	6.3	8.7	10.5	10.9
HUMIDITY/%	79	78	74	71	71	72	73	76	76	78	79	80
BLOOM SEASON		*	*	*	*							
DAYS CLR @ 10AM	3	1	2	1	1	2	1	0	0	1	1	1
RAIN/MM	254	152	64	25	25	28	53	84	160	221	267	277
°C AVG MAX	22.4	23.0	23.6	24.7	25.2	25.2	25.8	25.8	25.8	25.2	24.1	23.6
°C AVG MIN	17.4	17.4	18.6	19.7	20.2	20.8	20.8	20.8	20.2	19.7	19.1	18.6
DIURNAL RANGE	5.0	5.6	5.0	5.0	5.0	4.4	5.0	5.0	5.6	5.5	5.0	5.0
S/HEMISPHERE	JUL	AUG	SEP	OCT	NOV	DEC	JAN	FEB	MAR	APR	MAY	JUN

Cultural Recommendations

LIGHT: 2000–3000 fc. Diffused light is suggested. Reports from the collecting sites indicate that *P. sargentianum* grows both in deep shade and fully exposed to available light, but that the roots are always shaded.

TEMPERATURES: Summer days average 76–78°F (25–26°C), and nights average 67-69°F (20–21°C), with a diurnal range of 8–9°F (4–5°C).

HUMIDITY: 70–80%.

WATER: Plants should be constantly moist while actively growing. The rainfall pattern is wet/dry, with the dry period occurring in late spring and early summer.

FERTILIZER: ¼–½ strength, applied weekly to biweekly while the plants are actively growing.

REST PERIOD: Winter days average 72–76°F (22–25°C), and nights average 63–67°F (17–20°C), with a diurnal range of 9–10°F (5–6°C). In the habitat, temperatures and diurnal range are slightly lower during the wet winter. Fertilizer should be reduced when plants are not actively growing.

GROWING MEDIA: A rapidly draining, moisture-retaining medium is needed. Repotting is best done after flowering, just as new roots begin to grow.

MISCELLANEOUS NOTES: Growers report that the somewhat cooler rest is necessary to initiate blooming but indicate that lows of 67–68°F (19–21°C) might be adequate. In nature, blooming occurs at the end of the wet season when temperatures are cool.

Collectors indicate that *Oncidium gravesianum, Cattleya labiata,* and high-elevation *Cattleya granulosa* grow in the same area as *Phragmipedium sargentianum.*

Plant and Flower Information

PLANT SIZE AND TYPE: A 30–48 in. (76–122 cm) sympodial terrestrial. The plant may be somewhat smaller in cultivation.

PSEUDOBULB: None.

LEAVES: 4–6 per growth. The leaves are 24–36 in. (61–91 cm) long, straplike, smooth, and glossy. Depending on light, they may be dark green or grass-green.

INFLORESCENCE: 24–48 in. (61–122 cm) long. The erect spike emerges from the center of the leaf fan.

FLOWERS: 5–12. The blossoms open in succession, but 2–3 are usually open at a time. The green petals are wavy margined and slightly twisted. They are marked with red on the veins and at the apex, base, and margins. The dorsal sepal is green with red veins, as is the pouch, which is densely speckled with red in the center.

HYBRIDIZING NOTES: N/A.

REFERENCES: 72, 90, 93, 148.

PHOTOS/DRAWINGS: 72, *90, 93, 138.*

Phragmipedium schlimii (Linden and Rchb.f.) Rolfe

AKA: *Selenipedium schlimii.*

ORIGIN/HABITAT: Medellín and Ocaña, Colombia. The plants are usually found on eastern mountain slopes in areas with continuous water seepage, often near rivers at 4800–6200 ft. (1463-1890 m).

CLIMATE: Station # 80110, Medellín, Colombia, Lat. 6.2°N, Long. 75.6°W, at 4916 ft. (1498 m). The record high is 92°F (33.3°C), and the record low is 41°F (5.0°C).

N/HEMISPHERE	JAN	FEB	MAR	APR	MAY	JUN	JUL	AUG	SEP	OCT	NOV	DEC
°F AVG MAX	82	82	84	82	82	82	83	82	82	80	81	81
°F AVG MIN	59	60	59	60	60	58	59	60	60	60	60	61
DIURNAL RANGE	23	22	25	22	22	24	24	22	22	20	21	20
RAIN/INCHES	2.7	3.5	3.3	6.5	7.7	5.5	4.1	4.6	6.2	6.7	5.2	2.5
HUMIDITY/%	69	70	72	74	75	73	69	69	73	77	77	72
BLOOM SEASON	*	*	*	*	*	*	*	*	**	***	**	**
DAYS CLR @ 7AM	0	1	0	0	0	1	1	0	0	0	0	1
DAYS CLR @ 1PM	2	3	0	0	1	1	1	0	1	0	0	1
DAYS CLR @ 7PM	3	4	0	1	0	1	0	2	3	1	0	2
RAIN/MM	69	89	84	165	196	140	104	117	157	170	132	64
°C AVG MAX	27.8	27.8	28.9	27.8	27.8	27.8	28.3	27.8	27.8	26.7	27.2	27.2
°C AVG MIN	15.0	15.6	15.0	15.6	15.6	14.4	15.0	15.6	15.6	15.6	15.6	16.1
DIURNAL RANGE	12.8	12.2	13.9	12.2	12.2	13.4	13.3	12.2	12.2	11.1	11.6	11.1
S/HEMISPHERE	JUL	AUG	SEP	OCT	NOV	DEC	JAN	FEB	MAR	APR	MAY	JUN

Cultural Recommendations

LIGHT: 2500–4000 fc. Diffused light is suggested since the habitat is usually cloudy.

TEMPERATURES: Days average 80–84°F (27–29°C), and nights average 59–61°F (14–16°C), with a diurnal range of 20–25°F (11–14°C).

HUMIDITY: 70–75% throughout the year.

WATER: Plants should be constantly moist. The rainfall pattern is wet year-round, with a slightly drier period in winter. Evening showers with strong winds occur frequently in mistforest zones.

FERTILIZER: ¼–½ strength, applied weekly to biweekly while plants are actively growing.

REST PERIOD: Growing conditions should be maintained throughout the year. Water and fertilizer could be reduced slightly, and light levels raised a little; but fluctuations in the habitat are only minor, and the changes are probably insignificant in cultivation. The information on the climate table represents the warmest of the plant's habitats. Growers report that *P. schlimii* is the most cold-tolerant species of the genus, and winter lows of 50–55°F (10–13°C) should not harm it.

GROWING MEDIA: A rapidly draining, moisture-retaining medium is necessary. Repotting is best done after flowering, just as new roots begin to grow.

MISCELLANEOUS NOTES: Plants may bloom more than once a year, but the bloom initiator is unknown.

Two growers report that plants in cultivation regularly survive winter lows of 35°F (1.7°C), providing the plants are kept dry as temperatures drop to 45°F (7°C) or colder. However, regularly exposing the plants to temperatures below the habitat's record low is not advisable. Should the plants be exposed accidentally to unusually low temperatures, they would be more likely to survive if dry.

Plant and Flower Information

PLANT SIZE AND TYPE: A 12–20 in. (30–51 cm) sympodial lithophyte or terrestrial.

PSEUDOBULB: None.

LEAVES: 7–9 per growth. The linear-lanceolate leaves are 9–13 in. (23–33 cm) long, rigid, and suberect. Bright grass-green, they are purple on the underside.

INFLORESCENCE: 12 in. (30 cm) long. The spike is erect, very hairy, pale greenish purple, and sometimes branching.

FLOWERS: 5–10. The fragrant blossoms are 1.5–3.0 in. (4–8 cm) across which is small for the genus. They may be white, greenish white tinged or mottled with pink, or deep rose, and all segments are covered with a velvety down. The egg-shaped lip is white with violet spots and veins. The petals are round and wide-opening. The southern Colombia form is reported to have larger flowers.

HYBRIDIZING NOTES: Chromosome count is 2n = 30. The flowers are often self-pollinating, which can result in a steady decline in the plant's constitution. *P. schlimii* is frequently used for hybridizing since the round petal form and pink and white color are dominant. It is a very potent pollen parent. Hybrids are generally vigorous growers, and some clones are fragrant.

REFERENCES: 14, 90, 112, 129, 148, 174, 205.

PHOTOS/DRAWINGS: *14, 90,* 129, 148, *180,* 205, *210.*

Phragmipedium vittatum (Vell.) Rolfe

AKA: *Cypripedium vittatum.*

ORIGIN/HABITAT: 186 mi. (300 km) from Brasília, Brazil. The plant grows on the banks of small rivers in highly organic soil with a pH of 7.5. It has also been found growing with acid-loving pitcher plants in bogs of swampy peat soil with a high ratio of organic material, which would certainly have a very low pH. Whether the plants are adaptable, or whether plants from the 2 areas must be treated differently, is not known. In both locations they grow intermingled with tall grasses which provide shade to the roots.

CLIMATE: Station # 83377, Brasília, Brazil, Lat. 15.9°S, Long. 47.9°W, at 3481 ft. (1061 m). The record high is 93°F (33.9°C), and the record low is 46°F (7.8°C).

N/HEMISPHERE	JAN	FEB	MAR	APR	MAY	JUN	JUL	AUG	SEP	OCT	NOV	DEC
°F AVG MAX	78	82	87	82	82	78	80	81	82	82	79	77
°F AVG MIN	51	55	60	64	66	64	65	64	64	62	56	52
DIURNAL RANGE	27	27	27	18	16	14	15	17	18	20	23	25
RAIN/INCHES	0.0	0.0	1.3	4.9	9.7	11.7	9.0	7.8	4.8	3.4	1.4	0.0
HUMIDITY/%	61	54	48	66	71	84	80	78	71	72	70	63
BLOOM SEASON						*	*	*	*			
DAYS CLR	N/A											
RAIN/MM	0	0	33	124	246	297	229	198	122	86	36	0
°C AVG MAX	25.6	27.8	30.6	27.8	27.8	25.6	26.7	27.2	27.8	27.8	26.1	25.0
°C AVG MIN	10.6	12.8	15.6	17.8	18.9	17.8	18.3	17.8	17.8	16.7	13.3	11.1
DIURNAL RANGE	15.0	15.0	15.0	10.0	8.9	7.8	8.4	9.4	10.0	11.1	12.8	13.9
S/HEMISPHERE	JUL	AUG	SEP	OCT	NOV	DEC	JAN	FEB	MAR	APR	MAY	JUN

Cultural Recommendations

LIGHT: 2000–3000 fc. Dappled shade or diffused light is recommended. In the habitat, the plants are shaded by the tall grass with which they grow.

TEMPERATURES: Summer days average 78–82°F (25–30°C), and nights average 64–66°F (18–19°C), resulting in a diurnal range of 14–18°F (8–10°C).

HUMIDITY: 70–80%.

WATER: Plants should be constantly moist. Although the rainfall pattern is wet/dry, the plants grow in bogs or on stream banks where the roots are permanently wet.

FERTILIZER: ¼–½ strength, applied weekly to biweekly. An organic fertilizer is highly recommended. In nature, the plants often grow in bogs with so much decaying vegetation that the area smells like sewage.

REST PERIOD: For 3 months, winter days average 77–79°F (25–26°C), and nights average 51–55°F (11–13°C), with a diurnal range of 25–27°F (14–15°C). The warmest temperatures occur at the end of the dry period. Water, humidity, and fertilizer may be reduced, while light levels should be maintained or raised slightly. The number of clear days in the habitat is not recorded, but the lack of rainfall and the low humidity suggest that clear weather is more frequent in winter.

GROWING MEDIA: A moisture-retaining medium is needed. One successful grower indicates that plants from the locations with alkaline soils did not survive in cultivation unless dolomite was added to bring the pH of the medium to 7.5. In nature, however, the plants are also found in very acid habitats. Repotting is best done after flowering, just as new roots begin to grow.

MISCELLANEOUS NOTES: N/A.

Plant and Flower Information

PLANT SIZE AND TYPE: A 32 in. (81 cm) sympodial terrestrial.

PSEUDOBULB: None.

LEAVES: 4–8 per growth. The leaves are 18–24 in. (46–61 cm) long, erect to arching, straplike, and uniformly green.

INFLORESCENCE: 36 in. (91 cm) long. Greenish brown and erect, the spike emerges from the center of the leaf fan.

FLOWERS: 1–4. The blossoms are somewhat small in relation to plant size. Flowers are pale greenish yellow to greenish white. The twisted petals are 2–3 in. (5–8 cm) long and marked with brown at the edge and brownish purple at the base. The lip is ungrooved, rounded in front, and deep brown-purple with a greenish tinge.

HYBRIDIZING NOTES: N/A.

REFERENCES: 60, 90, 138, 205.

PHOTOS/DRAWINGS: *60, 90, 138*, 205.

Phragmipedium wallisii (Rchb.f.) Garay

AKA: *P. caudatum* var. *wallisii, Selenipedium wallisii. Phragmipedium wallisii*, with its slipper–shaped lip, was once considered the normal form of the species, while *P. lindenii*, which has a third petal instead of a lip, was considered a peloric version. They are now considered separate species for horticultural reasons and because both species breed true.

ORIGIN/HABITAT: Colombia. It grows fully exposed on granite rocks and cliff faces at elevations of 4000–7000 ft. (1219–2134 m).

CLIMATE: Station # 80234, Villavicencio, Colombia, Lat. 4.2°N, Long. 73.6°W, at 1414 ft. (431 m). Temperatures are calculated for an elevation of 4000 ft. (1219 m), resulting in probable extremes of 97°F (36.1°C) and 40°F (4.4°C).

N/HEMISPHERE	JAN	FEB	MAR	APR	MAY	JUN	JUL	AUG	SEP	OCT	NOV	DEC
°F AVG MAX	82	81	80	79	77	78	77	78	79	82	80	81
°F AVG MIN	62	64	64	61	62	61	60	61	60	61	60	60
DIURNAL RANGE	20	17	16	18	15	17	17	17	19	21	20	21
RAIN/INCHES	1.6	3.9	5.7	19.8	20.0	20.4	17.9	15.2	15.9	15.2	13.9	6.4
HUMIDITY/%	73	72	75	81	82	84	81	82	79	80	80	76
BLOOM SEASON	*	*	*	*							*	*
DAYS CLR @ 7AM	3	1	1	0	1	1	0	1	1	1	2	3
DAYS CLR @ 1PM	1	2	2	0	0	0	0	0	2	1	0	1
RAIN/MM	41	99	145	503	508	518	455	386	404	386	353	163
°C AVG MAX	28.0	27.5	26.9	26.4	25.3	25.8	25.3	25.8	26.4	28.0	26.9	27.5
°C AVG MIN	16.9	18.0	18.0	16.4	16.9	16.4	15.8	16.4	15.8	16.4	15.8	15.8
DIURNAL RANGE	11.1	9.5	8.9	10.0	8.4	9.4	9.5	9.4	10.6	11.6	11.1	11.7
S/HEMISPHERE	JUL	AUG	SEP	OCT	NOV	DEC	JAN	FEB	MAR	APR	MAY	JUN

Cultural Recommendations

LIGHT: 2400–3500 fc. Fairly high diffused light is recommended since the plants are not shaded, but clear weather is essentially nonexistent.

TEMPERATURES: Summer days average 77–79 °F (25–26 °C), and nights average 60–62 °F (16–17 °C), with a diurnal range of 15–19 °F (8–11 °C). The coolest daytime temperatures occur in summer because of the heavier cloud-cover associated with the heavy rainfall.

HUMIDITY: 80–85% during the growing season.

WATER: Plants should be constantly moist while actively growing. Although the rainfall pattern is wet/dry, the high humidity levels and low number of clear days indicate that moisture is continuously available in the habitat from dew, mist, or low clouds.

FERTILIZER: ¼–½ strength, applied weekly to biweekly while the plants are actively growing.

REST PERIOD: Winter days average 80–82 °F (27–28 °C), and nights average 60–62 °F (16–17 °C), with a diurnal range of 16–21 °F (9–12 °C). The increase in diurnal range is caused by warmer days rather than cooler nights.

GROWING MEDIA: A rapidly draining, moisture-retaining medium is needed. Repotting is best done after flowering, just as new roots begin to grow.

MISCELLANEOUS NOTES: The heaviest blooming occurs during the warmer winter dry period, but plants may bloom anytime during the year.

Plant and Flower Information

PLANT SIZE AND TYPE: A 14–24 in. (36–61 cm) sympodial lithophyte.

PSEUDOBULB: None.

LEAVES: 10–12 per growth. The leaves are 6–12 in. (15–30 cm) long, distichous, stiff, and yellow-green.

INFLORESCENCE: 14–16 in. (36–40 cm) long. The erect spike emerges from the base of the leaf fan.

FLOWERS: 2–4. The large, showy, velvety blossoms open simultaneously. The pendent petals are greenish and flushed with red-brown near the apex. Continuing to elongate for several days after the flowers open, they may grow to 24 in. (61 cm) in length. The sepals are ivory-white to yellow-green with green to yellowish green veins. The lip is flushed with pale rose at the base of the pouch but is yellow-green at the edges.

HYBRIDIZING NOTES: N/A.

REFERENCES: 89, 90, 205.

PHOTOS/DRAWINGS: 89, *90, 179.*

Phragmipedium warscewiczianum (Rchb.f.) Garay

AKA: *Cypripedium warscewiczianum, Phragmipedium caudatum* var. *warscewiczii.* This species is frequently labeled as *P. caudatum,* which is a species native to Peru and Ecuador.

ORIGIN/HABITAT: The Pacific watershed from Costa Rica to Colombia. In Chiriquí, Panama, it is found only at the tops of tall trees 60–100 ft. (18-30 m) above the ground. Collectors from other areas indicate it is also found on rocks in decayed vegetable matter.

CLIMATE: Station # 78793, David, Panama, Lat. 8.4 °N, Long. 82.4 °W, at 89 ft. (27 m). Temperatures are adjusted to 5742 ft. (1750 m), resulting in probable extremes of 81 °F (27.2 °C) and 41 °F (5.0 °C).

N/HEMISPHERE	JAN	FEB	MAR	APR	MAY	JUN	JUL	AUG	SEP	OCT	NOV	DEC
°F AVG MAX	72	74	75	74	71	69	69	69	69	67	68	69
°F AVG MIN	48	49	50	53	52	52	52	52	51	51	51	50
DIURNAL RANGE	24	25	25	21	19	17	17	17	18	16	17	19
RAIN/INCHES	4.0	0.4	1.0	3.1	10.9	13.8	11.3	12.6	12.2	18.9	10.2	4.5
HUMIDITY/%	78	67	68	77	85	88	88	88	88	90	89	86
BLOOM SEASON									*	*		
DAYS CLR @ 7 AM	13	13	18	9	2	2	1	1	1	0	1	6
DAYS CLR @ 1 PM	5	9	14	3	0	0	1	0	0	0	0	0
RAIN/MM	102	10	25	79	277	351	287	320	310	480	259	114
°C AVG MAX	22.4	23.5	24.1	23.5	21.9	20.7	20.7	20.7	20.7	19.6	20.2	20.7
°C AVG MIN	9.1	9.6	10.2	11.9	11.3	11.3	11.3	11.3	10.7	10.7	10.7	10.2
DIURNAL RANGE	13.3	13.9	13.9	11.6	10.6	9.4	9.4	9.4	10.0	8.9	9.5	10.5
S/HEMISPHERE	JUL	AUG	SEP	OCT	NOV	DEC	JAN	FEB	MAR	APR	MAY	JUN

Cultural Recommendations

LIGHT: 2500–3500 fc. Direct sunlight should be avoided, since clear weather is rare in the habitat.

TEMPERATURES: Summer days average 69 °F (21 °C), and nights average 52 °F (11 °C), with a diurnal range of 17 °F (9 °C). The coolest days during the year are in summer because of the heavy cloud-cover during the rainy season.

HUMIDITY: 85–90%.

WATER: Plants should be constantly moist while actively growing. The rainfall pattern is wet/dry.

FERTILIZER: ¼–½ strength, applied weekly to biweekly while the plants are actively growing.

REST PERIOD: Winter days average 69–74 °F (21–24 °C), and nights average 48–50 °F (9–10 °C), with the diurnal range increasing to 19–25 °F (11–14 °C). A short, 2-month dry rest is indicated by the climate, but rainfall and cloud-cover are much greater in the higher mountainous habitat, and additional moisture is available from heavy dew and mist. In cultivation, water and fertilizer may be reduced somewhat, but the plant should never be allowed to become dry. Humidity may be reduced to 75–80%, and light may be increased slightly; but in the habitat, light probably remains relatively low since the cloud-cover is heavy.

GROWING MEDIA: A rapidly draining, moisture-retaining medium is recommended. Repotting is best done after flowering, just as new roots begin to grow.

MISCELLANEOUS NOTES: The bloom season shown in the climate table is based on collection records.

Plant and Flower Information

PLANT SIZE AND TYPE: A 24 in. (61 cm) sympodial terrestrial or epiphyte. The plant is very similar to *P. caudatum*.

PSEUDOBULB: None.

LEAVES: 5–7 per growth. The deep green leaves are 20–24 in. (51–61 cm) long and arranged in a fan. They tend to be shorter and broader than *P. caudatum*.

INFLORESCENCE: 16–24 in. (41–61 cm) long. The spike emerges from the center of the leaf fan.

FLOWERS: Few. The blossoms open simultaneously. They are described as deeper and brighter than the blooms of *P. caudatum*. The sepals are greenish yellow with pale orange veins giving a pinkish suffusion, while the petals are dull rose-purple. Many times longer than the sepals, the petals continue to elongate for several days after the flowers open. The lip is deep yellow-brown in front and yellow-green underneath.

HYBRIDIZING NOTES: N/A.

REFERENCES: 90, 205.

PHOTOS/DRAWINGS: *90*.

Phragmipedium xerophyticum Soto, Salazar, and Hágsater

AKA: N/A.

ORIGIN/HABITAT: Endemic to a single, restricted region in Oaxaca, Mexico, at 1050 ft. (320 m) on eastern slopes that form part of the watershed for the Gulf of Mexico. *P. xerophyticum* grows on rocks in warm, humid conditions with other tropical, xerophytic vegetation such as *Agave* and *Plumeria*. Fearing over-collection, the describers gave no precise habitat loca-

tion. They did, however, indicate that the habitat receives 98 in. (2500 mm) of rainfall per year and has an average annual temperature of 77°F (25°C). The climate for Minatitlan, Mexico, was selected as representative of the general area, and the data agrees with the habitat description.

CLIMATE: Station # 76781, Minatitlan, Mexico, Lat. 18.0°N, Long. 94.5°W, at 90 ft. (27 m). Temperatures are calculated for an elevation of 1050 ft. (320 m), resulting in probable extremes of 102°F (38.9°C) and 47°F (8.3°C).

N/HEMISPHERE	JAN	FEB	MAR	APR	MAY	JUN	JUL	AUG	SEP	OCT	NOV	DEC
°F AVG MAX	73	77	80	83	86	84	83	83	82	80	76	73
°F AVG MIN	63	64	66	67	70	70	71	70	70	68	65	64
DIURNAL RANGE	10	13	14	16	16	14	12	13	12	12	11	9
RAIN/INCHES	3.4	2.5	1.5	1.9	3.7	9.4	10.7	12.1	20.0	14.9	17.6	4.1
HUMIDITY/%	90	88	85	82	82	86	87	87	88	87	88	90
BLOOM SEASON									*			
DAYS CLR	N/A											
RAIN/MM	86	64	38	48	94	239	272	307	508	378	447	104
°C AVG MAX	22.7	24.9	26.6	28.2	29.9	28.8	28.2	28.2	27.7	26.6	24.4	22.7
°C AVG MIN	17.1	17.7	18.8	19.4	21.0	21.0	21.6	21.0	21.0	19.9	18.2	17.7
DIURNAL RANGE	5.6	7.2	7.8	8.8	8.9	7.8	6.6	7.2	6.7	6.7	6.2	5.0
S/HEMISPHERE	JUL	AUG	SEP	OCT	NOV	DEC	JAN	FEB	MAR	APR	MAY	JUN

Cultural Recommendations

LIGHT: 2500–3500 fc. Good air movement should be provided at all times.

TEMPERATURE: Summer days average 83–84°F (28–29°C), and nights average 70–71°F (21–22°C), with a diurnal range of 12–14°F (7–8°C).

HUMIDITY: 80–90% year-round.

WATER: In the habitat, water is moderate in late spring and early winter and heavy for 6 months in summer and autumn, with a 3-month dry period from midwinter to spring.

FERTILIZER: ¼–½ recommended strength, applied weekly to biweekly while the plants are growing.

REST PERIOD: Winter days average 73–77°F (23–25°C), and nights average 63–64°F (17–18°C), with a diurnal range of 9–13°F (5–7°C). Water should be reduced for 2–3 months in winter, but plants should not be allowed to dry out completely. The very high humidity in the habitat causes heavy deposits of dew, which makes more moisture available than the rainfall averages indicate. This condition may be simulated in cultivation by occasional early morning misting between waterings, especially on days that will be bright and sunny. Fertilizer should be eliminated in winter. When new growth is evident, water should be increased and fertilizer applications resumed.

GROWING MEDIA: The lithophytic growth habit and the heavy summer rains in the habitat indicate that a fast-draining medium that will remain moist but not soggy should be used. Fine-grade fir bark with moisture-retaining additives such as perlite should work well in most growing conditions.

MISCELLANEOUS NOTES: This species was only recently discovered and was first described in 1990. No information is available from growers, and the above cultural recommendations are based entirely on analysis of the regional climatic conditions.

Plant and Flower Information

PLANT SIZE AND TYPE: A 4–5 in. (10–13 cm) sympodial lithophyte.

PSEUDOBULB: None. New growths are spaced widely, about 1–3 in. (3–8 cm) apart, on a large, coarse, elongated rhizome.

LEAVES: 5–6 per growth. The short, fleshy leaves are rigid, persistent, distichous, and arranged in a fan shape. They may reach a length of 4.7 in. (12 cm), though they are often much shorter.

INFLORESCENCE: 2.6–5.3 in. (6.5–13.5 cm) long. The tall inflorescence, which arises from the center of the leaf fan, commonly produces 2 abbreviated racemes. It is covered with hairs along its entire length.

FLOWERS: 1–2 per inflorescence. The small, pink and white flowers are 0.6–0.8 in. (1.5–2.0 cm) across. The backs of the sepals are covered with hairs and often flushed with pink. The white pouch is suborbicular with a pink, hairy patch at the base. Flowers may be short-lived.

HYBRIDIZING NOTES: N/A.

REFERENCES: Soto, M. A., G. A. Salazar, and E. Hágsater. 1990. *Phragmipedium xerophyticum*, una nueva especie del Sureste de México. *Orquidea* (Méx.) 12:1-10.

PHOTOS/DRAWINGS: Soto et al., 1990.

7
Pleione
General Information

SUBFAMILY: Epidendroideae.

TRIBE: *Coelogyneae.*

SUBTRIBE: *Coelogyninae.*

GENUS: *Pleione* D. Don.

AKA: Most *Pleione* were originally classified as *Coelogyne,* but they are now separated into their own genus on the basis of their growth habit.

SPECIES: The recent review of the genus in *The Genus Pleione* (1988), by Phillip Cribb and Ian Butterfield, has been used as the taxonomic basis for the 15 species included here.

ORIGIN/HABITAT: *Pleione* habitats range from central Nepal, across southern China to Taiwan, and southward into India, Burma, Thailand, and Laos.

CLIMATE: Subtropical alpine climates are normal throughout the range. Most *Pleione* will not survive without a fairly severe cool rest.

Cultural Recommendations

LIGHT: Rather bright, diffused light to moderate shade is generally appropriate.

TEMPERATURES: Individual climate records are provided for each species. These provide the best guide to the cultivation requirements of individual species. In general, summer highs should not exceed 80 °F (26 °C). Most *Pleione* will survive short periods at 90 °F (32 °C) providing that high humidity and excellent air circulation are available. Wide seasonal variations are necessary for plant survival.

HUMIDITY: High humidity is required during the growing season. Excellent air circulation is necessary, and species that grow at high altitudes in nature are healthiest in cultivation when placed directly in front of a fan or evaporative cooler.

WATER: *Pleione* do not tolerate drying while actively growing, nor do they tolerate wet conditions during the winter rest period.

Watering should be resumed very gradually in the spring. Since new growths are very susceptible to rot, plants should not be watered from above until after flowering, when the new growths begin to mature.

Once active growth resumes in spring, the plants need constant moisture and may be watered freely, providing that drainage is excellent. During warm weather, *Pleione* reportedly respond well to evening misting, but some growers indicate that this practice causes leaf-spotting.

Watering should cease after leaf fall. The roots on spring-blooming species die back within 3 weeks of leaf fall, and even the fall-blooming species enter their dormant period by late autumn. If live moss is used as the medium, it may be misted enough to keep it alive during the rest period, but the base of the pseudobulb should never be water-soaked.

FERTILIZER: A ½-strength solution of 3–2–2 fertilizer with trace elements should be applied weekly while plants are actively growing. Beginning in the middle of Jul. (Jan.) and continuing until leaf fall, a ½-strength solution of 2–3–3 fertilizer is recommended, as it helps the bulbs to mature and set flowers for the following bloom season. In addition to the liquid fertilizer, sieved manure and steamed bone meal added to or layered in the medium help plants to thrive.

REST PERIOD: *Pleione* should be kept cool and either dry or barely moist from the time leaves drop until new growth begins. Winter light does not appear to be important in the habitat, as the bulbs are dormant and many are covered with snow. After the plants are repotted, they need lower temperatures of 32–36 °F (0–2 °C) for at least part of the winter. Growers often rest *Pleione* outside, but the plants should be screened or protected in some way, as mice may damage the bulbs.

In warm climates, some species may be rested in the refrigerator or freezer (depending on the temperature required) for at least part of the winter. Since humidity is extremely low in most refrigerators and freezers, the potted bulbs should be sealed in a plastic bag. The bag is rinsed in water, then all the water is shaken out, leaving just a few beads of moisture clinging to the inside of the plastic. The bag is then sealed. When the plant is cooled in the refrigerator, this small amount of moisture is enough to raise the humidity to nearly 100%. Check the medium for moisture a day or so after refrigerating the plant; the medium shoud feel barely damp. The moisture level can be adjusted by adding small amounts of water or by leaving the bag open to allow evaporation. When the plants are removed from the refrigerator, they should be removed from the plastic bag.

GROWING MEDIA: Thick moss is usually the substratum in the plant's natural habitat. In cultivation, any moss- or humus-based medium that retains moisture and is free-draining is acceptable. Garden dirt should not be used. Growers report that including a layer of bone meal or sieved manure in the medium helps produce a healthy plant. Charcoal may be incorporated in the medium to help absorb and neutralize excess salts.

All *Pleione* species should be repotted each autumn. Fall-blooming plants should be repotted about 2 weeks after blooming, while spring-blooming plants should be repotted after the leaves drop. Repotting should not be delayed, since the new roots generally begin to grow almost immediately and are very fragile. If the non-branching roots are broken, they will not regrow.

Recommended media include the following:

A mixture of peat, loam, and sand, covered with a layer of live sphagnum moss. If loam is used, it should cover only the bottom ¼ of the bulb.

A mixture of 6 parts mixed bark, 1 part coarse perlite, 1 part snipped sphagnum moss, and 1 part coarse peat moss should be used for the bottom of the pan. The bulbs are then covered with the same blend of ingredients mixed with small or seedling-size bark.

It is often difficult to moisten peat moss adequately for use in potting. For perfectly moistened peat, mix 4 cups of peat moss with 1.5 cups of water in a large plastic bag, then shake the bag to distribute the moisture and thoroughly mix the peat.

During potting, bulbs should be placed ½ in. (1 cm) apart on a layer of coarse medium. The pan should be filled with a finer grade medium to approximately ½ the bulb's depth with the roots ½ in. (1 cm) below the surface for most species. Remaining old roots should not be removed, since they help anchor the bulbs in the medium. A pot 6 in. (15 cm) in diameter will hold about 12 bulbs.

Shallow bulb pans are highly recommended, as *Pleione* roots are near the surface, and shallow containers help reduce the risk of overwatering. If a deep container is used, the bottom half should be filled with broken crockery or styrofoam nuggets such as those used as packing material. The pots should have extra drainage holes added. A bulb pan 10 in. (25 cm) across should have 20 or more 0.25 in. (6 mm) holes in the bottom.

After the plants are repotted, they should be given a cool, dry rest until new growth appears.

Seedlings and bulbils should be mass-planted in a shallow pan of fine-grade medium with moss added. Steamed bone meal should be dusted on the surface, and the young bulbs should be barely covered with the potting mix. They should then be given the same growing conditions as mature plants, except that young seedlings should not be exposed to temperatures below 38°F (3°C). Constant moisture is particularly important for young plants.

MISCELLANEOUS NOTES: Many *Pleione* do well grown outdoors in most areas where camellias and rhododendrons grow, providing that temperatures remain within the recommended range and assuming that the bulbs can be kept quite dry in winter. In the summer, outdoor plants also need careful watering and fertilizing, and drainage must be excellent year-round. In cold weather, particularly, the plants cannot tolerate soggy conditions. *Pleione* should not be planted where they receive direct sun in winter, as they do not tolerate rapid or frequent freezing and thawing.

Root rot is normally caused by soggy medium or poor drainage and may kill the plant. Affected plants should be treated immediately with a systemic fungicide mixed at the recommended rate, and watering practices should be modified. Fungicide solutions that are stronger than recommended are known to cause premature dormancy.

Plant and Flower Information

PLANT SIZE AND TYPE: Notes regarding individual growth habits are included for each species. *Pleione* are all dwarf species, and they may be terrestrials, lithophytes, or epiphytes in their native habitats. All species seem healthiest when grown as semiterrestrials in cultivation.

PSEUDOBULB: The small, annual pseudobulbs are seldom over 1.5 in. (4 cm) long. Each mature bulb produces at least one new flowering-size replacement bulb, providing that conditions are adequate. Well-grown plants of some species may produce up to 3 new bulbs per year.

Bulb rot may result from insufficient rest during the preceding winter. Once rot begins to develop, it is nearly always fatal.

LEAVES: 1 or 2 per growth. The leaves are thin, plicate, and deciduous.

The following symptoms may indicate cultural problems:

Black lesions on the leaves are reportedly caused by inadequate water during early growth.

Black or brown tips on new shoots reportedly result from inadequate water.

Brown leaf tips in species of other genera are usually caused by insufficient water, overfertilizing, or salt buildup in the pot. The precise cause in *Pleione* has not been identified, but the condition seldom occurs when plants receive appropriate water and fertilizer.

Spotting on the underside of leaves may indicate infestation by spider mites, particularly during hot, dry weather. As a remedy, plants should be sprayed with an appropriate miticide.

Sunburn should be avoided, as a severe case may cause the loss of the plant. Because new leaves are extremely sensitive to direct sun, sunburn usually occurs when spring brings a rapid increase in light.

INFLORESCENCE: Spring flower spikes emerge from the apex of the new growth; fall spikes emerge from the apex of the mature pseudobulb.

Browning of the stem near the pseudobulb is an indication of rot, which spreads rapidly. This condition is usually caused by overwatering or poor drainage. Increased air circulation is the best preventative measure.

Damaged spikes and new growths are usually caused by slugs and snails.

FLOWERS: *Pleione* are normally single-flowered, but well-grown plants of some species may produce up to 3 flowers in cultivation.

Blossoms usually last about 2 weeks and are longest lived when kept cool but above 45°F (7°C). The time of spring flowering may be accelerated or delayed by controlling the timing of the cold winter conditions. Precisely how long it takes for the plants to flower after warm temperatures begin is unknown.

Flower symptoms of cultural problems include the following:

Deformed flowers may result from aphid damage. To prevent the problem, a regular control program should be started in early spring.

Short-lived flowers often result from early pollination by stray bumblebees or from temperatures which are too warm.

HYBRIDIZING NOTES: Normal chromosome count is x = 20. Seeds are mature in approximately 220 days. Seedlings usually require 4–5 years to bloom after pollination, but bulbils may reach blooming size in 2–3 years.

Pleione are often difficult to breed beyond the first generation since hybrids may not carry the normal number of chromosomes.

Hybrids between spring- and autumn-blooming species tend to flower in winter, in between the flowering seasons of the parent species. Fragrance is often transmitted to the progeny.

REFERENCES: 8, 33.

PHOTOS/DRAWINGS: See species listings.

Species Culture

Pleione alba. See *P. forrestii.* This synonym is listed with a *?* by Dr. Cribb. REFERENCES: 33.

Pleione albiflora Cribb and C. Z. Tang

AKA: Specimens were classified as either *P. grandiflora* or *P. humilis* before 1983, when the describers identified *P. albiflora* as a separate species.

ORIGIN/HABITAT: Northern Burma and Yunnan, China. It is found in the Ta-Li (Da-Li) Mountains at 7800–11,500 ft. (2377–3505 m) and usually grows in thick moss on shady tree trunks, rocks, or cliffs.

CLIMATE: Station # 56751, Ta-Li, China, Lat. 25.7°N, Long. 100.2°E, at 6430 ft. (1960 m). Temperatures are calculated for an elevation of 7800 ft. (2377 m), resulting in probable extremes of 85°F (29.4°C) and 23°F (-5.0°C).

N/HEMISPHERE	JAN	FEB	MAR	APR	MAY	JUN	JUL	AUG	SEP	OCT	NOV	DEC
°F AVG MAX	55	55	62	69	71	72	72	70	70	64	60	56
°F AVG MIN	32	35	39	45	50	56	58	57	53	48	38	33
DIURNAL RANGE	23	20	23	24	21	16	14	13	17	16	22	23
RAIN/INCHES	1.3	1.9	3.5	1.6	3.9	8.9	10.4	9.5	7.3	4.8	1.2	0.3
HUMIDITY/%	51	51	48	49	59	74	80	82	79	77	64	60
BLOOM SEASON				*	*							
DAYS CLR @ 7AM	25	16	18	12	9	5	2	2	8	10	22	26
DAYS CLR @ 1PM	23	10	14	8	4	4	2	2	6	6	19	23
RAIN/MM	33	48	89	41	99	226	264	241	185	122	30	8
°C AVG MAX	13.0	13.0	16.9	20.8	21.9	22.5	22.5	21.4	21.4	18.0	15.8	13.6
°C AVG MIN	0.0	1.9	4.2	7.5	10.3	13.6	14.7	14.2	11.9	9.2	3.6	0.8
DIURNAL RANGE	13.0	11.1	12.7	13.3	11.6	8.9	7.8	7.2	9.5	8.8	12.2	12.8
S/HEMISPHERE	JUL	AUG	SEP	OCT	NOV	DEC	JAN	FEB	MAR	APR	MAY	JUN

Cultural Recommendations

LIGHT: 2000–3000 fc. Diffused light is suggested.

TEMPERATURES: Summer days average 70–72°F (21–23°C), and nights average 50–58°F (10–15°C), with a diurnal range of 13–21°F (7–12°C). The probable extreme high is 85°F (30°C), so summer heat could be detrimental to plant health.

HUMIDITY: 60-80% during the growing season.

WATER: Plants should be constantly moist while actively growing. The rainfall pattern is wet/dry.

FERTILIZER: A ½-strength solution of 3–2–2 with trace elements should be applied weekly while plants are actively growing. A ½-strength 2–3–3 solution is recommended from mid-Jul. (Jan.) to leaf drop.

REST PERIOD: Winter days average 55–62°F (13–17°C), and nights average 32–39°F (0–4°C), with a diurnal range of 20–24°F (11–13°C). The rest period lasts 2-3 months, from leaf fall to new growth. In nature the dormant pseudobulbs may be protected by snow cover in winter, so plants should not be subjected to long, hard freezes or freezing/thawing conditions. Water should be reduced, but plants may be misted occasionally to prevent desiccation. Fertilizer should be eliminated. In the habitat, light is much higher in winter, but apparently winter light levels are not critical in cultivation.

GROWING MEDIA: The medium should retain moisture and drain rapidly. Repotting is best done after the leaves drop.

MISCELLANEOUS NOTES: This species is not currently available for cultivation, but a climate table is included since Chinese plants are becoming more accessible.

Plant and Flower Information

PLANT SIZE AND TYPE: A 12 in. (30 cm) epiphyte or lithophyte.

PSEUDOBULB: 1.2–1.8 in. (3.0–4.6 cm) long. The bulb is ovoid-conical with an elongated neck.

LEAVES: 1 per growth. The mature size of the lanceolate leaf was not recorded.

INFLORESCENCE: Size unknown. The spike emerges with the new growth.

FLOWERS: 1. The flower is normally 3–4 in. (8–10 cm) across, but size and color are variable. The nodding, fragrant blossoms are usually pure white, but they may be streaked with pale mauve. The white lip is fringed along the front edge and is sometimes marked with crimson or brown.

HYBRIDIZING NOTES: N/A.

REFERENCES: 33.

PHOTOS/DRAWINGS: 33.

Pleione amoena Schlechter. A little-known species which is not currently available for cultivation. REFERENCES: 33.

Pleione aurita Cribb and Pfenning

AKA: N/A.

ORIGIN/HABITAT: Yunnan Province, China. This species was described in 1988, but precise location and habitat details were not recorded. The plants may have been collected in western Yunnan, since they were shipped as *P. forrestii*.

CLIMATE: The habitat information now available is inadequate to select a specific climate, but the following guidelines are typical of fairly high elevations in the region where most species of *Pleione* are found.

Cultural Recommendations

LIGHT: 2400–3600 fc. Diffused light is probably appropriate, since summers in the habitat are generally cloudy.

TEMPERATURES: Summer days probably average 70–74°F (21–23°C), and nights average 47–59°F (8–15°C), with a diurnal range of 15–22°F (8–11°C).

HUMIDITY: 70–80%.

WATER: Plants should be constantly moist while actively growing. The rainfall pattern is generally wet in summer and dry in winter.

FERTILIZER: A ½-strength solution of 3–2–2 with trace elements should be applied weekly while plants are actively growing. A ½-strength 2-3-3 solution is recommended from mid-Jul. (Jan.) to leaf drop.

REST PERIOD: Winter days probably average 55–60°F (13–16°C), and nights average 31–40°F (-1–4°C), with a diurnal range of 22–28°F (12–16°C). The lows are probably necessary for at least part of the lengthy winter rest. In the habitat, light is probably higher in winter; but since the plants are dormant, increased light may not be critical. This habitat is clear, cold, and dry in winter, when even the humidity is very low. Water should be reduced to occasional misting to prevent the bulbs from withering, and fertilizer should be eliminated.

GROWING MEDIA: The medium should retain moisture but drain rapidly. Repotting is best done in autumn after the leaf drops.

MISCELLANEOUS NOTES: N/A.

Plant and Flower Information

PLANT SIZE AND TYPE: A 6–7 in. (15–18 cm) terrestrial.

PSEUDOBULB: 1.0–1.6 in. (2.5–4.0 cm) long. The bulbs are conical and uniformly green or pale green.

LEAVES: 1 per growth. The leaf is approximately 5–6 in. (13–15 cm) long; however, mature leaves were not available when the plants were described.

INFLORESCENCE: 2–3 in. (5–8 cm) long. The erect spike emerges from the new growth, which arises from the base of the old pseudobulb.

FLOWERS: 1 per growth. The showy blossoms are 2.5–3.0 in. (6.4–7.6 cm) across, but they are not wide-spreading. They may be pale pink, rose-pink, or purple and are usually darker at the tips. The petals are sharply reflexed, the dorsal sepal is somewhat hooded, and the lip is ruffled at the margin and has 4–5 lines of long hairs in the center.

HYBRIDIZING NOTES: N/A.

REFERENCES: 33.

PHOTOS/DRAWINGS: 33.

Pleione birmanica. See *P. praecox.* REFERENCES: 33.

Pleione bulbocodioides (Franch.) Rolfe

AKA: *Coelogyne bulbocodioides* and *C. pogonioides.* Other synonyms include *Pleione communis, P. delavayi, P. fargesii, P. ganchuenensis, P. henryi, P. mairei, P. pogonioides* Rolfe, *P. rhombilabia,* and *P. smithii.* Dr. Cribb considers *P. saxicola* a possible variation of *P. bulbocodioides.* Some *P. bulbocodioides* plants were erroneously identified as *P. yunnanensis* when imported in 1906. Their offspring, often mislabeled, are still in cultivation.

ORIGIN/HABITAT: Southern China at 2952–11,808 ft. (900-3600 m). The widespread plants often grow under rhododendron shrubs in deep leaf litter. They reportedly grow in profusion at Ta-Li, an area of open pine forests, where the *Pleione* are usually found on rapidly draining banks and ridges.

CLIMATE: Station # 56751, Ta-Li, China, Lat. 25.7°N, Long. 100.2°E, at 6430 ft. (1960 m), which is midrange for the plant's habitat. The record high is 90°F (32.2°C), and the record low is 28°F (-2.2°C).

N/HEMISPHERE	JAN	FEB	MAR	APR	MAY	JUN	JUL	AUG	SEP	OCT	NOV	DEC
°F AVG MAX	60	60	67	74	76	77	77	75	75	69	65	61
°F AVG MIN	37	40	44	50	55	61	63	62	58	53	43	38
DIURNAL RANGE	23	20	23	24	21	16	14	13	17	16	22	23
RAIN/INCHES	1.3	1.9	3.5	1.6	3.9	8.9	10.4	9.5	7.3	4.8	1.2	0.3
HUMIDITY/%	51	51	48	49	59	74	80	82	79	77	64	60
BLOOM SEASON	*	**	***	**	*							
DAYS CLR @ 7AM	25	16	18	12	9	5	2	2	8	10	22	26
DAYS CLR @ 1PM	23	10	14	8	4	4	2	2	6	6	19	23
RAIN/MM	33	48	89	41	99	226	264	241	185	122	30	8
°C AVG MAX	15.6	15.6	19.4	23.3	24.4	25.0	25.0	23.9	23.9	20.6	18.3	16.1
°C AVG MIN	2.8	4.4	6.7	10.0	12.8	16.1	17.2	16.7	14.4	11.7	6.1	3.3
DIURNAL RANGE	12.8	11.2	12.7	13.3	11.6	8.9	7.8	7.2	9.5	8.9	12.2	12.8
S/HEMISPHERE	JUL	AUG	SEP	OCT	NOV	DEC	JAN	FEB	MAR	APR	MAY	JUN

Cultural Recommendations

LIGHT: 2400–4000 fc. Diffused or dappled light is suggested. Clear days are uncommon in the habitat.

TEMPERATURES: Summer days average 74–77°F (23–25°C), and nights average 50–63°F (10–17°C), with a diurnal range of 13–24°F (7–13°C).

HUMIDITY: 60–80%.

WATER: Plants should be constantly moist while actively growing. The rainfall pattern is wet/dry.

FERTILIZER: Weekly applications of a ½-strength solution of 3–2–2 with trace elements is recommended until mid-Jul. (Jan.), when a ½-strength 2–3–3 solution should be used. Regular feeding is necessary to produce pseudobulbs large enough to flower the following year.

REST PERIOD: Winter days average 60–67°F (16–23°C), and nights average 37–44°F (3-7°C), with a diurnal range of 20–24°F (11–13°C). These lows are probably the warmest lows that this plant will tolerate and are absolutely necessary for at least part of the dormant period. The winter rest should last from leaf fall until new growth in the spring. This species regularly survives below-freezing temperatures in some portions of its native habitat, but the bulbs may be protected from severe freezes by a layer of snow. Plants that are dry survive freezing in cultivation. Occasional very light misting prevents withering of the bulbs. Fertilizer should be eliminated until new growth is evident.

GROWING MEDIA: The medium should retain moisture and drain rapidly. Unlike other *Pleione*, these bulbs should be planted beneath the surface of the medium. Repotting should be done immediately after the leaf drops.

MISCELLANEOUS NOTES: This species is slow to increase even under ideal growing conditions. It seldom produces more than one new flowering-size bulb, but 2–3 bulbils may be formed near the apex of the pseudobulb.

P. bulbocodioides is considered difficult to flower in cultivation, and bloom initiators have not been identified. A bulb that fails to bloom may not have reached full maturity during the preceding growing season. Growers speculate that this may occur when nutrients are deficient or when climatic conditions are incorrect, but other, as yet unknown factors may also influence blooming.

Plant and Flower Information

PLANT SIZE AND TYPE: A 5–6 in. (13–15 cm) terrestrial or lithophyte.

PSEUDOBULB: 0.8–1.0 in. (2.0–2.5 cm) long. The bulb is roughly conical with a distinct neck.

LEAVES: 1 per growth. The narrowly elliptical leaf is 6–7 in. (15–18 cm) long.

INFLORESCENCE: 8 in. (20 cm) long. The spike arises from the base of the old pseudobulb in the spring.

FLOWERS: 1 per growth. The showy blossoms are 2–3 in. (5–8 cm) across and may be pink, rose-purple, or magenta. The lip is marked with darker purple and is toothed along the front edge.

HYBRIDIZING NOTES: N/A.

REFERENCES: 7, 14, 33, 112, 174.

PHOTOS/DRAWINGS: 7, 14, 33, 174.

Pleione chiwuana. See *P. yunnanensis.* REFERENCES: 33.

Pleione chunii Tso. Considered by Dr. Cribb to be a little-known or doubtful species. REFERENCES: 33.

Pleione communis. See *P. bulbocodioides.* REFERENCES: 33.

Pleione concolor. See *P. praecox.* REFERENCES: 33.

Pleione × confusa. See *P. forrestii.* REFERENCES: 33.

Pleione coronaria Cribb and C. Z. Tang

AKA: N/A.

ORIGIN/HABITAT: Central Nepal, north of Kathmandu. It grows on mossy trunks and branches near ground level in rhododendron woodlands at 9348-9840 ft. (2850-3000 m). The range is extremely limited, and the species may be endangered in its natural habitat.

CLIMATE: Station # 44454, Kathmandu, Nepal, Lat. 27.7°N, Long. 85.3°E, at 4342 ft. (1323 m). Average temperatures are calculated for the plant elevation of 9750 ft. (2972 m). Records of extreme temperatures, humidity, and sky cover are not available for this station.

N/HEMISPHERE	JAN	FEB	MAR	APR	MAY	JUN	JUL	AUG	SEP	OCT	NOV	DEC
°F AVG MAX	44	47	55	60	63	64	63	63	62	58	52	46
°F AVG MIN	20	24	30	38	46	51	51	51	50	41	30	22
DIURNAL RANGE	24	23	25	22	17	13	12	12	12	17	22	24
RAIN/INCHES	0.6	0.9	1.3	1.9	2.3	9.9	14.8	13.9	5.1	2.2	0.3	0.1
HUMIDITY/%	N/A											
BLOOM SEASON	N/A											
DAYS CLR	N/A											
RAIN/MM	14	22	32	48	58	252	377	352	129	56	8	2
°C AVG MAX	6.5	8.6	12.8	15.6	17.1	17.7	17.4	17.2	16.5	14.3	11.1	7.7
°C AVG MIN	-6.8	-4.2	-1.1	3.4	7.7	10.5	10.7	10.5	9.8	4.9	-1.1	-5.6
DIURNAL RANGE	13.3	12.8	13.9	12.2	9.4	7.2	6.7	6.7	6.7	9.4	12.2	13.3
S/HEMISPHERE	JUL	AUG	SEP	OCT	NOV	DEC	JAN	FEB	MAR	APR	MAY	JUN

Cultural Recommendations

LIGHT: 2400–4000 fc. Diffused light is recommended. At other stations in this part of the Himalayas, clear days are rare during the summer and common in winter.

TEMPERATURES: The uniformly cool summer days average 60–64°F (16–18°C), and nights average 41–51°F (5–11°C), with a diurnal range of 12–17°F (7–9°C). Cool average temperatures could be critically important for this species.

HUMIDITY: 75–85% except in winter, when the humidity may drop to 60%. Although humidity records are not available for Kathmandu, these averages are reported at the nearest station with a similar rainfall pattern.

WATER: Plants should be constantly moist while actively growing. The rainfall pattern is wet/dry.

FERTILIZER: A ½-strength solution of 3–2–2 with trace elements, applied weekly while plants are actively growing. A ½-strength 2–3–3 solution should be used from mid-Jul. (Jan.) to leaf drop.

REST PERIOD: Winter days average 44–55°F (7–13°C). For 5 months, nights average 20–30°F (-1 to -6°C), with a diurnal range of 22–25°F (12–14°C). Freezing nights might be necessary for at least part of the winter. The plants should certainly survive freezing; but in nature, they may be protected from extremes. Water should be restricted to infrequent misting, and fertilizer should be eliminated. Clear weather and increased light occur in the habitat but may be unimportant in cultivation.

GROWING MEDIA: The medium should retain moisture and drain rapidly. *P. coronaria* bulbils are best grown in garden moss that is moist but not wet. Growers report that the bulbils tend to rot in sphagnum moss. Repotting is best done after the leaves drop.

MISCELLANEOUS NOTES: Only recently introduced into cultivation, this plant originates in a very limited natural habitat and may not prove to be adaptable. The short growing season suggests that rapid growth during the growing season should be encouraged.

Plant and Flower Information

PLANT SIZE AND TYPE: An 8 in. (20 cm) epiphyte.

PSEUDOBULB: 1.5 in. (4 cm) long. The closely clustered bulbs are conical-ovoid.

LEAVES: 1 per growth. The single leaf is 6 in. (15 cm) long, lanceolate, and spreading.

INFLORESCENCE: 3–4 in. (8-10 cm) long.

FLOWERS: 1–2. The blossoms are 2.5–3.5 in. (6–9 cm) across and are pale mauve-pink with red or purple spotting near the apex of the toothed lip.

HYBRIDIZING NOTES: N/A.

REFERENCES: 33.

PHOTOS/DRAWINGS: 33.

Pleione delavayi. See *P. bulbocodioides.* REFERENCES: 33.

Pleione diantha. See *P. humilis.* REFERENCES: 33.

Pleione diphylla. See *P. maculata.* REFERENCES: 33.

Pleione fargesii. See *P. bulbocodioides.* REFERENCES: 33.

Pleione formosana Hayata

AKA: *P. hui.* The synonym *P. pricei* is still in use for hybrid registration purposes.

ORIGIN/HABITAT: Eastern China to Taiwan, where it grows in moss on sunny rocks and fallen logs or on tree trunks in moist, foggy places at 4920–6560 ft. (1500–2000 m).

CLIMATE: Station # 46753, Ali-Shaw, Taiwan, Lat. 23.5°N, Long. 120.9°E, at 7891 ft. (2405 m). Temperatures are calculated for an elevation of 5000 ft. (1524 m), resulting in probable extremes of 85°F (29.4°C) and 28°F (-2.2°C).

N/HEMISPHERE	JAN	FEB	MAR	APR	MAY	JUN	JUL	AUG	SEP	OCT	NOV	DEC
°F AVG MAX	63	63	68	70	72	74	75	76	76	74	70	65
°F AVG MIN	45	46	50	54	57	61	59	60	57	55	50	47
DIURNAL RANGE	18	17	18	16	15	13	16	16	19	19	20	18
RAIN/INCHES	3.7	3.3	3.0	12.9	35.9	28.2	25.3	29.9	8.5	6.4	3.8	1.8
HUMIDITY/%	78	84	82	86	90	91	90	92	89	87	79	80
BLOOM SEASON	*	**	***	**	*							
DAYS CLR @ 8AM	15	13	15	6	10	4	5	9	14	16	16	15
DAYS CLR @ 2PM	7	3	2	0	0	0	0	0	0	1	4	7
RAIN/MM	94	84	76	328	912	716	643	759	216	163	97	46
°C AVG MAX	17.0	17.0	19.7	20.9	22.0	23.1	23.6	24.2	24.2	23.1	20.9	18.1
°C AVG MIN	7.0	7.5	9.7	12.0	13.6	15.9	14.7	15.3	13.6	12.5	9.7	8.1
DIURNAL RANGE	10.0	9.5	10.0	8.9	8.4	7.2	8.9	8.9	10.6	10.6	11.2	10.0
S/HEMISPHERE	JUL	AUG	SEP	OCT	NOV	DEC	JAN	FEB	MAR	APR	MAY	JUN

Cultural Recommendations

LIGHT: 2400–4000 fc. Diffused light is suggested. Although this species is apparently adaptable, direct sun should be avoided.

TEMPERATURES: Summer days average 70–76°F (21–24°C), and nights average 54–61°F (12–16°C), with a diurnal range of 13–16°F (7–16°C).

HUMIDITY: 80–90%.

WATER: Plants should be constantly moist while actively growing. The rainfall pattern is wet/wetter with a brief dry period in winter.

FERTILIZER: A ½-strength solution of 3-2-2 with trace elements should be applied weekly while plants are actively growing. A ½-strength 2-3-3 solution is recommended from mid-Jul. (Jan.) to leaf drop.

REST PERIOD: Winter days average 63–70°F (17–21°C), and nights average 45–50°F (7–10°C), with a diurnal range of 17–19°F (9–11°C). *P. formosana* is the warmest-growing *Pleione*, but it still requires at least occasional drops to 32–36°F (0–2°C) during part of the winter. Despite the relatively wet winter in the habitat, in cultivation water should be reduced to occasional light misting to help prevent problems with rot. Fertilizer should be eliminated.

GROWING MEDIA: The medium should retain moisture but drain rapidly. Repotting is best done after the leaves drop.

MISCELLANEOUS NOTES: *P. formosana* is vigorous, hardy, adaptable, free-flowering, and easy to grow if it receives a cool rest. However, it will decline and die out if grown at temperatures that are too warm. Each growth normally produces 2 new flowering-size pseudobulbs each year. Plants are often grown outside in peat beds in areas with moderate winters. When dry, the plant reportedly survives surprisingly severe freezes of 18–20°F (-6 to -8°C). These lows exceed the probable extremes calculated for the plant's habitat.

Plant and Flower Information

PLANT SIZE AND TYPE: A 6–12 in. (15–30 cm) epiphyte or lithophyte.

PSEUDOBULB: 0.4–1.2 in. (1–3 cm) long. The ovoid pseudobulbs range in color from green to dull, dark red.

LEAVES: 1 per growth. The elliptical leaf is 4–10 in. (10–25 cm) long, and usually drops in Sep. (Mar.).

INFLORESCENCE: 10 in. (25 cm) long. The spike emerges with the new growth in the spring.

FLOWERS: 1–2. The faintly fragrant flowers are 3–4 in. (8–10 cm) across. Normally lilac to rose-pink, the blossoms are extremely variable in size and color, and many varieties have been named. The lip is deeply fringed, flushed with yellow in the center, and marked with red or brown.

HYBRIDIZING NOTES: Chromosome count is x = 20. *P. formosana* transmits vigor, free-flowering characteristics, and the ability to produce bulbils to its progeny.

REFERENCES: 7, 24, 33, 114, 125, 132, 133, 181, 210.

PHOTOS/DRAWINGS: 7, 24, 33, 114, 125, 132, 133, 181, 210.

Pleione forrestii Schlechter

AKA: *P. alba* is a possible synonym. *P. forrestii* is known to hybridize naturally with *P. albiflora*, forming *P.* × *confusa*. Some plants grown as *P. forrestii* are actually the natural hybrid *P.* × *confusa*.

ORIGIN/HABITAT: Northern Burma through western Yunnan, China. Plants grow between 7800–10,100 ft. (2377–3078 m) on exposed or semishady, mossy granite boulders, in deep shade on mossy cliffs, and, rarely, on tree trunks.

CLIMATE: Station # 56651, Lichiang (Likiang), China, Lat. 27.0°N, Long. 100.3°E, at 7926 ft. (2416 m). The record high is 85°F (29.4°C), and the record low is 19°F (-7.2°C).

N/HEMISPHERE	JAN	FEB	MAR	APR	MAY	JUN	JUL	AUG	SEP	OCT	NOV	DEC
°F AVG MAX	57	56	64	70	74	74	74	73	72	67	63	59
°F AVG MIN	31	34	40	47	52	57	59	57	54	48	37	31
DIURNAL RANGE	26	22	24	23	22	17	15	16	18	19	26	28
RAIN/INCHES	0.3	0.2	0.4	0.6	2.5	5.7	10.8	9.9	7.3	2.4	0.2	0.0
HUMIDITY/%	42	49	45	47	55	73	80	82	79	71	56	50
BLOOM SEASON			**	*	*							
DAYS CLR @ 7AM	23	15	19	13	10	4	1	3	4	11	22	25
DAYS CLR @ 1PM	21	10	12	7	3	1	2	2	3	6	18	23
RAIN/MM	8	5	10	15	64	145	274	251	185	61	5	0
°C AVG MAX	13.9	13.3	17.8	21.1	23.3	23.3	23.3	22.8	22.2	19.4	17.2	15.0
°C AVG MIN	-0.6	1.1	4.4	8.3	11.1	13.9	15.0	13.9	12.2	8.9	2.8	-0.6
DIURNAL RANGE	14.5	12.2	13.4	12.8	12.2	9.4	8.3	8.9	10.0	10.5	14.4	15.6
S/HEMISPHERE	JUL	AUG	SEP	OCT	NOV	DEC	JAN	FEB	MAR	APR	MAY	JUN

Cultural Recommendations

LIGHT: 2400–4000 fc. Diffused light is indicated by the cloudy summers in the habitat.

TEMPERATURES: Summer days average 70–74°F (21–23°C), and nights average 47–59°F (8–15°C), with a diurnal range of 15–22°F (8–13°C).

HUMIDITY: 55–80% during the growing season.

WATER: Plants should be constantly moist while actively growing. The rainfall pattern is wet/dry.

FERTILIZER: A ½-strength solution of 3–2–2 with trace elements, applied weekly while plants are actively growing. A ½-strength 2-3-3 solution may be used from mid-Jul. (Jan.) to leaf drop.

REST PERIOD: For 3 months in winter, days average 56-59°F (13-15°C), and nights average 31–34°F (-0.6–1.0°C), with a diurnal range of 22–28°F (12–16°C). Temperatures in the climate table represent the warmer limit of the plant's habitat. Plants should tolerate winter lows that are 6–8°F (3–4°C) cooler than shown, but they must be kept dry when temperatures are below 45°F (7°C). Very cool nights are necessary for at least part of the lengthy winter rest. In winter, the habitat is clear, cold, and dry with humidity below 50%, so in cultivation, water should be reduced to occasional light misting to prevent withering, and fertilizer should be eliminated.

GROWING MEDIA: The medium should retain moisture and drain rapidly. Repotting is best done after the leaves drop.

MISCELLANEOUS NOTES: N/A.

Plant and Flower Information

PLANT SIZE AND TYPE: A 6 in. (15 cm) lithophyte or epiphyte. The plants tend to slowly form a large mat or cluster. Each bulb normally produces only one flowering-size replacement bulb, but the plant also produces 2–3 bulbils.

PSEUDOBULB: 0.6–1.0 in. (1.5–2.5 cm) long, the bulbs are conical.

LEAVES: 1 per growth. The leaf is 6 in. (15 cm) long and narrowly elliptic-lanceolate.

INFLORESCENCE: 2–4 in. (5–10 cm) long. The spike emerges in the spring before the leaf.

FLOWERS: 1 per growth. The sometimes fragrant blossoms are 2.0–2.5 in. (5–6 cm) across. The flowers are shorter-lived than those of other species. Blooms are commonly deep yellow to orange-yellow with red-orange to brown markings on the lip, but the coloring is variable. Rare ivory-white forms are known.

HYBRIDIZING NOTES: Chromosome count is 2n = 40.

REFERENCES: 7, 14, 33, 112, 174.

PHOTOS/DRAWINGS: 7, 33.

Pleione ganchuenensis. See *P. bulbocodioides.* REFERENCES: 33.

Pleione grandiflora (Rolfe) Rolfe

AKA: Specimens of *P. albiflora* were classified as *P. grandiflora* until 1983.

ORIGIN/HABITAT: Southern Yunnan in southwest China on rocks in mountain forests at 8700-9300 ft. (2652-2835 m).

CLIMATE: Station # 56985, Mengtze (Meng-tzu), China, Lat. 23.3°N, Long. 103.4°E, at 4262 ft. (1299 m). Temperatures are calculated for an elevation of 9000 ft. (2743 m), resulting in probable extremes of 81°F (27.2°C) and 12°F (-11.1°C).

N/HEMISPHERE	JAN	FEB	MAR	APR	MAY	JUN	JUL	AUG	SEP	OCT	NOV	DEC
°F AVG MAX	49	51	61	67	69	66	66	65	65	59	57	51
°F AVG MIN	29	33	39	45	50	51	52	50	47	43	38	31
DIURNAL RANGE	20	18	22	22	19	15	14	15	18	16	19	20
RAIN/INCHES	0.2	1.0	1.2	1.5	5.4	6.9	10.2	9.3	2.9	2.7	2.2	0.5
HUMIDITY/%	68	69	62	61	64	74	78	79	74	74	71	70
BLOOM SEASON				•	•							
DAYS CLR @ 7AM	13	11	13	11	7	2	2	3	5	4	12	14
DAYS CLR @ 1PM	12	10	10	11	3	1	1	1	2	2	7	13
RAIN/MM	5	25	30	38	137	175	259	236	74	69	56	13
°C AVG MAX	9.6	10.8	16.3	19.6	20.8	19.1	19.1	18.5	18.5	15.2	14.1	10.8
°C AVG MIN	-1.5	0.8	4.1	7.4	10.2	10.8	11.3	10.2	8.5	6.3	3.5	-0.4
DIURNAL RANGE	11.1	10.0	12.2	12.2	10.6	8.3	7.8	8.3	10.0	8.9	10.6	11.2
S/HEMISPHERE	JUL	AUG	SEP	OCT	NOV	DEC	JAN	FEB	MAR	APR	MAY	JUN

Cultural Recommendations

LIGHT: 2400–4000 fc. Diffused light is suggested. In the habitat, clear days are rare during the growing season.

TEMPERATURES: Summer days average 65–69°F (19–21°C), and nights average 45–52°F (7–11°C), with a diurnal range of 14–19°F (8–11°C).

HUMIDITY: 60–80%.

WATER: Plants should be constantly moist while actively growing. The rainfall pattern is wet/dry.

FERTILIZER: A ½-strength solution of 3-2-2 with trace elements should be applied weekly while plants are actively growing. A ½-strength 2–3–3 solution is recommended from mid-Jul. (Jan.) to leaf drop.

REST PERIOD: For several months, winter days average 49–61°F (9–16°C), and nights average 29-39°F (-2 to

4 °C), with a diurnal range of 18–22 °F (10–12 °C). Water should be reduced to occasional light misting, but humidity should remain above 60%. Fertilizer should be eliminated.

GROWING MEDIA: The medium should retain moisture but drain rapidly. Repotting is best done after the leaves drop.

MISCELLANEOUS NOTES: This species is not currently available for cultivation, but a climate table is included since Chinese plants are becoming more accessible.

Plant and Flower Information

PLANT SIZE AND TYPE: A 6 in. (15 cm) lithophyte.

PSEUDOBULB: 1.2–2.7 in. (3–7 cm) long.

LEAVES: 1 per growth. The leaf is described as lanceolate, but measurements of mature size are not recorded.

INFLORESCENCE: 3–5 in. (8–13 cm) long. The spike emerges from the base of the bulb before the leaf.

FLOWERS: 1 per growth. The large blossom is 2.0–3.5 in. (5–9 cm) across and is white to pink with a fringed lip.

HYBRIDIZING NOTES: N/A.

REFERENCES: 33, 36, 112.

PHOTOS/DRAWINGS: 33, 36.

Pleione henryi. See *P. bulbocodioides*. REFERENCES: 33.

Pleione hookeriana (Lindley) Moore

AKA: *P. laotica*, *P. schilleriana*.

ORIGIN/HABITAT: Central Nepal, southern China, northern Burma, and India at 7900–13,800 ft. (2407–4206 m). This widespread plant often grows in large clumps up to 40 in. (1 m) across in thick moss pads in rhododendron forests.

CLIMATE: Station # 44454, Kathmandu, Nepal, Lat. 27.7 °N, Long. 85.3 °E, at 4342 ft. (1323 m). Temperatures are calculated for an elevation of 9750 ft. (2972 m). Records of extreme temperatures, humidity, and sky cover are not available for this station.

N/HEMISPHERE	JAN	FEB	MAR	APR	MAY	JUN	JUL	AUG	SEP	OCT	NOV	DEC
°F AVG MAX	44	47	55	60	63	64	63	63	62	58	52	46
°F AVG MIN	20	24	30	38	46	51	51	51	50	41	30	22
DIURNAL RANGE	24	23	25	22	17	13	12	12	12	17	22	24
RAIN/INCHES	0.6	0.9	1.3	1.9	2.3	9.9	14.8	13.9	5.1	2.2	0.3	0.1
HUMIDITY/%	N/A											
BLOOM SEASON			*	**	**							
DAYS CLR	N/A											
RAIN/MM	14	22	32	48	58	252	377	352	129	56	8	2
°C AVG MAX	6.5	8.6	12.8	15.6	17.1	17.7	17.4	17.2	16.5	14.3	11.1	7.7
°C AVG MIN	-6.8	-4.2	-1.1	3.4	7.7	10.5	10.7	10.5	9.8	4.9	-1.1	-5.6
DIURNAL RANGE	13.3	12.8	13.9	12.2	9.4	7.2	6.7	6.7	6.7	9.4	12.2	13.3
S/HEMISPHERE	JUL	AUG	SEP	OCT	NOV	DEC	JAN	FEB	MAR	APR	MAY	JUN

Cultural Recommendations

LIGHT: 2400–4000 fc. Diffused light is recommended. Clear summer days are rare, while clear winter days are commonly reported at other stations in this part of the Himalayas.

TEMPERATURES: Summer days average 60–64 °F (15–18 °C), and nights average 46–51 °F (8–11 °C), with a summer diurnal range of 12–17 °F (7–9 °C). Cool growing temperatures and excellent air circulation may be critically important for this species. At high elevations in the Himalayas, spring, summer, and autumn last 6 months of the year, and the other 6 months are wintry.

HUMIDITY: 75–85% except in winter, when it can drop to 60%. While records are not available for Kathmandu, these figures are reported at the nearest station with similar rainfall patterns.

WATER: Plants should be constantly moist while actively growing. The rainfall pattern is wet/dry.

FERTILIZER: A ½-strength solution of 3–2–2 with trace elements should be applied weekly while plants are actively growing. A ½-strength 2–3–3 solution may be used from mid-Jul. (Jan.) to leaf drop. This species requires regular fertilizing and ideal growing conditions to reach maturity during the short growing season.

REST PERIOD: Winter days average 44–55 °F (7–13 °C), and nights average 20–30 °F (-1.0 to -6.0 °C), with a diurnal range of 22–25 °F (12–14 °C). Cold conditions are necessary for 5–6 months in cultivation, and below-freezing conditions for at least part of the winter are probably mandatory. Growers report that plants should be kept cold until late Apr. (Oct.) or mid-May (Nov.). The habitat elevation ranges 5000 ft. (1524 m). Consequently, some plant populations may be exposed to more than 4 months of below-freezing temperatures while other groups may be exposed to below-freezing conditions for less than 4 months. All populations are exposed to these conditions for at least part of the winter. In nature, the plants may be protected from freezing and thawing and from the severest extremes. Water should be restricted to infrequent, light misting to prevent withering, and fertilizer should be eliminated. Increased light occurs in the habitat but may be unimportant in cultivation.

GROWING MEDIA: The medium should retain moisture but drain rapidly. Growers recommend a covering of live sphagnum. Repotting is best done after the leaves drop.

MISCELLANEOUS NOTES: Considered one of the more difficult species in cultivation, *P. hookeriana* has a short, 6-month growing season during which careful attention should be paid to its requirements.

Plant and Flower Information

PLANT SIZE AND TYPE: A 4–5 in. (10–13 cm) epiphyte or lithophyte.

PSEUDOBULB: 0.4–1.2 in. (1–3 cm) long. This is the only *Pleione* whose growths are spread by stolons. The bulbs are conical to oval, smooth or pitted, and pale green or purple. When properly cultivated, the plant produces one new flowering-size bulb plus 2–3 bulbils each year.

LEAVES: 1 per growth. The leaf is 2–8 in. (5–20 cm) long.

INFLORESCENCE: 2.8–5.5 in. (7–14 cm) long. The spike emerges with the new growth, appearing later in the spring than spikes of other species.

FLOWERS: 1. The somewhat small flowers are 2 in. (5 cm) across and are normally lilac to bright rose, but they may be white. The lip is paler and blotched at the apex with pale brownish purple. Rare occurrences of very large flowers are probably the result of polyploid clones.

HYBRIDIZING NOTES: N/A.

REFERENCES: 9, 14, 17, 33, 36, 112, 157, 206, 211.

PHOTOS/DRAWINGS: 9, *14*, *33*, 36.

Pleione hui. See *P. formosana.* REFERENCES: 33.

Pleione humilis (J. E. Smith) D. Don

AKA: *P. diantha.* Specimens of *P. albiflora* were classified as *P. humilis* until 1982.

ORIGIN/HABITAT: Nepal, northern India and Burma. It grows in moss and on smooth-barked rhododendrons at 5900–10,500 ft. (1798–3200 m).

CLIMATE: Station # 44454, Kathmandu, Nepal, Lat. 27.7°N, Long. 85.3°E, at 4342 ft. (1323 m). Temperatures are calculated for an elevation of 7000 ft. (2134 m). Records of extreme temperatures, humidity, and sky cover are not available for this station.

N/HEMISPHERE	JAN	FEB	MAR	APR	MAY	JUN	JUL	AUG	SEP	OCT	NOV	DEC
°F AVG MAX	53	57	64	69	72	73	72	72	71	67	61	55
°F AVG MIN	29	33	39	47	55	60	60	60	59	50	39	31
DIURNAL RANGE	24	23	25	22	17	13	12	12	12	17	22	24
RAIN/INCHES	0.6	0.9	1.3	1.9	2.3	9.9	14.8	13.9	5.1	2.2	0.3	0.1
HUMIDITY/%	N/A											
BLOOM SEASON	***	**	**	*								
DAYS CLR	N/A											
RAIN/MM	14	22	32	48	58	252	377	352	129	56	8	2
°C AVG MAX	11.6	13.6	17.9	20.6	22.1	22.7	22.2	22.2	21.6	19.3	16.1	12.8
°C AVG MIN	-1.7	0.8	4.0	8.4	12.7	15.5	15.5	15.5	14.9	9.9	3.9	-0.5
DIURNAL RANGE	13.3	12.8	13.9	12.2	9.4	7.2	6.7	6.7	6.7	9.4	12.2	13.3
S/HEMISPHERE	JUL	AUG	SEP	OCT	NOV	DEC	JAN	FEB	MAR	APR	MAY	JUN

Cultural Recommendations

LIGHT: 2400–4000 fc. Diffused or dappled light is suggested, as clear summer days are very rare in the habitat.

TEMPERATURES: Summer days average 69–73°F (21–23°C), and nights average 47–60°F (8–16°C), with a summer diurnal range of 12–17°F (7–9°C).

HUMIDITY: 70–80% is recommended during the growing season, dropping to 60% in the winter.

WATER: Plants should be constantly moist while actively growing. Water should be increased very gradually in spring, since new growths often do not produce roots until after the flowers have faded. The rainfall pattern is wet/dry.

FERTILIZER: A ½-strength solution of 3-2-2 fertilizer with trace elements, applied weekly while plants are actively growing. A ½-strength 2-3-3 solution is recommended from mid-Jul. (Jan.) to leaf drop.

REST PERIOD: Winter days average 55–65°F (13–18°C), and nights average 29–39°F (-1.7 to 4°C), with a diurnal range of 22–25°F (12–13°C). Freezing to near-freezing temperatures last for about 3 months in the habitat, and these conditions are needed in cultivation for at least part of the winter rest. Water should be reduced to occasional light misting to prevent desiccation, and fertilizer should be eliminated. New roots do not start growing until after the flower withers, so the medium should be kept just slightly damp until root growth begins.

GROWING MEDIA: A medium that retains moisture but drains rapidly is required; it should be covered with live sphagnum moss. Repotting is best done after the leaves drop.

MISCELLANEOUS NOTES: The bloom season shown in the climate table is based on cultivation records and does not correlate with the temperatures given for the habitat. *P. humilis* is, however, a very early, spring-blooming plant.

This species is more difficult to maintain in cultivation than most *Pleione*. A plant may produce as many as 50 bulbils at the apex of well-grown bulbs, but these are difficult to bring to maturity. Bulbils should be grown in damp but not wet garden moss, as growers report that they tend to rot in sphagnum. The plants are slow to increase, since they do not always produce 2 new flowering-size bulbs each year.

Plant and Flower Information

PLANT SIZE AND TYPE: At 4–5 in. (10–13 cm), this species is one of the smallest of the genus. It may be an epiphyte or a lithophyte.

PSEUDOBULB: 0.8–2.4 in. (2–6 cm) long. The olive-green bulbs are ovoid with inconspicuous ridging at the apex.

LEAVES: 1 per growth. The elliptic, dark green leaf is 3–6 in. (8–15 cm) long.

INFLORESCENCE: 3–5 in. (8–13 cm) long. The spike emerges from the base of the pseudobulb.

FLOWERS: 1–2. The faintly fragrant blossoms are 2–4 in. (5–10 cm) across. They are spreading, nodding, and white, sometimes tinged with rose. The fringed lip is marked with rich crimson or yellow-brown streaks or spots and has a pale yellow callus in the center. Blossom size and color are variable. The flowers last 2–3 weeks or longer if kept cool.

HYBRIDIZING NOTES: Chromosome count is 2n = 40. The white color, fringed and attractively marked lip, and nodding habit are normally transmitted to hybrids. When *P. humilis* is crossed with *P. formosana*, the progeny may produce up to 3 flowers per inflorescence.

REFERENCES: 7, 9, 14, 17, 33, 36, 112, 148, 157, 211.

PHOTOS/DRAWINGS: 7, 9, *17, 33, 36*, 211.

Pleione × *lagenaria.*

Pleione × *lagenaria.* A natural hybrid between *P. praecox* and *P. maculata*. This plant is considered the easiest and most adaptable of the fall-blooming *Pleione*, but it only rarely produces bulbils. REFERENCES: 33.

Pleione laotica.

Pleione laotica. See *P. hookeriana*. REFERENCES: 33.

Pleione lauterbachiana.

Pleione lauterbachiana. Now considered a synonym of *Hologyne lauterbachiana*. REFERENCES: 33.

Pleione limprichtii Schlechter

AKA: N/A.

ORIGIN/HABITAT: Burma and southwest China east of K'ang-ting, where it grows in a narrow range at 9500–10,000 ft. (2896–3048 m) on cliffs or limestone outcroppings in a thin layer of humus-rich soil covered by a thin layer of moss.

CLIMATE: Station #56462, Chiulung, China, Lat. 29.0°N, Long. 101.6°E, at 9449 ft. (2880 m). The record high is 84°F (28.9°C), and the record low is 7°F (-13.9°C). Rainfall figures are for Station #56571, Hsi-ch'ang/Hsicha, China, Lat. 27.9°N, Long. 102.3°E, at 5346 ft. (1629 m), which is the nearest station with rainfall records. It has a comparable topographical location and a pattern of clear days similar to that found at Chiulung, so it should have a similar rainfall pattern.

N/HEMISPHERE	JAN	FEB	MAR	APR	MAY	JUN	JUL	AUG	SEP	OCT	NOV	DEC
°F AVG MAX	52	53	61	68	70	69	72	70	68	62	58	53
°F AVG MIN	19	23	28	35	43	50	53	51	48	40	28	21
DIURNAL RANGE	33	30	33	33	27	19	19	19	20	22	30	32
RAIN/INCHES	0.3	0.4	1.1	1.2	3.4	10.7	7.1	8.2	9.1	4.4	1.3	0.1
HUMIDITY/%	52	50	43	47	58	73	76	76	75	71	57	50
BLOOM SEASON			**	*	*							
DAYS CLR @ 7AM	22	16	18	15	10	3	4	3	5	8	18	23
DAYS CLR @ 1PM	20	12	9	7	4	3	4	3	5	8	20	23
RAIN/MM	8	10	28	30	86	272	180	208	231	112	33	3
°C AVG MAX	11.1	11.7	16.1	20.0	21.1	20.6	22.2	21.1	20.0	16.7	14.4	11.7
°C AVG MIN	-7.2	-5.0	-2.2	1.7	6.1	10.0	11.7	10.6	8.9	4.4	-2.2	-6.1
DIURNAL RANGE	18.3	16.7	18.3	18.3	15.0	10.6	10.5	10.5	11.1	12.3	16.6	17.8
S/HEMISPHERE	JUL	AUG	SEP	OCT	NOV	DEC	JAN	FEB	MAR	APR	MAY	JUN

Cultural Recommendations

LIGHT: 2400–4000 fc. Diffused light is suggested. In the habitat, clear summer days are infrequent.

TEMPERATURES: Days average 62–72°F (17–22°C), and nights average 40–53°F (4–12°C), with a summer diurnal range of 19–27°F (11–15°C).

HUMIDITY: 60–75% in summer.

WATER: Plants should be constantly moist while actively growing, but drainage must be excellent. The rainfall pattern is wet/dry.

FERTILIZER: A ½-strength solution of 3–2–2 fertilizer with trace elements should be applied weekly while plants are actively growing. A ½-strength 2–3–3 fertilizer may be used from mid-Jul. (Jan.) to leaf drop.

REST PERIOD: Winter days average 52–61°F (11–16°C), and nights average 19–28°F (-2 to -7°C), with a diurnal range of 30–33°F (17–18°C). The below-freezing temperatures, which continue for 5 months, are probably necessary for at least part of the winter rest. In nature, plants may be protected from freezing and thawing. Water should be reduced to occasional misting if needed to prevent desiccation. Fertilizer should be eliminated.

GROWING MEDIA: The medium should retain moisture but drain rapidly. The bulbs should be completely covered by the medium. Repotting is best done after the leaves drop.

MISCELLANEOUS NOTES: One of the first *Pleione* to die back in the fall and one of the last to bloom in the spring, *P. limprichtii* is said to be the hardiest *Pleione*. In cultivation, plants with snow protection are known to have survived temperatures of -4°F (-20°C). Flowers should be kept cool and dry, as water ruins them. This plant reportedly grows extremely well in a garden peat-bed.

Plant and Flower Information

PLANT SIZE AND TYPE: A 6–7 in. (15-18 cm) terrestrial or lithophyte.

PSEUDOBULB: 1.2–1.6 in. (3–4 cm) long. The conical-ovoid bulbs may be either green or purple.

LEAVES: 1 per growth. The lanceolate leaf is 5–6 in. (13–15 cm) long.

INFLORESCENCE: 4–5 in. (10–13 cm) long.

FLOWERS: 1–2. The blossoms are 1.6–2.2 in. (4.0–5.5 cm) across and may be pink to dark rose with brick-red spotting on the lip.

HYBRIDIZING NOTES: N/A.

REFERENCES: 33.

PHOTOS/DRAWINGS: 33.

Pleione maculata (Lindley) Lindley

AKA: *P. diphylla*.

ORIGIN/HABITAT: Northern Burma and Thailand at 1968–5248 ft. (600–1600 m). The range extends north into China and west into India and Nepal.

CLIMATE: Station # 48001, Putao, Burma, Lat. 27.3°N, Long. 94.4°E, at 1342 ft. (409 m). Temperatures are calculated for an elevation of 3000 ft. (914 m), resulting in probable extremes of 87°F (30.6°C) and 31°F (-0.6°C).

N/HEMISPHERE	JAN	FEB	MAR	APR	MAY	JUN	JUL	AUG	SEP	OCT	NOV	DEC
°F AVG MAX	55	58	64	69	73	74	75	76	74	69	62	56
°F AVG MIN	39	43	48	55	63	67	68	67	66	62	50	42
DIURNAL RANGE	16	15	16	14	10	7	7	9	8	7	12	14
RAIN/INCHES	0.3	2.6	2.8	3.7	8.1	24.7	39.9	33.4	18.3	4.2	1.1	0.2
HUMIDITY/%	92	91	88	85	87	92	93	94	93	93	92	92
BLOOM SEASON									**	***	**	
DAYS CLR @ 6AM	0	0	0	1	1	0	0	0	1	1	1	0
DAYS CLR @ 6PM	5	2	3	2	2	2	2	3	2	1	2	4
RAIN/MM	8	66	71	94	206	627	1013	848	465	107	28	5
°C AVG MAX	12.5	14.2	17.5	20.3	22.5	23.1	23.6	24.2	23.1	20.3	16.4	13.1
°C AVG MIN	3.6	5.8	8.6	12.5	17.0	19.2	19.7	19.2	18.6	16.4	9.7	5.3
DIURNAL RANGE	8.9	8.4	8.9	7.8	5.5	3.9	3.9	5.0	4.5	3.9	6.7	7.8
S/HEMISPHERE	JUL	AUG	SEP	OCT	NOV	DEC	JAN	FEB	MAR	APR	MAY	JUN

Cultural Recommendations

LIGHT: 2400–3000 fc. Diffused light is recommended. In the habitat, clear days are extremely rare.

TEMPERATURES: Summer days average 70–76°F (21-24°C), and nights average 55–68°F (13–20°C), with a narrow diurnal range of 7–10°F (4–6°C).

HUMIDITY: 85–95% throughout the year.

WATER: Plants should be constantly moist while actively growing, as continuous moisture is available in the plant's habitat. Although the rainfall pattern is wet/dry, the frequency of fog, low clouds, dew, and high humidity precludes any drying-out in the habitat. The plants are highly susceptible to root rot in early spring, so they should not be overwatered.

FERTILIZER: A ½-strength solution of 3–2–2 fertilizer with trace elements, applied weekly while plants are actively growing. A ½-strength 2–3–3 solution is recommended from mid-Jul. (Jan.) to leaf drop.

REST PERIOD: Winter days average 55–64°F (13-18°C), and nights average 39–48°F (4–9°C), with a diurnal range of 14–16°F (8–9°C). The climatic conditions are less severe for this species; colder temperatures should be avoided. Growers report that temperatures of 37–41°F (3–5°C) are ideal for plants from Thailand. Kew Gardens grows plants from India at a winter minimum of 64°F (18°C). Water should be reduced to light misting as needed to keep the medium just damp. Fertilizer should be eliminated.

GROWING MEDIA: The medium should retain moisture and drain rapidly. Repotting is best done after the leaves drop.

MISCELLANEOUS NOTES: *P. maculata* is the warmest-growing *Pleione*. Each well-grown pseudobulb will produce at least 2 new bulbs each year. Plants from Thailand reportedly produce flowers ½ the size of those produced by plants from India.

Plant and Flower Information

PLANT SIZE AND TYPE: A 10 in. (25 cm) epiphyte.

PSEUDOBULB: 1 in. (2.5 cm) long. The glossy, dark green bulb is turban-shaped.

LEAVES: 2 per growth. The elliptic-lanceolate leaves are 4-10 in. (10–25 cm) long.

INFLORESCENCE: 2.5–3.5 in. (6.4–7.6 cm) long. The spike arises from the base of the pseudobulb in autumn after the leaves fall, and blooms appear later than those of *P. praecox*.

FLOWERS: 1. The blossoms are 1.6–2.5 in. (4–6 cm) across with creamy white sepals and petals sometimes streaked with pink. The wavy-margined lip is white with yellow in the center. Flowers last 3–4 weeks and are apple-scented. This is a variable species with several named varieties.

HYBRIDIZING NOTES: N/A.

REFERENCES: 9, 14, 17, 33, 112, 157, 205, 206, 211.

PHOTOS/DRAWINGS: 9, *14*, *17*, *33*.

Pleione mairei. See *P. bulbocodioides*. REFERENCES: 33.

Pleione pogonioides. See *P. bulbocodioides* and the note under "AKA" for *P. speciosa*. REFERENCES: 33.

Pleione praecox (J. E. Smith) D. Don

AKA: *P. birmanica*, *P. concolor*, *P. reichenbachiana*, *P. wallichii*.

ORIGIN/HABITAT: Northern India and Thailand at 3936–11,152 ft. (1200–3400 m) and the hills around Kathmandu, Nepal, at 7000 ft. (2133 m). It grows in colonies on rocky, roadside slopes and nearly vertical cliffs, where it is usually found in moss- or humus-filled pockets in the rocks.

CLIMATE: Station #42314, Mohanbari, India, Lat. 27.5°N, Long. 95.0°E, at 360 ft. (110 m). Temperatures are calculated for an elevation of 5500 ft. (1676 m), resulting in probable extremes of 85°F (29.4°C) and 20°F (-6.7°C).

N/HEMISPHERE	JAN	FEB	MAR	APR	MAY	JUN	JUL	AUG	SEP	OCT	NOV	DEC
°F AVG MAX	54	56	62	64	68	70	70	70	69	67	63	57
°F AVG MIN	33	38	44	49	54	57	58	59	58	53	43	34
DIURNAL RANGE	21	18	18	15	14	13	12	11	11	14	20	23
RAIN/INCHES	1.5	2.4	4.1	9.5	12.1	19.7	21.1	17.8	13.9	6.0	1.3	0.6
HUMIDITY/%	81	78	72	76	84	86	87	88	85	84	80	81
BLOOM SEASON									*	**	***	***
DAYS CLR @ 6AM	2	2	6	5	2	1	0	1	3	7	5	3
DAYS CLR @ 12PM	13	7	11	8	3	1	0	1	3	9	14	15
RAIN/MM	38	61	104	241	307	500	536	452	353	152	33	15
°C AVG MAX	12.2	13.4	16.7	17.8	20.0	21.1	21.1	21.1	20.6	19.5	17.2	13.9
°C AVG MIN	0.6	3.4	6.7	9.5	12.2	13.9	14.5	15.0	14.5	11.7	6.1	1.1
DIURNAL RANGE	11.6	10.0	10.0	8.3	7.8	7.2	6.6	6.1	6.1	7.8	11.1	12.8
S/HEMISPHERE	JUL	AUG	SEP	OCT	NOV	DEC	JAN	FEB	MAR	APR	MAY	JUN

Cultural Recommendations

LIGHT: 4000 fc. Growers indicate that *P. praecox* prefers higher light than most *Pleione*.

TEMPERATURES: Summer days average 64–70°F (18–21°C), and nights average 49–59°F (9–15°C), with a diurnal range of 11–15°F (6–8°C).

HUMIDITY: 75–85%.

WATER: Constant moisture is necessary while plants are actively growing, but drainage must be excellent. The rainfall pattern is wet/dry.

FERTILIZER: A ½-strength solution of 3–2–2 with trace elements, applied weekly while plants are actively growing. A ½-strength 2–3–3 solution may be used from mid-Jul. (Jan.) to leaf drop.

REST PERIOD: Winter days average 54–63°F (12–17°C), and nights average 33–44°F (0.6–7.0°C), with a diurnal range of 18–23°F (10–13°C). The very cool temperatures are necessary for at least part of the winter rest. Habitat temperatures drop below freezing though averages are above this level. Water should be reduced, but the habitat is damp and highly humid throughout the year, so the plants benefit from occasional light misting. Fertilizer should be eliminated.

GROWING MEDIA: The medium should retain moisture but drain rapidly. Repotting is best done after the leaves drop.

MISCELLANEOUS NOTES: *P. praecox* is usually the first *Pleione* to bloom in the fall.

Plant and Flower Information

PLANT SIZE AND TYPE: A 5–10 in. (13–25 cm) epiphyte or lithophyte.

PSEUDOBULB: 0.6–1.2 in. (1.5–3.0 cm) long. The tightly clustered bulbs are either turban- or barrel-shaped. They are green with purple or reddish brown mottling.

LEAVES: 2 per growth. The leaves are 6–10 in. (15–25 cm) long, pointed, and narrowly elliptical.

INFLORESCENCE: 3–6 in. (8–15 cm) long. The spikes are the first to emerge in the fall, sometimes before the leaves have fallen. Plants usually produce a single spike, but when they are well-grown, they may produce 2.

FLOWERS: 1, rarely 2. The blossoms are 2–4 in. (5–10 cm) across. The sepals and petals are wide-opening and may curl back at the tip. They range in color from rose-purple to white flecked with lilac, and albino forms have been found. The lip may be white, pink with purple spots, or purple with a yellow streak down the center. When warm, the blooms have a spicy, primrose-like fragrance. This species is variable in size and color, and several varieties have been named.

HYBRIDIZING NOTES: N/A.

REFERENCES: 7, 9, 14, 17, 33, 36, 112, 148, 157, 174, 205, 206, 211, 217.

PHOTOS/DRAWINGS: *7, 9, 14, 17, 33, 36, 205, 217.*

Pleione pricei. See *P. formosana.* REFERENCES: 33.

Pleione reichenbachiana. See *P. praecox.* REFERENCES: 33.

Pleione rhombilabia. See *P. bulbocodioides.* REFERENCES: 33.

Pleione saxicola T. Tang and Wang ex S. C. Chen.
Recently described as originating in Yunnan, China, at 7900–8200 ft. (2400–2500 m), but no specific locality was given. Dr. Cribb considers it a possible variation of *P. bulbocodioides*. The climate information provided for *P. albiflora, P. forrestii,* or *P. yunnanensis* might also apply to plants labeled *P. saxicola.* REFERENCES: 33.

Pleione schilleriana. See *P. hookeriana.* REFERENCES: 33.

Pleione scopulorum W. W. Smith
AKA: N/A.

ORIGIN/HABITAT: Northern Burma and northeast India at 9184–13,776 ft. (2800–4200 m). It also grows in the mountains near the Mekong River in western Yunnan, China. It is found on shady, grassy cliffs, on humus-covered boulders near streams in ravines, in pine forests, and in subalpine meadows. Its distribution is very limited.

CLIMATE: Station # 56651, Lichiang, China, Lat. 27.0°N, Long. 100.3°E, at 7926 ft. (2416 m). Temperatures are calculated for an elevation of 10,000 ft. (3048 m), resulting in probable extremes of 78°F (25.6°C) and 12°F (-11.1°C).

N/HEMISPHERE	JAN	FEB	MAR	APR	MAY	JUN	JUL	AUG	SEP	OCT	NOV	DEC
°F AVG MAX	50	49	57	63	67	67	67	66	65	60	56	52
°F AVG MIN	24	27	33	40	45	50	52	50	47	41	30	24
DIURNAL RANGE	26	22	24	23	22	17	15	16	18	19	26	28
RAIN/INCHES	0.3	0.2	0.4	0.6	2.5	5.7	10.8	9.9	7.3	2.4	0.2	0.0
HUMIDITY/%	42	49	45	47	55	73	80	82	79	71	56	50
BLOOM SEASON				*	*							
DAYS CLR @ 7AM	23	15	19	13	10	4	1	3	4	11	22	25
DAYS CLR @ 1PM	21	10	12	7	3	1	2	2	3	6	18	23
RAIN/MM	8	5	10	15	64	145	274	251	185	61	5	0
°C AVG MAX	10.1	9.5	14.0	17.3	19.5	19.5	19.5	19.0	18.4	15.6	13.4	11.2
°C AVG MIN	-4.4	-2.7	0.6	4.5	7.3	10.1	11.2	10.1	8.4	5.1	-1.0	-4.4
DIURNAL RANGE	14.5	12.2	13.4	12.8	12.2	9.4	8.3	8.9	10.0	10.5	14.4	15.6
S/HEMISPHERE	JUL	AUG	SEP	OCT	NOV	DEC	JAN	FEB	MAR	APR	MAY	JUN

Cultural Recommendations

LIGHT: 2400–4000 fc. Diffused light is suggested. Light levels should be lower when temperatures are warm.

TEMPERATURES: Summer days average 60–67°F (16–20°C), and nights average 40–52°F (4–11°C), with a diurnal range of 15–23°F (8–13°C).

HUMIDITY: 55–80% during the growing season.

WATER: Plants should be constantly moist while actively growing. The rainfall pattern is wet with a 5-6 month very dry season.

FERTILIZER: A ½-strength solution of 3–2–2 with trace elements, applied weekly while plants are actively growing. A ½-strength 2–3–3 solution is recommended from mid-Jul. (Jan.) to leaf drop.

REST PERIOD: For 5 months, winter days average 50-57°F (10–14°C), and nights average 24–33°F (-4 to 1°C), with a diurnal range of 24–28°F (14–16°C). Whether below-freezing temperatures are necessary in cultivation is unknown, but a cold, dry rest is certainly required. In the habitat, water and humidity are very low in winter. Fertilizer should be eliminated after leaf fall until growth begins in the spring.

GROWING MEDIA: The medium should retain moisture but drain rapidly. Repotting is best done after the leaves drop.

MISCELLANEOUS NOTES: N/A.

Plant and Flower Information

PLANT SIZE AND TYPE: A 7–9 in. (18–23 cm) lithophyte or terrestrial.

PSEUDOBULB: 1 in. (2.5 cm) long. The bulbs are ovoid with a long, slender neck.

LEAVES: 2 per growth. The leaves are 5 in. (13 cm) long and roughly lanceolate.

INFLORESCENCE: 5–6 in. (13–15 cm) long. The tall, erect spike emerges with the new growth in the spring.

FLOWERS: 1, rarely 3. The blossoms are 1.5–2.5 in. (4–6 cm) across, which is small for *Pleione*. They are normally scarlet-rose to vivid magenta, but rare white and yellow forms have been recorded. The toothed lip is spotted and streaked with dark purple, yellowish at the base, and white in the center. It is also marked with a few purple spots near the yellow callus.

HYBRIDIZING NOTES: N/A.

REFERENCES: 33.

PHOTOS/DRAWINGS: 33.

Pleione smithii. See *P. bulbocodioides.* REFERENCES: 33.

Pleione speciosa Ames and Schlechter

AKA: *The Handbook on Orchid Nomenclature and Registration* published by the International Orchid Commission in 1985 indicates that some *P. speciosa* plants in cultivation today may be erroneously labeled as *P. pogonioides.*

ORIGIN/HABITAT: Hubei, Sichuan, and Kweichow Provinces, China, at 5740–7380 ft. (1750–2250 m).

CLIMATE: Station # 57707, Pi-Chieh, China, Lat. 27.3°N, Long. 105.2°E, at 4836 ft. (1474 m) elevation. Temperatures are calculated for an elevation of 6000 ft. (1829 m), resulting in probable extremes of 87°F (30.6°C) and 14°F (-10.0°C).

N/HEMISPHERE	JAN	FEB	MAR	APR	MAY	JUN	JUL	AUG	SEP	OCT	NOV	DEC
°F AVG MAX	40	42	57	65	68	72	77	77	71	58	52	45
°F AVG MIN	27	30	39	46	52	56	61	58	54	46	39	32
DIURNAL RANGE	13	12	18	19	16	16	16	19	17	12	13	13
RAIN/INCHES	0.4	0.6	1.1	2.5	4.1	6.9	6.8	5.0	4.0	2.7	0.8	0.5
HUMIDITY/%	81	84	77	75	77	79	78	78	78	85	84	85
BLOOM SEASON				*	*							
DAYS CLR @ 7AM	2	2	3	6	3	2	3	7	9	3	3	2
DAYS CLR @ 1PM	6	4	9	5	2	3	1	2	4	3	4	5
RAIN/MM	10	15	28	64	104	175	173	127	102	69	20	13
°C AVG MAX	4.5	5.6	14.0	18.4	20.1	22.3	25.1	25.1	21.8	14.5	11.2	7.3
°C AVG MIN	-2.7	-1.0	4.0	7.9	11.2	13.4	16.2	14.5	12.3	7.9	4.0	0.0
DIURNAL RANGE	7.2	6.6	10.0	10.5	8.9	8.9	8.9	10.6	9.5	6.6	7.2	7.3
S/HEMISPHERE	JUL	AUG	SEP	OCT	NOV	DEC	JAN	FEB	MAR	APR	MAY	JUN

Cultural Recommendations

LIGHT: 2400–4000 fc. Diffused or dappled light is recommended.

TEMPERATURES: Summer days average 72–77°F (22–25°C), and nights average 56–61°F (13-16°C), with a diurnal range of 16–19°F (9–11°C).

HUMIDITY: 75–80%. Although winter rainfall is low in the habitat, humidity is highest in winter, with frequent mist, fog, and dew.

WATER: Plants should be constantly moist while actively growing. The rainfall pattern is wet/dry.

FERTILIZER: A ½-strength solution of 3–2–2 with trace elements, applied weekly while plants are actively growing. A ½-strength 2–3–3 solution is recommended from mid-Jul. (Jan.) to leaf drop.

REST PERIOD: In nature, winter days average 40–57°F (5–14°C), and nights average 27–39°F (-3 to 4°C), with a low diurnal range of 12–18°F (7–10°C) for 5 months. While the lows average well below freezing for 3 months, growers indicate that average night temperatures of 32–36°F (0–2°C) may be sufficient in cultivation. The winter diurnal range is lower than the summer diurnal range. This pattern, very unusual for *Pleione*, is more typical of tropical habitats than of high-elevation habitats with cold winters. Water should be reduced, but misting may be beneficial to prevent desiccation. Fertilizer should be eliminated.

GROWING MEDIA: A medium that retains moisture but drains rapidly is required. Repotting is best done after leaf fall.

MISCELLANEOUS NOTES: *P. speciosa* is easy to cultivate providing that it is given a cool rest. Plants normally produce 2 new pseudobulbs from each mature growth. When introduced into cultivation in 1912, it was mislabeled as *P. pogonioides*. Some erroneously labeled clones of the original plant are still in cultivation.

Plant and Flower Information

PLANT SIZE AND TYPE: A 6–7 in. (15–18 cm) terrestrial.

PSEUDOBULB: 1.0–1.3 in. (2.5–3.3 cm) long. The bulb has a very rough surface.

LEAVES: 1 per growth. The leaf is 6 in. (15 cm) long and among the first to die back in the fall.

INFLORESCENCE: 9 in. (23 cm) long. The spikes, usually 1 and rarely 2, emerge from the base of the bulb either with or before the leaf.

FLOWERS: 1–2 per inflorescence. The faintly fragrant flowers are generally rose-purple or magenta with yellow or white ridges on the lip. They are variable in size, color, and extent of spotting.

HYBRIDIZING NOTES: As a parent, *P. speciosa* transmits its color and fragrance. The keels on the lip of the progeny are often orange-yellow on a dark red background. Hybrids often produce 2 flowers per stem.

REFERENCES: 33.

PHOTOS/DRAWINGS: *33.*

Pleione wallichii. See *P. praecox.* REFERENCES: 33.

Pleione yunnanensis (Rolfe) Rolfe

AKA: *P. chiwuana.*

ORIGIN/HABITAT: The northern extremity of Burma and western Yunnan, China, at 5000–10,500 ft. (1524–3200 m). It is found in grassy, subalpine meadows, under rhododendron shrubs in deep leaf-litter, among rocks in shady locations, and in open pine forests. The bulbs are buried 0.5–2.0 in. (1–5 cm) deep.

CLIMATE: Station # 56985, Mengtze (Meng-tzu), China, Lat. 23.3°N, Long. 103.4°E, at 4262 ft. (1299 m) elevation. Temperatures are calculated for an elevation of 8500 ft. (2591 m), resulting in probable extremes of 83°F (28.3°C) and 14°F (-10.0°C).

N/HEMISPHERE	JAN	FEB	MAR	APR	MAY	JUN	JUL	AUG	SEP	OCT	NOV	DEC
°F AVG MAX	51	53	63	69	71	68	68	67	67	61	59	53
°F AVG MIN	31	35	41	47	52	53	54	52	49	45	40	33
DIURNAL RANGE	20	18	22	22	19	15	14	15	18	16	19	20
RAIN/INCHES	0.2	1.0	1.2	1.5	5.4	6.9	10.2	9.3	2.9	2.7	2.2	0.5
HUMIDITY/%	68	69	62	61	64	74	78	79	74	74	71	70
BLOOM SEASON		**	***	**	*							
DAYS CLR @ 7AM	13	11	13	11	7	2	2	3	5	4	12	14
DAYS CLR @ 1PM	12	10	10	11	3	1	1	1	2	2	7	13
RAIN/MM	5	25	30	38	137	175	259	236	74	69	56	13
°C AVG MAX	10.6	11.7	17.2	20.6	21.7	20.0	20.0	19.5	19.5	16.1	15.0	11.7
°C AVG MIN	-0.5	1.7	5.0	8.3	11.1	11.7	12.2	11.1	9.5	7.2	4.5	0.6
DIURNAL RANGE	11.1	10.0	12.2	12.3	10.6	8.3	7.8	8.4	10.0	8.9	10.5	11.1
S/HEMISPHERE	JUL	AUG	SEP	OCT	NOV	DEC	JAN	FEB	MAR	APR	MAY	JUN

Cultural Recommendations

LIGHT: 3500–4000 fc. Dappled light is recommended. Growers indicate that *P. yunnanensis* prefers higher light than most *Pleione*.

TEMPERATURES: Summer days average 67–71°F (20–22°C), and nights average 52–54°F (11–12°C), with a diurnal range of 14–19°F (8-11°C).

HUMIDITY: 65–80% during the summer.

WATER: Plants should be constantly moist while actively growing. The rainfall pattern is wet/dry, but in the habitat, winter dew, fog, or mist provides moisture during the dry season.

FERTILIZER: A ½-strength solution of 3-2-2 with trace elements, applied weekly while plants are actively growing. A ½-strength 2-3-3 solution is recommended from mid-Jul. (Jan.) to leaf drop.

REST PERIOD: Winter days average 51–63°F (11–17°C), and nights average 31–41°F (-1 to 5°C), with a diurnal range of 19–22°F (10–12°C). Growers indicate that this species is healthy if night temperatures average 32–36°F (0–2°C) for at least part of the winter. The maximum diurnal range occurs in the spring. Water should be reduced to occasional misting in order to prevent desiccation. Fertilizer should be eliminated.

GROWING MEDIA: A medium that retains moisture but drains rapidly is required. Repotting is best done after the leaves drop.

MISCELLANEOUS NOTES: The bloom season shown in the climate table is based on cultivation records. In the habitat, blooming probably does not occur as early in the spring. Many cultivated plants labeled as *P. yunnanensis* are in fact *P. bulbocodioides*.

Plant and Flower Information

PLANT SIZE AND TYPE: An 8–11 in. (20–28 cm) lithophyte or terrestrial.

PSEUDOBULB: 0.4–0.8 in. (1–2 cm) long. The bulbs are conical.

LEAVES: 1 per growth. The leaf is 6–10 in. (15–25 cm) long, erect, and lanceolate.

INFLORESCENCE: 3–6 in. (8–15 cm) long. The spike emerges from the base of the pseudobulb before the leaf.

FLOWERS: 1, rarely 2. The blossoms are 2.0–3.5 in. (5–9 cm) across and spreading. The flowers may be pale lavender-pink to rose with vivid red streaks or blotches. The lip is spotted with purple.

HYBRIDIZING NOTES: N/A.

REFERENCES: 7, 33, 112.

PHOTOS/DRAWINGS: 7, 33.

Appendix A
Orchid Growing Problems

Appendix Contents

I. Preventing Disease
    Disease Development 179
    Techniques for Avoiding Orchid Diseases 179

II. Identifying and Treating Plant Problems
    Glossary of Terms 181
    Guide to Symptoms
        Flowers (Including Buds, Fruit, and Sheaths) 182
        Leaves 183
        New Leads, Pseudobulbs, Rhizomes, Roots, and Stems 189
    Pathogens
        General Information 191
        List of Pathogens 191
        Disease Treatment Summary 213
    Pests
        General Information 219
        List of Pests 220
        Orchid Pests Summary 224
    Nutrients
        General Information 226
        List of Nutrients 226
        Nutrients Summary 230

III. Using Chemicals Safely
    Chemical Toxicity 233
    General Rules for Chemical Use 233
    Chemical Classifications and Methods of Application 235

I. Preventing Disease

Disease Development

Plant scientists take a broad view of disease, defining it as any plant abnormality due to a causative agent. Thus, in the broad sense, disease includes problems resulting from unfavorable environmental conditions, pests, and nutrient imbalances as well as infection by pathogens, whether bacteria, fungi, or viruses.

The environmental and cultural requirements of individual orchid species have been the primary focus of this book, because vigorous, healthy plants grow and bloom better. Despite growers' best efforts, however, problems occasionally arise. This is when the most important benefit of paying careful attention to cultural requirements becomes apparent. When insects or disease attack, healthy plants usually survive, while stressed or sickly plants often die.

Disease caused by a pathogen requires 4 elements in order to become established:

1. The disease-producing organism must be present in the environment. All pathogens are not necessarily present in all areas.

2. The pathogen must be in the infectious stage of development and must come in contact with the host plant.

3. Environmental conditions must be suitable for the growth and reproduction of the disease-producing organism. Cool, wet weather increases the likelihood of infection by some pathogens, while warm weather increases the likelihood of infection by others.

4. The host plant must be susceptible to the infecting pathogen. Some plants are naturally resistant.

Plants cannot become infected if any one of these preconditions is missing. A strong, healthy plant exposed to a disease pathogen may ward off infection. Growers are usually unaware of this process, just as we are not always aware when our immune system protects us from disease.

Infectious diseases develop in 5 distinct phases. Understanding this progression may help growers more effectively prevent and control infections. When the risk of inoculation is high, preventive action is a far better approach than allowing the disease to develop and then attempting to treat it after the plant is damaged. On the other hand, when the risk is low, preventive sprays are unnecessary and potentially harmful to the plant. Treating plants after the problem has progressed to the point that signs or symptoms are evident is the least effective way of dealing with disease.

Inoculation occurs when the pathogen is introduced to the plant tissue. The infecting agents may be carried by environmental elements such as wind, rain, or dripping water. They may also be carried from one plant to another by insects or people.

Incubation is the period during which the pathogen changes to a form that can infect or penetrate the plant. Fungi, for instance, develop a structure called a penetration peg which grows through cell walls.

Penetration may be active or passive. It is the process whereby the pathogen enters the plant, which may be accomplished by penetrating the surface or by entering through openings in the leaves.

Infection occurs when a parasitic relationship is established between the pathogen and the host plant.

Disease is the final stage of infection and may be described as the host plant's response to the pathogen. It is at this stage in disease development when symptoms such as chlorosis (yellow discoloration of tissue), necrosis (death of tissue), or spotting begin to show. This is also the time when treatment often begins.

Plants respond to disease in a limited number of ways, and different problems frequently cause similar symptoms. Moreover, a given problem does not necessarily affect all plants the same way, nor do the same diseases attack all orchid species or genera around the world. Unfortunately, there is no simple means of diagnosis. But a careful analysis of plant signs and symptoms is a necessary step in dealing with plant abnormalities. Symptoms of plant diseases are discussed in Section II of this Appendix.

Treatment involves such actions as removing an infected portion of a plant or applying curative chemicals. Both techniques help control disease within the plant as well as reducing the risk that infection will spread to other plants. Eradication is usually impossible once a pathogen has been introduced, but control may be achieved through the use of general disinfectants. Control is possible only if plants with serious infections are removed or destroyed and the growing area is carefully disinfected. Treatments for controlling individual pathogens are discussed in Section III of this Appendix.

Techniques for Avoiding Orchid Diseases

Avoidance measures include selecting plants that are not susceptible to prevailing pathogens, keeping infected plants out of the growing area, isolating new or diseased plants, applying preventive treatments to plants being introduced into the environment, or preventing inoculation by controlling insects or sterilizing contaminated tools.

Protection is best achieved through careful environmental control, which results in a strong, healthy plant able to protect itself. The environment may be manipulated within the range of plant tolerance so that temperature and moisture conditions are outside the range necessary for the pathogens' survival. Preventive applications of fungicides, bactericides, or disinfectants together with insect control measures are effective techniques for plant protection.

Greenhouse cleanliness and good cultural practices cannot be emphasized too strongly. Experts have found that good culture together with good sanitation measures, both in the growing area and with respect to the plants themselves, prevents the vast majority of infections.

The following practices help to reduce the risk of infection.

- Always use new or sterile potting medium.

- Avoid cutting roots unnecessarily.

- Avoid physical injury to the plants since this provides a point of entry for disease.

- Avoid working with plants when they are wet.

- Control insects that may transmit diseases from plant to plant.

- Do not crowd plants.

- Identify and remove or isolate any diseased plants.

- Intermix plants so that susceptible plants are not close together.

- Keep greenhouses clean and free from plant debris.

- Keep new plants in isolation until a healthy new growth emerges. An isolation period of 3–4 months is recommended.

- Keep plants clean. Old sheaths, leaves, or other plant tissue should be removed. These serve as hiding places for various pests and allow infections or infestations to develop unnoticed.

- Maintain excellent air movement.

- Never allow water to drip from one plant to another.

- Observe plants carefully for signs of stress, particularly during seasonal shifts in temperature, light, and moisture. Whenever environmental conditions change, a preventive application of a disinfectant to the plants and growing area might be beneficial.

- Sterilize pots and tools after each use.

Sterilizing tools and equipment after each use is critically important to prevent the transmission of disease pathogens. As a safeguard, trays and benches (especially wooden ones) should be disinfected any time a diseased plant is discovered. Sterilizing every surface the plants might touch prevents the spread of bacterial diseases which are transmitted through splashing or dripping water.

Greenhouse disinfectants are available commercially. They must be mixed according to the instructions on the label, as different concentrations are recommended for sterilizing tools, pots, and trays, washing benches, and spraying plants.

Flaming has been the standard method for sterilizing tools. Heat destroys pathogens and is considered by many to be the surest means of deactivating viruses. Single-edged razor blades may be dipped in denatured or isopropyl alcohol then passed over a flame to ignite the alcohol. The blade should be cooled before reuse.

The University of California at Riverside recommends the following method as an alternative to flaming.

- Dip tool for 2 seconds in a fresh solution of

  1 part sodium hypochlorite (household bleach)
  5 parts water

- Immediately dip the tool into a neutralizing mixture consisting of

  1 part vinegar
  5 parts water

  1 tsp. salad oil

- Dry the tool before reusing or storing it.

The vinegar in the second dip neutralizes the corrosive action of the bleach, and the oil lubricates the tool. The same technique, with the oil omitted from the neutralizing mixture, should be used to sterilize pots and trays.

II. Identifying and Treating Plant Problems

Using the plant pathologist's definition of disease as any plant abnormality due to a causal agent means that disease must be considered the rule rather than the exception, for all plants are subject to disease. It also means that in determining the cause of a plant problem, symptoms of inappropriate light, temperature, and moisture levels must be considered together with other causal agents such as physical or chemical injury, disease pathogens, pests, or nutrient imbalances. This Appendix is designed as a tool to help growers identify the cause of plant problems and find possible solutions quickly, in order to reduce damage to their plants.

Signs and symptoms of many plant problems are described briefly in the following lists. Each symptom is classified under the plant part affected; thus the symptoms appear under 3 headings:

Flowers (Including Buds, Fruit, and Sheaths)

Leaves

New Leads, Pseudobulbs, Rhizomes, Roots, and Stems

In the symptom lists, which are arrannged alphabetically, the color of the affected area is a primary clue to identifying the probable source of the problem. Symptoms are further described in terms of size, shape, or location of the abnormality. Growers noticing a problem should carefully examine the particular plant, note the plant parts showing symptoms, then scan the lists for the description which most closely matches the observed abnormality. Cross-references are provided to the general information in Chapter 1; to individual species listings; and to the headings **Pathogens, Pests,** and **Nutrients** in this Appendix. For further information on prevention and recommended treatments or controls, we urge you to contact your local universities, agricultural agents, or other local growers.

The process of describing symptoms and matching them with causal agents is at best an uncertain science. Descriptive lists are subjective and require interpretation, as different observers would no doubt describe the same symptoms in different words. It is also important to remember that symptoms may differ from species to species and genus to genus. Still, the effort of careful analysis and interpretation is well worth making, since symptoms provide the grower's best clues to plant problems.

Glossary of Terms

The following terms are used repeatedly in symptom descriptions.

Chlorosis or *chlorotic*. Yellow or faded tissue that is normally green. The change in color results from the loss of chlorophyll.

Color break. A streaking or separating of flower color, usually caused by viral infections. It normally occurs on the sepals and petals as intensified streaks of color. White streaking on lavender *Cattleya* petals is usually caused by a genetic disorder rather than a virus.

Lesions. Abnormal tissue caused by disease or injury.

Mosaic mottling. A pattern of yellow or pale green tissue separated by areas of green tissue which appears normal. The overall effect resembles mosaic tile.

Mycelia. Hairlike filaments that are the vegetative growths of fungi and some bacteria.

Necrosis or *necrotic*. Dead or dying tissue which may be white, brown, or black. Necrotic spots may occur in larger chlorotic patches.

Pathogen. A specific cause of disease (such as a bacterium, fungus, or virus).

Pustules. Blisters or pimples, usually raised, which develop on diseased tissue.

Ringspot. Yellowish or dead tissue, usually circular, which surrounds green tissue.

Rosetting. Abnormal whorls formed by the leaves.

Sclerotia. Hardened masses of fungal threads which often remain dormant for an extended period.

Spores. Reproductive bodies which are capable of developing into new individual fungi. They are the fungal equivalent of seeds.

Sporing or *fruiting bodies*. Small, raised fungal structures where spores are produced. They are the fungal equivalent of seed pods and the fungi's means of propagation .

Guide to Symptoms

Flowers (Including Buds, Fruit, and Sheaths)

Black necrotic flecks. See Pathogens—*Alternaria alternata*.

Black or brown watery pustules. The raised areas usually occur on the underside of the sepals and petals of older flowers. See Pathogens—*Colletotrichum gloeosporioides*.

Black or light brown water-soaked spots. The spots start very small but may enlarge and cover the entire flower. See Pathogens—*Botrytis cinerea*; *Vanda* transit rot.

Black spots on the lip. The petals may also be discolored. See Pathogens—*Colletotrichum* species; *Glomerella* species.

Black spots or streaks on flower sheaths. Several fungi may also cause rotting of flower buds. See Pathogens—*Botrytis cinerea*, *Colletotrichum* species; *Curvularia geniculata*; *Glomerella* species.

Black to dark brown lesions. Usually sunken, the lesions are often covered with white, powdery mycelia and small pink sporing bodies. See Pathogens—*Fusarium moniliforme*.

Bleached spots on flowers. See Pathogens—*Cymbidium* mosaic.

Brown lesions. The areas may be light or dark, circular or oval. They appear on the sepals, petals, or flower spikes. See Pathogens—*Curvularia geniculata*.

Brown spots on the blossoms. They may be caused by water droplets. See Chapter 1—Flowers.

Brown spots on *Vanilla* flowers and beans. See Pathogens—*Nectria vanillae*.

Brown streaks or spots which develop on flowers approximately 1 week after the buds open. See Pathogens—Blossom necrotic streak.

Buds that develop improperly. See Nutrients—Calcium (deficiency); Cobalt (deficiency); Copper (deficiency); Iron (deficiency); Magnesium (excess); Manganese (excess); Potassium (excess); Zinc (deficiency or excess).

Buds that drop. The flower buds drop before opening. This is usually caused by incorrect temperatures or air pollution. See Chapter 1—Flowers; Species listings—Rest period; Temperatures.

Buds that fail to open properly. See Pests—Thrips.

Buds that rot. The flower buds rot before opening. See Pathogens—*Botrytis cinerea*; *Colletotrichum* species; *Curvularia geniculata*; *Glomerella* species; *Pseudomonas aeruginosa*.

Buds that yellow and drop. Symptoms are usually caused by incorrect light or temperature. See Chapter 1—Flowers; Pathogens—*Fusarium moniliforme*; Species listings—Light; Temperatures.

Color break. Particularly in *Vanda* flowers, color break may be caused by insect damage. See Pests—Thrips.

Color break (mild) in flowers. See Pathogens—Cucumber mosaic; *Odontoglossum* mosaic.

Color break with mottling and distortion of flowers. See Pathogens—*Odontoglossum* ringspot.

Color break with symmetrical variegations. The colored areas of the petals and the margins of the sepals are most likely to be affected. The center of the petals is not normally affected. See Pathogens—Flower break, symmetrical.

Color variegation and distortion of flowers. See Pathogens—*Cymbidium* bar mottle.

Damaged flowers. The damage may result from mechanical injury or inappropriate growing conditions. See Pests—Thrips; Species listings—Light; Rest period; Temperatures.

Few flowers. Poor flowering is usually caused by low light levels, incorrect photoperiods, or a lack of phosphorus. See Nutrients—Phosphorus (deficiency); Species listings—Light; Rest period.

Grey fungus on diseased or decaying flowers. See Pathogens—*Botrytis cinerea*.

Holes and notches in flowers. See Pests—Slugs and snails.

Malformed flowers. See Chapter 1—Flowers; Pathogens—Tobacco rattle.

Misshapen buds, flowers, or new growths. Affected areas may become stunted or distorted. See Pests—Aphids.

Necrotic flecks on sepals and petals. See Pathogens—*Alternaria alternata*; *Botrytis cinerea*; *Vanda* transit rot.

Necrotic specks with water-soaked margins on sepals and petals. See Pathogens—*Pseudomonas aeruginosa*.

Necrotic streaks and spots on flowers. Symptoms do not show on the leaves. See Pathogens—Flower necrosis.

Necrotic veins. See Pathogens—*Dendrobium* vein necrosis.

No flowers. Failure to flower usually indicates a cultural problem such as inappropriate growing temperatures or a lack of diurnal or seasonal temperature fluctuations. See Chapter 1—Flowers; Species listings—Rest period; Temperatures.

Orange spots on flower spikes. The oval spots are raised and often have a yellow halo. See Pathogens—*Coleosporium bletiae*.

Pink sporing bodies. These are usually associated with powdery, white mycelia and black to dark brown, sunken lesions. See Pathogens—*Fusarium moniliforme*.

Raised, watery pustules. Usually black or brown, they normally occur on the underside of aging sepals and petals. See Pathogens—*Colletotrichum gloeosporioides*.

Sepal wilt or premature aging. See Chapter 1—Flowers.

Sheaths that brown or discolor. The damaged sheath may prevent normal flowering. See Pathogens—Fungi species; *Paphiopedilum* flower sheath browning.

Sunken, black to dark brown lesions. White, powdery mycelia and small pink sporing bodies often cover the lesions. See Pathogens—*Fusarium moniliforme*.

Tan or light brown watery spots. They may have somewhat darker centers. See Pathogens—*Phytophthora cactorum*.

Tan to dark brown lesions. The circular or oval areas are usually slightly sunken and approximately 0.02 in. (0.5 mm) across. Sepals, petals, and flower spikes may be affected. See Pathogens—*Botrytis cinerea; Curvularia geniculata.*

Vanilla beans with brown spots. See Pathogens—*Nectria vanillae.*

Vanilla beans with brown tips. They are eventually covered with a white powder. See Pathogens—*Phytophthora jatrophae.*

Vein necrosis. See Pathogens—*Dendrobium* vein necrosis.

Water-soaked spots. The very small, black to light brown spots may enlarge and cover the entire flower. See Pathogens—*Botrytis cinerea.*

Watery pustules. The raised black or brown spots appear on the underside of sepals and petals, normally on older flowers. See Pathogens—*Colletotrichum gloeosporioides.*

White cell necrosis. The cause may be ethylene gas or other air pollutants. See Chapter 1—Flowers.

White cell necrosis on *Cattleya.* See Pathogens—*Cymbidium* mosaic.

White, powdery mycelia. Small pink sporing bodies may also be present on the black to dark brown, sunken lesions. See Pathogens—*Fusarium moniliforme.*

White streaks on flowers. (White streaks on lavender *Cattleya* petals are usually caused by a genetic disorder, not a virus.) See Pathogens—*Dendrobium* white streak.

Wilting flowers. Sepal wilt is usually caused by ethylene gas, but premature aging may occur if pollinia are dislodged or the flower is injured. See Chapter 1—Flowers.

Yellow buds in winter. These may indicate incorrect light or temperature. See Chapter 1—Flowers; Pathogens—*Fusarium moniliforme;* Species listings—Light; Temperatures.

Leaves

Black flecks and streaks on older leaves. As spots enlarge, they become necrotic and merge, forming hieroglyphic patterns. Leaves may show reddish purple ring lesions or elongated, mottled, diamond-shaped chlorotic areas. Plants may be stunted or develop abnormally. See Pathogens—*Odontoglossum* ringspot.

Black leaf tips on new leaves. Affected area may have an advancing yellow band. See Nutrients—Calcium (deficiency).

Black lesions. These are dry and appear old. See Pathogens—*Phytophthora cactorum.*

Black newer and older leaves. See Nutrients—Nitrogen (excess).

Black or orange pustules. The spots are arranged in concentric rings on the leaf undersurface. See Pathogens—*Sphenospora kevorkianii.*

Black spots, streaks, or lines. See Pathogens—Black streak.

Black spots that are usually sunken. See Pathogens—*Cymbidium* mosaic; *Erwinia chrysanthemi.*

Black streaks, lines, or spots that are usually sunken. See Pathogens—Black streak.

Black streaks or flecks which develop on older leaves. As the spots enlarge, they become necrotic and merge to form hieroglyphic patterns. Leaves may show reddish purple ring lesions or elongated, mottled, diamond-shaped chlorotic areas. Plants may be stunted and develop abnormally. See Pathogens—*Odontoglossum* ringspot.

Black tissue between veins. See Nutrients—Boron (excess).

Black to brown lesions which are small and usually sunken. See Pathogens—*Fusarium moniliforme.*

Black to brown rings, streaks, or blotches. They usually occur first on older leaves. See Pathogens—*Cymbidium* mosaic.

Black to brown spots or lesions which appear greasy. See Pathogens—*Diplodia laeliocattleyae.*

Black to brown spots or lesions which are circular or irregularly shaped. See Pathogens—*Septoria selenophomoides.*

Black to brown spots that ooze liquid. They are most common near the leaf tip. See Pathogens—*Pseudomonas cattleyae.*

Black to brown spots which are ring-shaped. See Pathogens—*Dendrobium* viral disease.

Black to brown spots which are usually sunken and oval. Often arranged in concentric rings, they usually occur on the underside of leaves. Plants may be stunted. See Pathogens—*Cymbidium* mosaic.

Black to brown spots which occur first on the leaf tips. The areas enlarge and merge until the entire leaf tip dies. They may be covered with powdery spore masses. See Pathogens—*Botrytis* species.

Black to dark brown lesions. The tiny spots may be circular or irregular and are usually sunken. They are yellow initially but darken with age. See Pathogens—*Septoria selenophomoides.*

Black to dark brown spots surrounded by a water-soaked brown area. They may ooze water if pressed. The affected area is usually small and irregular with a yellowish advancing margin. See Pathogens—*Phytophthora cactorum.*

Black to dark grey patchy deposits on the leaves. Discolored areas may be wiped off with a damp cloth. See Pathogens—*Gloeodes pomigena.*

Black to reddish brown areas. They may be spots, streaks, necrotic rings, or diamond-shaped lesions that begin as chlorotic tissue. Leaves may drop prematurely. See Pathogens—*Spathoglottis* diamond spot.

Blistered leaf cells, particularly on the underside of leaves. See Pests—Thrips.

Bronze leaves. See Nutrients—Chlorine (deficiency).

Brown areas which are dried and shriveled. See Pathogens—*Erwinia cypripedii.*

Brown blotches. Normally found on older leaves, the areas are watery. They are round or elongated and about 1.4–2.0 in.

(3.5–5.0 cm) across. The blotches usually have a pale brown margin. See Pathogens—*Penicillin thomii*.

Brown circular areas on the underside of leaves. The spots have an advancing orange margin. See Pathogens—*Uredo oncidii*.

Brown circular areas which appear suddenly on a curved leaf surface. These are usually caused by sunburn. See Chapter 1—Leaves; Species listings—Light.

Brown leaf tips or leaf margins. These are usually caused by accumulated fertilizer salts, or the symptoms may result from applying chemicals inappropriately. See Chapter 1—Fertilizer.

Brown leaf tips which proceed from the tip toward the base. See Nutrients—Chlorine (excess); Pathogens—*Glomerella cincta*.

Brown leaves. They start by yellowing and end by dying back. This may be a normal process for plants with deciduous leaves. See Nutrients—Calcium (deficiency); Cobalt (deficiency); Copper (deficiency); Iron (deficiency); Potassium (excess); Magnesium (excess); Manganese (deficiency); Zinc (deficiency or excess).

Brown lesions. The areas are watery and usually located at the base of the stem. The roots and leaf bases often collapse rapidly. See Pathogens—*Sclerotium rolfsii*.

Brown pustules. The areas are usually raised, often have reddish borders, and occur on the underside of leaves. With age, the pustules become purple-black. See Pathogens—*Uredo epidendri*.

Brown spots on either leaf surface. They start small and develop into round, oval, or irregular lesions. They become discolored in the center, and sporing bodies appear on older spots. See Pathogens—*Selenophoma dendrobii*.

Brown spots on the leaves. See Nutrients—Iron (deficiency); Manganese (excess); Zinc (excess).

Brown spots on the leaves which increase in size. The leaves turn yellow, and the tissue between the veins may collapse. See Pathogens—Short orchid rhabdovirus.

Brown spots on the underside of leaves. They are tiny and slightly raised. See Pathogens—*Cercospora angraeci; Cercospora* species I–IV.

Brown to grey areas in concentric zones or rings. The discolorations usually occur near the leaf apex. See Pathogens—*Colletotrichum gloeosporiodes*.

Brown to light grey areas without concentric zones or rings. See Pathogens—*Botryodiplodia theobromae*.

Brown to tan areas with well-defined margins. They often have a yellow outer band and with time develop black or dark brown sporing bodies. See Pathogens—*Phyllostictina citricarpa*.

Brown to tan spore pustules. See Pathogens—*Uredo nigropuncta*.

Brown to tan spots. The tiny spots have a slightly raised, red to purple-black margin, a tan or brown center, and raised black spore structures. See Pathogens—*Phyllostictina pyriformis*.

Brown, water-soaked spots on the leaves. See Pathogens—*Erwinia chrysanthemi*.

Brown, water-soaked spots that may ooze water if pressed. The spots are small and irregular and often have a yellowish advancing margin. The center becomes dark brown or black as the lesions age. See Pathogens—*Phytophthora cactorum*.

Burned leaves. A sudden increase in light levels or severe overexposure to excessive light may result in burning. See Chapter 1—Light; Species listings—Light.

Chestnut-brown areas on the leaves. See Pathogens—*Erwinia cypripedii*.

Chlorosis. Some forms of chlorosis may result from inappropriate use of chemicals. Also see listings beginning with the words "Yellow" or "Light green."

Chlorosis and ringspots on the leaves. The discolorations are sometimes quite faint. See Pathogens—*Cymbidium* ringspot.

Chlorosis between the veins on newer leaves. Affected leaf tissue is usually light yellow to white. See Nutrients—Zinc (deficiency).

Chlorosis between the veins on older leaves, usually light yellow. See Nutrients—Molybdenum (deficiency).

Chlorosis, light yellow. See Nutrients—Molybdenum (deficiency).

Chlorosis on middle or older leaves. Light yellow discoloration between veins or along the leaf margins is usually caused by a magnesium deficiency. See Nutrients—Calcium (excess); Cobalt (deficiency); Copper (deficiency); Iron (deficiency); Magnesium (deficiency); Manganese (deficiency); Potassium (excess); Zinc (deficiency or excess).

Chlorosis on new leaves. See Nutrients—Zinc (deficiency).

Chlorosis on new leaves which often produces mild discolorations. See Pathogens—*Cymbidium* mosaic.

Chlorosis on older leaves. The discoloration is usually light yellow and is usually caused by a nitrogen deficiency. See Nutrients—Cobalt (deficiency); Copper (deficiency); Iron (deficiency); Manganese (deficiency); Nitrogen (deficiency); Phosphorus (excess); Potassium (excess); Zinc (deficiency or excess).

Chlorosis with deep furrowing and ridging. The necrotic, water-soaked areas are most pronounced on the underside of leaves. Leaves may drop. See Pathogens—*Cymbidium* mosaic.

Chlorotic areas which are elongated or diamond-shaped. The areas may be mottled with pale, reddish purple ring lesions. As the spots enlarge, they become necrotic and merge to form hieroglyphic patterns. Older leaves may develop black flecks and streaks. Plants may be stunted and develop abnormally. See Pathogens—*Odontoglossum* ringspot.

Chlorotic areas which become large, dark brown or black, ring-shaped spots. See Pathogens—*Dendrobium* viral disease.

Chlorotic or dark areas on the leaves. Plants appear unhealthy. See Pests—Mealybugs; Scale.

Chlorotic patches and rings which are usually faint. They have a subtly different appearance from chlorosis caused by *Cymbidium* mosaic. See Pathogens—Cucumber mosaic.

Chlorotic patches on the upper leaf surface. Orange-yellow patches in a roughly circular pattern may cover the lower surface. See Pathogens—*Uredo behickiana*.

Chlorotic patches which are diamond-shaped and become necrotic. See Pathogens—*Cymbidium* mosaic.

Chlorotic spots and streaks. The necrotic rings or diamond-shaped lesions become reddish brown or black with age. Leaves may drop prematurely. See Pathogens—*Spathoglottis* diamond spot.

Chlorotic spots, streaks, or stippling. The area eventually becomes sunken and turns brown. See Pests—Mites.

Chlorotic streaks. Usually faint, the basal necrotic streaking may cause premature leaf drop. See Pathogens—Tomato ringspot.

Collapsed leaf bases and roots. Watery brown lesions appear at the base of the stem. See Pathogens—*Sclerotium rolfsii*.

Creamy-yellow discoloration which soon turns brown. See Pathogens—*Sclerotium rolfsii*.

Curled, desiccated leaves. Fungal growth and brown rot may be evident on the roots. See Pathogens—*Rhizoctonia solani*.

Curled or cupped mature leaves. These may result from inappropriate use of chemicals. Also see Nutrients—Calcium (deficiency or excess); Cobalt (deficiency); Copper (deficiency); Iron (deficiency); Magnesium (deficiency); Manganese (deficiency); Potassium (excess); Zinc (deficiency or excess).

Dark green leaves which are often succulent and brittle. See Nutrients—Nitrogen (excess); Potassium (deficiency).

Dark green leaves with purplish coloring along the veins. Affected plants are usually also stunted. See Nutrients—Phosphorus (deficiency).

Dark green or limp leaves. Soft leaves often indicate that the plant is receiving insufficient light or that temperatures are too low. See Chapter 1—Leaves; Species listings—Light; Temperatures.

Dark or chlorotic areas on the leaves. Plants appear unhealthy. See Pests—Mealybugs; Scale.

Dark streaks. They may rapidly cover the entire leaf. See Pathogens—*Erwinia carotovora*.

Dead tissue. The underside of leaves shows irregular, elongated streaks. See Pathogens—*Cymbidium* mosaic.

Dead tissue between veins. See Nutrients—Boron (excess).

Die-back of mature leaves. Even evergreen plants have a few leaves that die back each year. If all leaves die back, the plant may be deciduous. See Species listings—Leaves.

Die-back of new leaves. Apical buds, growing tips, or terminal leaves may be affected. Symptoms may result from inapropriate use of chemicals. See Nutrients—Boron (deficiency).

Distorted or deformed leaves. Symptoms usually result from inappropriate use of chemicals.

Dry, black lesions that look old. See Pathogens—*Phytophthora cactorum*.

Faded leaves or wilted terminal shoots. See Nutrients—Copper (deficiency).

Flyspeck-like spots. They appear in large groups on leaf surfaces and may be wiped off with a damp cloth. See Pathogens—*Microthyriella rubi*.

Furrowing and ridging. Chlorosis and necrotic, water-soaked areas also appear. See Pathogens—*Cymbidium* mosaic.

Grey to black patchy deposits on the leaves. They may be removed with a damp cloth. See Pathogens—*Gloeodes pomigena*.

Grey to brown areas. They have no concentric zones or rings. See Pathogens—*Botryodiplodia theobromae*.

Grey to brown concentric zones or rings. They occur primarily near the leaf apex. See Pathogens—*Colletotrichum gloeosporiodes*.

Greasy-looking black to brown spots or lesions. See Pathogens—*Diplodia laeliocattleyae*.

Green mosaic on older leaves. The mosaic forms concentric ring patterns. See Pathogens—*Dendrobium* mosaic.

Green veins on yellow mature leaves. See Nutrients—Magnesium (deficiency).

Holes and notches in new leaves. See Pests—Cockroaches; Grasshoppers; Slugs and snails.

Holes in the center of dark spots. See Pathogens—*Cercospora angraeci*; *Cercospora* species I–IV.

Irregular streaks and spots on the leaves. See Pathogens—*Oncidium* severe mosaic streaking.

Leaf drop. Premature leaf drop, sometimes resulting in plant death, may result from high night temperatures. See Species listings—Rest period; Temperatures.

Leaf drop of middle and older leaves. Leaves fall prematurely. See Nutrients—Calcium (deficiency or excess); Cobalt (deficiency); Copper (deficiency); Iron (deficiency); Manganese (deficiency); Nitrogen (deficiency); Phosphorus (deficiency); Potassium (excess); Zinc (deficiency or excess).

Leaf drop which may be accompanied by chlorosis. Other symptoms include deep furrowing and ridging and necrotic, water-soaked areas which are most pronounced on the underside of leaves. See Pathogens—*Cymbidium* mosaic.

Leaf drop with faint chlorotic streaks or basal necrotic streaking. The streaking is usually the first symptom. See Pathogens—Tomato ringspot.

Leaf drop with rotting leaves. See Pathogens—*Pseudomonas andropogonis*.

Leaf-tip die-back is frequently caused by a lack of moisture. Other causes of similar symptoms include excess water resulting in root loss, chemical damage from salt buildup or chemical applications, or overfertilization. See Chapter 1—Fertilizer; Leaves; Nutrients—Calcium (deficiency); Species listings—Water.

Light green. Also see listings beginning with the words "Chlorosis" and "Yellow."

Light green mosaic mottling. See Pathogens—*Oncidium* light green mosaic mottle.

Light green mosaic patches. Other symptoms include chlorosis on the leaves, tissue collapse, necrosis, broad chlorotic furrows, or water-soaked areas on the underside of leaves. See Pathogens—*Phalaenopsis* mosaic.

Light green to yellow rings. The rings may be small and irregular and may turn reddish black with age. See Pathogens—*Odontoglossum* streak.

Limp leaves. They are usually dark green, indicating that the plant is receiving insufficient light. See Chapter 1—Leaves; Species listings—Light.

Malformed leaves which may be mottled. Plants become stunted and weak and produce few flowers. See Pathogens—*Cymbidium* bar mottle.

Mold. Usually found on dead plant material, mold may spread to living tissue. See Pathogens—*Saprophytic* fungi.

Mosaic mottling on leaf tips. Usually inconspicuous, the mottling is often first noticed as a problem with the blossoms. See Pathogens—*Vanda* mosaic.

Mosaic mottling on older leaves. Usually green, it appears in concentric rings. See Pathogens—*Dendrobium* mosaic.

Mosaic mottling on the leaves which is usually light green. See Pathogens—*Oncidium* light green mosaic mottle.

Mosaic mottling on the leaves which may be very faint. See Pathogens—Flower break, symmetrical.

Mosaic mottling on the underside of leaves. It may be accompanied by diffuse, light green or yellow patches, tissue collapse, broad chlorotic furrows, or water-soaked areas. Necrosis and light green chlorosis may show on the upper surface. See Pathogens—*Phalaenopsis* mosaic.

Mosaic mottling on young leaves. It is usually quite pale. See Pathogens—*Cymbidium* bar mottle; *Dendrobium* mosaic.

Mosaic mottling, rings, or streaks. See Pathogens—*Paphiopedilum* viral infection.

Mosaic mottling, usually sunken. See Pathogens—Bean yellow mosaic.

Necrosis. Symptoms frequently result from inappropriate use of chemicals.

Necrotic concentric rings. They surround apparently healthy tissue and may merge to form faint mosaic patterns, chlorotic streaks, or diamond mottling. See Pathogens—*Odontoglossum* mosaic.

Necrotic lines or semicircular rings on the leaves. See Pathogens—*Laelia* etch.

Necrotic or chlorotic flecks on the leaves. See Pathogens—Orchid fleck.

Necrotic streaking and premature leaf drop. See Pathogens—Tomato ringspot.

Necrotic veins on the leaves and flowers. See Pathogens—*Dendrobium* vein necrosis.

Orange pustules in concentric rings on the underside of leaves. The pustules become black with age. See Pathogens—*Sphenospora kevorkianii*.

Orange pustules on both leaf surfaces. Affected areas often have a yellow halo. See Pathogens—*Coleosporium bletiae*.

Orange pustules on the underside of leaves. The pustules are small, and the affected area is usually circular. See Pathogens—*Uredo oncidii*.

Orange pustules which become black with age. See Pathogens—*Uredo nigropuncta*.

Orange to rust-brown pustules. The tiny, raised spots appear on the underside of leaves and turn dark brown with age. See Pathogens—*Sphenospora saphena*.

Orange-yellow patches on the underside of leaves. Patches appear in roughly circular patterns. The top surface develops chlorotic patches. See Pathogens—*Uredo behickiana*.

Pale leaves. They are also desiccated and curl inward. The roots may have fungal growth and brown rot. See Pathogens—*Rhizoctonia solani*.

Purple-black old-looking pustules. The spots, which appear on the underside of leaves, may have started as raised, brown pustules with reddish borders. See Pathogens—*Uredo epidendri*.

Purple-brown sunken spots on the underside of leaves. See Pathogens—*Cercospora angraeci; Cercospora* species I–IV.

Purple-brown to purplish black patches. Often irregularly shaped, they sometimes have either an advancing yellow margin or a darker raised margin. See Pathogens—*Cercospora angraeci; Cercospora* species I–IV.

Purple lesions. Usually elongated and parallel to the veins, the lesions become streaks, irregular blotches, or diamond-shaped areas. With age, the center turns tan and becomes raised, and black fungal structures develop. See Pathogens—*Guignardia* species.

Purplish to dark green leaves. Red coloring is strongest along the veins. Affected plants are usually stunted. See Nutrients—Phosphorus (deficiency).

Raised black spore structures on tiny brown to tan spots. The pustules may have a slightly raised, red to purple-black margin. See Pathogens—*Phyllostictina pyriformis*.

Raised black spore structures which develop in the brown center of purple lesions. They are usually elongated and parallel to the veins. They may become streaks, irregular blotches, or diamond-shaped areas. See Pathogens—*Guignardia* species.

Raised brown pustules, often with reddish borders. They occur on the underside of leaves, and with age, the pustules become purple-black. See Pathogens—*Uredo epidendri*.

Raised brown spots. Usually tiny, they appear on the underside of seedling leaves. See Pathogens—*Cercospora angraeci*; *Cercospora* species I–IV.

Raised orange to rust-brown pustules on the underside of leaves. Usually tiny, they turn dark brown with age. See Pathogens—*Sphenospora saphena*.

Reddish black deposits. See Pests—Thrips.

Reddish black rings. These may be small or irregular and often start as light green or yellow discolorations. See Pathogens—*Odontoglossum* streak.

Reddish brown or black areas. These may show as spots, streaks, necrotic rings, or diamond-shaped lesions that begin as chlorotic areas. Leaves may drop prematurely. See Pathogens—*Spathoglottis* diamond spot.

Reddish brown spots. They are sunken and well defined. Usually small initially, they may grow and merge, killing the leaf. The first spots usually appear near the leaf tip. See Pathogens—*Gloeosporium* species.

Reddish purple lesions. They may be ring-shaped or elongated, diamond-shaped chlorotic areas which may be mottled. As the areas enlarge, they become necrotic and merge to form hieroglyphic patterns. Older leaves may develop black flecks and streaks, and plants may be stunted and develop abnormally. See Pathogens—*Odontoglossum* ringspot.

Reddish purple spots. Usually sunken, they occur on the underside of leaves and may have a slightly raised, tan center. See Pathogens—*Cercospora angraeci*; *Cercospora* species I–IV.

Red or purple coloring along the veins. See Nutrients—Phosphorus (deficiency).

Red or purple coloring on the leaves. The chief causes are excessive light and macronutrient imbalances. See Chapter 1—Leaves; Nutrients—Cobalt (deficiency); Copper (deficiency); Iron (deficiency); Manganese (deficiency); Nitrogen (deficiency); Phosphorus (excess); Potassium (excess); Zinc (deficiency or excess); Species listings—Light.

Red spots on mature leaves. The spots eventually disappear, leaving sunken areas. See Pathogens—*Laelia* red leaf spots.

Ringspot, usually very distinct. See Pathogens—Ringspot.

Ringspot with faint chlorotic areas. Plants may be stunted, and old growths may die. See Pathogens—*Cymbidium* ringspot.

Rings which may be black to brown. See *Dendrobium* viral disease.

Rings which may be small or irregular and reddish black, light green, or yellow. See Pathogens—*Odontoglossum* streak.

Rosetting of the leaves. See Nutrients—Zinc (deficiency).

Rotting, dropping leaves. See Pathogens—*Pseudomonas andropogonis*.

Silvery sheen on the topside of leaves. It eventually becomes sunken and turns brown. See Pests—Mites; Thrips.

Small leaves. See Nutrients—Zinc (deficiency).

Small leaves on normally large-leaved species. See Chapter 1—Leaves.

Soft leaves. They may result from high moisture, low light, or high night temperatures. See Species listings—Light; Rest period; Temperatures; Water.

Soft rot of the leaves. See Pathogens—*Erwinia chrysanthemi*.

Spots on *Vanilla* leaves. See Pathogens—*Seuratia coeffeicola*.

Stippled streaks on the leaves. See Pathogens—*Oncidium* stippled streak.

Streaking, stippling, or spotting. Due to the loss of chlorophyll, the affected areas eventually become sunken and brown. See Pests—Mites.

Streaks of dead tissue on the underside of leaves. The areas are usually elongated and irregular. See Pathogens—*Cymbidium* mosaic.

Streaks, usually dark, that rapidly cover the entire leaf. See Pathogens—*Erwinia carotovora*.

Stunted plants. See Nutrients—Boron (deficiency); Calcium (deficiency).

Sunken mosaic mottling. See Pathogens—Bean yellow mosaic.

Sunken, purple-brown spots on the underside of leaves. See Pathogens—*Cercospora angraeci*; *Cercospora* species I–IV.

Sunken streaks or pebbling on new leaves in early spring. Initially yellow, the streaks become tan, and black pits develop with age. Although the damage resembles a virus, it is caused by low temperatures and occurs only on new leaves. Subsequent leaves are normal. See Species listings—Rest period; Temperatures.

Tan areas on the underside of leaves. Pitting and irregular depressions may also be present. See Pathogens—*Cymbidium* mosaic.

Tan growths resembling mustard seeds. See Pathogens—*Sclerotium rolfsii*.

Tan patches with dark brown borders. See Pathogens—*Macrophomina phaseolina*.

Tan spots with a purple margin. See Pathogens—*Cercospora angraeci*; *Cercospora* species I–IV.

Tan spots with darker brown margins. They are usually elongated. See Pathogens—*Sphaeropsis* species.

Tan, sunken streaks or pebbling on new leaves in early spring. Initially yellow, the streaks become sunken, and black pits develop with age. Although the damage resembles a virus, it is caused by low temperatures and occurs only on new leaves. Subsequent leaves are normal. See Species listings—Rest period; Temperatures.

Tan to dark brown areas with yellow margins. The margins are well defined, and black or dark brown sporing bodies may be present. See Pathogens—*Phyllostictina citricarpa*.

Tan to dark brown spore pustules. See Pathogens—*Uredo nigropuncta.*

Tan to dark brown spots. The tiny spots have a slightly raised, red to purple-black margin and a tan or brown center. Black, raised spore structures may be present. See Pathogens—*Phyllostictina pyriformis.*

Tan, water-soaked spots. They are often located near the middle of the leaf. See Pathogens—*Erwinia cypripedii.*

Translucent blisters. They may have a yellowish or pale green halo. See Pathogens—*Pseudomonas cattleyae.*

Translucent, water-soaked areas. Usually small and soft, they eventually turn brown or black and become sunken. The affected areas ooze liquid, especially near the leaf tip. See Pathogens—*Pseudomonas cattleyae.*

Translucent, water-soaked areas on the underside of leaves. See Pathogens—*Cymbidium* mosaic.

Translucent, water-soaked patches on the leaves. See *Erwinia chrysanthemi.*

Translucent, water-soaked spots on seedlings. The areas turn yellow then black. See Pathogens—*Phytophthora cactorum.*

Translucent, water-soaked spots on the upper leaf surface. See Pathogens—*Pseudomonas cypripedii.*

Translucent, water-soaked spots which are usually small. See Pathogens—*Erwinia carotovora.*

Twisted leaves. See Nutrients—Molybdenum (deficiency).

Unopened leaves. See Nutrients—Molybdenum (deficiency).

Water-soaked areas. Affected plants may also show light green chlorosis, mosaic patches, tissue collapse, or broad, chlorotic furrows on the underside of leaves. Necrosis and light green chlorosis may show on the upper surface. See Pathogens—*Phalaenopsis* mosaic.

Water-soaked areas on the underside of leaves. The leaves are usually chlorotic or necrotic with deep furrowing or ridging. They may drop prematurely. See Pathogens—*Cymbidium* mosaic.

Water-soaked brown spots. Usually small and irregular, they may have a yellowish advancing margin. The center becomes dark brown or black as the lesions age, and the spots may ooze water if pressed. See Pathogens—*Phytophthora cactorum.*

Water-soaked brown spots on the leaves. See Pathogens—*Erwinia chrysanthemi.*

Water-soaked tan spots. Affected areas are often located near the middle of the leaf. See Pathogens—*Erwinia cypripedii.*

Water-soaked, translucent areas on the underside of leaves. See Pathogens—*Cymbidium* mosaic.

Water-soaked, translucent lesions. Usually small and soft, they eventually become sunken, turn brown to black, and ooze liquid, especially from the leaf tip. See Pathogens—*Pseudomonas cattleyae.*

Water-soaked, translucent patches on the leaves. See Pathogens—*Erwinia chrysanthemi.*

Water-soaked, translucent spots. They turn yellow then black. See Pathogens—*Phytophthora cactorum.*

Water-soaked, translucent spots on the upper leaf surface. See Pathogens—*Pseudomonas cypripedii.*

Water-soaked, translucent spots which are usually small. See Pathogens—*Erwinia carotovora.*

Water-soaked, yellow leaves. See Pathogens—*Erwinia chrysanthemi.*

Water-soaked, yellow spots. Usually small and round, they eventually become reddish brown and sunken. See Pathogens—*Erwinia cypripedii.*

Watery brown blotches on older leaves. The round or elongated spots are 1.4–2.0 in. (3.5–5.0 cm) across with a pale brown margin. See Pathogens—*Penicillin thomii.*

Watery brown lesions at the base of the stem. The roots and leaf bases collapse rapidly. See Pathogens—*Sclerotium rolfsii.*

Wavy leaf margins. See Nutrients—Zinc (deficiency).

Webs. They are usually small and inconspicuous. See Pests—Mites.

Wet rot with a foul odor. See Pathogens—*Erwinia carotovora.*

White fungal mycelia. The filaments cover *Vanilla* plants and turn brown with age. See Pathogens—*Sporoschisma* species.

White leaves or streaks. New leaves may be pale or white, and older leaves may develop white streaks. Growth is often stunted. See Nutrients—Zinc (deficiency).

White to yellow mottling on new leaves. Veins usually remain green. Most frequent cause is lack of iron. See Nutrients—Copper (excess); Iron (deficiency); Zinc (excess).

Wilted, dying leaves. See Pests—Thrips.

Wilted leaf tips. Leaves do not become erect when the plants are watered. See Nutrients—Chlorine (deficiency).

Wilted terminal shoots or faded leaves. See Nutrients—Copper (deficiency).

Wrinkled or hard leaves. Inadequate moisture or high light may cause this problem. See Chapter 1—Leaves; Species listings—Light; Rest period; Water.

Wrinkling between the leaf veins. See Nutrients—Potassium (deficiency).

Yellow. Also see listings beginning with the words "Chlorosis," "Light green," and "Necrotic."

Yellow area with well-defined margins. The areas often have a yellow outer band and turn to brown. Black or dark brown sporing bodies may be present. As the lesion gets larger, the adjacent tissue becomes sunken and may become yellow or pale green. See Pathogens—*Phyllostictina citricarpa.*

Yellow areas on the underside of leaves. The affected areas are usually round or irregular and sunken. A chlorotic spot may show on the upper surface. See Pathogens—

Cercospora angraeci; Cercospora species I–IV.

Yellow between green veins. Stems are often yellowish green. See Nutrients—Manganese (deficiency).

Yellow blotches and streaks. The blotches may be pronounced rectangular chlorotic areas or broken lines of bar-shaped discolorations. The discolored area is usually yellow or light to dark green at first and later becomes necrotic. It may be ridged and bumpy. See Pathogens—*Cymbidium* bar mottle.

Yellow chlorosis. See Nutrients—Molybdenum (deficiency).

Yellow chlorotic areas. They may become large, dark brown or black, ring-shaped spots. See Pathogens—*Dendrobium* viral disease.

Yellow chlorotic streaks. The leaves may be ridged, thickened, or curled. See Pathogens—Chlorotic leaf streak of *Oncidium*.

Yellow-green leaves. If the leaves are normally dark green, the change may indicate inappropriate light levels. See Chapter 1—Leaves; Species listings—Light.

Yellow, irregular patches. See Pathogens—*Cymbidium* mosaic.

Yellow leaves. The cause is usually inappropriate light or nitrogen deficiency. A sudden increase in light, prolonged high light levels, severe light deprivation, or incorrect photoperiods all cause leaves to yellow. See Chapter 1—Light; Nutrients—Molybdenum (deficiency); Nitrogen (deficiency); Pathogens—Mycoplasmal diseases; Species listings—Light.

Yellow leaves that turn brown and die with age. See Nutrients—Calcium (deficiency); Cobalt (deficiency); Copper (deficiency); Iron (deficiency); Magnesium (excess); Manganese (deficiency); Nitrogen (deficiency); Potassium (excess); Zinc (deficiency or excess).

Yellow leaves which are thin, shriveled, and twisted. See Pathogens—*Rhizoctonia solani*.

Yellow leaves which may be thin, shriveled, or wilted and eventually turn grey. See Pathogens—*Fusarium oxysporum*.

Yellow leaves with collapsed tissue between the veins. The problem first shows as brown spots on the leaves. See Pathogens—Short orchid rhabdovirus.

Yellow lesions. The circular or irregular lesions are normally tiny and sunken. They become dark brown or black with age. See Pathogens—*Septoria selenophomoides*.

Yellow margins on the leaves. See Nutrients—Potassium (deficiency).

Yellow mature leaves with green veins. See Nutrients—Magnesium (deficiency).

Yellow rings and spots. The affected area increases in size as the leaf grows. See Pathogens—*Stanhopea* yellow spot.

Yellow spots on both leaf surfaces. The spots are usually tiny. See Pathogens—*Coleosporium bletiae*.

Yellow spots on either leaf surface. As they enlarge, they become greasy, brown or black lesions. See Pathogens—*Diplodia laeliocattleyae*.

Yellow streaks or pebbling on new leaves in early spring. The affected area is usually slightly sunken. With age, the streaks become tan, and black pits develop. Although it resembles a virus, it is caused by low temperatures and occurs only on new leaves. Subsequent leaves are normal. See Species listings—Rest period; Temperatures.

Yellow streaks which are long and irregular. See Pathogens—Blossom necrotic streak.

Yellow to light green leaves. The stem is often slender. See Nutrients—Sulfur (deficiency).

Yellow to light green rings. They are small and irregular and become reddish black with age. See Pathogens—*Odontoglossum* streak.

Yellow to light green spots. Circular, sunken spots appear on the leaves and pseudobulbs. The spots may merge to cover the leaf tip. With age, they turn light brown, and darker spots of fungal sporing bodies may appear. See Pathogens—*Gloeosporium affine*.

Yellow to white mottling on new leaves. Veins usually remain green. The primary cause is lack of iron. See Nutrients—Copper (excess); Iron (deficiency); Zinc (excess).

Yellow, water-soaked leaves. See Pathogens—*Erwinia chrysanthemi*.

Yellow, water-soaked spots which are usually small and round and eventually become reddish brown and sunken. See Pathogens—*Erwinia cypripedii*.

Yellow, wilted leaves which may be dying. See Pathogens—*Phytophthora cactorum; Sclerotium rolfsii*.

New Leads, Pseudobulbs, Rhizomes, Roots, and Stems

Black or brown roots or pseudobulbs. They soften and rot. See Pathogens—*Pythium ultimum*.

Black stems. See Nutrients—Boron (deficiency).

Black to dark brown pseudobulbs. The bulbs are usually soft and shriveled. The rot expands, and the advancing margin is water-soaked. See Pathogens—*Erwinia carotovora*.

Brown areas on pseudobulbs. Affected tissue may be light to dark brown with well-defined margins and often has a yellow or pale green outer band. As the lesion gets larger, the adjacent tissue becomes sunken. Black or dark brown sporing bodies may be present. See Pathogens—*Phyllostictina citricarpa*.

Brown rot on the leaves. The cause is a root disease which is often first noticed on aerial parts of the plant. See Pathogens—*Rhizoctonia solani*.

Chewed or missing growing tips or roots. See Pests—Cockroaches; Grasshoppers; Millipedes; Sowbugs.

Chlorotic blotches. Mild discolorations develop on new shoots. See Pathogens—*Cymbidium* mosaic.

Collapsed roots. See Pathogens—*Phytophthora cactorum.*

Creamy yellow discolorations. They occur on one or both sides of *Cattleya* family pseudobulbs. See Pathogens—*Pythium ultimum.*

Damaged or unhealthy-looking new growths. See Pests—Whiteflies.

Dead growing tip or bud. Symptoms usually result from inappropriate use of chemicals. See Section III of this Appendix.

Dead root-tips. These are probably caused by salt buildup resulting from hard water or excess fertilizer. See Chapter 1—Leaves; Nutrients—Calcium (deficiency); Cobalt (deficiency); Copper (deficiency); Iron (deficiency); Magnesium (excess); Manganese (deficiency); Potassium (excess); Zinc (deficiency or excess).

Deformed roots. See Nutrients—Chlorine (deficiency).

Distorted or stunted new growths. See Pests—Aphids.

Fungal mycelia on *Vanilla* stems. See Pathogens—*Fusicladium vanillae.*

Hard, mummified pseudobulbs. See Pathogens—*Pythium ultimum.*

Holes in canes or pseudobulbs. A yellow margin or chlorotic area surrounds the small, shot-sized holes. See Pests—Orchid beetle.

Malformed, twisted, or shriveled pseudobulbs. See Pathogens—*Fusarium oxysporum.*

Pale green or yellowish plants. See Nutrients—Sulfur (deficiency).

Poor growth or vigor. Often caused by nutrient problems, poor growth may also result from high night temperatures. See Nutrients—Calcium (deficiency); Cobalt (deficiency); Copper (deficiency); Iron (deficiency); Magnesium (excess); Manganese (deficiency); Nitrogen (deficiency); Phosphorus (deficiency or excess); Potassium (excess); Zinc (deficiency or excess); Species listings—Rest period; Temperatures.

Purple band or circle on the rhizome or roots. The symptom usually occurs on recently divided plants. A pinkish-purple discoloration may show on the connective tissue. See Pathogens—*Fusarium oxysporum.*

Purple or purplish-brown areas on new growths. The areas are sharply defined and have a yellowish, advancing margin. See Pathogens—*Phytophthora cactorum.*

Root die-back. The problem is often first noticed when the disease affects the stem. See Pathogens—*Pseudomonas aeruginosa.*

Rotting *Cattleya* pseudobulbs. See Pests—Orchid beetle.

Soft rot of pseudobulbs. See Pathogens—*Erwinia chrysanthemi.*

Soft, shriveled pseudobulbs. A dark brown or black progressive rot with a water-soaked advancing margin. See Pathogens—*Erwinia carotovora.*

Stunted growths. Leaves are dark green. See Nutrients—Phosphorus (deficiency).

Stunted plants or new growths. Growths may be distorted and lack vigor. Symptoms usually result from inappropriate use of chemicals. Also see Nutrients—Boron (deficiency); Calcium (deficiency); Cobalt (deficiency); Copper (deficiency); Iron (deficiency); Magnesium (excess); Manganese (deficiency); Nitrogen (deficiency); Phosphorus (excess); Potassium (deficiency or excess); Zinc (deficiency or excess).

Stunted roots. They are often poorly developed. See Nutrients—Boron (deficiency); Calcium (deficiency); Cobalt (deficiency); Copper (deficiency); Iron (deficiency); Magnesium (excess); Manganese (deficiency); Potassium (deficiency or excess); Sulfur (deficiency); Zinc (deficiency or excess).

Swollen pseudobulbs with an exit hole. See Pests—Wasps.

Tan to dark brown areas on pseudobulbs. The margins are red to purple-black and slightly raised, while the center is tan or brown. Tiny, black, raised spore structures may be present. See Pathogens—*Phyllostictina pyriformis.*

Tan to dark brown areas on pseudobulbs, usually with well-defined margins. The areas often have a yellow outer band. Black or dark brown sporing bodies may be present. See Pathogens—*Phyllostictina citricarpa.*

Tan, watery lesions at the base of the stem. The roots, stems, and leaf bases may collapse rapidly. See Pathogens—*Sclerotium rolfsii.*

Thin stems. See Nutrients—Phosphorus (deficiency); Sulfur (deficiency).

Watery, tan lesions at the base of the stem. The roots, stems, and leaf bases may collapse rapidly. See Pathogens—*Sclerotium rolfsii.*

Weak, spindly growth. See Nutrients—Nitrogen (excess); Potassium (deficiency).

Wet rot with a foul odor on any plant part. See Pathogens—*Erwinia carotovora.*

White, powdery growth on organic potting media. See Pathogens—*Ptychogaster* species.

Withered new pseudobulbs. The cause is insufficient water. See Species listings—Rest period; Water.

Yellowish green stems. See Nutrients—Manganese (deficiency).

Yellowish or pale green plants. See Nutrients—Sulfur (deficiency).

Yellow or pale green areas on the pseudobulb. The well-defined margins often have a yellow outer band. They become light to dark brown with age. Black or dark brown sporing bodies may be present. As the lesion enlarges, the adjacent tissue becomes sunken. See Pathogens—*Phyllostictina citricarpa.*

Yellow, shriveled new growths. Usually thin and twisted, the growths are progressively smaller. See Pathogens—*Rhizoctonia solani.*

Yellow, sunken lesions on any plant part. The round to oval spots are usually tiny and turn tan to dark brown with age. They have slightly raised, red to purple-black margins and a tan or brown center. Tiny, black, raised spore structures may be present. See Pathogens—*Phyllostictina pyriformis.*

Pathogens

General Information

Diseases known to affect one species or genus often occur in closely related species and genera. If one plant in the growing area is infected by a particular pathogen, species not normally considered susceptible may also become infected. It is important to note that symptoms may be distinctly different depending on the plant part affected. Symptoms may also differ from one plant to another and from one genus to another.

Infectious organisms may be divided into the following categories.

Bacteria are single-celled, microscopic organisms without chlorophyll that reproduce by division. They are usually the infecting agent in oozing or soft, wet-rot orchid diseases. Bacteria frequently spread rapidly and are often quickly fatal.

Fungi are filamentlike plant organisms without chlorophyll that reproduce and spread by means of sporing bodies. In orchids, they cause diseases ranging from deadly root and rhizome rots to annoying leaf and flower spotting. During the sexual stage of the fungal life cycle (when the fungus is known by a different Latin name), each sporing body produces enough spores to infect the entire growing area. Common fungi include molds, yeasts, and mushrooms.

The vast majority of infectious plant diseases are caused by fungi. Visible sporing bodies or mycelia (masses of fungal threads) confirm the presence of a fungal infection. The rate at which the infection spreads depends on the stage of fungal growth.

Mycoplasa are microscopic organisms similar to bacteria which lack cell walls, causing them to appear filamentlike. They are uncommon in orchids, but when present, they interfere with plant metabolism. Mycoplasa may be controlled and destroyed in the growing area, but they cannot be eliminated once they have invaded a plant.

Viruses are submicroscopic, subcellular organisms that require a host cell in which to multiply. They cause a number of diseases in cultivated orchids but are rare or nonexistent in the wild. While viral infections may be prevented, they cannot be cured once a plant is infected.

Only 2 orchid viruses are known to occur world-wide: *Cymbidium* mosaic virus (CyMV) and *Odontoglossum* ringspot virus, which is the orchid strain of tobacco mosaic (TMV-O).

Viral diseases are transmitted by insects, mites, nematodes, fungi, parasitic plants, and human handling. They may also be spread by contact between plants and contaminated pots, benches, and tools, or through exchange of pollen, dripping sap, or the sale or exchange of infected plant divisions. Several practices help prevent the spread of viruses: sterilizing tools and pots after each use, eliminating insect carriers, removing or destroying infected plants, eliminating weeds which might be infected, and isolating new plants so that viruses are not brought into the growing area. Unfortunately, infected plants may appear free from symptoms, so that other plants become infected before symptoms of the disease show in the host plant.

Propagating virus-infected *Cymbidium* plants through shoot-tip culture is considered a means of salvaging a valuable plant; but the procedure is difficult to do correctly, and when done incorrectly, it results in spreading infected plants. Meristeming genera such as *Cattleya* does not result in virus-free plants. Using dry pollen from infected plants was once considered a safe means of propagation. Since infected pollen has been found, this is no longer considered a safe technique.

Indicator plants are sometimes used to detect viruses. When an indicator plant is inoculated with sap from a diseased orchid, it develops symptoms which confirm the presence of a virus. In the following list, known indicator plants are included under "Miscellaneous Notes" for each pathogen. Among orchids, *Spathoglottis* species are often used as indicators since they are highly susceptible to infection by viruses which attack other orchid genera. The *Handbook on Orchid Pests and Diseases* published by the American Orchid Society in 1986 discusses indicator plants, methods of inoculation, and the symptoms produced.

Symptoms of viral infection often resemble symptoms of other problems. Before assuming that a problem is a virus, it is wise to consider other possible causes. For example, chemicals may be toxic to some plants, so consider whether the symptoms are showing on the first new growth following treatment with a chemical. Because symptoms vary from plant to plant, it is nearly impossible to confirm viral infection without using indicator plants or obtaining a laboratory analysis. To prevent possible contamination of other plants, isolate any plant suspected of infection until a determination is made.

Viroids are particles which resemble viruses but lack the protein coat of a virus. They frequently cause abnormalities in coloration, often in the form of chlorotic streaking or mosaic patterns, and they may also cause stunting and growth distortion. Like mycoplasa and viruses, viroids may be controlled and destroyed in the growing area before plants are infected, but they cannot be eliminated once they have invaded a plant.

List of Pathogens

The following list corresponds to pathogens named in the preceding "Guide to Symptoms." For information about suggested chemical treatments, refer to the "Disease Treatment Summary" at the end of the list of pathogens. Note that numbers denoting classes of bactericides, fungicides, and so on correspond to this table. Thus "Fungicide-7" refers to several different chemicals and brand-name products which are grouped together in the table for ease of reference. "N/A" following any heading indicates that information is not available. See Section III of this Appendix for information about using chemicals.

Alternaria alternata (fungus). The following pathogens cause similar symptoms and respond to similar treatment: *Bipolaris setariae, Bipolaris sorokiniana, Bipolaris urochloae, Botrytis cinerea, Exserohilum rostratum,* and *Stemphylium* species of fungi.

COMMON NAMES: Necrotic flecks.

PLANTS AFFECTED: *Dendrobium.*

SYMPTOMS: Dark necrotic flecks on the flowers.

TREATMENT: Apply Fungicide-7.

CONTROL/PREVENTION: Methods of control are not established, but the information given for *Botrytis cinerea* may be helpful.

MISCELLANEOUS NOTES: The symptoms are thought to be aborted infections caused by one of the fungi listed. The disease is a common problem in Hawaii. Also see *Vanda* transit rot.

American anthracnose. See *Colletotrichum gloeosporiodes.*

Anthracnose orchid spot. See *Colletotrichum gloeosporiodes.*

Bacterial brown rot. See *Erwinia cypripedii.*

Bacterial brown spot. See *Pseudomonas cattleyae.*

Bacterial leaf rot. See *Erwinia chrysanthemi.*

Bacterial rot. See *Pseudomonas aeruginosa.*

Bacterial soft rot. See *Erwinia cartovora.*

Bacterial tip burn. See *Miltonia* scorch.

Bacterium cattleyae. See *Pseudomonas cattleyae.*

Bar mottle. See *Cymbidium* bar mottle.

Bean yellow mosaic (virus)

COMMON NAMES: Abbreviated BYMV.

PLANTS AFFECTED: *Calanthe, Masdevallia.*

SYMPTOMS: The leaves show a sunken mosaic or mottled pattern. The flowers are apparently unaffected.

TREATMENT: Destroy the plant when infection is confirmed.

CONTROL/PREVENTION: Isolate any plant suspected of infection. Sterilize cutting tools, control insects, and disinfect the growing area.

MISCELLANEOUS NOTES: The virus is reported in Japan and the United States. *Chenopodium quinoa* and *Vicia faba* are known indicator plants.

Bipolaris setariae. See *Alternaria alternata.*

Bipolaris sorokiniana. See *Alternaria alternata.*

Bipolaris urochloae. See *Alternaria alternata.*

Black rot. See *Phytophthora cactorum.*

Black sheath. See Fungi species.

Black spot on *Vanda*. See *Colletotrichum* and *Glomerella* species.

Black streak. See *Cymbidium* mosaic.

Blossom brown necrotic streak. See *Cymbidium* ringspot.

Blossom necrosis. See *Cymbidium* ringspot.

Blossom necrotic streak (virus)

COMMON NAMES: N/A.

PLANTS AFFECTED: *Cattleya.*

SYMPTOMS: Flowers develop brown streaks or spots approximately a week after opening. Leaves may develop long, irregular, yellowish streaks.

TREATMENT: Destroy the plant when infection is confirmed.

CONTROL/PREVENTION: Isolate any plant suspected of infection. The pathogen is known to be spread by contaminated cutting tools, so it is possible that insects also transmit the disease. Disinfect the growing area.

MISCELLANEOUS NOTES: *Chenopodium amaranticolor* is an indicator plant. Also see *Odontoglossum* ringspot.

Botryodiplodia theobromae (fungus)

COMMON NAMES: Brown spot.

PLANTS AFFECTED: N/A.

SYMPTOMS: Similar to those of anthracnose (*Colletotrichum gloeosporiodes*) without the concentric zones.

TREATMENT: Apply Fungicide, germicide-2. Also see treatments for *Colletotrichum gloeosporiodes.*

CONTROL/PREVENTION: Normal sanitation with good air movement in the growing area.

MISCELLANEOUS NOTES: A weak fungus that seldom attacks healthy plants, *B. theobromae* usually invades a cut or broken surface.

Botrytis cinerea (fungus). Pathogens known to cause similar symptoms include *Sclerotinia fuckeliana* (the sexual stage of *Botrytis)* and *Cladosporium oxysporum.* Other fungi may cause similar problems. Also see *Alternaria alternata* and *Vanda* transit rot.

COMMON NAMES: *Botrytis* blossom blight, *Botrytis* rot, *Dendrobium* blossom blight, flower blight, flower brown rot, flower brown speck, flower speck, flower spotting, petal blight, petal speck, *Vanilla* fruit deformation.

PLANTS AFFECTED: *Cattleya, Cymbidium, Dendrobium, Oncidium, Phalaenopsis, Spathoglottis, Vanda,* and older, fading flowers of many other genera.

SYMPTOMS: Very small, black or light brown, water-soaked spots on the flowers. The spots may enlarge and cover the entire flower. If conditions are moist, a grey fungal growth may appear on severely infected or decaying flowers. Also see *Curvularia geniculata. Vanilla* beans may be deformed.

TREATMENT: Remove infected flowers, then treat the plant with Bactericide, fungicide, nematocide-1, Fungicide-7, or Systemic fungicide-1 or -3.

CONTROL/PREVENTION: Remove and destroy affected flowers and old or infected plant material, since these are reservoirs of infection. In general, infection by these common grey molds may be reduced through careful sanitation, increased air circulation, reduced humidity, and warmer night temperatures. The fungus is most active during damp, cool weather but may occur anytime. It is common and cannot be eradicated. Since it is often transmitted by scale and insects, the growing area should be treated to control these pests as well as to control the fungus itself.

MISCELLANEOUS NOTES: N/A.

Botrytis species (fungus)

COMMON NAMES: *Cymbidium* tip burn.

PLANTS AFFECTED: *Cymbidium.*

SYMPTOMS: Dark spots that enlarge and merge until the entire leaf tip dies. Tips may be covered by powdery spore masses.

TREATMENT: Remove infected tissue and treat the plant with a fungicide. Bactericide, fungicide, nematocide-1, Fungicide-3 or -7, and Systemic fungicide-1 or -3 are recommended.

CONTROL/PREVENTION: Some growers believe the symptoms occur when salts are concentrated in the leaf tips, suggesting that *Botrytis* infection may be a particular problem in areas with hard water or when excess chemical fertilizers are used, damaging leaf tissues and making the plants more susceptible. If *Botrytis* disease is a recurring problem, flush the pots frequently and reduce the strength and frequency of fertilizer applications.

MISCELLANEOUS NOTES: *Botrytis* disease is reported world-wide.

Brown rot. See *Erwinia cypripedii.*

Brown spot. See *Botryodiplodia theobromae.*

Capnodium **species.** See *Gloeodes pomigena.*

Cattleya **flower disease.** See *Cymbidium* ringspot.

Cattleya **leaf necrosis.** See *Cymbidium* mosaic.

Cattleya **severe flower break.** See *Cymbidium* bar mottle.

Cercospora angraeci (fungus). Other *Cercospora* pathogens listed below cause similar symptoms and require similar treatment.

COMMON NAMES: *Cercospora* leaf spot.

PLANTS AFFECTED: *Angraecum, Dendrobium, Odontoglossum.*

SYMPTOMS: Infection shows first as a yellow spot on the underside of the leaf. As the spots enlarge in irregular patterns, they become sunken and turn purplish brown to purplish black. The top surface of the leaf first becomes chlorotic and finally necrotic.

TREATMENT: Remove and burn affected tissue. Spray or soak plants with Fungicide-2, -7, or -18 or Systemic fungicide-1 with a wetting agent. If fungicides are applied as a spray, the underside of the leaves must be treated in order for the fungicide to be effective. Three fungicide applications at intervals of 7–15 days should control the fungus.

CONTROL/PREVENTION: Normal sanitation with good air movement in the growing area. Apply a preventive spray at monthly intervals if needed, or when new plants are brought into the growing area.

MISCELLANEOUS NOTES: The disease is reported in England, France, Malaysia, and Florida in the United States. It is known to affect *Dendrobium* only in Malaysia. In Florida, only *Angraecum* infections are reported. Spider-mite damage is easily confused with *Cercospora* leaf spots.

Cercospora dendrobii (fungus)

COMMON NAMES: N/A.

PLANTS AFFECTED: *Dendrobium, Odontoglossum.*

SYMPTOMS: The first symptom is light yellow spots on the underside of leaves. Soon after infection occurs, the yellow-green area may be noted on the top surface of the leaf. The spots continue to enlarge in a circular or irregular pattern and may eventually cover the entire leaf. With age, the spots become slightly sunken and necrotic and change to purple-brown or purple-black. The advancing margin remains yellow. Heavily infected leaves usually fall from the plant prematurely, especially if the infection started near the base of the leaf.

TREATMENT: Remove and burn infected tissue. Plants may be sprayed or soaked with Fungicide-2, -7, or -18. Systemic fungicide-1 with a wetting agent is effective against most *Cercospora* species. It should be applied weekly until the infection is controlled. If fungicides are applied as a spray, the underside of the leaves must be treated in order for the fungicide to be effective.

Other susceptible plants should receive at least 3 fungicide applications at intervals of 7–15 days to control the fungus. Repeat the spray at monthly intervals if needed, or when new plants are brought into the growing area.

CONTROL/PREVENTION: Normal sanitation with good air movement in the growing area.

MISCELLANEOUS NOTES: This pathogen affects only *Dendrobium*—both deciduous and evergreen—and *Odontoglossum.* Spider-mite damage is easily confused with *Cercospora* leaf spots. The disease is reported in Florida and Japan.

Cercospora epipactidis (fungus)

COMMON NAMES: N/A.

PLANTS AFFECTED: *Anguloa, Ansellia, Bletia, Brassia, Calanthe, Catasetum, Coelogyne, Cycnoches, Cyrtopodium, Dendrochilum, Epipactis, Eulophia, Gongora, Lycaste, Maxillaria, Monomeria, Neomoorea, Phaius, Spathoglottis, Stanhopea, Xylobium, Zygopetalum.*

SYMPTOMS: On *Phaius tankervilleae*, the initial symptoms are tiny, sunken yellow spots on the underside of leaves. As the disease progresses, the spots continue to enlarge to approximately ¼ in. (6 mm) across. They then turn purplish black with a somewhat darker, slightly raised margin. The spots may merge to form large, irregular lesions. The center of the spots may fall out with age.

TREATMENT: Spraying or soaking the plants with Fungicide-2, -7, or -18 or Systemic fungicide-1 with a wetting agent is effective against some *Cercospora* species. Other susceptible plants should receive 3 fungicide applications at intervals of 7–15 days to control the fungus. If fungicides are applied as a spray, the underside of the leaves must be treated in order for the fungicide to be effective.

CONTROL/PREVENTION: Normal sanitation with good air movement in the growing area. If the fungus is a continuing problem, monthly fungicide sprays may offer effective prevention. New plants should be treated before they are brought into the growing area.

MISCELLANEOUS NOTES: Spider-mite damage is easily confused with *Cercospora* leaf spots. This pathogen is reported in Italy, Germany, Mexico, Russia, and numerous areas in the United States.

Cercospora leaf spot. See *Cercospora angraeci*.

Cercospora odontoglossi (fungus)

COMMON NAMES: N/A.

PLANTS AFFECTED: *Brassavola, Broughtonia, Cattleya, Caularthron, Epidendrum, Laelia, Schomburgkia, Sophronitis.*

SYMPTOMS: This is the most serious leaf-spotting fungus that attacks the *Cattleya* family. Seedlings and small plants first show signs of infection as tiny, slightly raised, dark brown spots on the underside of leaves. The spots are first chlorotic and finally necrotic. The disease spreads rapidly, eventually affecting and killing the entire leaf. Seedlings and small plants may be killed by this fungus. If all the leaves on small seedlings become infected, the plant dies. If the infected seedling is strong enough, it may produce a new growth; but if the disease is untreated, the new growth is also infected.

Older seedlings and mature plants first show symptoms as slightly sunken, yellow, round or irregular areas on the underside of leaves. With age these spots turn purplish black. The top surface is chlorotic initially but becomes necrotic. The disease is seldom fatal to mature plants.

TREATMENT: Remove and destroy affected tissue. Spray or soak plants with Fungicide-2, -7, or -18 or Systemic fungicide-1 with a wetting agent. Three fungicide applications at intervals of 7–15 days should control the fungus. If fungicides are applied as a spray, the underside of the leaves must be treated in order for the fungicide to be effective.

CONTROL/PREVENTION: Normal sanitation with good air movement in the growing area. Preventive fungicide sprays may be applied at monthly intervals if reinfection is a problem. New plants should be treated before they are brought into the growing area.

MISCELLANEOUS NOTES: Both species and hybrids may be affected. Infections are reported in Brazil, France, Venezuela, and several areas in the United States. Spider-mite damage is easily confused with *Cercospora* leaf spots.

Cercospora peristeriae (fungus)

COMMON NAMES: N/A.

PLANTS AFFECTED: *Peristeria elata* is the only known host.

SYMPTOMS: Infections show first on the lower leaf surface as yellowish to pale brown oval or elongated spots. Within a few days, spots may appear on both surfaces of the leaf. As the disease progresses, the spots become tan with a purple border and enlarge to 0.2–2.0 in. (5–50 mm) across. Sporing bodies develop on the underside of the leaf.

TREATMENT: Remove and destroy affected tissue. Spray or soak affected plants with Fungicide-2, -7, or -18 or Systemic fungicide-1 with a wetting agent. Three applications at intervals of 7–15 days should control the fungus in a growing area. If fungicides are applied as a spray, the underside of the leaves must be treated in order for the fungicide to be effective.

CONTROL/PREVENTION: Normal sanitation with good air movement in the growing area. Fungicide sprays may be used at monthly intervals if needed. New plants should be treated before they are brought into the growing area.

MISCELLANEOUS NOTES: Spider-mite damage is easily confused with *Cercospora* leaf spots.

Cercospora species I (fungus)

COMMON NAMES: N/A.

PLANTS AFFECTED: *Aerides, Arachnis, Ascocentrum, Doritis, Phalaenopsis, Renanthera, Rhynchostylis, Vanda.*

SYMPTOMS: Purple-brown spots appear on the underside of leaves. The tiny, sunken spots are usually less than 0.05 in. (1 mm) across but may merge to form a larger spot. The upper leaf surface is initially yellow-green but may become purple-brown with age.

TREATMENT: Soak or spray plants with Fungicide-2, -7, or -18 or Systemic fungicide-1 with a wetting agent. Three applications at 15-day intervals should control the fungus. If fungicides are applied as a spray, the underside of the leaves must be treated in order for the fungicide to be effective.

CONTROL/PREVENTION: Normal sanitation with good air movement in the growing area. If infection is a continuing problem, monthly preventive sprays may be applied. New plants should be treated before they are brought into the growing area.

MISCELLANEOUS NOTES: The symptoms may be slightly different depending on the genus infected. Spider-mite damage is easily confused with *Cercospora* leaf spots.

Cercospora species II (fungus)

COMMON NAMES: N/A.

PLANTS AFFECTED: *Cattleya* and related genera.

SYMPTOMS: Tiny, purple-brown spots occur on the underside of leaves. They are usually slightly sunken and 0.05 in. (1 mm) or less in diameter. The upper leaf surface is light yellow-green. When entire leaves are infected, they may fall prematurely. The oldest leaves are usually the most severely infected, but leaves which are not fully mature may also be attacked.

TREATMENT: Spraying or soaking the plants with Fungicide-2, -7, or -18 or Systemic fungicide-1 with a wetting agent is effective against some *Cercospora* species. Three applications at 15-day intervals should eradicate the fungus from a growing area. Repeat the spray at monthly intervals if needed, or when new plants are brought into the growing area. If fungicides are applied as a spray, the underside of the leaves must be treated in order for the fungicide to be effective.

CONTROL/PREVENTION: Normal sanitation with good air movement in the growing area.

MISCELLANEOUS NOTES: Reported primarily in the southern United States, the disease has also been found in the northeastern states. Spider-mite damage is easily confused with *Cercospora* leaf spots.

Cercospora species III (fungus)

COMMON NAMES: N/A.

PLANTS AFFECTED: *Comparettia, Miltonia, Oncidium, Rodriguezia.*

SYMPTOMS: Tiny, sunken spots appear on the underside of leaves. Usually less than 0.05 in. (1 mm) across, they are reddish purple with a slightly raised tan center. With age, the spots merge and become longer, but they retain the reddish purple color.

TREATMENT: Remove and burn infected tissue. Plants may be soaked or sprayed with Fungicide-2, -7, or -18 or Systemic fungicide-1 with a wetting agent. Three applications at intervals of 7–15 days should control the fungus. If fungicides are applied as a spray, the underside of the leaves must be treated in order for the fungicide to be effective.

CONTROL/PREVENTION: Normal sanitation with good air movement in the growing area. Repeat the spray at monthly intervals if needed, or when new plants are brought into the growing area.

MISCELLANEOUS NOTES: The symptoms may differ slightly depending on the genus infected. The disease affects both species and hybrids and is reported in the southern United States. Spider-mite damage is easily confused with *Cercospora* leaf spots.

Cercospora species IV (fungus)

COMMON NAMES: N/A.

PLANTS AFFECTED: *Cymbidiella, Cymbidium, Grammatophyllum.*

SYMPTOMS: Tiny, round spots appear on the underside of leaves. The slightly sunken spots are dark brown and usually less than 0.05 in. (1 mm) across, but several spots may merge to form a larger spot. A yellow-green spot shows on the upper leaf surface; with age, it becomes brown with a slight yellow halo. The symptoms are usually more severe on older leaves.

TREATMENT: Spraying or soaking the plants with Fungicide-2, -7, or -18 or Systemic fungicide-1 with a wetting agent is effective against many *Cercospora* species. Three applications at intervals of 7–15 days should control the fungus. If fungicides are applied as a spray, the underside of the leaves must be treated in order for the fungicide to be effective.

CONTROL/PREVENTION: Normal sanitation and good air movement in the growing area may help reduce the spread of this disease. Preventive sprays may be applied at monthly intervals if needed, and new plants should be treated before they are placed in the growing area.

MISCELLANEOUS NOTES: Symptoms may be slightly different depending on the genus infected. The symptoms are easily confused with spider-mite damage. The disease is reported in the southern United States.

Chlorotic leaf streak of *Oncidium* (virus)

COMMON NAMES: N/A.

PLANTS AFFECTED: The hybrid *Oncidium* Golden Shower is the primary host, but *Cattleya, Phalaenopsis,* and *Renanthera* have also been infected.

SYMPTOMS: Chlorotic streaks of varying length, often with ridging, thickening, or curling of the leaves.

TREATMENT: Destroy the plant when infection is confirmed.

CONTROL/PREVENTION: Isolate any plant suspected of infection. Sterilize cutting tools, control insects, and disinfect the growing area with Algicide, bactericide, fungicide-1 or with a disinfectant.

MISCELLANEOUS NOTES: These symptoms are caused by *Cymbidium* mosaic (CyMV) and tobacco mosaic–orchid strain (TMV-O) in combination. The disease is currently reported only in the Philippines.

Cladosporium oxysporum. See *Botrytis cinerea.*

Coleosporium bletiae (fungus)

COMMON NAMES: Rust.

PLANTS AFFECTED: *Phaius.*

SYMPTOMS: Orange rust pustules on either leaf surface or on the flower spike. The earliest symptom is the appearance of tiny yellow spots, which become orange spore masses in just a few days. The spots enlarge in a circular pattern. The outside margin is orange, due to the spore masses, while the center turns brown and often falls out. A yellow halo surrounds the spots. Individual lesions on the leaves are usually less than ½ in. (13 mm) across. The oval lesions on the flower stalks are often larger.

TREATMENT: Isolate infected plants and remove all affected tissue. Spray plants with Fungicide-7 or -18 mixed with a wetting agent. New chemicals effective against rust are being introduced and may soon be approved for orchids: consult your local agricultural agents or fellow orchid growers.

CONTROL/PREVENTION: Isolate the plant and disinfect the growing area.

MISCELLANEOUS NOTES: N/A.

Colletotrichum and *Glomerella* species (fungus)

COMMON NAMES: Black spot of *Vanda* flowers.

PLANTS AFFECTED: *Vanda tricolor.*

SYMPTOMS: Discoloration of the petals with black spots on the lip. Also see *Vanda* transit rot.

TREATMENT: Spray blossoms with Disinfectant-4.

CONTROL/PREVENTION: Normal sanitation with good air movement in the growing area.

MISCELLANEOUS NOTES: The disease is reported in the United States. The same fungi may also cause other orchid diseases.

Colletotrichum cinctum. See *Colletotrichum gloeosporiodes.*

Colletotrichum gloeosporiodes (fungus). Other pathogens which cause similar symptoms include *Calospora vanillae, Colletotrichum cinctum, Colletotrichum orchidearum, Gloeosporium orchidearum, Glomerella cincta, Glomerella cingulata,* and *Glomerella vanillae.* The *Colletotrichum* pathogens are the most destructive and are nearly always those responsible for disease in orchids.

COMMON NAMES: American anthracnose, Anthracnose orchid spot.

PLANTS AFFECTED: *Aerides, Angraecum, Brassia, Cattleya, Coelia, Coelogyne, Cymbidium, Cypripedium, Dendrobium, Dichaea, Epidendrum, Eria, Gongora, Isochilus, Laelia, Lycaste, Malaxis, Maxillaria, Miltonia, Odontoglossum, Oncidium, Ornithidium, Paphiopedilum, Phaius, Phalaenopsis, Pholidota, Pleurothallis, Polystachya, Sobralia, Spiranthes, Stanhopea, Tetramicra, Trichopilia, Vanda, Vandopsis, Vanilla, Xylobium, Zygopetalum,* and other genera.

SYMPTOMS: This disease infects the aerial portion of the plant. Flowers develop watery, black or brown pustules which are usually raised and occur on the underside of older sepals and petals. The spots may merge and cover the entire flower. The leaves are most often attacked. Leaf tips turn brown beginning at the apex and proceeding toward the base. Dark brown or light grey patches develop, sometimes as concentric rings or as numerous dark bands across the leaf. The affected area is usually sharply defined and somewhat sunken, while the remainder of the leaf appears normal. Sporing bodies develop in the infected area.

TREATMENT: Remove dead tissue by cutting through healthy tissue 1–2 in. (2.5–5.0 cm) below the diseased area. Paint the cut surface with Systemic fungicide-1 mixed with a wetting agent, or paint it with Fungicide, germicide-2. In addition to treating the cut surface, spray or drench plants with Systemic fungicide-3 or Fungicide-1, -2, -7, or -18. Spraying with Systemic fungicide-1 is also effective for *Fusarium,* which often attacks the flowers of plants weakened by *Colletotrichum.*

CONTROL/PREVENTION: Normal sanitation, good air movement, lower temperatures, and increased light may help reduce the spread of this disease.

MISCELLANEOUS NOTES: The pathogen is most active in warm weather when light is low and moisture is high. Conditions which increase plants' susceptibility to attack include excessive nitrogen, exposure to some chemicals, and generally poor cultivation. *Colletotrichum gloeosporiodes* always infects the aerial portion of the plant and tends to invade weak or injured plants. It often spreads rapidly toward the base of the plant, which may die if left untreated. The disease symptoms occur world-wide but may be caused by different pathogens in different regions.

Colletotrichum orchidearum. See *Colletotrichum gloeosporiodes.*

Color break. See *Cymbidium* ringspot.

Crown rot. See *Phytophthora cactorum.*

Cucumber mosaic (virus)

COMMON NAMES: Abbreviated CMV.

PLANTS AFFECTED: *Dendrobium, Miltonia.*

SYMPTOMS: Flowers may be affected with mild color break. The leaves show faint chlorotic patches and rings. The appearance is different from that of chlorosis caused by *Cymbidium* mosaic (CyMV).

TREATMENT: Destroy the plant when infection is confirmed.

CONTROL/PREVENTION: Isolate any plant suspected of infection. This highly infectious pathogen is present in sap and easily transmitted by aphids or contaminated tools. Sterilize cutting tools, control insects, and disinfect the growing area.

MISCELLANEOUS NOTES: The disease is reported in Korea and Japan. Fortunately, this virus does not cause infection in *Cattleya, Cymbidium, Oncidium,* or *Zygopetalum.* Known indicator plants include *Chenopodium amaranticolor, Citrullus vulgaris, Datura stramonium,* and *Sesamum.*

Curvularia **flower blight.** See *Curvularia geniculata.*

Curvularia geniculata (fungus)

COMMON NAMES: *Curvularia* leaf spot, flower blight.

PLANTS AFFECTED: N/A.

SYMPTOMS: Many tiny, slightly sunken, light to dark brown, circular or oval lesions on either or both surfaces of sepals, petals, or flower spikes. Similar symptoms are caused by *Botrytis cinerea.* Infections are usually first noticed on the flowers.

TREATMENT: Remove damaged tissue and paint the cut with Systemic fungicide-1. Spray leaves and flowers with Systemic fungicide-1 or Fungicide-7, or use the treatments listed for *Colletotrichum gloeosporiodes.*

CONTROL/PREVENTION: Increasing air movement and decreasing humidity may help prevent the disease from spreading.

MISCELLANEOUS NOTES: The disease invades the plant through damaged leaf tissue. It is reported world-wide.

Curvularia **leaf spot.** See *Curvularia geniculata.*

Cymbidium **bar mottle** (virus)

COMMON NAMES: Bar mottle, *Cattleya* severe flower break.

PLANTS AFFECTED: *Cattleya, Cymbidium,* and possibly other orchid genera.

SYMPTOMS: *Cattleya* plants are most likely to show signs of infection in the flowers. Symptoms include strong color variegation, mottling, distortion, and malformation. Weakened plants become stunted and produce few flowers. In *Cymbidium* plants, the infection usually shows first in the leaves.

Affected leaves show yellow blotches or streaks or bar-shaped discolorations which may be yellow or light to dark green. The discolorations often appear in broken lines. The affected area later becomes necrotic and develops ridges and bumps.

TREATMENT: Destroy the plant when infection is confirmed.

CONTROL/PREVENTION: Remove infected plants from the growing area, control aphids, screen greenhouse vents, and disinfect the growing area. The disease is spread from area to area through propagation of infected plants. The green peach aphid is the only insect known to carry the disease from plant to plant.

MISCELLANEOUS NOTES: Symptoms may result from *Cymbidium* mosaic (CyMV) alone or in combination with other viruses.

Cymbidium chlorotic leaf streak. See Tomato ringspot.

Cymbidium diamond mottle. See *Cymbidium* ringspot.

Cymbidium mild mosaic (virus). Abbreviated CyMMV, this virus is known to affect *Cymbidium*, but information on symptoms is not available. The primary means of transmission is infected sap, carried by insects or contaminated tools. *Chenopodium amaranticolor* is an indicator plant. The virus is reported in Korea.

Cymbidium mosaic (virus)

COMMON NAMES: Often abbreviated CyMV, this virus may be called black streak, *Cattleya* leaf necrosis, mosaic, necrotic mosaic, necrotic spot, necrotic streak, orchid mosaic, or white cell necrosis.

PLANTS AFFECTED: *Ada, Aerides, Angraecum, Arundina, Brassavola, Calanthe, Catasetum, Cattleya, Cymbidium, Dendrobium, Epidendrum, Gongora, Grammatophyllum, Laelia, Lycaste, Miltonia, Odontoglossum, Oncidium, Peristeria, Phaius, Phalaenopsis, Phragmipedium, Pleurothallis, Rhynchostylis, Schomburgkia, Selenipedium, Spathoglottis, Trichopilia, Vanda, Vanilla, Zygopetalum,* and probably other genera.

SYMPTOMS: The disease has variable symptoms depending on the species, the plant part affected, and the environmental conditions. This variability has resulted in numerous common names for a single disease organism.

Flowers on infected plants may be symptom-free. White *Cattleya* flowers show necrotic spots and streaks. Infected flowers may appear healthy until several days after they open, when the symptoms begin to show. Lavender *Cattleya* flowers show white cell necrosis, usually along the center rib of the petals, 1–2 weeks after the flowers open. However, bleached spots on lavender *Cattleya* flowers may result from air pollution rather than a virus, while color breaking in lavender *Cattleya* is consistently associated with tobacco mosaic–orchid strain (TMV-O). *Dendrobium superbum* may have color break in the flowers. *Phalaenopsis* flowers show symptoms similar to those of *Cattleya. Cymbidium, Dendrobium, Epidendrum, Laelia,* and *Vanda* flowers are also affected.

In the early stage of infection, the leaves usually develop irregular yellow patches known as chlorotic mosaic. Later, irregular, elongated streaks of dead tissue are often found on the underside of leaves, and some leaves may die. Black necrotic spots may develop, and the area is sometimes sunken. Other patterns may appear; or, in the right environment, infected plants may be symptom-free.

The leaves of *Cattleya* and related orchids show light brown pitting and irregular sunken areas on the underside of leaves, particularly near the tip. Black or brown rings, streaks, or blotches are usually the first symptoms on older leaves, but the leaves are eventually covered with spots and blotches. Infected plants may die within a few months. When the disease is indicated by these symptoms, it is often called *Cattleya* leaf necrosis.

Cymbidium develop mild chlorotic mosaic or blotches in new shoots about 3 weeks after infection. The affected areas enlarge, and symptoms become more pronounced as the leaves mature. *Dendrobium* leaves and flowers may show symptoms similar to those described for *Cattleya.* Sometimes, however, *Dendrobium* plants show no symptoms yet test positive for the virus.

Infected *Epidendrum* plants are very stunted, with sunken, brown or black, oval spots which usually occur on the underside of leaves.

Oncidium Golden Shower plants show the infection as sunken brown or black spots on the underside of leaves. The spots sometimes appear in concentric rings, with a few spots breaking through to the upper leaf surface.

Phalaenopsis symptoms are highly variable; they include light green and chlorotic patches, deep furrowing and ridging, and necrotic, water-soaked areas. Necrosis is more pronounced on the underside of leaves. Leaves may drop if the infection is severe. Sometimes, however, *Phalaenopsis* plants show no symptoms yet test positive for the virus.

Spathoglottis plants usually show diamond-shaped chlorotic patches which become necrotic.

TREATMENT: Destroy the plant if infection is confirmed.

CONTROL/PREVENTION: Isolate any plant suspected of infection. Infected cutting tools are the most common means of transmission, but the virus is present in the sap and may be transmitted by contaminated pots, dripping water, and insects. Disinfect the growing area. Because plants may carry CyMV without showing symptoms, other plants may be contaminated before the grower is aware of a problem. Careful sanitation is important.

MISCELLANEOUS NOTES: Unlike many viruses, CyMV occurs naturally only in orchids. *Cassia occidentalis* (and possibly other *Cassia* species), *Chenopodium amaranticolor, Chenopodium quinoa, Datura stramonium,* and *Tetragonia expansa* can be artificially infected and therefore serve as indicator plants.

Cymbidium ringspot (virus)

COMMON NAMES: Abbreviated CyRV, this virus is sometimes called necrotic ringspot or severe leaf necrosis. Apparently it is a form of white clover virus.

PLANTS AFFECTED: *Cymbidium* is the primary host, but *Cattleya, Spathoglottis,* and *Trichosma* may also be susceptible.

SYMPTOMS: Leaves may have faint chlorotic ringspot patterns. Plants may be stunted, and old shoots may die. No symptoms were reported for flowers.

TREATMENT: Destroy the plant.

CONTROL/PREVENTION: Isolate any plant suspected of infection. The virus is carried in sap and soil. Sterilize cutting tools, control insects, and disinfect the growing area.

MISCELLANEOUS NOTES: Reported in southern England, this disease is severe, highly contagious, and often lethal to plants. Fortunately, it is uncommon. *Chenopodium amaranticolor, Emilia sangitota, Nicotiana clevelandii,* and *Phaseolus vulgaris* 'The Prince' are indicator plants.

Cymbidium **soft rot.** See *Erwinia carotovora.*

Cypripedium filamentous (virus). Abbreviated CF, this virus was reported in Germany in *Cypripedium calceolus.* Information on symptoms or means of transmission is not available.

Damping off. See *Fusarium; Phytophthora cactorum; Pythium ultimum; Rhizoctonia.*

Dendrobium **blossom blight.** See *Botrytis cinerea.*

Dendrobium **leaf spot.** See *Septoria selenophomoides;* Short orchid rhabdovirus.

Dendrobium **mosaic** (virus)

COMMON NAMES: Abbreviated DeMV.

PLANTS AFFECTED: *Dendrobium.*

SYMPTOMS: Sharply defined mosaic and green concentric ring patterns on older leaves. Young leaves may show light mottling, but flowers are not affected.

TREATMENT: Destroy the plant when infection is confirmed.

CONTROL/PREVENTION: Isolate any plant suspected of infection. The virus is transmitted by aphids and contaminated cutting tools. Sterilize cutting tools, control insects, and disinfect the growing area.

MISCELLANEOUS NOTES: *Chenopodium amaranticolor* and *C. quinoa* serve as indicator plants. This virus, currently reported only in Japan, does not cause infection in *Cattleya, Cymbidium, Miltonia, Oncidium,* or *Zygopetalum* even when these plants are deliberately inoculated.

Dendrobium **vein necrosis** (virus). Abbreviated DVN, this virus was reported in Germany in *Dendrobium* plants. Flowers and leaves develop vein necrosis. The disease is uncommon.

Dendrobium **viral disease** (virus)

COMMON NAMES: Abbreviated DV.

PLANTS AFFECTED: *Dendrobium ionoglossum* and *D. antennatum* are the primary hosts, but other *Dendrobium* species and hybrids may also be susceptible.

SYMPTOMS: Yellow chlorotic areas and large, dark brown or black, ring-shaped spots appear on the leaves.

TREATMENT: Destroy the plant when infection is confirmed.

CONTROL/PREVENTION: Isolate any plant suspected of infection. Sterilize cutting tools, control insects, and disinfect the growing area.

MISCELLANEOUS NOTES: DV is reported in New Guinea and Germany.

Dendrobium **white streak** (virus). This disease is reported in Hawaii. *Dendrobium* is the primary host, but *Phalaenopsis* may also be susceptible. The virus causes white streaks on the flowers. Information on means of transmission or indicator plants is not available.

Diplodia laeliocattleyae (fungus)

COMMON NAMES: *Diplodia* leaf spot, leaf spot.

PLANTS AFFECTED: *Cattleya* and related genera.

SYMPTOMS: Small yellow spots on either leaf surface. They enlarge with age and become greasy, brown to black lesions. Black sporing bodies may be visible on older lesions.

TREATMENT: Apply Fungicide-1.

CONTROL/PREVENTION: Normal sanitation measures should prevent the spread of this disease.

MISCELLANEOUS NOTES: This fungus is rare and affects only old or damaged tissues.

Diplodia **leaf spot.** See *Diplodia laeliocattleyae.*

Erwinia carotovora (bacterium)

COMMON NAMES: Bacterial soft rot, *Cymbidium* soft rot, soft rot.

PLANTS AFFECTED: *Brassavola, Cattleya* and closely related genera, *Cymbidium, Cycnoches, Lockhartia, Odontoglossum, Oncidium, Paphiopedilum, Phalaenopsis,* and probably other orchid genera.

SYMPTOMS: Small, water-soaked spots appear on the leaves and eventually become dark streaks. If unchecked, the infection may rapidly cover the entire leaf. The rot spreads rapidly in the leaves and roots and more slowly in the rhizomes or pseudobulbs. This wet rot may have a foul odor.

Pseudobulbs or crown develop a progressive rot which has a water-soaked advancing margin, while the tissues behind it are brown. The oldest portion of the infection may be black. Infected bulbs are often soft, shriveled, and dark.

In *Phalaenopsis,* the disease spreads so rapidly that plants may be completely rotted in 2–3 days. Bacteria enter the plant through wounds.

TREATMENT: If the plant is valuable and the disease is localized, remove the plant from the growing area, then cut off and destroy all tissue showing infection. Spray or paint cuts with Algicide, bactericide, fungicide-1 or a paste of Fungicide, germicide-1. Localized infection may be swabbed with mercuric chloride (1 : 1,000 dilution).

CONTROL/PREVENTION: *Erwinia carotovora* is a highly contagious disease. Destroy affected plants, and immediately disinfect the entire growing area with a 10% sodium hypochlorite (bleach) solution or a 1 : 1000 (¾ tsp. per gal.—0.98 ml/liter) mercuric chloride solution. Wear protective clothing when using mercuric chloride, and handle the compound very cautiously.

Avoid overhead watering if the disease is present, as the infection is spread when fluids from infected plants drip on other plants. Treat nearby plants as well as those that are diseased, and take measures to control insects. Periodic sprays of Algicide, bactericide, fungicide-1 help to prevent infection.

When dividing plants, use careful sanitation measures to prevent the slower rot of pseudobulbs and rhizomes. Disinfect tools after each cut. Paint cut surfaces with a paste of Fungicide-9 or asphaltum paint.

MISCELLANEOUS NOTES: The disease is rare in orchids, affecting *Cattleya* most seriously. But it affects many vegetables and ornamentals and is so devastating that infected plants are best destroyed. Infection enters the plant through wounds or breaks in the plant's outer skin, which may result from insects, mechanical injury, or fungal infection.

Erwinia chrysanthemi (bacterium)

COMMON NAMES: Bacterial leaf rot, *Erwinia chrysanthemi* soft rot.

PLANTS AFFECTED: *Cymbidium, Dendrobium, Grammatophyllum, Oncidium, Phalaenopsis, Vanda.*

SYMPTOMS: Soft rot of the leaves and pseudobulbs. *Dendrobium* leaves appear yellow and water-soaked and become black and sunken. *Vanda* leaves develop translucent patches which become black and sunken. *Grammatophyllum* leaves have water-soaked, brownish spots which become black and sunken.

TREATMENT: Remove diseased tissue and spray with Fungicide, germicide-2 or Algicide, bactericide, fungicide-1. Disinfectant-2 is specifically recommended for *Cymbidium, Oncidium,* and *Phalaenopsis,* as are Bactericide-1 and -2. Bactericides are toxic to many orchids and should be used cautiously.

CONTROL/PREVENTION: Normal sanitation and increased air movement may reduce the risk of infecting other plants. Preventive sprays of Fungicide, germicide-2 may be applied before and during wet weather.

MISCELLANEOUS NOTES: This disease occurs primarily in Hawaii.

Erwinia chrysanthemi soft rot. See *Erwinia chrysanthemi.*

Erwinia cypripedii (bacterium)

COMMON NAMES: *Erwinia* f. *cypripedii,* commonly called bacterial brown rot, brown rot, *Paphiopedilum* brown rot, *Paphiopedilum* brown spot.

PLANTS AFFECTED: *Cypripedium, Paphiopedilum.* The disease also occurs occasionally in *Brassia* and *Miltonia* hybrids, *Phalaenopsis, Phragmipedium,* and many other orchid genera.

SYMPTOMS: Water-soaked spots appear, often near the center of the leaf. They are usually small and may be either round or oval. As the disease progresses, the color of the spot changes from light brown to very dark chestnut-brown. The spot enlarges in all directions and may reach the growing crown before the leaf tip is affected. If untreated, the disease quickly spreads throughout the plant, leaving it a dark, shriveled mass. *Paphiopedilum* leaves develop small, round spots that are initially yellow and water-soaked but eventually become reddish brown and sunken.

TREATMENT: Remove infected tissue down to the rhizome, and disinfect tools after each cut. Soak the plant for several hours in Fungicide, germicide-2 or Disinfectant-4. Repeat this treatment 2–3 times every few days. An alternative treatment is spraying with Algicide, bactericide, fungicide-1.

CONTROL/PREVENTION: The pathogen favors warm, moist conditions, so if infection occurs, keep leaves dry, reduce temperature and humidity if possible, and increase air circulation. Give adjacent plants a preventive spray with Fungicide-3 or Algicide, bactericide, fungicide-1, since the disease can be devastating if not controlled. Periodic sprays with Algicide, bactericide, fungicide-1 may be used throughout the year to help prevent infection.

MISCELLANEOUS NOTES: The symptoms are easily confused with the disease caused by *Pseudomonas cypripedii.*

European anthracnose. See *Gloeosporium affine.*

Exserohilum rostratum. See *Alternaria alternata.*

Flower blight. See *Botrytis cinerea; Fusarium moniliforme.*

Flower break. See *Cymbidium* ringspot; *Vanda* mosaic.

Flower break, symmetrical (virus)

COMMON NAMES: N/A.

PLANTS AFFECTED: *Cattleya* and possibly other orchids.

SYMPTOMS: Symmetrical variegations appear in colored areas of the petals and at sepal margins. The center of the petals is not usually affected. Leaves may develop a light mosaic mottling.

TREATMENT: Destroy the plant when infection is confirmed.

CONTROL/PREVENTION: Isolate any plant suspected of infection. Infections are transmitted by insects and contaminated cutting tools. Sterilize cutting tools, control insects, and disinfect the growing area.

MISCELLANEOUS NOTES: The unnamed virus that causes this condition occurs world-wide.

Flower brown rot. See *Botrytis cinerea.*

Flower brown speck. See *Botrytis cinerea.*

Flower necrosis (virus). White-flowered *Cattleya* develop necrotic streaks and spots on the flowers without foliage symptoms. Symptoms are apparently caused by a strain of *Cymbidium* mosaic (CyMV), perhaps in combination with *Odontoglossum* ringspot. Also see *Cymbidium* ringspot. The disease occurs in Europe, Italy, and the United States.

Flower speck. See *Botrytis cinerea.*

Flower spotting. See *Botrytis cinerea.*

Fly speck. See *Microthyriella rubi.*

Fungi species

COMMON NAMES: Black sheath.

PLANTS AFFECTED: All orchids that produce flowers in sheaths.

SYMPTOMS: The sheath is discolored and may rot, spreading the infection to flower buds.

TREATMENT: Remove the sheath, and allow the area to dry. Apply Fungicide-2 or -17 or Fungicide, germicide-2.

CONTROL/PREVENTION: This disease usually occurs when water, from either excessively high humidity or careless watering, is allowed to soak the sheath or stand in the area between the leaf and the sheath.

MISCELLANEOUS NOTES: If the sheath is treated quickly and kept dry, the infection may not spread to the buds. The problem is reported in the United States and probably occurs world-wide.

Fusarium batatis var. *vanillae* (fungus)

COMMON NAMES: *Vanilla* root rot, *Vanilla* wilt.

PLANTS AFFECTED: *Vanilla planifolia. Vanilla barbellata* and *V. pompona* are also susceptible, while *V. phaeantha* is somewhat resistant.

SYMPTOMS: The roots turn brown and rot. Depending on available moisture, the rot may be dry or soft and watery. Underground roots are usually destroyed before the aerial roots begin to show signs of infection. When the infection is firmly established, growth slows, and the plant eventually dies.

TREATMENT: Systemic fungicide-1 is being used experimentally.

CONTROL/PREVENTION: Use only disease-free plants for propagating or stem cuttings.

MISCELLANEOUS NOTES: The disease was originally thought to be caused by *Fusarium oxysporum*. It occurs in commercial *Vanilla*-growing areas of the world.

Fusarium flower blight. See *Fusarium moniliforme*.

Fusarium moniliforme f. *cattleyae* (fungus)

COMMON NAMES: Flower blight, *Fusarium* flower blight.

PLANTS AFFECTED: *Arachnis, Dendrobium*, and perhaps others.

SYMPTOMS: Flowers, buds, and inflorescences develop sunken, dark brown to black lesions which are often covered with powdery white mycelia and small pink sporing bodies. Severe infections cause the flowers to yellow and drop, usually in the bud stage. This pathogen is related to the fungi known to cause wilt.

Dendrobium leaves develop small spots, as do the leaves of several other orchids. The disease organism usually invades through wounded tissue. The symptoms are similar to those found on the flowers, except that sporing bodies are not usually present.

TREATMENT: Remove infected areas, and spray plants every 4–7 days with Fungicide-1, -2, or -18. For additional control measures, see *Colletotrichum gloeosporiodes*.

CONTROL/PREVENTION: Normal sanitation with good air movement in the growing area.

MISCELLANEOUS NOTES: The disease is prevalent throughout the United States and is reported world-wide. It is apparently one of the causes of bud drop in Singapore.

Fusarium oxysporum (fungus). *Fusarium oxysporum* f. *cattleyae*, f. *vanillae*, and f. *vasinfectus* cause similar problems. *Fusarium, Phytophthora, Pythium,* and *Rhizoctonia* all cause damping off and much the same symptoms.

COMMON NAMES: *Fusarium* rot, *Fusarium* wilt, *Paphiopedilum* wilt.

PLANTS AFFECTED: *Ascocenda, Brassavola, Catasetum, Cattleya* and most related genera, *Cirrhopetalum, Coelogyne, Cymbidium, Dendrobium, Doritis, Encyclia, Oncidium, Paphiopedilum, Phalaenopsis,* and *Vanilla* are specifically listed. The disease is widespread and may affect all orchid genera.

SYMPTOMS: Infected leaves are yellow, thin, shriveled, or wilted and eventually die. Leaf margins may become grey or greyish green.

Symptoms on aerial portions of the plant are similar to those of *Rhizoctonia solani*, but *Fusarium* wilt produces a circle or band of purple or pinkish-purple discoloration on the outer layers of the rhizome. If the disease is extensive, the entire rhizome may turn purple, and the discoloration may extend to the pseudobulbs. The pathogen attacks the plant through roots or through the cut ends of rhizomes on recently divided plants. Severely infected plants may die in 3–9 weeks, while mildly infected plants gradually decline over a year or so.

Pseudobulbs may be malformed, twisted, or shriveled, symptoms very similar to those caused by root rot. Rot eventually sets in and extends an inch (2.5 cm) or so up the pseudobulb after the disease reaches an advanced stage. The rot may be the result of invasion by other organisms.

Vanilla plants become yellow then wither and die. Wilting is often an early symptom which öccurs when the pathogen affects the roots. The roots blacken on the outside and are stained brown in the center.

TREATMENT: Remove all parts of the plant that show purple discoloration, sterilizing the cutting tool after each cut. Then treat the plant, repot it, and destroy the old medium. Systemic fungicide-1 may be used as a drench or soak for the entire plant. Alternatively, Fungicide-8 may be used as a spray on the diseased plant, bench, and nearby plants; use it cautiously as the chemical is toxic. Repeat sprays every 3 days, for 3 applications. Repot only in new potting material with good drainage. If osmunda is used as the medium, pre-drench with 4% formalin solution, since osmunda can carry *Fusarium* spores.

CONTROL/PREVENTION: Burn diseased plant tissue. Disinfect benches in areas of possible contamination with a 4% formalin solution. Decrease moisture levels in the growing area. Excellent drainage and good air movement help prevent the spread of the disease.

MISCELLANEOUS NOTES: The disease is reported in Australasia and the United States and probably occurs world-wide.

Fusarium rot. See *Fusarium oxysporum*.

Fusarium wilt. See *Fusarium oxysporum*.

Fusicladium vanillae (fungus). *Vanilla* stems are covered with fungal mycelia. The disease is reported in Java, but no information about controls or treatment is available.

Gloeodes pomigena (fungus). *Capnodium* species and *Meliola* species cause similar problems and require the same treatment.

COMMON NAMES: Sooty blotch, sooty mold.

PLANTS AFFECTED: This pathogen is thought to affect *Vanilla* and numerous other orchid genera.

SYMPTOMS: Patchy, dark grey or black residue on the leaves that may be removed by wiping with a damp cloth.

TREATMENT: Wipe leaves or spray with Systemic fungicide-1. Other fungicides are also effective. The fungus usually dies out when plants are moved to a new location.

CONTROL/PREVENTION: Good air movement in the growing area may be beneficial.

MISCELLANEOUS NOTES: *Gloeodes pomigena* often occurs with *Microthyriella rubi*. Both pathogens live on aphid honeydew on the leaf surface and seldom invade healthy plant tissue. They generally appear during warm, humid weather or when the plants are grown outdoors, particularly under trees infested with aphids and affected with sooty mold. The pathogen usually affects the aerial portions of plants. It apparently affects *Vanilla* in Madagascar and probably in other *Vanilla*-growing areas.

Gloeosporium affine (fungus)

COMMON NAMES: European anthracnose.

PLANTS AFFECTED: *Aerides, Angraecum, Brassia, Cattleya, Coelia, Coelogyne, Cymbidium, Cypripedium, Dendrobium, Dichaea, Epidendrum, Eria, Gongora, Isochilus, Laelia, Lycaste, Malaxis, Maxillaria, Miltonia, Odontoglossum, Oncidium, Ornithidium, Paphiopedilum, Phaius, Phalaenopsis, Pholidota, Pleurothallis, Polystachya, Sobralia, Spiranthes, Stanhopea, Tetramicra, Trichopilia, Vanda, Vandopsis, Vanilla, Xylobium, Zygopetalum,* and other orchid genera.

SYMPTOMS: Slightly sunken, yellow to light green circular areas develop on leaves and pseudobulbs. As the lesions dry, black spots (fungal sporing bodies) develop. The spots develop in concentric rings, circular patches, or diamond-shaped areas, which at first glance resemble a virus infection. As the infected area spreads and the spots merge, the area becomes thin, dry, and light brown, while the outer portion dies. Infections spread rapidly in *Dendrobium, Odontoglossum,* and *Oncidium.*

TREATMENT: Remove infected areas and spray with Fungicide-2 or -3 or Systemic fungicide-1 mixed with a wetting agent. Repeat sprays at the recommended interval until the disease is under control. See *Colletotrichum gloeosporiodes* for additional treatment options.

CONTROL/PREVENTION: This fungus is most active when temperatures are warm, moisture is high, and light is low. If plants develop symptoms, lower temperatures and reduce the humidity in the growing area. Careful sanitation and in-

creased air movement are also important. When infection occurs, apply a preventive spray of a long-acting systemic fungicide to other orchids in the area.

MISCELLANEOUS NOTES: *Gloeosporium affine* usually infects the aerial portions of weak plants. It seldom invades healthy plants except through injured tissue. Also see *Colletotrichum gloeosporiodes* (American anthracnose) and *Vanda* transit rot.

Gloeosporium species (fungus)

COMMON NAMES: *Gloeosporium* leaf spot.

PLANTS AFFECTED: *Cattleya, Pholidota,* and other orchid genera.

SYMPTOMS: Prominent, reddish-brown spots on leaves are well defined and sunken. The spots usually start small, frequently near the tip of the leaf, but they may merge to cover the entire leaf.

TREATMENT: See recommended treatments for *Colletotrichum gloeosporiodes.*

CONTROL/PREVENTION: Avoid damp conditions, and do not allow water to stand on the leaves.

MISCELLANEOUS NOTES: The disease is reported in Hawaii and Singapore.

Glomerella cincta. See *Colletotrichum gloeosporiodes.*

Glomerella cingulata. See *Colletotrichum gloeosporiodes.*

Glomerella orchidearum. See *Colletotrichum gloeosporiodes.*

Grammatophyllum bacilliform (virus). Abbreviated GBV, this virus was reported in *Grammatophyllum* in the United States. Information on symptoms and means of transmission is not available.

Guignardia species (fungus)

COMMON NAMES: N/A.

PLANTS AFFECTED: *Ascocentrum* and *Vanda,* and their hybrids.

SYMPTOMS: The first signs of infection are tiny, dark purple, elongated lesions on either leaf surface. These lesions run parallel to the veins and elongate into purple streaks or diamond-shaped areas. Spots often merge to form large, irregular lesions that may affect a large part of the leaf. With age, the center of the lesions turns tan. Raised, black sporing bodies develop in the affected area.

TREATMENT: Definite control measures have not been established for this disease.

CONTROL/PREVENTION: Protect other plants from contamination by practicing good sanitation and increasing air movement in the growing area. Preliminary tests indicate that Systemic fungicide-1 helps control the spread of the disease.

MISCELLANEOUS NOTES: See *Phyllostictina citricarpa.*

Heart rot. See *Phytophthora cactorum.*

Laelia etch (virus). *Laelia anceps* foliage is marked with necrotic lines and semicircular rings. This unnamed virus occurs primarily in California and may prove to be *Cymbidium* mosaic (CyMV).

Laelia red leaf spots (virus)

COMMON NAMES: Abbreviated LRLS.

PLANTS AFFECTED: *Laelia purpurata*, other *Laelia* species, *Laelia* and *Cattleya* hybrids. The virus may also affect *Cymbidium*.

SYMPTOMS: Leaves are marked with dark red, 0.05–0.20 in. (1–5 mm) spots which eventually disappear, leaving sunken areas on the mature leaves.

TREATMENT: Destroy the plant when infection is confirmed.

CONTROL/PREVENTION: Isolate any plant suspected of infection. Sterilize cutting tools, control insects, and disinfect the growing area.

MISCELLANEOUS NOTES: This virus, reported in Germany, may also occur elsewhere.

Leaf blight. See *Sphaeropsis* species.

Leaf necrotic fleck. See Orchid fleck.

Leaf spot. See *Diplodia laeliocattleyae*; *Macrophomina phaseolina*; *Phyllostictina pyriformis*.

Leptothyrium pomi. See *Microthyriella rubi*.

Long orchid rhabdovirus (virus). Abbreviated LORV, it was found in *Cattleya*, *Epidendrum*, *Laelia*, *Paphiopedilum*, and *Phragmipedium* plants in Germany. Information on symptoms or means of transmission is not available.

Macrophomina leaf spot. See *Macrophomina phaseolina*.

Macrophomina phaseolina (fungus)

COMMON NAMES: Leaf spot, *Macrophomina* leaf spot.

PLANTS AFFECTED: *Calanthe* and probably other orchid genera.

SYMPTOMS: Light brown patches with dark brown borders on the leaves.

TREATMENT: N/A.

CONTROL/PREVENTION: Normal sanitation and good air movement in the growing area.

MISCELLANEOUS NOTES: This common root fungus, normally found in tropical areas, is reported in Southeast Asia.

Masdevallia isometric (virus). Known as MI-virus unnamed, it was reported in *Masdevallia* in Colombia. Information on symptoms and treatment is not available.

Meliola species. See *Gloeodes pomigena*.

Microthyriella rubi (fungus)

COMMON NAMES: Flyspeck. *Leptothyrium pomi* is the sexual stage of the fungus.

PLANTS AFFECTED: *Cattleya*, *Dendrobium*, *Epidendrum*, *Vanda*, and other orchid genera.

SYMPTOMS: Large groups of flyspeck-sized spots appear on leaf surfaces.

TREATMENT: Any common fungicide or Systemic fungicide-1 is recommended.

CONTROL/PREVENTION: Move the plants to a different location. Good air movement in the growing area may be beneficial.

MISCELLANEOUS NOTES: Reported primarily in Florida in the United States, *Microthyriella rubi* often occurs with *Gloeodes pomigena*. Both pathogens live on aphid honeydew on the leaf surface and seldom invade healthy plant tissue. They generally appear during warm, humid weather when the plants are grown outdoors, particularly under trees infested with aphids and affected with sooty mold. The pathogen usually affects the aerial portions of plants.

Mild flower break. See *Cymbidium* ringspot.

Miltonia leaf scorch. See *Miltonia* scorch.

Miltonia scorch (bacterium)

COMMON NAMES: Bacterial tip burn, *Miltonia* leaf scorch, and streak are some of the common names given to this unidentified pathogen.

PLANTS AFFECTED: *Miltonia*.

SYMPTOMS: Water-soaked spots develop on the tips or margins of the leaves. When the disease spreads to the pseudobulbs, they become yellow to orange with necrotic areas that appear burned or injured.

TREATMENT: Remove and destroy infected leaves or growths. Soak plants in a solution of Disinfectant-4 or Fungicide, germicide-2 for several hours.

CONTROL/PREVENTION: This is a cool-temperature disease that is highly infectious, dictating extremely careful sanitation. Increase temperatures and air circulation, and decrease moisture in the growing area.

MISCELLANEOUS NOTES: N/A.

Mosaic. See *Cymbidium* mosaic.

Mycoplasmal disease. Known as yellowing, this uncommon disease causes yellowing of the leaves. It was isolated from a *Dactylorhiza majalis* plant in Germany. Further information is not available.

Necrotic fleck. See *Alternaria alternata*; Orchid fleck.

Necrotic mosaic. See *Cymbidium* mosaic.

Necrotic ringspot. See *Cymbidium* ringspot.

Necrotic spot. See *Cymbidium* mosaic.

Necrotic streak. See *Cymbidium* mosaic.

Nectria vanillae (fungus). *Nectria vanillicola* and *Negria tjibodensis* cause similar symptoms. These pathogens cause malformed *Vanilla* buds and brown spots on *Vanilla* flowers and beans. *Nectria vanillae*, reported only from Réunion in the Mascarene Islands, is thought to be a saprophytic fungus and may respond to treatment with Fungicide-14. No treatment information is available.

Nectria vanillicola. See *Nectria vanillae*.

Negria tjibodensis. See *Nectria vanillae.*

Odontoglossum mosaic (virus)

COMMON NAMES: N/A.

PLANTS AFFECTED: *Cattleya, Cymbidium, Odontoglossum.*

SYMPTOMS: Concentric rings of necrotic tissue may develop around apparently healthy green tissue. The rings often merge to form a variety of patterns. Symptoms are frequently more pronounced in the early stages of infection and may cause the leaves to drop. Although the plant appears to improve with time, it is still infected with the virus. *Cymbidium* leaves may show faint mosaic patterns, chlorotic streak, or diamond mottle. This virus may cause a form of mild color break in *Cattleya* flowers.

TREATMENT: Destroy the plant when infection is confirmed.

CONTROL/PREVENTION: Isolate any plant suspected of infection. Sterilize cutting tools, control insects, and disinfect the growing area.

MISCELLANEOUS NOTES: This unidentified virus is known to occur in Europe and the United States and may occur world-wide. It affects a wide variety of orchids and may have different strains.

Odontoglossum ringspot (virus). A form of tobacco mosaic–orchid strain (TMV-O).

COMMON NAMES: This virus often occurs in combination with *Cymbidium* mosaic (CyMV), the virus that causes *Cymbidium* diamond mottle and mild flower break. In some cases, a combination of these 2 viruses causes other conditions known as blossom brown necrotic streak, blossom necrosis, *Cattleya* flower disease, color break, flower break, flower necrosis, and mild flower break.

PLANTS AFFECTED: *Cattleya, Cymbidium, Epidendrum, Odontoglossum, Oncidium.* The disease is common in *Cattleya.* Similar problems are recorded for *Angraecum, Arundina, Brassavola, Calanthe, Catasetum, Cochleanthes, Dendrobium, Grammatophyllum, Laelia, Miltonia, Phaius, Phalaenopsis, Vanda, Vanilla, Zygopetalum,* and probably other orchid genera.

SYMPTOMS: The leaves are marked with elongated, diamond-shaped chlorotic areas and may be mottled with light red-purple, ring-shaped lesions. As the disease progresses, the spots enlarge, become necrotic, and merge to form hieroglyphic patterns. Older leaves may develop black flecks and streaks. Other common symptoms include mottling, color breaking, and flower distortion. The plants may be stunted and develop abnormally.

Plants which test positive for infection may not show symptoms in the flowers. *Cattleya, Cymbidium, Odontoglossum, Phalaenopsis,* and plants of other genera show the infection as broken or variegated flower color, usually described as mild color break. Sepals and petals are generally not deformed, and any symptoms on the leaves are mild and scarcely noticeable.

TREATMENT: Destroy the plant when infection is confirmed.

CONTROL/PREVENTION: The virus is transmitted by insects and contaminated cutting tools. Isolate any plant suspected of infection. Sterilize cutting tools, control insects, and disinfect the growing area.

MISCELLANEOUS NOTES: *Odontoglossum* ringspot is considered the same as tobacco mosaic–orchid strain (TMV-O) for cultivation purposes. It is reported in Europe, Japan, and the United States and may occur world-wide.

Indicator plants may be used to confirm infection by this virus. *Chenopodium amaranticolor* and *Gomphrena globosa* are indicators for mild flower break caused by *Odontoglossum* ringspot. *Chenopodium quinoa* is an indicator for the form of the virus that causes *Cattleya* blossom brown necrotic streak. *Tetragonia expansa* is an indicator for all forms of the disease.

Odontoglossum streak (virus). In *Odontoglossum* it causes yellow to light green rings on the leaves. The rings may be small or irregular and turn reddish black with age. The virus is currently reported in the United States but may also occur elsewhere. Information on means of transmission is not available.

Oncidium light green mosaic mottle (virus). This pathogen was reported in *Oncidium altissimum* in the United States. The virus causes light green mosaic mottling on the leaves. Information on means of transmission is not available.

Oncidium severe mosaic streaking (virus). Reported in *Oncidium concolor* and *Oncidium varicosum* in the United States, the virus causes irregular streaks and spots on the leaves. This may be the same virus which causes *Cymbidium* mosaic and *Cattleya* mild flower break. Information on means of transmission is not available.

Oncidium stippled streak (virus). Reported in *Oncidium flexuosum* in the United States, this virus causes stippled streaks on the leaves. No additional information is available.

Orchid fleck (virus). In Japan, orchid fleck is the common name given to short orchid rhabdovirus.

COMMON NAMES: Leaf necrotic fleck, necrotic fleck.

PLANTS AFFECTED: *Anguloa, Cymbidium, Dendrobium, Odontoglossum, Oncidium, Pescatorea,* and probably other orchid genera. Leaf spots on *Dendrobium* and *Phalaenopsis* may result from this virus.

SYMPTOMS: Necrotic or chlorotic flecks on the leaves.

TREATMENT: Destroy the plant when infection is confirmed.

CONTROL/PREVENTION: The disease may be spread by infected sap. Isolate any plant suspected of infection. Sterilize cutting tools, control insects, and disinfect the growing area.

MISCELLANEOUS NOTES: Reported in Brazil, Europe, and Japan. Indicator plants include *Chenopodium amaranticolor, Chenopodium quinoa, Nicotiana glutinosa,* and *Nicotiana tabacum.*

Orchid mosaic. See *Cymbidium* mosaic.

Orchid wilt. See *Sclerotium rolfsii.*

***Paphiopedilum* brown rot.** See *Erwinia cypripedii.*

***Paphiopedilum* brown spot.** See *Erwinia cypripedii.*

Paphiopedilum flower sheath browning (fungus?)

COMMON NAMES: N/A.

PLANTS AFFECTED: *Paphiopedilum* and possibly other orchids that produce flower sheaths.

SYMPTOMS: Flower sheaths turn brown and die, preventing normal blooming.

TREATMENT: N/A.

CONTROL/PREVENTION: These symptoms may also be caused by wide temperature fluctuations, excessive humidity, waterlogging, and air pollution. Correcting these conditions in the growing area may help to prevent the disease.

MISCELLANEOUS NOTES: Fungal infection is the suspected cause, but specific microorganisms have not been identified.

Paphiopedilum leaf blotch. See *Penicillin thomii*.

Paphiopedilum viral infection (virus). Mosaic rings and streaks have been reported on *Paphiopedilum* leaves in the United States and elsewhere. Viral diseases in *Paphiopedilum* have not been confirmed, and viruses that attack other orchids—such as *Cymbidium* mosaic (CyMV) and tobacco mosaic–orchid strain (TMV-O)—are the suspected cause of these symptoms.

Paphiopedilum wilt. See *Fusarium oxysporum*.

Pellicularia filamentosa. See *Rhizoctonia solani*.

Penicillin thomii (fungus)

COMMON NAMES: *Paphiopedilum* leaf blotch.

PLANTS AFFECTED: *Paphiopedilum*.

SYMPTOMS: Watery, deep brown blotches 1.4–2.0 in. (3.5–5.0 cm) across occur on older leaves. The blotches are usually round or elongated with a pale brown margin.

TREATMENT: Spray with a standard fungicide.

CONTROL/PREVENTION: Normal sanitation and good air movement in the growing area.

MISCELLANEOUS NOTES: This pathogen normally infects plants only through unhealthy or injured tissue.

Pestalotiopsis disseminata (fungus). *Pestalotiopsis versi* causes similar symptoms and requires similar controls.

COMMON NAMES: *Pestalotiopsis* leaf spot.

PLANTS AFFECTED: *Cymbidium aloifolium* and possibly other orchid species. A wide variety of other plants are affected by this pathogen.

SYMPTOMS: N/A.

TREATMENT: N/A.

CONTROL/PREVENTION: Normal sanitation and good air movement in the growing area.

MISCELLANEOUS NOTES: The disease occurs in India.

Pestalotiopsis leaf spot. See *Pestalotiopsis disseminata*.

Pestalotiopsis versi. See *Pestalotiopsis disseminata*.

Petal blight. See *Botrytis cinerea*.

Phalaenopsis mosaic (virus)

COMMON NAMES: N/A.

PLANTS AFFECTED: *Cymbidium, Phalaenopsis, Spathoglottis*.

SYMPTOMS: Leaves are marked with a diffuse mosaic consisting of light green or chlorotic patches. Leaf tissue collapses, and broad chlorotic furrows or water-soaked areas appear on the underside of leaves, while the upper surface shows necrosis or light green chlorosis.

TREATMENT: Destroy the plant when infection is confirmed.

CONTROL/PREVENTION: Isolate any plant suspected of infection. Sterilize cutting tools, control insects, and disinfect the growing area.

MISCELLANEOUS NOTES: The symptoms are apparently caused by a combination of *Cymbidium* mosaic (CyMV) and tobacco mosaic–orchid strain (TMV-O). The disease is reported in the United States and elsewhere.

Phyllosticta citricarpa. See *Phyllostictina citricarpa*.

Phyllosticta leaf spot. See *Phyllostictina citricarpa*.

Phyllostictina citricarpa (fungus). *Guignardia citricarpa* is the sexual stage. In Hawaii, *Phyllostictina capitalensis* and *P. pyriformis* are said to cause similar symptoms.

COMMON NAMES: *Phyllosticta, Phyllosticta* leaf spot, *Phyllostictina* leaf spot.

PLANTS AFFECTED: *Dendrobium, Vanilla*, and numerous other orchid genera.

SYMPTOMS: Areas on the leaves and pseudobulbs turn yellow; with age, the spots become light to dark brown. The discolorations have a well-defined margin, often with a yellow outer band. As the infection progresses, black or dark brown sporing bodies may appear. The lesions increase in size, and the adjacent tissue becomes yellow or pale green and sunken.

TREATMENT: Spray with Systemic fungicide-1.

CONTROL/PREVENTION: Normal sanitation and good air movement help prevent the infection.

MISCELLANEOUS NOTES: Not normally a devastating disease, *P. citricarpa* may become serious in *Dendrobium*. It is reported in Asia and the United States and probably occurs world-wide. It is known to affect *Vanilla* in Madagascar.

Phyllostictina leaf spot. See *Phyllostictina citricarpa*.

Phyllostictina pyriformis (fungus)

COMMON NAMES: Leaf spot.

PLANTS AFFECTED: *Aerides, Angraecum, Arachnis, Ascocenda, Ascocentrum, Aspasia, Bifrenaria, Brassavola, Brassia, Broughtonia, Catasetum, Cattleya, Caularthron, Chondrorhyncha, Cochleanthes, Cymbidiella, Cymbidium, Cyrtopodium, Cyrtorchis, Dendrobium, Encyclia, Epidendrum, Eulophiella, Gongora, Grammatophyllum, Isochilus, Laelia, Laeliopsis, Lockhartia, Masdevallia, Maxillaria, Miltonia, Odontoglossum, Oncidium, Paphiopedilum, Pescatorea,*

Phalaenopsis, Pleurothallis, Renanthera, Rhynchostylis, Schomburgkia, Spathoglottis, Stanhopea, Stelis, Trichopilia, Vanda, Vanilla, Xylobium, Zygopetalum.

SYMPTOMS: Spotting may start anywhere on the leaf or pseudobulb. The lesions are tiny, yellow, and slightly sunken. As they enlarge, they become round to oval and more sunken, especially if the infection is on the leaves. With age, they turn tan to dark brown and develop a slightly raised, red to purple-black margin. Eventually, tiny, black, raised spore structures develop in the center of the spots. Individual spots are about ¼ in. (6 mm) across. Severely infected leaves may drop prematurely.

TREATMENT: Spray with Systemic fungicide-1 mixed with a wetting agent.

CONTROL/PREVENTION: Normal sanitation with good air movement in the growing area.

MISCELLANEOUS NOTES: The disease is reported in Australasia, the Caribbean islands, Central America, India, the Pacific islands, the Netherlands, South America, and the United States. It probably occurs world-wide.

Phytomonas cattleyae. See *Pseudomonas cattleyae.*

Phytophthora cactorum (fungus). *Phytophthora omnivora* and *P. palmivora* cause similar symptoms and require the same treatment.

COMMON NAMES: Black rot, crown rot, damping off, and heart rot are some common names for infections caused by *Phytophthora* pathogens. Other pathogens such as *Fusarium, Pythium,* or *Rhizoctonia* may also cause damping off.

PLANTS AFFECTED: *Brassavola, Cattleya, Coelogyne, Cymbidium, Dendrobium, Epidendrum, Gongora, Grammatophyllum, Laelia, Oncidium, Paphiopedilum, Phaius, Phalaenopsis, Rhynchostylis, Rodriguezia, Trichocentrum, Vanda, Vanilla,* and other, less commonly cultivated genera. *Phalaenopsis* and *Vanda* are particularly susceptible.

SYMPTOMS: Symptoms vary with plant age. The infection usually starts on the leaves, new leads, or roots, though all plant parts are susceptible.

On flowers, the infection shows as light brown, watery spots with a somewhat darker center.

Leaves usually show the first signs of infection. Symptoms first appear on the underside as small, irregular, watery, brown spots which rapidly become purplish brown or purplish black. The spots may have a yellowish advancing margin. The lesions enlarge with age and may ooze water if pressed. Old lesions sometimes become dry and black, often allowing other diseases to attack the plant. The disease may spread rapidly to the rhizome and roots, particularly when the humidity is high.

New leads show a purple or purple-brown area with a yellowish advancing margin and may be pulled off easily. Only under extremely wet conditions does the infection start in the shoot tip.

Pseudobulbs, roots, or rhizomes show infection as a purplish-black, often sharply delineated, discolored area in the center of the plant. The infection often starts in the roots and may spread to the base of the pseudobulb or leaf, causing the plant to wilt. Sometimes the leaves do not appear infected but become brittle and fall from the plant.

The seedlings of many species are susceptible, but the disease is a particular problem with *Cattleya* and semiterete *Vanda* seedlings. It first appears as small, water-soaked spots which turn yellow and then black. Infected roots collapse, killing the seedlings.

TREATMENT: Remove infected tissue, then spray the plant with a disinfectant or with Fungicide-2 or -9. An alternative treatment is to dip the entire plant in Fungicide-3 or Disinfectant-2. Recommended drenches include Fungicide, germicide-1 and Fungicide-9 or -13. Plants may be dusted with Fungicide-3. Spraying regularly with Fungicide-1, -7, or -17 is reported to be an effective protective measure.

Seedlings in community pots are particularly susceptible and may be lost in 1–2 days. The disease is most devastating when soft-tissued young plants are crowded and conditions are moist. Infected seedlings rarely recover. Very dilute solutions of Fungicide, germicide-2 or drenches of Fungicide-9 or -13 may be applied weekly to control the spread of the disease.

CONTROL/PREVENTION: Unless the plant is valuable, the best approach is to remove and burn it, as the disease is highly contagious. If left untreated, the disease spreads from plant to plant when contaminated water splashes from the plant or drips through the growing medium. Warm temperatures, high humidity, and water-soaked medium all contribute to the spread of this disease.

MISCELLANEOUS NOTES: If the growing tip of *Vanda* is infected, cut well below the infected site to promote growth of a healthy side shoot. If the newest growth of a sympodial orchid becomes infected, remove the growth. The disease is specifically reported in Asia, the Caribbean, Europe, New Zealand, and the United States, but it probably occurs world-wide.

Phytophthora jatrophae (fungus). Commonly called *Vanilla* mildew, the fungus causes the tips of *Vanilla* beans to turn brown. Eventually the beans are covered with a white powder. No treatment information is available, but the treatments recommended for *Phytophthora cactorum* might be effective. The disease is reported in the Cormoro Islands, Java, Madagascar, Puerto Rico, and on Réunion in the Mascarene Islands.

Phytophthora omnivora. See *Phytophthora cactorum.*

Phytophthora palmivora. See *Phytophthora cactorum.*

Pseudomonas aeruginosa (bacterium). *Pseudomonas fluorescens* causes similar symptoms and requires similar treatment.

COMMON NAMES: Bacterial rot.

PLANTS AFFECTED: *Cattleya, Cymbidium, Paphiopedilum.*

SYMPTOMS: Buds may rot, and the sepals and petals may develop small necrotic specks with water-soaked margins.

Infected roots die back, but the infection often goes unnoticed until it spreads upward to the base of the stem.

TREATMENT: See *Pseudomonas cattleyae.*

CONTROL/PREVENTION: Normal sanitation with good air movement in the growing area.

MISCELLANEOUS NOTES: *Pseudomonas* is normally a secondary infection that does not invade healthy plants.

Pseudomonas andropogonis (bacterium). Also called *Vanda* firm rot, it affects *Dendrobium, Phalaenopsis, Vanda*, and possibly other orchids. The leaf rots and drops. The disease occurs primarily in Hawaii. No additional information is available.

Pseudomonas cattleyae (bacterium). *Bacterium cattleyae* and *Phytomonas cattleyae* cause similar symptoms and require the same treatment.

COMMON NAMES: Bacterial brown spot.

PLANTS AFFECTED: *Aerides, Ascocenda, Ascocentrum, Brassia, Catasetum, Cattleya* and related genera, *Cymbidium, Cyrtopodium, Dendrobium, Doritaenopsis, Epidendrum, Oncidium, Ornithocephalus, Paphiopedilum, Phalaenopsis, Phragmipedium, Renanthopsis, Rhynchostylis, Rodriguezia, Sophronitis, Vanda,* and other, less commonly cultivated orchid genera.

SYMPTOMS: The infection may appear anywhere on the leaf as a small, soft, water-soaked blister. Initially dirty green in color, the infected spot enlarges and eventually becomes brown or black and sunken. It oozes a bacteria-laden liquid, particularly when the disease reaches the tip of the leaf.

In *Cattleya*, the infection enters through wounds on older plants and usually affects only older leaves. It advances slowly and is rarely fatal.

In *Phalaenopsis*, the blister-like spots may be surrounded with a yellowish or pale green halo. Spots coalesce, and the infection spreads rapidly. If the diseased area invades the crown, the plant will die.

In seedlings, infection is particularly severe. Young leaves need not be damaged for infection to occur, since the pathogen is able to enter directly through the stomata. The disease rapidly kills young *Phalaenopsis* plants.

TREATMENT: Remove infected plants from the growing area. Cut away infected tissue, leaves, and growths, and soak the entire plant for several hours in Algicide, bactericide, fungicide-1 or Fungicide, germicide-2. Fungicide, germicide-2 is suggested for seedlings since Algicide, bactericide, fungicide-1 is sometimes harmful. Diseased plants should also be drenched or thoroughly sprayed with broad-spectrum, systemic fungicide since secondary infections are likely to develop in weakened plants. Several repeat treatments a few days apart are usually necessary.

CONTROL/PREVENTION: Reduce humidity, and avoid overhead watering. *Pseudomonas cattleyae* is a water-borne pathogen which prefers warm, moist conditions. Increase air circulation and reduce temperatures if possible. Sterilize wooden benches by painting them with a copper naphthenate compound. The exudate from diseased tissue is laden with infectious bacteria, which are easily spread to other plants through dripping or splashing water, insect carriers, or contaminated tools.

MISCELLANEOUS NOTES: This is the most common and severe disease affecting *Phalaenopsis*. It is reported in Asia, the Philippines, and the United States.

Pseudomonas cypripedii (bacterium)

COMMON NAMES: *Paphiopedilum* brown spot.

PLANTS AFFECTED: *Paphiopedilum.*

SYMPTOMS: Soft, water-soaked spots appear on the upper leaf surface. These enlarge and eventually destroy the plant.

TREATMENT: Cut out infected tissue down to the rhizome, and soak plants for several hours in Fungicide, germicide-2 or Disinfectant-4. Repeat this treatment several times. Another recommended treatment is spraying with Algicide, bactericide, fungicide-1.

CONTROL/PREVENTION: Normal sanitation procedures and good air movement are important protective measures. Plants and the entire growing area should be sprayed with Algicide, bactericide, fungicide-1.

MISCELLANEOUS NOTES: Symptoms are easily confused with those of *Erwinia cypripedii*, and treatment is similar. The disease is reported in the United States and probably occurs elsewhere.

Pseudomonas fluorescens. See *Pseudomonas aeruginosa.* Although these are different bacteria, they cannot be differentiated without laboratory diagnosis. Plant symptoms and recommended treatments are the same for both pathogens.

Ptychogaster species (fungus)

COMMON NAMES: Snow mold.

PLANTS AFFECTED: Plants grown in organic potting media are subject to infection. In some regions, snow mold is a problem for *Vanda* growers.

SYMPTOMS: White, powdery growth on the medium or near the base of the stem. The mold, which repels water, covers the roots and rhizome, suffocating and dehydrating the plant.

TREATMENT: Unpot the plant, then treat it with Fungicide-14 mixed with a suitable wetting agent, or soak it in Algicide, bactericide, fungicide-1. Inspect and treat nearby plants also. Several treatments may be necessary, as the fungus is quite water repellent. After treatment, repot the plant in new medium.

CONTROL/PREVENTION: Repot plants according to the recommended schedule, as this problem seldom occurs when plants receive regular care.

MISCELLANEOUS NOTES: Plant symptoms may be similar to those caused by *Fusarium oxysporum* f. *cattleyae* and *Rhizoctonia solani*. Other molds in the potting medium respond to similar treatment. Also see Saprophytic fungi.

Pythium rot. See *Pythium ultimum.*

Pythium ultimum (fungus). *Pythium* is one of the fungi which cause damping off. Other pathogens such as *Fusarium,*

Phytophthora, and *Rhizoctonia* also cause damping off and similar symptoms.

COMMON NAMES: Black rot, *Cattleya* soft rot, damping off, *Pythium* rot.

PLANTS AFFECTED: *Cattleya, Cymbidium, Epidendrum, Oncidium,* and other orchid genera.

SYMPTOMS: The infection usually starts in the roots then spreads to the rhizome, pseudobulbs, and leaves. Information on the symptoms of *Phytophthora* rot also applies to *Pythium* rot: see *Phytophthora cactorum.* When infected, the tissue of the pseudobulb often remains firm and gradually dries, becoming hard and mummified.

Cattleya may show a creamy yellow discoloration on one or both sides of the pseudobulbs. The discoloration eventually turns black or brown and softens, and the bulb rots.

Seedlings are particularly susceptible to infection and die rapidly unless treated immediately. The affected plants turn translucent brown, sometimes with black spots near the base.

TREATMENT: Destroy seriously infected seedlings and isolate other infected plants. Older plants may recover if infected tissue is cut away well beyond the affected area. Soak plants, particularly *Phalaenopsis* and seedlings, for several hours in Fungicide, germicide-2. In the case of seedlings or plants in community pots, even unaffected plants should be soaked.

CONTROL/PREVENTION: Destroy or carefully isolate the plant. A water-borne mold, *Pythium ultimum* is often carried from plant to plant through dripping or splashing water. As a preventive measure, growers suggest watering seedlings and plants in community pots each month using Disinfectant-4 or Fungicide, germicide-2. *Pythium* is most active when humidity is high and temperatures are cool, so reducing humidity and raising temperatures should help prevent the infection from spreading.

MISCELLANEOUS NOTES: Reported in Asia and the United States, this disease probably occurs world-wide.

Rhizoctonia solani (fungus). The names *Pellicularia filamentosa* and *Thanatephorus cucumeris* apply to the sexual stage of the fungus. *Rhizoctonia* is one of the fungi thought to cause damping off and other symptoms similar to those caused by *Fusarium, Phytophthora,* and *Pythium.*

COMMON NAMES: Root rot, *Paphiopedilum* root rot.

PLANTS AFFECTED: Seedlings of *Cattleya* and related genera, *Oncidium, Paphiopedilum,* and *Phalaenopsis.* Adult plants of *Brassavola, Cattleya, Cypripedium, Dendrobium, Epidendrum, Oncidium, Paphiopedilum, Phalaenopsis, Trichocentrum,* and *Vanda.*

SYMPTOMS: *Rhizoctonia* is primarily a root disease, but the symptoms are usually first noticed on aerial parts of the plant. The symptoms are similar to those caused by *Fusarium oxysporum.* If the disease is not controlled, infected plants develop brown rot and die. The process is quite gradual in mature plants.

Leaves and pseudobulbs become yellow, shriveled, thin, and twisted, and new growths become progressively smaller. *Paphiopedilum* leaves become pale and desiccated and curl inward.

The roots usually show a brown rot with white or brown fungal growth. In severe infections, the fungus girdles and kills the plant. The infection quickly invades the lower leaves and rhizomes of small seedlings.

TREATMENT: Remove infected portions of the roots and leaves, and repot the plant in sterile medium. Drench several times with Systemic fungicide-1 or -3 or Fungicide, germicide-2 or spray with Fungicide-2 or -3. To treat seedlings, submerge them in Fungicide, germicide-2 or Fungicide-2 or -17.

CONTROL/PREVENTION: *Rhizoctonia solani* is very contagious. If not controlled immediately, it spreads rapidly, causing severe damage. When disease is suspected in other plants or when repotting is overdue, unpot the plants and check their roots. If the roots are not firm and healthy, they should be trimmed, and the plants should be treated with a fungicide then repotted in new, sterile medium.

Root rot usually occurs when the medium breaks down, drainage is poor, or plants are overwatered. Rot sets in quickly when roots are damaged by injury or salt buildup from hard water or overfertilizing. In hard-water areas, pots should be flushed at least monthly to prevent root damage.

MISCELLANEOUS NOTES: N/A.

Ringspot (virus). This disease is known to affect *Aspasia, Bifrenaria, Brassia, Dendrobium, Hormidium, Miltonia, Oncidium, Phalaenopsis,* and *Trigonidium.* Distinct ringspots develop on the leaves. The virus is currently reported in Europe and Brazil. No additional information is available.

Rust. See *Sphenospora kevorkianii, Sphenospora saphena, Uredo behickiana, Uredo epidendri, Uredo nigropuncta, Uredo oncidii.*

Saprophytic fungi (fungus). These are species that live on dead matter.

COMMON NAMES: Molds.

PLANTS AFFECTED: All dead or dying vegetable matter.

SYMPTOMS: These fungi are usually found on dead plant material, but they may spread to living tissue. The mycelia and fruiting bodies may appear on potting medium or other organic material.

TREATMENT: Treat the plant with Fungicide-14, then repot it in new, sterile medium.

CONTROL/PREVENTION: Remove dead plant material, increase spacing between plants, and spray with a fungicide. Excessively wet or humid conditions are conducive to the spread of the infection, so moisture levels should be reduced. General cleanup of the growing area is indicated, including removal of dead plant parts. Avoid mold in seedling flasks by maintaining sterile conditions.

MISCELLANEOUS NOTES: Saprophytic fungi are seldom serious except for young plants in seedling flasks or community pots.

Sclerotinia fuckeliana. See *Botrytis cinerea.*

Sclerotium rolfsii (fungus). This is the asexual stage of the fungus *Pellicularia rolfsii* (*Corticium rolfsii*), which occurs only rarely. *Sclerotium vanillae* and other closely related *Sclerotium* fungi cause symptoms similar to those caused by *Botrytis cinerea* and respond to the same treatments.

COMMON NAMES: Basal rot, collar rot, crown rot, *Cymbidium* collar rot, *Cymbidium Sclerotium* rot, orchid wilt, southern blight, *Vanilla* bean deformation.

PLANTS AFFECTED: *Cattleya, Cycnoches, Cymbidium, Oncidium, Phaius, Phalaenopsis, Spathoglottis, Vanda, Vanilla,* and probably other orchid genera.

SYMPTOMS: Roots, pseudobulbs, leaf bases, and the lower part of stems turn cream-yellow. The affected tissue becomes brown (resulting from invasion by secondary pathogens), collapses, and rots very rapidly. The disease eventually girdles and destroys the entire basal portion of the plant and attacks young leaves. Affected leaves become yellow, wilt, and die. If left untreated, the infection leads to the death of the entire plant. In *Vanilla,* the beans may be deformed. Seedlings are particularly susceptible to infection.

Small yellow or tan sclerotia about the size and color of mustard seed form on the affected tissue. This is the resting form of the fungus and often persists for years in soil, in medium, and on benches or other surfaces in the growing area.

TREATMENT: If this disease becomes established in the growing area, it can be devastating and difficult to eradicate. Remove and burn diseased plants. If the infected plant is very valuable, and if the infection is just starting, remove the affected plant parts, and dip the entire plant in a solution of Fungicide, germicide-2 or Disinfectant-2 for at least an hour. This treatment sometimes controls the disease.

CONTROL/PREVENTION: Isolate the plant until it is disease-free. Sterilize the pot with a solution of 4% formalin or 10% bleach before reusing it. Also sterilize benches and the surrounding area with a 2% formalin solution or with Fungicide-14. Temperatures below 85°F (29°C), good sanitation, and increased air movement help limit the spread of this disease.

MISCELLANEOUS NOTES: Reported world-wide, *Sclerotium* is most prevalent in warmer climates, where it also affects beans, peppers, marigolds, and phlox.

Sclerotium vanillae. See *Sclerotium rolfsii.*

Selenophoma dendrobii (fungus)

COMMON NAMES: *Selenophoma* leaf spot.

PLANTS AFFECTED: *Dendrobium.*

SYMPTOMS: Small brown spots on the leaves which rapidly develop into round, oval, or irregular lesions. The spots may occur on either side of the leaves and eventually become discolored in the center. Sporing is evident on older spots. Severely infected leaves drop off.

TREATMENT: N/A.

CONTROL/PREVENTION: Normal sanitation with good air movement in the growing area.

MISCELLANEOUS NOTES: This disease is reported only in Japan.

Selenophoma **leaf spot.** See *Selenophoma dendrobii.*

Septoria **leaf spot.** See *Septoria selenophomoides.*

Septoria selenophomoides (fungus)

COMMON NAMES: *Dendrobium* leaf spot, *Septoria* leaf spot.

PLANTS AFFECTED: *Brassia, Bulbophyllum, Coelogyne, Cymbidium, Dendrobium, Encyclia, Laelia, Masdevallia, Miltonia, Odontoglossum, Oncidium, Paphiopedilum, Pleurothallis, Stanhopea, Stenocoryne. Dendrobium nobile* and its hybrids are extremely susceptible.

SYMPTOMS: The tiny spots may start on either leaf surface as sunken, yellow lesions. They continue to enlarge, becoming dark brown to black, circular or irregular lesions. Spots may merge to form large, irregular patches on the leaf. Heavily infected leaves fall prematurely.

TREATMENT: Spray the plant with Fungicide-2 or Systemic fungicide-1.

CONTROL/PREVENTION: Water on the leaves may lead to infection by this pathogen.

MISCELLANEOUS NOTES: The disease is most frequently reported in Hawaii and Japan, but it also occurs in Brazil, Colombia, Costa Rica, the Dominican Republic, England, Guatemala, India, Mexico, the Philippines, Thailand, and Florida in the United States. In the United States it most often appears on recently imported orchids, which should be given a preventive fungicide treatment.

Seuratia coeffeicola (fungus). *Seuratia pinicola* and *S. vanillae* cause similar problems and require the same treatment.

COMMON NAMES: *Vanilla seuratia.*

PLANTS AFFECTED: *Vanilla.*

SYMPTOMS: Sporing bodies on the leaves and stem.

TREATMENT: Treating the plant with Fungicide-14 may be helpful.

CONTROL/PREVENTION: Excessively wet or humid conditions are conducive to the spread of this saprophytic fungus. Thus planting in areas with improved air circulation might be beneficial.

MISCELLANEOUS NOTES: This is a rare disease from Madagascar that is not normally parasitic.

Seuratia pinicola. See *Seuratia coeffeicola.*

Seuratia vanillae. See *Seuratia coeffeicola.*

Severe leaf necrosis. See *Cymbidium* ringspot.

Short orchid rhabdovirus (virus)

COMMON NAMES: N/A.

PLANTS AFFECTED: *Coelogyne, Dendrobium, Dendrobium phalaenopsis, Miltonia, Odontoglossum, Oncidium, Paphiopedilum, Phalaenopsis, Renanthera, Stanhopea, Vanda, Zygopetalum.* This virus has been found in more than 26 orchid genera throughout the world. It may be a single strain or multiple strains of the virus.

SYMPTOMS: Brown spots on the leaves. As the spots increase in size, the leaves turn yellow, and the tissues between the veins may collapse.

TREATMENT: Destroy the plant when infection is confirmed.

CONTROL/PREVENTION: Isolate any plant suspected of infection, since the infection is transmitted through contaminated sap.

MISCELLANEOUS NOTES: This virus was first reported during a study of *Fusarium moniliforme*, a fungus that causes flower blight. Symptoms of the fungal infection may hide the symptoms of the viral infection. Possible indicator plants include *Chenopodium amaranticolor*, *Chenopodium quinoa*, and *Nicotiana clevelandii*. The disease occurs in Denmark, Germany, and Japan. In Japan it is called orchid fleck.

Snow mold. See *Ptychogaster* species.

Soft rot. See *Erwinia carotovora*; *Pythium ultimum*.

Sooty blotch. See *Gloeodes pomigena*.

Sooty mold. See *Gloeodes pomigena*.

Spathoglottis diamond spot (virus)

COMMON NAMES: N/A.

PLANTS AFFECTED: *Cattleya, Cymbidium, Dendrobium, Miltonia, Spathoglottis, Vanda.*

SYMPTOMS: The leaves develop chlorotic streaks or spots, necrotic rings, or diamond-shaped lesions. With age, the affected areas become reddish brown or black, and leaves drop prematurely.

TREATMENT: Destroy the plant when infection is confirmed.

CONTROL/PREVENTION: Isolate any plant suspected of infection. Sterilize cutting tools, control insects, and disinfect the growing area.

MISCELLANEOUS NOTES: *Spathoglottis* may be used as an indicator plant since it is highly susceptible to infection by viruses which attack other orchid genera. Symptoms are fairly consistent regardless of the host plant being tested, although several different viruses cause similar symptoms. The disease is reported in the United States.

Sphaeropsis species (fungus)

COMMON NAMES: Leaf blight.

PLANTS AFFECTED: *Spathoglottis.*

SYMPTOMS: Light brown, linear markings with darker brown margins. With age, the spots increase in size to cover most of the leaf.

TREATMENT: Fungicides used for other blights or leaf spots may be effective. See *Cercospora angraeci*.

CONTROL/PREVENTION: Normal sanitation with good air movement in the growing area.

MISCELLANEOUS NOTES: The disease is reported in Assam.

Sphenospora kevorkianii (fungus)

COMMON NAMES: Rust.

PLANTS AFFECTED: *Batemania, Bletia, Brassia, Bulbophyllum, Capanemia, Catasetum, Caularthron, Cycnoches, Cyrtopodium, Epidendrum, Gongora, Hexisea, Huntleya, Ionopsis, Laelia, Leochilus, Lockhartia, Lycaste, Masdevallia, Maxillaria, Miltonia, Mormodes, Notylia, Odontoglossum, Oeceoclades, Oncidium, Ornithocephalus, Pelexia, Peristeria, Pescatorea, Pleurothallis, Plocoglottis, Polystachya, Rodriguezia, Schomburgkia, Sigmatostalix, Stanhopea, Trichoceros, Trichopilia, Trigonidium, Xylobium, Zygopetalum, Zygostates,* and probably other orchid genera.

SYMPTOMS: Small, orange spore pustules appear on the underside of leaves. The disease rarely infects the stem. As the lesion enlarges, the pustules eventually break through to the top leaf surface. The orange pustules, which turn black with age, often develop in a concentric pattern, giving the infected area the appearance of a target spot.

TREATMENT: Remove and burn all leaves that show infection. If all plant parts are infected, destroy the entire plant. Spray plants with Fungicide-7 or -18 mixed with a suitable wetting agent. Because rust is capable of infecting numerous genera, it is usually best to destroy infected plants. New chemicals effective against rust are being introduced and may soon be approved for orchids. For more information, consult with local agricultural agents or orchid growers.

CONTROL/PREVENTION: Isolate or destroy the plant and disinfect the growing area. Periodically inspect plants for symptoms of this disease.

MISCELLANEOUS NOTES: Rust seldom kills a plant but weakens it, reducing or eliminating flowering. The disease is known to occur in the Caribbean islands, Central America, Florida in the United States, and northern South America.

Sphenospora mera (fungus)

COMMON NAMES: Rust.

PLANTS AFFECTED: *Bletia, Bletilla, Cycnoches, Epidendrum, Ionopsis, Mormodes, Oncidium, Pleurothallis, Rodriguezia.*

SYMPTOMS: Only leaves are affected. The tiny, raised spots are cinnamon brown and appear on the underside of leaves. The sporing bodies rupture when mature, dispersing the spores via wind or splashing water.

TREATMENT: Remove and burn all leaves showing infection. Spray plants with Fungicide-7 or -18 mixed with a suitable wetting agent. New chemicals effective against rust are being introduced and may soon be approved for orchids. For more information, consult with local agricultural agents or orchid growers.

CONTROL/PREVENTION: Isolate infected plants until they are disease-free. Give plants in susceptible genera a preventive spray, and periodically inspect them for symptoms of this disease.

MISCELLANEOUS NOTES: This pathogen is reported in Brazil, Central America, and Mexico.

Sphenospora saphena (fungus)

COMMON NAMES: Rust.

PLANTS AFFECTED: *Cochlioda, Epidendrum, Ionopsis, Laelia, Masdevallia, Oncidium, Pescatorea, Rodriguezia, Sobralia.*

SYMPTOMS: Tiny, raised, orange or rust-brown pustules appear on the underside of leaves, which eventually become covered with these spore-bearing pustules. The spots turn dark brown with age.

TREATMENT: Because rust is capable of infecting numerous genera, it is usually advisable to destroy infected plants. To treat a plant, isolate it and remove and burn all leaves showing infection. Spray the plant with Fungicide-7 or -18 mixed with a suitable wetting agent. New chemicals effective against rust are being introduced and may soon be approved for orchids. For more information, consult local agricultural agents or orchid growers.

CONTROL/PREVENTION: Disinfect the growing area and apply a preventive spray to other plants in the growing area. Periodically inspect plants for symptoms of this disease.

MISCELLANEOUS NOTES: The disease occurs from Brazil to Mexico.

Sporoschisma species (fungus)

COMMON NAMES: *Vanilla sporoschisma.*

PLANTS AFFECTED: *Vanilla.*

SYMPTOMS: White fungal mycelia cover the plant and turn brown with age.

TREATMENT: N/A.

CONTROL/PREVENTION: Plant debris in the growing area may encourage disease development, since this fungus is apparently saprophytic.

MISCELLANEOUS NOTES: Reported only in *Vanilla planifolia* in Indochina, the disease does not weaken the plant severely.

Stanhopea yellow spot (virus). *Stanhopea* leaves develop yellow rings and spots that increase in size as the leaf grows. The disease is uncommon. It was reported in California in the United States on plants imported from an unnamed location. No information on the virus is available.

Stemphylium species. See *Alternaria alternata.*

Streak. See *Miltonia* scorch.

Thanatephorus cucumeris (fungus). This is the sexual stage of *Rhizoctonia solani.*

Tobacco mosaic (virus). Abbreviated TMV, this virus, unlike Cymbidium mosaic, has many strains and variants and infects numerous plant families. Tobacco mosaic–orchid strain (TMV-O) has many of the same properties as TMV, but it has a unique chemical makeup and infects only a few plants other than orchids. Similarly, most vegetable strains of TMV do not invade orchids. TMV-O often occurs with other viruses and causes somewhat different symptoms in different orchid genera. For further information, see Chlorotic leaf streak of *Oncidium, Odontoglossum* ringspot, *Paphiopedilum* viral infection, and *Phalaenopsis* mosaic.

Tobacco rattle (virus). Abbreviated TRV, it was reported to affect *Orchis* in Germany. The virus causes misshapen flowers and is transmitted by contaminated tools. Indicator plants include *Nicotiana tabacum* 'Xanthi' and 'Samsun'. A strain of this virus is common in crop plants, but no other instances of orchid infection have been recorded.

Tomato ringspot (virus)

COMMON NAMES: Abbreviated TRSV, it is also known as *Cymbidium* chlorotic leaf streak.

PLANTS AFFECTED: *Cymbidium.*

SYMPTOMS: Faint chlorotic streaks on leaves, basal necrotic streaking, and premature leaf drop. No flower symptoms were reported. Plants with no visible symptoms sometimes test positive for the virus.

TREATMENT: Destroy the plant when infection is confirmed.

CONTROL/PREVENTION: Isolate any plant suspected of infection. Sterilize cutting tools, control insects, and disinfect the growing area.

MISCELLANEOUS NOTES: *Cassia quinoa, Nicotiana tabacum* 'Kentucky 35', *Vigna sinensis,* and *Vigna unguiculata* are indicator plants. The infected sap can be transmitted to indicator plants but not back to orchids. The disease is reported in the United States.

Trichopilia isometric (virus). Known as TI—virus unnamed, this virus was isolated in Germany from a *Trichopilia* plant. It is probably uncommon. No further information is available.

Turnip mosaic (virus). Abbreviated TuMV, this virus was isolated in Germany from an *Orchis* plant. It is apparently transmitted by contaminated tools. Information on symptoms is not available. *Nicotiana clevelandii* is an indicator plant.

Unnamed bacilliform (virus). Abbreviated PhBV, this virus reportedly affects *Phalaenopsis* in Germany. Information on symptoms and means of transmission is not available.

Unnamed rhabdovirus (virus). Known as RV—unnamed, this virus reportedly affects *Bifrenaria harrisoniae, Brassia, Hormidium fragrans, Miltonia,* and *Oncidium* plants in Brazil. Information on symptoms and means of transmission is not available.

Uredo behickiana (fungus)

COMMON NAMES: Rust.

PLANTS AFFECTED: *Cattleya, Bletia, Dendrobium, Encyclia, Hexisea, Laelia, Masdevallia, Maxillaria, Oncidium, Phaius, Pleurothallis, Schomburgkia, Spathoglottis, Stanhopea.*

SYMPTOMS: Orange-yellow patches enlarge in a roughly circular pattern, eventually covering the entire underside of the leaf. The top surface of the leaf becomes chlorotic. Even severely infected plants may bloom, but the inflorescences are smaller than normal, with fewer and smaller flowers.

TREATMENT: Cut off and destroy all leaves showing infection. A chemical control for this disease has not been established.

CONTROL/PREVENTION: Isolate or destroy infected plants, and disinfect the growing area. Inspect plants frequently for signs of reinfection.

MISCELLANEOUS NOTES: Rust is seldom fatal, but it weakens the plant, thus reducing or eliminating flowering. This fungus is reported from Brazil to Mexico and in the Caribbean islands. It is sometimes found in the United States in imported plants.

Uredo epidendri (fungus)

COMMON NAMES: Rust.

PLANTS AFFECTED: *Caularthron, Encyclia, Epidendrum, Ionopsis, Laelia, Oncidium, Rodriguezia, Trigonidium.*

SYMPTOMS: The first symptoms, which appear on the underside of leaves, are raised brown pustules, often with a reddish border. As the disease progresses, the developing spore pustules break through to the upper leaf surface. With age, the pustules change from brown to purple-black. Only the leaves are affected.

TREATMENT: Cut off and burn all leaves showing infection, and spray plants with Fungicide-7 or -18 mixed with a suitable wetting agent.

CONTROL/PREVENTION: Because rust is capable of infecting many plant genera, it is usually best to destroy infected plants. Disinfect the growing area, and periodically inspect plants for signs of reinfection. To treat a plant, isolate it, remove all infected tissue, and spray with Fungicide-7 or -18. New chemicals effective against rust are being introduced and may soon be approved for orchids. For more information, consult with local agricultural agents or orchid growers.

MISCELLANEOUS NOTES: Rust is seldom fatal, but it weakens the plant, thus reducing or eliminating flowering.

Uredo nigropuncta (fungus)

COMMON NAMES: Rust.

PLANTS AFFECTED: *Bletia, Cyrtopodium, Encyclia, Stanhopea.*

SYMPTOMS: On *Stanhopea*, the symptoms are light to dark brown spore pustules on the underside of the leaf. As the infection progresses, the pustules break through to the upper leaf surface. In other orchid genera, the symptoms are similar, but the pustules may be orange and turn black with age.

TREATMENT: Cut off and burn all leaves showing infection, and spray plants with Fungicide-7 or -18 mixed with a suitable wetting agent. New chemicals effective against rust are being introduced and may soon be approved for orchids. For more information, consult with local agricultural agents or orchid growers.

CONTROL/PREVENTION: Because rust is difficult to control once it becomes established, it is usually best to destroy infected plants. Disinfect the growing area, and inspect plants periodically for signs of this disease.

MISCELLANEOUS NOTES: Rust is seldom fatal, but it weakens the plant, thus reducing or eliminating flowering.

Uredo oncidii (fungus)

COMMON NAMES: Rust.

PLANTS AFFECTED: *Epidendrum, Lycaste, Odontoglossum, Oncidium.*

SYMPTOMS: Small orange pustules appear on the underside of leaves. The infected area is usually circular with an advancing orange margin. With age, the center turns brown.

TREATMENT: Cut off and burn all leaves showing infection, and spray plants with Fungicide-7 or -18 mixed with a suitable wetting agent. New chemicals effective against rust are being introduced and may soon be approved for orchids. For more information, consult with local agricultural agents or orchid growers.

CONTROL/PREVENTION: Because rust is capable of infecting numerous genera, it is usually best to destroy infected plants. Disinfect the growing area, and inspect plants periodically for signs of this disease.

MISCELLANEOUS NOTES: Rust is seldom fatal, but it weakens the plant, thus reducing or eliminating flowering. This pathogen is reported from Brazil to Mexico and in the Caribbean islands.

Uredo scabies (fungus)

COMMON NAMES: Rust, *Vanilla* rust.

PLANTS AFFECTED: *Vanilla.*

SYMPTOMS: Small pustules appear on the underside of leaves. The infected area is usually circular with an advancing margin of infected tissue. With age, the spots may change color.

TREATMENT: It is usually best to burn infected plants. If infection is just beginning, cut off and burn all leaves showing infection, sterilizing the tool after each cut. Spray plants with Fungicide-7 or -18 mixed with a suitable wetting agent. New chemicals, effective against rust are being introduced and may soon be approved for use on orchids. For more information, consult with local agricultural agents or orchid growers.

CONTROL/PREVENTION: Periodically inspect plants for signs of this disease.

MISCELLANEOUS NOTES: Rust is the most serious disease affecting *Vanilla* plantations. It seldom kills plants but weakens them, thus reducing or eliminating flowering. The disease is reported in all commercial *Vanilla*-growing areas.

Vanda firm rot. See *Pseudomonas andropogonis.*

Vanda mosaic (virus)

COMMON NAMES: Flower break.

PLANTS AFFECTED: *Vanda.*

SYMPTOMS: Symptoms include distorted sepals and petals, variegated flower color, and faint or inconspicuous mosaic on the leaf tips.

TREATMENT: Destroy the plant when infection is confirmed.

CONTROL/PREVENTION: Isolate any plant suspected of infection. Sterilize cutting tools, control insects, and disinfect the growing area.

MISCELLANEOUS NOTES: This virus is different from other flower break viruses. It occurs wherever *Vanda* is grown.

***Vanda* transit rot** (fungus). This is a complex of fungi including *Alternaria, Botrytis,* and *Gloeosporium.*

COMMON NAMES: N/A.

PLANTS AFFECTED: *Vanda.*

SYMPTOMS: Small, chocolate brown spots appear 3–5 days after cut flowers have been packed for shipping. The spots continue to enlarge until they cover the blossom.

TREATMENT: Before *Vanda* flowers are packed for shipping, they should be sprayed with Fungicide, germicide-2, diluted to 1 : 2000.

CONTROL/PREVENTION: Pretreat blossoms before shipping.

MISCELLANEOUS NOTES: The disease probably occurs worldwide.

***Vanilla* anthracnose.** See *Colletotrichum gloeosporiodes.*

***Vanilla* astérinées.** See *Gloeodes pomigena.*

***Vanilla* bud malformation.** See *Nectria vanillae.*

***Vanilla* fruit deformation.** See *Botrytis cinerea.*

***Vanilla* mildew.** See *Phytophthora jatrophae.*

***Vanilla* root rot.** See *Fusarium batatis* var. *vanillae.*

***Vanilla* rouille or rust.** See *Uredo scabies.*

***Vanilla* seuratia.** See *Seuratia coeffeicola.*

***Vanilla* sporoschisma.** See *Sporoschisma* species.

***Vanilla* wilt.** See *Fusarium oxysporum.*

White cell necrosis. See *Cymbidium* mosaic.

Yellowing. See Mycoplasmal disease.

Disease Treatment Summary

Despite all efforts at prevention, orchid growing problems that require more drastic measures occur from time to time. A wide variety of chemicals are specifically formulated to deal with these problems. Given the ever-changing nature of the chemical arsenal and the complexity of regulations regarding their sale and use, we do not recommend specific chemical compounds but urge readers instead to consult their local agricultural agents for information on accepted chemical preventatives and their use. For information on interpreting product labels and using chemicals safely, see Section III of this Appendix.

To facilitate cross-referencing, we have divided widely used chemicals into the following broad classifications: bactericides, disinfectants, fungicides, and systemic fungicides.

Bactericides, as used in horticulture, are broad-spectrum antibiotics that effectively destroy a wide variety of bacteria that cause plant diseases.

Disinfectants, which kill pathogens on contact, are used for general control of a variety of organisms. They have a short residual effect but may be highly toxic to plants. Sterilizing with a disinfectant kills viruses on pots, tools, benches, and equipment in the growing area, but no chemical is selective enough to kill only a virus once it has infected plant cells.

Fungicides kill fungi on contact.

Systemic fungicides provide longer-term protection but are sometimes not effective until they are absorbed by the plant.

The products listed in the following tables may be available and approved for use only in certain parts of the world. The inclusion of a chemical on this list does not indicate that it has been registered for use on orchids. Other, equally effective products may be available. Consult with local agricultural agents for the names of products currently approved for use on orchids.

The use of product names implies no endorsement by the authors or publisher, nor do the authors or publisher assume liability for any accidents resulting from use of the chemicals named. *The information on applications given below is not a substitute for the information on the product label.* It is the responsibility of the user to comply with the directions on the container of the product used and with the laws of the area in which the chemical is applied.

The following list of chemicals known to be effective against particular pathogens was compiled from information in the following works:

American Orchid Society, Inc. 1986. *Handbook on orchid pests and diseases.* American Orchid Society, Inc., 6000 South Olive Ave., West Palm Beach, FL, U.S.A. 33405.

Extension Services of Oregon State University, Washington State University, and the University of Idaho. 1988. *Pacific Northwest disease control handbook.* Pacific Northwest Extension Services, c/o Agricultural Communications, Oregon State University, Corvallis, OR, U.S.A. 97331-2119.

Hadley, G., M. Arditti, and J. Arditti. 1987. Orchid diseases—a compendium. In: *Orchid biology: reviews and perspectives.* Vol. IV. Edited by J. Arditti. Comstock Publishing, Cornell University Press, Ithaca, N.Y.

Disease Treatment Summary

Chemical Type	Chemical Name—Active Ingredient	Product Names	Product Applications
Treatment categories used in the preceding list of pathogens.	The primary active ingredient. Information on chemical composition is followed by more general chemical names.	Generic and brand-name products containing the primary active ingredient.	General information on usage.
Algicide, bactericide, fungicide-1	dimethyl benzyl ammonium chlorides *or* dimethylethyl-benzyl ammonium chlorides	Consan Consan 20 Physan 20 RD-20 Triconsan	A broad-spectrum bactericide and fungicide used to treat *Erwinia, Phytophthora, Pseudomonas,* and *Pythium* infections. Used as a disinfectant, it helps prevent the spread of all pathogens, including viral pathogens.
Bactericide-1	4-(dimethylamino)-1,4,4a,5,5a-6,11,12-octahydro-3, 5,6,10,12,12a-hexahydroxy-6-methyl-1,11-dioxo-2-naphthacenecarboxamide	Oxytetracycline Terramycin	Available as a dust or a wettable powder, this compound is an antibiotic used specifically to treat bacterial infections caused by *Erwinia* and *Pseudomonas.*
Bactericide-2	o-2-deoxy-2-(methylamino)-a-L-glucopyranosyl-(1d)-o-5-deoxy-3-C-formyl-a-L-lyxofuranosyl-(1d 4)-N, N^2-bis (ammoniomethyl)-a-streptamine *or* cycloheximide *or* streptomycin sulfate, sometimes combined with oxytetracycline (terramycin)	Agrimycin Agristrep Phytomycin Streptomycin	Available as a dust or a wettable powder, this compound is an antibiotic used specifically to treat bacterial infections caused by *Erwinia* and *Pseudomonas.*
Bactericide, fungicide, nematocide-1	2,4,5,6-tetrachloro-1,3-benzenedicarbonitrile *or* tetrachloroisophthalonitrile	Bravo Chlorothalonil DAC-2787 Daconil Exotherm-Termil Forturf	Available as a liquid or a wettable powder, this compound is a broad-spectrum fungicide that is effective against *Botrytris* infections.
Disinfectant-1	8-quinolinol	8-hydroxyquinoline	Used to sterilize pots, tools, benches, and the growing area.

Chemical Type	Chemical Name—Active Ingredient	Product Names	Product Applications
Disinfectant-2	8-quinolinol sulfate *or* oxyquinoline sulfate	8-hydroxyquinoline sulfate 8-quinol sulfate Chinosol Quinosol	Used to treat petal blights and Erwinia, *Phytophthora, Pseudomonas, Pythium,* and *Sclerotium* infections.
Disinfectant-3	37% formaldehyde solution	Formaldehyde Formalin Karsan Steriform	Used to sterilize pots, tools, benches, and the growing area.
Disinfectant-4	oxyquinolinol benzoate *or* quinolinol benzoate	8-hydroxyquinoline benzoate Wilson's Anti-Damp	Used to treat *Colletotrichum, Erwinia,* and *Glomerella* species and to counteract *Miltonia* scorch.
Disinfectant-5	sodium hypochlorite	Clorox Purex	Common household bleach, used to sterilize pots, tools, benches, and the growing area.
Fungicide-1	1,2-ethanediylbis[carbamo-dithioato](2-)manganese *or* 80% manebmanganese ethylene *or* bisdithio carbamate with manganese or zinc ions	Dithane M-22 Dithane M-45 Fore Mancozeb Maneb Maneba Manesan Manzate	Available as a dust, liquid, or wettable powder, these compounds are used to treat blight, *Diplodia* leaf spot, *Fusarium, Phytophthora,* rust, and *Septoria* leaf spot.
Fungicide-2	1,2-ethanediylbis[carbamo-dithioato](2-) zinc *or* zinc ethylene bisdithiocarbamate	Aspor Curit Dithane Z-78 Dithane Z-79 Pamazol-Z Polyram Z Triofterol Trisan Tritogot Z Zebenide Zinate Zineb	Available as a dust or a wettable powder, these compounds have a long residual action. They are used to treat Cercospora, Colletotrichum, fungi species, *Fusarium, Gloeosporium, Phytophthora, Rhizoctonia, Sclerotium,* and *Septoria.*

Fungicide-3	1,4,-dichloro-2,5-dimethoxybenzene *or* tetramethylthiuram disulfide *or* thiram	Chloroneb Polyram-M Tersan-LSR Tersan SP Thiram Trimangol Trimanoc Tritogol	Available as a dust or a wettable powder, these compounds are used to treat Phytophthora.
Fungicide-4	3-(3,5-dichlorophenyl)-5-ethenyl-5-methyl-2,4-oxazolidinedione	Ornalin Ronilan Vinclozolin 50% WP	Available as a wettable powder, this compund is used to control *Botrytis*.
Fungicide-5	3-(3,5-dichlorophenyl)-N-(1-methyl-ethyl)-2,4-dioxo-1-imidzolidine-carboxamide	Chipco 26019 Fungicide VI Iprodione Roval 50W	Effective as a preventative for *Diplodia*, other dark-spored fungi, and *Rhizoctonia*. The compound reportedly offers particularly dependable protection when rotated with Systemic fungicide-1.
Fungicide-6	3a,4,7,7a-tetrahydro-2-[(1,1,2,2-tetra-chloroethyl)thiol]-1H-isoin-dole-1,3(2H)-dione	Capatafol Difolatan	Available as a liquid. No information on specific applications.
Fungicide-7	3a,4,7,7a-tetrahydro-2-[(trichloromethyl)thiol]-1H-isoin-dole-1,3(2H)-dione *or* N-[(trichloromethyl)thiol]-4-cyclohexene-1,2,dicarboxamide *or* N-trichloromethyl-thiotetrahydrophthalimide	Bygone Captan Captane Merpan Ortho 5865 Orthocide Trimegol	Available as a liquid, dust, or wettable powder, this compound is a broad-spectrum fungicide used to treat *Alternaria*, black spot, *Botrytis*, *Cercospora*, *Colletotrichum*, *Curvularia*, *Gloeosporium*, leaf spot, *Phytophthora*, rust, *Sphenospora*, *Uredo*, and perhaps other infections.
Fungicide-8	4-[2-(3,5-dimethyl-2-oxocyclohexyl)-2-2-hydroxyethyl]-2,6-piperidinedione *or* cycloheximide	Actidione Cycloheximide Naramycin A	Used to treat *Fusarium*.
Fungicide-9	5-ethoxy-3-trichloromethyl-1,2,4-thiadiazole *or* ethazol	Terrazole Truban ETAT Truban 30WP	Compound should be applied as a drench. This fungicide is best used for preventing rather than treating infections. It is reported to be effective against black rot diseases such as damping off or against infections caused by *Phytophthora* and *Pythium*. One application is effective for 12 weeks.

Disease Treatment Summary

Chemical Type	Chemical Name—Active Ingredient	Product Names	Product Applications
Fungicide-10	5,6-dihydro-2-methyl-1, 4-oxathion-3-carboxanilide-4,4-dioxide *or* 2,3-dihydro-5-carboxanilide-4, 4-dioxide-6-methyl-1,4-oxathion	Oxycarboxin Plantvax	No information on specific applications.
Fungicide-11	methylmercury dicyandiamide	Mosodren	Used to treat *Phytophthora*.
Fungicide-12	N-alkyl dimethyl benzyl and ethyl ammonium chlorides *or* N-alkyl methyl isoquinolinium chlorides	Shield 10WP	Used as a drench to treat *Ptychogaster* and other molds that occur in the medium.
Fungicide-13	p-(dimethylamino) benzenediazo sodium sulfonate *or* sodium [4-(dimethylamino) phenyl] diazene sulfonate *or* fenaminosulf	Dexan Lesan	Used to treat *Phytophthora* and *Pythium*, this compound is more effective against the latter. It deteriorates rapidly in sunlight and should be used immediately after it is mixed. After the roots are drenched, it should be watered in.
Fungicide-14	pentachloronitrobenzene	Avicol Brassicol Earthside Quintozene Teraclor Terraclor Tri-PCNB	Available as a liquid, dust, or wettable powder, this compound should be used as a drench. It is reported to be an effective treatment for *Rhizoctonia* and *Sclerotium*. Only one application is required.
Fungicide-15	propylenebis (dithiocarbamato) zinc	Airone Antracol Bayer 46131 Methylzineb Mezineb	No information on specific applications.
Fungicide-16	tetrachloroisophthalonitrile	Bravo Chlorothalonil	Available as a liquid or a wettable powder. No information on specific applications.
Fungicide-17	tetramethylthioperoxydicarbonicdiamide *or* tetramethyl thiuran disulfide + 2% methoxychlor	Polyram Forte Pomarsol Forte Tersan-F Thiram Tripomol	Available as a dust or a wettable powder, this compound is used to treat *Phytophthora* and other fungal species.

216

Fungicide-18	tris (dimethylcarbamodithoato-S,S') iron *or* ferric dimethyl dithiocarbamate	Carbamate WDG Ferbam Ferbame Fermspray Niacide Tricarbamix Trifungol	Available in several forms, this compound is used to treat *Cercospora*, *Coleosporium*, *Colletotrichum*, *Fusarium*, *Gloeosporium*, *Rhizoctonia*, rust, *Sphenospora*, *Uredo*, and probably other infections.
Fungicide, germicide-1	cupric hydroxide *or* cupric sulfate + lime *or* micronized tribasic copper sulfate	Bordeaux Mix Coxysan Cuprax Kocide 101 Microcop OrthoCop-53 Perenox Vitigran	Copper compounds are available as water suspensions or dusts, since fixed copper is insoluble. Copper is used to treat *Erwinia*, *Phytophthora*, and *Pseudomonas* infections, but it is toxic to some orchids and should be used cautiously. Copper-based compounds should never be mixed with other chemicals. Most copper compounds require repeat applications at 7–10 day intervals.
Fungicide, germicide-2	o-phenylphenol, sodium salt tetrahydrate *or* sodium 2-hydroxy diphenyl *or* sodium orthophenylphenate *or* sodium o-phenylphenate	Dowicide A Natriphene Stopmold	Compound is used as a drench or soak. It is a stable chemical with short residual effects. Compatible with most water-soluble chemicals, it is effective in treating bacterial infections such as *Miltonia* scorch or those caused by *Erwinia* and *Pseudomonas*. It is used to treat *Phytophthora*, *Pythium*, and other fungal diseases such as *Colletotrichum*, *Rhizoctonia*, and *Sclerotium*.
Systemic fungicide-1	[1-[(butylamino) carbonyl]-1H-benzi-midazol-2-yl] carbamic acid methyl ester	Benlate Benomyl DuPont 1991 Tersan 1991	A broad-spectrum fungicide effective against most orchid diseases except those caused by *Pythium ultimum*, *Phytophthora cactorum*, and bacteria. It both cures and prevents infections of black spot, *Botrytris*, *Cercospora*, *Colletotrichum*, *Curvularia*, *Fusarium*, *Gloeodes*, *Gloeosporium*, *Guignardia*, *Microthyriella*, *Phyllostictina*, *Rhizoctonia*, *Septoria*, and others. Treatments must be repeated at 10–14 day intervals until the disease is controlled.
Systemic fungicide-2	1-(4-chlorophenxy)-3,3 dimethyl-1-(1H-1,2,4-triazol-1-yl)-2 butanone	Bayleton 50WP Tridimefon	An effective treatment for rust diseases. Applied as a spray, the chemical enters plants through the foliage.

217

Chemical Type	Chemical Name—Active Ingredient	Product Names	Product Applications
Systemic fungicide-3	15% 5-ethoxy-3-(trichloromethyl)-1,2,4-thiadiazole plus 25% dimethyl 4,4'-O-phenylene bis (3-thicallophanate) *or* thiophanate methyl, 5-ethoxy-3-trichloromethyl-1, 2-thiadiazole	Banrot (40WP) ETMT	Available as a wettable powder, this compound contains the active ingredient in Fungicide-9 together with a systemic fungicide. It is used to treat *Botrytis, Colletotrichum, Fusarium, Gloeosporium, Pythium, Phytophthora, Rhizoctonia, Sclerotinia,* and other infections.
Systemic fungicide-4	aluminum tris-o-ethyl phosphate *or* fosetyl aluminum	Aliette Fosetyl-A1	A plant-activated compound considered very safe for the environment, this fungicide reportedly improves or enhances plant resistance and is effective as both preventative and curative for *Phytophthora* and *Pythium.* Although it is absorbed by both roots and leaves, it should be sprayed on the foliage since it only moves down the plant.
Systemic fungicide-5	N-(2,6-dimethylphenyl)-N-(methoxyacetyl) alanine methyl ester	Metalaxyl Ridomil 2E Subdue 2E	Supplied as a liquid, this compound should be applied as a drench. Although it is absorbed by both roots and leaves, it moves only up the plant. It is effective as both preventative and curative for *Phytophthora* and *Pythium.*
Systemic fungicide-6	N,N-[1,4-piperazinediyl bis (2,2,2-trichloroethylidene)]-bis(formamide)	Funginex Saprol Triforine	An effective treatment and systemic protectant against rust diseases, this compound should be applied as a spray, since plants take it up through the foliage.
Systemic fungicide-7	propamocarb	Banol	Effective as both preventative and curative for *Phytophthora* and *Pythium.*
Systemic fungicide-8	thiophanate-methyl, (dimethyl [(1,2-phenylene) bis (iminocarbonothioyl)] bis [carbamate]), with zinc++ ions and manganese++ ethylenebis dithiocarbamate	Zyban	A contact and systemic fungicide that should be applied as a foliar spray. It is reportedly effective against *Alternaria, Botrytis, Cercospora, Colletotrichum, Curvularia, Fusarium, Gloeosporium, Rhizoctonia,* and *Septoria.*
Systemic fungicide-9	triadimefon	Bayleton	A systemic protectant against rust diseases, this compound is applied as a spray and taken up by the foliage.

WARNING: READ AND FOLLOW THE INSTRUCTIONS ON THE LABEL.

Growers are warned that chemicals may damage plants if applied in a manner or to a plant not specifically recommended on the label. Chemicals may alter a plant's sensitivity to light or cause damage that results in deformed new growths. See the discussion under "General Rules for Chemical Use" in Section III.

Pests

General Information

Greenhouse pests usually fall into one of 2 groups: the phylum *Arthropoda*, which includes insects, mites, and millipedes, and the phylum *Mollusca*, which includes slugs and snails. Insects may be the oldest, most numerous creatures on earth, and the vast majority are either beneficial or harmless to plants.

The few insects that pose problems in horticulture often cause considerable damage by chewing and sucking. In addition to direct injury, insects play a role in transferring disease pathogens. There is evidence that insects contribute to the spread of approximately 150 viral diseases, 25 fungal diseases, and 15 or more bacterial diseases.

Overall health is a plant's first line of defense against pests. Most gardeners have seen weak plants devastated by attack while nearby healthy plants were completely unaffected. Our understanding of the means by which healthy plants protect themselves from insects and diseases is currently quite limited. Scientists have learned that plant varieties which are resistant to certain insects or diseases naturally produce more chemicals than those which are affected. Recent research further indicates that forest trees rapidly increase their production of chemical defenses when a nearby tree is under attack. While a similar phenomenon has not been confirmed for orchids, it is a fascinating possibility.

Protective, preventive measures are the grower's second line of defense against pests. When plants are growing in an enclosed area, all vents and openings should be screened. In addition, new plants should be inspected and sprayed before they are introduced into the growing area. Plants that are summered outside should be carefully sprayed before they are reintroduced into the enclosed growing area.

An option available to greenhouse owners is using positive pressure (fans that blow air in) rather than negative pressure (fans that pull air out). Growers with positive-pressure greenhouses experience dramatically fewer problems with insects and hypothesize that the pests are destroyed as they are blown through the fan. Even in a positive-pressure greenhouse, however, the safest approach is to screen the air vents.

Applying chemicals should be the last pest-control option considered by a grower. Pesticide applications should be carefully timed to coincide with the appropriate phase of the insect's life-cycle. The only effective time to spray for armored scale, for example, is when eggs are hatching in spring. One way to monitor insect populations is to install and periodically inspect sticky strips or yellow boards coated with a sticky substance such as Stick-em or Tangle-foot. The panels may be cleaned with turpentine and recoated as needed. The time to apply control sprays is just as insect populations begin to increase.

Beneficial insects are sometimes used to help keep pest populations under control in the garden. Ladybugs and praying mantises are familiar predatory insects, and parasitic insects may be available locally. Beneficial insects should not be released until after the pest population begins to increase, or they will simply move on to other gardens where food is available. Using beneficial insects is less practical in a greenhouse, since most orchid growers prefer to control pests before their numbers increase to this level.

Small frogs are very effective at controlling insects. Growers can encourage green frogs to take up residence by providing places where the frogs are safe during the day. Hiding places must be shaded, moist, and protected. A pot turned upside down and buried with the drainage holes above the surface of the ground is an ideal frog-house.

Local agricultural agents are an excellent source of information regarding local pest populations, recommended pesticides, and effective timing of pest-control measures.

Adding a spreader-sticker or wetting agent often increases the effectiveness of a spray. Follow the label directions. An alternative to a commercial spreader-sticker is liquid dishwashing soap (not detergent) mixed at ½ tsp. per gal. (2.5 ml per 3.8 liters) of water.

Pesticides are classified as either botanical or synthetic, indicating whether they are derived from plants or manmade. Regardless of their source, pesticides should be used cautiously and conservatively. Even natural pesticides are potent chemical substances that are as devastating to beneficial insects as they are to pests.

Botanical Pesticides

Botanical pesticides are natural pesticidal products which often act rapidly but tend to have a short life. Because of their short life, they are generally considered safer to use than synthetic pesticides. Unlike many of the latter, botanical pesticides are not stored in the tissue of plants, so they are potentially less harmful to the environment.

Insecticidal soap is considered the least toxic form of insect control. A special formulation of fatty acids, it is effective against aphids, mealybugs, mites, scale, thrips, and whiteflies. Some formulations include pyrethrum. Orchid growers commonly use insecticidal soaps successfully.

The following botanical insecticides are powerful natural chemicals that should be used carefully. The general rules for using chemicals included in Section III of this Appendix, "Using Chemicals Safely," also apply to the use of botanical insecticides.

Pyrethrum, derived from *Chrysanthemum cinerariaefolium*, is a contact insecticide that kills rapidly by paralyzing insects. It is available as a dust. Pyrethrum is considered a safe insecticide for people and other warm-blooded animals, but the dust should not be inhaled. Cats are sometimes sensitive to pyrethrum, and it is toxic to fish. Synthetic or concentrated pyrethrum, shown on the label as "pyrethrin," is usually formulated as a liquid and is available under a variety of brand names. It is effective against aphids, beetles, mealybugs, exposed thrips, mites, and whiteflies. Orchid growers commonly use it successfully.

Rotenone is another strong pesticide derived from plants, including the roots of *Tephrosia virginiana* (a weed commonly called devil's shoe string), which contain 5% rotenone. This chemical works as a slow-acting poison, and a 1% solution should kill any insect. Rotenone is often adulterated with other chemicals, however, so read the label. It also has a short period of effectiveness with little residual effect. Pyrethrum and rotenone, the most frequently used botanicals, are often combined to form a strong, effective, short-lived insecticide which is considered safe for warm-blooded animals. Rotenone should not be inhaled, and it is extremely toxic to fish. Orchid growers commonly use it successfully.

Ryania and *Sabadilla* are less commonly available botanicals. Ryania is usually sold as a dust, which is sometimes mixed with water for spraying. It is a mildly alkaline insecticide known to be effective against many moths, borers, larvae, and other insects. Information regarding its effect on orchids is not available. Sabadilla, also sold as a dust, is derived from a lily originating in Mexico and South America. It is also effective against many pest larvae as well as aphids and some beetles.

Nicotine is derived from *Nicotiana tabacum* (commonly known as tobacco). It kills by fumes and on contact. Unlike most botanicals, however, it is extremely toxic to warm-blooded animals, including people and pets. It should be used with great caution. Nicotine is available commercially as a dust or in a liquid formulation called nicotine sulfate. In contrast to many synthetic compounds, it does not cause discoloration when sprayed directly on blossoms, and it is used by many orchid growers. No insect has ever developed a tolerance or immunity to nicotine.

Nicotine pesticide solutions were originally made by soaking tobacco leaves in water. Orchid growers thinking of preparing their own nicotine solution should remember that one of the viral diseases which affects orchids is tobacco mosaic–orchid strain (TMV-O). While orchids are not a host for the form of tobacco mosaic virus that affects tobacco, viruses do mutate, and there is no point in risking contamination.

Veratrum or *false hellebore*, also called skunk cabbage or Indian poke, is derived from several species of *Veratrum*. The roots of all plants in this genus are extremely poisonous. All parts of the plant known as Indian poke (*V. viride*) are also poisonous. Veratrum is applied to garden plants as a spray—0.5 oz. (15 ml) of hellebore dissolved in 1 gal. (3.8 liters) of water. Information regarding its effect on orchids is not available. It is a stomach poison that is effective against many chewing insects such as beetles, caterpillars, grasshoppers, and sawflies.

Wormwood tea, made from the leaves of *Artemesia* species, is sometimes used as a pesticide and also serves as a repellent for pests such as flea beetles and butterflies. Information regarding its effect on orchids is not available. (Note that *A. absinthium* should not be used as a companion plant since it also produces a growth retardant which inhibits the growth of nearby plants.)

Synthetic Pesticides

Synthetic pesticides are chemical compounds made by man. They are sometimes designed to resemble a botanical. Synthetic chemicals are readily available, easy to use, and specifically labeled for approved uses. They are sometimes very selective, often particularly effective, and frequently long-lasting, but many are considered potentially more dangerous than botanicals. Systemic insecticides should not be used with orchids. They can cause severe damage, particularly to soft-leaved orchids.

Except for synthetic baits, such as those used for slugs and snails, we have found that botanical insecticides are as effective as synthetics, and we prefer to use pesticides with the shorter life of these natural chemicals.

Laws concerning the use and registration of synthetic insecticides vary enormously from region to region. Consequently, we do not recommend specific chemicals. Consult a local nursery or agricultural agent for information on specific synthetic insecticides.

List of Pests

The most common pests affecting orchids—pests which occur world-wide—are listed below. A summary of pests and treatment information follows this list.

Ants

DESCRIPTION: Ants, which belong to the family Formicidae, are usually 1/6–1/4 in. (4–6 mm) long and may be black, brown, or red. They have an enlarged abdomen and are true insects. During certain periods, female ants may have wings.

SYMPTOMS: Ants may cause spotting on flowers but do little direct damage. Apparent damage is usually caused by the insects exuding the honeydew to which the ants are attracted.

TREATMENT: Controlling aphids, mealybugs, or scale usually solves any problem with ants. Pyrethrum is reportedly effective. Honey placed strategically around the greenhouse lures ants from orchids.

MISCELLANEOUS NOTES: When ants are present, plants should be inspected for aphids, mealybugs, or scale.

Aphids

DESCRIPTION: Aphids that attack orchids belong to several genera in the suborder Homoptera. Also called plant lice, these small, soft-bodied, slow-moving pests are 0.05–0.35 in. (1–6 mm) long. They cause damage by sucking plant juices and, more importantly, by transmitting disease from plant to plant. Aphids are somewhat pear-shaped and may be pale green, yellow, brown, or black. They mature rapidly, so that numerous generations are produced each season.

SYMPTOMS: Aphids attack buds, flowers, or new growths, which may become stunted or distorted. Buds or flowers may fail to open. Leaves may have a sticky deposit.

TREATMENT: The simplest approach is to wash aphids from the plant with a jet of water. Botanical insecticides such as pyrethrum, rotenone, and nicotine are particularly effective against aphids. Applying a systemic fungicide may help prevent a fungal infection from developing in plant tissue damaged by aphids.

MISCELLANEOUS NOTES: Various aphid species occur in most parts of the world. The honeydew excreted by aphids and other sucking insects is very attractive to ants and is also an ideal medium for sooty mold. When sooty mold or ants are present, plants should be inspected for aphids, mealybugs, or scale.

Cockroaches

DESCRIPTION: Members of the order Orthoptera, cockroach species are usually flattened and broadly oval. They are active at night and hide in dark, moist places during the day.

SYMPTOMS: Cockroaches occasionally cause damage to orchid flowers, roots, and new growths.

TREATMENT: Treatment is usually unnecessary unless populations are very high. Reported botanical controls include pyrethrum and nicotine. One method of reducing populations is to trap the insects in the dark nooks where they customarily hide.

MISCELLANEOUS NOTES: The damage caused by cockroaches may be similar to that caused by grasshoppers.

Grasshoppers

DESCRIPTION: Grasshoppers or locusts are classified as *Acrididae* and belong to the order Orthoptera. Varied in size and color, they have narrow wings and strong, oversized back legs. While many species are capable of flying, these pests usually move by jumping. Grasshoppers are active during the day.

SYMPTOMS: These chewing insects can quickly destroy orchid leaves and roots. They are unlikely to be a problem unless conditions are dry and other vegetation is not available.

TREATMENT: Partially bury jars which contain a mixture of molasses and water. These will attract grasshoppers, which fall into the water and drown. Other controls are probably unnecessary unless the population increases rapidly and conditions are dry. Veratrum is the only botanical pesticide reported to be effective.

MISCELLANEOUS NOTES: The damage caused by grasshoppers may be similar to that caused by cockroaches.

Mealybugs

DESCRIPTION: Mealybugs belong to several genera in the suborder Homoptera and are closely related to scale. Mealybugs are 0.1–0.2 in. (2–5 mm) long and tend to live in colonies. They are most mobile when young but become sluggish as their bodies develop a characteristic waxy coating. These soft-bodied, sucking insects may be recognized by the soft, mealy covering, which makes them appear white and waxy.

SYMPTOMS: Severe infestations cause darkened or chlorotic areas on the leaves. Plants appear unhealthy, and symptoms may be more obvious than the insects themselves. Plant damage is similar to that caused by scale.

TREATMENT: Mealybugs need constant attention, as many generations are produced each year. Mealybugs may attack any part of the plant, but they tend to stay tucked away at the junction of the leaf and stem. Old leaf and pseudobulb sheaths should be removed regularly.

Treatments with insecticidal soap, nicotine, or a cotton swab dipped in soapy water, rubbing alcohol, kerosene, or methylated spirits (turpentine, paint thinner, or mineral spirits) dissolve the waxy covering that normally protects the insect. It is difficult to control mealybugs effectively by spraying, since their waxy covering tends to repel liquids. Mixing a spreader-sticker or wetting agent with the insecticide solution helps it to penetrate the waxy covering and remain in place long enough to be effective. The underside of leaves should be thoroughly coated with the spray. Repeat applications may be necessary to control overlapping generations.

MISCELLANEOUS NOTES: Various mealybug species occur in most parts of the world. Ants may signal a mealybug infestation since mealybugs deposit a sweet honeydew which attracts the ants. The honeydew is also an ideal medium for sooty mold. When sooty mold or ants are present, plants should be inspected for aphids, mealybugs, or scale.

Millipedes

DESCRIPTION: Commonly called thousand-legged worms, millipedes may have up to 400 legs. Classified as Diplopoda, they are hard-bodied and coil like a spring when disturbed. These pests may be brown, pinkish brown, or grey.

SYMPTOMS: Millipedes may occasionally damage orchid roots, though they feed primarily on dead plant material.

TREATMENT: Reduce watering. The presence of millipedes indicates that plants may need repotting. A nicotine drench is reportedly an effective control.

MISCELLANEOUS NOTES: Millipedes contribute to the breakdown of natural media. They prefer moist places and are unlikely to be a problem unless plants are overwatered. The greatest threat they pose to orchids is the possibility of transmitting fungal infection.

Mites

DESCRIPTION: Often called spider mites, these sucking insects are closely related to spiders, ticks, and scorpions and belong to the class Arachnida. They usually appear in spring during warm, dry weather. They multiply rapidly if left unchecked; at 60°F (16°C) new generations mature in approximately 3 weeks, while at 90°F (32°C) they mature in 6 days. Mites are red to brown, very small, and difficult to see without a hand lens.

SYMPTOMS: Damage to the upper surface of the leaves is often the first symptom of mite infestation. The affected area may be darkened or develop a silvery sheen that eventually becomes sunken and turns brown. The leaves may be streaked, stippled, or spotted due to loss of chlorophyll. Small webs may be present, and damaged leaves may drop prematurely.

TREATMENT: Insecticidal soap, pyrethrum, rotenone, nicotine, and commercial miticides are effective. To control mites, it is often necessary to make 6–8 applications repeated at intervals of 2–4 days. Treating once or twice is not enough to control the pest. Hosing off the plants washes away mites and breaks down their webs. Increasing humidity and lowering temperatures help prevent infestations. Applying a systemic fungicide may help prevent a fungal infection from developing in the damaged tissue.

MISCELLANEOUS NOTES: Various mite species occur in most parts of the world. Spider-mite damage is easily confused with *Cercospora* leaf spots. To check a plant for mites, rub a piece of white paper or cloth on the underside of the leaves. If it is streaked with red or brown, mites are present.

Orchid beetles

DESCRIPTION: These members of the genus *Xylosandrus* are classified as Coleoptera. They are also called black twig borers and dendrobium beetles. Mature beetles measure about 0.2–0.4 in. (4–10 mm) long. These chewing pests bore into plant tissue to lay their eggs, causing unusual swelling in *Dendrobium* canes and *Cattleya* pseudobulbs.

SYMPTOMS: Old pseudobulbs may be abnormally swollen with small, shot-sized holes. A yellow or chlorotic margin surrounds the infested area. *Dendrobium* are not normally killed by the insect, but rot often follows infestation of *Cattleya* pseudobulbs.

TREATMENT: Adult beetles are easily seen and may be picked off the plants; but they tend to fall off the leaf when they feel threatened, so it is best to hold a container under the leaf during inspection. Pyrethrum, rotenone, and nicotine are effective against mature beetles. If new growths become abnormally swollen, they should be removed and burned to prevent the maturation of hidden beetle larvae.

MISCELLANEOUS NOTES: If these pests become established in the growing area, they can be extremely difficult to control. Various species occur in most tropical areas. The beetles seldom appear in temperate areas unless they are imported along with a new plant. The canes and pseudobulbs of plants imported from infested areas should be carefully examined. Remove old leaf and pseudobulb sheaths to inspect for abnormal swelling, chlorotic areas, or small holes that may otherwise be hidden.

Orchid fly. See Wasps.

Scale

DESCRIPTION: Scale refers to several species of sucking insects belonging to various genera of the suborder Homoptera. Usually smaller than 0.1 in. (1–2 mm) in length, these insects attach to and feed on the underside of leaves and are often hidden under old leaf and pseudobulb sheaths.

Female armored scale secrete a waxy protective coating that is raised, nearly round, often with concentric ridges, and feels hard to the touch. Different species vary in color and may be brown, grey, reddish, white, or yellow. The males are usually smaller, with a protective shell that is often oval with ridges rather than concentric rings. Once the insects attach to a plant, they remain in the same location throughout their life.

Soft scale (such as mealybugs, which are listed separately) also damage by sucking. These insects are smaller than 0.2 in. (1–5 mm) in length. Some species are fully exposed, while others are protected by a soft, waxy covering.

SYMPTOMS: Severe infestations cause darkened or chlorotic areas to appear on the leaves. The leaves may yellow and drop prematurely. Plants appear unhealthy, and leaf symptoms, which are similar to those caused by mealybugs, may be more obvious than the insects themselves.

TREATMENT: Scale is best removed immediately. It may be scraped off or wiped away with a cotton swab soaked in methylated spirits (turpentine, paint thinner, or mineral spirits). The mature scale may be scrubbed off with a toothbrush dipped in any pesticide which will kill young scale in the crawler stage. When plants are inspected regularly, scale is unlikely to become a serious problem. Old leaf and flower sheaths should be removed and the exposed surfaces checked for scale and mealybugs. New plants should be carefully inspected before they are introduced into the growing area. If it is necessary to treat scale with chemicals, they should be applied just as the young hatch and begin to move from plant to plant (i.e., at the crawler stage). The underside of leaves must be carefully sprayed in order for the treatment to be effective. Repeat applications are usually necessary to control overlapping generations.

MISCELLANEOUS NOTES: Various scale species occur in most parts of the world. Ants may signal a scale infestation since these pests deposit a sweet honeydew of plant sap which attracts ants. The honeydew is also an ideal medium for sooty mold. When sooty mold or ants are present, plants should be inspected for aphids, mealybugs, or scale.

Slugs and snails

DESCRIPTION: These familiar chewing pests belonging to the phylum *Mollusca* may be grey, black, or brown, often with spots or stripes. Their soft bodies are usually 0.5–3 in. (13–76 mm) long. Snails are protected by a hard shell, but slugs do not have a protective covering. These pests can cause considerable damage, particularly to young seedlings and tender new growths.

SYMPTOMS: Slugs and snails leave holes and notches in the leaves and may chew off growing tips. Chewed areas may also appear on buds. These nocturnal pests travel on a layer of slime which they excrete to protect their undersides, and this trail is evidence of a potential problem.

TREATMENT: Chemical baits are commercially available. Growers who prefer not to use chemicals may bait slugs and snails with a saucer of beer. The pests are attracted to the beer, in which they drown. Nicotine dust or wormwood (*Artemesia* species) tea may offer effective control. The tea should be applied as a drench, though we have no knowledge of the effect wormwood may have on orchids. Slugs and snails can be difficult to eradicate from the growing area because they enter pots through the drainage holes and stay safely hidden in the damp medium. These pests are often found in damp debris and under rocks or boards. They can be attracted to pieces of cut potato where they can be crushed or killed with salt or ammonia (substances which should not be applied directly to plants).

MISCELLANEOUS NOTES: Various slug and snail species occur in most parts of the world. Slugs and snails frequently return each night to the same plant to feed—a characteristic growers can use to good advantage in setting out bait or hand-picking.

Sowbugs

DESCRIPTION: Sowbugs or pillbugs have hard, segmented, greyish brown bodies and roll into a ball when disturbed. They are classified as Crustacea.

SYMPTOMS: Sowbugs may occasionally damage orchid roots and leaves, though they feed primarily on dead plant material.

TREATMENT: Reduce watering. Many botanical pesticides, including pyrethrum, rotenone, and nicotine, control sowbugs if applied as a drench. The presence of sowbugs may indicate that plants need repotting.

MISCELLANEOUS NOTES: Sowbugs contribute to the breakdown of natural media. They prefer moist places and are unlikely to be a problem unless plants are overwatered.

Thrips

DESCRIPTION: A number of different insects of the order Thysanoptera are known as thrips, a term used for tiny, slender, winged insects measuring 0.02–0.20 in. (0.5–5.0 mm) long. They are usually dark brown or black, but at least one species is yellowish white. Most species produce 3–5 generations per year. These sucking insects are barely visible. They move rapidly when disturbed.

SYMPTOMS: Infested buds may not open properly, and flowers may be deformed. Flowers are damaged when the insects break through cell walls and suck the plant juices. Flowers may appear to have a virus-caused color break that is actually the result of thrip damage. Damaged flowers, buds, and new leaves appear pitted, stippled, silvery, or bleached. Some species feed on the underside of leaves, moving to the upper surface as populations increase. When damage is extensive, the leaves may wilt and die. The leaves may also be spotted with reddish black deposits of excrement. Some species lay eggs in the leaf cells, causing small blisters.

TREATMENT: Insecticidal soaps, pyrethrum, rotenone, and nicotine are very effective against exposed thrips, but because these pests often remain hidden, sprays frequently fail to reach them. Repeat applications are often necessary to control overlapping generations. Applying a systemic fungicide may help prevent a fungal infection from developing in damaged tissue.

MISCELLANEOUS NOTES: Various species of thrips occur in most parts of the world, particularly in warmer climates and in greenhouses. Flowers, beans, and fruit, particularly citrus, are common hosts. Thrips are especially bothersome in that they carry disease from plant to plant.

Wasps

DESCRIPTION: A chalcid wasp, of the order Hymenoptera, has transparent wings and lays its eggs in plant tissue. It is 0.1 in. (1.5–3.0 mm) long. Sometimes called the orchid fly, this insect is not a true fly.

SYMPTOMS: Pseudobulbs are enlarged or swollen, and old canes and pseudobulbs have an exit hole, usually near the base. The wasp pierces the plant tissue to lay its eggs. As the eggs mature, the larvae feed inside the canes and pseudobulbs, causing abnormal swelling. If the insect becomes established in the growing area, it can be extremely difficult to control.

TREATMENT: Pyrethrum, rotenone, and nicotine are effective controls for adult wasps, but killing larvae in the pseudobulb is more difficult. Swollen new growths should be removed and destroyed to prevent the larvae from maturing.

MISCELLANEOUS NOTES: Plant damage results when the larvae feed on the pseudobulb and cut their way out as they mature.

Whiteflies

DESCRIPTION: *Trialeurodes vaporariorum* is commonly known as the greenhouse whitefly. This mothlike sucking insect is tiny, usually less than 1/16 in. (1.6 mm) long, with wings covered by a white, powdery substance.

SYMPTOMS: New growth may appear damaged or unhealthy. Whitefly attacks weaken the plant, making it more susceptible to disease. Fungal infections often invade plants where whiteflies have punctured the tissue.

TREATMENT: Insecticidal soap, pyrethrum, rotenone, and particularly nicotine are effective. Sprays repeated at 4-day intervals are necessary for control of overlapping generations. Applying a systemic fungicide may help prevent a secondary infection.

MISCELLANEOUS NOTES: The insect lays eggs on the underside of leaves. Initially yellow, the eggs become white or grey, which results in a chalky-looking spot. Many broods are produced each year. Various whitefly species occur in most parts of the world.

Orchid Pests Summary

Pests	Plant Symptoms	Miscellaneous Notes	Botanical Pesticides in order of increasing toxicity to humans
Ants	Damaged flowers	Honey placed strategically around the greenhouse lures ants from orchids.	Pyrethrum
Aphids	Buds or flowers that fail to open. Distorted or stunted flowers, buds, or new leaves. Sticky deposits on leaves	Aphids may be washed off flowers and foliage.	Insecticidal soap, Pyrethrum, Rotenone, Nicotine
Cockroaches	Damaged flowers, roots, and new growths	These nocturnal pests may be controlled by trapping.	Pyrethrum, Nicotine
Grasshoppers	Damaged roots and new growths	Grasshoppers may be baited with jars of molasses water.	Veratrum
Mealybugs	Chlorotic or darkened areas on leaves. Sticky deposits on leaves	Mealybugs appear as a white, cottony-looking mass. Treat with compounds that dissolve the waxy protective covering. Repeat applications to control overlapping generations.	Insecticidal soap, Nicotine
Millipedes	Damaged roots	Millipedes prefer moist places and may indicate that plants are overwatered or in need of repotting.	Nicotine
Mites	Darkened areas on leaves. Leaves that are pitted, stippled, bleached, white, or silvery. Sunken areas on leaves	Mites may be washed off foliage. Reducing temperatures and increasing humidity help prevent infestations. Mites are seldom visible, but minute webs may be evident. Sprays should be repeated at 2–4 day intervals 6–8 times.	Insecticidal soap, Pyrethrum, Rotenone
Orchid beetles	Swollen pseudobulbs with small, visible holes	Pesticides are effective only against adults. Abnormally swollen new growths indicate the presence of larvae. The growths should be removed and burned.	Pyrethrum, Rotenone, Nicotine
Scale	Chlorotic or darkened areas on leaves. Leaves that appear yellow and drop prematurely. Sticky deposits on leaves	These sucking insects attach to leaves and pseudobulbs. A cotton swab dipped in methylated spirits (paint thinner) may be used to remove scale. Sprays should be repeated to control overlapping generations.	Insecticidal soap, Nicotine

Pest	Symptoms	Notes	Controls
Slugs and snails	Chewed areas on buds, leaves, young roots, and new growths	Slugs and snails are nocturnal, but shiny slime trails confirm their presence. They may be baited with beer or pieces of cut potato. Damp debris, rocks, and boards serve as hiding places. Commercial baits are available.	Nicotine dust Wormwood tea
Sowbugs	Damaged roots and leaves	Sowbugs prefer moist places and may indicate that plants are overwatered or in need of repotting.	Pyrethrum Rotenone Nicotine
Thrips	Blossoms with color break Buds that fail to open Deformed buds or flowers Flowers, buds, and new leaves that are stunted, pitted, stippled, or blistered Leaves that wilt and die prematurely Reddish black deposits of excrement on leaves	Thrips, which are barely visible, often hide deep in buds and may be difficult to eradicate. Sprays should be repeated to control overlapping generations.	Rotenone Nicotine
Wasps	Swollen pseudobulbs with small, visible holes	Pesticides are effective only against adults. Abnormally swollen new growths indicate the presence of larvae. The growths should be removed and burned.	Pyrethrum Rotenone Nicotine
Whiteflies	Chalky spots on the underside of leaves New growths that are damaged or unhealthy looking	The tiny, sucking insects are white and mothlike. Sprays should be repeated at 4-day intervals to control overlapping generations.	Insecticidal soap Pyrethrum Rotenone Nicotine

WARNING: READ AND FOLLOW THE INSTRUCTIONS ON THE LABEL.

Growers are warned that chemicals may damage plants if applied in a manner or to a plant not specifically recommended on the label. Chemicals may alter a plant's sensitivity to light or cause damage that results in deformed new growths. See the discussion under "General Rules for Chemical Use" in Section III.

Nutrients

General Information

Adequate nutrition is normally provided by the fertilizer applications recommended in the species listings throughout this volume. Nutrition is not a simple matter, however, since plants differ widely in their nutritional needs and the availability of different nutrients varies with pH. Though individual orchid species may have different nutrient requirements, these differences are often subtle and are seldom identified.

Essential plant nutrients are classified as either macronutrient or micronutrients. Macronutrients, required in relatively large amounts, include carbon (C), hydrogen (H), and oxygen (O), which are available directly from the atmosphere.

Other macronutrients needed in large quantities are

Nitrogen (N)

Phosphorus (P)

Potassium (K)

Also classified as macronutrients but needed in much smaller quantities are

Calcium (Ca)

Magnesium (Mg)

Sulfur (S)

Micronutrients, needed in minute quantities, include

Boron (B)

Chlorine (Cl)

Cobalt (Co)

Copper (Cu)

Iron (Fe)

Manganese (Mn)

Molybdenum (Mo)

Zinc (Zn)

Cultivated orchids are much more likely to suffer from an excess of nutrients than from a deficiency. Fertilizers and micronutrient supplements are readily available and easy to apply. The tendency to apply too much fertilizer must be avoided as diligently as the tendency to overwater. Recommended fertilizer type, strength, and frequency of application are discussed in Chapter 1 under the heading "Fertilizer."

Accidental overfertilization may be remedied by immediately flushing the pot several times to leach the fertilizer from the medium. This prevents the plants from absorbing the nutrients. Growers often include charcoal in the medium to help remedy slight to moderate overfertilization. Once a plant has absorbed the nutrients, nothing will draw the nutrients out of the plant. Repotting will prevent the plant from absorbing still more, but only time will tell whether the plant is able to survive.

Macronutrients are usually mobile in the plant, while most micronutrients are not. When nutrients are mobile in the plant, they are pulled from older growths and used for new growth anytime they are in short supply. Consequently, deficiencies of mobile nutrients show first in older leaves or mature growths. On the other hand, nutrients that are not mobile in the plant are locked up in older growths and cannot be further utilized by the plant. Deficiencies of these elements usually show first in the new leaves or growths.

Micronutrients are generally available from organic media in amounts adequate for orchids. The stored nutrients are released by the microbial action that breaks down the medium. Little work has been done on which micronutrients are available from different media. In addition to these naturally occurring micronutrients, many fertilizers contain micronutrients in varying amounts which may not be shown on the label. Many micronutrients are mutually antagonistic in such a way that an excess of one crowds out another and shows as a deficiency of the nutrient no longer available.

Brief descriptions of the various nutritional elements and symptoms of both excesses and deficiencies are given below to assist growers in determining and correcting possible nutritional problems. Although various plant species react differently to imbalances, most indicate an excess or deficiency of a particular nutrient with a variation of the symptoms given.

Research has shown that symptoms of micronutrient deficiencies, which might show in days or weeks in garden plants, usually do not occur for several months in orchids. Symptoms of excess are more common. High levels of micronutrients are toxic to all plants, but orchids are particularly sensitive. If a commercial micronutrient supplement is used, care must be taken to ensure that recommended levels are not exceeded. In fact, since orchids are very efficient at absorbing nutrients, it is a good practice to make 1 or 2 applications at $\frac{1}{4}$–$\frac{1}{2}$ the recommended strength. Toxicity is more likely if micronutrients are applied to any dry medium, but this is particularly true of dry rock wool. An excess of micronutrients is much worse for a plant than a deficiency.

List of Nutrients

For ease of reference, all nutrients are listed alphabetically below. When imbalances of several macro- or micronutrients could cause a plant symptom, macronutrients are most likely to be the problem. A summary of nutrients and problems related to nutrient balance follows this list.

Boron (B). Not mobile in the plant.

Boron, a micronutrient, is required as a catalyst in plant nutrition and metabolism, and it is essential for flowering and fruiting.

SYMPTOMS OF EXCESS: Excess boron causes blackening or death of tissue between veins. Boron in excessive amounts is very toxic to all plants, but it is especially harmful to orchids.

SYMPTOMS OF DEFICIENCY: Boron deficiency can lead to failure to set seed and to death of apical buds, terminal leaves, or growing tips. Plants are usually stunted, roots may be short, and stems may be black and dying. Boron is less available when the pH is above 7. Excess calcium can reduce a plant's ability to use boron.

MISCELLANEOUS NOTES: Boron balance is unlikely to be a problem in orchid cultivation, since adequate amounts of boron are normally available to plants from natural media, regularly applied natural fertilizers, or 1–2 applications each year of a micronutrient supplement. Boron is potentially so toxic that a laboratory tissue analysis should be performed and deficiency determined before boron is added.

Calcium (Ca). Somewhat mobile in the plant.

Calcium, a lesser macronutrient, is used to build cell walls, helps plants neutralize certain toxic acids produced as by-products of plant metabolism, and raises the pH of the medium.

SYMPTOMS OF EXCESS: Excess calcium interferes with magnesium absorption. Consequently, symptoms of magnesium deficiency such as chlorosis on middle or older leaves, light yellow discoloration between the veins or along the leaf margins, curled or cupped mature leaves, or leaf drop of middle and older leaves may indicate a calcium excess. High calcium levels may raise the pH to such a level that some micronutrients are unavailable to the plant.

SYMPTOMS OF DEFICIENCY: Deficiencies usually occur in spring and summer during periods of active growth. Possible symptoms range widely.

Poor growth or vigor are early symptoms; however, these symptoms can result from other cultural problems including root rot due to overwatering or deteriorated medium, high night temperatures, and inappropriate rest-period conditions. Plants should be unpotted and the roots examined for damage before fertilizer is increased.

New leaves may turn black at the tips. The affected area has an advancing yellow band. How far the discoloration extends down the leaf depends on the severity of the deficiency. Similar symptoms are caused by lack of water or excess fertilizing, so it is important to review watering and fertilizing practices before increasing nutrients.

Yellow leaves may turn brown and die prematurely.

Mature leaves may become cupped. A similar symptom may be caused by chemical damage.

Bud growth may be inhibited, or buds may develop improperly. Buds that yellow and drop prematurely usually indicate light or temperature problems rather than a nutrient imbalance, while deformed buds usually result from insect or chemical damage.

A calcium deficiency may cause death of root tips.

Excess potassium or magnesium may cause symptoms of calcium deficiency. Likewise, too much or too little water can cause symptoms of calcium deficiency in the growth which occurred during the period of water stress. At low pH, calcium binds with other elements and is unavailable to the plant.

MISCELLANEOUS NOTES: Calcium is seldom included in commercial fertilizers or micronutrient preparations because the calcium content in water varies so greatly that calcium levels may already be excessive in some hard-water areas. If calcium is needed, 1 Tbs. of dolomitic limestone may be added to each gal. (3.8 liters) of medium to provide both calcium and magnesium in the correct ratio. Dolomite lime has a natural balance of calcium and magnesium. Using garden lime, which

contains no magnesium, can result in an excess of calcium which interferes with the plant's ability to absorb magnesium. Other sources of calcium include steamed bone meal and crushed shells. Growers in soft-water areas often add dolomitic limestone as a rapidly available form of calcium and crushed shells for a longer term calcium supply.

Chlorine (Cl). Not mobile in the plant.

Chlorine, a micronutrient, is required in extremely small amounts.

SYMPTOMS OF EXCESS: Excess chlorine shows as salt injury and may cause leaves to turn brown from the tip toward the base. Soft-leaved orchids are sometimes extremely sensitive to chlorinated water. If chlorinated water is the suspected cause of brown leaf tips, try storing water overnight in an open container, which allows the chlorine to dissipate before the water is applied to sensitive plants.

SYMPTOMS OF DEFICIENCY: Leaves become bronze then chlorotic and finally die. Wilted leaf tips that do not become erect when watered usually indicate insufficient chlorine. A deficiency may also cause deformed roots. Chlorine deficiency is very unlikely, since chlorine is normally available in adequate quantities from natural media or from the water supply. A laboratory tissue analysis should be performed before chlorine is added.

MISCELLANEOUS NOTES: Chlorine balance is unlikely to be a problem in orchid cultivation.

Cobalt (Co). Degree of mobility is not known.

Only recently established as a necessary micronutrient, cobalt is required for nitrogen fixation.

SYMPTOMS OF EXCESS: N/A.

SYMPTOMS OF DEFICIENCY: Cobalt deficiency may cause chlorosis in older leaves or red or purple coloring on the leaves. Excess phosphorus or potassium may interfere with cobalt availability.

MISCELLANEOUS NOTES: Cobalt balance is unlikely to be a problem in orchid cultivation. Cobalt should be added only as part of a micronutrient supplement.

Copper (Cu). Not mobile in the plant.

Copper, a micronutrient, is essential for plant growth and serves as a catalyst in plant respiration and the utilization of iron.

SYMPTOMS OF EXCESS: Excess copper may be toxic to orchids. It often shows as symptoms of iron deficiency, such as yellow to white mottling on new leaves with green veins. The condition may occur at low pH levels.

SYMPTOMS OF DEFICIENCY: New growths may be small and misshapen. Terminal shoots may wilt, and leaf color may be faded. Excess potassium interferes with copper utilization, causing symptoms of copper deficiency.

MISCELLANEOUS NOTES: Copper balance is unlikely to be a problem in orchid cultivation. Copper should be applied only as part of a micronutrient supplement, as it can be highly toxic to orchids. When the pH is above 7, copper is less available to the plant.

Iron (Fe). Not mobile in the plant.

Iron, a micronutrient, is used in chlorophyll and carbohydrate production.

SYMPTOMS OF EXCESS: Excess iron is rarely a problem in cultivated plants. Research indicates that excess iron is particularly harmful to orchids, but no information on symptoms is available.

SYMPTOMS OF DEFICIENCY: Interveinal chlorosis (yellowing) usually occurs in new leaves. If the deficiency continues, the yellow tissue may become white. Brown spots on the leaves, which may indicate iron deficiency, are more likely to be caused by fungal infection or insect damage. Iron deficiencies may occur, even in a natural medium, if oxygen is deficient or if the pH is 7 or greater.

MISCELLANEOUS NOTES: Iron balance is unlikely to be a problem in orchid cultivation. Iron is pH sensitive and is more likely to be deficient at extremely high or low pH levels. It is normally available to the plant in sufficient amounts from natural media. Orchids are known to be extremely sensitive to excess iron. Since iron is available in many fertilizers and commercial micronutrient supplements, additional iron should be applied only if a tissue analysis has determined a deficiency.

Magnesium (Mg). Mobile in the plant.

Magnesium, a lesser macronutrient, is necessary for the production of chlorophyll. In addition, it aids in protein formation, corrects plant pH, and is necessary to the plant's utilization of other nutrients.

SYMPTOMS OF EXCESS: Excess magnesium interferes with calcium uptake, so plants may show signs of calcium deficiency.

SYMPTOMS OF DEFICIENCY: Cupped leaves, reduction in growth, and marginal or interveinal chlorosis (yellow along leaf edges or between veins) are symptoms of deficiency in some species. Deficiencies usually show in the middle or older leaves. If the local water supply is high in calcium but low in magnesium, plants may benefit from increased magnesium.

MISCELLANEOUS NOTES: Like calcium, magnesium is seldom included in commercial fertilizers. In addition, it is easily leached from the medium. Magnesium may be applied alone in the form of Epsom salts, mixed at the rate of 1 tsp. per gal. of water (1 tsp. per 3.8 liters), every few weeks during periods of active growth. Adding 1 Tbs. of dolomitic limestone to each gal. (3.8 liters) of medium provides both calcium and magnesium in the correct ratio. Dolomite lime has a calcium to magnesium ratio of 62 to 38. At very low pH levels, plants are unable to use magnesium.

Manganese (Mn). Not mobile in the plant.

Manganese, a micronutrient, is necessary as a catalyst in plant nutrition and influences growth and maturation.

SYMPTOMS OF EXCESS: An excess of manganese causes reduced growth and brown spotting on the leaves. An excess usually occurs under acid conditions (low pH). It may show as symptoms of iron deficiency, since too much manganese can interfere with iron uptake.

SYMPTOMS OF DEFICIENCY: Manganese deficiency causes interveinal chlorosis of new leaves. The yellowing occurs between green veins. Later, the discolored areas become brown, producing a checked or mottled effect. Stems may be yellowish green. Symptoms of manganese deficiency can be caused by excess potassium. Plants are less able to use manganese when the pH is above 7.

MISCELLANEOUS NOTES: Manganese balance is unlikely to be a problem in orchid cultivation. Manganese is seldom deficient in orchids grown in organic media, and growers using inorganic media can provide adequate supplies with a micronutrient supplement. Extremely high or low pH levels may cause poor manganese utilization.

Molybdenum (Mo). Somewhat mobile in the plant.

Molybdenum, a micronutrient, is normally considered a pollutant, but plants need it in very small amounts in order to utilize nitrogen.

SYMPTOMS OF EXCESS: N/A.

SYMPTOMS OF DEFICIENCY: Molybdenum deficiency may cause pale yellow interveinal chlorosis on older leaves. Leaves may be twisted or fail to expand. Plants are seldom deficient in molybdenum unless the pH is below 5.2.

MISCELLANEOUS NOTES: Molybdenum balance is unlikely to be a problem in orchid cultivation. A laboratory tissue analysis should be performed and deficiency determined before molybdenum is added.

Nitrogen (N). Mobile in the plant.

Nitrogen, a macronutrient, is directly used in the growth of green, leafy portions of the plant. Plants with an appropriate supply are sturdy and mature rapidly.

SYMPTOMS OF EXCESS: When nitrogen levels are too high, new growth is weak, spindly, and dark green. It may also be brittle, especially when temperatures are high. An imbalance of nitrogen and potassium is a possible cause of dark green leaves, but nutrient imbalances are unlikely if a balanced fertilizer is used at the recommended frequency. Excess nitrogen combined with low light can cause leaf curl in some plants, as can any chemical injury. Leaves may turn black when nitrogen is grossly excessive. Exceedingly low temperatures may produce a similar plant response.

Excess nitrogen results in soft, rapid growth that is more susceptible to disease. In agriculture, *high nitrogen with moderate levels of phosphate is known to increase many plants' susceptibility to fungal, bacterial, and mosaic diseases.* High nitrogen may be one of the reasons viral diseases are found in cultivated orchids, while they are seldom found in plants growing in the wild.

SYMPTOMS OF DEFICIENCY: Inadequate nitrogen results in reduced growth, poor vigor, and yellowing (chlorosis) of the older growth. Low light or excess moisture are other possible causes. Red or purple coloring may intensify in the leaves of some plants. A different fertilizer mix should be considered since nitrogen is seldom deficient when a balanced fertilizer is applied regularly. An excess of phosphorus or potassium may cause symptoms of nitrogen deficiency.

MISCELLANEOUS NOTES: The best nitrogen to potassium (N/K) ratio is 1/1 unless a medium requiring high nitrogen is used. Orchids need much less nitrogen than most plants, and fertilizers should normally be diluted to ¼–½ the strength recommended for garden plants. Growers report good success with most orchids when an even weaker solution is applied every watering.

Phosphorus (P). Mobile in the plant.

Phosphorus, a macronutrient, is needed for cell division, is essential to root growth, and is particularly important in producing flowers, fruit, and seed.

SYMPTOMS OF EXCESS: Excess phosphorus prevents plants from taking up micronutrients, resulting in deficiencies of zinc, iron, or cobalt. It may also cause symptoms of nitrogen deficiency. Phosphorus is unlikely to be excessive if a balanced fertilizer is used regularly.

SYMPTOMS OF DEFICIENCY: Common plant responses to phosphorus deficiency are reduced growth, stunted plants with dark green leaves, and red to purple coloring along leaf veins. The leaves of some plants develop intensified color, while the leaves of other plants become brown or purple. Reddish or purplish leaves also may be caused by high light.

Thin stems and spindly growth may be caused by phosphorus deficiency but usually result from low light levels.

Older leaves may drop prematurely. Unless a high-nitrogen fertilizer is used exclusively, light levels are probably the problem.

Phosphorus deficiency may result in reduced flowering, but this symptom is more likely to result from low light levels, incorrect photoperiods, insufficient rest, or inappropriate temperatures.

A deficiency seldom occurs if a balanced fertilizer is used at the recommended frequency.

MISCELLANEOUS NOTES: Phosphorus is especially critical for seedlings and young or actively growing plants. A periodic application of high-phosphorus fertilizer is sometimes suggested for young plants, and many growers use a high-phosphate fertilizer near the end of the growing season to promote blooming the following year. Phosphorus leaches easily from a medium which is high in bark or peat. In acid (low pH) conditions, it combines with other elements and is unavailable to the plant. In alkaline conditions (pH above 7), phosphorus binds with other elements, forming compounds which the plant cannot use. High levels of phosphorus interfere with micronutrient and nitrogen absorption.

Potassium (K). Mobile in the plant.

Potassium, a macronutrient, is necessary for the production of plant sugars. It also increases resistance to disease, reduces dehydration during dry weather, increases resistance to cold, and helps to counteract the effects of excess nitrogen.

SYMPTOMS OF EXCESS: Excess potassium shows as a deficiency of other nutrients (including nitrogen, magnesium, calcium, iron, zinc, copper, manganese, and cobalt) because it interferes with a plant's ability to use those nutrients.

SYMPTOMS OF DEFICIENCY: Common symptoms of potassium deficiency are reduced growth, dwarfed plants, and shortened internodes. Other symptoms include chlorosis, burned leaf margins, and necrotic or dead spots on the leaf. Leaves may be wrinkled between the veins.

MISCELLANEOUS NOTES: The nitrogen/potassium balance is important. High nitrogen/low potassium favors vegetative growth; low nitrogen/high potassium promotes reproductive (flowering and fruiting) growth.

Potassium is seldom deficient if a balanced fertilizer is applied at the recommended strength and frequency. If other symptoms of macronutrient deficiency are present, fertilizer should be applied more frequently. Increasing the frequency of application is preferable to increasing strength. If a high-nitrogen fertilizer has been used exclusively, a more balanced formula should be considered.

Sulfur (S). Not mobile in the plant.

Sulfur, a micronutrient, helps plants to produce chlorophyll.

SYMPTOMS OF EXCESS: Excess sulfur is rarely a problem. Since sulfur is acidifying, an excess would probably show as micronutrient deficiencies resulting from low pH.

SYMPTOMS OF DEFICIENCY: Stunted or reduced roots, slender stems, light green leaves, or a general yellowing of the leaves or the entire plant may indicate a sulfur deficiency. Sulfur is rarely deficient, however, since it may be absorbed from the air, and it is often used as a carrier or an impurity in fertilizers.

MISCELLANEOUS NOTES: Sulfur balance is unlikely to be a problem in orchid cultivation. In agriculture, sulfur is used as a fungicide and to lower the soil pH.

Zinc (Zn). Not mobile in the plant.

Zinc, a micronutrient, is critical in the production of amino acids.

SYMPTOMS OF EXCESS: Zinc excess usually shows as iron or magnesium deficiency, since too much zinc interferes with the utilization of these nutrients.

SYMPTOMS OF DEFICIENCY: Symptoms of zinc deficiency include wavy, distorted, or puckered leaf margins; rosetting of the leaves; small or white-streaked leaves; and leaves that are necrotic or chlorotic, with yellowing between the veins on newer leaves. Shortened internodes may result in stunted plants. Excess phosphorus or potassium may cause symptoms of zinc deficiency.

MISCELLANEOUS NOTES: Zinc balance is unlikely to be a problem in orchid cultivation. Zinc is seldom deficient when a natural medium is used or a micronutrient supplement is applied to inorganic media. A laboratory tissue analysis should be performed and deficiency determined before zinc is added. A pH above 7 may interfere with a plant's ability to use zinc, but this is unlikely in orchid cultivation.

Nutrients Summary

Nutrient	Symptoms of Excess	Symptoms of Deficiency	Miscellaneous Notes
Boron	Black or dead tissue between veins	Black stems Die-back of apical buds or terminal leaves Failure to set seed Short roots Stunted plants	Boron balance is unlikely to be a problem in orchid cultivation. Excess boron is highly toxic. Deficiency of boron seldom occurs, since boron is usually available from natural media and is included in most micronutrient preparations. A laboratory tissue analysis should be performed and deficiency determined before boron is added.
Calcium	Chlorosis on middle or older leaves, between veins, or along leaf margins Curled or cupped mature leaves Leaf drop of middle and older leaves Leaves that fall prematurely	Black leaf tips on new leaves Buds that develop improperly Cupped leaves Dying root tips Poor growth or vigor Yellow leaves that turn brown and die prematurely	Excess calcium blocks magnesium absorption and causes symptoms of magnesium deficiency. It may also raise the pH to such a level that some micronutrients are unavailable to the plant. Deficiency of calcium usually occurs during periods of active growth and is more likely to be a problem than most other nutrient imbalances. Before adding calcium, growers should review other possible causes of symptoms. Dark leaf tips may be caused by too little water or too much fertilizer. Bud problems are usually caused by improper light or temperature, while deformed buds usually result from insect or chemical damage. Poor growth or yellow leaves may be caused by various nutrient deficiencies or root damage. Imbalances of magnesium and phosphorus are other possible problems.
Chlorine	Browning of leaves from the tip toward the base	Bronze leaves Chlorotic, dying leaves Deformed roots Wilted leaf tips that do not become erect when plants are watered	Chlorine balance is unlikely to be a problem in orchid cultivation. Excess chlorine may be a problem with soft-leaved orchids. Store water overnight in an open container to allow the chlorine to dissipate before watering sensitive plants. Deficiency of chlorine occurs rarely. A laboratory tissue analysis should be performed and deficiency determined before chlorine is added.
Cobalt	N/A	Chlorosis in older leaves Red or purple coloring on leaves	Cobalt balance is unlikely to be a problem in orchid cultivation. Excess cobalt seldom occurs. Deficiency of cobalt is very rare. Cobalt should be added only as a part of a micronutrient supplement.
Copper	Signs of iron deficiency Yellow to white mottling on new leaves with green veins	Faded leaves New growths that are small or misshapen Wilted terminal shoots	Copper balance is unlikely to be a problem in orchid cultivation. Excess copper can be highly toxic to orchids. Deficiency of copper may be caused by excess potassium. Copper should be added only as a part of a micronutrient supplement.

Nutrient	Symptoms	Notes
Iron	N/A Brown spots on leaves Yellow or white leaf tissue	Iron balance is unlikely to be a problem in orchid cultivation. Excess iron can be highly toxic to orchids. Deficiency of iron seldom occurs. A laboratory tissue analysis should be performed and deficiency determined before iron is added.
Magnesium	Signs of calcium deficiency Cupped leaves Reduced growth Yellow mature leaves with green veins	Excess magnesium can be highly toxic to orchids. Deficiency of magnesium is more likely to be a problem than most other nutrient imbalances. If the water supply is low in magnesium but high in calcium, plants may benefit from increased magnesium.
Manganese	Brown spotting on leaves Reduced growth Signs of iron deficiency Brown discoloration on leaves Yellow between green veins on new leaves Yellowish green stems	Manganese balance is unlikely to be a problem in orchid cultivation. Excess manganese may occur under very acid conditions (low pH). Too much manganese can interfere with iron uptake. Deficiency of manganese seldom occurs. Manganese should be added only as part of a micronutrient supplement.
Molybdenum	N/A Pale yellow chlorosis between veins on older leaves Twisted leaves that fail to open	Molybdenum balance is unlikely to be a problem in orchid cultivation. Excess molybdenum can be highly toxic to orchids. Deficiency of molybdenum seldom occurs. A laboratory tissue analysis should be performed and deficiency determined before molybdenum is added.
Nitrogen	Blackened leaves Brittle new growth Dark green leaves New growth that is weak and spindly Chlorosis of older growth Red or purple coloring on leaves Reduced growth	Excess nitrogen is a fairly common problem resulting from poorly balanced fertilizer. Moderately high levels may increase the plant's susceptibility to disease. Grossly excessive nitrogen causes blackened leaves, which may also result from very cold temperatures. Deficiency of nitrogen is unlikely to occur when a balanced fertilizer is used at the recommended frequency. An excess of phosphorus or potassium may cause symptoms of nitrogen deficiency.
Phosphorus	Signs of deficiencies in other nutrients Dark green leaves with reddish or purplish coloring along veins Premature leaf drop Purplish leaves Reduced flowering Spindly new growth Stunted plants Thin stems	Excess phosphorus is unlikely to be a problem. Deficiency of phosphorus seldom occurs if a balanced fertilizer is applied at the recommended frequency. Unless a high-nitrogen fetilizer is used exclusively, spindly growth and discolored leaves probably result from problems with light levels. Poor flowering is usually due to low light levels, incorrect photoperiods, insufficient rest, or inappropriate temperatures.

Nutrient	Symptoms of Excess	Symptoms of Deficiency	Miscellaneous Notes
Potassium	Signs of deficiencies in other nutrients	Burned leaf margins Chlorosis of leaves Dead spots on leaves Dwarfed plants Shortened internodes Wrinkling between leaf veins Yellow leaf margins	Excess potassium is unlikely to be a problem. Deficiency of potassium seldom occurs if a balanced fertilizer is applied at the recommended strength and frequency. If a high-nitrogen fertilizer has been used exclusively, a more balanced formula should be considered. The nitrogen/potassium balance is important.
Sulfur	Signs of deficiencies in other nutrients	Slender stems Stunted or reduced roots Yellowish to pale green plants or leaves	Sulfur balance is unlikely to be a problem in orchid cultivation. Excess sulfur seldom occurs. Deficiency of sulfur is rare. Discoloration of leaves is more likely to result from inappropriate light or macronutrient imbalances; short roots, from insufficient watering; and slender stems, from phosphorus deficiency.
Zinc	Signs of iron or magnesium deficiency	Chlorosis between the veins on newer leaves Chlorotic leaves Pale or white new leaves Rosetting of the leaves Small leaves Stunted growth Wavy leaf margins White streaks on older leaves	Zinc balance is unlikely to be a problem in orchid cultivation. Excess zinc seldom occurs. Deficiency of zinc rarely occurs if a natural medium is used or a micronutrient supplement is applied to inorganic media. A laboratory tissue analysis should be performed and deficiency determined before zinc is added.

WARNING: READ AND FOLLOW THE INSTRUCTIONS ON THE LABEL.

Growers are warned that chemicals may damage plants if applied in a manner or to a plant not specifically recommended on the label. Chemicals may alter a plant's sensitivity to light or cause damage that results in deformed new growths. See the discussion under "General Rules for Chemical Use" in Section III.

III. Using Chemicals Safely

Chemical Toxicity

Chemicals are designed to kill—treat them with the respect they deserve.

Chemicals are best avoided if possible. When their use is appropriate, remember that most pathogen-related plant diseases are caused by fungi which are a form of plant life. Any chemical applied to save the host plant is a chemical designed to kill another plant form. This is why some chemicals may be fatal to young seedlings and sometimes damage adult plants.

An important rule of thumb is to select *the least toxic chemical that will do the job.* All chemicals are rated with an LD_{50} number. This number sounds innocuous until one realizes that it means the amount given was a Lethal Dose to **50%** of the animals tested. Thus, if the LD_{50} number is 1–5 mg, the chemical is extremely toxic. In human terms, this means that for someone weighing 154 lbs. (70 kg), about 6 drops could be fatal 50% of the time. For a 50 lb. (23 kg) child, 2 drops could be fatal 50% of the time. For a toddler or small family pet, less than a drop could be fatal. An LD_{50} of 5000 mg indicates that an amount equal to a pint of chemical for a 154 lb. (70 kg) person killed 50% of the test animals. LD_{50} ratings are not printed on labels, but this information is available from local agricultural agents. The lower the LD_{50} number, the more dangerous the chemical, and the stronger the precautionary statement on the label.

Danger—Poison with a skull and crossbones symbol means that the substance is highly toxic, and the lethal dosage ranges from a taste to a teaspoon. Children might be killed by merely putting the bottle to their mouth.

Warning indicates that the chemical is moderately toxic. A dose lethal to humans ranges from a single teaspoon to a single tablespoon.

Caution indicates that the toxicity level is relatively low. A dose lethal to humans ranges from an ounce to more than a pint.

The importance of the information on the label cannot be over-emphasized: *Read the label, and follow the instructions.* Labels indicate the dangers of the particular chemical and whether swallowing it, inhaling it, or bringing it into contact with skin or eyes can result in serious injury or accidental poisoning. Emergency first-aid measures are printed on the label. If accidental poisoning should occur, the pesticide label is the most important information you can take to the physician.

In addition to indicating toxicity, the label should also provide information about environmental hazards such as the risk of fire or explosion or physical dangers, including the risk of harming the eyes or inhaling fumes. Local agricultural agents are the best source of information regarding toxicity ratings.

Another aspect of toxicity is the long-term carcinogenic effect of certain chemicals. Dr. Bruce Ames, Chairman of the Biochemistry Department, University of California at Berkeley, is one of the leading researchers exploring the possible mutagenic effects of chemical substances. His research has shown that we are continuously exposed to mutagens from such common substances as citrus oil, peanut butter, and broiled steak. Until the interactions between our immune systems and these potentially carcinogenic substances is more fully understood, however, it is unlikely that definitive standards or a danger-rating system will be established. In the meantime, growers should be aware of the serious possible side effects from exposure to chemicals and take every possible precaution when mixing or applying any chemical.

General Rules for Chemical Use

Protect yourself and others. Read and follow the precautionary statements on the label. Always remember that these chemicals are designed to be toxic to living things. Recent evidence indicates that agricultural workers may develop severe health problems as a result of regular or prolonged exposure to many of the chemicals used in greenhouses.

When using chemicals, the most dangerous phase is during mixing, when the chemical is still in concentrated form. An accidental spill or splash of the concentrate on exposed skin can easily result in a dangerous amount of the chemical being rapidly absorbed through the skin. It is therefore important to wear protective clothing. The grower who mixes and applies a spray wearing only shorts or lightweight summer clothing is running a great risk.

Gloves which are impervious to chemicals should be worn during all phases of pesticide use, but most particularly when the chemical concentrate is being measured.

A respirator, designed to prevent the inhalation of fumes and vapor, should be considered a necessity, not a luxury.

Goggles or face shields to protect the eyes and face are also critical, since the optic nerves may be permanently damaged if even dilute mixtures of certain chemicals are absorbed through the eyes.

Many chemicals are specifically designed to be absorbed through the living "skin" of the plant or insect. Long-sleeved shirts and long-legged pants or coveralls help prevent absorption through the skin. Clothing should be changed and washed separately immediately after chemicals are used. After the clothes are removed from the machine, it should be run through another complete cycle with soap before it is again used for the family wash.

Do not ignore illness which occurs during or shortly after exposure to or use of pesticides. Read the label, follow the instructions for emergency first-aid, and contact a doctor, hospital, or poison control center immediately.

Protect your plants. The risk of chemical damage to orchid plants is high. These general guidelines will help reduce that risk.

- Avoid spraying stressed plants. They are more likely to be damaged than healthy, actively growing plants.

- Do not apply aerosols at less than the recommended distance. If the can indicates spraying at 12 in. (30 cm), and it is held at 8 in. (20 cm), it is very likely to cause damage.

- Do not spray during cool, humid weather. The risk of injury increases when plants do not dry quickly after they are sprayed.

- Do not spray during hot, sunny weather. The risk of plant injury increases when temperatures are warm or light levels are high. When air or plant temperatures are as high as 90 °F (32 °C), damage is likely since some chemical actions are intensified.

- Do not apply chemicals more frequently than recommended.

- Mix at the correct strength, and avoid overdosing plants.

- Water plants thoroughly before spraying. Dry plants absorb more chemical than is needed, which often causes injury.

- Spray only to the point of runoff. Excess chemicals do not benefit the plant but may increase the risk of chemical damage.

- Spray early in the day, preferably between 6 and 10 a.m.

- Use only chemicals that are known to be safe for the particular plant.

Avoid noxious fumes, which harm plants. Some chemicals produce fumes that are quickly fatal to many plants. Weed control compounds containing 2-4-D should not be sprayed in the vicinity of orchids. Other chemical compounds also produce fumes, often for an extended period, that are extremely harmful to orchids. Fumes from tar oil (sometimes found in rust preventatives used on greenhouse pipes) can injure orchids in a closed greenhouse. Likewise, fumes from wood preserved with Penta compounds or creosote may be toxic, particularly in winter when air circulation is reduced. Fumes from some preservative paints may also affect plants adversely. Use paints designated for greenhouse use.

Use caution in combining chemicals. Mixing chemicals in an attempt to control several diseases or pests in a single application may change a plant's response to chemicals that are safe when used separately. Information regarding chemical compatibility is sometimes found on the product label, but generally, wettable powders may be mixed with other wettable powders and emulsifiable concentrates with other emulsifiable concentrates. Chemical compatibility charts are published annually by the Meister Publishing Co., Willoughby, OH, U.S.A. 44094.

Pesticides are often mixed as a convenience, allowing a grower to apply treatments for several pests at one time, and in many instances mixing may be done safely. When there is any room for doubt, however, it is safer to make separate applications of the different chemicals, spaced a few days apart. Chemical brands from a single manufacturer are more likely to be compatible than those from different manufacturers. Only chemicals of similar toxicity—such as the group marked "Danger," the group marked "Warning," and the group marked "Caution"— should be mixed. Growers sometimes make the mistake of diluting each chemical separately then combining the 2 solutions in a sprayer. This dilutes each chemical to less than the recommended strength. If each chemical should be mixed in a gallon of water, only one gallon of water should be used.

Symptoms of phytotoxicity (plant toxicity) normally show within 18–72 hours and nearly always within a week. Chemical toxicity may cause problems such as burn, necrosis, or chlorosis. Injury is most likely to be evident at leaf tips and margins, but the damage may also show as spotting or discoloration of the entire leaf, and growing tips or buds may die. Distortion such as crinkling, cupping, or curling of the leaves may occur quickly, while stunting or abnormal growth appears more gradually.

Sprays are more likely to damage new leaves, while drenches are more likely to damage older leaves and roots.

If many plants of a single species are to be sprayed, it is wise to test spray a few plants before making a general application.

Follow the package instructions, and mix chemicals at the recommended strength. This is important because the recommended application strength is necessary to kill the pathogen without harming the orchid. Using a single chemical exclusively for a prolonged period may result .in the survival of only strains of pathogens that are unaffected by that chemical. It is always wise to complete a treatment with one chemical, then to use a different chemical if the problem continues.

Mix only what you need. Most chemicals rapidly lose their effectiveness after being mixed, so mix only the amount that can be used that day. Never put mixed chemicals in a food-storage container. These are not child-proof, and if accidentally left out, they could easily lead a curious child to sample the contents.

Store chemicals safely. Safe storage means always keeping the chemical in the original container, which was designed with safety in mind. Also, when chemicals are kept in the original container, the label is available to be read before each use. A locked cabinet is highly recommended. This protects both people and the chemicals, since the effective life of a chemical can be prolonged by storage in a cool, dark place.

Dispose of containers and extra solution as instructed. Rinse empty containers several times by filling them with water and emptying the rinse into the solution being mixed. Dispose of the empty, well-rinsed container and any leftover solution as the label advises.

Clean sprayers and mixing containers. After using chemicals, it is very important to thoroughly clean mixing containers and spraying equipment. When wettable powders or other suspended solids are used, the containers are easily cleaned by carefully rinsing and flushing the spray mechanism with fresh, clean water. For some chemicals, however, especially liquids using an oil base or those mixed with sticker/spreaders, rinsing may not be sufficient to remove all the chemical from the equipment. Any chemical solution left clinging to the equipment may be neutralized by first rinsing with a solution of 2 parts household ammonia and 1 part water. The ammonia reacts with most agricultural and horticultural chemicals, changing them into substances that are safe for plants and animals. This solution should be pumped through the spray mechanism, and the equipment allowed to stand for 24 hours then given a final rinsing with clean water. The equipment is then safe to use with another chemical.

Chemical Classifications and Methods of Application

Pesticides are categorized by their intended use. All chemicals used to control pests (such as disease and insects) are considered pesticides.

Acaricides control mites, ticks, and spiders.

Attractants lure pests.

Bactericides control bacteria.

Fungicides control fungi.

Herbicides kill plants (not just weeds).

Insecticides control insects.

Miticides control mites.

Repellents keep pests away.

Pesticides are further classified by how they work.

Broad-spectrum formulations kill a wide variety of pests.

Contact poisons kill by touching.

Disinfectants are used to sterilize and normally kill on contact.

Fumigants are gasses which kill when inhaled or absorbed.

Selective chemicals are designed to treat only specific problems.

Stomach poisons kill when swallowed by the pest.

Systemic poisons circulate through the plant, killing pests when they attack.

Treatments are applied in several ways, and the application method is often critical. Chemicals absorbed by the leaves should be applied as a spray, while chemicals absorbed by plant roots should be used as a drench. Spraying a chemical that should be applied as a drench provides little benefit to the plant.

The following terms are used in labeling to describe application methods.

Band: Apply in a strip.

Broadcast: Scatter over the surface.

Dip: Submerge the entire plant.

Direct: Aim at a specific location.

Drench: Saturate the medium.

Side dress: Place beside the plant.

Spot treat: Apply to the affected area.

Spray or foliar spray: Apply to both sides of the leaves until the chemical drips off the tips of the leaves.

Chemicals are available in various forms depending on how they should be applied. Following is a list of formulation types. Common abbreviations that may appear on labels are included in parentheses.

Aerosol (A): A low concentrate applied as a fine mist.

Bait (B): A solid or liquid, often with an attractant, used to combat slugs and snails.

Dust (D): A powder which is dusted on the leaves or surface of the medium.

Emulsified concentrate (EC or E): An oil-based solution designed to be diluted with water.

Flowable (F or L): A liquid which forms a suspension when mixed with water.

Granules (G): Coarse particles which are usually broadcast. The pesticide is often mixed with clay for easy handling.

Soluble powder (SP): A powder which dissolves when mixed with water.

Wettable powder (WP or P): A dust designed to be mixed with water and sprayed. Wettable powders are held in suspension rather than dissolved, so the solution must be continuously agitated during spraying. These powders should first be mixed with a small quantity of water to form a slurry, then diluted to the required strength.

Certain products, called surfacants or simply additives, are mixed with some chemicals to improve dispersal of the spray, alter droplet size, increase coverage, keep the chemical in suspension, or allow oil and water to mix. Different brand-name products have different formulations; the brand recommended on the label is the one designed to be compatible with that pesticide formulation. Follow the instructions on the label.

Spreaders increase the deposit and coverage on plant surfaces. Often used with wettable powder insecticides, they improve contact between the pesticide and the plant surface.

Stickers are compounds which help the spray adhere to the leaf surface. They are particularly beneficial when used with wettable powders and are frequently recommended for use with fungicides.

Wetting agents are usually oily additives which prevent the droplets from beading up and rolling off the leaf surface, thereby allowing the pesticide to dry on the plant.

Chemicals are valuable tools that should be used only when necessary. This approach makes the chemicals more effective and is safer for people, pets, plants, and the environment. We hope the information in this Appendix will help growers understand and identify plant problems that may occur. We also hope that it will assist the grower in selecting the safest and most effective possible remedial action when intervention is required.

English and Metric-System Equivalents

1 inch	=	25.4 millimeters
1 foot	=	30.48 centimeters
1 yard	=	91.44 centimeters
1 mile	=	1.609 kilometers
1 gallon	=	3.785 liters
1 ounce	=	28.35 grams
1 pound	=	453.6 grams
1 millimeter	=	0.03937 inches
1 centimeter	=	0.3937 inches
1 meter	=	39.37 inches
1 kilometer	=	0.62137 miles
1 liter	=	1.057 quarts
1 gram	=	15.43 grains
1 kilogram	=	2.205 pounds

Metric Prefixes

Names of multiples of metric and other units are formed by adding a prefix (representing a power of 10) to "meter," "gram," "liter," and so on.

tera	=	one trillion	or 10^{12}	or	1,000,000,000,000
giga	=	one billion	or 10^{9}	or	1,000,000,000
mega	=	one million	or 10^{6}	or	1,000,000
kilo	=	one thousand	or 10^{3}	or	1,000
hecto	=	one hundred	or 10^{2}	or	100
deka	=	ten	or 10^{1}	or	10
deci	=	one tenth	or 10^{-1}	or	0.1
centi	=	one hundreth	or 10^{-2}	or	0.01
milli	=	one thousandth	or 10^{-3}	or	0.001
micro	=	one millionth	or 10^{-6}	or	0.000001
nano	=	one billionth	or 10^{-9}	or	0.000000001
pico	=	one trillionth	or 10^{-12}	or	0.000000000001

NOTE: The special case of one millionth of a meter is called a micron.

Abbreviations

BTU	=	British thermal unit		Tbs.	=	tablespoon
CFM	=	cubic feet per minute		tsp.	=	teaspoon
cu.	=	cubic		yd.	=	yard
ft.	=	foot		cm	=	centimeter
gal.	=	gallon		g	=	gram
in.	=	inch		kg	=	kilogram
lb.	=	pound		km	=	kilometer
oz.	=	ounce		l	=	liter
pt.	=	pint		l/sec	=	liters per second
qt.	=	quart		m	=	meter
sec.	=	second		ml	=	milliliter
sq.	=	square		mm	=	millimeter

Approximate Conversion Factors and Relationships Among Units of Measure

Liquid Measure

1 ounce (fluid) = 2 Tbs. = 6 tsp. = 1.805 cu. in. = 29.54 ml

1 teaspoon = 50–60 drops = 0.33 Tbs. = 0.167 oz. = 0.301 cu. in. = 4.93 ml

1 tablespoon = 3 tsp. = 0.5 oz. = 0.0625 cup = 0.9025 cu. in. = 14.79 ml

1 cup = 16 Tbs. = 8 oz. = 0.5 pt. = 0.25 qt. = 14.44 cu. in. = 236.32 ml

1 pint = 32 Tbs. = 16 oz. = 2 cups = 0.5 qt. = 28.88 cu. in. = 472.65 ml

1 quart = 64 Tbs. = 32 oz. = 4 cups = 0.25 gal. = 57.76 cu. in. = 946 ml

1 gallon = 4 qt. = 8 pt. = 16 cups = 128 oz. = 231 cu. in. = 3.785 liter

1 milliliter = 1 cu. cm = 0.001 liter = 0.203 tsp.

1 liter = 1000 cu. cm = 1.057 qt. = 0.2642 gal. = 61.02 cu. in.

Dry Measure

1 teaspoon = 0.33 Tbs.	1 quart = 2 pt.
1 tablespoon = 3 tsp.	1 gallon = 4 qt.
1 cup = 16 Tbs. = 48 tsp.	1 peck = 2 gal.
1 pint = 2 cups	

Weight

1 ounce = 0.0625 lb. = 28.35 g = 3 Tbs. (dry) = 2 Tbs. (liquid)

1 pound = 16 oz. = 453.6 g = 2 cups

1 gram = 15.43 grains = 0.0353 oz. = 0.1058 Tbs. = 0.3175 tsp.

1 kilogram = 1000 g = 2.205 lb. = 35.28 oz.

Length

1 inch = 25.4 mm = 2.54 cm = 0.0833 ft.

1 foot = 12 in. = 30.48 cm = 0.333 yd. = 0.3048 m

1 yard = 36 in. = 3 ft. = 91.44 cm = 0.914 m

1 mile = 5280 ft. = 1609.344 m = 1.609 km

1 millimeter = 0.001 m = 0.03937 in.

1 centimeter = 0.01 m = 0.3937 in.

1 meter = 1000 mm = 100 cm = 0.001 km = 39.37 in. = 3.281 ft.

1 kilometer = 1000 m = 3281 ft. = 0.62137 mile

Square Measurements

1 square inch (in.^{2}) = 6.452 sq. cm = 0.0069 sq. ft.

1 square foot (ft.^{2}) = 144 sq. in. = 929.03 sq. cm = 0.0929 sq. m = 0.1109 sq. yd.

1 square meter (m^2) = 1550 sq. in. = 10.765 sq. ft.

1 square mile = 27,878,400 sq. ft. = 2.59 sq. km = 640 acres

1 acre = 43,560 sq. ft. = 4,045.13 sq. m = 0.4 hectare

1 hectare = 10,000 sq. m = 2.47 acres

Cubic Measurements

1 cubic inch (in.^{3}) = 0.03463 pt. = 0.01732 qt. = 16.39 cu. cm = 0.01639 l

1 cubic foot (ft.^{3}) = 1728 cu. in. = 0.028 cu. m = 0.03704 cu. yd. = 7.4805 gal. = 29.92 qt. = 28.32 liter = 1.25 bushels

1 cubic yard (yd.^{3}) = 27 cu. ft. = 808 qt. = 202 gal. = 764.6 liter = 0.7646 cu. m = 22 bushels

1 cubic centimeter (cm^3) = 1 ml = 0.001 liter = 0.06102 cu. in. = 0.002113 pt.

1 cubic meter (m^3) = 1,000,000 cu. cm = 1000 liter = 35.31 cu. ft. = 1.308 cu. yd. = 2113 pt. = 1057 qt. = 264.2 gal.

Miscellaneous Measurements

1 palm = 3 in.
1 hand = 4 in.
1 span = 6 in.
1 cubit = 18 in.
1 biblical cubit = 21.8 in.
1 furlong = 660 ft. = 0.125 mile
1 league = 3 miles

Per-Gallon Equivalents for Diluting Concentrated Fertilizers and Chemicals

Some commercial products give dilution rates per 100 gal. (380 liters). Listed below are the approximate equivalents for 1 gal. (3.8 liters).

Liquids

2 gal./100 gal.	=	5 Tbs./gal.
1 gal./100 gal.	=	7.5 tsp./gal.
2 qt. /100 gal.	=	3.75 tsp./gal.
1 qt. /100 gal.	=	2 tsp./gal.
1 pt. /100 gal.	=	1 tsp./gal.
8 oz. /100 gal.	=	0.5 tsp./gal.
4 oz. /100 gal.	=	0.25 tsp./gal.

Solids

5 lb./100 gal.	=	4.75 tsp./gal.
4 lb./100 gal.	=	3.75 tsp./gal.
2 lb./100 gal.	=	2 tsp./gal.
1 lb./100 gal.	=	1 tsp./gal.
8 oz./100 gal.	=	0.5 tsp./gal.

Dilutions

For some chemicals, dilution rates are given as a ratio. The following are approximate equivalent rates for a single gallon.

1:100	=	2 Tbs. + 2 tsp./gal.	=	10.0 ml/l
1:200	=	4 tsp./gal.	=	5.2 ml/l
1:400	=	2 tsp./gal.	=	2.6 ml/l
1:800	=	1 tsp./gal.	=	1.3 ml/l
1:1000	=	¾ tsp./gal.	=	1.0 ml/l
1:2000	=	⅜ tsp./gal.	=	0.5 ml/l

For some chemicals, dilution rates are given as parts per million (ppm). The following are approximate equivalents.

%sol.*	dilution	ppm[†]	tsp./gal.			ml/l
0.001	1:100,000	10	0.00768	or	¾ tsp./100 gal.	0.01
0.005	1:50,000	20	0.0154	or	¾ tsp./50 gal.	0.02
0.01	1:10,000	100	0.0768	or	¾ tsp./10 gal.	0.1
0.02	1:5000	200	0.1536	or	¾ tsp./5 gal.	0.2
0.05	1:2000	500	0.384	or	⅜ tsp./gal.	0.5
0.10	1:1000	1000	0.768	or	¾ tsp./gal.	1.0
1.00	1:100	10,000	7.68	or	7⅔ tsp./gal.	10.0

* This assumes an initial concentration of 100%. To use with different concentrations, divide 100 by the % of concentration and multiply the tsp./gal. or ml/l by the answer. For example, when using a fertilizer containing 20% nitrogen, divide 100 by 20, which yields 5. Then multiply 5 by the amount shown under **tsp./gal.** or **ml/l**.

[†]If a solution of 100 ppm is desired when using a 20% concentration, multiply 0.0768 tsp./gal. or 0.1 ml/l by 5. In other words, it requires 0.0768 tsp./gal. or 0.1ml/l of 100% concentrate to give a solution with 100 ppm; but it takes 5 times these amounts of 20% concentrate to produce a mixture with the same strength.

Approximate Pot Volumes

The following volumes are approximate. Pot volumes vary dramatically depending on pot shape. These volumes may be used to approximate the amount of medium needed or to estimate the quantity of a supplement that is appropriate for small to medium-sized pots.

Round Azalea Pots (height = ¾ diameter of top)

4 in. (10 cm) = 1½ cups (354 ml)
5 in. (13 cm) = 3⅝ cups (857 ml)
6 in. (15 cm) = 5½ cups (1300 ml)
7 in. (18 cm) = 8 cups (1890 ml)

Round Bulb Pans (height = ½ diameter of top)

5 in. (13 cm) = 2¾ cups (473 ml)
6.5 in. (17 cm) = 5¾ cups (1359 ml)
8 in. (20 cm) = 8 cups (1890 ml)

Round Standard Pots (height = diameter of top)

1.5 in. (4 cm) = ⅛ cup (29.5 ml)
2 in. (5 cm) = ¼ cup (59 ml)
2.5 in. (6 cm) = ⅜ cup (89 ml)
3 in. (8 cm) = ¾ cup (178 ml)
3.5 in. (9 cm) = 1¼ cup (295 ml)
4 in. (10 cm) = 1⅞ cup (443 ml)
5 in. (13 cm) = 3¾ cup (886 ml)
6 in. (15 cm) = 6½ cup (1536 ml)

Square Pots (height = width of top)

2¼ in. (5.7 cm) = ⅜ cup (89 ml)
2½ in. (6 cm) = ½ cup (118 ml)
3 in. (8 cm) = ⅞ cup (206 ml)
3½ in. (9 cm) = 1¼ cup (295 ml)
4 in. (10 cm) = 1¾ cup (413 ml)
4½ in. (11 cm) = 2¾ cup (532 ml)

Temperature Conversions

Conversion Formulas

$$°C = (\tfrac{5}{9})(°F - 32) \qquad °F = (\tfrac{9}{5})(°C) + 32$$

Conversion Table

Fahrenheit to Celsius and Celsius to Fahrenheit

°F	0	1	2	3	4	5	6	7	8	9
	°C	°C	°C	°C	°C	°C	°C	°C	°C	°C
-10	-23	-24	-24	-25	-26	-26	-27	-27	-28	-28
-0	-18	-18	-19	-19	-20	-21	-21	-22	-22	-23
0	-18	-17	-17	-16	-16	-15	-14	-14	-13	-13
10	-12	-12	-11	-11	-10	-9	-9	-8	-8	-7
20	-7	-6	-6	-5	-4	-4	-3	-3	-2	-2
30	-1	-1	0	1	1	2	2	3	3	4
40	4	5	6	6	7	7	8	8	9	9
50	10	11	11	12	12	13	13	14	14	15
60	16	16	17	17	18	18	19	19	20	21
70	21	22	22	23	23	24	24	25	26	26
80	27	27	28	28	29	29	30	31	31	32
90	32	33	33	34	34	35	36	36	37	37
100	38	38	39	39	40	41	41	42	42	43
110	43	44	44	45	46	46	47	47	48	48

To convert from °F to °C, find the appropriate tens line on the left and move to the right to the column under the appropriate units digit (the line of numbers at the top of the table). The number at the intersection of the column and the line is the °C value. For example, to convert 64°F, locate the 60 line and move to the right to the column under 4. The number at this intersection is 18. Thus 64°F = 18°C.

To convert from °C to °F, simply work backwards. Find the desired °C value in the table and determine the corresponding °F value by combining the numbers at the left and the top of the table. For example, 13°C falls at the intersection of the 50 line and the 5 and 6 columns. Consequently, 13°C = 55–56°F. (If it is desirable to find °F in tenths of degrees, the best procedure is to use the formula given above. Thus, for the present example, °F = (⅖)(13°C) + 32 = 55.4.)

Some Equations Useful in Greenhouse Management

$$Watts = Amps \times Volts \qquad Volts = \frac{Watts}{Amps}$$

$$Amps = \frac{Watts}{Volts}$$

1 BTU = 0.252 kilocalorie   1 CFM = 0.472 liters per second

Greenhouse Ventilation

Due to the engineering constants in the following equations, they are appropriate only for use with English units of measure.

Fans used for greenhouse ventilation should be of sufficient size to provide a complete exchange of air every 1.5 minutes. The following equation gives the fan size necessary to meet this requirement:

$$V \times 0.7 = CFM$$

where V is the volume of the greenhouse, obtained by multiplying the length times the width times the average height of the structure, and where CFM is the required fan size given in cubic feet per minute.

Air removed by a fan must be replaced if the fan is to operate properly, so inlet vents that allow passage of the required volume of air should be provided. To determine the size of the necessary vent area, divide the CFM (as determined above) by 250. This will give the total shutter area in square feet. Divide this number by the number of shutters that will be used to determine the size of each shutter.

Greenhouse Heating

The following formula determines the approximate heating requirements of a greenhouse:

$$A \times D \times 1.1 = BTU$$

where A is the total wall and roof area of the greenhouse in square feet, D is the °F difference between the coldest outdoor winter temperature and the night temperature desired in the greenhouse, and BTU is the required output of the heater expressed in British thermal units. Subtract 30% from this value if the greenhouse is double-glazed or has a polyethylene liner.

239

Bibliography
References

Citations of journal articles include name(s) of author(s), year of publication, article title, and journal name, followed by volume number, issue number (in parentheses), and page numbers. The issue number corresponds to the month of publication, or in the case of quarterlies, the 3-month period for which the issue was released.

1 American Orchid Society, Inc. 1974. *An orchidist's glossary*. American Orchid Society, Inc., 6000 S. Olive Ave., West Palm Beach, FL, U.S.A. 33405.

2 Ames, O. [1920] 1982. *Orchidaceae*. Fascicles I–VII. Merrymount Press, Boston. Reprint, Twin Oaks Books, Greenfield, Wis.

3 ———. [1922] 1983. *Schedulae orchidianae*. Vols. 1–10. Merrymount Press, Boston. Reprint, Twin Oaks Books, Greenfield, Wis.

4 Ames, O., and D. S. Correll. [1952, 1953, 1965] 1985. Orchids of Guatemala and Belize. Parts 1–3. *Fieldiana: Botany* 26(1), 26(2), 31(7). Chicago Natural History Museum Press, Chicago. Reprint, Dover Publications, New York.

5 Arditti, J. 1982. Orchid seed germination and seedling culture—a manual. Appendix in *Orchid biology: reviews and perspectives*. Vol. II. Edited by J. Arditti. Comstock Publishing, Cornell University Press, Ithaca, N.Y.

6 Australasian Native Orchid Society (Victoria Group). 1984. *Cultivation of Australian native orchids*. Australasian Native Orchid Society, Melbourne, Australia.

7 Bailes, C. 1988. *Pleione*—a neglected genus. 1, The species. *American Orchid Society Bulletin* 57(5):493.

8 ———. 1988. *Pleione*—a neglected genus. 2, How to grow them. *American Orchid Society Bulletin* 57(6):594.

9 Banerji, M. L., and P. Pradhan. 1984. *The orchids of Nepal Himalaya*. J. Cramer, Vaduz, India.

10 Batchelor, S. R. 1980. The Butterworth Prize for most outstanding specimen plant. *American Orchid Society Bulletin* 49(8):871.

11 ———. 1982. Beginner series, 20. *Phalaenopsis*, Part 1. *American Orchid Society Bulletin* 51(12):1267.

12 ———. 1983. Beginner series, 21. *Phalaenopsis*, Part 2. *American Orchid Society Bulletin* 52(1):4.

13 ———. 1983. Beginner series, 24. *Phalaenopsis*, Part 5. *American Orchid Society Bulletin* 52(4):364.

14 Bechtel, H., P. Cribb, and E. Launert. 1980. *Manual of cultivated orchid species*. MIT Press, Cambridge, Mass.

15 Bergstrom, B. 1988. The great *Phragmipedium bessae* caper. *Orchid Digest* 52(1):22–24.

16 Berkeley, E. S. 1971. Notes on orchids in the jungle—*Phalaenopsis speciosa*. *Orchid Digest* 35(2):49.

17 Bhattacharjee, S. K. 1984. A note on the native *Pleione* species of India. *Orchid Digest* 48(4):143–146.

18 Birk, L. 1973. The *Orchid Digest* guide on the culture of orchids: *Phalaenopsis*. *Orchid Digest* 37(6):215–217.

19 ———. 1976. The capture and cultivation of *Vanda hookeriana*. *Orchid Digest* 40(3):101–105.

20 Bose, T. K., and S. K. Bhattacharjee. 1980. *Orchids of India*. Naya Prokash, Calcutta, India.

21 Bosser, J. 1971. Revision du genre *Phaius* Lour. *Adansonia*, Series 2 (3):519–543.

22 Cantwell, E. 1987. Windowsill orchids: the easy way. *American Orchid Society Bulletin* 56(4):361.

23 Chen, Sing-Chi, and T. Tang. 1982. A general review of the orchid flora of China. *Orchid biology: reviews and perspectives*. Vol. II. Edited by J. Arditti. Comstock Publishing, Cornell University Press, Ithaca, N.Y.

24 Cheng, Chow. *Chow Cheng orchids*. Missouri Botanical Garden, St. Louis, Mo.

25 Cheong, C. K. 1974. *Phalaenopsis* and its culture. *Orchid Digest* 38(4):142.

26 Christenson, E. A. 1989. The living legacy of Marie Selby, 2. *American Orchid Society Bulletin* 58(4):354.

27 Coleman, R. A. 1986. Propagating *Phaius* by flower stem cuttings. *Orchid Digest* 50(6):196–197.

28 Collins, R. 1983. Some thoughts on contemporary *Phalaenopsis* hybridizing. *American Orchid Society Bulletin* 52(8):792.

29 Comber, J. B. 1972. A habitat note on *Paphiopedilum chamberlainianum* and *Phalaenopsis sumatrana*. *Orchid Digest* 36(1):25.

30 ———. 1976. The rediscovery of *Phalaenopsis viridis* on a limestone ridge in Sumatra. *Orchid Digest* 40(3):84–89.

References

31   ———. 1980. The genus *Phaius* in Java. *Orchid Digest* 44(1):35–37.

32   ———. 1983. The genus *Pholidota* in Java. *Orchid Digest* 47(2):72–77.

33   Cribb, P. J., and I. Butterfield, with C. Z. Tang. 1988. *The genus* Pleione. Timber Press, Portland, Ore.; Christopher Helm, Bromley, Kent, United Kingdom.

34   Dassanayake, M. D., and E. R. Fosberg. 1981. *Flora of Ceylon. A revised handbook*. Oxford and IBH Publishing Co., New Delhi, India.

35   De la Bathie, H. Perrier. [1939, 1941] 1981. *Flora of Madagascar*. Vols. I–II. The Government of Madagascar and the National Museum of Natural History, Paris. Translated and published in one vol., Steven D. Beckman, 621 Palm Ave., Lodi, CA, U.S.A. 95240.

36   Deva, S., and H. B. Naithani. 1986. *Orchid flora of N.W. Himalaya*. Print & Media Assoc., New Delhi, India.

37   De Vogel, E. F. 1988. *Orchid monographs*. Vol. 3, Revisions in Coelogyninae *(Orchidaceae)* III: *the genus* Pholidota. E. J. Brill/Rijksherbarium, Leiden, The Netherlands.

38   Dockrill, A. W. 1967. *Australian Sarcanthinae*. Australasian Native Orchid Society, Sydney, Australia.

39   ———. 1969. *Australian indigenous orchids*. Society for Growing Australian Plants, Halstead Press, Sydney, Australia.

40   Dodson, C. H., and P. M. de Dodson. 1980–1982. Orchids of Ecuador. *Icones Plantarum Tropicarum*. Marie Selby Botanical Gardens, Sarasota, Fla.

41   Dodson, C. H., and J. Kuhn. 1981. *Phragmipedium besseae:* a new species from Peru. *American Orchid Society Bulletin* 50(11):1308.

42   Duardo, Dr. 1974. *Phalaenopsis violacea*. *Orchid Digest* 38(4):128–130.

43   Dunsterville, G. C. K. 1980. Orchids of Venezuela, new names for old. *American Orchid Society Bulletin* 49(3):223.

44   ———. 1982. Orchids of Venezuela: hunting *Phragmipedium klotzscheanum*—an agony in eight fits. *American Orchid Society Bulletin* 51(7):709.

45   Dunsterville, G. C. K., and E. Dunsterville. 1983. Blackwaters. Acid rain and blackwater orchids. *Orchid Digest* 47(3):85–90.

46   Dunsterville, G. C. K., and L. A. Garay. 1959. *Venezuelan orchids illustrated*. Orchid Herbarium of Oakes Ames, Botanical Museum, Harvard University, Cambridge, Mass.

47   ———. 1979. *Orchids of Venezuela: an illustrated field guide*. Orchid Herbarium of Oakes Ames, Botanical Museum, Harvard University, Cambridge, Mass.

48   Durheim, L. 1987. Growing orchids in the home: pests and diseases, more specifics. *Orchid Digest* 51(3):153-154.

49   Embree, A., and J. A. Fowlie. 1989. Notes on *Phragmipedium bessae* Dodson and Kuhn including cultural hints. *Orchid Digest* 53(3):119–122.

50   Fischer, C. E. C. [Not dated] 1984. *Orchidaceae*. Vol. III in *Flora of the Presidency of Madras*. Edited by J. S. Gamble. Adlard & Son, London. Reprint, Bishen Singh Mahendra Pal Singh, Dehra Dun, India.

51   Fitch, C. M. 1979. Orchids at Bogor Botanic Gardens of Indonesia. *American Orchid Society Bulletin* 48(5):459.

52   ———. 1980. Indonesian orchid species specialist, 2. *American Orchid Society Bulletin* 49(3):261.

53   ———. 1980. Color variations of *Phalaenopsis violacea*. *American Orchid Society Bulletin* 49(8):860.

54   ———. 1983. Malaysian orchid conservationist. *American Orchid Society Bulletin* 52(7):705.

55   ———. 1989. Techniques for photographing orchid flowers in the field. *American Orchid Society Bulletin* 58(4):373.

56   Flowers, R. W. 1981. Orchids at Fortuna, Panama. *American Orchid Society Bulletin* 50(8):920.

57   Fowlie, J. A. 1968. Key and annotated checklist to the genus *Pescatorea*. *Orchid Digest* 32(3):86–91.

58   ———. 1968. The quest for *Phalaenopsis sanderiana*. *Orchid Digest* 32(10):315–316.

59   ———. 1972. In search of *Phragmipedium caudatum* Rolfe emend. *Orchid Digest* 36(2):47–48.

60   ———. 1973. With Ghillany in Brazil, Part V. In search of *Phragmipedium vittatum* in the peat bogs of the Planato. *Orchid Digest* 37(3):111–113.

61   ———. 1979. Two additional lost species of *Phalaenopsis* refound in Indonesia, *Phalaenopsis psilantha* Schlechter and *Phalaenopsis modesta* J. J. Smith. *Orchid Digest* 43(6):212–213.

62   ———. 1981. Speciation amongst the Orchidaceae as a function of climate change and topophysiography.

Orchid Digest 45(2):44–49.

63 ———. 1981. Malaya revisited, Part XVIII. The occurrence of *Paphiopedilum virens* (Rchb.f.) Pfitz. on granite boulders with leaf detritus on Mt. Kinabalu, Sabah, North Borneo. *Orchid Digest* 45(3):84–90.

64 ———. 1982. Malaya revisited, Part XXI. *Phalaenopsis corningiana* on sapling and streamside trees near waterfalls. *Orchid Digest* 46(4):138–142.

65 ———. 1983. Malaya revisited, Part XXII. A visit to the habitat of *Paphiopedilum argus*. *Orchid Digest* 47(1):5–6.

66 ———. 1983. A new *Phalaenopsis* species of the section *Zebrinae* from central Sumatra, *Phalaenopsis inscriptiosinensis* Fowlie sp. nov. *Orchid Digest* 47(1):11–12.

67 ———. 1985. Malaya revisited, Part XXVII. *Paphiopedilum curtisii* in the Barisan Mountains of Sumatra. *Orchid Digest* 49(2):49.

68 ———. 1985. Malaya revisited, Part XXVIII. *Paphiopedilum liemianum* and *Paphiopedilum tonsum* on a limestone ridge in northern Sumatra. *Orchid Digest* 49(3):84–90.

69 ———. 1985. Malaya revisited, Part XXIX. Rediscovering the habitat of *Paphiopedilum dayanum* on serpentine cliffs of Mt. Kinabalu in eastern Malaysia (formerly North Borneo). *Orchid Digest* 49(4):125,185.

70 ———. 1985. A new species of *Spathopetalum* from central Sumatra, *Paphiopedilum tortipetalum* Fowlie. *Orchid Digest* 49(4):155.

71 ———. 1985. Malaya revisited, Part XXXI. *Paphiopedilum victoria-mariae* (Sander ex Masters) Rolfe: refound in Sumatra at high elevations on andesite lava cliffs. *Orchid Digest* 49(6):207.

72 ———. 1986. In Brazil, Part XXXIII. *Phragmipedium sargentianum* atop granite chapadas in Pernambuco. *Orchid Digest* 50(3):105–109.

73 ———. 1986. Malaya revisited, Part XXXIII. *Paphiopedilum stonei* on limestone cliffs in Sarawak. *Orchid Digest* 50(5):157–162.

74 ———. 1987. A peculiar means of vegetative reproduction by *Phalaenopsis stuartiana*. *Orchid Digest* 51(2):93–94.

75 ———. 1987. Growing orchids in live moss, Part II. A visit with Ernie Campuzano of Butterfly Orchids. *Orchid Digest* 51(3):155–157.

76 Fowlie, J. A., with L. Holguin. 1968. A rediscovery note on *Phragmipedium boissieranum*. *Orchid Digest* 32(3):82.

77 Fowlie, J. A., and T. Lamb. 1980. Malaya revisited, Part XVIII. The climate of Sabah, North Borneo, with cultural hints on the cultivation of certain *Paphiopedilum* and *Phalaenopsis* species which grow there. *Orchid Digest* 44(5):187–189.

78 Frank, D. W. 1988. Control of bacterial soft rot caused by *Pseudomonas cattleya* in the culture of *Phalaenopsis*. *Orchid Digest* 52(2):66.

79 Freed, H. 1968. Breeding pink *Phalaenopsis*. *Orchid Digest* 32(9):262–265.

80 ———. 1972. *Phalaenopsis violacea* breeding has come of age. *Orchid Digest* 36(1):5–7.

81 ———. 1973. Breeding novelty *Phalaenopsis*. *Orchid Digest* 37(1):4–10.

82 ———. 1975. The exquisite semi-alba *Phalaenopsis*. *Orchid Digest* 39(1):4–6.

83 ———. 1976. Those golden gems: the yellow *Phalaenopsis*. *Orchid Digest* 40(6):204–211.

84 ———. 1979. *New horizons in orchid breeding.* Day Printing Corp., Pomona, Calif.

85 ———. 1980. Novelty *Phalaenopsis* species and their hybrids, 1. *Phalaenopsis amboinensis*. *American Orchid Society Bulletin* 49(5):468.

86 ———. 1981. Novelty *Phalaenopsis* species and their hybrids, 4. The unpredictable *Phalaenopsis fuscata*. *American Orchid Society Bulletin* 50(8):937.

87 ———. 1981. Novelty *Phalaenopsis* species and their hybrids, 5. The versatile *Phalaenopsis lueddemanniana*, Part 1. *American Orchid Society Bulletin* 50(9):1077.

88 ———. 1981. Novelty *Phalaenopsis* species and their hybrids, 7. *Phalaenopsis stuartiana*. *American Orchid Society Bulletin* 50(12):1458.

89 Garay, L. A. 1978. *Orchidaceae* 225 (1). *Flora of Ecuador*, No. 9. Edited by G. Harling and B. Sparre. *Opera Botanica*, Swedish Natural Science Research Council, Stockholm, Sweden.

90 Garay, L. A. 1979. The genus *Phragmipedium*. *Orchid Digest* 43(4):133–148.

91   Garay, L. A., and H. Sweet. 1974. *Orchids of the southern Ryukyu Islands.* Botanical Museum, Harvard University, Cambridge, Mass.

92   Geernick, D. 1984. *Flore d'Afrique central: Orchidaceae.* Jardin botanique national de Belgique, Meise, Belgium.

93   Ghillany, B. A. 1972. In search of the elusive *Phragmipedium sargentianum* in Brazil. *Orchid Digest* 36(3):111–115.

94   Glicenstein, L. 1988. Reminiscences of orchids. *American Orchid Society Bulletin* 57(5):500.

95   Goh, Chong Jin, M. Strauss, and J. Arditti. 1982. Flower induction and physiology in orchids. In: *Orchid biology: reviews and perspectives.* Vol. II. Edited by J. Arditti. Comstock Publishing, Cornell University Press, Ithaca, N.Y.

96   Gordon, B. 1985. *Culture of the* Phalaenopsis *orchid.* Laid-Back Publications, Rialto, Calif.

97   ———. 1988. *Phalaenopsis* culture: a beginners' guide, 1. *American Orchid Society Bulletin* 57(1):17.

98   ———. 1988. *Phalaenopsis* culture = pest control. *Orchid Digest* 52(3):107–115.

99   ———. 1989. The breedin' o' the green (*Phalaenopsis* that is). *American Orchid Society Bulletin* 58(3):226.

100   Gorinsky, P. 1972. Habitat notes from a collection in Guyana of *Phragmipedium klotzscheanum. Orchid Digest* 36(4):151–153.

101   ———. 1973. Habitat notes from a collection in Guyana of *Phragmipedium lindleyanum. Orchid Digest* 37(2):47–52.

102   Grant, B. [1895] 1966. *Orchids of Burma and the Andaman Islands.* Hanthawaddy Press, Rangoon, Burma. Reprint, Twin Oaks Books, Greenfield, Wis.

103   Griesbach, J. 1983. Orchid flower color: genetic and cultural interactions. *American Orchid Society Bulletin* 52(10):1056.

104   ———. 1983. *Phalaenopsis mariae* as a parent. *Orchid Digest* 47(6):204–209.

105   Griesbach, R. J. 1981. Genetics and taxonomy. *Orchid Digest* 45(6):219–221.

106   Hadley, G., M. Arditti, and J. Arditti. 1987. Orchid diseases—a compendium. In: *Orchid biology: reviews and perspectives.* Vol. IV. Edited by J. Arditti. Comstock Publishing, Cornell University Press, Ithaca, N.Y.

107   Hallé, N. 1977. *Flore de la Nouvelle Calédonie et Dépendencies.* Vol. 8, *Orchidacées.* Musée national d'histoire naturelle, Paris, France.

108   Hamilton, R. M. [1980] 1988. *Orchid doctor.* Robert M. Hamilton, 9211 Beckwith Road, Richmond, B.C., Canada V6X 1V7.

109   ———. 1988. *New orchid doctor.* Robert M. Hamilton, 9211 Beckwith Road, Richmond, B.C., Canada V6X 1V7.

110   ———. 1988. *When does it flower?* 2nd ed. Robert M. Hamilton, 9211 Beckwith Road, Richmond, B.C., Canada V6X 1V7.

111   Harper, T. 1985. *Phalaenopsis* culture for beginners. *American Orchid Society Bulletin* 54(8):947.

112   Hawkes, A. D. [1965] 1987. *Encyclopaedia of cultivated orchids.* Faber and Faber, London.

113   Heeseler, R. 1987. *Orchid species culture guide.* Richard C. Heeseler, P.O. Box 1525, Seaford, NY, U.S.A. 11783.

114   Helleiner, M. 1984. Growing more orchids in a windowsill greenhouse. *American Orchid Society Bulletin* 53(3):266.

115   Hernandez, M. O. 1958. *Orquideas Colombianas.* Publicaciones Tecnicas, Bogota, Colombia.

116   Hetherington, E. 1981. *Phalaenopsis* hybridizing—today and tomorrow. *Orchid Digest* 45(3):95–97.

117   Hillerman, F. E., and A. W. Holst. 1986. *An introduction to the cultivated* Angraecoid *orchids of Madagascar.* Timber Press, Portland, Ore.

118   Holttum, R. E. 1964. *A revised flora of Malaya.* Vol. 1, *Orchids.* Government Printing Office, Singapore.

119   Hooker, J. D. [1895] 1967. *A century of Indian orchids.* Annals of the Royal Botanic Garden, Calcutta. Reprint, J. Cramer, Lehre, Germany.

120   Hu, Shiu-Ying. 1977. *The genera of Orchidaceae in Hong Kong.* The Chinese University Press, Hong Kong.

121   Hunt, D. R. 1981. *Orchids from* Curtis's Botanical Magazine. Bentham-Moxon Trust, Curwen Books, Plaistow, London.

122   *Index Kewensis.* 1983. Microfiche compilation. Royal Botanic Gardens, Kew, London.

123   International Orchid Commission. 1985. *Handbook on orchid nomenclature and registration.* 3rd ed., rev. International Orchid Commission, London.

124 Joseph, J. 1982. *Orchis of Nilgiris*. Vol. XXII of the *Records of the botanical survey of India*. P.O. Botanic Garden, Howrah, India.

125 Jouseau, M. R. 1981. *Pleione formosana:* species and what we need to know about them. *American Orchid Society Bulletin* 50(1):21.

126 Kamemoto, H., and R. Sagarik. 1975. *Beautiful Thai orchid species.* Orchid Society of Thailand, Aksornsampan Press, Bangkok, Thailand.

127 Kehew, K. A. 1989. Growing paphiopedilums and phragmipediums in your home. *American Orchid Society Bulletin* 58(9):866.

128 Kennedy, G. C. 1977. Peloric orchids. *Orchid Digest* 41(5):169.

129 Lager, J. E. 1979. Reminiscences of an orchid collector. *Orchid Digest* 42(6):231–232.

130 Lamb, A. 1982. The wild orchid species of Sabah. *Orchid Digest* 46(1):25.

131 Lavarack, P. S., and B. Gray. 1985. *Tropical orchids of Australia*. Thomas Nelson, Melbourne, Australia.

132 Lin, Tsian-Piao. 1975. *Native orchids of Taiwan*. Vol. 1. Southern Materials Center, P.O. Box 13-342, Taipei, Taiwan, Republic of China.

133 Mark, F. 1980. The *Pleione* of Taiwan—*Pleione formosana* Hayata with temperature and rainfall data of Taiwan. *Orchid Digest* 44(6):236–237.

134 Martin, J. G. 1985. In search of red *Phalaenopsis*. *American Orchid Society Bulletin* 54(4):411.

135 Mattes, P. 1982. A discovery trip to the Philippines with notes on the habitat of *Paphiopedilum fowliei* on Palawan Island. *Orchid Digest* 46(1):4–10.

136 McCorkle, J. K. 1971. Comments on certain infectious diseases of orchids: *Phalaenopsis* bacterial rot. *Orchid Digest* 35(7): 224.

137 McQuerry, M. N. 1976. Ramblings on a collecting trip to Bolivia and the rediscovery of *Phragmipedium caricinum*. *Orchid Digest* 40(6):224–227.

138 Menzes, L. C. 1989. *Phragmipedium vittatum* (Vell.) Rolfe. An orchid in the process of extinction. *Orchid Digest* 53(2):76–78.

139 Millar, A. 1978. *Orchids of Papua, New Guinea: an introduction*. University of Washington Press, Seattle, Wash.

140 Miller, J., and J. A. Fowlie. 1974. Notes on the distribution of *Phalaenopsis* in the Philippines—with a useful climate summary. Part I, *Phalaenopsis lueddemanniana* and the miniature species most often confused with it. *Orchid Digest* 38(4):139-141.

141 ———. 1974. Notes on the distribution of *Phalaenopsis* in the Philippines—with a useful climate summary. Part II, The large white-flowered species, *P. aphrodite* and *P. amabilis*. *Orchid Digest* 38(5):191–193.

142 ———. 1974. Notes on the distribution of *Phalaenopsis* in the Philippines—with a useful climate summary. Part III, The large colored species, *P. schilleriana, P. stuartiana*, and *P. sanderiana. Orchid Digest* 38(6):219–221.

143 ———. 1975. Notes on the distribution of *Phalaenopsis* in the Philippines— with a useful climate summary. Part IV, *P. lindenii, P. equestris*, and *P. micholitzii. Orchid Digest* 39(1):24–25.

144 Moses, J. R. 1980. *Phalaenopsis:* the search for pink. *American Orchid Society Bulletin* 49(4):363.

145 Nax and Butterworth Winners. 1989. *American Orchid Society Bulletin* 58(3):255.

146 New and recently named orchids. 1988. *Orchid Digest* 52(4):165.

147 Nicholls, W. H. 1969. *Orchids of Australia*. Edited by D. L. Jones and T. B. Muir. Nelson Publishing, Melbourne, Australia.

148 Northen, R. T. 1970. *Home orchid growing*. Van Nostrand Reinhold, New York.

149 ———. 1980. *Miniature orchids*. Van Nostrand Reinhold, New York.

150 ———. 1988. The Kingdom of Lilliput: miniature orchids. *American Orchid Society Bulletin* 57(2):116–124.

151 North Shore Orchid Society of Australia. 1983. *World of orchids*. North Shore Orchid Society of Australia, Sydney, Australia.

152 Obata, J. K. 1987. Native and naturalized orchids of Hawaii. *American Orchid Society Bulletin* 56(7):695.

153 Parham, J. W. 1972. *Plants of the Fiji Islands: Orchidaceae*. Rev. ed. The Government Printer, Suva, Fiji.

154 Peterson, K. E. 1988. The F.C.C.'s of 1987. *American Orchid Society Bulletin* 57(8):842.

155 Pradhan, G. M. 1981. *Phalaenopsis* species of northern India. *American Orchid Society Bulletin* 50(1):30.

156 Pradhan, U. C. 1977. The natural conditions of *Phalaenopsis mannii* and *Phalaenopsis parishii* (with notes on

their jungle mimics). *Orchid Digest* 41(3):94–97.

157 ——. 1979. *Indian orchids: guide to identification and culture.* Vols. I–II. Udai C. Pradhan, Kalimpong, India.

158 Random thoughts on the judging of orchids. 1972. *American Orchid Society Bulletin* 41(11):1007.

159 Rolfe, R. A. 1898. Orchideae. In: *Flora of Tropical Africa.* Vol. VII, *Hydrocharideae to Liliaceae.* Edited by W. T. Thiselton-Dyer. Royal Botanic Gardens, Kew, London, United Kingdom; Lovell Reeve and Co., Covent Garden, London.

160 ——. 1910. XXII.—New orchids: decade 35. *Kew Bulletin:* 158–162. Royal Botanic Gardens, Kew, London.

161 ——. 1913. XXI.—New orchids: decade 40. *Kew Bulletin:* 141–145. Royal Botanic Gardens, Kew, London.

162 Santapau, H., and Z. Kapadia. 1964. *The orchids of Bombay.* Government of India Press, Calcutta, India.

163 Schlechter, R. R. 1911. Zur kenntnis der orchidaceen von Celebes. *Feddes Repertorium* X. Berlin.

164 Schlechter, R. R. [1911–1914] 1982. *The Orchidaceae of German New Guinea.* Translated by D. F. Blaxell, H. J. Katz, and J. T. Simmons. Australian Orchid Foundation, Melbourne, Australia.

165 Schweinfurth, C. 1983. Orchids of Peru. *Fieldiana: Botany* 30(1). Chicago Natural History Museum Press, Chicago.

166 Seidenfaden, G. 1972. An enumeration of Laotian orchids. *Bulletin du Musée national d'histoire naturelle botanique* 71(5):141–142.

167 ——. 1975. *Contributions to a revision of the orchid flora of Cambodia, Laos, and Vietnam.* Kai Olsen, 10 Helstedsvej, DK-3480, Fredensborg, Denmark.

168 ——. 1986. Orchid genera in Thailand, XIII. Thirty-three epidendroid genera. *Opera Botanica* 89, Copenhagen, Denmark.

169 Sheehan, T., and M. Sheehan. 1979. Orchid genera, illustrated–69–*Pescatorea. American Orchid Society Bulletin* 48(5):456.

170 Shim, Phyau Soon, and J. A. Fowlie. 1983. A new species of *Phalaenopsis* from Sulawesi (Celebes)—formerly confused with *Phalaenopsis psilantha* Schlechter, *Phalaenopsis venosa* Shim and Fowl., sp. nov. *Orchid Digest* 47(4):124–128.

171 Shuttleworth, H., H. Zim, and G. Dillon. 1970. *Orchids, a golden guide.* Golden Press, New York.

172 Simpson, P. D. 1988. Observations on *Phragmipedium* species near Tingo Maria, Peru. *Orchid Digest* 52(2):81–84.

173 Singh, F. 1979. An exquisite orchid from western Ghats. *American Orchid Society Bulletin* 48(4):345.

174 Skelsey, A. 1979. Orchids. In: *Time-Life encyclopedia of gardening.* Time-Life Books, Alexandria, Va.

175 Smith, J. J. [1905] 1984. *Die orchideen von Java.* J. Brill, Leiden, The Netherlands. Reprint, Bishen Singh Mahendra Pal Singh, Dehra Dun, India.

176 Some novelty *Phalaenopsis* species, relatively new on the scene for consideration in breeding. 1987. *Orchid Digest* 51(3):102.

177 South Florida Orchid Society. 1984. *Introduction to orchids.* South Florida Orchid Society, Miami, Fla.

178 Stermitz, F. R. 1980. Orchids from Iquitos to Cuzco to Tingo Maria, Peru. *American Orchid Society Bulletin* 49(12):361.

179 Stermitz, F. R., N. Fink, and L. S. Hegedus. 1981. A comparison of alkaloid content in some *Phragmipedium* species. *American Orchid Society Bulletin* 50(11):1346.

180 Stermitz, F. R., L. S. Hegedus, and L. Richard. 1983. A remake (?) of *Phragmipedium stenophyllum.* Some comments on the *Himantopetalum* section of *Phragmipedium. American Orchid Society Bulletin* 52(10):1040.

181 Su, Horng-Jye. 1975. *Taiwan orchids.* 2nd ed. Horng-Jye Su, Department of Forestry, National Taiwan University, Taipei, Republic of China.

182 Summerhayes, V. S. 1964. African orchids: XXIX. *Kew Bulletin* 17(3). Royal Botanic Gardens, Kew, London.

183 Sweet, H. R. 1971. Observations on the genus *Phalaenopsis.* Part III, The miniature white-flowered species. *Orchid Digest* 35(2):45–46.

184 ——. 1971. Observations on the genus *Phalaenopsis.* Part IV, *Phalaenopsis amabilis* and *Phalaenopsis aphrodite. Orchid Digest* 35(4):123–125.

185 ——. 1971. Notes on the habitat of *Phalaenopsis speciosa* var. *tetraspis. Orchid Digest* 35(7):201–204.

186 ——. 1971. Observations on the genus *Phalaenopsis.* Part V, The colored large-flowered species. *Orchid Digest* 35(8):247–250.

187   ———. 1971. Observations on the genus *Phalaenopsis*. Part VI, *Phalaenopsis mariae* and *Phalaenopsis maculata*. *Orchid Digest* 35(10):307–308.

188   ———. 1972. Observations on the genus *Phalaenopsis*. Part VII, *Phalaenopsis violacea* Witte. *Orchid Digest* 36(1):11–12.

189   ———. 1972. Observations on the genus *Phalaenopsis*. Part VIII, *Phalaenopsis gigantea*. *Orchid Digest* 36(2):67–68.

190   ———. 1972. Observations on the genus *Phalaenopsis*. Part IX, *Phalaenopsis amboinensis* and *P. sumatrana*. *Orchid Digest* 36(3):87–88.

191   ———. 1972. Observations on the genus *Phalaenopsis*. Part X, *Phalaenopsis cornu-cervi* and *Phalaenopsis mannii*. *Orchid Digest* 36(5):167.

192   ———. 1972. Observations on the genus *Phalaenopsis*. Part XI, *Phalaenopsis equestris* and *Phalaenopsis lindenii*. *Orchid Digest* 36(6):207–208.

193   ———. 1973. Observations on the genus *Phalaenopsis*. Part XII, *P. fuscata* and its related species. *Orchid Digest* 37(3):107–108.

194   ———. 1973. Observations on the genus *Phalaenopsis*. Part XIII, *Phalaenopsis parishii* var. *lobbii* Rchb.f. *Orchid Digest* 37(5):167–168.

195   ———. 1980. *The genus* Phalaenopsis. The Orchid Digest, Inc., 1739 Foothill Blvd., La Cañada, CA, U.S.A. 91011.

196   Tang, C. Z., and C. J. Cheng. 1986. Two new *Phaius* species from China, *Phaius hainensis* and *Phaius columnaris*. *Orchid Digest* 50(6):199–202.

197   Teo, C. K. 1985. *Native orchids of peninsula Malaysia*. Times Books International, Singapore.

198   Teoh, E. S. 1980. *Asian orchids*. Times Books International, Singapore.

199   Tharp, A. G., J. A. Fowlie, and C. Z. Tang. 1987. A recently described *Phalaenopsis* species from the Philippines: *Phalaenopsis philippinensis* Golamco ex Fowlie and Tang, C. Z. *Orchid Digest* 51(2):87–92.

200   Thorne, A., and P. Cribb. 1984. *Orchids of the Solomon Islands and Bougainville—a preliminary checklist*. Royal Botanic Gardens, Kew, London.

201   Thornton, F., and B. Thornton. 1968. Breeding characteristics of *Phalaenopsis*. *Orchid Digest* 32(3):84–85.

202   Valdivisieso, P. O., with A. M. Martinez and G. M. Urreta. 1982. *Ornamental orchids of Colombia*. Carlos Valencia, Bogota, Colombia.

203   Valmayor, H. 1984. *Orchidiana Philippiniana*. Vols. 1–2. Eugenio Lopez Foundation, Manila, Philippines.

204   Van Delden, R. J. 1979. The new hybrid genus *Doriellaopsis*. *Orchid Digest* 43(3):100–101.

205   Veitch, James, and Sons. [1887-1894] 1963, 1981. *Manual of orchidaceous plants*. Vols. I–II. James Veitch and Sons Royal Exotic Nursery, Chelsea, London, United Kingdom. Reprint, Vol. I, A. Asher and Co., Amsterdam, The Netherlands; reprint, Vol. II, Bishen Singh Mahendra Pal Singh, Dehra Dun, India.

206   Watson, W., and W. Bean. [1890] 1979. *Orchids: their culture and management*. L. Upcott Gill, London.

207   Werkhoven, M. C. M. 1986. *Orchids of Surinam*. VACO, Uitgeversmaatschappij, Paramaribo, Surinam.

208   Wie, Liem Khe. 1977. The rediscovery of *Phalaenopsis viridis*. *Orchid Digest* 41(5):177.

209   ———. 1979. In search of the lost species *Phalaenopsis javanica*. *Orchid Digest* 43(3):57.

210   Williams, B., with Jack Kramer. 1987. *Orchids for everyone*. W. H. Smith Publishers, New York.

211   Williams, B. S. [1894] 1973. *Orchid growers' manual*. 7th ed. Victoria and Paradise Nurseries, London. Reprint, Weldon & Wesley, Codicote, Herts, United Kingdom, and Verlag J. Cramer, Lehre, Germany.

212   Williams, L. O., and P. H. Allen. 1980. *Orchids of Panama*. Vol. 4 of *Monographs in systematic botany*. Missouri Botanical Garden, St. Louis, Mo.

213   Williams, T. 1984. Yellow *Phalaenopsis*: 86 years of hybridizing. *American Orchid Society Bulletin* 53(3):238.

214   Wilson, K. S. 1980. The difference between alba, alba form, and white. *American Orchid Society Bulletin* 49(8):863.

215   Wimber, D. E. 1983. *Phragmipedium* cytology. 1, Diploidy and polyploidy in the hybrids. *American Orchid Society Bulletin* 52(9):933.

216   Winter, L. 1989. A pouch fetish. *American Orchid Society Bulletin* 58(5):461.

217   Wishinski, P. 1978. Some orchids of the Nepal Himalayas. *American Orchid Society Bulletin* 47(7):623.

218   Wisniewski, J. 1980. Fluorescent light culture for orchids. *American Orchid Society Bulletin* 48(7):691.

219 Young, R. 1979. The discovery of *Phalaenopsis gigantea* in Sabah. *Orchid Digest* 43(1):28.
220 Zetterstrom, G. 1988. Growing phragmipediums. *American Orchid Society Bulletin* 57(4):361.

List of Sources

The following indexes, books, and articles are helpful.

Dietrich, Helga. 1980, 1981, 1985, 1988. *Bibliographia orchidacearum*. Vols. 2.1, 2.2, 3, 4. Bibliographische Mitteilungen der Universiatsbibliothek, Friedrich-Schiller-Universitat, Jena, Germany.

Hamilton, Robert M. 1972. *Index to plant illustrations*. 1932–1971. Vols. 1–40 of the *American Orchid Society Bulletin*. R. M. Hamilton, 9211 Beckwith Road, Richmond, B.C., Canada V6X 1V7.

———. 1986. *Supplementary index to plant illustrations*. 1972–1985. Vols. 41–54 of the *American Orchid Society Bulletin*. R. M. Hamilton, 9211 Beckwith Road, Richmond, B.C., Canada V6X 1V7.

Index Kewensis. 1983. Microfiche compilation. Royal Botanic Gardens, Kew, London.

Index to plant chromosome numbers. 1975–1978. Missouri Botanical Garden, St. Louis, Mo. Reprint, Twin Oaks Books, Greenfield, Wis.

Index to plant chromosome numbers. 1979–1981. Missouri Botanical Garden, St. Louis, Mo. Reprint, Twin Oaks Books, Greenfield, Wis.

Oertle, Charles F. (ed.). 1987. *Index periodicarum orchidacearum*. Tipografia Poncioni, Lausanne, Switzerland.

Tanaka, R., and H. Kamemoto. 1984. Chromosomes in orchids: counting and numbers. Appendix in *Orchid biology: reviews and perspectives*. Vol. III. Edited by J. Arditti. Comstock Publishing, Cornell University Press, Ithaca, N.Y.

On Geographic Names

The following maps and gazetteers were used to correlate obsolete or uncommon place names with names in current usage.

Gazetteers. 1955–present. U.S. Board of Geographic Names. Prepared and published by the U.S. Defense Mapping Agency, Washington, D.C. The *Gazetteers*, in numerous volumes, are updated periodically.

O.N.C. aeronautical navigation charts. Prepared and published by the U.S. Defense Mapping Agency, Washington, D.C. The charts are updated periodically as additional mapping is accomplished.

The Times atlas of the world. 7th ed. 1988. Times Books, Random House, New York.

Webster's new geographical dictionary. 1977. G. and C. Merriam Co., Springfield, Mass.

On Specific Climates

Published weather records appear in the following publications.

World weather records, 1961–1970. 1979–1985. Vols. 1–5. U.S. Department of Commerce, National Oceanic and Atmospheric Administration, National Climatic Center, Asheville, N.C.

World wide airfield summaries. 1967, 1968, 1974. Vols. I–VII, IX, XII. U.S. Naval Weather Service, National Technical Information Service, Washington, D.C.

Readers seeking weather data for special projects are invited to contact Margaret and Charles Baker, c/o Timber Press, 9999 S.W. Wilshire, Portland, OR, U.S.A. 97225.

On Botanical Names

The following volume offers general information on botanical names.

Coombes, A. J. 1985. *Dictionary of plant names*. Timber Press, Portland, Ore.

On Foreign-language Publications

The following references are useful in translating botanical terms from various languages.

Davydov, N. N. 1962. *Botanical dictionary, Russian—English—German—French—Latin*. Central Editorial Board, Foreign-Language Scientific and Technical Dictionaries, Moscow.
Stearn, W. T. 1986. *Botanical Latin*. 3rd ed. David and Charles, North Pomfret, Vt.

Suppliers of Books on Botany and Horticulture

American Orchid Society, 6000 S. Olive Ave., West Palm Beach, FL, U.S.A. 33405. Catalog available.
Equatorial Plant Company, 73 Dundas Street, Edinburgh EH3 6RS, United Kingdom. Catalog available.
McQuerry Orchid Books, 5700 W. Salerno Road, Jacksonville, FL, U.S.A. 32244. Catalog available.
Orchid Digest Book Department, The Orchid Digest, 4336 Laurelwood Way, Sacramento, CA, U.S.A. 95864.
RHS Enterprises, RHS Garden, Wisley, Woking, Surrey GU23 6QB, United Kingdom. Catalog available.
Timber Press, 9999 S.W. Wilshire, Portland, OR, U.S.A. 97225. Catalog available.
Touchwood Books, P.O. Box 610, Hastings, New Zealand. Catalog available.
Twin Oaks Books, P.O. Box 20940, Greenfield, WI, U.S.A. 53220. Catalog available.

Orchid Societies

Members of the following regional orchid societies and libraries may be able to provide detailed information on cultural techniques for particular climates as well as approved treatments for insect or disease problems. Organizations wishing to be listed in future volumes of *Orchid Species Culture* are invited to send names and address to Margaret and Charles Baker, c/o Timber Press, 9999 S.W. Wilshire, Portland, OR, U.S.A. 97225.

Australia: Australian Orchid Council, c/o *The Australian Orchid Review*, Mr. David Wallace, 90 Great Western Hwy., Blaxland, N.S.W. 2774, Australia.
Austria: Osterreichische Orchideen-Gesellschaft, Postfach 300, 1222 Vienna, Austria.
Belgium: Orchika Orchideenklub Antwerpen, c/o Mr. G. Verhulst, H. De Braeckeleerlaan 48, B2630 Aartselaar, Belgium.
Bermuda: Bermuda Orchid Society, c/o Mr. R. Mercer, P.O. Box HM 19, Hamilton 5, Bermuda.
Brazil: Coordenadoría das Associaçaes Orquidófilas do Brasil, Rue 5, Number 1515, Caixa Postal, 129, 13500 Rio Claro, São Paulo, Brazil.
Canada: Canadian Orchid Society, c/o Mr. T. I. Smith, Brisbane Avenue, Winnipeg, Manitoba, Canada R3T 0T2.
Cayman Islands: Grand Cayman Orchid Society, c/o Mrs. Joyce Hylton, Box 86, Grand Cayman, Cayman Islands, British West Indies.
China (Taiwan): See Taiwan.
Colombia: Sociedad Colombiana de Orquideología, c/o Sr. Alvaro Arango M., Apartado Aereo 4725, Medellín, Colombia.
Costa Rica: Asociación Costarricense de Orquideología, c/o Jorge Miranda, Apartado Postal 6351, 1000 San José, Costa Rica.
Czechoslovakia: Zahrada Ostrava, c/o M. Sembol, P.O. Box 74, 70800 Ostrava Poruba, Czechoslovakia.
Denmark: Orchid Club of Denmark, c/o Mr. Jørgen Listov-Sâabye, Solsikkevej 7, DK-4600, Køge, Denmark.
Dominican Republic: Sociedad Dominicana de Orquideología, c/o Mr. D. Dod, P.O. Box 1053, Santo Domingo, Dominican Republic.
Ecuador: Asociación Ecuatoriana de Orquideología, c/o Mr. Max Konanz, Apartado 1033, Guayaquil, Ecuador.
El Salvador: Asociación Salvadorena de Orquideología, c/o Mr. H. C. Clason, Apartado Postal (01) 276, San Salvador, El Salvador.
France: Société Française d'Orchidophilie, c/o Mme. Nicole Bellone, 31 Rue Victor Clément, 92160, Antony, France.
Germany: Deutsche Orchideen-Gesellschaft Bibliothek, Siesmayer Str. 61, D-6000, Frankfurt, Germany.
Guatemala: Asociación Guatemalteca de Orquideología, c/o Dr. Alberto Behar A., P.O. Box 151-A, Guatemala City, Guatemala.
Holland: See The Netherlands.
Hong Kong: Hong Kong Orchid Society, c/o Dr. T. Lee, 610A Champion Building, 301–309 Nathan Road, Kowloon, Hong Kong.

India: *The Orchidologist*, Orchid Reserve and Development Center, Forest Department, Gov. Arunachal Pradesh, Tipi, Bhalukpong–790 114, Assam, India.

Indonesia: Pusat Perpustakaan Pertanian, National Library of Agricultural Sciences, Jalan Ir. H. Juanda 20, Bogor, Indonesia.

Ireland: Northern Ireland Orchid Society, c/o Mrs. A. Laming, 80 Greyston, Belfast BT9 6UL, Northern Ireland.

Israel: Central Library of Agricultural Science, P.O. Box 12, Rehovot 76100, Israel.

Italy: Società Italiana Orchidee, Via Macaggi 17-9, 16121 Genoa, Italy.

Jamaica: Jamaica Orchid Society, c/o Dr. S. I. Terry, 38 Hope Blvd., Kingston 6, Jamaica.

Japan: Japan Orchid Society, c/o Japan Orchid Growers Assn., No. 19-14, Hachimanyama, 3-Chone, Setagaya-Ku, Tokyo 156, Japan.

Kenya: Kenya Orchid Society, c/o Mr. M. H. Vincent, Box 24744, Nairobi, Kenya.

Malaysia: Orchid Society of South East Asia, Maxwell Road, P.O. Box 2363, Singapore 9043.

Mauritius: Orchid Society of Mauritius, c/o Dr. A. Majeedk Khadaroo, 3 Ave. Bernardin de Saint Pierre, Quatre-Bornes, Mauritius.

Mexico: Asociación Mexicana de Orquideología, c/o Mr. Eric Hagsater, Apartado Postal 53-123, 11320 Mexico, D.F. Mexico.

Netherlands Antilles: Curaçao Orchid Club, c/o Mr. de Groot, Cassandraweg 27, Curaçao, Netherlands Antilles.

Netherlands, The: V.K.C. Proefatation Voor de Bloemisterij, Linnaeslaan 2A,1431 J V Aalsmeer, The Netherlands.

New Caledonia: Société Nouvelle-Calédonienne d'Orchidophilie, BP 23, Noumea, New Caledonia.

New Guinea: Orchid Society of Papua–New Guinea, c/o Ms. Alexa Burns, Box 147, Post Office Port Moresby 212167, Port Moresby, Papua–New Guinea.

New Zealand: Council of New Zealand, c/o R. A. Claburt, 18 Littlejohn Street, Hillsborough 4, Auckland, New Zealand.

Okinawa: Okinawa Orchid Society, c/o Mr. T. Amano, Aza, Hantagawa 373, Haha City, Okinawa-ken, Japan.

Panama: Asociación Chiriqui de Orquideas, c/o Feria de Las Flores, Boquete Chiriqui, Republic of Panama.

Peru: Club Pervano de Orquideas, c/o Ms. Ida Hamer De Fernandex, Apartado Postal 042, Lima 12, Peru.

Philippines: Philippine Orchid Society, c/o Dr. V. R. Potenciano, The Polymedic General Hospital, 163 E. Delos Santos, Mandaluyong, Metro-Manila, Philippines.

Poland: Krakow Botanical Institute U.J., c/o Prof. Jadwiga Dyakowska, UL Lubicz 46, 31-512 Krakow, Poland.

Romania: Familia Savel Ichimescu, Scara A., Ap. 7, Aleea J.O.R. No. 7, Bolc G2, R 74402, Bucharest, Romania.

Singapore: Orchid Society of South East Asia, Maxwell Road, P.O. Box 2363, Singapore 9043.

South Africa: Orchid Society of Northern Transvaal, c/o Mr. N. J. Broekhuysen, 265 Eridanus Street, Waterkloof Ridge, Waterkloof, 0191 Pretoria, Republic of South Africa.

South Korea: Kangwom-Do Hallym College Library, 1 Ockchon Dong, Chunchon City, Kangwom-Do 200, South Korea.

Spain: Club Amigo de las Orquideas, c/o P. Bourguignon, c/Montearagon, 8, 28033 Madrid, Spain.

Sri Lanka (Ceylon): Orchid Circle of Ceylon, Gamini Goonesekara, c/o The Editor, *Orchidologia*, Zeylanica, Coconut Research Institute, Lunuwila, Sri Lanka.

Sweden: Orchid Club of Stockholm, c/o Mr. A. Sanridsson, Satrangsvagen 56, S-182, 36 Danderyd, Sweden.

Switzerland: Schweizerische Orchideen-Gesellschaft, c/o O. Feistle, Rueteliweg 4, CH-4304 Giebenach, Switzerland.

Taiwan: Orchid Society of the Republic of China (Taiwan), No. 12, Lane 356, SEC 2, Pei Mem Road, Tainan, Taiwan, Republic of China.

Thailand: Orchid Society of Thailand, 6 Soi 41, Pahol-Yothin Road, Bangkhen, Bangkok 9, Thailand.

U.S.A. (including Puerto Rico and the Virgin Islands): American Orchid Society, 6000 S. Olive Ave., West Palm Beach, FL, U.S.A. 33405.

U.S.S.R: Library of Natural Sciences, Exchange Dept., U.S.S.R. Academy of Sciences, 119890 GSP, Moscow G 19, U.S.S.R.

United Kingdom: Royal Horticultural Society, Vincent Square, London SW1P 2PE, United Kingdom.

Venezuela: Sociedad Venezolana de Ciencias Naturales Comité de Orquideología, c/o E. Indorf, Apartado 99110, Terrazas Cluib Hipico, Caracas 1080, Venezuela.

West Indies: Trinidad and Tobago Orchid Society, c/o Alex Gibson, 6 Sinclair Hill, Diego Martin, Port of Spain, Trinidad, West Indies.

Zimbabwe: Bulawayo Orchid Society, c/o Mr. A. Abel, P.O. Box 1772, Bulawayo, Zimbabwe.